TV Gothic

TV Gothic

*The Golden Age
of Small Screen Horror*

HOWARD MAXFORD

McFarland & Company, Inc., Publishers
Jefferson, North Carolina

ISBN (print) 978-1-4766-7975-4
ISBN (ebook) 978-1-4766-4553-7

LIBRARY OF CONGRESS AND BRITISH LIBRARY
CATALOGUING DATA ARE AVAILABLE

Library of Congress Control Number 2022024473

Front cover: Ronnie Scribner as the young vampire Ralphie Glick
in the 1979 miniseries *Salem's Lot* (Warner Bros./Photofest)

Printed in the United States of America

*McFarland & Company, Inc., Publishers
Box 611, Jefferson, North Carolina 28640
www.mcfarlandpub.com*

Table of Contents

Introduction   1

**Section One. In the Beginning: Horror
in Television's Stone Age (the 1930s and 1940s)**   5
   Live from Ally Pally   5
   The Big Apple Bites Back   10
   The Rise of Poe   14
   Picture Perfect   18
   Questions in the House   23
   The Pepsi Challenge   25

Section Two. The Monsters Arrive (the 1950s)   29
   Cue Frankenstein   29
   Enter Professor Quatermass   34
   Vamping It with Vampira   40
   A Hitch in Time   43
   The Great Beyond   50
   Entering the Zone   54

Section Three. The Genre Takes Hold (the 1960s)   60
   Beloved Boris   60
   Who?   73
   Canned Laughter   75
   Mysterious Imaginings   83
   Tales from Europe   89
   A Rum Collins   92
   A Fateful Whistle   97
   Strange Journeys   100
   Scooby and the Gang   104
   And Now the Gallery   108

**Section Four. The American TV Movie
Comes of Age (the 1970s)**   112
   Movie of the Week   112
   Kolchak Scores a Hit   120
   The Devil to Pay   128
   Creature Feature   136
   A Fetish for Horror   143

MTM Goes for the Jugular   151
The True Story   159
Bringing In the Harvest   171
Gargoyles   181
Up at the Marsten House   191
Meet the Hardy Boys   201
More Tales from Europe   210

Section Five. Enter the Brits (the 1970s)   216
The Doomsday People   216
The Play's the Thing   217
Festive Frissons   225
Dead of Night   243
Country Matters   250
A Party with Barty   259
Teatime Terrors   266
What Music They Make   274
Mrs. Amworth Pays a Visit   279
An Old Master   286

Section Six. New Realms (the 1980s)   291
Hammer Has Risen from the Grave   291
Venturing into the Darkside   304
The Spielberg Touch   308
Ready for Freddy   317
Tut, Tut   323
The Music of the Night   328
Raising Caine   337
Further Tales from Europe   343

Section Seven. The End of an Era (the 1990s)   349
The Anthology Lives On   349
Duped by Auntie   356
The X Factor   358
The Color Purple   361
It   366
Corman Quickies   373
King of the Airwaves   378

Epilogue: A New Era (the 2000s and 2010s)   384
Bibliography   389
Index   391

"Oh, Daddy, I *hate* being dead."
—Mary Constable (Pamelyn Ferdin),
Daughter of the Mind (1969, TVM)

Introduction

The history of the horror film has been chronicled in book form many times over, from its early stirrings in such silent offerings as *The Cabinet of Dr. Caligari* (1920) and *Nosferatu* (1922) to the Universal classics of the thirties and forties, among them such longstanding favorites as *Dracula* (1931), *Frankenstein* (1931), *The Mummy* (1932) and *The Wolf Man* (1941). The work of RKO producer Val Lewton, noted for such fare as *Cat People* (1942) and *I Walked with a Zombie* (1943), has also been the subject of detailed analysis, as has the output of the fabled British studio Hammer, with its luridly colored remakes of the Universal films as well as such stand-alone pieces as *The Kiss of the Vampire* (1963) and *The Devil Rides Out* (1968). Equally admired is the work of director Roger Corman, best known for his Poe adaptations, among them *House of Usher* (1960) and *The Masque of the Red Death* (1964), and the producers Max J. Rosenberg and Milton Subotsky who, through their company Amicus, turned out a series of popular all-star compendiums, taking in the likes of *Dr. Terror's House of Horrors* (1965) and *Tales from the Crypt* (1972). The output of such directors as John Carpenter and Wes Craven, responsible for the *Halloween* and *Nightmare on Elm Street* franchises, respectively, has also been well documented. In fact, from big-budget extravaganzas such as Roman Polanski's *The Fearless Vampire Killers* (1967, aka *Dance of the Vampires*) to grade-Z schlock, there seems to be little that hasn't been chronicled and celebrated, be it the emergence of the Italian *giallo* movement in the sixties or the stalk-and-slash cycle of the seventies and eighties. The nineties even saw a number of Hollywood's finest begin to embrace the often critically maligned genre, among them Jack Nicholson with *Wolf* (1994) and Tom Cruise with *Interview with the Vampire: The Vampire Chronicles* (1994). They were in turn followed by Nicolas Cage with *Ghost Rider* (2007), Johnny Depp with *Dark Shadows* (2012) and Cruise again with yet another remake of *The Mummy* (2017), whose $125 million budget could hardly be described as paltry. The genre's two most prolific characters also got the red-carpet treatment with *Bram Stoker's Dracula* (1992) and *Mary Shelley's Frankenstein* (1994), which were directed in turn by Francis Ford Coppola and Kenneth Branagh.

Yet an equally prolific parallel universe of small screen horror is also out there, though its history barely seems to have been acknowledged, despite the fact that it has embraced all the major characters of the genre, including Dracula, Frankenstein and Dr. Jekyll and Mr. Hyde, plus the work of many major genre writers, among them Edgar Allan Poe, Robert Louis Stevenson and Sheridan Le Fanu. In fact, from

1

the early days of broadcasting in Britain and America, one-off plays, TV movies and series with a horror bias have played an increasing role in the schedules. Their content may initially have been mild beer compared to their larger screen counterparts, owing to the strict censorship guidelines of the day, yet genre TV has recently become as visceral as the movies playing in the multiplexes thanks to such series as *The Vampire Diaries* (2009–2017, TV), *The Walking Dead* (2010–, TV) and *Ash vs. Evil Dead* (2015–2018, TV), whose violence and bloodletting make the horror films of yesteryear seem tame indeed.

In fact, British and American television has provided almost as many memorable genre productions as the large screen and has attracted some highly respectable names in the process. While in the cinema the role of Count Dracula has primarily been defined by Bela Lugosi and Christopher Lee, the character's small screen interpreters have included Denholm Elliott, Jack Palance and Louis Jourdan. Likewise, Colin Clive and Peter Cushing may be considered the cinema's definitive portrayers of Baron Frankenstein, yet on the small screen the role has been played by Anton Diffring, Leonard Whiting and Patrick Bergin, while the Monster, the domain of Boris Karloff and Christopher Lee on the big screen, has been brought to life by Ian Holm, Michael Sarrazin and Randy Quaid on the small. Fredric March may have won the genre's first best actor Oscar for playing both Dr. Jekyll and Mr. Hyde back in 1931, yet the roles have since been played on television by Kirk Douglas, David Hemmings and Michael Caine, which is hardly slumming it.

The work of M.R. James has been a frequent source for television adaptation, particularly in the BBC's highly regarded *A Ghost Story for Christmas* (1971–1978, 2005–2021, TV) strand, yet the venerated author has been almost entirely ignored by the cinema, save for *Night of the Demon* (1957, aka *Curse of the Demon*), a celebrated version of *Casting the Runes*, which went on to be adapted for television in 1968 and 1979. Many series have embraced horror in one form or another down the decades too, including *Lights Out* (1946–1952, TV), *The Twilight Zone* (1959–1964, TV), *Mystery and Imagination* (1966–1970, TV), *Dark Shadows* (1966–1971, TV), *Thriller* (1973–1976, TV), *Beasts* (1976, TV) and *Tales from the Darkside* (1983–1988, TV) to name but a few, while Hammer itself even got in on the act with *Journey to the Unknown* (1968, TV), *Hammer House of Horror* (1980, TV) and *Hammer House of Mystery and Suspense* (1984, TVM), not to mention an early aborted series titled *Tales of Frankenstein* (1958, TV). There have also been countless TV movies, whose content has frequently provided shudders equal to their large screen counterparts, among them *The Night Stalker* (1972, TVM), *Gargoyles* (1972, TVM), *Something Evil* (1972, TVM), *The Eyes of Charles Sand* (1972, TVM), *Haunts of the Very Rich* (1972, TVM), *The Night Strangler* (1973, TVM), *The Cat Creature* (1973, TVM), *Scream Pretty Peggy* (1973, TVM), *The Possessed* (1977, TVM), *The Dark Secret of Harvest Home* (1978, TVM), *Deadly Messages* (1985, TVM) and *Bay Coven* (1987, TVM), many of which have either been forgotten or neglected or perhaps are unknown to younger audiences, despite featuring contributions from such names as Steven Spielberg, Bette Davis, Harrison Ford and Hammer scribe Jimmy Sangster, who also enjoyed a prolific career in Hollywood.

And just as the cinema has its genre gods in the form of directors James Whale and Terence Fisher, it can be claimed that the small screen has its own roll call of top talent, among them directors Dan Curtis, Lawrence Gordon Clark and John Llewellyn Moxey, and such writers as Nigel Kneale, Robert Muller, Richard Matheson, Rod Serling, David Rudkin and John Bowen. One can't underestimate the contributions of such composers as Bob Cobert and Billy Goldenberg, either, while producers with a track record with the genre include Irene Shubik and, perhaps surprisingly, Aaron Spelling and Leonard Goldberg, despite being better known for such mainstream fare as *Charlie's Angels* (1976–1981, TV) and *Fantasy Island* (1977–1984, TV).

So, with horror, fantasy and science fiction presently big hitters on TV, perhaps now is the time to chronicle the genre's glorious past on the small screen. The main focus of the book is the fifties, sixties and seventies of the last century, but I have not neglected to provide a lead up to these decades, to which end I have included an overview of the very early days of genre television in the thirties and forties. However, given that much of the material broadcast during these pioneering days went out live and is therefore unavailable for study, I have provided as much pertinent information as is available about these programs. Consequently, given the nature of the beast, this section reads like a glorified checklist, though I have done my best to make it seem otherwise. But from the fifties onwards, when the monsters began to show their faces, things undeniably become rather more fun, and from here on, the studies include plot synopses, critical evaluations and, where available, press coverage (note that my reaction to these films and series is inevitably a personal one and therefore may, on occasion, be at variance with the reader's own heartfelt opinions, for which I appreciate your indulgence).

My own favorite sections are four and five, both of which cover the seventies and deal primarily with the American TV movie and Britain's small screen output, respectively, and for which I have watched as much as is available from the period, which has been done via TV, video (good old VHS), DVD and Blu-ray as well as online (YouTube), where a surprising number of obscurities can be found, among them many forgotten or half-remembered gems. "But surely I can look all this stuff up myself on IMDb?" you might argue, to which my reply would be "Yes, you can, but if you don't know *what* to look up genre-wise on IMDb and YouTube, how do you know what goodies are actually hiding out there in the shadows?" Hopefully, the following pages will help to fill in those gaps and introduce you, possibly for the first time, to such jewels as *The Ghost of Sierra de Cobre* (1964, TVM), *Sweet, Sweet Rachel* (1971, TVM), *La Cabina* (1972, TV) and *Mrs. Amworth* (1978, TV), as well as such all time classics as *Whistle and I'll Come to You* (1968, TV), *Frankenstein: The True Story* (1973, TVM), *The Norliss Tapes* (1973, TVM), *Salem's Lot* (1979, TVM) and *Schalcken the Painter* (1979, TVM), all of which feature in my top 20 (see below).

And while it might be said that the classic days of TV's *first* golden age of horror began to peter out towards the end of the seventies, I have nevertheless gone on to provide an overview of the eighties and nineties (which produced several highlights of their own), again noting all series and TV movies with a genre leaning. A number of thrillers, science fiction films and fantasy hybrids have also been included throughout the book for the sake of completeness, along with notable productions from Canada, Australia and Europe. Things are then rounded out with a brief overview of genre output in the noughties (arguably TV's *second* golden age), which is so prolific, it deserves a volume all of its own.

As a child growing up in Britain in the sixties and seventies, I became, like most of my generation, used to hiding behind the sofa during the scarier moments in *Doctor Who* (1963–1989, TV), particularly when the Daleks were involved. The much-loved cartoon series *Scooby-Doo, Where Are You!* (1969–1970, TV) also provided some early childhood shudders, while in the seventies, I was lucky to catch the first-run broadcasts of such landmark productions as *Frankenstein: The True Story* (1973, TVM), *Count Dracula* (1977, TVM) and *Salem's Lot* (1979, TV), all of which made me realize one very important thing: that TV horror could be *just* as good and *just* as scary as what the movies had to offer (*Salem's Lot* in particular had me reaching for the light switch, with the surprise arrival of Kurt Barlow being the talk of the school playground the next day). Quality productions such as the aforementioned *A Ghost Story for Christmas* meanwhile taught me it could be quite classy on occasion, too, and a lot more subtle. I also discovered plenty to enjoy in the TV movies of the seventies care of NBC, CBS and, in particular, ABC via their *Movie of the Week* strand, most of which played in the UK and proved that you didn't need massive budgets and special effects to produce a good horror movie (or at least a reasonably diverting one), as was the case with *When Michael Calls* (1972, TVM), *The Eyes of Charles Sand* (1972, TVM), *The Devil's Daughter* (1973, TVM), *A Cold Night's Death* (1973, TVM), *Don't Be Afraid of the Dark* (1973, TVM) and *Satan's Triangle* (1975, TVM) among many others … and all beamed directly into our living rooms.

Indeed, TV has produced classics every bit as rich and worthy of study as those to be found on the silver screen (as well as dreck comparable to any drive-in triple bill), and here, at last, they get to share a little of the love and attention that their big screen counterparts have so far hogged. So make a cuppa, turn down the lights and prepare to grab a cushion for comfort as we enter the golden age of TV horror.…

A brief note on the text: All programs, telefilms and series are followed by the year(s) in which they originally aired, with dates of the month provided within the critique. Series are noted as TV, while movies are noted as TVM. Theatrically released films simply feature a bracketed date. Generally speaking, the book takes the form of a year-by-year narrative, with occasional jumps forwards and backwards in time, the reasons for which will become apparent during reading.

Author's top 20:

Salem's Lot (1979, TVM)
A Ghost Story for Christmas (1971–1978, 2005–2021, TV)
Whistle and I'll Come to You (1968, TV)
Frankenstein: The True Story (1973, TVM)
Count Dracula (1977, TVM)
Schalcken the Painter (1979, TVM)
The Night Stalker (1972, TVM)
The Night Strangler (1973, TVM)
The Norliss Tapes (1973, TVM)
Mrs. Amworth (1978, TV)

Sweet, Sweet Rachel (1971, TVM)
Scooby-Doo, Where Are You! (1969–1970, TV)
La Cabina (1972, TV)
The Twilight Zone (1959–1964, TV)
The Ghost of Sierra de Cobre (1964, TVM)
The Eyes of Charles Sand (1972, TVM)
Daughter of the Mind (1969, TVM)
Gargoyles (1972, TVM)
The Spirit of Dark and Lonely Water (1973, TV)
Crowhaven Farm (1970, TVM)

In the Beginning

*Horror in Television's Stone Age
(the 1930s and 1940s)*

Live from Ally Pally

Launched on 2 November 1936, the BBC (British Broadcasting Service) began broadcasting in black and white in the UK from two studios in Alexandra Palace (affectionately known as "Ally Pally") to a potential audience of less than 19,000 homes within a 40-kilometer radius of the transmitter (18,999 television sets were manufactured between 1936 and 1939, though people could watch in what were termed "public viewing rooms"). The first program broadcast was *Opening of the BBC Television Service* (1936, TV), which went out at three o'clock in the afternoon to what must have been a minuscule audience, given that most people would have been at work at the time.

Programming was pretty primitive during this period, given the limits of the camera equipment, and the fact that everything was live. Programs were thus very much studio bound and consisted mainly of cookery demonstrations, fashion parades, variety items (singers, comedians, dancers) and potted versions of popular plays, although there were occasional outside broadcasts, among the first being the coronation of George VI and a relay from the dog show Crufts. Among the early plays screened were a ten minute scene from *Much Ado About Nothing* (1937, TV) starring Margaretta Scott and Henry Oscar as Beatrice and Benedick, a 25-minute version of *A Midsummer Night's Dream* titled *Pyramus and Thisbe* (1937, TV) starring Wilfrid Walter as Bottom, *The School for Scandal* (1937, TV) starring Greer Garson, and a previously unperformed Agatha Christie play *The Wasp's Nest* (1937, TV), in which the detective Hercule Poirot (played by Francis L. Sullivan) made his small screen debut. There was even a version of J.B. Priestley's *When We Are Married* (1938, TV) transmitted live from a West End theater. Feature films were also shown, among them the Harry Carey western *The Last of the Clintons* (1935), which was first broadcast on 23 August 1937, and the allegorical fantasy *Der Student von Prag* (1935, aka *The Student of Prague*) starring Anton Walbrook, which went out (complete with subtitles) a year later on 14 August 1938, with a rerun following on 5 September.

However, specifically produced fantasy and horror programs were in short supply during these very early years, among them a 35-minute version of Karel Capek's 1920 science fiction play *R.U.R.* (1938, TV, aka *Rossumovi Univerzalni Roboti* and *Rossum's Universal Robots*), which was first performed in 1921, and remains of passing note for introducing the word "robot" into the English language (the word was actually devised by Capek's older brother Josef). Set in a factory that produces artificial people from synthetic matter, the piece culminates in a rebellion of the initially servile replicants that ultimately leads to the extinction of the human race. Broadcast at 3:20 p.m. on 11 February 1938 (with a repeat later the same day at 9:20 p.m.), the program featured Evan John, Larry Silverstone, Connaught Stanley, Derek Bond, Harvey Braban and Cherry Cottrell, and was produced by Jan Bussell, who would also go on to write, produce and direct a remake (again for the BBC) in 1948, this time featuring Anthony Eustrel, Pamela Stirling and future *Doctor Who* star Patrick Troughton as one of the disaffected robots (the play had previously been filmed for the big screen in the Soviet Union as *Gibel sensatsii* [1935, aka *Loss of Feeling*]).

A prolific hand during TV's early years, Jan Bussell was behind the broadcast of many teleplays, among them the aforementioned *Pyramus and Thisbe* (1937, TV), as well as a version of F. Anstey's popular 1882 age reversal fantasy *Vice Versa* (1937, TV), in which a father and son (Richard Goolden and Nigel Stock) find themselves swapping places, and a 40-minute presentation of the 1923 Arnold Ridley classic *The Ghost Train* (1937, TV), in which a disparate group of travellers (among them John Counsell, Hugh Dempster and Daphne Riggs) find themselves stranded at an apparently haunted rural train station overnight (in its review, *The Times* seems to have been particularly impressed by the production's sound effects, notably "the wind-machine working overtime from the start, doors opening spontaneously as on the best-ordered stages, bells tinkling ominously," along with "an excellent train flying madly by beyond the waiting-room windows").

I, robot. A moment from the early tele-fantasy *R.U.R.* (1938, TV), in which the cast sport costumes designed by Mary Allan, whose contribution was deemed important enough to rate a credit in the *Radio Times*. From left to right: Connaught Stanleigh, Derek Bond, Larry Silverstone and (sitting) Evan John (BBC).

Other programs with a fantasy or horror theme made by the BBC during this period include a version of Edgar Allan Poe's 1843 short story *The Tell-Tale Heart* (1939, TV), which was adapted by Michael Hogan and directed by Frank Wisbar, who would later go on to direct and astonishing 214 episodes of the American series *Fireside Theatre* (1949– 1955, TV). In the program the central character attempts to convince himself that he remains sane despite having murdered an old man with a "vulture eye" whose body he has dismembered and hidden underneath his floorboards, only to become convinced that he can still hear the man's heart beating, all of which leads to his inevitable downfall. Featuring Ernest Milton as the guilty party and A. Harding Steerman as the victim, the 25-minute drama was produced by Dallas Bower and contained music by James Hartley, which was performed by The BBC Television Orchestra. Broadcast on 4 January 1939, the story became something of a TV staple, being remade a number of times down the decades.

A half-hour version of W.W. Jacobs' 1902 story *The Monkey's Paw* (1939, TV) followed on 17 April 1939. In it, a grieving couple (Eliot Makeham and Olive Walter) use a talisman to wish for the return of their recently deceased son. The story was adapted by Louis N. Parker from his 1907 stage version and produced by Moultrie R. Kelsall, who was also responsible for a presentation of the 1930 James Birdie play *The Anatomist* (1939, TV), which aired on 2 June 1939. In it, 19th-century physician Dr. Knox (Andrew Cruickshank) uses the services of two grave robbers, Burke and Hare (W.G. Fay and Harry Hutchinson), to procure cadavers for him to experiment upon, but when bodies start to run low, they resort to dastardly measures in order to keep up the supply. Another play by Karel Capek was also presented on 30 May 1939. This was a version of his 1921 allegory *The Insect Play* (1939, TVM [original title *Ze zivota hmyzu*]), which had been written in collaboration with his brother Josef. Produced by Stephen Thomas, it starred Edmund Willard as a tramp who falls asleep in the woods and has a strange dream about insects, each of which represents a human characteristic. Among those playing the bugs and creepy crawlies were Wendy Toye, Geoffrey Wincott, Wilfrid Grantham and Leslie French, who sported elaborate costumes by Hugh Stevenson. Featuring music by Frederic Austin, again played by the BBC Television Orchestra, and sets by Malcolm Baker-Smith, the production seems to have been a fairly extravagant affair.

Unfortunately, just as it was getting going, the BBC ended its fledgling service on 1 September 1939, two days before the outbreak of war, primarily over fears that the transmissions could act as a beacon for enemy aircraft (the Ally Pally transmitter was actually used during the war to send signals to disrupt the navigation systems of enemy aircraft in what was termed the "battle of the beams"). The service remained off air for the duration as a consequence, the last item to be relayed being a Mickey Mouse cartoon, *Mickey's Gala Premier* (1933), which was repeated just 20 minutes after broadcasting started again on 7 June 1946! However, despite the resumption of transmission following the cessation of hostilities, programming initially fell back into its uninspired pre-war mix of musical items, talks and demonstrations.

But as time progressed, the ambitions of the program makers gradually began to widen, among first the plays presented during this initial return to broadcasting being an adaptation of Alexander Pushkin's 1834 story *Pikovaya dama*, better known to English speaking audiences as *The Queen of Spades* (1946, TVM), which was broadcast on 2 August 1946. In it Martita Hunt starred as the ancient Countess Anna Fedorovna, whose ability to always win at cards is keenly sought by a young army officer (Guy Verney). Unfortunately, she dies of fright during his attempt to wrest the secret from her but returns to extract a ghostly revenge. Adapted by

Mervyn Mills and directed by John Glyn-Jones (who also produced with Denis Johnston), the play also starred Ronald Adam, Geoffrey Wincott and Philippa Hyatt, and featured music from Tchaikovsky's opera version of the story conducted by Walter Goehr. All very tantalizing, but sadly now lost owing to the fact that it was broadcast live.

Likewise missing is a version of the 1939 Robert Ardrey play *Thunder Rock* (1946, TV), in which a lighthouse keeper (Robert Sansom), who has taken the job to escape a world on the brink of war, is haunted by idealists from the past. Adapted by Peter Sims and produced by the prolific Jan Bussell, it also featured Frederick Valk, Elsie Wagstaff and Robert Berkeley, and was broadcast on 29 October 1946 (a film version had been made in 1942 starring Michael Redgrave, while the BBC produced a remake in 1955 with Stephen Murray now as the haunted lighthouse keeper).

Broadcast the following year was an adaptation of the 1894 George L. Du Maurier warhorse *Trilby* (1947, TVM), in which a young woman (Sally Rodgers) is hypnotized by the mystical Svengali (Abraham Sofaer) into becoming a great singer. Dramatized by Paul M. Potter and produced by Fred O'Donovan, it also featured Bryan Coleman, Jack Lambert and Morris Sweden, and was aired on 23 October 1947. This was followed a month later by *Sweeney Todd* (1947, TVM), a presentation of the 1847 play *The String of Pearls* by the prolific actor-manager-playwright George Dibdin-Pitt. Another actor-manager, Todd Slaughter, had toured the hoary melodrama in the provinces for years, and had appeared in a film version titled *Sweeney Todd, the Demon Barber of Fleet* Street (1936), which sees a barber avenge himself over past grievances with a cut-throat razor and a chair that tips his victims into the cellar below his shop. Here the title role was taken on by Valentine Dyall in a production that also featured Selma Vaz Dias, Keith Pytott, Erik Chitty and Julian Somers. Produced by John Glyn-Jones, it was broadcast on 6 November 1947 (earlier the same year, Glyn-Jones had produced another melodrama previously filmed by Slaughter in 1935: *Maria Marten, or The Murder in the Red Barn* [1947, TVM]). The next month, the BBC staged television's first production of *Hamlet* (1947, TV). Clearly as prestigious affair, it starred John Byron as the brooding Dane, Sebastian Shaw as Polonius, Margaret Rawlings as Gertrude, Patrick Troughton as Horatio, Patrick Macnee as Laertes, Hay Petrie as the gravedigger and W.E. Holloway as the ghost. Adapted by George More O'Ferrall (who also produced) and Basil Adams (who also directed), it aired on 9 December 1947.

A restaging of *The Monkey's Paw* (1948, TV) appeared on 18 February 1948, this time starring Jack Livesey and Beatrice Varley as the grieving parents wishing for the return of their dead son (Varley would go on to appear in yet another version of the story for the BBC in 1954, this time opposite Henry Oscar). This was followed later in the year by a version of Noel Coward's celebrated 1941 comedy *Blithe Spirit* (1948, TV), which aired on 16 November 1948 under the direction of George More O'Ferrall. In it, novelist Charles Condomine (Frank Lawton) and his second wife Ruth (Marian Spencer) are haunted by the playful spirit of his fist wife Elvira (Betty Ann Davies) after a séance conducted by the dotty medium Madame Arcati (Beryl Measor) conjures her from the beyond (the play had been filmed for the cinema three years earlier by David Lean).

Another favorite also came to the small screen in 1948. This was *Berkeley Square* (1948, TVM), which was based upon Henry James' posthumously published 1917 novel *The Sense of the Past*, which had been successfully adapted for the stage in 1926 by John L. Balderston, who would go on to co-write the popular 1933 film version starring Leslie Howard, as well as such genre favorites as *Dracula* (1931), *Frankenstein* (1931) and *The Mummy* (1932). In it, a young American man named Peter Standing (Manning Wilson) finds himself transported back in time to London during the American Revolution, where he meets his ancestors. Adapted by J.C. Squire and produced by Joel O'Brien, the production also featured Isabel Dean, Maxine Audley, Campbell Singer and Howard Marion-Crawford, and was broadcast on 13 June 1948.

The same year, the BBC broadcast excerpts from *Macbeth* under the title *Scenes from Twelfth Night and Macbeth* (1948, TV), albeit without the witches, who wouldn't make their small screen debut until the following year in a fuller two-hour version of the text which aired on 20 February 1949, in which the characters were played by Rosamund Greenwood, Michael Martin Harvey and Ernest Thesiger, the latter best known for his performance as Doctor Pretorious in *Bride of Frankenstein* (1935). Adapted and directed by George More O'Ferrall, it starred Stephen Murray in the title role, supported by Ruth Lodge as Lady Macbeth, Patrick Macnee as Malcolm, Esmond Knight as Banquo and Mark Dignam as Macduff. Since then, the play has been broadcast multiple times on television around the world, with the witches portrayed by the likes of Jane Rose, Elsie Wagstaff and Eileen Way. *Hamlet* has likewise proved a staple, with the ghost being played by such respected names as Malcolm Keen, Henry Oscar, John Gielgud and Patrick Allen.

The year 1948 also saw the broadcast of *Thark* (TV), a version of Ben Travers' 1927 farce about a supposedly haunted house and its jittery occupants, which had already been filmed for the big screen in 1932 with its original stage cast, among them such noted *farceurs* as Ralph Lynn, Robertson Hare, Tom Walls and Claude Hulbert. Produced by Eric Fawcett, the production aired on 24 April 1948 with a cast that here included Erik Chitty, Gibb McLaughlin, Joan Mundy, Muriel George, Eleanor Summerfield and Kenneth Kove. Later the same year also saw the transmission of *The Case of Mr. Pelham* (1948, TV), in which a dull businessman (William Mervyn) begins to suspect that a doppelganger is gradually taking over his life. Adapted by Duncan Ross from a 1940 story by Anthony Armstrong, itself taken from an idea by Ian Messiter, it was produced by Ian Atkins and also featured Eleanor Summerfield, Erik Chitty and Gordon Tanner. Broadcast on 30 October 1948, it was later remade by the BBC in 1955 (using the same script) with Richard Wattis in the role of Pelham. This slightly pre-empted another version, made as an installment of *Alfred Hitchcock Presents* (1955–1962, TV), more of which in due course.

The following year, the corporation staged an hour-long adaptation of H.G. Well's 1895 novel *The Time Machine* (1949, TVM), which was written and produced by Robert Barr, and aired on 25 January 1949. According to the *Radio Times*' description of the program, Russell Napier played "a time traveller who projects himself into the year 802,701 A.D., and journeys onwards into the twilight of the world." A fairly ambitious affair, the program was designed by Barry Learoyd, and also featured Mary Donn, Christopher Gill, Eugene Leahy, Anthony Nicholls, George

Stanford and Dilys Laye. This was succeeded by a presentation of J.B. Priestley's 1937 play *I Have Been Here Before* (1949, TVM), which aired on 29 May 1949. In it, an elderly German professor (Gerard Heinz) helps to change the lives of several guests at a Yorkshire inn following a precognitive dream, preventing an impending suicide as a result of his intervention. Produced by Harold Clayton, it also featured Bernard Lee, Gwen Bacon, Arthur Hambling and John Robinson.

The Big Apple Bites Back

Meanwhile, in America, television had begun to air commercially in New York in 1941 via NBC and CBS, with programming not dissimilar to that of the BBC. Likewise, broadcasting was, save for a handful of minor stations, suspended once the U.S. became involved in the war, though by 1944, new licenses were already being granted. However, an earlier experiment with the medium via what was termed "mechanical television" (a low-resolution scanning system) had produced *The Television Ghost* (1931–1933, TV), a 15-minute talking head series produced by CBS and broadcast in New York City via W2XAB, in which the ghosts of murder victims recount how they came to be killed. Featuring George Kelting (later Artells Dickson) as the weekly storyteller, the series was little more than a fixed shot of the actor sporting white make-up and a bed sheet as he narrated each episode (the program's visual limitations were such that it was also broadcast on radio via W2XE). The show is generally regarded as one of the world's first dramatic series and was shown in a 9:15–9:30 p.m. timeslot between 21 July 1931 and 20 February 1933. Sadly, save for a publicity shot and a few related press cuttings, nothing remains of the show (heralded one newspaper, which ran a copy of the photograph, "Halloween will be a busy night for this television ghost who stalks up and down the wave of W2XAB to prove that spirits are in the air even in this day and age," while another reported that "a woman fainted when the 'Television Ghost' was made up for his appearance over W2XAB").

Halloween Will Be a Busy Night for This Television Ghost, Who Stalks Up and Down the Wave of W2XAB to Prove That Sprites Are in the Air Even in This Day and Age.

Not the best image in the world (nor the best costume for that matter), but this rare still, in need of some serious tuning, features George Kelting in his bed sheet garb as *The Television Ghost* (1931–1933, TV) (CBS/W2XAB).

What we might regard as regular network television (albeit in its most basic form) began broadcasting in the U.S. in New York and Philadelphia from 1944 following a number of experimental broadcasts (among them an hour-long adaptation of Charles Dickens' 1843 classic *A Christmas Carol* [1943, TV] starring William Podmore as Ebenezer Scrooge, which aired on W2XWV New York City on 22 December 1943), and by 1947 it was estimated that there were 30,000 TV sets in the New York area (at a cost of around $400 each), while by 1951, TV had reached the West Coast. The same year, CBS even experimented with color for a period. Notable programs made during this time include the NBC variety show *Texaco Star Theatre* (1948–1956, TV) starring Milton Berle, the ABC western adventure *The Lone Ranger* (1949–1957, TV), and the CBS sitcom *I Love Lucy* (1951–1957, TV), which starred Lucille Ball, and which was notable for being shot on 35mm film by three cameras. Genre programming was still thin on the ground during this period and found it hard to find a place amid the glut of variety shows and westerns, but very gradually, it began to raise its head above the parapet.

The first genre series to leave a mark was *Lights Out* (1946–1952, TV), which began with four specials in 1946 before becoming more of a mainstay in 1949. Produced by Fred Coe for NBC, it was based upon a long running and phenomenally popular radio series which had begun airing in January 1934, and which offered listeners "a midnight mystery serial" (as *Variety* had it) featuring stories involving crime and the supernatural. The inaugural episode of the TV show, *First Person Singular* (1949, TV), which aired on 30 June 1946, focused on an unseen murderer out to kill his nagging wife. Voiced by actor Carl Frank, his actions were relayed by the use of subjective camera, a daring conceit given that the program went out live. Penned by Wyllis Cooper (who had created the radio series) and directed by Coe himself, the episode was described by *Variety* as being "undoubtedly one of the best dramatic shows yet seen on a television screen." By the time it became more of a staple in 1949, the half-hour program had acquired a host (Frank Gallop, later Jack La Rue), a sponsor (Admiral) and a regular director (Lawrence Schwab, Jr.). It was also attracting such established big screen names as Boris Karloff (who appeared in a 1950 episode titled *The Leopard Lady*), Basil Rathbone (who appeared in *Dead Man's Coat* in 1951) and Vincent Price (who appeared in *Third Door* in 1952). Coe was clearly smitten with the use of subjective camera work and went on to produce an entire series titled *First Person Singular* (1952–1953, TV, aka *The Gulf Playhouse*) featuring stories using the technique.

Lights Out also provided opportunities for such upcoming talent as Anne Bancroft, Eva Marie Saint, Jack Palance and Leslie Nielsen, the latter of whom appeared in a total of four episodes, prime among them *The Lost Will of Dr. Rant* (1951, TV) a version of the 1911 M.R. James story *The Tractate Middoth*. Aired on 7 May 1951, it was adapted by Doris Halman, and tells the story of a librarian (Nielsen) who finds himself inveigled in a tall tale involving a lost will that is seemingly hidden in a rare edition of the *Talmud* known as *The Tractate Middoth*, only to find himself haunted by the will's author, Dr. John Rant, a strange, diminutive man with spider webs for eyes. By no means a classic adaptation, the story is crudely presented in long unadventurous takes, as was the wont of the period, yet remains of archival interest for being TV's first M.R. James adaptation, for Nielsen's keen-to-please performance as the unfortunate librarian, and the brief but mildly effective appearances of the ghostly doctor, whose creepy presence is provided by former stage and film star Fred

Ardath in his only television role. Yet despite its deficiencies, the episode somehow maintains one's interest, if only to see what happens next (as of writing, it can be seen in all its glory on YouTube, along with several other examples from the show).

Other entries in the 160-episode series included three Edgar Allan Poe adaptations—*The Fall of the House of Usher* (1949, TV), *The Masque of the Red Death* (1951, TV) and *The Pit* (1952, TV [taken from *The Pit and the Pendulum*])—as well as stories by Ray Bradbury, Dorothy L. Sayers and Robert Louis Stevenson, whose 1891 story *The Bottle Imp*, about a cursed bottle and the imp inside it, was featured in a 1951 episode. Other installments included *The Martian Eyes* (1950, TV), an adaptation of Henry Kuttner's 1948 story *Don't Look Now*, in which a professor (Burgess Meredith) claims he can spot Martians masquerading as humans (this was restaged in 1951 with the same director and much the same cast); *Dr. Heidegger's Experiment* (1950, TV), an adaptation of Nathan Hawthorne's 1837 story about a doctor who has been sent some water from the Fountain of Youth which he tests on some elderly friends (among them Billie Burke and Halliwell Hobbes) with startling effects; *Beware This Woman* (1950, TV), in which a girl (Veronica Lake) claims to be the subject of poltergeist activity; and *Dark Image* (1951, TV), a haunted mirror story in which a husband's second wife (Ann Shepherd) is traumatized by the image of his first (Beatrice Kraft). Along with Lawrence Schwab, Jr., the program also attracted such directors as Delbert Mann and Fred Coe, as well as such contributing writers as Milton Subotsky (who would go on to co-found the horror studio Amicus with Max J. Rosenberg) and Ira Levin (whose novels would include *Rosemary's Baby* [1967], which would be memorably filmed by Roman Polanski in 1968). Arch Oboler, another writer and producer involved with the series, even attempted to revive the show in 1972 with an hour long pilot. Written by himself and Alvin Boretz, the program told the story of a toymaker who creates dolls with the ability to kill. Sadly, despite starring Laurence Luckinbill and Joan Hackett, and featuring a score by Jerry Goldsmith, it failed to find any takers as a series, and has since disappeared into the ether.

Other American TV shows whose remit was drama in general as opposed to horror in particular also now began looking to the work of noted genre writers for adaptation. For example, *The Chevrolet Tele-Theatre* (1948–1950, TV), whose 82-episode run began airing on NBC on 27 September 1948, presented a version of Robert Louis Stevenson's 1878 story *The Suicide Club* (1949, TV) on 2 May 1949, in which Prince Florizel of Bohemia (Bramwell Fletcher) and his friend Colonel Geraldine (Oliver Thorndike) discover and infiltrate a macabre club which helps its unhappy members to end their lives. This was followed by an adaptation of Alexander Pushkin's *The Queen of Spades* on 6 March 1950 (as *Queen of Spades*), in which Basil Rathbone this time starred as the army officer out to gain the secret of winning at cards from an ancient countess (Margaret Wycherly).

However, it was Edgar Allan Poe who proved to be a particularly popular choice given his name recognition, and *The Tell-Tale Heart*, was frequently put before the cameras, perhaps because its limited setting (generally one room) made for an easy life technically during a live transmission. It first appeared on American television in 1947 in a now lost 20-minute version presented by WBKB Chicago. Directed by Helen Carson and written by Bill Vance, who also starred, the program aired on 27

February at 8:30 p.m., and was staged in front of a live studio audience minus commercial breaks. *Billboard* described the program as "a masterful television adaptation" and went on to reveal that "in the public audience at WBKB were two children who started crying with fright at one of the more forceful points in the show." Two further versions of the story followed in 1949. The first of these aired on ABC on 20 February as an episode of *Actors Studio* (1948–1950, TV) and starred Warren Stevens and Russell Collins. A series of 30-minute potted dramas, other episodes broadcast during the show's run included versions of H.G. Wells' 1902 piece *The Story of the Inexperienced Ghost* as *The Inexperienced Ghost* (1948, TV), James Thurber's 1933 story *The Night the Ghost Got In* (1948, TV) and Oscar Wilde's *The Canterville Ghost* (1949, TV). The second version of the Poe story followed eight months later as an installment of *Fireside Theatre* (1949–1955, TV) under the title of *Heartbeat* (1949, TV). Broadcast on 25 October, it starred Richard Hart as the tormented murderer, and was directed by the acclaimed production designer William Cameron Menzies, whose occasional feature credits in this capacity had already taken in *Chandu the Magician* (1932) and *Things to Come* (1936). Menzies had previously helmed a double bill of *The Stronger* (1949, TV) and *A Terribly Strange Bed* (1949, TV) for the show, which were based on stories by August Strindberg and Wilkie Collins, respectively, and which had aired back in June. *Heartbeat* was actually double billed with another story (a piece titled *Mardi Gras*), all of which must have made for a busy 30-minute show (not including commercials).

Broadcast on NBC from the Hal Roach Studios and produced by Bill Finney (who would go on to work with Menzies on a 1950 TV short titled *The Marionette Mystery*), *Fireside Theatre* was made by General Television Enterprises. Amazingly, it notched up a total of 271 episodes during its run, among them the tantalizingly titled *Ghost Story* (1949, TV), which starred Dorothea Jackson and Eda Heinemann, but about which little else is known; *Germelshausen* (1949, TV, restaged 1950), which told the tale of a legendary German city which rises to the surface of the Earth every 100 years; a version of Oscar Wilde's *The Canterville Ghost* (1950, TV); *The Lottery* (1951, TV), a presentation of the disturbing 1948 Shirley Jackson story about a ritual stoning; an adaptation of Charles Dickens' perennial ghost story *A Christmas Carol* (1951, TV), which featured Ralph Richardson as Ebenezer Scrooge and Arthur Treacher, Melville Cooper, Pat Malone and Malcolm Keen as the various ghosts; and *Phantom of the Bridge* (1953, TV), which revolved round a reporter's investigation of an allegedly haunted bridge.

The Tell-Tale Heart next appeared as an installment of *Monodrama Theater* (1953, TV) in an adaption by two-time Edgar winner Jay Bennett starring Martin Kosleck (who simply read the piece before a black drape), while the Canadians had a crack at it in 1955 as an episode of *On Camera* (1954–1958, TV), this time featuring future horror star Donald Pleasance, who also adapted the story. It also appeared as an episode of *Matinee Theater* (1955–1958, TV) in 1956, this time with John Carradine and John Abbott appearing under the direction of the prolific Boris Sagal, who worked from an adaptation by William Templeton, and as a 1960 episode of *The Robert Herridge Theater* (1960–1961, TV) starring Michael Kane as the narrator/madman in an adaptation by Herridge himself. The popular British series *Mystery and*

Imagination (1966–1970, TV) also added it to its list of classic adaptations in 1968, also among them a version of Poe's *The Fall of the House of Usher* (1960, TV), of which more in due course.

Other versions of the story meanwhile popped up around the world, including in Brazil as *Coracao delator* (1953, TV); in Argentina as a 1959 episode of *Obras maestras del terror* (1959–1962, TV [*Masterworks of Terror*]) under the title *El corazon delator* (this particular series also included versions of Poe's *The Facts in the Case of M. Valdemar* and *The Cask of Amontillado*, along with adaptations of work by Robert Louis Stevenson, M.M. Jacobs, Gaston Leroux and Guy de Maupassant); in Germany as *Das verraterische Herz* (1961, TV); in Australia (1961, TV) as a ballet, with the male protagonist now recast as a female (portrayed by dancer Ruth Galene); in France as a 44-minute opera titled *Le coeur révélateur* (1966, TV), with a libretto by Philippe Soupault; in Denmark as *Hjertet der sladrede* (1971, TV); in Poland as *Bicie serca* (1972, TV [*Heartbeat*]); and in Germany again as *Dar verraterische Herz* (1979, TV) featuring Ferdy Mayne as the old man. As well as television, the story has also been filmed countless times as a short subject on film and video.

The Rise of Poe

In fact Poe proved to be something of a go-to author during TV's developing years, and many of his other stories also ended up on screen in some form or another. The half-hour series *Suspense* (1949–1954, TV), which aired on CBS from 6 January 1949, and which was based on a popular radio show of the same name which ran between 1942 and 1962, presented a series of mini plays in which the protagonists frequently found themselves in threatening situations. The show (sponsored by Auto-Lite) clocked up 262 episodes during its run and was directed by the likes of Robert Stevens (who helmed an amazing 105 episodes) and Robert Mulligan (somewhat slacking with 31), among them a version of *The Cask of Amontillado* which aired as *A Cask of Amontillado* (1949, TV) on 11 October 1949 under the guiding hand of Stevenson. In Poe's original 1846 story, a nobleman relates how he murdered his friend over an unspecified insult by walling him up in a wine cellar. Here, the action is updated to Italy at the end of World War II, with Count Montressor (Romney Brent) recalling how he walled up his former stable boy Fortunato (Bela Lugosi) who has become a ruthless Nazi general who has not only murdered his sister, but also stolen his wife. A rather hesitant piece accompanied by cheesy organ music, its most amusing moment comes when the two main characters descend to the cellar by using the same few steps multiple times. It also remains of passing note for a rare TV appearance by horror legend Lugosi, whose only other work on the box included gag cameos as Count Dracula in both *The Milton Berle Show* (1948–1956, TV) and *The Paul Winchell and Gerry Mahoney Show* (1950–1956, TV), and a guest shot on *The Red Skelton Show* (1951–1971, TV), in which he appeared as Professor Lugosi.

The other Poe story to feature on *Suspense* was the non horror piece *The Purloined Letter* (1952, TV), a tale of blackmail involving unscrupulous behavior in the French government starring the once prolific but now barely remembered television actress Mary Sinclair, who appeared in a total of nine episodes of the series, as well as episodes of *Lights Out* (1946–1952, TV), *Fireside Theatre* (1949–1955, TV) and practically every other anthology drama series then playing. Other stars who appeared in the series included Cloris Leachman, George Reeves, Walter Slezak, John Forsythe, Pat Hingle, Sidney Blackmer, John Kerr and Eva Gabor, while the rest of the stories came from the likes of Wilkie Collins, Emile Zola, Agatha Christie, Ray Bradbury and Gore Vidal, the latter of whom won an Edgar for his episode *Smoke* (1954, TV). Other episodes with a genre flavor to them included a version of *The Monkey's Paw* (1949, TV), in which the couple grieving for the return of their dead son were played by Boris Karloff and Mildred Natwick; this was restaged for the series in 1950 with Stanley Ridges now joining Natwick as the grieving parents. There would also be another version in 1953 care of *Your Jeweler's Showcase* (1952–1953, TV) starring Nolan Leary and Una Merkel.

The most important episodes presented by *Suspense*, however, were undoubtedly its two versions of Robert Louis Stevenson's 1886 novella *The Strange Case of Dr. Jekyll and Mr. Hyde*, which aired under the more usual title of *Dr. Jekyll and Mr. Hyde* in 1949 and 1951. The first of these starred Ralph Bell as the scientist who changes his personality after imbibing a potion of his own concoction and proved to be TV's first version of the oft-told story. Adapted by Halsted Welles and directed by Robert Stevens, the program aired on 20 September 1949, while in the second version, which aired on 6 March 1951, Basil Rathbone starred in the dual role, which was again adapted and directed by Welles and Stevens. Sadly, both appear to be lost. In between these two versions, the BBC also had a go at the story in the UK on 14 November 1950 with the fuller titled *The Strange Case of Dr. Jekyll and Mr. Hyde* (1950, TVM), a 69-minute adaptation by John Keir Cross (also lost), in which Alan Judd played Jekyll and Desmond Llewelyn (later to find fame as Q in the Bond films) played Hyde, presumably to make an easier job of the transformation sequences (the cast also included Jack Livesey and Patrick Macnee).

Other shows to "go with Poe" included *Your Favorite Story* (1953–1955, TV), which ran with his 1843 treasure hunt adventure *The Gold Bug* (1953, TV), generally regarded as an early form of detective fiction, the German series *Die Galerie der groken Detektive* (1954–1955, TV), which presented another version of *The Purloined Letter* (1954, TV), and Britain's long running *Armchair Theatre* (1956–1974, TV), which produced a more faithful take on *The Cask Amontillado* (1957, TV). This time the one-hour episode, broadcast on 17 March 1957, featured Paul Stassino as the unfortunate Fortunato who succumbs to Raymond Huntley's Carlo Montressor in the wine cellar below the count's palazzo. Adapted by Juan Cortés and directed by John Knight, it co-starred Adrienne Corri and Lorenza Colville. Meanwhile, *Matinee Theater* (1955–1958, TV), which had already shown *The Tell-Tale Heart* (1956, TV), also presented its own version of *The Cask of Amontillado* (1957, TV), this time starring Eduardo Ciannelli under the directorial reins of Walter Grauman, prior to both of which it had aired an hour-long adaptation of *The Fall of the House of Usher* (1956, TV), with Tom Tyron as the troubled Roderick Usher, who finds himself succumbing to a mysterious malady, just as his sister Madeline (Joan Elan) falls prey to catalepsy, resulting in her being buried alive in the family tomb. Directed by Boris

Sagal, who would go on to helm *The Tell-Tale Heart* (1956, TV) for the series, the program, which aired on 6 August 1956, was notable for being shot in color by Roger Shearman, and though talkative at times, is a surprisingly atmospheric presentation. Tryon is undoubtedly a little too young and handsome to be playing the brooding lead (Vincent Price would make the role his own in Roger Corman's classic 1960 film version), yet it benefits from some unexpectedly lavish art direction care of Spencer Davies and a solidly staged climax in which the crumbling house collapses around the protagonists.

Other stories presented by *Matinee Theater* included adaptations of Nathaniel Hawthorne's 1851 gothic novel *The House of the Seven Gables* (1951, TV), which revolved around the dark deeds a feuding family whose past (in the novel at least) is tainted by suggestions of witchcraft; Robert Louis Stevenson's *The Bottle Imp* (1956, TV); Elsie Milnes' 1951 story *The Ghost of Greenwich Village* (1956, TV); John Cecil Holmes' 1951 play *Gramercy Ghost* (1956, TV), in which a young woman inherits a house that is haunted by the ghost of a soldier from the American Revolution (this had already appeared as a 1949 episode of *Kraft Television Theatre* [1947–1958, TV], which would go on to present a second version in 1955); and *The Hex* (1957, TV), in which a young boy asks a woman to use her voodoo powers to help pull his father from a streak of melancholy. As we shall later see, *Matinee Theater* also presented a number of major genre titles, among them television's first version of *Dracula*.

Other programs to occasionally take in fantasy and horror stories back in the era of live television included the aforementioned *Kraft Television Theatre* (1947–1958, TV), which broadcast a version of *Berkeley Square* (1948, TV) on 21 July 1948. In this presentation, which made used of the BBC script by J.C. Squire, Ralph Nelson starred as the young American Peter Standish, who finds himself transported back in time to meet his ancestors. The series, which was produced by the J. Walter Thompson Agency for NBC, also presented two versions of Barré Lyndon's *Dorian Gray*–style 1939 play *The Man in Half Moon Street*, the story of a scientist who has discovered a means by which to prolong his life to the age of 120 while maintaining the appearance of youth, all of which results in the expected catastrophe when things finally go wrong. The first version, broadcast on 21 September 1949, starred Will Hare as the ill-fated scientist, while the second, which aired on 30 April 1952, starred John Newland, with Anne Jackson appearing in both as the love interest. A film version had been made by Paramount in 1945 starring Nils Asther, which itself was remade by Hammer as *The Man Who Could Cheat Death* (1959), with Anton Diffring in the lead, the actor having already essayed the role in an episode of the British series *Hour of Mystery* (1957, TV) on 22 June 1957, which itself had been preceded by an American adaptation aired on 9 January the same year care of *Matinee Theater* (1955–1958, TV).

Kraft Television Theatre also produced a version of the festive staple *A Christmas Carol* (1952, TV), which it broadcast on Christmas Eve, with Malcolm Keen starring as Scrooge. The show's later follow-up, *Kraft Mystery Theater* (1959–1963, TV), though primarily concerned with twist-in-the-tail thrillers, did nevertheless "buy in" the British second feature *House of Mystery* (1961) to show as part of its run. In it a young couple viewing a house gradually come to realize that the woman showing them the property is actually a ghost. A mildly diverting piece written and directed by the prolific Vernon Sewell (from the play *L'angoisse* [*Anguish*] by Pierre Mille and Celia de Vylars), it starred Nannette Newman and Maurice Kaufmann as the young couple, while Jane Hylton took on the ghostly duties as the mysterious Stella Lemming, who ends the film by disappearing into the building's walls. A further series, *Kraft Suspense Theatre* (1963–1965, TV), stuck closer to its remit, however, simply providing stories of intrigue and suspense.

Elsewhere, *Hands of Murder* (1949–1952, aka *Hands of Destiny* and *Hands of Mystery*), although a crime series primarily devoted to hoary murder plots, occasionally relished in such titles as *The Fetish* (1950, TV), *The Hiroshima Ghost* (1950, TV) and *The Flying Saucers* (1950, TV). Likewise, *Robert Montgomery Presents* (1950–1957, TV), although chiefly concerned with drama, occasionally embraced something a little more fantastical, such as a version of Oscar Wilde's *The Canterville Ghost* (1950, TV). In this particular adaptation of Wilde's 1887 story, Cedric Parker played Simon de Canterville, who was cursed back in the 17th century for an act of cowardice, and for which he will remain doomed as a ghost until one of his descendants performs an act of bravery. Befriended by a young girl who moves into his ancestral home with her family, Sir Simon eventually finds redemption thanks to her intervention. Made by Neptune Productions and broadcast on 20 November from the NBC Studios at Rockefeller Plaza, the hour-long program was of note primarily for featuring child actress Margaret O'Brien as the young girl, a role she had already played in the 1944 film version, in which Charles Laughton had essayed the role of Sir Simon.

Other stories with a genre leaning presented in the series included an adaptation of Nathaniel Hawthorne's *The House of the Seven Gables* (1951, TV), which revolved round the dark deeds of a feuding family (among them Gene Lockhart and June Lockhart); *Nostradamus Berry* (1952, TV), in which a man (Vaughn Taylor) discovers he has the ability to predict the future; *The Outer Limit* (1953, TV), in which a military pilot (Jackie Cooper) returns from the outer atmosphere safe and well an hour after he should have run out of oxygen and fuel; *The Man Who Vanished* (1956, TV), in which a successful middle-aged businessman (Leslie Barrett), pining for his carefree youth, begins to disappear before the eyes of his colleagues; and *Faust '57* (1957, TV), the show's final episode, in which a scientist (Robert Montgomery himself) sells his soul to the Devil in order to resolve a formula, which ultimately proves to be useless to him.

The Canterville Ghost meanwhile continued to do service elsewhere, appearing twice in 1953 as episodes of *Your Favorite Story* (1953–1955, TV), this time with the show's regular host Adolph Menjou playing the ghostly Sir Simon, and *Medallion Theatre* (1953–1954, TV). It resurfaced again in 1957 in a German-made puppet version titled *Das Gespenst von Canterville* care of the Augsburger Puppenkiste in which Sir Simon was voiced by Hans Baur, in 1958 as an installment of *Matinee Theater* (1955–1958, TV), in 1960 as the German *Das Gespenst von Canterville* with Josef Krastel, in 1961 as the Portuguese *O Fantasma de Canterville*, and four times in 1962: as the Swedish *Spoket pa Canterville* starring Stig Gustavsson, as an episode of the

French-made *La théatre de la jeunesse* (1960–1968, TV) under the title *Le fantome de Canterville* with Claude Rich in the lead, the Yugoslavian *Kentervilski duh*, and as a 1962 installment of the prestigious *BBC Sunday-Night Play* (1960–1963, TV), with comedy favorite Bernard Cribbins appearing as the ghost. These were followed by the Spanish *El fantasma de Canterville* (1964, TV), which aired as an episode of the long running drama series *Novela* (1963–1978, TV), the West German *Das Gespenst von Canterville* (in both 1964 and 1965), the Portuguese *O Fantasma de Canterville* (1967, TV) and the Polish *Duch z Canterville* (1968, TV). As we shall see, there was also a 1966 American version, which aired as an episode of *ABC Stage 67* (1966–1967, TV), which was likewise followed by several other versions thereafter.

Picture Perfect

As well as his 1895 play *The Importance of Being Earnest* ("a trivial comedy for serious people"), Wilde's epithet strewn Faustian novel *The Picture of Dorian Gray*, first published in the monthly magazine *Lippincott's* in 1890 and in book form the following year, also proved a popular mainstay with television producers keen for material to fill their anthology shows. The focus of the story is a handsome English aristocrat who wishes away his soul in order to maintain the appearance of youth, while a full-length portrait that has been painted of him begins to record every sin in his increasingly depraved and hedonistic life. Already the subject of several silent films, as well as a highly regarded 1945 version starring Hurd Hatfield and George Sanders, the story first appeared on the small screen in a lost 1953 installment of the sci-fi/horror series *Tales of Tomorrow* (1951–1953, TV). Sadly, little remains known about the episode other than it starred John Newland.

Wilde's story also did service as an episode of the Canadian made *General Motors Presents* (1952–1961, TV [known in the U.S. as *Encounter*]), which was broadcast by ABC. Adapted by John Bethune and directed by David Greene, the program, which aired on 26 October 1954, starred Lloyd Bochner as the corrupt Dorian Gray, Douglas Rain (later to find fame as the voice of HAL in *2001: A Space Odyssey* [1968]) as the portrait's artist Basil Hallward and Donald Davis as Lord Henry Wotton, under whose influence Gray begins to savor the darker aspects of life with increasing fervor. The series went on to rack up an astonishing 303 episodes during its run, among them a version of Pushkin's *The Queen of Spades* as *Queen of Spades* (1956, TV) starring Lloyd Bochner as the army officer keen to learn the secret of winning at cards from an ancient countess played by Mary Savidge (earlier the same year, the Brazilians had had a crack at the story under the title *A Dama de Espadas* as part of their own ongoing drama series *Grande Teatro Tupi* [1951–1964, TV] starring Carlos Zara and Nydia Licia, while the year before, *NBC Television Opera Theatre* [1949–1964, TV] had presented Tchaikovsky's opera version). Other installments in the series included *The Invaders* (1958, TV), in which a young couple (Patrick Macnee and Jill Showell) find themselves warned by a mysterious stranger (Gillie Fenwick) of a curse placed upon the abandoned cottage which they have decided to make their home, and *Children of the Sun* (1958, TV), in which survivors of a nuclear war (among them Lorne Greene and Kate Reid) venture out of their bunker for water, only to encounter mutated humans with glowing eyes.

Dorian Gray was also pressed into service as an episode of the Argentinean *Cuentos para mayors* (1960, TV) under the title *El retrato de Dorian Gray*; as a German TV movie *Das Bildnis des Dorian Gray* (1961, TVM) starring Sebastian Fischer; and as the opening episode of *Golden Showcase* (1961–1964 TV), which was broadcast on CBS on 6 December 1961. A starry occasion, this version featured John Fraser in the title role, George C. Scott as Lord Henry Wotton and Louis Hayward as Basil Hallward, while Cedric Hardwicke was the narrator (as he was for the 1945 film version). Future TV horror star Jonathan Frid also featured in the cast in the supporting role of Mercutio. Executive produced by David Susskind and produced by Jacqueline Babbin (who also adapted the book along with Audrey Gellen), the program, which was clearly a prestige affair, was directed by Paul Bogart, and featured special make-up effects by the legendary Dick Smith, who would go on to work on such large screen horrors as *The Exorcist* (1973) and *Ghost Story* (1981). Sadly, the surviving copy of the program (currently available on YouTube) is bedeviled by horrendous picture problems, yet the dialogue track preserves the strong performances of both Fraser (whom the program purports to introduce) and Scott. Like *The Canterville Ghost*, *The Picture of Dorian Gray* continued to be a television staple for years to come, appearing in versions in 1961 (as an episode of the British series *Armchair Theatre* [1956–1974, TV] starring Jeremy Brett as Gray), 1968 (in a Russian adaptation titled *Portret Doriana Greya* starring Valeri Babyatinsky) and 1969 (as a three-part Mexican series titled *El retrato de Dorian Gray* starring Enrique Alvarez Félix).

Other literary figures to find their work adapted for anthology series include Victor Hugo, whose 1831 magnum opus *The Hunchback of Notre Dame* has likewise proved to be a staple. Memorably filmed in 1923 (with Lon Chaney) and 1939 (with Charles Laughton), it first appeared on television as an episode of *Monodrama Theater* (1953, TV), which featured classics from literature performed as monologues before a black drape accompanied by music. Produced by the DuMont Television Network, the series included readings of, among others, *The Man in the Iron Mask* (1953, TV), *Great Expectations* (1953, TV), *Jane Eyre* (1953, TV) and, as has already been noted, Poe's *The Tell-Tale Heart* (1953, TV). Like the latter, Hugo's novel was adapted by Jay Bennett,

Charm offensive. John Fraser and Susan Oliver get close as Louis Hayward (right) looks on in *The Picture of Dorian Gray* (1961, TV) (CBS/Talent Associates).

and was broadcast on 8 June. *Robert Montgomery Presents* (1950–1957, TV) also broadcast a two-part version of *The Hunchback of Notre Dame* (1954, TV), which was shown on 8 and 15 November, with Robert Ellenstein starring as the deformed bell ringer Quasimodo and Celia Lipton as Esmeralda, the object of his veneration. It was also produced as a Brazilian series under the title of *O Cordcunda de Notre Dame* (1957, TV), with Douglas Norris in the role of Quasimodo, while in 1966 the BBC presented a seven-part version starring Peter Woodthorpe as Quasimodo, Gay Hamilton as Esmeralda and Wilfrid Lawson as the King of the Gypsies. Produced by Douglas Allen and directed by James Cellan Jones from a script by Vincent Tilsely, the complete series is sadly now lost, though as we shall see, further versions have since followed.

Like Edgar Allan Poe, another American literary giant, Henry James, also had his work become something of a staple on the networks. One of his most regularly performed stories was his time travel piece *Berkeley Square* (taken from *The Sense of the Past*), which, as has been noted, had already appeared twice in 1948. It also did service as a 1949 installment of *Studio One* (1948–1958, TV), in which William Price played Peter Standish, the young American who finds himself transported back in time to London where he meets his ancestors; a 1951 episode of *The Prudential Family Playhouse* (1950–1951, TV), with Richard Green as Standish; and a 1959 episode of *Hallmark Hall of Fame* (1951–, TV, aka *Hallmark Television Playhouse*), with John Kerr now in the role. James' 1898 novella *The Turn of the Screw*, the story of a Victorian governess who gradually comes to realize that her two seemingly angelic charges may not be quite what they seem, also appeared several times, notably as a 1955 adaptation by Gore Vidal for *Omnibus* (1952–1961, TV), which starred Geraldine Page as the governess; a 1957 episode of *Matinee Theater* (1955–1958, TV) under the title *The Others* (1957, TV) starring Sarah Churchill; and a 1958 episode of the Canadian series *Folio* (1955–1959, TV) with Theresa Gray. Benjamin Britten's celebrated 1954 opera version of the story has also been presented several times on television, most notably in 1959, 1982, 1990 and 1994. *Omnibus* also offered its viewers *The Horn Blows at Midnight* (1953, TV), in which an angel (Jack Benny, repeating his 1945 film role) is sent to Earth to destroy it with a blow on a trumpet, while *Folio* also featured *The Haunted Post Office* (1956, TV) and the fantasy musical *Salad Days* (1959, TV) by Julian Slade.

Meanwhile, *Studio One*, which went on to accumulate a mighty 467 episodes, beginning with the body in the basement shocker *The Storm* (1948, TV), which it restaged in 1949 and 1953, also included such genre-centric installments as *The Medium* (1948, TV), in which a bogus medium (Marie Powers) feels hands around her neck during one of her séances; *The Rival Dummy* (1949, TV), in which a ventriloquist (Paul Lukas) finds himself increasingly dominated by his doll, which he finally destroys with an axe (this was a remake of the Erich von Stroheim film *The Great Gabbo* [1929], here helmed by Franklin J. Schaffner, who directed an incredible 110 episodes of the show); *Mrs. Moonlight* (1949, TV), in which a young wife wishes herself perpetually young as everyone else around her ages; a forgotten version of *Mary Poppins* (1949), in which Mary Wickes played P.L. Travers' magical nanny 15 years before Julie Andrews won an Oscar for the role in the celebrated Disney film;

The Inner Light (1949, TV), in which a doctor discovers a cure for blindness; a version of *Trilby* (1950, TV), in which a young woman (Priscilla Gillette) is hypnotized into becoming a great singer by a mystic (Arnold Moss); *The Devil in Velvet* (1952, TV), in which a professor (Whit Bissell) travels back in time to save a 17th-century woman from poisoning; *A Connecticut Yankee in King Arthur's Court* (1952, TV), in which an American (Thomas Mitchell) likewise travels back in time, albeit to the court of King Arthur (Boris Karloff), where he does battle with Merlin the magician (Salem Ludwig); *1984* (1953, TV), an adaptation of George Orwell's 1949 novel about a totalitarian society, with Eddie Albert starring as Winston Smith and Lorne Green as his interrogator, Minister of Truth O'Brien; *Cinderella '53* (1953, TV), an update of the classic fairytale, this time set in New York; *U.F.O.* (1954, TV), a Rod Serling original about the editor of a small town newspaper who attempts to put the place on the map by concocting a farfetched story; *An Almanac of Liberty* (1954, TV), in which time stops during a town hall meeting after a stranger (Sandy Kenyon), who has been looking for work, has been beaten up simply for being different; *Donovan's Brain* (1955, TV), an adaptation of the 1942 Curt Siodmak novel about a doctor (Wendell Corey) who keeps a dying man's brain alive in a jar from whence it begins to exert a malignant influence (the novel had already been filmed in 1953); *The Incredible World of Horace Ford* (1955, TV), in which a middle-aged man (Art Carney) travels back to his childhood, only to discover it wasn't the idyll he remembers; *The Staring Match* (1957, TV), in which two angels (one good, one bad) agree to resolve their differences in a staring match in a small town church; and *The Night America Trembled* (1957, TV), an account of Orson Welles' notorious 1938 broadcast of H.G. Wells' *The War of the Worlds*, which co-starred such upcoming names as James Coburn, Warren Beatty, Warren Oates and John Astin.

Other series to delve into the realms of fantasy and horror included *The Philco Television Playhouse* (1948–1956, TV), which presented a version of Dickens' *A Christmas Carol* (1948, TV) starring Dennis King as Scrooge, as well as *Mr. Mirgethwirker's Lobblies* (1949, TV), in which Vaughn Taylor played the title character, who is the only person able to see a race of fairy creatures. Other genre items in the series included *Dark of the Moon* (1949, TV), in which a witch boy (Richard Hart) falls in love with a beautiful girl and requests to become human so as to marry her; an adaptation of Nathaniel Hawthorne's *The House of the Seven Gables* (1949, TV), in which one brother attempts to frame another of murder; *The Strange Christmas Dinner* (1949, TV), a modern day take on *A Christmas Carol* with Melvyn Douglas in the Scrooge role; *High Tor* (1950, TV), an adaptation of Maxwell Anderson's 1936 play in which the owner of a mountain (Alfred Ryder) is helped by the 200-year-old ghost of a Dutchwoman to overcome a group of ruthless businessmen who wish to acquire it for commercial purposes; and *Dear Guest and Ghost* (1950, TV), in which a ghost helps a mother with her troublesome children. Other versions of *A Christmas Carol* made during this period include a 1947 adaptation starring John Carradine as Scrooge, which was produced and aired by the DuMont Television Network on 25 December 1947, and a 25-minute 1949 production made via Jerry Fairbanks Productions titled *The Christmas Carol*, which was narrated by Vincent Price and starred Taylor Holmes as Ebenezer Scrooge (spelled Ebeneezer in the opening and closing credits), and which aired in syndication on 22 stations across America on 25 December 1949.

Another spook was featured in a 1951 episode of *Showtime U.S.A.* (1950–1951, TV), which presented a version of *Gramercy Ghost* (the story was subsequently expanded into a Broadway play by its author John Cecil Holm for the 1951 season). Meanwhile, among the expected crime dramas and murder mysteries of its 222 live installments, *Danger* (1950–1955, TV) presented *The Fearful One* (1950, TV), about a young girl who believes that a ferret she has been given has supernatural powers (!); *The Ghost Is Your Heart* (1951, TV), about which no plot summary survives, so it may not actually feature any supernatural elements; and, most tantalizingly, a version of Daphne Du Maurier's *The Birds* (1955, TV), made some eight years before Hitchcock's big screen adaptation. Like all the other episodes, this installment sadly no longer exists, the only information remaining being that it starred Betty Lou Holland, Michael Strong and Ian Tucker, and was adapted by James P. Cavanagh, who would later become a regular writer on Hitchcock's TV show *Alfred Hitchcock Presents* (1955–1962, TV).

Elsewhere, *Pulitzer Prize Playhouse* (1950–1952, TV) presented the 1924 Owen Davis play *The Haunted House* (1951, TV), a comedy melodrama in which an apparent murder is solved with the use of a truth potion, while *Lux Video Theatre* (1950–1959, TV), which began life by showcasing a series of original dramas and mysteries, went on to present a number of Hollywood remakes, among them new versions of *The Heiress* (1954, TV), *Sunset Boulevard* (1955, TV) and *The Enchanted Cottage* (1955, TV), in the latter of which a plain maid and a battle scarred soldier marry and come to see each other as beautiful in the seemingly magical cottage in which they live. *Broadway Television Theatre* (1952–1954, TV) had also presented a potted version of the original 1921 Arthur Wing Pinero play (first performed in 1923) on which it was based back in 1952 starring Judith Evelyn. Other genre pieces presented by the hour-long program included versions of Alberto Cassella's 1924 play *Death Takes a Holiday* (1953, TV [original title *La morte in vacanza*]), in which Death (Nigel Green) poses as a mortal being for three days to see what it's like; Karel Capek's *Rossum's Universal Robots* (1953, TV) starring Dorothy Hart and Hugh Reilly; Augustus Thomas's 1907 play *The Witching Hour* (1953, TV), in which a gambler (Warren Wade) uses his skills as a clairvoyant to help him win at cards; Mary Roberts Reinhart and Avery Hopwood's 1920 play *The Bat* (1953, TV), taken from Reinhart's 1907 magazine serial (novelized in 1908), in which guests in an old dark house are terrorized by a masked criminal dressed as a bat; Bayard Veiller's 1916 play *The Thirteenth Chair* (1953, TV), in which a medium helps to expose a murderer; and yet another version of John Cecil Holmes' *The Gramercy Ghost* (1954, TV), this time starring Richard Hylton and Veronica Lake. The long running Canadian series *On Camera* (1954–1958, TV), whose 179 episodes began airing on CBC 2 October 1954, meanwhile presented yet another version of Robert Louis Stevenson's *The Bottle Imp* (1954, TV) along with (as has already been noted) an adaptation of *The Tell-Tale Heart* (1955, TV), as well as a version of James Thurber's 1933 story *The Night the Ghost Got In* (1956, TV).

Questions in the House

Over in the UK, the prestigious *BBC Sunday-Night Theatre* (1950–1959, TV) presented versions of such novels and plays as Josef and Karel Capek's *The Insect Play* (1950, TV), in which Bernard Miles plays the tramp who falls asleep and dreams of insects with human characteristics; a controversial adaptation by Nigel Kneale of George Orwell's *1984* (1954, TV) starring Peter Cushing as Winston Smith and André Morell as O'Brien, whose interrogation scenes were deemed so disturbing that the program actually raised questions in the House of Commons; *The Creature* (1955, TV), a Nigel Kneale original in which explorers (among them Peter Cushing and Stanley Baker) search for the mythical Yeti in the Himalayas and encounter more than they bargained for (the program was subsequently filmed by Hammer as *The Abominable Snowman* [1957, TV], also starring Cushing); Ben Travers' haunted house comedy *Thark* (1957, TV), which starred the noted *farceur* Brian Rix (the play would go on to appear as episodes of *Comedy Matinee* [1961, TV] and *The Jazz Age* [1968, TV]); *Mary Rose* (1959, TV), a version of J.M. Barrie's 1920 play about a girl who vanishes twice, once as a child and later as an adult, only to return with no knowledge of where or with whom she has been (this had already been presented as a 1957 episode of *ITV Television Playhouse* [1955–1967, TV] and would go on to be remade in Spain in 1960 as an episode of *Gran teatro* [1960–1965, TV] and West Germany in 1961); and another dusting down of *Berkeley Square* (1959, TV), this time starring David Knight as Peter Standish, the American who travels back in time to meet his forbears. The program's follow up, *BBC Sunday-Night Play* (1960–1963, TV), brought audiences another version of *The Insect Play* (1960, TV), with Patrick McAlinney as the dreaming tramp; *The Critical Point* (1960, TV), in which a guilt ridden doctor (Owen Holder) involved with cryogenics volunteers to be a human guinea pig for the process after murdering his wife; and the aforementioned version of *The Canterville Ghost* (1962, TV) starring Benard Cribbins.

The BBC also aired two M.R. James adaptations during this period, both of which went out the same night under the umbrella title of *Two Ghost Stories* (1954, TV) on 14 October 1954. These were *Canon Alberic's Scrapbook*, which

Big Brother is watching you! Yvonne Mitchell and Peter Cushing share a tender moment in the controversial *1984* (1954, TV).

was first published in 1895, and *The Mezzotint*, which followed in 1904, both of which were "adapted and presented for television by Tony Richardson," as the *Radio Times* listing had it, and read by Robert Farquarson and George Rose respectively (Richardson would go on to direct such acclaimed films as *A Taste of Honey* [1961] and *Tom Jones* [1963], winning Oscars for best director and best picture for the latter).

The BBC's rival broadcaster, ITV, meanwhile launched their own flagship drama series *ITV Television Playhouse* (1955–1967, TV), which went on to notch up an astonishing 387 episodes, among them a version of Karel Capek's 1921 play *The Makropulos Affair*, here re-titled *The Macropulos Secret* (1958, TV), about an opera singer, Emilia Marty (Eva Bartok), who has lived 300 years thanks to the benefits of a life extending elixir (this had already been performed earlier the same year as an episode of *Matinee Theater* [1955–1958, TV] under the title *The Makropoulos Incident*); *2000 Minus 60* (1958, TV), in which London looks set to be destroyed by a runaway rocket on the eve of the new millennium; and *The Two Wise Virgins from Hove* (1960, TV) by Robin Maugham, in which two spinsters (Margaret Rutherford and Martita Hunt) believe they are about to be visited by Christ.

Another long runner from the same source, *ITV Play of the Week* (1955–1974, TV), managed to notch up an incredible 610 episodes, among them an adaptation of Edgar Wallace's popular 1927 play *The Terror* (1956, TV), about the mysterious goings on at a supposedly haunted manor; a new version of *The Anatomist* (1956, TV), in which the good Dr. Knox (Alastair Sim) employs Burke and Hare (Diarmuid Kelly and Michael Ripper) to dig up fresh corpses from the graveyard for him to experiment upon; Jan Wiers Jenson's witch hunt drama *The Witch* (1958, TV); a version of Thornton Wilder's 1942 play *The Skin of Our Teeth* (1959, TV), a freewheeling drama that switches between the present and the ice age, with the family at its focus having dinosaurs as pets (the play had already been staged for television in America as a 1955 episode of the prestigious *Producers' Showcase* [1954–1957, TV]); *The Night of the Big Heat* (1960, TV), a version of the 1959 John Lymington novel starring Bernard Cribbins, Melissa Stribling and Lee Montague about a remote village on the Salisbury Plain which is invaded by aliens whose arrival is accompanied by an intense heat wave (the story was subsequently filmed in 1967 with Peter Cushing and Christopher Lee under the direction of Terence Fisher); an adaptation of Conrad Aiken's 1931 short story *Mr. Arcularis* (1959, TV), in which the title character (Robert Eddison) goes on an ocean voyage to recover from an operation only to encounter a series of increasingly strange happenings; and *Countdown at Woomera* (1961, TV), a germ warfare thriller set against the first manned mission to the moon in 1968.

Back in the U.S., *Goodyear Playhouse* (1951–1957, TV) ran with Gore Vidal's *Visit to a Small Planet* (1955, TV), in which Cyril Ritchard played Kreton, a visitor from another world who seems eager to instigate a war (the program was subsequently turned into a Broadway play by Vidal in 1957, again starring Ritchard, and a 1960 movie starring Jerry Lewis, albeit without Vidal's involvement). *Four Star Playhouse* (1952–1956, TV) meanwhile featured the fantasy *The Man Who Walked Out on Himself* (1953, TV), in which a man's mirror image walks out on him in disgust when he divorces his wife for a younger model; pretty much a one man vehicle, the episode starred Ronald Colman and was helmed by Robert Florey, whose film credits included *Murders in the Rue Morgue* (1932) and *The Beast with Five Fingers* (1946). *Four Star* also presented *The Devil to Pay* (1955, TV), in which the Devil (Florenz Ames) enlists the skills of an aggressive businessman (Charles Boyer) to overhaul the administration of Hell.

Elsewhere, *The Unexpected* (1952, TV), though it generally involved itself with twist-in-the-tail dramas, occasionally dipped its toe into the slightly more fantastical, as with *Born Again* (1952, TV), in which a man (Billy Halop) suffers nightmares after being told by a fortune teller (Mira McKinney) that he is a reincarnation of someone else; *The Witch of the Eight Islands* (1952, TV), in which a seaman tries to dispose of a cursed bottle (this was a version of Robert Louis Stevenson's *The Bottle Imp*); *The Eyeglasses* (1952, TV), in which a woman (Gertrude Michael) discovers that her husband (Philip Terry) is planning to murder her after donning a pair of spectacles that she has found; and *Beyond Belief* (1952, TV), in which a student helps scientists to create a mechanical mind.

The Pepsi Challenge

Meanwhile, the first season of *The Pepsi-Cola Playhouse* (1953–1955, TV) included such episodes as *Farewell Performance* (1954, TV), in which a ventriloquist murders his wife only to be betrayed by his dummy; *The Psychophonic Nurse* (1954, TV), which sees an electronics expert (Lee Marvin) develop a humanoid nurse to look after his baby; and *The Whistling Room* (1954, TV), in which a Englishman (Edmund Purdom), who has moved to a castle in Ireland so as to be near his fiancée (Barbara Bestar), finds himself plagued by wailing sounds which require the services of Carnacki (Alan Napier), a so-called ghost finder, to quiet them (Napier had previously appeared as Carnacki in a 1952 version of the story made for *Chevron Theatre* [1952–1953, TV]). The show's second season went on to include *A Husband Disappears* (1955, TV), in which a wife fails to recognize her husband when he returns from a hunting trip, and *Petersen's Eye* (1955, TV), in which a lab technician loses his sight during an atomic experiment only to find that he can see 24 hours into the future. The long running *General Electric Theater* (1953–1962, TV), which was hosted by Ronald Reagan, also occasionally ventured into the genre, as per *The Victorian Chaise-Longue* (1957, TV), in which a woman (Joan Fontaine) recovering from an illness on a day bed finds herself possessed by the spirit of a former occupant from 80 years earlier, and *Imp on a Cobweb Leash* (1957, TV), in which a Madison Avenue executive (Fred Astaire) finds himself gifted a mischievous (albeit invisible) imp by a grateful panhandler to whom he has given some change, but the imp compels him to behave increasingly out of character. Other installments in the series included *The Trail to Christmas* (1957, TV), a western take on *A Christmas Carol* directed by James Stewart, with John McIntire in the role of Scrooge (the episode hailed from Stewart's radio series *The Six Shooter* [1953–1954], on which it went out under the title *Britt Ponset's Christmas Carol*), and *The Unfamiliar* (1958, TV), in which an unearthly-looking man rescued at sea may be an alien.

The United States Steel Hour (1953–1963, TV) also got in on the act with *The Man Who Knew Tomorrow* (1960, TV), in which a writer (Cliff Robertson) discovers he has the ability to make his characters come to life, and *The Two Worlds of Charlie Gordon* (1961, TV), an adaptation of Daniel Keys' 1959 short story *Flowers for Algernon*, in which a retarded man (Cliff Robertson again) becomes a genius after an operation, only to gradually slide back to his former mental status (Robertson later filmed the story as *Charly* [1968] and won a best actor Oscar for his performance). Elsewhere, *Ponds Theater* (1953–1956, TV) presented another take on *A Christmas Carol* (1953, TV), which it broadcast on Christmas Eve, with Noel Leslie starring as Scrooge, as well as a versions of Alberto Cassella's *Death Takes a Holiday* (1954, TV) and Robert Ardrey's *Thunder Rock* (1955, TV), in which a lighthouse keeper is haunted by idealists from the past (this had already been presented by the BBC in 1946 and again in 1955 one month following the *Ponds* version. The previously mentioned *Your Favorite Story* (1953–1955, TV), as well as producing versions of *The Gold Bug* (1953, TV) and *The Canterville Ghost* (1953, TV), also included such fantastical tales as Rudyard Kipling's *The Phantom Rickshaw* (1953, TV), Adelbert von Chamisso's *The Man Who Sold His Shadow* (1953, TV), F. Anstey's *Vice Versa* (1953, TV), which was also the subject of a two-part series care of the BBC the same year, Frank R. Stockton's *A Tale of Negative Gravity* (1953, TV) and *The Magic Egg* (1954, TV).

Studio 57 (1954–1958, TV) meanwhile kicked off its second season with *Young Couples Only* (1955, TV), a version of Richard Matheson's 1952 short story *Shipshape Home* in which a husband and wife (Barbara Hale and Bill Williams) come to realize that their weird janitor (Peter Lorre) is actually an alien who is building a spaceship in their tenement's basement, while *Shower of Stars* (1954–1958, TV) presented a version of Dickens' *A Christmas Carol* (1954, TV) starring Fredric March as Scrooge and Basil Rathbone as Marley's ghost, with a score by Bernard Herrmann. Elsewhere, *Conrad Nagel Theater* (1955, TV) kicked off the first of its 26 episodes with a version of Pushkin's *The Queen of Spades* (1955, TV), while *The Alcoa Hour* (1955–1957, TV) contained *The Archangel Harrigan* (1956, TV), in which a man (Darren McGavin) claims that he can fly. It also presented *The Stingiest Man in Town* (1956, TV), an elaborate musical version of *A Christmas Carol*, which was directed by Daniel Petrie and starred Basil Rathbone as Scrooge, and which was originally broadcast in color.

With *Screen Directors Playhouse* (1955–1956, TV), the premise was that noted film directors (among them William Dieterle, John Ford, Ida Lupino and Frank Borzage) took on a television half-hour. Among these was a version of Robert Louis Stevenson's 1885 story *Markheim*. Broadcast on 11 April 1956, it told the tale of a penurious thief (Ray Milland) who kills a shopkeeper on Christmas Day in order to steal his money, only to find himself bargaining with the Devil (Rod Steiger) as a result of his crime. Directed by Fred Zinnemann and shot on film by Paul Ivano at the Hal Roach Studios, it was one of the better pocket-sized dramas broadcast at the time. This was not the first time *Markheim* had appeared on television, however.

It had also done service as a 1952 episode of *Suspense* (1949–1954, TV) under the title *All Hallows Eve* (1952, TV), this time starring Franchot Tone as Markheim and Romney Brent as the Stranger, and would go on to be featured as a 1957 episode of *On Camera* (1954–1958, TV) with Lloyd Bochner as Markheim and Jack Creley as the Stranger, and a 1961 episode of *Rendezvous* (1957–1961, TV), now with Charles Drake as Markheim and Anthony Dawson as the Stranger. Other episodes of *Screen Directors Playhouse* that took on a fantastical air included *Life of Vernon Hathaway* (1955, TV), in which a daydreamer (Alan Young) finds his imaginings coming true; *The Dream* (1956, TV), a period piece set in 1887 France in which a young man (Sal Mineo) is haunted by a nobleman (George Sanders) who may be his dead father; and *The Carroll Formula* (1956, TV), in which a professor (Michael Wilding) discovers a formula that can shrink anything.

Another anthology series, *Star Tonight* (1955–1956, TV), presented Ray Bradbury's 1951 alien invasion story *Zero Hour* (1955, TV), while *Ford Star Jubilee* (1955–1956, TV) featured a color version of *Blithe Spirit* (1956, TV) starring its author, Noel Coward, as the novelist who finds himself haunted by the playful spirit of his fist wife (Lauren Bacall) after a séance conducted by the medium Madame Arcati (Mildred Natwick), much to the chagrin of his second wife (Claudette Colbert). The starry cast had already played together in a touring version of the play, which they also recorded for LP (the play had previously been presented on American TV as early as 1946 as an episode of *NBC Television Theatre* [1946–1947, TV], pre-empting the BBC's version by two years; it also aired as an episode of the Brazilian series *Grande Teatro Tupi* [1951–1964, TV] as *Espirito Travesso* [1953, TV] and would later appear as a 1964 episode of *ITV Play of the Week* [1955–1974, TV] and as a 1978 TV movie [recorded in South Africa]). *Ford Star Jubilee* also presented a musical version of the Maxwell Anderson fantasy *High Tor* (1956, TV), previously presented "straight" by *The Philco Television Playhouse* (1948–1956, TV) in 1950, this time starring Bing Crosby (who also executive produced) and Julie Andrews, with music by Arthur Schwartz. Filmed in just 12 days, it is generally regarded as the first telefilm ever made, but critical reaction wasn't exactly warm (writing in *The New York Times*, Jack Gould described the production as "embarrassingly awkward and inept").

Star power. From left to right, Lauren Bacall, Noel Coward and Claudette Colbert pose for the cameras during the recording of *Blithe Spirit* (1956, TV) (CBS).

The prestigious *Playhouse*

90 (1956–1961, TV), as well as producing such standout dramas as *Requiem for a Heavyweight* (1956, TV) and *The Miracle Worker* (1957, TV), also occasionally turned its hand to fantasy with the likes of *The Star Wagon* (1957, TV), an adaptation of Maxwell Anderson's 1937 play in which an inventor (Eddie Bracken) creates a time machine with which he decides to make a few changes to his personal history (a second version produced by *NET Playhouse* [1964–1972, TV] followed in 1966 starring Orson Bean and Dustin Hoffman). Another time travel story appeared in *Westinghouse Desilu Playhouse* (1958–1960, TV). Titled *The Time Element* (1958, TV), it revolved round a man who continually dreams that he is sent back to Honolulu on 6 December 1941 where he tries to warn people about the imminent Japanese invasion of Peal Harbor. Written by Rod Serling, who would go on to create *The Twilight Zone* (1959–1964, TV), for which this acted as an unofficial pilot, the program starred William Bendix as the time traveller Peter Jenson and Martin Balsam as his psychiatrist, though the twist ending in which Jenson disappears and the psychiatrist learns that his patient is dead, having actually been killed in the Peal Harbor attack, apparently left some critics and viewers somewhat frustrated.

With the BBC's *Saturday Playhouse* (1958–1961, TV), audiences received another version of *Trilby* (1959, TV), this time starring Jill Bennett in the title role and Stephen Murray as the manipulative Svengali, along with an adaptation of John Willard's 1922 spooky house thriller *The Cat and the Canary* (1959, TV), with comedian Bob Monkhouse in the role that Bob Hope had played in the classic 1939 film version. With *Sunday Showcase* (1959–1960, TV), audiences were meanwhile offered an episode titled *Murder and the Android* (1959, TV), in which Rip Torn appeared as the android, and a version of Stephen Vincent Benet's 1936 short story *The Devil and Daniel Webster* (1960, TV), which had already been filmed in 1941, in which a New Englander (Edward G. Robinson) sells his soul to the Devil (David Wayne) in order to save his farm. Finally, *Startime* (1959–1961, TV) presented another version of *The Turn of the Screw* (1959, TV) in which a suitably tense Ingrid Bergman, making her TV debut, played the jittery governess under the direction of John Frankenheimer. Other episodes included *Cindy's Fella* (1959, TV), a western take on *Cinderella* starring Lois Smith and James Stewart, and another version of *Mr. Arcularis* (1960, TV).

Many of the above episodes are now lost or unavailable, and in most cases all we can do is note their existence, while a good many of those that *have* survived are undeniably primitive in their staging, and not always watchable in the modern sense. However, while we must applaud many of the old-style anthology series for at least occasionally including genre items in their weekly schedules, we must note that such pieces were more often the exception rather than the rule. As we've seen, there *were* a few series that specifically focused on fantasy and horror themes, such as *Lights Out* (1946–1952, TV). But other examples gradually emerged from the shadowy corners of the studios, and with them, finally, came the monsters....

Section Two

The Monsters Arrive
(the 1950s)

Cue Frankenstein

During the early years of American broadcasting, programs with a fantasy flavor tended towards science fiction rather than out and out horror, among them such low-budget kiddie fare as *Captain Video and His Video Rangers* (1949–1955, TV), which began airing on the DuMont Television Network on 27 June 1949. Described by its creator Lawrence Menkin as "a western in outer space," it often featured some form of menace, as per the episode *I, Tobor* (1953, TV), in which the Video Rangers find themselves under threat from a giant robot (this particular installment was penned by none other than Isaac Asimov). This was followed by a companion series, *The Secret Files of Captain Video* (1953–1955, TV), which began airing on DuMont on 5 September 1953, in which our hero (played, as before, by Al Hodge), recalls some of his earlier adventures, among them *Revolt of the Machines* (1953, TV), in which a megalomaniac hopes to take over the world with machines, and *The Wendigo* (1954, TV), in which our hero seeks out a mythic creature in the wastes of the North. Other shows that favored science fiction included *Space Patrol* (1950–1955, TV), in which the cast find themselves doing battle with a variety super villains and aliens, among the latter the humanoid Thormanoids who are intent on galactic domination in the installment titled *Threat of the Thormanoids* (1952, TV).

As we've already noted, *Tales of Tomorrow* (1951–1953, TV), which began its 85-episode run on ABC on 3 August 1951, had broadcast a now lost version of Oscar Wilde's *The Picture of Dorian Gray* starring John Newland in 1953. Like other fantasy shows of the period, it also tended to lean towards science fiction, but occasionally embraced a full-on horror subject. Shown on Friday evenings between 9:30 and 10 p.m., the series was the brainchild of Mort Abrahams and Theodore Sturgeon, their idea being to dramatize material from the Science Fiction League of America, which numbered various novels and some 2,000 short stories in its library. Working with the producers Richard Gordon and George Foley, the duo selected a number of established classics as well as new writing for adaptation, which they brought to the screen with the help of a long serving team of personnel, among them technical director Walter Kubilus (who worked on 73 episodes), sound engineer Nick Carbonaro (who worked on 64) and set designer James Trittipo (who worked on 53).

29

The series kicked off with *Verdict from Space* (1951, TV), which was written by Sturgeon himself (from his own story), in which a man (Lon McCallister) on trial for the murder of a scientist (Martin Brandt) reveals the discovery of an alien recording device in a cave, its purpose being to inform those monitoring us when man has achieved the level of intelligence required to enter the atomic age, which would prove to be a threat to them, resulting in action on their part. Inevitably, the authorities disbelieve his story ("The state contends that you deliberately invented this non-existent cave and incredible machine to cover up a sordid case of murder for profit," hounds the prosecutor), but by the installment's conclusion, the young man has been vindicated ("Look, look up there in the sky—thousands of spaceships! The sky is full of ships!"). Despite its hints of *2001: A Space Odyssey* (1968) to come, the program is a fairly unremarkable affair, with cheap sets and declamatory acting, yet it has enough going on to adequately fill its half-hour running time, including a flashback to the discovery of the cave and the machine, and an ending in which the aliens conveniently arrive above the courthouse (if only on the soundtrack).

Other episodes in season one included *Blunder* (1951, TV), in which a scientist's experiments prove to be a threat to the existence of Earth; *The Last Man on Earth* (1951, TV), in which Martians experiment on the last two humans alive; *The Crystal Egg* (1951, TV), in which the title artifact proves to be a live conduit to life on Mars; *Test Flight* (1951, TV), in which a businessman uses his wealth to construct a rocket to take him to Mars; and *The Invader* (1951, TV), in which a scientist's mild-mannered son undergoes a change after diving down to investigate a UFO which has crashed into the sea. Horror legend Boris Karloff also appeared in two episodes, *Memento* (1952, TV) and *Past Tense* (1953, TV), in the latter of which he plays a scientist who has invented a time machine via which he hopes to travel to an earlier period so as to sell penicillin to a pharmaceutical company and thus make a fortune. However, all eyes were on episode 16, which aired on 18 January 1952. This eschewed the show's usual obsessions with Martians and UFOs to present TV's very first version of *Frankenstein* (1952, TV), starring none other than Lon Chaney, Jr., as the Monster, a role he had already played on the big screen in *The Ghost of Frankenstein* (1942).

With just 30 minutes to play with (including ads), Henry Myers' teleplay telescopes Mary Shelley's much-filmed 1818 novel into a to-the-point scenario which sees Victor Frankenstein (John Newland) working from a 16th-century castle on an island in the middle of a Swiss lake, where he has created what he hopes will be the perfect human being, only for something to go wrong and the result of his experiments turn into a rampaging Monster. As directed by Don Medford (who would total 36 episodes of the show, of which this was his fourth), this is a straightforward modernization of the story which nevertheless does attempt to introduce a few moments of style into the proceedings, including a number of from-the-rafters shots as Frankenstein prepares to infuse his creation with life, plus several roving shots which follow the Monster about the castle as he threatens the servants (as he attacks a maid in a corridor, he looms straight into the camera at one point).

As Frankenstein, Newland makes for a rather bland hero, while the actors playing the servants (Peggy Allenby and Farrell Pelly) irritate more than they amuse. The same can also be said of Mary Alice Moore as Frankenstein's concerned fiancée

Elizabeth and Raymond Bramley as his former professor (and Elizabeth's father), though top marks for bravery go to Michael Mann as Victor's young cousin William, who is somewhat brutally manhandled by the Monster during a scene in front of a mirror. Despite his obviously short stature, Chaney makes a strong impression as the Monster, and lumbers quite threateningly about the set in Vin Kehoe's excellent make-up, which eschews Jack P. Pierce's copyrighted square forehead and bolts in the neck look of the Universal films, and instead opts for some convincing scars over the Monster's face and pate. According to legend, Chaney, supposedly drunk, thought the live broadcast was actually a full dress rehearsal, and so when it came to smashing up a chair in a corridor, he picks it up then carefully puts it down, then mimes smashing it, at the same time, saying, "Break, break." Someone, it would appear, had a quick word with him off camera after this sequence, and Chaney completes his role by smashing everything he was required to, including a window through which he takes a backwards fall to his death, and from which he inevitably returns, only to be fried by Frankenstein's electrical equipment, bringing things to a hasty conclusion with another overhead shot.

Other episodes in season one of the show include a two-part version of Jules Verne's *Twenty Thousand Leagues Under the Sea* (1952, TV) starring Thomas Mitchell as Captain Nemo; *Plague from Space* (1952, TV), in which a plague carrying Martian spaceship lands at a USAF base; *World of Water* (1952, TV), in which a scientist develops a solvent which turns everything to water; *Appointment on Mars* (1952, TV), in which three astronauts (among them Leslie Nielsen) land on Mars in search of valuable minerals, only for one of them to feel that they are being watched; and *Ice from Space* (1952, TV), in which a missing test rocket finally returns to Earth carrying a block of ice capable of freezing everything within its proximity (among the cast dealing with the peril is a very young Paul Newman). Meanwhile, season two went on to feature *The Cocoon* (1952, TV), in which a cocoon discovered in a jungle crater is found to contain a dangerous creature (this was the first of eight teleplays for the show by Frank DeFelitta, future author of *Audrey Rose* [1975] and *The Entity* [1978]); *Substance "X"* (1952, TV), in which a community becomes reliant on an experimental food substitute; *The Tomb of King Tarus* (1952,

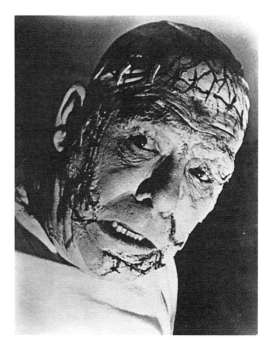

Scarface. Lon Chaney, Jr., as the Monster in *Frankenstein* (1952, TV), TV's first adaptation of the famous story, which appeared as an episode of *Tales of Tomorrow* (1951–1953, TV). In this publicity pose, the make-up is markedly different to that worn by the star in the actual broadcast (ABC/George F. Foley).

TV), in which a team of archaeologists discover an Egyptian tomb containing a king who is 4,000 years old; *The Fatal Flower* (1952, TV), in which a botanist produces a carnivorous flower (shades of *Little Shop of Horrors* [1960] to come); *The Great Silence* (1952, TV), in which a remote community loses the use of their vocal cords; *The Evil Within* (1953, TV), in which a scientist (Rod Steiger) and his lab assistant (James Dean [yes, *the* James Dean]) produce a serum capable of releasing people's baser instincts; and, finally, *What Dreams May Come* (1953, TV), in which a woman learns of her future murder after receiving telepathic thoughts.

Another program that ostensibly focused on science fiction, but occasionally veered into the realms of horror, was *Out There* (1951–1952, TV), which began broadcasting on CBS on 28 October 1951 with an episode titled *Outer Limit* (1951, TV), about which little remains known other than it was adapted by Elihu Winer from a *Saturday Evening Post* story by Graham Doar and starred Wesley Addy who played a character called Commander Xeglon. Other titles in the series included *Ordeal in Space* (1951, TV), *Seven Temporary Moons* (1951, TV) and *The Castaway* (1952, TV). With a story budget of just $650 per episode and a recording budget of $10,000, the programs were hardly lavish, yet story editor Arthur Heinemann managed to make use of material by such writers as Ray Bradbury, Robert A. Heinlein and Theodore Sturgeon, while the casts featured such names as Whit Bissell, Eileen Heckart, Leslie Nielsen, Kim Stanley, Rod Steiger, Robert Webber and Jack Weston.

Another low-budget production was *CBS Television Workshop* (1952, TV), whose 14 episodes began airing on 13 January 1952. Inspired by the radio series *Columbia Workshop*, its half-hour dramas were promoted as "a proving ground for new ideas, new techniques, new personalities," among the latter such upcoming names as Sidney Poitier, Audrey Hepburn and James Dean. The series began with a potted version of Cervantes' *Don Quixote* (1952, TV) starring Boris Karloff and Grace Kelly, which was directed by Sidney Lumet. It went on to include *The Sound Machine* (1952, TV), which was based upon a 1949 Roald Dahl story about an inventor who creates a machine capable of recording the slightest of sounds, including the cries of flowers when they are cut, and *The Gallows Tree* (1952, TV), which presented an account of the hangings that took place during the Salem witchcraft trials.

Although primarily concerned with drama, the long running *Douglas Fairbanks, Jr. Presents* (1953–1957, TV, aka *Rheingold Theatre*), which went on to clock up 156 half-hour episodes during its five-season run, inevitably found space for more macabre stories. Made in Britain at Elstree Studios via Douglas Fairbanks, Jr. Productions for broadcast on NBC (as well as other networks around the world), it featured scripts by the likes of Miles Malleson, Berkely Mather, Hugh Walpole, Nelson Gidding and Gordon Wellesley, and attracted such directors as Terence Fisher, Lance Comfort, Arthur Crabtree, Leslie Arliss, Francis Searle and Bernard Knowles, who found themselves working with such actors as Christopher Lee (who appeared in 16 episodes), André Morell, Robert Beatty, Lois Maxwell, Michael Ripper, Clifford Evans, Wilfrid Hyde-White, Harold Goodwin and Dulcie Gray. The show began its run on 7 January 1953 with *The Accused* (1953, TV), in which an insurance agent and his wife find their lives changed by a murder.

Stories of a darker or more fantastical hue that followed included *The Scream*

(1953, TV), in which a couple (Douglas Fairbanks, Jr., and Constance Cummings) buy a house which is haunted by the agonized cries of a woman; *Happy Birthday* (1953, TV), in which a Frenchwoman (Anouk Aimée) believes that she will die before her 30th birthday; *A Priceless Pocket* (1953, TV), in which a man (James Hayter) finds a pound note every time he puts his hand in his pocket; *The Genie* (1953, TV), in which a young woman (Yvonne Furneaux) discovers that her grandfather possesses the magical lamp that once belonged to Aladdin; *Pardon My Ghost* (1956, TV), in which a Canadian financier (MacDonald Parke) buys a Scottish castle only to discover it to be haunted by a 350-year-old ghost; *The Man Who Heard Everything* (1956, TV), in which a man (Michael Gough) finds that he can hear everything after he suffers an accident; *Goodbye Tomorrow* (1957, TV), in which a writer (Phil Brown) passes off an old manuscript as his own, only to find himself haunted; and *Johnny Blue* (1957, TV), in which a musician (Lee Patterson) is offered a mysterious trumpet to play, on the understanding that he must never hit the highest note.

Over in the UK, the BBC presented a well received production of *The Bespoke Overcoat* (1954, TV), in which a poor tailor finds himself visited by the ghost of a client for whom he was making an overcoat before he died. Adapted by Wolf Mankowitz from his 1953 play (itself taken from an 1842 story by Nikolai Gogol titled *The Overcoat*, aka *The Cloak*), it was directed by Eric Fawcett (who also produced) and broadcast live from Alexandra Palace on 17 February 1954, with Alfie Bass appearing as the ghostly Fender and David Kossoff as the tailor Morry. This in turn led to a 1955 film version, again starring Bass and Kossoff, which was likewise adapted by Mankowitz, directed by Jack Clayton (who also produced) and photographed by Wolfgang Suschitzky. The best regarded version of the tale ("A triumph of talent," praised the *New Statesman*), it went on to win the Oscar for best two-reel short subject at the 1957 Academy Awards. The half-hour Canadian anthology series *Playbill* (1953–1959, TV), which began airing on 9 June 1953, and which went on to notch up 50 episodes, also dipped into the supernatural on occasion, and presented its own version of *The Bespoke Overcoat* (1954, TV), again adapted by Mankowitz, which aired on 29 June 1954. Executive produced by Silvio Narizzano, it starred Paul Kligman, Alfie Scopp, Jacob Reinglass and Isaac Swerdlow. Unfortunately, it now seems to be lost. A variation on the story was also presented as an installment of *Douglas Fairbanks, Jr. Presents* (1953–1957, TV, aka *Rheingold Theatre*) under the title *The Awakening* (1956, TV), this time starring Buster Keaton in an adaptation by Lawrence B. Marcus, while a spoof version titled *Son of Bespoke Overcoat*, appeared as a 1962 episode of the Alfie Bass sitcom *Bootsie and Snudge* (1960–1974, TV).

Back in the U.S. the lighter side of things that go bump in the night was explored in the sitcom *Topper* (1953–1958, TV), in which a banker named Cosmo Topper (Leo G. Carroll) finds himself haunted by a recently deceased married couple, George and Marion Kerby (real life couple Anne Jeffreys and Robert Sterling), who were swallowed by an avalanche on their fifth wedding anniversary, and whom only he can see. Based upon the 1926 novel *The Jovial Ghosts* by Thorne Smith, this had already produced three highly popular films, *Topper* (1937), *Topper Takes a Trip* (1939) and *Topper Returns* (1941), in which the hapless title character had been played by Roland

Young ("Ectoplasm runs riot and blazes a trail of hilarity from 5th Avenue to the French Riviera," ran the tagline for the second film). Notching up a respectable 78 episodes over its two-season run, the program, which was produced by John W. Loveton for CBS, began airing on 9 October 1953, and was very much of its period, featuring familiar domestic situations and misunderstandings, a canned laugh track and endorsement by the cast in the opening and closing sequences of the sponsor's product, in this case Camel cigarettes ("You know the sensible way to find out about cigarette mildness is to try the thirty day test," encourages Jeffreys during one closing segment). All very tame these days, but ably enough performed by its likeable cast, and with surprisingly good trick effects for a weekly TV show.

Enter Professor Quatermass

However, it was the Brits who truly broke new boundaries in genre television with their science fiction epic *The Quatermass Experiment* (1953, TV), which catapulted its writer Nigel Kneale into the stratosphere and led to an internationally successful film version care of Hammer, which not only put the company on the map, but also led directly to such genre defining classics as *The Curse of Frankenstein* (1957) and *Dracula* (1958). Yet as Kneale noted, the six-part series, which ran between 18 July and 22 August 1953, began in somewhat humble circumstances. A lowly contributing writer at the time with only a handful of credits to his name, among them the children's puppet series *Vegetable Village* (1951, TV) and one or two play adaptations and rewrites, he was swiftly pressed into service to pen something of his own choosing when it was realized by the BBC that they had a gap in their up-coming schedules. And so he set to work on "a thriller for television in six parts," as the opening titles have it, dealing with the first manned flight into space, from which only one of the three astronauts involved returns, the other two having somehow disappeared from the sealed spacecraft in which they were travelling. The survivor, Victor Carroon (Duncan Lamont), meanwhile begins to mutate into something rather nasty, much to the concern of the boffin supervising the mission, Professor Bernard Quatermass (Reginald Tate), who has to act quickly if he is to save mankind from the threat.

The writer found his hero's surname in the London phone directory, to which he added Bernard in tribute to Bernard Lovell, the man behind the Jodrell Bank telescope. And such was the intensity of Kneale's schedule, he was still writing the final two episodes as the first were being broadcast live across the nation. By the time these final installments were aired, however, the country had become glued to its TV sets, and the program was deemed something of an event, clearing the streets and pubs each evening of its run. More a think piece than an out-and-out action adventure, audiences nevertheless thrilled to its then-radical concepts and forgave it any shortcomings engendered by its meager budget (said to have been just £4,000). Indeed, such was the strength of the writing, audiences were completely hooked, from the opening title card (accompanied by a blast of Holt's ominous *Mars* theme) to the climax in Westminster Abbey, by which time Carroon has transformed into a giant, plant-like monster (achieved via a glove puppet performing in front of a photographic blow-up of the Abbey's interior!).

Primitive stuff now (the film version is far slicker, despite its own budgetary deficiencies), the program nevertheless remains of historical interest regardless of its crude production values, which modern day audiences might not be so ready to forgive, notwithstanding its status. That said, as the head of the British Experimental Rocket Group, Reginald Tate exudes tweedy authority as Quatermass, while as the unfortunate Carroon, Duncan Lamont appears suitably delirious and angst ridden during his hospital scenes, in which Kneale includes a flashback involving the astronaut and the launch of the rocket, presented care of a previously filmed segment cleverly inserted into the live broadcast ("I've got a Union Jack in case we happen to land on Mars!" he jovially comments during the scene). Elsewhere, the sets by Richard R. Greenough and Stewart Marshall are somewhat restricted and not always entirely convincing, while the occasionally inventive handling by the respected Austro-Hungarian director Rudolph Cartier (who is credited as the show's producer, as was the wont at the time), is at times hampered by the lumbering camera equipment he had to work with (this was Cartier's second collaboration with Kneale following an adaptation of the 1950 Albrecht Goes novel *Arrow to the Heart* [1952, TV] for the flagship drama series *BBC Sunday-Night Theatre* [1950–1959, TV]). Yet none of these shortfalls mattered to audiences at the time—they'd never seen anything like this on the box before, and the show became a national talking point, pulling in an impressive five million viewers for its climactic episode.

Sadly, only the first two installments of the series are available for viewing today, having been recorded by the BBC care of a primitive kinescope process via which the live transmissions were filmed on a special TV monitor. Unfortunately, the results were deemed so poor that the recordings were halted, thus depriving future audiences of a chance to see one of the most important genre programs ever broadcast. Of the subsequent film version, which starred Hollywood actor Brian Donlevy as Quatermass, the BBC agreed to split any potential profits with Hammer. Given that he was only a contributing writer, Kneale himself was excluded from the deal, and even from writing the screenplay, not being considered important enough! However, things soon changed when a sequel was called for, and he and Cartier went on to even greater heights with the follow up *Quatermass II* (1955, TV), by which time Kneale was a staff writer, albeit now with an agent strong enough to stand his corner over the film rights of any material he might pen for the Beeb.

This time, alien life forms are invading Earth via showers of small artificial meteors, of which exposure to the noxious gas within results in the victim's mind being taken over. Quatermass discovers that this has been going on for some time, so much so that the government has already been infiltrated by the alien beings, which have authorized the building of a vast plant on the wilds of Winnerden Flats supposedly to manufacture artificial food, but which in fact is being used to acclimatize a number of larger creatures to the Earth's atmosphere. To his chagrin, the plant (one of several being built across the globe, it transpires) is based on one of the professor's own designs, intended to help man live on the moon, and it is only after infiltrating the site himself, which is patrolled by zombie-like guards, that he formulates a plan to destroy the invaders, which he and his assistant do by travelling to the asteroid from which they are making their advances, the professor's aim being to blow it up before more of the creatures can reach the Earth.

Broadcast from the BBC's Lime Grove Studios from 22 October, the six-part sequel contains more filmed inserts than its predecessor (including location work at the Shell Haven Refinery, which doubles for the acclimatization plant). It is also technically more confident, has more ambitious effects work (care of Jack Kine and Bernard Wilkie), and benefits from a generally quicker pace. Unfortunately, Reginald Tate, who had previously played Quatermass, had died a month prior to transmission, and his hastily sought replacement, John Robinson, is somewhat on the dull side, but he is surrounded by a strong supporting cast, among them Hugh Griffith as the professor's technical assistant Dr. Leo Pugh, future *Steptoe* star Wilfrid Brambell as a tramp who has observed the building of the plant ("The men they've got working in there—*thousands* of them!"), Rupert Davies as Vincent Bromhead, a bluff northern MP who offers to help the professor look into the new specialist unit in the House of Commons, and Derek Aylward as Rupert Ward, who joins Quatermass when he investigates the plant, only to find himself covered in the deadly slime its domes contain when curiosity gets the better of him. This sees him slithering down some steps outside one of the silos, leaving a handprint of the poisonous goo as he does so. Heady stuff for 1955. In fact so potent was some of the program's content considered to be by the BBC (among those scenes in question being one in which pipes at the plant are discovered to have been blocked with "human pulp") that the corporation felt obliged for the first time to issue a warning to viewers prior to certain episodes: "Before we begin the fourth episode of *Quatermass II*, we'd like to say in our opinion that it is not suitable for children or those of you who may have a nervous disposition." Again, audiences thrilled to the series (which was fully tele-recorded), and the screen rights were quickly acquired by Hammer, who filmed it as *Quatermass 2* (1957), with Kneale this time being allowed to write the screenplay (which was nevertheless reworked by the film's director, Val Guest, much to his chagrin). As he had for Hammer's first Quatermass film, Brian Donlevy again played the role of the professor.

By now, Kneale and Cartier were on something of a roll, and a third series was put into production by the BBC. Titled *Quatermass and the Pit* (1958–1959, TV), it began its six-episode run on 22 December 1958 and proved to be the most imaginative yet, its focus being the discovery during building excavations in London of a number of pre-human skulls and a tube-shaped craft, which is at first thought to be a World War II bomb, but in fact turns out to contain several insect-like creatures. Quatermass is brought in by a paleontologist named Roney to help solve the mystery of their origins, his shocking deduction being that they are in fact locust-like Martians who came to Earth five million years ago to genetically engineer primitive mankind, the legacy of which it is discovered is still very much with us today when it manifests itself in several disturbing ways among those involved with the dig, climaxing with riots, mass psychosis and the emergence of a "devil" in the skies of the city.

Having decided to recast the role of Quatermass yet again, Cartier at first approached Alec Clunes (father of *Doc Martin* star Martin Clunes), who turned him down. He next approached André Morell, who had in fact turned down the original series, but who now, thankfully, was happy to take on the role, providing the most authoritative interpretation of it yet. Supporting him was Cec Linder as Roney, Christine Finn as Roney's assistant Barbara Judd, who turns out to have a pivotal role in the developments, and Anthony Bushell as the blinkered Colonel Breen, who has been sent by the military to oversee operations, much to the irritation of Quatermass and Roney, given his various unhelpful interferences.

Broadcast live from the BBC's Riverside Studios (with filmed segments having been pre-recorded at the company's Elstree Studios), the series was a fairly lavish affair compared to its predecessors, having a budget of approximately £17,500. It also contained some of Kneale's most potent concepts, freely mixing science fiction with the occult, the supernatural and the paranormal to almost dizzying effect (*The Times* described his script as "an excellent example of Mr. Kneale's ability to hold an audience with promises alone"). It also featured some impressive sets care of production designer Clifford Hatts, among them the large-scale excavation site and the eye-catching interior of the space tube, and some disturbing special effects, again by Kine and Wilkie, including a rippling floor effect, which is seen during one particularly unsettling sequence involving a seemingly possessed workman who has been drilling into the spacecraft, who trips and falls while running to gain sanctuary in a nearby church.

As before, audience reaction was strong, with the final episode pulling in an impressive 11 million viewers. Again, Hammer made a film of the series, though this time the gestation period was somewhat longer than before, and it didn't emerge until 1967, with Andrew Keir now in the role of Quatermass, Morell having turned down the opportunity to reprise it, though Kneale did get at least to write the screenplay without interference. Following this, the professor went into a period of hibernation, despite talk of Hammer making what was tentatively titled *Quatermass 4*, which was announced in 1969. This finally emerged ten years later as another television series simply titled *Quatermass* (1979, TV), though not before the BBC had begun pre-production on a subsequently abandoned version of the tele-play in 1973 set to be produced by Joe Waters, and for which some effects test sequences were made by Ian Scoones. Euston Films eventually picked up the package on behalf of ITV, and the admired film star John Mills was cast in the title role.

Set in the near future, in which society has broken down and violent gangs rule the debris strewn streets, the story sees the now retired professor searching for his missing granddaughter, who has run away to join a group called The Planet People who, led by the charismatic Kickalong, travel between England's ancient stone circles in a bid to be "taken up" by a mysterious alien force which turns out not to be quite so benign as its followers believe. The series was directed by Piers Haggard and co-starred Simon MacCorkindale as scientist Joe Kapp, whose satellite dish has been monitoring the mysterious signals from space, and which Quatermass eventually makes use of to destroy the force, sacrificing himself for the common good in order to do so, taking his granddaughter, with whom he is finally reunited, with him in the process.

Shot on 35mm film by Ian Wilson, the four-part series was by far the best look-ing of the TV serials, and benefited enormously from Mills' pulling power as Quater-mass, with able support provided by Ralph Arliss as Kickalong, Barbara Kellerman as Joe's wife Clare, and Margaret Tyzack as Annie Morgan, a crusading district com-missioner who helps Quatermass in his plight. Not everything works (an elongated sequence involving a group of elderly people forced to live underground in a scrap yard holds up the action somewhat), but overall the intentions are honorable, and the show builds to a suitably satisfying climax. A high-profile advertising campaign to launch the series in September 1979 proved to be a waste of money, however, as the original broadcast dates had to be abandoned following a strike by ITV technicians, so that when it finally started to air on 24 October without much fanfare, its poten-tial audience was somewhat diminished. And while the series received mixed reac-tions from audiences and critics at the time, it has since grown in status down the years, and is certainly no better or worse than some of its predecessors.

After a trimmed down film version of the series was prepared for foreign distri-bution under the title *The Quatermass Conclusion* (1979), it looked like Kneale was done and dusted with the professor. However, in 1993 Hammer announced their ambitions to make a new version of *The Quatermass Xperiment* (1955) in league with Warner Bros., with either Sean Connery or Anthony Hopkins playing the profes-sor, but sadly nothing came of the proposals. The character eventually emerged from the shadows in the guise of Andrew Keir again in the radio drama *The Quatermass Memoirs*, which was aired by the BBC in 1996, and in which the professor recalled his previous adventures (the series marked Kneale's first return to radio since 1952). The character then appeared more fully formed in *The Quatermass Experi-ment* (2005, TV), a new version of Kneale's original television scripts, edited down to a manageable 90-plus minutes by executive producer Richard Fell. Directed by Sam Miller, and featuring Jason Flemyng as the Professor, supported by the likes of Adrian Dunbar, Mark Gatiss, David Tennant and Andrew Tiernan (the latter as the doomed astronaut Victor Carroon), the program was broadcast live from a disused defense base on 2 April by BBC4 with all the old pitfalls that that entails (fudged lines, missed cues, visible cameras, etc.). Nevertheless, despite its imperfections, the professor's return was generally given a warm reception by the critics, with *The Times* noting that it served "as a reminder of how a clever story, a good script and some decent acting can be just as effective as millions of pounds worth of special effects."

The success of the original *Quatermass Experiment* inevitably produced a hand-ful of British imitators and wannabes which likewise blended science fiction and horror to more variable effect. The first, produced by the BBC's new rival ATV (which had gone on air in 1955), was *The Strange World of Planet X* (1956, TV), a six-part adventure which began airing on 15 September 1956, and was the first series to go out under the umbrella title *Saturday Serial* (1956–1959, TV). In it, scientists discover a means of accessing the fourth dimension (the unification of time and space) via a new formula, which allows them to be transported to the mysterious Planet X. Told via such chapter titles as *The Formula*, *The Unholy Threshold* and *The Dimension Discovered*, the 30-minute installments were written by René Ray, a British stage and screen actress who had also turned her hand to writing short stories and novels (among the latter the 1946 fantasy *Wraxton Marne*). Directed by Arthur Lane (who helmed the first and third episodes, which he also produced) and Quentin Lawrence (who directed and produced the other four), it starred Helen Cherry, William Lucas and David Garth, and was deemed enough of a success for Ray to novelize it and for film producer George Maynard to turn it into a (very) low-budget movie in 1958 (aka *Cosmic Monsters*) starring American import Forrest Tucker, but if another success on the level of the big screen version of *The Quatermass Experiment* was hoped for, it failed to materialize.

The Strange World of Planet X concluded its run 20 October and was followed by the second *Saturday Serial* some two months later on 15 December 1956 with another six-parter, *The Trollenberg Terror* (1956–1957, TV). Written by Peter Key and this time wholly directed by Quentin Lawrence (who also produced), it starred Sarah Lawson, Ronan O'Casey, Rosemary Miller, Stuart Saunders and Laurence Payne, and focused on the investigation of a number of mysterious deaths on a Swiss mountain (the Trollenberg of the title), which prove to be the work of telepathic aliens hiding within a radioactive cloud. Luxuriating in such chapter headings as *The Mind of Ann Pilgrim*, *First Blood* and *The Power of the Ixodes*, it proved to be another ratings success, and likewise prompted its own (slightly better) film version in 1958 (aka *The Crawling Eye*), which again starred Forrest Tucker, along with series holdovers Laurence Payne and Stuart Saunders. This was also directed by Quentin Lawrence and had a screenplay by Hammer's very own Jimmy Sangster.

Saturday Serial continued its run with such thrillers as *McCreary Moves In* (1957, TV), *Web* (1957–1958, TV), *The Truth About Melandrinos* (1958, TV), *The Man Who Finally Died* (1959, TV), which also garnered its own film version in 1963 directed by Quentin Lawrence, *Epilogue to Capricorn* (1959, TV) and *The Voodoo Factor* (1959–1960, TV), in the latter of which a scientist working in the tropics does battle with a spider goddess who has created a disease capable of turning people into arachnids! Penned by Lewis Greifer and directed and produced by *Saturday Serial* regular Quentin Lawrence, the six-parter featured such familiar names as Maurice Kaufmann, Maxine Audley, Anna May Wong (not *the* Anna May Wong), Ric Young and, further down the cast list, Jill Ireland.

Meanwhile, picking up our story again back in 1950s America, the half-hour anthology series *Inner Sanctum* (1954, TV) occasionally presented something a little more off kilter amid its more usual weekly offerings of crime and murder. Made via Galahad Productions, it was based upon a popular radio series of the same name (1941–1952, aka *Inner Sanctum Mystery*), which had been created and produced by Himan Brown, and which featured stories taken from Simon & Schuster's imprint of mystery novels (Universal also produced a series of six *Inner Sanctum* second features in the forties [1943–1946] starring Lon Chaney, Jr.). Brown took on the same duties for the TV show, whose 39-episode run began on NBC on 9 January 1954 with *The Stranger* (1954, TV), in which a young man registering at a hotel finds himself accused of murdering three people (this was preceded by an unaired pilot, *Dead Level* [1954, TV], in which a hearse driver finds himself drawn into a murder plot).

Once settled, the series went on to include *Cat Calls* (1954, TV), in which an architect finds himself suffering from nightmares as a consequence of the cats that constantly howl beneath his window; *Watcher by the Dead* (1954 TV), in which a practical joker bets a friend $10,000 that he can spend a night in a supposedly haunted house accompanied by a corpse; *Ghost Male* (1954, TV [not *Ghost Mail* as sometimes listed]), in which the ghost of an aviator seemingly turns up at his own funeral; *Third Fate* (1954, TV), in which a woman is told in her dreams by a dead killer that she will soon die; and *The Skull Beneath* (1954, TV), in which a man proves that he is able to predict a person's death. There was even an uncredited modern-day variation on *The Queen of Spades*—as *Queen of Spades* (1954, TV)—in which a man bets his life during a game of cards. Each episode began with the opening of a creaking door over which the host (Paul McGrath, later House Jameson) welcomed viewers across the threshold before introducing the week's story ("Come on in for the crime of your life"). A typical studio production of its day, it starred such names as Martin Balsam, Jack Albertson, Barbara Baxley, Everett Sloane, Jack Klugman, Joseph Wiseman and Harry Dean Stanton, was helmed by Alan Neuman and Mende Brown (among others), and featured new writing from the likes of Nelson Gidding, Louis Vittes and John Roeburt, as well as adaptations of stories by Edgar Wallace and Guy de Maupassant ("Remember, a *fiend* in need is a *fiend* indeed. Good night. Pleasant dreams," ran the sign off).

Vamping It with Vampira

Horror also had a new face (and body) in the form of the voluptuous Maila Nurmi who, as her alter ego Vampira, hosted the late-night horror slot *The Vampira Show* (1954–1955, TV), which began airing with a preview titled *Dig Me Later, Vampira* on KABC-TV Channel 7 in Los Angeles on 30 April 1954. The show proper began on 1 May 1954, in which the wasp-waisted Finnish-born actress introduced the Italian melodrama *The Charge Is Murder* (1954, aka *Atto di accusa*). Further films featured during the show's 50-episode run included a mix of ropey second feature thrillers and cheapjack horror, among them *Revenge of the Zombies* (1943), *White Zombie* (1932), *Corridor of Mirrors* (1948), *Bluebeard* (1944), *King of the Zombies* (1941) and *The Woman Who Came Back* (1945). However, it was as much for Vampira's humorous intros as it was for the movies themselves that fans tuned in (quipped the hostess during one intro: "Do you know I've often been asked why I don't light my attic with electricity. Ridiculous—everyone knows electricity is for *chairs*"). Consequently, Nurmi, with her Morticia Addams look (first worn for a masquerade contest which she subsequently won), became something of a cult figure, generating much press attention and going on to appear in Edward D. Wood, Jr.'s, notorious *Plan 9 from Outer Space* (1959) and several other B-movies. Her time in the limelight turned out to be brief, but she has gone down in history as TV's first horror hostess, inspiring many who followed in her footsteps (she later sued the actress Cassandra Petersen, claiming that her own horror hostess personality Elvira, as seen in the series *Movie Macabre* [1981–1993, TV], was based upon her creation). While here, we should also mention Bob Hersh who, as The Advisor, also came to fame for a period as the host of a handful of horror movie shows. These were *Shock* (1958–1959, TV), *Double Shock* (1958–1959, TV), which aired on Milwaukie's Channel 6, and *The Advisor's Mystery Theater* (1959–1960, TV), which aired on Channel 18, and which between them clocked up 120 episodes.

Meanwhile, with *Captain Midnight* (1954–1958, TV, later *Jet Jackson, Flying Commando*), Richard Webb starred as the title character in a 40-episode run of half-hour adventures which began on CBS on 4 September 1954. Produced by George Bilson and made by Screen Gems, the show sees our hero, aided and abetted by his sidekick Ichabod Mudd (Sid Melton), lead a government group known as the Secret Squadron. Based atop a mountain from which they launch their Silver Dart jet via a special runway, they travel the world to vanquish the villainous plans of "evil men everywhere," as the jaunty intro has it. Playing like a Saturday morning serial, the programs mostly dealt with kidnappings, espionage and acts of theft by dastardly foreign agents, and usually ended in a bout of fisticuffs, but occasionally leaned toward the slightly more fantastical, as with such episodes as *The Walking Ghost* (1954, TV), in which the team investigate an apparently haunted mansion, where a local legend has been revived to mask the smuggling of spies into the country, and *The Curse of the Pharaohs* (1954, TV), in which they find themselves sealed in an Egyptian tomb while trying to solve the disappearance of an archaeologist, who had been warned away from the ruins he had discovered by a weird voice speaking out of the darkness. Mostly directed by D. Ross Lederman, the series (which had its origins in a radio program [1938–1949], a film serial [1942] and a comic book [1942–1948]) was pretty much everything a ten-year-old boy could wish for in the fifties.

It was back to the anthology format with *Climax!* (1954–1958, TV), which began its 166-episode run on CBS on 7 October 1954. Like most anthology shows, it offered the expected mix of dramas and thrillers (some of them new, some of them old and familiar), with an occasional dip into horror. It launched with the Raymond Chandler thriller *The Long Goodbye* (1954, TV), with Dick Powell repeating the role of detective Philip Marlowe, which he'd already played to acclaim in the big screen feature *Farewell My Lovely* (1944, aka *Murder, My Sweet*). This was followed by a version of the séance thriller *The Thirteenth Chair* (1954, TV), already presented as a 1953 episode of *Lux Video Theatre* (1950–1959, TV), and a historically notable but dramatically disappointing adaptation of the Ian Fleming James Bond adventure *Casino Royale* (1954, TV), with Barry Nelson in the role of Bond.

Behind the screams. Everyone's favorite ghoulfriend prepares for an appearance on *The Vampira Show* (1954–1955, TV) (KABC-TV Channel 7).

Other installments in the first season included a surprisingly well mounted version of Robert Louis Stevenson's much filmed *Dr. Jekyll and Mr. Hyde* (1955, TV). This version, written by Gore Vidal and directed by Allen Reisner (who would helm an impressive 31 episodes of the show) stars Michael Rennie as the sociable Dr. Jekyll, whose experiments in alchemy (and the accidental use of an "impure salt") result in the splitting of his soul and the emergence of the more sociopathic side of his personality who goes by the name of Mr. Hyde. Co-starring Cedric Hardwicke as Jekyll's friend Mr. Utterson and Mary Sinclair as the girl who becomes the focus of Hyde's desires, the program features music by the young Jerry Goldsmith (who'd already scored *Casino Royale*), and despite being live, is reasonably innovative in its telling, among its devices being a pre-recorded voiceover narration and an effective transformation sequence involving the use of a double (shot from the back), a handful of overhead shots, and a distracting "bulging wall" effect as Rennie was being swiftly made up off camera as Mr. Hyde (though sadly, the make-up itself is somewhat unremarkable). A later transformation meanwhile involved the insertion of a pre-filmed sequence in which Rennie changes into Hyde via several crossfades and the use of a rippling effect (the shot was reversed for a third transformation). As both Jekyll and Hyde, Rennie is sadly a little dull, and the rest of the cast likewise bring little to their roles. Yet thanks to its clever staging, this remains a surprisingly tolerable version of the story, proving that live television could tackle fantastic themes involving visual effects as long as the process was thought through with a certain degree of imagination as it was done here (note that yet another version of the story appeared the following year in the UK; made by ABC Weekend Television for broadcast on the ITV network, it starred Dennis Price, was adapted by James Parish and directed by Philip Saville [who also produced], but its six 30-minute episodes, which included such titles as *Good Evening, Mr. Hyde* and *Mr. Utterson's Encounter*, are sadly lost).

Following this experiment with innovation, *Climax!* returned to its established mix of dramas, thrillers and literary adaptations, leaving it to *Science Fiction Theatre* (1955–1957, TV) to pick up the baton care of Ivan Tors Productions. The show began its 78-episode run on ZIV TV on 9 April 1955 with *Beyond* (1955, TV), which focuses on the testing of a super speed jet. Starring William Lundigan and Bruce Bennet, the program was introduced by regular host Truman Bradley and was shot in color (as was all of season one) and set the tone for what was to follow: a mix of experiments gone wrong and alien encounters, with the emphasis on dull chat and exposition rather than action and effects. Among those contributing scripts and stories to the show were the likes of Jack Finney (whose 1955 novel *The Body Snatchers* has been filmed several times) and Ivan Tors (who penned 23), while directors involved in handling what action there was included future horror king William Castle, Herbert L. Strock (who took on the most episodes, with 19 to his credit), Tom Gries and Jack Arnold (already known for helming such big screen features as *It Came from Outer Space* [1953] and *Creature from the Black Lagoon* [1954]). Guest stars included Whit Bissell, DeForest Kelley, Vincent Price, Beverly Garland and Basil Rathbone, and while the weekly remit was clearly more sci-fi than horror, it did occasionally teeter towards the latter, as in *Legend of Crater Mountain* (1956, TV), in which a teacher

(Marilyn Erskine) finds herself the subject of increasingly violent telekinetic assaults by three siblings, and *Killer Tree* (1957, TV), in which a tree uses a deadly gas to kill people (no, really, that *is* the plot).

A Hitch in Time

The anthology show took a true leap forward with its next incarnation, however. With *Alfred Hitchcock Presents* (1955–1962, TV), which began broadcasting on CBS on 2 October 1955, the Master of Suspense himself hosted and also occasionally directed a weekly half-hour twist-in-the-tail drama which benefited not only from top notch production values, A-list guest stars and excellent writing, but also from being shot on 35mm film, thus allowing for greater directorial control (it also had a catchy title theme: Charles Gounod's *Funeral March of a Marionette*, which became indelibly associated with Hitchcock). If anything was responsible for the decline in cinema attendance in America during this period, then it was shows such as this and *I Love Lucy* (1951–1957, TV), also shot on 35mm, which not only brought the stars directly into the living rooms of the average home, but also began to treat TV as being halfway equal to the big screen, albeit in 4:3 (hence the cinema's rush to embrace such widescreen come-ons as CinemaScope, Cinerama and Todd-AO, not to mention 3D and stereophonic sound).

Unlike many directors of standing, Hitchcock refused to ignore TV, and instead fully embraced the medium. Indeed, he was very much the star of the show, thanks to his comedic introductions and moralistic conclusions, all of which were penned by Jimmy Allardice; as its executive producer, he was also fully in command (the series was filmed at the Revue Studios via Hitchcock's own company, Shamley, named after a Tudor cottage he bought in England in 1928 as a weekend retreat). Among the stars featured in the 268-episode run (the day-do-day producing of which was handled by Joan Harrison and, later, Norman Lloyd) were Joseph Cotten, Ann Todd, Peter Lorre, Claude Rains and Joan Fontaine, all of whom had appeared for the director on the big screen; a number of up-and-coming actors also got a helping hand onto the ladder to stardom via the show, including Charles Bronson, Lee Majors, Joanne Woodward, Robert Redford and Roger Moore. Among those contributing scripts and stories to the program were Ray Bradbury, Sterling Silliphant, Alec Coppel, Roald Dahl, Robert Bloch and Charles Beaumont, while its directors included Sydney Pollack, Boris Sagal, Gordon Hessler, Robert Florey, Paul Henreid, Robert Altman, William Friedkin and Robert Stevenson, all of whom helped to establish it as the Rolls-Royce of anthology shows which others subsequently aimed to emulate (though it did sometimes fall below its own high standards and produce the occasional Model-T).

Hitch himself helmed the first episode, *Revenge* (1955, TV), which featured Vera Miles and Ralph Meeker in a story in which a husband seeks revenge upon a man suspected of attacking his wife. The following episodes followed the established Hitchcock formula that had served his films so well, and featured psychological dramas, thrillers and crime stories involving blackmail, insanity plots and murder for profit. Some, such as *Breakdown* (1955, TV), which Hitchcock again directed, teetered towards horror, with its story of a man (Joseph Cotten) so paralyzed after a traffic accident that he gives every outward appearance of being dead.

Other episodes which embraced more fantastical elements included *The Case of Mr. Pelham* (1955, TV), another Hitchcock installment, in which a dull businessman (Tom Ewell) comes to suspect that a more dynamic doppelganger is gradually taking over his life. The episode was scripted by Francis M. Cockrell from a story by Anthony Armstrong, itself taken from an idea by Ian Messiter, which had already done service on the BBC in 1948 and 1955, the latter of which aired less than a month before the Hitchcock version. Here, given that the episode was filmed rather than broadcast live, Hitchcock was able to make use of a split screen effect for the finale, enabling the confused Pelham to eventually meet his alter ego, during which the doppelganger turns the tables and fully takes over his life, the dull Pelham ending up in an asylum ("Poor fellow, he's been put away ever since, you know"). As for the explanation as to why all this has happened: "No reason. It just did, you see," the interloper flatly explains to his hapless victim. Benefiting from a strong performance by Tom Ewell, who presents well defined versions of both the dull and dynamic Pelham, the episode, though a little on the talkative side, is very much the essence of the whimsical twist-in-the-tail thriller that would soon become a TV staple (the story would later be used as the basis of the film *The Man Who Haunted Himself* [1970], in which Roger Moore gave one of his best performances as the increasingly disorientated Pelham).

Further episodes in the series veering towards fantasy and horror include *Whodunit* (1956, TV), in which a recently deceased mystery writer (John Williams) gets to relive his last day so as to discover who, out of many suspects, actually murdered him; *The Gentleman from America* (1956, TV), in which a wealthy tourist (Biff McGuire) visiting London bets that he can survive a night in a room supposedly haunted by a headless ghost; *The Glass Eye* (1957, TV), in which a woman (Jessica Tandy) falls for a handsome ventriloquist (Tom Conway), only to discover that the dummy is in fact a dwarf in disguise who has been manipulating the "man" she has fallen for; *And So Died Riabouchinska* (1957, TV), in which a detective (Charles Bronson) investigating a murder at a vaudeville theater is helped to solve the case by the intervention of a ventriloquist's dummy; *The Canary Sedan* (1958, TV), in which a psychic (Jessica Tandy) discovers her husband's affair with a countess after hearing a voice while being chauffeured about Hong Kong in a car that formerly belonged to the woman; *Design for Loving* (1958, TV), a near future piece (care of the 1949 Ray Bradbury short story

A lending hand. Alfred Hitchcock appears in one of his introductions for *Alfred Hitchcock Presents* (1955–1962, TV) (CBS/Revue Studios/Shamley Productions/Alfred J. Hitchcock Productions).

Marionettes, Inc.) in which a bored businessman (Norman Lloyd) purchases a robot that looks exactly like himself so that he can escape his wife and job and live the high life in Rio; *Murder Me Twice* (1958, TV), in which a woman (Phyllis Thaxter) murders her husband (Alan Marshal) while under hypnosis at a party, claiming to be a woman from 1853 who, it transpires, had carried out the same crime; *Six People, No Music* (1959, TV), in which a recently deceased department store owner (Howard Smith) revives long enough to let the mortician (John McGiver) know that he wants the cheapest funeral possible; *The Waxwork* (1959, TV), in which a writer (Barry Nelson) spends the night in a wax museum where one of the dummies appears to come to life; *Banquo's Chair* (1959, TV), in which a retired detective (John Williams) hopes to catch a murderer (Kenneth Haigh) by inviting him to a dinner party at which an actress pretending to be the ghost of his victim will appear, but the former copper proves to be the only person able to see the so-called apparition; *Human Interest Story* (1959, TV), in which a newspaperman (Steve McQueen) interviews a man (Arthur Hill) who claims to be a Martian; *The Blessington Method* (1959, TV), a sci-fi piece set in 1980 when people have a life expectancy of 125, which prompts a man (Henry Jones) into accepting an offer to have his increasingly demanding mother-in-law bumped off by a specialist in such matters; *Special Delivery* (1959, TV), a Ray Bradbury story about a young boy (Peter Lazer) whose quick growing mushrooms may in fact be alien life forms responsible for a number of disappearances; *Specialty of the House* (1959, TV), in which a gourmand (Robert Morley) finds himself on the menu at an exclusive dining club; *An Occurrence at Owl Creek Bridge* (1959, TV), in which the noose around the neck of a man (Ronald Howard) being hanged from a bridge for sabotage during the American Civil War breaks and he seemingly makes his escape down river (or does he?); *Man from the South* (1960, TV), in which a young man (Steve McQueen) accepts a macabre bet that if his cigarette lighter won't strike ten times in a row the penalty will be the loss of a finger; *Across the Threshold* (1960, TV), in which a man (George Grizzard) persuades an old flame to impersonate a medium so that his mother (Patricia Collinge) can "contact" his dead father, with whom she is obsessed; *The Doubtful Doctor* (1960, TV), in which a man (Dick York) claims to his doctor that he recently travelled two years back in time following an argument with his wife; *Summer Shade* (1961, TV), in which a young girl (Veronica Cartwright) living in modern day Salem may have befriended the spirit of a witch; *The Greatest Monster of Them All* (1961, TV), in which a has been horror actor (Richard Hale) is cast in a cheap vampire film only to find himself being made a fool of, much to his chagrin; and *The Landlady* (1961, TV), in which a young man (Dean Stockwell) discovers that his landlady (Patricia Collinge) has a propensity for killing her guests and turning them into mannequins!

Once it had reached its conclusion on 26 June 1962, the series was re-launched as *The Alfred Hitchcock Hour* (1962–1965, TV), whose three-season run of 93 episodes began airing on CBS on 20 September 1962. This time the focus was more firmly on murder, mystery and intrigue, though an occasional story with supernatural leanings was slipped in, among them *The Magic Shop* (1964, TV), an adaptation of the 1903 H.G. Wells story in which a young boy (John Megna) disappears in a magic shop, only to return with supernatural powers which he uses to malevolent effect (this would later be remade for Russian TV as *Volshebnaya lakva* [1992, TV]); *Beyond the Sea of Death* (1964, TV), in which a recently married heiress (Diana Hyland) uses a swami to contact her husband after he is suddenly killed; *The Jar* (1964, TV), in which a man (Pat Buttram) buys a strange jar at a carnival whose contents resemble a deformed creature; *The Sign of Satan* (1964, TV), in which a lapsed Satanist (Christopher Lee) is offered a role in a horror film by a Hollywood studio; *The Life Work of Juan Diaz* (1964, TV), in which the mummified body of a Mexican peasant (Alejandro Rey) is exhumed and put on display with others when his family cannot pay the rent on his grave; *Where the Woodbine Twineth* (1965, TV), in which a young orphan (Eileen Baral) is given a doll with which she ultimately swaps places; and *The Monkey's Paw—A Retelling* (1965, TV), in which a businessman (Leif Erickson) uses a gypsy charm to change his luck with drastic consequences. However, what worked well in a half-hour format often seemed stretched at double the length, despite the polished production values and starry casts, yet the program remained popular thanks to the Hitchcock brand and his amusing intros. It was followed two decades later by a remake of *Alfred Hitchcock Presents* (1985–1989, TV), which began airing on NBC on 5 May 1985 with a two-hour pilot consisting of four stories. The following series notched up a total of 77 half-hour episodes, and featured colorized versions of Hitchcock's original intros, along with new versions of old stories from both *Presents* and *The Alfred Hitchcock Hour*, plus several new ones. Directors involved this time included Tim Burton, Joan Tewkesbury, Randa Haines and Atom Egoyan, while the list of guest stars featured Martin Sheen, Van Johnson, David McCallum, Edward Woodward, Barbara Hershey, Sandy Dennis, Dirk Benedict, Arsenio Hall and George Lazenby.

Meanwhile, *Matinee Theater* (1955–1958, TV), which, as we have already noted, would go on to present a number of literary horror stories in its daily hour-long broadcasts, among them versions of *The Baron and the Banshees* (1956, TV), *The Fall of the House of Usher* (1956, TV), *Gramercy Ghost* (1956, TV), *The Tell-Tale Heart* (1956, TV), *The Man in Half Moon Street* (1957, TV), *The Avenging of Anne Leete* (1957, TV), *The Cask of Amontillado* (1957, TV), *The Others* (1957, TV [taken from *The Turn of the Screw*]), *Queen of Spades* (1957, TV) and *The Canterville Ghost* (1958, TV), also aired television's very first version of *Dracula* (1956, TV) on 23 November 1956. Sadly now lost, doubly so given that it was shot in color, Bram Stoker's 1897 grand opus was adapted by Robert Esson and directed by Lamont Johnson, with John Carradine reprising the role of Dracula, which he had already played twice on the big screen in *House of Frankenstein* (1944) and *House of Dracula* (1945), with further interpretations to come in *Billy the Kid Versus Dracula* (1966) and *Nocturna* (1979). The episode also starred Lisa Daniels as Lucy Weston, was hosted by John Conte, and was produced by Albert McCleery. Not even any stills survive of the event. The following year, the show also tackled *Frankenstein* (1957, TV) in an adaptation again by Robert Esson, with the directorial reigns this time in the hands of Walter Grauman. Also shot in color, it starred Gene Raymond, Tom Tryon and Marcia Henderson, with former world heavyweight boxing champion Primo Carnera as the Monster, but it has likewise disappeared.

Other episodes of the show that dealt with horror themes included *Dr. Jekyll and*

Mr. Hyde (1957, TV), again adapted by Robert Esson, with Douglass Montgomery in the roles of Jekyll and Hyde, supported by Lumsden Hare, Lisa Daniels and Patrick Macnee; *The Invisible Man* (1957, TV), with Esson this time in charge of adapting H.G. Wells' 1897 serial (novelized the same year), with Chet Stratton in the title role as the mysterious scientist Griffin who has discovered a means of becoming invisible; *Daniel Webster and the Sea Serpent* (1957, TV), a sequel to Stephen Vincent Benet's *The Devil and Daniel Webster*, starring John Carradine and John McGiver; and a version of Alberto Cassella's *Death Takes a Holiday* (1958, TV), which had already done service on both *Broadway Television Theatre* (1952–1954, TV) and *Ponds Theater* (1953–1956, TV). All in all, not a bad running for an afternoon drama series aimed primarily at housewives.

Meanwhile, over at Disney, the company was churning out a number of kid friendly live action shows, among them *The Adventures of Spin and Marty* (1955, TV) and *Corky and White Shadow* (1956, TV), both of which aired as a segment in *The Mickey Mouse Club* (1955–1958, TV). Also included was a version of the popular Hardy Boys books (the characters had been created by Edward Straytemeyer while the books themselves were penned by Franklin W. Dixon, a pseudonym that covered several writers). The segment launched with *The Hardy Boys: The Mystery of the Applegate Treasure* (1956, TV), a 19-parter which began airing on ABC on 2 October 1956 in which the young detectives (Tim Considine and Tommy Kirk) attempt to solve the mystery of the missing Applegate treasure. This was followed by a second series, *The Hardy Boys: The Mystery of the Ghost Farm* (1957, TV), a 15-parter which began airing on 13 September 1957 in which the boys come across a farm where the owner has died, yet someone, somehow, has been looking after the animals. Mild stuff certainly, given its intended audience, the 12-minute programs were directed by R.G. Springsteen and produced by Bill Walsh, who would go on to co-produce *Mary Poppins* (1964) and *Blackbeard's Ghost* (1968) for the studio. The studio's flagship program *Disneyland* (1954–1997, TV, aka *The Magical World of Disney*), which had begun airing on 27 October 1954, also occasionally ventured into spookier realms, first with an airing of *The Legend of Sleepy Hollow* (1949) on 26 October 1955 (this was taken from the theatrical cartoon *The Adventures of Ichabod and Mr. Toad* [1949]) and then again the following year with *Our Unsung Villains* (1956, TV), in which the Slave of the Magic Mirror hosted a tribute to Disney villains.

Not all TV shows went to series, however. One that fell by the wayside was *The Unknown* (1956, TV), a pilot for an anthology series which was produced by movie mogul Samuel Goldwyn for The Samuel Goldwyn Company, and which appears to have aired on 10 July 1956 (although no broadcaster is named by IMDb). Scripted by Raphael Hayes from a story by Ray Bradbury, little else seems known about the production, save that it featured Leo Gordon, Barry Froner, Peter J. Votrian and Whitey Hautt, and had music by Hugo Friedhofer.

Over in Britain, *Hour of Mystery* (1957, TV) began its 20-episode run on 15 June 1957. Hosted by Donald Wolfit, the series was made by ABC for broadcast on the ITV network and began with a straightforward mystery drama *Duet for Two Hands* (1957, TV) before going on to present an adaptation of Barré Lyndon's *The Man in Half*

Moon Street (1957, TV). Written and directed by Wilfred Eades, the program, as previously noted, starred Anton Diffring as John Thackeray, a corrupt scientist who has found a way of prolonging his life to the age of 120 (the actor would go on to repeat the role in Hammer's big screen version of the story, *The Man Who Could Cheat Death* [1959], albeit as Dr. Georges Bonnet). Other installments in the show included versions of such staples as Emlyn Williams' 1935 play *Night Must Fall* (1957, TV) and Robert Louis Stevenson's *The Bottle Imp* (1957, TV).

Back in the States, another anthology series, *Suspicion* (1957–1958, TV), which ran for 42 episodes on NBC from 30 September 1957, offered pretty much the same mix of crime and murder plots as the highly successful *Alfred Hitchcock Presents* (1955–1962, TV). This was hardly surprising given that the series (which contained a mix of hour-long live and filmed episodes) was executive produced by Hitchcock (via Shamley again) and overseen by his regular *Presents* producer Joan Harrison. The crews (again working out of the Revue studios) were also on the familiar side, among the directors being Robert Stevens, John Brahm and Don Medford, as well as Hitchcock himself (who helmed the debut episode, a ticking bomb drama, *Four O'Clock* [1957, TV]), while the writers included Roald Dahl, Stirling Silliphant and James P. Cavanagh. It also boasted such stars as Bette Davis, Rod Steiger, Ray Milland (who also directed an episode) and Rod Taylor. Like *Presents*, it also dipped into horror on occasion. Among those episodes that did so were *The Other Side of the Curtain* (1957, TV), in which a woman (Donna Reed) suffers a recurring dream about a curtain hanging at the end of a long dark hallway, and *Voice in the Night* (1958, TV), in which two survivors of a shipwreck (Barbara Rush and James Donald) discover that a curious fungus grows on everything on the remote island they have landed upon, including, eventually, themselves (the man comes to resemble "a great, grey sponge," as one of the sailors attempting to rescue them observes). The latter was based upon a 1907 story by William Hope Hodgson, and though talkative, concludes in true *Tales from the Crypt* style (it was later filmed in Japan as *Matango* [1963, aka *Curse of the Mushroom People*]).

Although clearly aimed at children, *Shirley Temple's Storybook* (1958–1961, TV), which was hosted and narrated by the former child star (who also occasionally starred), sometimes veered towards the mildly horrific, given the material that some of its 41 episodes was drawn from. Initially produced by Alvin Cooperman for NBC, season one launched on 12 January 1958 with a lavish version of Jean-Marie Leprince de Beaumont's 1740 fairy tale *Beauty and the Beast* (1958, TV) starring Charlton Heston as the Beast and Claire Bloom as Beauty (the story had already been tackled by the BBC in the UK in 1952 with Brian Nissen and Judy Dyson, and four years later with Inia Te Wiata and Sally Bazely). Other stories featured during this inaugural season included Jacob and Wilhelm Grimm's 1820 story *Rumpelstiltskin* (1958, TV), which featured Shaike Ophir as the title character; Washington Irving's 1812 classic *The Legend of Sleepy Hollow* (1958, TV), starring Jules Munshin as Ichabod Crane, Boris Karloff as Father Knickerbocker and Temple herself as Katrina Van Tassel; and the Grimm's 1812 story *Rapunzel* (1958, TV), starring Carol Lynley as Rapunzel and Agnes Moorehead as the Witch. Season two, which initially moved to ABC before returning to NBC, contained versions of Nathaniel Hawthorne's 1851 novel

The House of the Seven Gables (1960, TV), about a 200-year-old New England house and its inhabitants (among them Temple as Phoebe Pyncheon and Agnes Moorhead as Hepzibah Pincheon); Jules Verne's 1854 short story *Master Zacharius*, broadcast as *The Terrible Clockman* (1961, TV), in which an alchemist (Eric Portman) terrorizes a Swiss village with a man-shaped walking clock; and George MacDonald's 1872 story *The Princess and the Goblin*, presented as *The Princess and the Goblins* (1961, TV), about a princess (Temple) living in a mountaintop castle who discovers a stairway leading down to a world of goblins ruled by the Goblin King (Jack Weston). Directors involved with the series, which was clearly a prestige production of its day, included Mitchell Leisen, Daniel Petrie, David Greene, Arthur Hiller and William Asher.

Horror was also occasionally embraced in *Target* (1958, TV), whose 41 episodes, most of which appear to be lost, were hosted by Hollywood star Adolph Menjou and produced by ZIV Television Programs, which was behind such fifties staples as *The Cisco Kid* (1950–1956, TV), *Boston Blackie* (1951–1953, TV) and *Highway Patrol* (1955–1959, TV), as well as the previously discussed *Science Fiction Theatre* (1955–1957, TV). Among those directors involved were horror veterans William Castle, who helmed the now lost opener, *Breaking Point* (1958, TV), and Terence Fisher, whose own installment *Temporary Escape* (1957, TV), which appears to have been filmed in the UK, is also no longer available. Other titles in the show, which was broadcast on Sunday nights at 10:30 p.m. from 15 March 1958, included *Edge of Terror* (1958, TV), *Death Has Many Faces* (1958, TV) and *The Unknown* (1958, TV). Even more short stories, among them science fiction, fantasy and horror, could be found in the half-hour Canadian series *The Unforeseen* (1958–1960, TV), which aired on CBC from 2 October 1958 and went on to clock up 58 episodes (initially two per week) over its two-season run, the first of which, *A Terribly Strange Bed* (1968, TV), was adapted by Vincent McConnor from the 1852 Wilkie Collins story about a young man who finds himself in danger after having won a fortune gambling in Paris. Other installments included *The Storm* (1959, TV), *The Monsters* (1960, TV) and *The Haunted* (1960, TV). Guest stars included Patrick Macnee, Robert Goulet, Barry Morse, John Bethune, James Doohan, John Colicos and Lloyd Bochner, while direction was in the hands of Charles Jarrott, Eric Till and Peter Francis among others. Unfortunately, like *Target* (1958, TV), most of the episodes now appear to be lost.

That old black magic. Agnes Moorehead as the witch in *Rapunzel* (1958, TV), an episode of *Shirley Temple's Storybook* (1958–1961, TV) (NBC/ABC/Screen Gems/Henry Jaffe Enterprises Inc.).

The Great Beyond

A variation on the anthology format followed next with *One Step Beyond* (1959–1961, TV, aka *Alcoa Presents One Step Beyond*), which differed from other shows given that, rather than fiction, its stories were re-enactments supposedly taken from actual supernatural experiences past and present. Created by Merwin Gerard (who also worked as the program's associate producer), the series' three-season run of 96 half-hour shows offered a mixture of science fiction, fantasy and horror involving ghosts, premonitions and unexplained events. Hosted by John Newland (billed as "our guide into the world of the unknown"), the programs, which were made via ABC Films and Joseph L. Schenck Enterprises on a budget of $40,000 per episode, were mostly written by Lawrence B. Marcus and directed by Newland himself, who, in addition to topping and tailing the stories, also stepped into the action on occasion to pass comment ("The amazing drama you are about to see is a matter of human record. You may believe it or not. But the real people who lived this story, they believe it. They *know*. They took that … one step beyond," he says at the top of each program).

Like most long running shows of the period, *One Step Beyond* attracted a number of loyal personnel, among them cinematographer Dale Deverman (who photographed 88 episodes), editor Henry Berman (who cut 79), art director George W. Davis (who designed 64) and composer Harry Lubin (who scored 88 [he also provided the theme tune, *Fear*]). It also attracted the usual roster of guest stars old and new, among them Jack Lord, Mike Connors, Sig Ruman, William Shatner, Charles Bronson, Warren Beatty, Joan Fontaine, Yvette Mimieux, Whit Bissell, Jocelyn Brando and Patrick O'Neal. Episode one, which aired on ABC on 20 January 1959, was titled *The Bride Possessed* (1959, TV), and starred Skip Homeier and Virginia Leith as Matt and Sally Conroy, a honeymooning couple who find their happiness marred somewhat when she takes on the personality of a murdered woman, previously thought to have been killed in a car accident ("I was murdered, I was murdered, I was *murdered*," she tells the local sheriff). A well mounted pocket-sized drama benefiting from a surprisingly strong performance from Leith in two contrasting roles, it got the series off to a solid start. Other episodes in season one included *Night of April 14th* (1959, TV), in which a woman (Barbara Lord) dreams of drowning just before learning that she is to spend her honeymoon on the *Titanic*; *The Dead Part of the House* (1959, TV), in which a young girl (Mimi Gibson) makes friends with three ghosts haunting the nursery of her new home; and *The Captain's Guests* (1959, TV), in which a couple (Robert Webber and Nancy Hadley) are haunted by a sadistic 19th-century sea captain.

Season two meanwhile featured *Ordeal on Locust Street* (1959, TV), in which a couple (Bart Burns and Augusta Dabney) seek the help of a hypnotist (David Lewis) to deal with their deformed son (Gary Campbell) who resembles a sea monster (only his hands, provided by make-up man William Tuttle, are briefly seen); *The Stone Cutter* (1959, TV), in which a man (Arthur Shields) believes he will die on a certain date because his gravestone has already been cut; and *The Storm* (1960, TV), in which a couple (Lee Bergere and Rebecca Welles) investigate a painting seemingly completed by the ghost of the artist. The first two seasons of the show were filmed entirely in Hollywood at MGM, though for season three, after 21 episodes, the series relocated to the UK and MGM's Borehamwood Studios for the final 13 programs, allowing Newland and his team to make use of such local acting talent as Christopher Lee, Roger Delgado, Donald Pleasence, Pamela Brown, Peter Wyngarde and André Morell. Episodes for this season included *The Gift* (1961, TV), in which a fake gypsy fortune teller (Betty Garde) discovers she has actually acquired second sight; *The Room Upstairs* (1961, TV), in which a woman (Lois Maxwell) is convinced that she can hear a child crying in the house that she and her husband (David Knight) have rented; and *The Tiger* (1961, TV), in which a young girl (Pauline Challoner [billed Challenor]) uses her stuffed tiger to extract revenge on her much hated governess (note that a variation on this story was later used as a segment of the compendium film *Tales That Witness Madness* [1973] under the title *Mr. Tiger*). Following its end, the series proved to be a popular filler in syndication for many years, while in the seventies, a follow up titled *The Next Step Beyond* (1978–1979, TV) appeared, with Newland again hosting and directing 18 of the 25 episodes, several of which were new versions of stories from the original series, among them *Possessed* (1978, TV), which was a remake of *The Bride Possessed* (1959, TV), whose storyline was also reused in *The Invasion of Carol Enders* (1973, TVM).

In Britain in the late fifties, fantasy and horror were still comparative rarities on TV, which perhaps made *The Invisible Man* (1959–1960, TV), which began airing on ITV on 13 June 1959, all the more welcome. Based upon the H.G. Wells novel and the landmark 1933 Hollywood film starring Claude Rains, the series (suggested for television by Larry White) top lined Tim Turner as scientist Dr. Peter Brady, who finds himself (and his clothes) rendered invisible following an accident during one of his experiments. Unfortunately, there seems to be no immediate cure for his predicament, and while working on an antidote, he finds himself called upon by British military intelligence to go on a number of special missions, among them trips to Europe and the Middle East, all of which make use of his newly acquired powers. Produced by Ralph Smart for ITC, the show, which racked up a respectable 27 episodes during its two-season run, was directed by C.M. Pennington-Richards, Peter Maxwell, Quentin Lawrence and, on occasion, Smart himself (who also contributed to a handful of the scripts). Like most ITC productions, it was a few marks up in quality on most programs of the period, given that they also aimed their product at the American market as well as the domestic (CBS aired the show in the States), and while the series couldn't be described as a full-on horror piece as per the original movie (Brady is more a hero in the mold of the later ITC series *The Saint* [1962–1969, TV]), it was nevertheless notable at the time for its (albeit minimal) effects and jaunty storylines, which see Brady involved with crooks and criminals of various types, including gunrunners and extortionists (note that the 1958 pilot featured Robert Beatty as Brady).

Also in the UK, Hammer Films was enjoying success after success with such genre films as *The Quatermass Xperiment* (1955), *The Curse of Frankenstein* (1957) and *Dracula* (1958). The company also hoped to diversify into television, and so approached Columbia—with whom they were then collaborating on *The Camp on*

Blood Island (1958), *The Snorkel* (1958) and *The Revenge of Frankenstein* (1958)—about a series focusing on the continuing exploits of Baron Frankenstein, who had been played by Peter Cushing in their first two features. Columbia took the bait and proposed the making of a pilot episode for the show, whose title was to be *Tales of Frankenstein* (1958, TV). Hammer's regular scribe, Jimmy Sangster, consequently produced a script, *The Single-Minded Blackmailer,* which Columbia nevertheless rejected, preferring to go with

I wear my sunglasses at night. Tim Turner makes an appearance (or rather not) as *The Invisible Man* (1959–1960, TV) (ITC/Peter Rodgers Organization).

their own teleplay, *The Face in the Tombstone Mirror*, which was penned by Catherine and Henry Kuttner, with additional work by Jerome Bixby. They also decided to forego Peter Cushing as the Baron and instead cast Anton Diffring, soon to work with Hammer on *The Man Who Could Cheat Death* (1959), and decreed that filming would take place in Hollywood rather than the UK under the direction of Curt Siodmak, whose own screenplays had included the genre landmark *The Wolf Man* (1941).

Unfortunately, the pilot (made by Columbia's TV arm Screen Gems, with little involvement from Hammer itself) was considered to be so bad that it only made it to air in a handful of late-night slots, and the series itself was quietly abandoned, despite preparations already being afoot for six programs (the second installment, *Frankenstein Meets Dr. Varno*, had already been scripted by Jerome Bixby). Its reputation aside, the episode actually offers a fair stab at a basic Frankenstein story, and the results are certainly no worse than the live 1952 episode of *Tales of Tomorrow* (1951–1953, TV) starring Lon Chaney, Jr. In the half-hour program, the Baron is working on his latest experiment, but needs a fresh brain with which to complete it to his satisfaction, procuring that of a terminally ill sculptor following his death, much to the chagrin of the artist's wife, who had previously approached the baron for help in curing him. Consequently, when she turns up at the castle to have it out with the Baron, the Creature recognizes his former spouse and attempts to abduct her, but in doing so catches sight of himself in a mirror and consequently attacks Frankenstein, chasing him back to the grave from whence his body had been removed, hurling himself back into its depths, leaving the Baron to answer some rather awkward questions about grave robbing from the pursuing authorities.

As the Baron, Diffring is his usual brusque, cold-eyed self, while Don Megowan's Creature lumbers about Carl Anderson's surprisingly lavish sets in the expected manner, smashing every test tube and bell jar to hand (his make-up, care of Clay Campbell, is notably close to Jack P. Pierce's iconic work for Boris Karloff in the original *Frankenstein* [1931], despite it being heavily copyrighted). As for the proceedings themselves, they certainly contain enough incident to keep one watching. Indeed, the handling by Siodmak is commendably brisk, given the amount of plot required to be covered in such a brief running time, and one can't accuse the program of skimping on the basics (its budget was a healthy $80,000). Sadly, despite its plus points, the results were deemed a disaster, and the episode was condemned to the vaults (a DVD finally emerged in 2001). As for Hammer, they instead concentrated their efforts on the big screen, their next Frankenstein outing being *The Evil of Frankenstein* (1964), which actually contained elements from a Peter Bryan synopsis prepared for the abandoned TV show. In fact the studio wouldn't attempt another TV series until the late sixties with *Journey to the Unknown* (1968, TV), which they made in conjunction with Twentieth Century–Fox, and which they filmed in the UK, where they could better control the end product.

Other American shows made during this period that also delved into the realms of science fiction, fantasy and horror included *World of Giants* (1959, TV), a variation on *The Incredible Shrinking Man* (1957), in which Marshall Thompson starred as Mel Hunter, a secret agent just six inches tall, the result of an incident behind the Iron Curtain. With episodes directed by the likes of Nathan Juran, Jack Arnold (director of *The Incredible Shrinking Man*), Byron Haskin and Eugene Lourié, the program, which was produced by ZIV, certainly had strong credentials, yet ran on CBS for only 13 episodes from 5 September 1959. With its low angle photography and large-scale sets of everyday objects and furniture, it benefited from a larger budget than most of its ilk, and though unsuccessful in itself must surely have laid the groundwork for such future shows as *Land of the Giants* (1968–1970, TV).

Running to 38 episodes and thus regarded as more of a success was *Men into Space* (1959–1960, TV), which began its run on CBS on 30 September 1959. Another ZIV production, it followed the exploits of Colonel Edward McCauley (William Lundigan) and his team of astronauts in their adventures on the moon and beyond. Budgeted at a healthy $50,000 an episode, the program benefited from strong art direction and effects work. The opening episode, *Moon Probe* (1959, TV), followed man's first orbit of the moon, but things don't go according to plan, and control of the spaceship is lost at a vital moment. Although the program took its space exploration angle seriously (there were no monsters hidden behind the moon rocks), certain episodes hinted at life elsewhere in the universe, among them *Is There Another Civilization?* (1960, TV), which revolved around the discovery of a meteorite that proves to have been artificially made, and *Mystery Satellite* (1960, TV), in which the mission's spaceship is pursued by a mysterious object which hails from somewhere other than Earth.

More macabre fare was meanwhile on offer in the anthology series *13 Demon Street* (1959, TV), which saw the return to television of horror star Lon Chaney, Jr., albeit purely in the capacity of the show's host. "Number thirteen Demon Street. I am condemned to live here, to suffer on this Earth forever, as a punishment for my crime. It is said that no greater outrage was ever committed by any mortal, but should I find a crime more terrible than mine, my punishment will end," intones the actor in his intro, following which that installment's story is introduced. An American-Swedish co-production made at the Nordisk Tonefilm Studios in

Stockholm by Herts-Lion Productions, the 30-minute show, which ran to 13 episodes, was directed by the likes of Jason Lindsay and Curt Siodmak, the latter of whom created the show and also penned several episodes. He'd also previously provided the screenplays for such big screen Chaney classics as *The Wolf Man* (1941), *Frankenstein Meets the Wolf Man* (1943) and *Son of Dracula* (1943), and had directed the star in *Bride of the Gorilla* (1951), which he'd also written.

Featuring such guest names as John Crawford, Lorri Scott and Alf Kjellin (whose career as a director would soon take off in the U.S.), the show kicked off with *A Gift of Murder* (1959, TV), in which a businessman (Charles Nolte) uses a voodoo doll to avenge himself against a colleague who has been flirting with his wife. The other episodes included *Murder in the Mirror* (1959, TV), in which an architect (Ben Breen) sees within a mirror a long ago murder committed in front of it; *The Black Hand* (1959, TV), in which a doctor (Sheldon Lawrence), whose hand was mangled in a car collision, replaces it with one taken from the victim in the other vehicle, who turns out to have been a serial killer; and *The Vine of Death* (1959, TV), in which an archaeologist (Ingemar Pallin) receives a number of 4,000-year-old plant bulbs from a Malaysian death vine, whose tendrils are capable of strangling humans. Unfortunately, the stories presented were of very variable quality, and the presentation (save for Chaney's atmospheric intros) lacked any particular flair, which perhaps explains why the show wasn't picked up for broadcast in the States (it played in Sweden with subtitles). However, three episodes (*The Photograph* [1959, TV], *The Girl in the Glacier* [1959, TV] and *Condemned in Crystal* [1959, TV]) were later edited together to form the feature film *The Devil's Messenger* (1961), for which Chaney filmed additional framing sequences as Satan. This subsequently played the U.S. drive-in circuit.

Entering the Zone

If *Alfred Hitchcock Presents* (1955–1962, TV) was considered the Rolls-Royce of dramatic anthology shows, then the one that set the benchmark for all future science fiction and horror anthologies was undoubtedly *The Twilight Zone* (1959–1964, TV), which began its 156- episode, five-season run on CBS on 2 October 1959. It was introduced by its creator Rod Serling, a preppy looking writer who'd been slaving away in the salt pits of television drama for almost a decade, contributing polished scripts for such series as *Stars Over Hollywood* (1950–1951, TV), *Lux Video Theatre* (1950–1959, TV) and *Climax!* (1954–1958, TV), earning a name for himself with such acclaimed pieces as the boardroom saga *Patterns* (1955, TV), which first appeared as an episode of *Kraft Theatre* (1947–1958, TV), and the boxing drama *Requiem for a Heavyweight* (1956, TV), which made its debut on *Playhouse 90* (1956–1960, TV), both of which had won him Emmys.

Serling had already skirted with fantastical themes with *U.F.O.* (1954, TV) for *Studio One* (1948–1958, TV) and *The Time Element* (1958, TV) for *Westinghouse Desilu Playhouse* (1958–1960, TV), but had given no real indication that this was where his true talent would eventually lie (the writer pitched the idea for the show via a specially filmed promotion aimed at sponsors and advertisers, commenting,

"All I can tell you is that we think *The Twilight Zone* is pretty unique. We think it will be much talked about, and we think it will also be enjoyed. We think it's the kind of a show that will put people on the edge of their seats, but only for that one half an hour; we fully expect they'll go to the stores on the following day and buy your products—we think it's that kind of a show.... So, gentlemen, sit back and take your first trip into *The Twilight Zone*").

The series, which ran 25 minutes for a half-hour slot (save for the 18-episode run of season four, which ran 51 minutes for an hour-long slot), was executive produced by Serling himself via Cayuga Productions (which he owned and named), and kicked off with *Where Is Everybody?* (1959, TV), a Serling penned piece in which a confused young man (Earl Holliman) suffering from memory loss wanders about a deserted township, gradually coming to the conclusion that he might well be the last person on Earth ("Was there a bomb? That must have been it, a bomb.... But if there was a bomb, everywhere would be destroyed, and nothing is destroyed"). But then paranoia begins to take over and he starts to feel that he is somehow being watched, especially when he comes across telltale signs of life (pies cooking on a stove, a movie projector suddenly coming to life). However, at the last moment it is revealed that he's actually been in an experimental deprivation tank, in training for the potentially lonely life of an astronaut ("The barrier of loneliness—that's one thing we haven't licked yet," he is told when he emerges).

Filmed on the back lot at Universal (primarily in the town square later to find fame as the setting for the *Back to the Future* movies), the episode benefits enormously from the cine-literate direction of Robert Stevens, the stark photography of Joseph LaShelle (an Oscar winner for his work on *Laura* [1944]) and the performance of Earl Holliman as the increasingly edgy and unhinged astronaut (the actor had already appeared in the Serling tele-play *The Dark Side of the Earth* [1957, TV] for *Playhouse 90* [1956–1961, TV]). The ace up its sleeve, however, is its score by the legendary Bernard Herrmann (known for his big screen associations with Alfred Hitchcock), who also provided an eerie main title theme (the universally known title tune by Marius Constant wasn't used until season two). Adding immeasurably to the unsettling atmosphere, the music helped to set the standard for the show, for which Herrmann would pen a total of seven original scores, many cues from which would subsequently be reused as stock music throughout the run (other composers providing original music for the series included such respected names as Jerry Goldsmith, Van Cleave, Fred Steiner, Franz Waxman, Lyn Murray and Leonard Rosenman).

Having set out its stall, the show went on to cover a wide range of themes, some horrific, some with a sci-fi slant and almost all of them with a strong moral to them. Among the writers contributing scripts and stories were Charles Beaumont, Richard Matheson and Ray Bradbury. The show also attracted such name directors as Jacques Tourneur, John Brahm, Robert Florey and Christian Nyby, whose big screen work included such genre gems as *Cat People* (1942), *The Lodger* (1944), *Murders in the Rue Morgue* (1932) and *The Thing from Another World* (1951), respectively. Those delivering long service to the series included day-to-day producer Buck Houghton (who worked on 102 episodes), cinematographer George T. Clemens (117 episodes), editor Bill Mosher (43 episodes), art director George W. Davies (143 episodes), set decorator

Henry Grace (116 episodes), assistant director E. Darrell Hallenbeck (53 episodes), production manager Ralph Nelson (139 episodes) and sound recordist Franklin Milton (148 episodes), all of whom contributed to the efficiency of the enterprise. The show was also noted for its title graphics, care of Sam Clayberger, Rudy Larriva and Joe Masserli, and its make-up effects by William Tuttle and Bud Westmore. And although it never attracted top rank stars as did the likes of the Hitchcock show (Serling and the stories were the real stars), it nevertheless featured such dependable performers as Robert McCord (who appeared in a total of 32 episodes), Burgess Meredith, William Shatner, Jack Klugman, Gladys Cooper, John Carradine, Robert Cummings, Cliff Robertson and Virginia Gregg, as well as such upcoming names as Robert Redford, Burt Reynolds, James Coburn and Charles Bronson.

Among the standout episodes of season one were *Perchance to Dream* (1959, TV), in which a man (Richard Conte) who hasn't slept for days seeks the help of a psychiatrist, claiming that if he falls asleep he will have a nightmare that will kill him (spoiler alert: it does); *And When the Sky Was Opened* (1959, TV), in which three astronauts (Rod Taylor, Jim Hutton and Charles Aidman) find themselves being erased from existence and the collective memory of everyone who ever knew or knew of them ("Someone or some *thing* took them somewhere," intones Serling in his conclusion); *The Hitch-Hiker* (1960, TV), in which a woman (Inger Stevens) driving across America keeps passing the same hitchhiker (Leonard Strong) along the way ("No matter how far I travel or how fast I go, he's ahead of me," she observes); and *People Are Alike All Over* (1960, TV), in which an astronaut (Roddy McDowall) crash lands on Mars, and though he finds the inhabitants he discovers there initially very pleasant, he nevertheless ends up as a specimen in their zoo.

Having established itself as a ratings success, as well as earning many critical plaudits, Serling and his team were thus emboldened to stretch their imaginations further for season two, which kicked off with *King Nine Will Not Return* (1960, TV), in which a downed bomber pilot (Robert Cummings) can't seem to find the rest of his crew after having landed in the African desert. Episodes that leant more towards horror this time included *The Howling Man* (1960, TV), in which a traveller (H.M. Wynant) seeking refuge in a monastery is told by the head monk (John Carradine) that a seemingly innocent man being held there is in fact the Devil (Robin Hughes), who makes a nice transformation at the climax passing behind a series of pillars before disappearing in a puff of smoke; *Eye of the Beholder* (1960, TV), in which a woman (Donna Douglas) hoping that an operation to correct a severe facial disfigurement so as to make her like everyone else gets a nasty surprise when the bandages are taken off (William Tuttle's make-ups for the disfigured nursing staff who represent the "real" world—disguised via clever lighting and camerawork until the big reveal—are superb); and *Will the Real Martian Please Stand Up?* (1961, TV), in which a couple of cops are sent to a snowed in roadside diner where a Martian (John Hoyt) who has survived a crash landing is apparently hiding out (the cheerful bartender [Barney Phillips], who is revealed to be a three-eyed Venusian during the twist climax, was another disturbing William Tuttle creation).

Season two also contained six episodes shot on videotape, which were then transferred to film for broadcast. This was done as a cost cutting exercise at the

Devil may care. Robin Hughes as *The Howling Man* (1960, TV) in *The Twilight Zone* (1959–1964, TV) (CBS/Cayuga).

insistence of CBC, much to Serling's chagrin, given that the saving amounted to just $5,000 per episode. The process involved using four cameras to shoot the action simultaneously, with the editing taking place in camera. However, having noted the resultant visual limitations, the exercise (which began with *The Lateness of the Hour* [1960, TV] and concluded with *Long Distance Call* [1961, TV]) was thankfully abandoned. Thus it was back to normal with season three, which kicked off with *Two* (1961, TV), a post-apocalyptic story involving two survivors (Charles Bronson and Elizabeth Montgomery) from opposing sides of the conflict. Horror naturally reared its head again, most specifically in the likes of *The Jungle* (1961, TV), in which a businessman (John Dehner) returning from Africa after a period discovers that the curse placed upon him there by a witch doctor has followed him home; the cunningly titled *To Serve Man* (1962, TV), in which an alien (Richard Kiel) lands on Earth with the promise that his people wish to serve man, but a mysterious book that he has left at the UN turns out to reveal their true intentions (spoiler alert: "It's a cook book!"); and *The Dummy* (1962, TV) in which a ventriloquist (Cliff Robertson) believes his dummy to be alive (don't they always?).

Season four, which switched to the hour-long running time, which seemed a little overgenerous for the format, kicked off with *In His Image* (1963, TV), in which a confused young man (George Grizzard) finds himself suffering from unaccountable murderous impulses. This time horror was represented by the likes of *Death Ship* (1963, TV), in which space explorers from Earth (among them Jack Klugman and Ross Martin) land on a distant planet only to find that an exact copy of their spaceship has already crash landed there, complete with bodies that look like themselves; *The New Exhibit* (1963, TV), in which the curator (Martin Balsam) of a waxwork museum attempts to preserve five figures from the murderer's row exhibit after the building has been closed to make way for a supermarket; and *Of Late I Think of Cliffordville* (1963, TV), in which a wealthy but bored executive (Albert Salmi) agrees to sell his business to Devlin Travel in order to go back in time to where his success started and do it all again, only things don't quite pan out the way he expected.

It was back to the better suited 30-minute slot for season five, which launched with *In Praise of Pip* (1963, TV), in which a bookie (Jack Klugman), whose son has been fatally wounded while serving in Vietnam, gets to spend an hour at an amusement park with the ten-year-old version of beloved his boy. The rest of the season produced such variable episodes as *Living Doll* (1963, TV), in which a frustrated stepfather (Telly Savalas) does battle with his daughter's verbally abusive talking doll; *Caesar and Me* (1964, TV), in which a ventriloquist (Jackie Cooper) is persuaded into a life of crime by his dummy; and *The Fear* (1964, TV), in which a woman and a policeman (Hazel Court and Mark Richman) believe that they are being stalked by giants.

This season did, however, produce two genuine humdingers. The first of these was *Nightmare at 20,000 Feet* (1963, TV), in which an increasingly panic stricken airline passenger (William Shatner), who has recently recovered from a nervous breakdown, becomes convinced that a gremlin is out on the wing, damaging the plane in which he and his wife are flying ("I'm not acting much like a cured man, am I?" he says to her before the plane has even taken off, giving a hint of the hysteria to come). Unfortunately, no one else can see the creature ("He jumps away whenever anyone might see him … except me"), all of which leads to the expected concern from his missus and the crew. To be honest, the monster, played by the acrobat Nick Cravat, is a rather unconvincing beast; looking like a demented teddy bear complete with slip resistant soled feet, it is, for once, something of a letdown from make-up man William Tuttle. Thankfully, the tight writing by Richard Matheson and Shatner's dynamic performance (an early career high) carry the piece superbly, while director Richard Donner (later to make a name for himself with *The Omen* [1976] and *Superman* [1978]) keeps the action moving along briskly to the inevitable moment when Shatner's character opens the emergency exit next to which he is conveniently sitting and shoots the creature with a gun he has furtively purloined from the air marshal.

The second highlight was *An Occurrence at Owl Creek Bridge* (1964, TV), in which a Confederate prisoner (Roger Jacquet) seemingly escapes being hanged when, luckily for him, the rope snaps as he falls from the titular bridge, after which he scrambles his way home through river and forest to his wife, only to be brought back to reality as he is about to kiss her. Based upon the celebrated 1890 Ambrose Bierce story which had already done service as a 1959 installment of *Alfred Hitchcock Presents* (1955–1962, TV), this episode was actually a buy in, being a 28-minute French film dating from 1961 which had won the Academy Award for best live action short subject, and for which Serling paid $20,000 to screen. Directed with quiet skill by Robert Enrico, with expert assistance from his cinematographer Jean Boffety, it makes the most of the story's verdant setting. A superbly crafted and edited piece, this remarkable miniature is put together with refreshing cinematic dexterity.

However, after season five's final episode, *The Bewitchin' Pool* (1964, TV), in which two kids (Mary Badham and Jeffrey Byron) escape from their quarrelling parents via a portal in their swimming pool which takes them to another land overseen by the seemingly benign Aunt T. (Georgia Simmons), CBS called time on the show. Serling, preferring to go out on a high, subsequently moved on to other things, among them further TV shows (more of which to come) and several noted screenplays, including *Seven Days in May* (1964) and *Planet of the Apes* (1968), which were directed by fellow television alumni John Frankenheimer and Franklin J. Schaffner, respectively. Yet this was far from the end of *The Twilight Zone*, which went into syndication, becoming cult viewing down the decades that followed, influencing several soon to emerge filmmakers along the way, a group of whom—John Landis,

Steven Spielberg, Joe Dante and George Miller—pooled their talents to bring to the big screen three stories from the show, along with some new material, in *Twilight Zone: The Movie* (1983). These were *Time Out*, a new piece care of writer-director John Landis (who had instigated the project), *Kick the Can* from season three, *It's a Good Life*, likewise from season three, and *Nightmare at 20,000 Feet* from season five. These were bookended by two brief new segments, *Something Scary* and *Even Scarier* ("Wanna see something *really* scary?"). The best episode is undoubtedly the remake of *Nightmare at 20,000 Feet*, in which the tension is cranked up to the *n*th degree (and then some) by director George Miller, aided and abetted by a dazzling performance by John Lithgow as the paranoid air passenger, who this time gets to vie with a rather more convincing gremlin care of make-up effects maestro Craig Reardon and his team. The rest of the package is something of a mixed bag, but is at least busied along by a lively score by series veteran Jerry Goldsmith, who naturally makes use of Marius Constant's iconic "Doo-doo-doo-doo" title theme.

Although the $10 million film met with mixed notices and a less than stellar box office, it nevertheless helped to reinvigorate interest in the show, to whit a color revival was launched by CBS on 27 September 1985. Running to 65 episodes over three seasons, the initial installments ran 45 minutes in length and offered two (sometimes three) stories per episode, while later episodes ran to 22 minutes and concentrated on a single story, among them remakes of old favorites, as well as lots of new material. Plenty of familiar names were inevitably among the writing and story credits, including Richard Matheson (who'd contributed to the film version), Ray Bradbury and Charles Beaumont, along with such new kids on the block as Stephen King, Steven Bochco and Rockne S. O'Bannon (who, as well as penning multiple episodes, also worked as a story consultant/editor on the show). Directors involved included such names of the moment as Wes Craven, Peter Medak, Jeannot Szwarc, William Friedkin, Joe Dante (who'd helmed a segment of the film version), Curtis Harrington, Martha Coolidge and John Milius, while stars lining up for an appearance included Morgan Freeman, Martin Balsam, Jeffrey Tambor, Piper Laurie, Bruce Willis, Helen Mirren, Elliott Gould and Adrienne Barbeau. The show (which *TV Guide* described as "an intriguing change from standard weekly series") concluded in 1989 and was followed by a second reboot which ran between 2002 and 2003, notching up 43 episodes (each running 43 minutes) care of New Line Television via a pool of directors that included Bob Balaban, Jonathan Frakes and Lou Diamond Phillips. A third reboot followed in 2019, whose episodes (which ran between 31 and 55 minutes) included yet another version of *Nightmare at 20,000 Feet*, albeit as *Nightmare at 30,000* (2019, TV), with Adam Scott now in the Shatner/Lithgow role, although this time there wasn't a gremlin in sight, save for the nice touch of having a toy from the 1963 version washed up on a beach.

Having established the pattern on how such things should be done, and that they could be popular with viewers *and* advertisers, *The Twilight Zone* (1959–1964, TV) led to a number of other genre series in the sixties, several of which similarly became household favorites, likewise surviving in syndication to this day....

SECTION THREE

The Genre Takes Hold
(the 1960s)

Beloved Boris

The anthology series continued apace into the sixties, the next of which to embrace the format being *The Dow Hour of Great Mysteries* (1960, TV), whose seven episodes, which began airing on NBC on 31 March 1960, included studio productions of such spooky house thrillers as *The Bat* (1960, TV) by Mary Roberts Rinehart and Avery Hopwood, and *The Cat and the Canary* (1960, TV) by John Willard, plus an adaptation of Sheridan Le Fanu's 1872 story *The Room in the Dragon Volant* (1960, TV). Produced by Robert Saudek and sponsored by Dow Chemical, the show featured such major names as Rex Harrison, Helen Hayes, Jason Robards, Jr., Farley Granger, Eva Gabor, Keith Michell, Hugh Griffith and Margaret Hamilton. Sadly, the series was curtailed following the death of its host, Joseph N. Welch.

Likewise, *The Chevy Mystery Show* (1960, TV, aka *Sunday Mystery Hour*), whose 18 episodes began airing on NBC on 29 May 1960, occasionally leaned toward the fantastical, as with its launch episode *The Machine Calls It Murder* (1960, TV), in which an insurance company's computer expert (Larry Blyden) works out a way of predicting who will be killed next in a series of apparent accidents involving young women (this was remade the following year in the UK as an episode of *Drama '61* [1961, TV] with Dave King in the Blyden role), and *The Suicide Club* (1960, TV), an adaptation of the Robert Louis Stevenson story about the discovery by Prince Florizel (Cesar Romero) and his friend Colonel Geraldine (Berry Kroeger) of a club which helps its unhappy members to end their lives. Hosted by Walter Slezak and later Vincent Price (who both also appeared in episodes), the show was produced by Himan Brown and Henry Jaffe (among others), featured writing by Gore Vidal, Richard Levinson and William Link, and starred such names as Zachary Scott, Agnes Moorehead, Everett Sloane, Bobby Driscoll and Jack Cassidy.

However, the first *major* anthology series of the decade proved to be *Thriller* (1960–1962, TV, aka *Boris Karloff's Thriller* and *Boris Karloff Presents*), which began its two season, 67-episode run on NBC on 13 September 1960. Filmed at the Revue Studios care of Hubbell Robinson Productions, the show hadn't actually set out to be a horror specific program, its original focus being mysteries, thrillers and crime dramas. However, with horror icon Boris Karloff onboard as the host (and occasional

60

guest star), the program's remit gradually morphed over its run to fully embrace the genre (contributing writers included Robert Bloch, Cornell Woolrich and Charles Beaumont). Karloff himself was already a horror icon thanks to his big screen work in *Frankenstein* (1931), in which he'd played the star making role of the Monster for the first time, *The Mummy* (1932) and *The Black Cat* (1934). More recently he'd also begun to work in TV, guesting in such series as *The Ford Theatre Hour* (1948–1951, TV), *Suspense* (1949–1954, TV), *Tales of Tomorrow* (1951–1953, TV), *Curtain Call* (1952, TV) and *General Electric Theater* (1953–1961, TV), among others.

He'd also fronted a handful of shows by this time, among them the mystery series *Starring Boris Karloff* (1949, TV, aka *The Boris Karloff Mystery Playhouse*), which he hosted, and the detective show *Colonel March of Scotland Yard* (1954–1956, TV), in which he played a one-eyed sleuth in charge of Scotland Yard's Department of Queer Complaints. The latter, which was based upon a series of stories by John Dickson Carr, was made in Britain at Southall Studios for broadcast on the recently launched ITV network, as well as for syndication in the U.S. The 26-episode series kicked off with a straightforward locked room murder mystery titled *The Sorcerer* (1955, TV), which was broadcast on 1 October, before going on to take on occasionally more fantastical episodes (all explained away), among them *The Abominable Snowman* (1955, TV), in which a Himalayan climbing club is apparently threatened by a vengeful Yeti; *Death in Inner Space* (1956, TV), in which a scientist claims he is receiving messages from Mars; *The Case of the Lively Ghost* (1955, TV), in which a fake spiritualist believes she has summoned a real ghost; and *The New Invisible Man* (1956, TV), in which a major claims to have seen a man shot dead by a pair of gloves. A rather typical production of its time, the series was helmed by the likes of Bernard Knowles, Arthur Crabtree and Terence Fisher, and featured such guest artistes as Anton Diffring, Christopher Lee and Eric Pohlmann, while its contributing writers included Paul Monash, Waldo Salt and Paul Tabori.

Rather more interesting in terms of horror content was *The Veil* (1958, TV), which Karloff hosted and also appeared in. Running to just 12 episodes, it was shot at the Hal Roach Studios, but sadly ran into financial difficulties during filming (the star claimed he was never paid for the series). Consequently, the full run of programs planned was abandoned and the show failed to get a network airing (it wasn't made available to the public until 1968, when several episodes were edited together to form three TV movies: *Jack the Ripper* [1968, TVM], *Destination Nightmare* [1968, TVM] and *The Veil* [1968, TVM]). Nevertheless, it remains of passing note for a handful of episodes (now available on DVD), among them *Vision of Crime* (1958, TV), in which a man (Karloff) on a boat trip to Paris has a vision of his brother's murder, and *Jack the Ripper* (1958, TV), in which a clairvoyant (Niall MacGinnis) suffers a series of dreams in which he witnesses a number of grisly murders (this was actually a UK buy-in for which Karloff simply added an intro, and thus did not appear in).

Karloff was on firmer footing then with *Thriller*, which launched with *The Twisted Image* (1960, TV), a psychological drama directed by Arthur Hiller in which a businessman (Leslie Nielsen) has to deal with a deranged female stalker who has become obsessed with him. It was hardly a hint of what was to come, but as the hour-long series progressed, it began to tackle slightly more genre specific stories, among the earliest being *The Purple Room* (1960, TV), in which a skeptic (Rip Torn) has to live a year in a supposedly haunted mansion in order to inherit the valuable property, only to suspect that greedy relatives are trying to scare him off (the mansion exteriors were actually the Bates house featured in the recently released *Psycho* [1960]). Other early episodes that veered towards the more fantastical included *The Prediction* (1960, TV), in which a fake stage mentalist (Karloff, making his series debut) begins to experience visions of violent deaths yet to occur, and which he subsequently attempts to prevent from happening; *The Cheaters* (1960, TV), in which a man (Henry Daniell) invents a pair of glasses capable of seeing the truth; and *The Hungry Glass* (1961, TV), in which a couple (William Shatner and Joanna Heyes) move into a house whose mirrors, hidden away in a locked attic, are able to deceive and influence those who look into them.

However, the series fully embraced the horrific with *Hay-Fork and Bill-Hook* (1961, TV), in which a London police detective (Kenneth Haigh) investigates a ritual murder in the Welsh village of Dark Woods, where the local hedge cutter (Lumsden Hare), thought to have been a witch, has been killed on St. Valentine's Day with a hay-fork and carved with a cross on his throat with his own bill-hook. Accompanied by his young wife Nesta (Audrey Dalton), with whom he is on honeymoon, the policeman finds himself confronted with superstition on all levels, while his missus apparently keeps seeing a black dog (an omen of death), leading the locals to assume that she herself is a witch, resulting in her being kidnapped and placed in a wicker basket ready for burning at the nearby druids' stones…. Although a little chatty at times, this episode has moments of genuine cinematic flair thanks to the involvement of veteran director Hershel Daugherty (whose credits at this stage already included 24 episodes of *Alfred Hitchcock Presents* [1955–1962, TV]), and opens with a highly effective nighttime scene in which the poor hedge cutter meets his doom. With its extreme close-ups and tilted shots care of cinematographer Benjamin H. Kline, it piles on the atmosphere with a spade, as does the following fog-shrouded scene in which the policeman and his wife arrive by night at the village and are confronted by a pitch-fork wielding local (who turns out to be the non too friendly village copper) by the druids' stones, where the action eventually concludes with the rescue of Nesta before she can be burned alive. Accompanied by an excellent Jerry Goldsmith score (complete with plenty of scratchy *danse macabre* string work), the program displayed what could be accomplished on a small budget if the talent involved was fully committed to the project at hand.

Having set such a high bar, season one went on to include such tales as *Well of Doom* (1961, TV), in which an heir (Ronald Howard) is kidnapped and placed in a dungeon by a mysterious man named Moloch (Henry Daniell, looking like Lon Chaney in *London After Midnight* [1927]) who, aided and abetted by his giant assistant Master Styx (Richard Kiel), is out to avenge himself for having had his land and position usurped by the victim's father; *Trio of Terror* (1961, TV), a three-story episode directed by Ida Lupino, one of which involves the murder of a warlock (Terence de Marney), who returns from the dead to avenge himself against his killer in a train carriage with what appears to be a giant cockerel claw; *Papa Benjamin* (1961, TV), in which a composer (John Ireland) resorts to voodoo melodies for inspiration,

Dapper Dan. Boris Karloff in a publicity pose for *Thriller* (1960–1962, TV) (NBC/ Hubbell Robinson Productions).

then wishes he hadn't; and *Yours Truly, Jack the Ripper* (1961, TV), in which it would seem an eternally young Jack the Ripper (Donald Woods) is presently alive and well and carrying on with his crimes in modern day New York. The latter was written by Barré Lyndon from a short story by Robert Bloch and was directed by Ray Milland, such was the caliber of talent the program now attracted (soundtrack enthusiasts might be interested to note that Jerry Goldsmith's quirky score for this particular episode somewhat resembles his later work for *The List of Adrian Messenger* [1963]).

Other horror themed episodes from the first season include *The Devil's Ticket* (1961, TV), in which a struggling artist (Macdonald Carey) pawns his soul to the Devil; *Parasite Mansion* (1961, TV), in which a young woman (Pippa Scott) finds herself being held captive in a spooky mansion presided over by an evil old woman after being involved in a car accident; *The Prisoner in the Mirror* (1961, TV), in which a professor (Lloyd Bochner) buys a blacked out mirror once belonging to the sorcerer Count Cagliostro, only to find himself possessed by the evil spirit contained therein once he scrapes the paint off it; and *The Grim Reaper* (1961, TV), in which an authoress (Natalie Schafer) purchases a painting of the Grim Reaper, despite warnings that many of its previous owners have come to a sticky end (this contains another excellent performance from the young William Shatner as the writer's nephew, who uses the painting's story to fulfill his own nefarious schemes, much to his inevitable regret).

With season two came a commitment to yet more horror themed episodes, among them *The Premature Burial* (1961, TV), in which a millionaire (Sidney Blackmer), prone to catalepsy and already the victim of one premature burial, finds himself the object of a scheme by his devious wife; *The Weird Tailor* (1961, TV), in which a grieving father (George Macready) has a special suit made to resurrect his dead son (written and based upon a short story by Robert Bloch, this later did service in the film *Asylum* [1972]); *God Grante That She Lye Stille* (1961, TV), in which a witch (Sarah Marshall), burned 300 years ago, returns to her ancestral pile to wreak revenge on the latest heir (also played by Marshall); *The Closed Cabinet* (1961, TV), in which a young woman (Olive Sturgess) staying at a spooky Victorian mansion attempts to solve the curse placed upon the family many years earlier; *Dialogues with Death* (1961, TV), in which a morgue attendant (Karloff) is able to communicate with the bodies in his charge (this was double billed with a second story involving an inheritance hidden in a mausoleum on a Southern plantation which also featured

Karloff, both of whose characters appear together via split screen during the intro, much to their surprise); *Waxworks* (1962, TV), in which it seems that the figures in a touring waxworks exhibition owned by Pierre Jacquelin (Oskar Homolka) are somehow responsible for a series of murders (based upon another Robert Bloch story, this one was later re-used in the film *The House That Dripped Blood* [1971]); *La Strega* (1962, TV), in which a painter saves a beautiful young witch (Ursula Andress) from being drowned by three peasants and falls in love with her, only to be cursed by her grandmother; *The Storm* (1962, TV), in which a woman (Nancy Kelly) discovers a body in her basement during a violent thunderstorm (this had already been staged three times by *Studio One* [1948–1958, TV] in 1948, 1949 and 1953, and by *The Unforeseen* [1959–1960, TV] in 1959, and would later be remade as *The Victim* [1972, TVM]); *Flowers of Evil* (1962, TV), in which a faithless wife (Luciana Paluzzi) sells her dead husband's skeleton to a medical school, only for it to keep returning; and *The Innocent Bystanders* (1962, TV), in which two Victorian body snatchers (John Anderson and George Kennedy) resort to murder in order to boost their supplies.

Note that while in the midst of *Thriller*'s second season, the ever-busy Karloff also appeared in a version of the classic 1939 Joseph Kesselring play *Arsenic and Old Lace* (first performed in 1941), which centers on the criminal activities of two spinster aunts (Dorothy Stickney and Mildred Natwick) who murder men with poisoned elderberry wine and bury them in the cellar. For the program, which aired on NBC on 5 February 1962 as an episode of *Hallmark Hall of Fame* (1951–, TV, aka *Hallmark Television Playhouse*), Karloff reprised the role of Jonathan Brewster, which he'd played on Broadway, and who is said to look like Boris Karloff. When the play was again staged for American television in 1969, Fred Gwynne took on the role, which he played in the style of Karloff, who had died earlier the same year (Karloff had also appeared as Brewster in a 1949 broadcast of the play for *The Ford Theatre Hour* [1949–1953, TV] and a 1955 version for *The Best of Broadway* [1954–1955, TV]; other versions of the play were presented as installments of such series as *TV de Vanguarda* [1952–1964, TV] in 1953, *BBC Sunday-Night Theatre* [1950–1959, TV] in 1957, *Grande Teatro Tupi* [1951–1964, TV] in 1958, *ITV Play of the Week* [1955–1974, TV] in 1958, *Gran teatro* [1960–1965, TV] in 1961, *Primera fila* [1962–1965, TV] in 1964, *Au théatre ce soir* [1966–1990, TV] in 1971, *Ahududu* [1974, TV] in 1974 and *To theatro tis Defteras* [1970–1994, TV] in 1981, as well as one-offs in 1955 [Italian], 1960 [Dutch], 1967 [Yugoslavian], 1971 [Belgian], 1981 [Greek], 1995 [Spanish] and 2002 [Danish], which makes for a valuable property indeed).

Thriller wasn't Karloff's only brush with horror on television during this period. As we've already seen, some drama series occasionally dipped their toes into more genre centric material, and this proved to be the case with the hour-long adventure series *Route 66* (1960–1964, TV), which began its four season, 116-episode run on CBS on 7 October 1960. Created by Stirling Silliphant (who wrote many of the episodes) and Herbert B. Leonard (who executive produced), it followed the exploits of two young drifters, Tod Stiles (Martin Milner) and Buz Murdock (George Maharis), as they wend their way across America in a Corvette ("Two soldiers of fortune ride the highway to adventure in this thrilling new series," ran the season one tagline). Shot on location across the States, the series was directed by the likes of David Lowell

Rich (who helmed 21 episodes), Arthur Hiller, Tom Gries, Jack Smight, James Goldstone, Richard Donner, Sam Peckinpah, Ted Post, Paul Wendkos and Frank Pierson, while the principal photographer was Jack A. Marta (who notched up an incredible 90 episodes). The series relied greatly on guest stars to fill out the various characters Tod and Buz encounter on the road, among them Edward Asner, Lee Marvin, Sylvia Sidney, Michael Rennie, Suzanne Pleshette, Leslie Nielsen, Robert Duval, Buster Keaton, Robert Redford, Rod Steiger, James Caan, Joan Crawford, Patrick O'Neal, Jack Warden, Janice Rule, Beatrice Straight, Diane Baker, Dorothy Malone and horror star Lon Chaney, Jr., the latter of whom notched up three episodes, the second of which was *Lizard's Leg and Owlet's Wing* (1962, TV), which cast him alongside fellow icons Boris Karloff and Peter Lorre who, playing themselves, make plans to meet up at the O'Hare Inn, a motel near Chicago, to discuss plans for a television series. Karloff wants to strike out in new directions. "We can't rely on hair on our faces, nodules on our foreheads or any of the old bag of tricks," he argues, while Lorre and Chaney want to stick with their tried and tested make-ups and costumes, to whit Tod, who is working as their liaison at the motel, suggests to Lorre they test them out on a group of hapless executive secretaries who have arrived for a conference.

Unfortunately, despite its highly promising scenario and the willingness of the three stars to lampoon themselves, the results, which were aired on 26 October 1962 (just in time for Halloween), are something of a squandered opportunity. The script by Stirling Silliphant is a surprisingly flabby and witless affair which devotes too much time to a subplot involving Buz and a lovelorn secretary (Jeannine Riley), while what Karloff, Chaney and Lorre are required to do is nothing out of the ordinary, save to argue with each other in a motel room with their imperious lawyer, Mrs. Baxter (Martita Hunt), with little in the way of real nostalgic reference to their past silver screen glories. Still, Chaney gets to don two of his classic make-ups, the Mummy and the Wolf Man (recreated by Maurice Seiderman), as well as that of Quasimodo, whom his father Lon Chaney played to great effect in the silent version of *The Hunchback of Notre Dame* (1923), in which guise he opens the episode, trying to get a scare out of his sleeping grandson, played by his real-life grandson Ron Chaney. Otherwise, he is reduced to running around the motel as the Wolf Man, growling at all and sundry in his bid to prove that he's still got what it takes (as it turns out, he *has*—all the secretaries faint, much to his satisfaction). The episode concludes with all three stars dressed in their horror garb, with Karloff wearing his celebrated Frankenstein Monster make-up for one last time and Lorre sporting a top hat and opera cape, yet given the bright lighting of the motel, they sadly lack the creep factor, as indeed does the whole episode, which is further diluted by an irritating "comedy" score care of series composer Nelson Riddle. Still, the show's audience was happy to see the trio of stars, and the results are still held in affectionate regard by fans.

Over in Britain, the spy series *The Avengers* (1961–1969, TV), which began its phenomenally popular seven series run on ITV on 18 March 1961, went on to have several brushes with the fantastic of its own. Created by Sidney Newman, the show went through various guises during its lifetime (including a change from black and white to color), and was developed into a series of wit, style and imagination by its two most frequent producers, Brian Clemens (who joined it in 1965, and also wrote many episodes) and Albert Fennell (who joined in 1967). Although the show's original leading man was Ian Hendry, who starred as Dr. David Keel, it was the character of John Steed played by Patrick Macnee, brought in by Keel to help avenge the death of his wife, who went on to dominate the series (he would appear in all 161 episodes). Over the years he was accompanied by a number of glamorous assistants, among them Honor Blackman as the judo kicking Cathy Gale, Diana Rigg as Emma Peel and Linda Thorson as Tara King, whose increasingly outrageous adventures went on to include such episodes as *Warlock* (1963, TV), in which a scientist turns out to be a member of a black magic cult; *Man with Two Shadows* (1963, TV), in which a government official is replaced by a doppelganger; *The Cybernauts* (1965, TV), in which a number of murders prove to be the work of an electronics expert's karate chopping robots; *A Surfeit of H₂O* (1965, TV), in which a scientist has discovered a means of controlling the weather; *Man-Eater of Surrey Green* (1965, TV), in which a carnivorous plant from outer space is menacing the home counties; *From Venus with Love* (1965, TV [the first episode in color]), in which members of a society devoted to the observation of Venus appear to have been killed by aliens; *Who's Who???* (1967, TV), in which a scientist has invented a mind swapping machine; *Return of the Cybernauts* (1967, TV), which sees the reappearance of the deadly (not to mention highly popular) automatons; *Fog* (1969, TV), which involves a modern-day Jack the Ripper, and *Thingumajig* (1969, TV), which features energy creatures capable of eating anything.

When the series was revived in the seventies, this time as *The New Avengers* (1976–1977, TV), which ran to 26 episodes over two seasons beginning on 22 October 1976 (again on ITV), Macnee was joined by Joanna Lumley as Purdey and Gareth Hunt as Mike Gambit. Like its predecessor, the new program sometimes featured fantastical elements. For example, the opening episode, *The Eagle's Nest* (1976, TV), revolved around the return of Adolf Hitler, while *The Last of the Cybernauts...?* (1976, TV) saw a disfigured double agent use cybernaut technology to avenge himself against Steed and his assistants. Elsewhere, *Cat Amongst the Pigeons* (1976, TV) featured a madman (played by go to villain Vladek Sheybal) who uses a special musical instrument to coerce birds into attacking his enemies; *Gnaws* (1976, TV) had a giant rat roaming the sewers; while *Forward Base* (1977, TV) saw the shoreline of Lake Ontario become the subject of some seemingly inexplicable changes.

The Avengers wasn't the only British crime show to veer towards the fantastical in the sixties. For example, *The Saint* (1962–1969, TV), in which Roger Moore played the debonair adventurer and ladies man Simon Templar, was occasionally confronted by out of the ordinary situations, as in *The Convenient Monster* (1966, TV), in which he becomes involved in a case in which the Loch Ness monster is implicated (despite giant footprints found on the shore, it proves to be a hoax), and *The House on Dragon's Rock* (1968, TV), in which he travels to a Welsh village where the inhabitants are apparently being attacked by a monstrous creature (in this case a giant ant). Meanwhile, in *The Champions* (1968–1969, TV), three agents (Stuart Damon, William Gaunt and Alexandra Bastedo), working for Nemesis, a Geneva based intelligence organization, use their supernatural powers (which include telepathy), acquired from a society in the Himalayas following a plane crash, to solve international intrigues, while in *Randall and Hopkirk (Deceased)* (1969–1971, TV, aka *My Partner the Ghost*), a private investigator (Mike Pratt) and his late partner (Kenneth Cope), killed in a hit and run accident, use the latter's abilities to pass through doors and walls, allowing him to eavesdrop and gather clues so as to help his colleague, who is the only person who can see him (a reboot followed in 2000 with Bob Mortimer and Vic Reeves now in the roles). All three series were made by ITC Entertainment, which was also responsible for such popular shows as *The Baron* (1965–1966, TV), *The Prisoner* (1967, TV) and *Department S* (1969–1970, TV) among many others.

Anthology series continued to prove popular in the sixties, and the British turned their own attention to the format with *Tales of Mystery* (1961–1963, TV), which began airing on the ITV network on 29 March 1961. Made by Associated-Rediffusion Television, the half-hour show, which notched up 29 episodes during its run, was based on the short stories of Algernon Blackwood, and was hosted by John Laurie in the guise of the author. Sadly, all of the episodes are now lost, among them such tantalizing titles as *The Terror of the Twins* (1961, TV), which launched the series, *The Woman's Ghost Story* (1961, TV), *Ancient Sorceries* (1962, TV), *Wolves of God* (1962, TV), *The Doll* (1963, TV), *Egyptian Sorcery* (1963, TV) and *Dream Cottage* (1963, TV). Featuring such names as Laurence Payne, Hugh Burden, Naunton Wayne, Raymond Huntley, Jennie Linden and Andree Melly, the series was directed by the likes of Peter Graham Scott (who also produced several episodes), John Frankau and Raymond Menmuir, while the adaptations were penned by Owen Holder, John Richmond and Barbara S. Harper among others.

Another series to embrace the format was *Thirty Minute Theatre* (1961–1963, TV), which began its 24-episode run on ITV on 31 October 1961, and went on to include a version of George Bernard Shaw's *Don Juan in Hell* (1962, TV), taken from act three, scene two of his 1903 play *Man and Superman*, which starred Alan Badel and Cyril Cusack as (respectively) Don Juan and the Devil, who indulge in a philosophical discussion in hell (other versions of the play were presented in 1960, as an episode of the American *Play of the Week* [1959–1961, TV], whose 67-episode run also included a version of Sholom Ansky's 1920 play *The Dybbuk* [1960, TV]; in 1962, as an episode of the British *ITV Play of the Week* [1955–1974, TV], again with Badel and Cusack; and as a 1971 episode of the British *BBC Play of the Month* [1965–1983, TV]). A slightly later series also titled *Thirty Minute Theatre* (1965–1973, TV), this time broadcast by the BBC from 7 October 1965, went on to notch up an astonishing 285 episodes, among them *Come Death* (1967, TV) by Peter S. Beagle (dramatized by John Wiles), in which Lady Neville (Pamela Brown) invites Death to a ball in 19th-century Rome as the plague rages about the city. Sadly, many episodes from both series are now missing, believed either lost or wiped, which is particularly tragic given that the likes of Tom Stoppard, David Mercer and John Mortimer wrote for the latter.

Meanwhile, with *Studio Four* (1962, TV), which was presented from the recently completed Studio 4, the BBC aimed to tackle more experimental dramas, among them adaptations of works by Graham Greene, Arthur Hailey, Doris Lessing and

Muriel Spark, all of which were selected by presiding story editor Roger Smith. A follow-up of sorts to an earlier series titled *Storyboard* (1961, TV), directors involved in the new 18-part series included James MacTaggart, Alan Bridges, Rudolf Cartier and Alvin Rakoff (all of whom produced for the series), while actors taking part included Alec McCowen, Donald Sutherland, Patricia Haines, Frank Finlay and Harry H. Corbett. The series launched on 22 January 1962 with *The Cross and the Arrow* (1962, TV) and went on to include *The Ballad of Peckham Rye* (1962, TV), an adaptation (by Roger Smith) of Muriel Spark's 1960 novel, in which it is thought that a troublesome man, Dougal Douglas (Ian MacNaughton), may in fact be the Devil, and *The Victorian Chaise-Longue* (1962, TV), an adaptation (by its director James MacTaggart) of Marghanita Laski's 1953 novel, in which a young woman, Melanie Langdon (Frances White), convalescing on a day bed, finds herself possessed by the spirit of a former occupant from 80 years earlier (this story had previously been presented as a 1957 episode of *General Electric Theater* [1953–1962, TV]). Unfortunately, much of the series is now lost (only two episodes survive), preventing a fuller appreciation.

A couple of months after he concluded his duties on *Thriller*, Boris Karloff found himself hosting another British anthology show, *Out of this World* (1962, TV), a science fiction series whose single season ran to 14 hour-long episodes. Made for ABC and on air from 24 June 1962, it featured stories by Philip K. Dick, Terry Nation and John Wyndham, and occasionally drifted into the realms of horror, as it did with *The Yellow Pill* (1962, TV), in which a homicidal maniac crosses swords with an eminent psychiatrist; *Vanishing Act* (1962, TV), in which a magician buys a trick box from which people and objects permanently vanish; *The Dark Star* (1962, TV), in which a mysterious disease gives its victims superhuman strength; and *The Tycoons* (1962, TV), in which a tax inspector investigating a company that manufactures novelties gets more than he bargained for. Sadly, only one episode, *Little Lost Robot* (1962, TV), based upon a 1947 story by Isaac Asimov, has survived.

Out of This World wasn't the only anthology show to disappear as quickly as it appeared, despite having strong credentials. One such was *'Way Out* (1961, TV [apostrophe correct]), which had aired in America the year before, and likewise ran to just 14 episodes on CBS (which produced it) from 31 March to 14 July. Hosted by short story specialist Roald Dahl, the half-hour show offered a self contained, blackly humorous tale of the macabre each week, and began its brief run with *William and Mary* (1961, TV), in which a domineering husband (Henry Jones) agrees to plans proposed by his doctor to have his brain kept alive in a tank after his death if only to irritate his wife (Mildred Dunnock), but she has a surprise up her sleeve for him: "Because from now on, you're going to do exactly what Mary tells *you!*" she warns before blowing cigarette smoke at him (ironically, the program was sponsored by L&M cigarettes, whose tagline was "Start fresh with L&M, stay fresh with L&M"). Penned by Dahl himself and directed by Marc Daniels, the episode is clearly a low-budget affair, plainly shot on just a handful of sets, and looking as if it had been made in the early fifties rather than the early sixties, yet its quirky qualities make for an amusing enough installment, despite its borrowings from *Donovan's Brain*. Other episodes in the run include *The Croaker* (1961, TV), in which a boy (a young Richard Thomas) befriends a mysterious new neighbor (John McGiver) whose collection of frogs grows exponentially while people in the area begin to disappear; *False Face* (1961, TV), in which a stage actor (Alfred Ryder) playing Quasimodo pays a deformed derelict in order to copy his face, but finds he can't get the make-up off after the show (the make-up was provided by the program's regular make-up artist Dick Smith); and *Soft Focus* (1961, TV), in which a vain photographer (Barry Morse) acquires a special touching up fluid which he discovers has the ability to remove real life wrinkles.

Another series that came and went pretty quickly was *Great Ghost Tales* (1961, TV), whose 12-episode run began on NBC on 6 July 1961. Produced via Talent Associates, the series launched with a version of Edgar Allan Poe's 1839 story *William Wilson* (1961, TV), in which a young man (Robert Duvall) finds himself being shadowed by a mysterious doppelganger with the same name. Other episodes included *Lucy* (1961, TV), in which a woman (Lee Grant) discovers she has inherited the magical powers of one of her forebears; another adaptation of W.W. Jacobs' *The Monkey's Paw* (1961, TV), in which a grieving couple (R.G. Armstrong and Mildred Dunnock) use a magical talisman to bring back their dead son; another version of Conrad Aiken's *Mr. Arcularis* (1961, TV), with John Abbott in the role of the recuperating title character; *Room 13* (1961, TV), a version of M.R. James' 1904 story *Number 13* in which a couple (William Redfield and Diana Van der Vlis) discover that a new room has materialized in the Austrian inn at which they are staying; and *The Wendigo* (1961, TV), in which a group of hunters (among them Walter Matthau) search for a mythic beast that has been abducting people in the wilds of the Canadian Northwest (this story had already been the subject of a 1954 episode of *The Secret Files of Captain Video* [1953–1955, TV]). Unfortunately, the series was not a success and came in for some carping ("*Great Ghost Tales* not so very scary," noted critic Fred Danzig), yet it remains of passing note for being the last regularly scheduled American drama series to be broadcast live. After this, actors and program makers could sigh with relief in the knowledge that if a line was flubbed or a wayward camera came into shot, they could at least go for another take.

Lasting rather longer—a healthy 88 episodes—was the Canadian series *Playdate* (1961–1964, TV), which began airing on CBC on 24 November 1961, and though it generally concentrated on heavier pieces, it occasionally strayed into genre territory, as per its productions of W.O. Mitchell's Faustian drama *The Black Bonspiel of Wullie MacCrimmon* (1962, TV), which featured Ed McNamara as the Devil out to trick a shoemaker (John Drainie), and yet another version of the Pushkin staple *The Queen of Spades* (1963, TV) starring John Colicos as the soldier keen to con an aged countess (Hilary Vernon) out of her secret of winning at cards. Initially hosted by Christopher Plummer, the series was executive produced by Ed Moser, and featured such names as Douglas Rain, Cec Linder, Heather Sears, Darren McGavin, Robert Goulet, James Shigeta, Michael Learned, Barry Morse and Murray Matheson.

Over in the UK, science fiction was the focus of *A for Andromeda* (1961, TV), albeit that of the more sobering variety. Written by John Elliott and Fred Hoyle (a noted Cambridge Professor of Astronomy), it sees a team of scientists intercept signals from outer space which carry instructions on how to build a super computer which, once made, provides further instructions on how to create a living organism, which takes on the form of a lab technician, Christine (Julie Christie), who has been compelled to commit suicide by the computer. The question remains whether the newly created being, named Andromeda, which the government is keen to use as an aid to industry and defense, is to be trusted, or has a hidden agenda, such as the taking over of humanity. Set between 1970 and 1972, the series, which began airing live on the BBC on 3 October 1961, was produced by Norman James and Michael Hayes, the latter of whom also directed the seven 45-minute episodes, which made a star of the young Julie Christie, who appeared in six of them. Featuring such episode titles as *The Message* (1961, TV), *The Monster* (1961, TV) and *The Last Mystery* (1961, TV), it was described by *The Evening News* as "a jolly good successor to *Quatermass*," and also starred Esmond Knight as Professor Ernest Reinhart, who was supported by Peter Halliday, Patricia Kneale, Noel Johnson, Frank Windsor, Anthony Valentine and John Nettleton, and although somewhat talkative, proved to be a big enough hit to warrant a six-part sequel, *The Andromeda Breakthrough* (1962, TV), also written by Elliot (who directed four episodes) and Hoyle, which nevertheless proved less compelling, perhaps because Julie Christie had moved on to bigger things, the role of Andromeda now being played by Susan Hampshire (note that a five-part Italian remake, *A come Andromeda*, care of RAI, followed in 1973, featuring Nicoletta Rizzi as Christine/Andromeda, while the BBC broadcast a live 90-minute remake in 2006 starring Tom Hardy and Kelly Reilly as Christine/Andromeda; only one episode of the original series, *The Face of the Tiger* [1961, TV], remains, along with clips from several others and the soundtrack to *The Last Mystery* [1961, TV]).

The BBC was also behind a half-hour adaptation of F. Antsey's age reversal fantasy *Vice Versa* (1961, TV), which aired on 3 December 1961, with William Mervyn and Graham Aza as the father and son who find themselves trading places (a fuller version of the novel appeared in 1981 care of rival channel ITV, which presented it as a seven-part series starring Peter Bowles and Paul Spurrier), while the following year they aired a four-part, 50-minute series titled *The Monsters* (1962, TV), which began on 8 November 1962. In this, William Greene starred as zoologist John Brent who, along with his new wife Felicity (Elizabeth Weaver), find themselves involved with the mysterious death of a government agent while honeymooning in a small lakeside village in the north of England. The locals believe the death attributable to the creatures that supposedly lurk in the depths of the lake, though Brent is more inclined to believe that Professor Cato (Robert Harris), who is working in the vicinity, is somehow responsible. Written by Evelyn Frazer and Vincent Tilsley, the series was directed by Mervyn Pinfield, and also featured Mark Dignam, Philip Madoc, Norman Mitchell, George Pravda and John Barrett, while the music was provided by Humphrey Searle. Unfortunately, all four episodes appear to be lost, and so further evaluation is not possible.

Drama series presenting plays (both old and new) for television were also still an integral part of the schedules in the UK in the sixties. Among such series was ATV's hour-long *Love Story* (1963–1974, TV), which began its 128-episode run on 3 June 1963, and though it primarily presented romantic dramas of varying hues, it occasionally went off piste, as with *It's a Long Way to Transylvania* (1967, TV) by

Robert Muller, in which Peter Wyngarde starred as Konrad Von Kroll, a long forgotten actor who finds himself in the public eye again when his old horror films are revived and take on cult status. Falling for a young admirer (June Barry), he attempts to woo her with a candlelit dinner and a coach ride, during which he recreates his vampire character with the aid of some plastic fangs, much to her amusement and, on occasion, fright. An affectionate lampoon of old-style horror films and performances, the program was directed by Valerie Hanson and also featured Irene Prador as Anna Von Kroll. Unfortunately, it is presently unavailable for further evaluation.

Another of these drama showcases was the BBC's *First Night* (1963–1964, TV), whose 33-episode run, which began on 22 September 1963, featured writing by Clive Exton, Willis Hall, Alun Owen, Arnold Wesker and Nigel Kneale among others. Mostly produced by John Eliott and directed by the likes of Alan Bridges, Ted Kotcheff, John Llewellyn Moxey and Peter Graham Scott, Kneale's episode, titled *The Road* (1963, TV), was helmed by Christopher Morahan, and involved an investigation into a reputedly haunted wood from which strange sounds have been emanating. Set in 1775, it sees the local squire (James Maxwell) request the assistance of Gideon Cobb (John Phillips), a scholar visiting from London, to use his scientific methods (such as they are) to determine whether the woods are indeed prey to supernatural phenomena, or if there is a more rational explanation. However, in the twist ending it is revealed that the wood is not haunted by events from the past, but by an echo from the future, which Cobb is unable to identify, given that the sounds—gridlocked traffic on a motorway in the aftermath of a nuclear war—are totally alien to him and the others who hear them. With sound effects care of Brian Hodgson and the BBC Radiophonic Workshop, it seems that the program, which also starred Ann Bell and Rodney Bewes, successfully achieved its aims. Unfortunately, although it was pre-recorded owing to its complex technical requirements, it was later wiped as a cost saving measure (videotape being too expensive to use just once at the time), and only the script itself now remains (note that the play was restaged for television in Australia in 1964, with Norman Kaye as the squire and Alexander Archdale as Gideon Cobb, although in this instance it was not so well received, with the *Sydney Morning Herald* describing it as being "too feeble to stand up to scrutiny," and likewise this version longer exists; the script was, however, later adapted for BBC radio by Tony Hadoke in 2018, with Adrian Scarborough as the squire and Mark Gatiss as Gideon Cobb).

Meanwhile, back in the States, and quickly making a mark for itself, was *The Outer Limits* (1963–1965, TV), an anthology show in the style of *The Twilight Zone* (1959–1964, TV), offering a mix of science fiction, fantasy and horror ("There is nothing wrong with your television set. Do not attempt to adjust the picture. We are controlling transmission," stated Vic Perrin's opening voice over, which concluded each program by informing audiences, "We now return control of your television set to you until next week at this same time when the Control Voice will take you to … *The Outer Limits*"). Running to 49 episodes over a two-season run, the show was created by jobbing writer and producer Leslie Stevens (who also executive produced), and featured scripts by the likes of Joseph Stefano (who also produced 32 episodes), Lou Morheim (who was also a story consultant on 31 episodes) and

Robert Towne (who would go on to win an Oscar for penning *Chinatown* [1974]), and like *The Twilight Zone*, it attracted a loyal production team, among them composer Dominic Frontiere (who worked on 31 episodes), cinematographers Kenneth Peach and Conrad L. Hall (25 episodes and 15 episodes each, respectively), editor Anthony DiMarco (18 episodes), effects man Jim Danforth (24 episodes), art director Jack Poplin (all 49 episodes) and make-up man Fred B. Phillips (likewise, all 49 episodes). It also brought in such established directors as Gerd Oswald (who helmed 14 episodes), Byron Haskin and James Goldstone, while visiting cast members included Robert Duvall, Robert Culp, Dabney Coleman, Martin Landau, June Havoc, Leonard Nimoy, Donald Pleasence, Mimsy Farmer, Adam West, Sally Kellerman and William Shatner.

The show began airing on ABC on 16 September 1963 with *The Galaxy Being* (1963, TV), which, like the show's title, was originally to have been *Please Stand By*. In it, a radio operator (Cliff Robertson) makes contact with a being from another galaxy, only for the alien to make its way to Earth via the radio waves after a DJ (Lee Philips) turns the power up too high! Written and directed by Leslie Stevens, the episode cost an astonishing $219,000 to make thanks to its involved effects work, which sees the glowing "electric" alien (achieved by using a reflective suit, which was subsequently turned to a negative image) have various run-ins with mankind during his visit. However, while science fiction was clearly the series' favored leaning, the program nevertheless often included horrific elements in its stories, which could be found in such season one installments as *Nightmare* (1963, TV), in which a group of soldiers from Earth are captured and experimented upon by aliens on the planet Ebon; *It Crawled Out of the Woodwork* (1963, TV), in which an experimental power station is taken over by an energy being; *Tourist Attraction* (1963, TV), in which an ancient monster is discovered in a Latin American lake; and *The Invisibles* (1964, TV), in which aliens plan to take over the Earth by taking over society's loners. However, the season's highlight was undoubtedly *The Sixth Finger* (1963, TV), in which a

scientist (Edward Mulhare) persuades a Welsh miner (David McCallum) to be a guinea pig in his experiments involving human evolution, only to find himself advancing by some 20,000 years into an egg-headed, six-fingered super genius care of make-up effects artist John Chambers.

Season two went on to present such titles as *Cold Hands, Warm Heart* (1964, TV), in which an astronaut (William Shatner) fresh back from a mission to Venus finds himself constantly cold; *Cry of Silence* (1964, TV), in which a couple (Eddie Albert and June Havoc), lost in a valley, find themselves under attack from the flora and

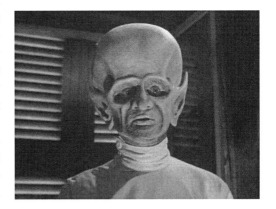

Egghead. An unrecognizable David McCallum in *The Sixth Finger* (1963, TV), an episode of *The Outer Limits* (1963–1965, TV) (ABC/ United Artists Television/Daystar Productions/Villa Di Stefano).

fauna; *The Invisible Enemy* (1964, TV), in which an alien kills off the members of man's first mission to Mars (among them Adam West and Rudy Solari); and, finally, *The Probe* (1965, TV), in which the crew of a crashed plane (among them Peggy Ann Garner, Ron Hayes and Peter Mark Richman) awake inside a strange chamber in which they are terrified by a rubber-like creature. The show was revived in 1995, and ran to 2002, clocking up a robust 152 episodes (compared to the original's 49), and while sci-fi always had the upper hand, horror occasionally showed its face, as with *Under the Bed* (1995, TV), about a missing boy (Joel Palmer) who, according to his sister, has been eaten by the Bogeyman, and *Ripper* (1999, TV), yet another variation on the Jack the Ripper legend, with Dr. John York (Cary Elwes) wrongly coming under suspicion for the crimes.

Who?

By the time the original *Outer Limits* was on air in the U.S., another science fiction show was making its mark in the UK. This was the perennially popular BBC series *Doctor Who* (1963–1989, TV), which follows the adventures of a Timelord simply known as the Doctor, who can hop about time and space in his Tardis, a police call box that is substantially bigger on the inside than it appears on the out. Created by Sydney Newman and originally starring William Hartnell, the show's epic 696-episode run began airing on 23 November 1963 with *An Unearthly Child* (1963, TV), in which two schoolteachers (William Russell and Jacqueline Hill) take an interest in the Doctor's granddaughter Susan (Carole Ann Ford), only to find themselves taken on a trip back to the time of the cavemen. Future adventures saw the Doctor encounter such celebrated opponents as the Daleks (the brainchild of long-standing contributor Terry Nation) and the Cybermen (the creation of Kit Pedler and Gerry Davis), as well as more familiar monsters, among them Count Dracula and the Frankenstein Monster in the adventure *Journey into Terror* (1965, TV), the Yeti in *The Abominable Snowmen* (1967, TV) and mummies in *Pyramids of Mars* (1975, TV). The Doctor's ability to conveniently "regenerate" himself saw the role subsequently played by Patrick Troughton, Jon Pertwee, Tom Baker, Peter Davison, Colin Baker and Sylvester McCoy (with Richard Hurndall standing in for the late Hartnell in *The Five Doctors* [1983, TV]). Noted for its eerie theme tune care of Ron Grainer (perfectly realized by the BBC's electronic music department, the Radiophonic Workshop), and for its inventive low-budget special effects, the program was aimed primarily at children, who would often find themselves taking refuge behind the sofa during its scarier moments, though it also attracted a sizeable adult following.

During its initial run, the program generated two theatrical features: *Dr. Who and the Daleks* (1965) and *Daleks—Invasion Earth 2150 A.D.* (1966), in which the character was played by horror star Peter Cushing. By the time the series was cancelled in 1989, it had become a cheap parody of itself. An attempt to revive it appeared in 1996 in the form of a TV movie, *Doctor Who* (1996, TVM), in which the title character was played by Paul McGann. A subsequent series failed to materialize, however, and it was left to super fan Russell T. Davies to reignite things in 2005, with Christopher Eccleston now in the title role. A popular hit, even more so when David Tennant took over the part the following season, it has remained on screen ever since, with Tennant subsequently followed by Matt Smith, Peter Capaldi, Jodie Whittaker and Ncuti Gatwa, while the Doctor's companions down the decades have included Billie Piper, Freema Agyeman, Catherine Tate, Bonnie Langford, Frazer Hines, Elisabeth Sladen, Lalla Ward, Peter Purvis and Louise Jameson. Sladen even had her own spin off series, *The Sarah Jane Adventures* (2007–2011, TV), which itself led to *SJA: Alien Files* (2010, TV), while another associate, Captain Jack Harkness, also generated his own show, *Torchwood* (2006–2011, TV), each of which featured monsters of various descriptions (Harkness also had a web series, *Torchwood: Web of Lies* [2011, TV]).

Other sixties series, ostensibly science fiction but not above featuring monsters or horror references, included such favorites as *Voyage to the Bottom of the Sea* (1964–1968, TV), whose 110 episodes, which began airing on ABC on 14 September 1964, included such self explanatory titles as *The Monster from Outer Space* (1965, TV), *Terror on Dinosaur Island* (1965, TV), *The Menfish* (1966, TV), *Werewolf* (1966, TV), *The Heat Monster* (1967, TV), *The Fossil Men* (1967, TV), *The Mummy* (1967, TV), *Deadly Amphibians* (1967, TV), *The Lobster Man* (1968, TV), *The Abominable Snowman* (1968, TV) and *Man-Beast* (1968, TV), whose creatures were created by make-up supervisor Ben Nye and his team. Based on his 1961 film, which he'd produced, directed and co-written, the show was created by Irwin Allen, whose TV output during this era also took in such sci-fi/fantasy shows as *Lost in Space* (1965–1968, TV [rebooted in 2018]), *The Time Tunnel* (1966–1967, TV) and *Land of the Giants* (1968–1970, TV), with the former the most likely to feature monsters, as per such installments as *Invaders from the Fifth Dimension* (1965, TV), *Attack of the Monster Plants* (1965, TV), *Ghost in Space* (1966, TV), *Space Creature* (1967, TV) and *The Dream Monster* (1970, TV). Likewise, *Star Trek* (1966–1969, TV), which was the creation of Gene Roddenberry, featured a number of monsters during its 80-episode run, but as the series was crammed with various races and alien species they were pretty much par for the course, among the more memorable being the rock eating Horta (as seen in *The*

Monster mash. The Frankenstein Monster (John Maxim) and Count Dracula (Malcolm Rogers) look on as the Daleks are lifted into position by the prop men during the filming of *Journey into Terror* (1965, TV) for *Doctor Who* (1963–1989, TV) (BBC).

Devil in the Dark [1967, TV]) and the cute but prodigiously reproductive Tribbles (as seen in *The Trouble with Tribbles* [1967, TV]).

Back to earlier in the decade now, and the British series *Detective* (1964–1969, TV), which began airing on the BBC on 30 March 1964. Clocking up 45 episodes over three seasons, the show presented adaptations of classic detective stories, among them works by Arthur Conan Doyle, G.K. Chesterton and Charles Dickens, as well as stories by more recent writers, among them *Carry On* composer Bruce Montgomery (writing as Edmund Crispin), whose 1946 novel *The Moving Toyshop* (1964, TV), which fea-

The howling. Charles Aidman plays the title character in *Werewolf* (1966, TV), one of the more memorable episodes of *Voyage to the Bottom of the Sea* (1964–1968, TV) (ABC/Irwin Allen Productions/Twentieth Century–Fox Television).

tured his recurring detective Gervase Fen (Richard Wordsworth), opened the series. In it a drunken poet (John Wood) sees a body in a toyshop window, only for both it and the shop to have disappeared by the time the police arrive. Among the other episodes (which included cases for Sherlock Holmes [Douglas Wilmer], Father Brown [Mervyn Johns] and Albert Campion [Brian Smith]) was an adaptation of Edgar Allan Poe's 1841 story *The Murders in the Rue Morgue* (1968, TV), in which Auguste Dupin (Edward Woodward) discovers that an ape was responsible for a series of grisly murders in Paris. Sadly, many of the 50-minute episodes have now been lost, preventing detailed evaluation (note that the fist season was introduced by Rupert Davies in the guise of Georges Simenon's Chief Inspector Jules Maigret).

Canned Laughter

In America, the 1964 season produced two popular sitcoms which, while by no means horrific in themselves, took a certain joy in poking fun at the genre, as well as the idealized American family. The first of these was *The Addams Family* (1964–1966, TV), which was based upon the popular cartoons by the artist Charles Addams, which had first appeared in *The New Yorker* in 1937. The immediate members of the ghoulish clan included the dashing Gomez Adams (John Astin), his vampire-like wife Morticia (Carolyn Jones), whose love of horticulture includes the rearing of carnivorous plants, their children Wednesday and Pugsley (Lisa Loring and Ken Weatherwax), their knife throwing grandmamma (Marie Blake), Morticia's bald-headed Uncle Fester (Jackie Coogan), whose idea of relaxation is to lie on his bed of nails, and the exceptionally hairy Cousin Itt (Felix Silla). Their servants meanwhile included the towering, harpsichord playing Lurch (Ted Cassidy), summoned by a hangman's noose bell pull that shakes the whole *Psycho*-like house they live in, and Thing, a disembodied hand which has the ability of turning up in the most unexpected of places. Created by David Levy, who also executive produced via Filmways Television, and noted for its finger snapping theme tune care of Vic Mizzy, the 64-episode series first aired on ABC on 18 September with *The Addams Family Goes to School* (1964, TV), in which, much to his inevitable regret, the local truant officer (Allyn Joslyn) visits the family to see why the children have been absent from school.

Surprisingly, the show ran to just two seasons, with a third (planned to be shot in color) cancelled at the planning stage, and while not exactly hilarious (the irritating canned laughter tends to kill the somewhat mild humor), it has remained a syndication stalwart ever since. It also produced a number of offshoots, among them a 16-episode Hanna-Barbera cartoon series, *The Addams Family* (1973, TV), for which Jackie Coogan and Ted Cassidy returned to voice Uncle Fester and Lurch; a one-off reunion special, *Halloween with the New Addams Family* (1977, TVM), which reunited the majority of the main cast in color (sadly, the intended new series failed to materialize); a second cartoon series, *The Addams Family* (1992–1993, TV), for which John Astin returned to voice Gomez for the show's 21 installments; and a TV movie, *Addams Family Reunion* (1998, TVM), starring Daryl Hanna as Morticia and Tim Curry as Gomez. There have also been two big-budget theatrical releases: *The Addams Family* (1991) and *Addams Family Values* (1993), which starred Anjelica Huston as Morticia, Raul Julia as Gomez and Christopher Lloyd as Uncle Fester, and a cartoon feature, *The Addams Family* (2019), with Gomez and Morticia voiced by Oscar Isaac and Charlize Theron (a sequel, *The Addams Family 2*, followed in 2021). There's also been a Broadway musical, *The Addams Family* (first performed in tryout in 2009), with songs by Andrew Lippa, while in 2021 Tim Burton helmed an eight-part series titled *Wednesday*, which observed the family's ghoulish activities from the young daughter's point of view.

The second genre spoofing sitcom to hail from 1964 was

Altogether ooky. From left to right (back row), Jackie Coogan, John Astin, Marie Blake and Ted Cassidy and (front row) Lisa Loring, Carolyn Jones and Ken Weatherwax in a publicity shot for *The Addams Family* (1964–1966, TV) (ABC/Filmways Television).

The Munsters (1964–1966, TV), which began its 72-episode run on CBS on 24 September with *Munster Masquerade* (1964, TV), just six days after the launch of *The Addams Family*, and like their contemporaries, they presented an oddball but loving family who couldn't quite understand why people reacted to them the way they did. Among them were father Herman (Fred Gwynne), a goofy Frankenstein Monster lookalike, his vampire wife Lily (Yvonne de Carlo), their were-boy son Eddie (Butch Patrick) and their niece Marilyn (Beverley Owen, later Pat Priest), the only one of them to look "normal." Also in residence was Lily's father, the Dracula-like Grandpa (Al Lewis [who was actually one year younger than de Carlo]). Created by Ed Haas and Norm Liebmann, the show was originally to have been shot in color but was switched to 35mm black and white as a cost saving exercise, which actually better suited its subject matter, given that the old Universal monster films it was spoofing were all in black and white (the series was actually filmed at Universal Studios). Helped along by another catchy theme tune, this time care of Jack Marshall, and committed playing by the cast (not to mention some impressive make-ups care of brothers Perc and Bud Westmore and their nephew Michael), the show was another hit, which has likewise remained a syndication favorite ever since (note that an unaired 15-minute pilot titled *My Fair Munster*, which was shot in color, featured Joan Marshall as Herman's wife Phoebe and Nate Derman as Eddie; a second 30-minute pilot shot in black and white and also titled *My Fair Munster* was then filmed with Yvonne De Carlo and Butch Patrick; a third version of *My Fair Munster* subsequently appeared as episode two of season one).

The series was followed by a theatrical feature *Munster, Go Home!* (1966), which sees Herman inherit an English castle from his uncle (thus making him Lord Munster, Fifth Earl of Shroudshire), much to the consternation of his cousins. The movie reunited the full original cast and also featured guest shots from Terry-Thomas, Hermione Gingold and John Carradine (who'd appeared in two of the TV episodes as Mr. Gateman). More importantly, it was shot in widescreen and Technicolor care of Benjamin H. Kline, thus revealing the green hue of the cast's monster make-up (in the U.S. the film was released on 15 June in support of the Don Knotts comedy *The Ghost and Mr. Chicken* [1966] while in the UK

A candid shot of Fred Gwynne in full Herman Munster regalia behind the scenes in *The Munsters* (1964–1966, TV) (CBS/Kayro-Vue Productions).

it went out on 30 December in support of the Norman Wisdom comedy *Press for Time* [1966]). A TV movie followed 15 years later titled *The Munsters' Revenge* (1981, TVM), which again featured Gwynne, de Carlo and Lewis, but the moment seemed to have passed. This time the Munsters find themselves accused of being behind a series of robberies committed by lookalike robots controlled by Dr. Diablo (Sid Caesar), all of which prompted *Variety* to comment, "All the fun of a trip on the *Titanic*, or a return to Vietnam." A series reboot followed in 1987 with *The Munsters Today* (1987–1991, TV), which starred John Schuck as Herman, Lee Meriwether as Lily and Howard Morton as Grandpa, and despite being a pale imitation of the original, it nevertheless stood its ground and racked up a surprising 73 episodes (one more than the sixties show). This was followed by another TV movie, *Here Come the Munsters* (1995, TVM), which aired on Halloween and starred Edward Herrmann as Herman, Veronica Hamel as Lily and Robert Morse as Grandpa (with gag cameos by Yvonne de Carlo, Al Lewis, Butch Patrick and Pat Priest). This in turn was followed by *The Munsters' Scary Little Christmas* (1996, TVM), this time with Sam McMurray as Herman, Ann Magnuson as Lily and Sandy Baron as Grandpa.

One could argue that there was a third genre spoofing comedy with *Bewitched* (1964–1972, TV), which began its epic 254-episode run on ABC on 17 September 1964, the day before *The Addams Family* first aired. Created by Sol Saks, the program starred Elizabeth Montgomery as Samantha Stephens, a suburban housewife who just happens to be a witch, and despite being urged by her husband Darrin (Dick York, later Dick Sargent) to keep her supernatural powers a secret, she can't help but use them to get herself out of various scrapes (which she does by wriggling her nose). Mildly amusing fun thanks to the efforts of its personable cast, among them Agnes Moorehead as Samantha's garishly gowned mother Endora, one couldn't really label it a horror spoof as such, despite its cast of witches and warlocks, primarily because it is so bright and cheerful, but its catchy theme tune, silly situations and simple trick effects made it popular with young and old alike, and it is included here for the sake of completeness. Shows with a similar theme include *I Dream of Jeannie* (1965–1970, TV), *Nanny and the Professor* (1970–1971, TV), *The Girl with Something Extra* (1973–1974, TV) and *Tabitha* (1976–1978, TV), the latter the sequel to *Bewitched* (1964–1972, TV), while both *Mr. Terrific* (1967, TV) and *Captain Nice* (1967, TV), which debuted on the same day, offered comedy takes on the Jekyll and Hyde theme, with our mild mannered heroes (Stephen Strimpell in the former [Alan Young in the unaired 1966 pilot] and William Daniels in the latter) taking on superhuman abilities after downing a pill and a formula, respectively, but we really are starting to veer off the road with these.

It's often the case, particularly today, that a pilot won't go to series, the reasons for which can be many and various (poor concept, bad handling, wrong cast, inappropriate content, lack of faith from the studio, change of management, etc.). One such show that fell at the starting gate was the anthology series *Haunted* (1964, TV), which was to have aired on CBS. It certainly had pedigree, given that it was created by Joseph Stefano, who not only wrote the feature-length pilot, *The Ghost of Sierra de Cobre* (1964, TVM), but also produced it (via Villa Di Stefano, which had been behind *The Outer Limits* [1963–1965, TV]) and took over the direction when TV veteran Robert Stevens fell ill during shooting and had to pull out. The set up is certainly intriguing and sees architect and part time paranormal investigator Nelson Orion (Martin Landau) invited to the estate of the wealthy Mandore family by Vivia Mandore (Diane Baker), whose blind husband Henry (Tom Simcox) wishes him to investigate a ghost who is haunting him by telephone. Could it be a prankster calling, or his mother, who died almost a year earlier, and had insisted in her will that a telephone be installed in the crypt within arm's reach of her open coffin, given her fear of being buried alive? And what does the mysterious new housekeeper, Paulina (Judith Anderson), have to do with it all? And how does the murder of an American schoolteacher in Sierra de Cobre fit into things?

At 80 minutes, the film (which was extended from a 52-minute original to create a feature) is a little stretched at times, but its opening scenes in the crypt are undeniably atmospheric thanks to the excellent work of art director McClure Capps and cinematographer Conrad L. Hall, whose lighting and roving camera is very much in the style of Italian horror maestro Mario Bava, while the appearance of the "bleeding ghost" which is accompanied by moaning and screeching sounds carries a genuine frisson (so much so that it was feared to be too strong for television audiences). Careful performances from the cast, all of whom are in tune with the material and prevent things from becoming overly melodramatic, meanwhile help to sell the story, as does a solid score care of Dominic Frontiere. Some of the dialogue is pretty good too (comments Vivia when she first meets Orion outside the imposing family tomb, "I've seen villages in Mexico, living people living in tin and mud—and here, dignity, protection from the rain, and even art, and all wasted on the dead"). The highly effective opening titles also help to set up the piece with some style, beginning with what appears to be a shot of gravestones, only for them to cross fade into the skyscrapers of LA, over which the ocean then laps. A lost gem which only now appears to be garnering recognition, the film doesn't seem to have aired in the U.S. at the time, but was shown on channels elsewhere around the globe, including Japan, the Philippines and Australia, hence the enthusiastic comments on IMDb from these parts of the world. It's certainly worth tracking down on YouTube or Blu-ray (care of Kino Lorber, whose disc contains both the longer and shorter versions), and it's a genuine shame that Orion didn't go on to investigate further cases (Landau would instead find a home on TV two years later with the long running *Mission: Impossible* [1966–1973, TV], in which he played Rollin Hand between 1966 and 1969).

By way of a brief stop off, we next encounter *Carol for Another Christmas* (1964, TVM), a one-off written by Rod Serling following the conclusion of his duties on *The Twilight Zone* (1959–1964, TV). Aired on ABC on 28 December 1964, this update of Charles Dickens' *A Christmas Carol* sees a wealthy industrialist, Daniel Grudge (Sterling Hayden), visited on Christmas Eve by three ghosts (Steve Lawrence, Pat Hingle and Robert Shaw) who try to persuade him to reconsider his staunchly held isolationist views, fermented by the grief and embitterment over the death of his son Marley 20 years earlier on Christmas Eve during World War II. Shown without commercial interruption, the 84-minute program (made for a 90-minute timeslot) was the first in a series of specials sponsored by Xerox to promote the UN and global cooperation, and as such it sometimes wears its sermonizing a little too obviously on its sleeve (the *LA Times* described the play as "more tract than drama," whist *The New York Times* labeled it an "exercise in garrulous ineptitude"). Nevertheless, it's clearly a prestige production given the talent involved, among them Joseph L. Mankiewicz (producer-director), Arthur J. Ornitz (cinematographer), Gene Callahan (production designer), Henry Mancini (composer) and Anna Hill Johnstone (costumes), while the supporting cast includes such high profile names as Eva Marie Saint, Ben Gazzara, Britt Ekland and Peter Sellers, the latter as Imperial Me, who appears in the Christmas Future sequence as an evangelist whose mission is to promote selfishness and xenophobia via mob politics ("the civilization of I," as he puts it), and on which count alone this rather oddball affair is worth a look. Intended for a one-time broadcast, it subsequently lay in the vaults for 48 years before eventually being resurrected on TCM in 2012, though clips from it had been featured in the documentary *The Unknown Peter Sellers* (2000, TV).

The Canadians also had a stab at the story the same year with *Mr. Scrooge* (1964, TVM), which aired on CBC during the festive period (air date unavailable). A musical version featuring songs by Dolores Claman, Richard Morris and Ted Wood, it starred Cyril Ritchard as Scrooge, Alfie Bass as Bob Cratchit, Tessie O'Shea as Mrs. Crachit, Eric Christmas as Jacob Marley and, as the Ghosts of Christmas Past, Present and Yet to Come, Gillie Fenwick, Norman Welsh and Eric Clavering, respectively. Sadly, it no longer seems to be available, but may, like *A Carol for Another Christmas*, reappear one day. The Czechs also presented a version of the story during this period titled *Mister Scrooge* (1967, TVM), which starred Vaclav Nouzovsky in the title role, and which aired on 25 December 1967, but this too seems to be no longer available. The Brits meanwhile took the comedic route with *Carry on Christmas* (1969, TV), which aired on ITV on 24 December 1969. A broad romp in the style of the much-loved *Carry On* movies, it was written by Talbot Rothwell and starred series regulars Sid James as Ebenezer Scrooge, Charles Hawtrey as the Spirit of Christmas Past, Barbara Windsor as the Spirit of Christmas Present and Bernard Bresslaw as the Spirit of Christmas Future. Bresslaw also played Frank N. Stein's Monster in the show, Terry Scott Dr. Frank N. Stein and Peter Butterworth Dracula, while Windsor also appeared as Cinderella, Hawtrey as Buttons, Frankie Howerd as Robert Browning and Hattie Jacques as Elizabeth Barrett, which gives a fair indication as to how far the story strayed from Dickens!

While we've pulled over, let's also take a quick look at *The Stately Ghosts of England* (1965, TV), a rather curious one-hour documentary special that aired on NBC on 25 January 1965. Written, produced and directed by Frank de Felitta from a 1963 book by Diana Norman (who provided the program with research and technical advice), it starred eccentric comedy favorite Margaret Rutherford and her husband Stringer Davis, who travel about England in the company of society clairvoyant Tom Corbett, calling at three stately homes (Longleat, Salisbury Hall and Beaulieu Abbey), where they discuss the ghostly sightings and "uncanny happenings" (as Lord Bath puts it at one point) that allegedly have taken place there. Nicely photographed in color by Leonard Waldorf, and featuring a plush score by Glenn Paxton, the program presents anecdotal evidence and photographs of ghosts and materializations as if gospel (they're certainly taken as such by our intrepid explorers, of whom we are informed that Rutherford is a true believer in ghosts). However, though told with a completely straight face, one can't help but suppress a smile as a be-caped Rutherford, in full Madame Arcarti mode, relays such stories as that of Nell Gwyn, and Corbett wanders about solemnly taking in the vibes, leaving Davis to look on in his usual state of befuddlement. Undeniably full of curiosity value (albeit for all the wrong reasons), this perhaps wasn't the kind of thing that NBC News, which was rather surprisingly behind the project, should have been putting its name to.

Over in the world of television animation, the myopic Mr. Magoo had an encounter with one the genre's major characters in *Mr. Magoo's Doctor Frankenstein* (1965, TV), a 30-minute version of the celebrated Mary Shelley novel made via UPA, which aired on NBC on 13 March 1965 as one of 26 episodes of *The Famous Adventures of Mr. Magoo* (1964–1965, TV) which, following its launch on 19 September 1964 with *Mr. Magoo's William Tell* (1964, TV), went on to include *Mr. Magoo's Gunga Din* (1964, TV), *Mr. Magoo's Rip Van Winkle* (1965, TV) and *Mr. Magoo's Sherlock Holmes* (1965, TV). Magoo had actually encountered Frankenstein before in one of his theatrical shorts, *Magoo Meets Frankenstein* (1959), in which he inadvertently stays at the good doctor's castle while driving through Europe; this had also aired as an episode of an earlier TV series *Mister Magoo* (1960–1961, TV). However, in this potted adaptation of the story, penned by Sloan Nibley, Magoo himself portrays Frankenstein, who recalls his experiments to the captain of a schooner, who has rescued him from a small boat adrift at sea during an attempt to reach the Monster, who has escaped to a remote island.

Remembering how he managed to produce "live muscle cell" Magoo/Frankenstein goes on to describe how he created a monstrous looking being which he teaches to speak, only for it to escape. But when its appearance causes shock among the locals, it retreats back to the castle. "I don't like the world of people," it tells the doctor, and demands others of his kind so as to show the world "the real meaning of fear and hatred." But when the doctor proves reluctant to carry out the Monster's request, it steals his notes so as to produce the beings himself ("You have done your work well, doctor. I now have it in my power to create a super race, and I will"), and disappears to a remote island to carry out its scheme, where, bringing the story full circle, the captain drops off Magoo, who hopes to prevent the Monster from achieving its plan, only to discover three new beings awaiting activation. The story concludes with Magoo blowing up the lab and himself with it ("I made their creation possible, and now, now I must redeem myself"), bringing the proceedings to a surprisingly nihilistic conclusion.

Directed by Abe Levitow (who'd co-directed *Magoo Meets Frankenstein* [1959]), this is a pretty straight condensation of the story, almost completely lacking comedy relief, with Magoo's usual bumbling, voiced as always by Jim Backus, kept to a minimum, and while the animation is fairly simple in typical UPA style, the backgrounds are often stylish, while the ghoulish appearance of the Monster, with its bellowing voice, may well have caused a few sleepless nights for younger viewers. This wasn't actually Magoo's first encounter with the supernatural. A couple of years earlier he'd also appeared in the holiday special *Mr. Magoo's Christmas Carol* (1962, TV), a musical version of the Dickens story with songs by Jule Styne and Bob Merrill. Broadcast on NBC on 18 December 1962, this featured the voices of Jim Backus (as Magoo/ Scrooge), Royal Dano (Marley's ghost), Paul Frees (Fezziwig) and Jack Cassidy (Bob Cratchit) and was also directed by Abe Levitow. Seven years later, another cartoon version, this time featuring songs by Richard Bowden, appeared. First aired in Australia in 1969, it was directed by Zoran Janjic via API (Air Programs International), with Ron Hadrick now providing the miser's vocals. This was shown in America the following year by CBS on 13 December 1970 (note that API was also behind such genre-centric cartoons as *Tales of Washington Irving* [1970, TV], *The Mysterious Island* [1975, TV] and *A Journey to the Center of the Earth* [1977, TV]).

Although it mostly presented serious works by such names as Samuel Beckett, Anton Chekhov and George Bernard Shaw, *New York Television Theatre* (1965–1970, TV), which launched its 30-episode run on WNDT on 18 October 1965 with a version of Jack Richardson's 1961 play *Gallows Humor* (1965, TV), took an occasional foray into the gothic with the likes of *The Sandbox* (1970, TV), a version of Edward Albee's absurdist 1959 piece about an old woman who is visited at the beach by the Angel of Death. Unfortunately, despite starring the likes of Rosemary Harris, Eileen Heckart, Hurd Hatfield, Morgan Freeman, Frances Sternhagen, Fred Gwynne and George Gaynes, it appears that many of the episodes, a number of which were produced and directed by Glenn Jordan, are no longer extant, preventing further comment.

In the UK, horror and science fiction melded again in the little remembered ABC series *Undermind* (1965, TV), in which a personnel officer (Jeremy Wilkin) discovers that his brother Frank (Jeremy Kemp) has been brainwashed by an alien force intent on using subversive acts to bring about the collapse of civilization prior to a full-scale invasion. With the help of his sister-in-law (Rosemary Nicols), they attempt to expose the threat and save mankind, but the task proves more difficult than they imagined. Written by Robert Banks Stewart (and others) and directed by the likes of Bill Bain and Peter Potter, the 11-part series began airing on 8 May, and though now finally available on DVD, seems somehow to have slipped through the net of cult worship, despite a cast featuring Denis Quilley, Peter Barkworth, Barrie Ingham, Patrick Allen, George Baker, Ewan Hooper, Philip Latham and Lally Bowers. Also pretty much forgotten is the BBC serial *Legend of Death* (1965, TV), a five-part modern day sci-fi reworking of the ancient Greek myth *Theseus and the Minotaur*. Written by Brian Hayles and directed by Gerald Blake, it bore such episode titles as *The Moving Maze* and *Death Switch* and began airing on BBC2 on 19 July 1965. Starring David Andrews as Theodore and John Hollis as Minolti, it also featured Andrew Sachs, Gerald Sim and Sarah Lawson. Unfortunately, it is now regarded as lost, preventing further evaluation.

Science fiction was also to the fore in the BBC's hour-long anthology series *Out of the Unknown* (1965–1971, TV), whose four season, 49-episode run offered stories by the likes of Ray Bradbury, Terry Nation, John Wyndham, Nigel Kneale, J.G. Ballard and Isaac Asimov. Season one kicked off on 4 October 1965 with a post apocalyptic piece *No Place Like Earth* (1965, TV), but as early as episode three, horror began to rear its head with *Stranger in the Family* (1965, TV), in which a young man (Richard Callaghan) with telepathic abilities is able to control others against their wills. Season two went on to include *Frankenstein Mark 2* (1966, TV), in which a divorcee (Rachel Roberts) begins to fear for her ex-husband's safety at the space research facility at which he works, while season three included *The Yellow Pill* (1969, TV), in which a psychiatrist (Francis Matthews) finds himself outwitted by a murderer he is examining (this story by Rog Phillips had already done service as an episode of *Out of This World* [1962, TV]). Season four more fully embraced the supernatural with *To Lay a Ghost* (1971, TV), in which the victim of a sexual assault (Lesley-Anne Down) moves into a house with her new husband, only to find herself pursued by the ghost of a rapist and murderer (that it is revealed that the young woman actually enjoyed her experience and seeks more of the same can no longer stand scrutiny; it also makes the episode's title all the more dubious). Other episodes in the final season included *Deathday* (1971, TV), in which a newspaper reporter (Robert Lang) plans to murder his cheating wife and blame it on a serial killer; *The Sons and Daughters of Tomorrow* (1971, TV), in which it is revealed that a village community is controlled by a witch; *Welcome Home* (1971, TV), in which a doctor (Anthony Ainley) returning home from a period in a psychiatric ward finds that he is no longer recognized and that another man has taken over his life; *The Last Witness* (1971, TV), in which a man (Anthony Bate) finds himself suffering visions from the future following his involvement in a shipwreck; *The Chopper* (1971, TV), a Nigel Kneale story in which the spirit of a dead motorcyclist possesses a lady journalist; *The Uninvited* (1971, TV), in which a couple (John Nettleton and June Ellis) are seemingly haunted by visions from the past which turn out to be a portent of things to come; and *The Shattered Eye* (1971, TV), in which a painter's life is turned upside down following an encounter with a mysterious old tramp (Freddie Jones). Sadly, a good many of the episodes, many of which were produced by Irene Shubik, were wiped by the Beeb as a cost saving exercise (though the surviving episodes are available on DVD care of the BFI).

Mysterious Imaginings

The horror-themed anthology show finally came into its own with the British series *Mystery and Imagination* (1966–1970, TV), which took upon itself the task of presenting a number of literature's key genre works, as well as a few choice lesser known items (it was billed as "Great Tales of the Supernatural"). Featuring adaptations of Bram Stoker, Edgar Allan Poe, Mary Shelley, Robert Louis Stevenson and Sheridan Le Fanu, this, finally, was the big hitter as far as a serious, fully-fledged, all-encompassing gothic horror omnibus was concerned. Primarily produced by Jonathan Alwyn, who took on 20 of the show's 24 episodes, it was shot on video for broadcast on the UK's independent television network ITV care of ABC between 1966 and early 1968, and, following a franchise change, by Thames Television thereafter.

The series began on Saturday, 29 January, at 10:05 p.m. with a 50-minute black and white presentation of the 1895 J. Meade Falkner story *The Lost Stradivarius* (1966, TV), the importance of which was marked by having a still from the program featured on the cover of the weekly listings magazine *TV Times*. Unfortunately, aside from a tantalizing domestic audio recording available on YouTube, this, along with many of the show's other episodes, is presently lost. Adapted by Owen Holder and directed by Bill Bain, the story top lined future Sherlock Holmes star Jeremy Brett as Sir John Maltravers, who discovers a violin hidden in a secret compartment in his Oxford college rooms, the playing of which appears to summon the ghost of its former owner, an evil occultist whose influence leads to a life of obsession and depravity. The program also starred David Buck in the role of Richard Beckett, whose character, taken from Le Fanu's 1872 story *The Room in the Dragon Volant*, acted as the show's host over 12 episodes. The program also featured Patricia Garwood as Maltravers' increasingly concerned sister Sophia, Franco De Rosa, Peter Ashmore and Angela Morant, had music by Robert Sharples and was designed by Stan Woodward. Otherwise, little else remains of this important moment in small screen gothic horror.

For episode two, Alwyn and his regular story editor Terence Feely turned to Robert Louis Stevenson's 1884 story *The Body Snatcher* (1966, TV), in which David Buck was this time joined by the likes of Ian Holm, Michael Gwynne, Dermot Tuohy, John Garrie and James Cossins in a production adapted by Robert Muller, designed by Voytek and helmed by Toby Robinson. Unfortunately, the program is likewise missing in action. In fact, only the following two installments (episodes three and four) from the first two ABC seasons survive, the first of them being a reasonably lavish version of Edgar Alan Poe's 1839 opus *The Fall of the House of Usher* (1966, TV), with Denholm Elliott in the role of the deranged Roderick Usher and Susannah York as his cataleptic sister Madeleine. Adapted by David Campton, designed by Assheton Gorton and directed by Kim Mills, this is a quality version of an albeit familiar story, given an air of class thanks to the acting talent on show. Rather less familiar to audiences would have been the following episode, *The Open Door* (1966, TV), taken from an 1882 short story by the prolific Margaret Oliphant, about a Colonel who is called home from a trip to London to discover that his young son is bedridden, having been traumatized by a wailing voice he heard on the way home from school. This time the star was British cinema stalwart Jack Hawkins, who plays the worried Colonel Mortimer. Accompanied by Rachel Gurney as his wife, John Laurie, Mark Dignam, Henry Beltram, Molly Weir and Amanda Walker (the latter as the

Cover story. *Mystery and Imagination* (1966–1970, TV) is launched in style by *TV Times* (ITP/TI Media/Time Inc. UK/Future plc).

unseen voice), the production was adapted by George F. Kerr, designed by Philip Harrison and directed by one of the few women working in this capacity at the time, Joan Kemp-Welch, who generates moments of genuine atmosphere as the Colonel's investigation into the matter in a nearby ruin proves the voice to be all too real.

The remaining episodes of season one took in a fresh version of M.R. James' *The Tractate Middoth* (1966, TV), an adaptation of the same author's 1895 story *Lost Hearts* (1966, TV), in which a kindly gentleman (Richard Pearson) is revealed to have a predilection for child sacrifice, and yet another version of Oscar Wilde's *The Canterville Ghost* (1966, TV), with entertainer Bruce Forsythe in the role of the ghostly Sir Simon. Tantalizing stuff, but all missing, save for some homemade audio recordings and the cherished memories of those who watched the programs at the time of broadcast. Season two began with *Room 13* (1966, TV), taken from the M.R. James story *Number 13* (already presented as an episode of *Great Ghost Tales* [1961, TV]), in which a room seems to appear and disappear in a small hotel (Joss Ackland, David Battley, George Woodbridge and Tessa Wyatt were this time among the cast). This was followed by *The Beckoning Shadow* (1966, TV), adapted from J.H. Riddell's 1882 story *Old Mrs. Jones*, about woman (Maureen Pryor) who returns to haunt the place where she was poisoned by her husband; *The Flying Dragon* (1966, TV), taken from Le Fanu's *The Room in the Dragon Volant*, in which David Buck's Richard Beckett comes into his own after becoming involved with the mysterious Countess de St. Valyre (Ann Bell) in a story about a number of disappearances at the titular inn; an adaptation of Le Fanu's 1872 novella *Carmilla* (1966, TV), in which a seemingly ageless vampire (Jane Merrow) returns to one of her previous haunts (Hammer would soon after film the story as *The Vampire Lovers* [1970] with Ingrid Pitt in the role of the voluptuous vampire); and *The Phantom Lover* (1966, TV), taken from the 1886 Vernon Lee novella *Oke of Okehusrt*, about a husband (Robert Hardy) who becomes jealous when his wife (Virginia McKenna) reveals that she has a ghostly admirer.

Following a break of some 14 months, season three returned on 22 March 1968 with another M.R. James adaptation, *Casting the Runes* (1968, TV), taken from his 1911 story of the same name, which had already been the subject of a well-regarded film *Night of the Demon* (1957, aka *Curse of the Demon*). In it, John Fraser starred as the hapless Dunning, who finds himself involved in the deadly machinations of a powerful demonologist named Karswell (Robert Eddison, best known for later playing the Grail Knight in *Indiana Jones and the Last Crusade* [1989]). Like the majority of the previous episodes, however, it remains lost, save for a few tantalizing "preview" moments in which Dunning discovers an advertisement on an omnibus commemorating his death in one month's time. The remainder of the season's episodes also remain missing in action, among them *The Listener* (1968, TV), based on a 1907 Algernon Blackwood story, in which a man (Edward Woodward) sensitive to noise finds himself quiet lodgings only to suspect that he is not quite alone in his rooms; *A Place of One's Own* (1968, TV), a take on the popular 1940 Oswell Sitwell novel (already the subject of a well regarded 1945 film) in which a couple (Joss Ackland and Megs Jenkins) move into a house haunted by a young woman who was murdered there; a version of Sir Walter Scott's *The Devil's Piper* (1968, TV), in which the Devil (Robert James) persuades a bagpipe player to literally go to hell to get a receipt for his rent from his recently deceased landlord; yet another version of Poe's ever popular *The Tell-Tale Heart* (1968, TV); and *Feet Foremost* (1968, TV), taken from the 1948 short story by L.P. Hartley, in which a man (Neil Stacy) staying with friends encounters a vengeful female ghost out to right an injustice.

Season four, which continued on 4 November the same year, and was now produced by Thames Television, upped the running time from 50 minutes to 75, thus allowing for more substantial material to be covered, among them the genre's two big hitters, *Frankenstein* and *Dracula*. These, however, were preceded by *Uncle Silas* (1968, TV), taken from the 1864 novel by Sheridan Le Fanu, which had already been filmed in 1947, with Derrick de Marney starring as the title character, out to menace his young niece, now in his care until she comes of age and is able to inherit her father's fortune. Here it is Robert Eddison who takes on the role of the dastardly uncle, with his vulnerable young charge played by Lucy Fleming. Adapted by Stanley Miller and directed by Alan Cooke, the program was designed by Stan Woodward, whose work takes in a series of suitably gloomy Victorian interiors, while the supporting cast includes Patience Collier as the girl's evil (and bald headed!) governess Madame de la Rougierre, Lally Bowers, Dudley Sutton, Michael Redd (as the young Silas), John Walsh and Gwendolyn Watts. A little talky a times, and perhaps lacking a knowing wink or two, the installment nevertheless racks up some moments of high melodrama and is accompanied by an imposing organ soundtrack care of composer James Stevens (a three-part remake of the story titled *The Dark Angel* followed in 1989 care of the BBC, starring Peter O'Toole as Uncle Silas).

The following week the series turned its attention to *Frankenstein* (1968, TV). This wasn't television's first stab at the story as we have noted, but was certainly the first seriously intentioned attempt to bring Mary Shelley's saga to the screen, two of the previous versions having been little more than escapades in the style of the later Universal films, which had begun seriously enough with *Frankenstein* (1931) and *Bride of Frankenstein* (1935) before descending to such B-level romps as *Frankenstein Meets the Wolf Man* (1943) and *House of Frankenstein* (1944), not to mention *Abbott and Costello Meet Frankenstein* (1948). Hammer had of course taken matters seriously with *The Curse of Frankenstein* (1957) and *The Revenge of Frankenstein* (1958), for which the selling point had been color, but even they had started to go down the path of the B-movie scenario with *The Evil of Frankenstein* (1964), and none of their screenplays could claim any particular adherence to the Shelley original above or beyond the central idea of a scientist attempting to create a new, super intelligent being from cadavers.

To this end, Robert Muller's adaptation clearly attempts to more fully return to the spirit of Shelley, but the results are somewhat po-faced as a consequence, taking matters a little *too* seriously (some knowing gallows humor would not have gone amiss). It also sticks to formula in some respects (Frankenstein has a hunchbacked assistant), and is not without its own gimmicks, among them the novelty of having the leading actor play both Frankenstein and The Being (as the Monster is listed in the credits), thanks to the use of split screen and a double (Keith Adrian) for the reverse angles. As the creator, Ian Holm makes for a suitably monomaniacal albeit rather dull Frankenstein, while as the created, he marginally better portrays the tortured nature of the Monster who, as per the book, is capable of increasingly cogent speech ("You despise me, you who gave me life!"). Of the supporting cast, Richard Vernon comes across best as Frankenstein's tutor, Professor Krempe, but the rest, among them Sarah Badel, Ron Pember and Robert Hunter, are rather bland and characterless. Ultimately, despite its lofty ambitions, for which full marks, this is nevertheless a disappointingly tedious production, with Voytek's direction lacking pace, visual flair and even thrills, all of which appear to have been sacrificed in the name of fidelity (in this regard, the creation scene is a particular disappointment). Originally broadcast in color, the program is now available only in black and white.

A far better affair is the series' production of *Dracula* (1968, TV). Despite the fact that Charles Graham's adaptation of the Stoker epic takes the usual licenses with the storyline, it benefits from a far stronger cast than its direct predecessor, among them Denholm Elliott as the title character, Bernard Archard as Professor Van Helsing, Corin Redgrave as Jonathan Harker, Suzanne Neve as Mina Harker, James Maxwell as Dr. Seward, Susan George as Lucy Weston and Joan Hickson as Mrs. Weston, not to mention Nina Baden-Semper, Valerie Muller and Margaret Nolan as three hissing vampires. The story begins *in media res* with the Count already in England being entertained in the home of Dr. Seward, when Jonathan Harker bursts through the window of the drawing room, having escaped from the good doctor's asylum (he is the sole survivor of the wrecked *Demeter* we are told), following which we briefly flash back to his dealings with Dracula in Transylvania. Wearing tinted glasses ("Daylight is painful to me"), the Count is very much a gentleman of society, and has clearly taken a liking to Miss Lucy, whom he eventually visits in her bedroom, where he sinks his rat-like teeth into her neck, draining her of blood. Having examined her, it's not long before Van Helsing is on Dracula's trail, eventually tracking down his resting place to a nearby unconsecrated grave to which he and Seward have inadvertently been led by Harker, who is in the Count's thrall.

While the less-well-known *Uncle Silas* benefits from the extended running time, both *Frankenstein* and *Dracula* do not, perhaps because their stories are so familiar from multiple tellings (this must have been the case even back in the sixties). As the Count, Elliott is perhaps a little full of face for the part, and his curious accent doesn't quite work, while Archard lacks the required eccentricity as Van Helsing, but Redgrave expertly chews the scenery as the deranged Harker, and George is pretty as a picture as the Count's unfortunate victim, whose return from the grave proves to be one of the program's highlights ("See, I am no spirit, but flesh transformed," she informs Mina, whom she encounters in the graveyard). She is eventually dispatched by Van Helsing after having returned to her coffin in the family crypt, while Dracula's demise follows soon after with the touch of a cross, which prompts him to crumble to dust before our eyes in one of the best disintegration scenes captured on camera (but is this really the conclusion of the story given that we see Mina holding Dracula's ring at the end?). A little slow at times, the program could have benefited from a little more visual flair from director Patrick Dromgoole, and while one might not be inclined to rate it as a classic telling of the story as a consequence, there are sequences along the way that aren't without atmosphere, despite the low-budget with which it has been saddled.

For the fifth and final season, which began airing on 9 February 1970, the running time remained at 75 minutes, and color became a permanent fixture. Things began with a somewhat dull presentation of Robert Louis Stevenson's *The Suicide Club* (1970, TV), which follows the attempts by Prince Florizel (Alan Dobie) to curtail the illicit activities of a club at which desperate men, keen to end it all, are able to gamble with their lives. Written by Robert Muller and directed by Mike Vardy, the program has a score by the well-regarded film composer Benjamin Frankell, and also starred Hildegard Neil, Ronald Adam, Jonathan Newth and Ivor Danvers. Again, the extra length is not necessarily a benefit to the proceedings, but they at least conclude with a well staged sword fight between the prince and the club's president (Bernard Archard), which takes place before an open coffin which lies in wait to accommodate the loser.

Rather more full-blooded was *Sweeney Todd* (1970, TV), which was adapted from the George Dibdin-Pitt play *The String of Pearls* by Vincent Tilsley. Earlier TV versions of the story include a previously noted 1947 BBC production starring Valentine Dyall, and an episode of *Gaslight Theatre* (1965, TV) with Alfred Marks in the lead. Here it is character star Freddie Jones who wields the razor and delivers the ham as the vengeful barber in one of the series' more obviously studio bound productions, whose art direction care of Frederick Pusey includes old style painted backdrops. Directed by Reginald Collin (who also produced, as he had *The Suicide Club*), it also features Lewis Fiander, Barry Stanton, Charles Morgan, Peter Sallis and Russell Hunter (the latter two playing multiple parts, as supporting actors would have been obliged to do in the original touring version).

The series finally came to a close with *Curse of the Mummy* (1970, TV), a version of Bram Stoker's 1903 novel *The Jewel of Seven Stars*, in which the daughter of an archaeologist appears to be possessed by Tera, the evil spirit of an Egyptian queen whose gold-painted body he has been responsible for unearthing. The program features Graham Crowden as the Egyptologist, Trelawny, and Isobel Black as his daughter Margaret, with support provided by Patrick Mower as Dr. Ross, the hero of the piece. Adapted by John Russell Taylor and directed by Guy Verney, the episode opens with a visually arresting sequence in which Margaret dreams of the death of Tera (whom she resembles) in a vaulted crypt, only for her to awake to discover that her father has been gassed and attacked, and had his hand almost severed. Expertly framed and edited, the scene gets the proceedings off to an exciting start, and if things become a little slow and talkative thereafter (events could very easily take place on a stage), they come to life again towards the end with a sequence in which Trelawny attempts to revive the Egyptian queen. That he has a room in his basement made to look like her tomb, complete with a sarcophagus to house her perfectly preserved body, stretches credulity somewhat, but once one accepts that this is nothing more than a load of old nonsense told with a straight face, it proves to be an enjoyable enough conclusion to a series that at least attempted big things, even if it didn't always bring them off with the required finesse. Interestingly, Hammer tackled the same story, to somewhat better effect, with *Blood from the Mummy's Tomb* (1971), which likewise didn't actually feature a marauding mummy (a tie in collection of stories titled *Great Stories of Mystery and Imagination* [1966] was published by Fontana; selected by Bryan Douglas, the cover featured an image from *The Trac-tate Middoth* ["Weird and gruesome tales from ABC Television's top-rating series," ran the cover blurb]).

In addition to *Mystery and Imagination*, the hour-long anthology series *ABC Stage 67* (1966–1967, TV), which began airing in the U.S. on ABC on 14 September 1966, also presented a version of *The Canterville Ghost* in 1966 (it aired on 2 November whereas the British version had been broadcast some months earlier on 12 March). The American program was actually filmed in the UK, where it made use of Allington Castle in Kent as a location. Written and produced by Bert Shevelove, it was a musical presentation of the story, with songs provided by Jerry Bock and Sheldon Harnick (best known for *Fiddler on the Roof*), among them "Canterville Hall," "Rattletrap" and "You're Super," the latter performed by British pop star Peter Noone, who plays the young Duke of Cheshire in the piece (the program purported to introduce the singer, despite the fact that he'd already appeared in a couple of movies). Other British cast members include Michael Redgrave, who plays both the current Sir Simon Canterville as well as his ghostly ancestor seeking release from an ancient curse, George Curzon and Madge Brindley as the castle's butler and house-keeper, and Frankie Howerd as the local copper, while the castle's visiting Ameri-cans are represented by Douglas Fairbanks, Jr., Natalie Schafer and Tippy Walker. Unfortunately, the program is a rather ham-fisted affair, slackly directed by John Robins and with a cast (save for Noone) seemingly chosen for their tone deafness. As for the songs, they tend to go in one ear and out the other ("A spiritless, soggy effort with few redeeming qualities," commented *Variety*).

Tales from Europe

Britain and the States weren't the only countries producing television content based on classic genre fiction in the sixties. West Germany produced versions of Henry James' *The Turn of the Screw* under the title *Die sundigen Engel* (1962, TVM), starring Gertrude Kuckelmann as the haunted governess, and Robert Louis Steven-son's *The Bottle Imp* under the title *Gluck und glas* (1964, TV). This seems to have been a popular story in Germany, as it also appeared on television under the same title in 1978 and 1980 (the former made by the West Germans, the latter by the East Germans). The Finns meanwhile tackled Edgar Allan Poe's *The Cask of Amontillado* as *Ett fat amontillado* (1963, TV), while the French presented the author's *The Pit and the Pendulum* under the title *Le puits et le pendule* (1964, TV), as well as a version of Gustav Meyrink's 1915 novel *Le golem* (1967, TVM). Elsewhere, the Australians pre-sented the J.B. Priestley *déjà vu* drama *I Have Been Here Before* (1964, TVM), which the *Sydney Morning Herald* praised for its "scrupulous craftsmanship," the Italians made their own version of *The Bottle Imp* as *Il diavolo nella bottiglia* (1966, TV) for the series *Avventure di mare et di costa* (1966, TV [*Adventures of Sea and Coast*]), while the Czechs produced a version of Karel Capek's *The Makropulos Affair* as *Vek Makropulos* (1967, TVM).

It was in France, however, that the celebrated film director Jean Renoir hoped to make a film that would play both on television and in cinemas at the same time. This was an uncredited modern-day adaptation of Robert Louis Stevenson's *Dr. Jekyll and Mr. Hyde* filmed under the title *Le testament du Docteur Cordelier* (1959, TVM, aka *Experiment in Evil*) which, following a screening at the Venice Film Festival on 31 August 1959, was eventually shown on TV throughout Europe during the early sixties (this following a delay over accusations of unfair competition from the Federation of French Film Exhibitors), beginning in Sweden on 4 July 1960. It eventually aired in France on RTF on 16 November 1961 and *was* finally released theatrically in some territories as intended, including France on 17 November 1961, albeit to a mixed reception (*Variety* noted that "Renoir has tried to make a pic to please both mediums and hasn't quite brought it off").

In it, Jean-Louis Barrault stars as the respected psychiatrist Dr. Cordelier, who surprises his lawyer (Teddy Bilis) by willing his entire estate to a delinquent named Opale, who is in fact Cordelier, who has been experimenting with mind altering drugs so as to create a separate personality for himself, through which he can indulge his various desires, both criminal and sexual, without taking responsibility for his actions, among them the murder of a fellow psychiatrist (Michel Vitold) who had challenged his theories. Starkly photographed in black and white in just ten days (Renoir and his cameraman Georges Leclerc used multiple cameras to help free up the actors), this is a sometimes talkative but occasionally striking take on the story, its major asset being Barrault's dynamic performance, particularly as the deranged Opale, whose criminal acts include sexual molestation, baby snatching and kicking the crutches from under a cripple! Further adaptations of the Stevenson story were also presented in Italy, as an episode of *Biblioteca di Studio Uno* (1964, TV [*Study Library One*]) under the title *Il dottor Jeckill e mister Hide* (1964, TV), and in Spain, twice, both as four-parters under the title *El hombre y la bestia* (1965, TV) for the horror series *Tras la puerta cerrada* (1964–1965, TV [*Behind the Closed Door*]) and *Mañana puede ser verdad* (1964–1965, TV [*Tomorrow May Be True*]).

In fact it was Spain that made the most notable contribution to the genre during this period with *Historias para no dormir* (1966–1968, TV [*Stories to Keep You Awake*]), an Iberian version of the anthology format, which was created and hosted by Narciso Ibanez Serrador, whose earlier credits as a writer included the biographical *Rasputin* (1958, TV), an adaptation of Edgar Allan Poe's 1838 story of death and transformation *Ligeia* (1959, TV), and a nine-part series based on Gaston Leroux's 1910 grand opus *The Phantom of the Opera* (originally published as a serial between 1909 and 1910) under the title *El fantasma del opera* (1960, TV), all of which top lined Serrador's father Narciso Ibanez Menta, who appeared as Erik the Phantom in the latter. A star name in his home country, Menta also appeared in a version of *The Monkey's Paw* during this period titled *La pata del mono* (1961, TV) which, along with *Ligeia*, *Phantom* and several other titles, was exported to Argentina where they appeared as part of the series *Obras maestras del terror* (1959–1962, TV, aka *Masterworks of Terror*). He must have liked *The Monkey's Paw*, as he appeared in it again in 1974 as an episode of the anthology series *Narciso Ibanez Serrador presenta a Narciso Ibanez Menta* (1974, TV), which also featured a couple of stories based on Poe, all of which were directed by his son, who also worked as a director on an earlier anthology series *Tras la puerta cerrada* (1964–1965, TV [*Behind the Closed Door*]), which likewise included stories by Edgar Allan Poe as well as Cornell Woolrich and Robert Louis Stevenson, while his father's other small screen genre credits included the series *El muneco maldita* (1962, TV [*The Cursed Doll*]), thus making horror very much a family business.

As for *Historias para no dormir* itself, it featured stories by such well known writers as Edgar Allan Poe (of course), Ray Bradbury and Robert Bloch, which Serrador adapted and directed, along with stories by such local talent as Juan Tébar, Carlos Buiza, Fernando Jiménez del Oso and Serrador himself (writing as Luis Penafiel). The series, usually half an hour in length though sometimes longer, began its two-season run of 26 episodes on TVE on 4 February 1966 with *El cumpleanos* (1966, TV [*The Birthday*]), which was based on the 1961 story *Nightmare in Yellow* by Fredric Brown, and concerns the meticulous plans of a man (Rafael Navarro) to rob his company, kill his wife (Josefina de la Torre) and abscond to a new life on his 50th birthday, but there is something he hasn't anticipated in his scheme. Atmospherically photographed in black and white on 16mm by Alfonso Nieva (the rest of the series would be shot on videotape), this is a neatly handled little story with a nicely judged surprise ending (literally) and is certainly the equal of any of the better episodes of *Alfred Hitchcock Presents* (1955–1962, TV) and *The Twilight Zone* (1959–1964, TV).

Season one then went on to include a number of Ray Bradbury adaptations, among them *La bodega* (1966, TV), a two-part version of his 1962 story *Come into My Cellar* (aka *Boys! Raise Giant Mushrooms in Your Cellar!*) about a young lad who grows mushrooms in his basement which turn out to be aliens (the story actually hailed from a 1959 episode of *Alfred Hitchcock Presents* [1955–1962, TV] under the title *Special Delivery* which Bradbury wrote); *El doble* (1966, TV), an adaptation of his 1949 story *Marionettes, Inc.*, about a man who orders a robot double of himself so that he can escape to a new life; and *El cohete* (1966, TV), a version of his 1950 story *The Rocket*, about an old man who dreams of travelling into space (other Bradbury adaptations included *La espera* [1966, TV], taken from the 1949 story *The One Who Waits*, and *La sonrisa* [1966, TV], taken from the 1952 story *The Smile*). The season also included *El pacto* (1966, TV [*The Deal*]), a version of Poe's 1845 story *The Facts in the Case of M. Valdemar*, about a mesmerist who hypnotizes a man at the moment of death, and *El asfalto* (1966, TV [*The Asphalt*]), taken from a story by Carlos Buiza in which a man (Narciso Ibanez Menta) finds himself gradually sinking into the asphalt of a sidewalk, made molten by the heat of the sun, yet despite his calls for help, no one steps forward to assist him. Season two went on to include *La zarpa* (1967, TV [*The Paw*]), an adaptation of W.W. Jacobs' *The Monkey's Paw*, and *El cuervo* (1967, TV), taken from Poe's 1845 poem *The Raven*.

On the strength of the series, Serrador was able to launch his film career with *La residencia* (1969, aka *The House That Screamed* and *The Boarding School*), which was based on a script originally intended for *Historias para no dormir*, after which he planned a follow up show titled *Historias para la noche* (*Stories for the Night*), which was intended for 1970, but its pilot episode was turned down. However, he did go on to make two stand-alone specials for *Historias para no dormir* titled *El lobo* (1972,

TV [*The Wolf*]) and *El televisor* (1974, TV [*The TV Set*]), following which he devised the highly successful quiz show *Un, dos, tres* (1972–2004, TV), which was exported to the UK as *3,2,1* (1978–1987, TV), and another feature film, *Quien puede matar a un nino?* (1976, aka *Island of the Damned* and *Who Can Kill a Child?*) before finally returning to *Historias para no dormir* in 1982 with four new color episodes. These were *Freddy* (1982, TV), which concerned a murderous ventriloquist's doll; *El caso del Senor Valdemar* (1982, TV), which was a remake of *El pacto* (i.e.: *The Facts in the Case of M. Valdemar*); *El fin empezo ayer* (1982, TV [*The End Started Yesterday*]), in which a university professor suspects a star pupil of committing several crimes on campus; and *El trapero* (1982, TV), a version of Richard Le Gallienne's 1920 poem *The Junkman*, about a ragman whose alcoholic son has profaned a number of tombs in the nearby cemetery. In 2005, Serrador oversaw *Peliculas para no dormir* (2005, TV [*Films to Keep You Awake*]), a six-part follow up series, of which he directed one episode himself, which proved to be his last film. This was *La culpa* (2005, TV [*Blame*]), a tragic story involving abortion, lesbianism and mental fragility, the most shocking moment of which sees a fetus flushed down a toilet.

Another Spanish series that occasionally dipped its toes into genre-centric waters was *Hora once* (1968–1974, TV [*Hour Eleven*]), which made its debut with an adaptation of Franz Kafka's 1915 novella *The Metamorphosis* (original title *Die Verwandlung*) as *La metamorfosis* (1968, TV), in which a young man awakes one morning to discover that he has transformed into a giant insect. The series went on to include adaptations of Nathaniel Hawthorne's Fountain of Youth story *Dr. Heidegger's Experiment* as *El experiment del doctor Heideger* [sic] (1970, TV), Sheridan Le Fanu 1839 story *Strange Event in the Life of Schalken the Painter* under the title *El extrano secreto de Shalken, el pintor* (1970, TV), albeit as a reading (the story would by tackled in definitive style by the BBC in 1979, of which more to come), and yet another version of Pushkin's *The Queen of Spades* as *La dama de los tres naipes* (1970, TV).

A Rum Collins

Back to America in the sixties now, and daytime drama took on a new guise with *Dark Shadows* (1966–1971, TV, working title *Shadows on the Wall*), a Maine-set gothic soap opera centered on the Collins family whose closet contains a number of surprising skeletons. Running to a stonking 1,225 episodes, the weekday series, which began airing on ABC at 4 p.m. on 27 June 1966, was created by Dan Curtis who also executive produced through his own company Dan Curtis Productions. Curtis, who would go on to be one the major names in genre television in the seventies, began his career in the fifties working for NBC as a syndication salesman before moving over to MCA and, finally, ABC, for whom he created the show, the success of which would lead to a number of important TV movies (among them versions of *Dracula*, *Frankenstein* and *Dr. Jekyll and Mr. Hyde*), following which he finally went "respectable" with the blockbusting mini-series *The Winds of War* (1983, TV) and its sequel, *War and Remembrance* (1988–1989, TV), the latter of which won him an Emmy (shared with Barbara Steele) for outstanding mini-series.

The 30-minute show, which was taped as live at the ABC studios in Manhattan, was originally broadcast in black and white before switching to color in 1967, and opened with the arrival of a new governess, Victoria Winters (Alexander Moltke), a former foundling who has been invited to work at the Collinwood estate by its matriarch Elizabeth Collins Stoddard, played by the former Hollywood star Joan Bennett, whose imperious presence certainly lends the proceedings an air of dignity. But Elizabeth's younger brother Roger Collins (Louis Edmonds) is wary of the girl's arrival ("With all our ghosts, we don't need any strangers in this house"), particularly as it transpires she may have a connection with the family. In fact, Victoria is met with veiled warnings from practically everyone she encounters on her journey to Collinwood. But she is not the only arrival in town, for Burke Devlin (Mitchell Ryan) is also on the same train, returning after a long absence, having served a sentence for manslaughter, and it is soon revealed that he too has his own interest in the Collins family.

Despite the spooky surroundings care of production designer Sy Tomashoff, an almost continual background score by Bob Cobert, which adds immeasurably to the atmosphere, and the careful, deliberately paced handling by director Lela Swift (who went on to helm an impressive 592 installments), the opening episode was described by *Variety* as "one big contemporary yawn," despite the fact that it is clearly setting up situations meant for future development. The early episodes did tend towards melodrama (the governess plotline has strong echoes of Charlotte Bronte's 1847 novel *Jane Eyre*), and it took audiences a while to warm to the show, which teetered on the brink of cancellation before fully embracing the supernatural in episode 211 (aired on 18 April 1967) with the arrival of Barnabas Collins, a cousin from England who has an uncanny likeness to an old portrait hanging in the hallway (right down to the same ring and singular haircut), and who, it transpires, is a vampire (albeit a reluctant one). As played by Jonathan Frid, a RADA-trained Canadian stage actor who would go on to rack up 594 episodes, Barnabas's arrival turned the show into a national talking point, and as well as housewives, it soon began to attract a sizeable younger audience, keen to indulge in the show's minor frissons and increasingly bizarre plotlines—which included a witch, ghosts and a werewolf, plus elaborate flashbacks—all of which were told with a surprising straight face, but undoubtedly appreciated for the load of camp old nonsense it actually was.

Also featuring Grayson Hall,

No oil painting. Jonathan Frid makes an appearance as Barnabas Collins in *Dark Shadows* (1966–1971, TV). Note the lighting equipment in the background (ABC/Dan Curtis Productions).

David Selby, Kathryn Leigh Scott, Lara Parker, Thayer David, Kate Jackson and David Henesy (as well as such upcoming names as Harvey Keitel and Frederic Forrest), the show went on to become cult viewing. In fact such was its success it even inspired two feature film spinoffs, both of which were produced and directed by Dan Curtis. These were *House of Dark Shadows* (1970), in which Barnabas is offered a normal existence via a series of serum injections care of Dr. Julia Hoffman (series regular Grayson Hall) only to be betrayed and resort to his old ways by the climax (spoiler alert: during which he is staked), and *Night of Dark Shadows* (1971), in which Quentin Collins (David Selby), the heir to the Collinwood estate, arrives with his bride Tracy (Kate Jackson, whom the film introduces, and who had previously played Daphne Harridge, later Collins, in the series), only to find himself plagued by dreams of a former existence. To make the films, regular cast members still involved in the show, which continued to tape at the same time, were temporarily written out of proceedings so as to be able to moonlight on the movies. The series itself eventually came to an end on 2 April 1971, in which the Collins family finally free themselves from the curse from which they have long been afflicted (*Night of Dark Shadows* was released a few months later on 4 August).

But this was by no means the end of *Dark Shadows*, which continued to haunt the airwaves in syndication (the first soap to do so) and developed a devoted fan base. As well as the two film spinoffs, there were also a number of novels by the romance writer Marilyn Ross (real name Dan Ross) based upon the show, among them *The Mystery of Collinwood* (1968) and *Barnabas Collins and the Gypsy Witch* (1969), while in 1991 the series was rebooted care of Dan Curtis Productions for MGM Television. The 45-minute show (made to fill an hour-long timeslot) now starred Ben Cross as Barnabas Collins and followed the original series' opening storyline involving the arrival of governess Victoria Winters (Joanna Going). Other cast members included Joseph Gordon-Levitt, Roy Thinnes, Lysette Anthony, horror icon (and Curtis associate) Barbara Steele (perfectly cast as Dr. Julia Hoffman) and Jean Simmons (as Elizabeth Collins Stoddard). Yet despite its higher production values, the show had the misfortune of being aired during the Gulf War and was pulled after just 12 episodes (four of which Curtis directed himself). A further attempt to reboot the show (again via Dan Curtis Productions) followed in 2005, this time starring Alec Newman as Barnabas Collins, Blair Brown as Elizabeth Collins Stoddard, Kelly Hu as Dr. Julia Hoffman and Marley Shelton as Victoria Winters, who yet again arrives at Collinwood to become a governess. Written by P.J. Hogan and directed by Mark Verheiden, it unfortunately failed to get beyond an unaired hour-long pilot, which only got shown only at a handful of *Dark Shadows* festivals. There was, however, a final spin of the dice with the release of director Tim Burton's $150 million homage *Dark Shadows* (2012), which featured Burton regular Johnny Depp as Barnabas Collins and Michelle Pfeiffer as Elizabeth Collins Stoddard, supported by the likes of Helena Bonham Carter, Eva Green and horror legend Christopher Lee, not to mention guest shots from original cast members Kathryn Leigh Scott, David Selby, Lara Parker and Jonathan Frid (whose film and television career, like Bela Lugosi's before him, had in the meantime been blighted by playing a vampire). Like all of Burton's films, the proceedings certainly looked good, but a multi-million dollar revamp of a TV show notable for its low budget didn't quite work, and though the film took a solid if unspectacular $245 million at the box office, *Dark Shadows*' moment finally seemed to have passed (note that other soaps occasionally dipped their toes in the supernatural; this was the case with the later *Port Charles* [1997–2003, TV], a spin off from *General Hospital* [1963–, TV], which went on to include storylines involving time travel and vampires).

While he was working on *Dark Shadows*, Dan Curtis made further inroads into the field of horror with *The Strange Case of Dr. Jekyll and Mr. Hyde* (1968, TVM), an adaptation of the Robert Louis Stevenson novella starring Jack Palance in the dual role. A co-production between Dan Curtis Productions (with Curtis himself producing) and the Canadian Broadcasting Corporation, the two-hour program was shot on videotape in Toronto, with Charles Jarrott (soon to be known for such films as *Anne of the Thousand Days* [1969] and *Mary, Queen of Scots* [1971]) in the director's chair. The teleplay was originally in the hands of Rod Serling, who left the production early on, to be replaced by Ian McLellan Hunter, best known for penning *Roman Holiday* (1953). Likewise, the original leading man, Jason Robards, Jr., was lost following a technicians' strike, compounded by his dislike of Serling's script (the show was originally set to be recorded in London in 1967). This left the door open for Palance, who would go on to play Dracula for Curtis a few years down the road.

Clearly a prestige production (it was budgeted at $900,000 and had a seven-week schedule), it benefits enormously from its top line cast, among them Denholm Elliott as George Devlin, Leo Genn as Dr. Lanyon, Torin Thatcher as Sir John Turnbull, Oskar Homolka as Stryker, Billie Whitelaw (whom the program "introduces") as Gwyn Thomas, Duncan Lamont as Sergeant Grimes and music hall star Tessie O'Shea as Tessie O'Toole. As in previous versions of the story, it follows Dr. Jekyll's experiments to separate the good and evil in man, which he does via the creation of a potion which he consumes himself, leading to a double life of crime and debauchery. To this end, the legendary Dick Smith was brought onboard not only to create the mono-browed make-up for the dastardly Hyde, but to make Palance as handsome as possible as Jekyll, for which he had to correct the actor's broken nose (Smith had already worked for Curtis on *Dark Shadows* [1966–1971, TV] and would go on to work for him again on *House of Dark Shadows* [1970]).

With its mobile camera work (including exterior location shots), excellent sets care of *Dark Shadows* contributor Trevor Williams (among them a $200,000 replication of Washington Square) and atmospheric music by Robert Cobert (which includes dramatic new cues as well as stock music cheekily borrowed from *Dark Shadows*), the program was clearly a labor of love for all concerned, yet at two hours, it does drag its heels at times and contains rather too many dialogue heavy scenes, but one can't discount Palance's committed performance, to which he brings a genuine maniacal charge when running about the streets as Hyde. Shown in America on ABC on 3 January 1968, the program was well received, and went on to garner four Emmy nominations, including one for Curtis for Outstanding Dramatic Program and one for Smith's make-up; McLellan Hunter meanwhile won an Edgar for his adaptation.

It should also be noted that while he was working on *Dark Shadows*, Dan

Curtis tried to instigate another horror themed series, *Dead of Night* (1969, TV), which he wrote with regular *Shadows* scribe Sam Hall for Dan Curtis Productions. Unfortunately, only the pilot, *A Darkness at Blaisedon* (1969, TV), which aired on ABC on 26 August 1969, was made ("If *Dark Shadows* gives you chills, then you'll scream for ... *A Darkness at Blaisedon*," ran the opening caption for the trailer). Other *Shadows* personnel involved in the project included director Lela Swift, composer Bob Cobert and costume designer Ramsey Mostoller, as well as such cast members as Thayer David and Louis Edmond. In it, Kerwin Matthews and Cal Bellini star as two investigators of the supernatural who are invited to a mansion by a young heiress (Marj Dusay) who cannot sell it because it is apparently haunted. Shot on videotape in the style of *Shadows*, the hour-long show is surprisingly atmospheric at times, thanks to some effective sets care of art director Trevor Williams, among them a cobweb strewn hallway and an overgrown graveyard. Sadly, there were no takers for a full series, though Curtis later made use of the series' title for a 1977 multi-story TV movie.

Meanwhile, over in Britain, investigations into the supernatural were the focus of *Haunted* (1967–1968, TV), whose hour-long episodes began airing on the ITV network on 19 August 1967. In it, Patrick Mower starred as university lecturer Michael West, who travels about the country investigating all manner of supernatural occurrences and paranormal phenomena that have been reported to him. Written by the likes of Robert Muller, Anthony Skene and Katharine Blake, who worked under the aegis of producer cum script editor Michael Chapman, the series, which was made via ABC Weekend Television, also featured recurring appearances by John Nettleton as Professor Alec Ritchie and Michael Barrington as Professor Gordon, as well guest turns from Jacqueline Pearce, Peter Barkworth, Ronald Lacey, Nigel Stock, Fabia Drake, George Coulouris and Peter Vaughan, who worked under such directors as Patrick Dromgoole, Don Leaver and Charles Jarrott. The series opened with *I Like It Here* (1967, TV), in which the young professor finds himself troubled by strange dreams in his new lodgings, and went on to include *The Girl on a Swing* (1967, TV), in which he investigates an abandoned old house whose weed strewn garden is haunted by a young girl, and *Through a Glass Darkly* (1968, TV), in which he learns about the power of suggestion. Unfortunately, the eight-part series is now considered lost, so further evaluation is presently not possible.

The anthology series also continued apace in the UK with *Late Night Horror* (1968, TV), which was broadcast on Friday evenings on BBC2 from 19 April 1968, and which the *Radio Times* described as "a new series of plays for people who enjoy a good honest scare." Sadly, five of its six episodes have been wiped, which is a shame given that it featured such tantalizing titles as *No Such Thing as a Vampire* (1968, TV), in which the wife of a doctor in a Transylvanian village shows signs of having been bitten by a vampire (based upon a 1959 story by Richard Matheson, this was directed by Paddy Russell, one of TV's few women directors at the time); *William and Mary* (1968, TV), in which a man's eye and brain are kept alive after he has died (written by Roald Dahl, this story had already done service as an episode of *'Way Out* [1961, TV]); *The Corpse Can't Play* (1968, TV), in which a strange boy introduces some unexpected games at a children's party (also directed by Paddy Russell, this is the only surviving episode); *The Triumph of Death* (1968, TV), which focuses on the haunting of an Elizabethan mansion (this was directed by Rudolph Cartier, for whom Paddy Russell formerly worked as a floor manager, including an episode of *The Quatermass Experiment* [1953, TV]); *The Bells of Hell* (1968, TV), in which a newlywed couple find themselves staying at a strange inn (this was directed by Naomi Capon, another of television's few female directors of the time); and *The Kiss of Blood* (1968, TV), in which a married woman has an affair behind her older husband's back, much to her regret. The wiping of the series (which featured such star names as Diane Cilento, Jean Anderson, Andrew Keir, Roy Dotrice and Claire Bloom) seems all the more puzzling in this case given that it was the first to be recorded in color by the BBC (it was taped in 1967).

A Fateful Whistle

Mercifully, there was no chance that the BBC's next brush with horror could be wiped, as luckily it was filmed on 16mm. Presented as an episode of the channel's long running arts program *Omnibus* (1967–2003, TV), which occasionally included dramas (among them several directed by Ken Russell), as well as documentaries and concerts. Titled *Whistle and I'll Come to You* (1968, TV), it was an adaptation of M.R. James' short story *Oh, Whistle, and I'll Come to You, My Lad*, which was first published in his 1904 collection *Ghost Stories of an Antiquary*. Written and directed by Jonathan Miller, it stars Michael Hordern as Professor Parkins, a self-absorbed university professor who, while holidaying in a remote part of Norfolk, discovers an ancient whistle half buried in an overgrown beachside graveyard, the blowing of which appears to summon a supernatural entity. That the professor avowedly does not ordinarily hold truck with such notions makes the experience all the more unsettling for him, given that there appears to be no rational explanation for the disturbing events that he subsequently experiences. As Miller explains in his introductory voiceover, "This is a tale of the supernatural…. It's the story of solitude and terror, and it has a moral, too. It hints at the dangers of intellectual pride and shows how a man's reason can be overthrown when he fails to acknowledge those forces inside himself which he simply cannot understand."

Although it does not follow the text of James' story to the letter, this is nevertheless a masterful adaptation which achieves its aims through the gradual accumulation of seemingly mundane detail and character observation. Indeed, the film concerns itself greatly with the professor's stay at the hotel (which may frustrate less patient viewers), with its unhurried attention to the monotonous regimen of bed making, bath taking and tedious meals through which he awkwardly mumbles and bumbles his way. Consequently, when the manifestations make their belated appearance, they have all the more impact, among them a distant lone figure on the beach following the professor's discovery of the whistle, his subsequent nightmares in which he is pursued along the shore by a rag-like wraith, and the disturbance of the sheets on the spare bed in his room.

As the inward-looking professor, Hordern is superb, never more so than in one particular breakfast scene during which he fussily eats half a grapefruit and a piece of haddock while patronizingly answering a fellow guest's inquiry as to whether or not he believes in ghosts. Prior to this, upon his arrival, he has a delightfully awkward encounter with the hotel porter (George Woodbridge), who displays the facilities of the room in which he will be staying in a breathless form of gobbledygook. The professor's first evening meal among the other guests, with whom eye contact (particularly with one female guest) clearly proves to be an uncomfortable experience for him, is equally well observed, as is his incremental disintegration over the following days as he begins to suspect that someone or some*thing* is coming for him ("Who is this who is coming?" reads the Latin inscription on the whistle). As for his reaction when he finally sees the ghostly disturbance in the spare bed, he sucks his thumb like a frightened child and repeatedly exclaims, "No, no, no!" Ironically, it is his fellow guest, the Colonel (Ambrose Coghill), whom he patronized at breakfast, who comes to his rescue, having heard his cries from across the hallway.

Expertly filmed in black and white by Dick Bush (who'd already worked with Miller on an adaptation of *Alice in Wonderland* [1966, TV] for the BBC), the 42-minute film is notable for its austere look and lack of music; instead, unsettling sound effects (care of Ron Hooper and John Ramsay) are brought to the fore during the professor's nightmares, while extreme close-ups of his half awake eyes help to create the sense that he is not alone in his room. It is the beach scenes, with their empty, wintry vistas, that stay in the mind, however, especially when that lone figure makes its first appearance. First broadcast on 7 May 1968, the film was much admired and led to several further M.R. James adaptations which subsequently went out annually in the seventies under the strand *A Ghost Story for Christmas* (1971–1978, revived 2005–2021, TV), of which more to come. Of the 2010 remake there is little to say, except that it disappoints on almost every level when compared to its well-regarded predecessor. In this needless present-day spin on the story, the professor (John Hurt) is staying at a hotel having just deposited his ailing wife in a nursing home. As before, he is troubled by a lone figure on the beach and unsettling occurrences in his bedroom after discovering a half-buried ring in the dunes. However,

Graveyard disturbance. Michael Hordern in the superb *Whistle and I'll Come to You* **(1968, TV) (BBC).**

this time it transpires that the manifestations emanate from his wife (Gemma Jones), whose spirit is very much alive, despite the outward appearances of Alzheimer's disease ("I'm still here, *I'm still here*," she cries repeatedly when she finally appears at the bottom of his bed). Adapted by Neil Cross and directed by Andy De Emmony, the 52-minute film contains a few minor frissons, but otherwise strives too hard to leave its own imprint on the material, which it overwhelms in the process (in 2014, the story was reworked as an episode of the long running daytime soap *Doctors* [2000–, TV]).

Back in the U.S. a failed pilot is our next port of call. Titled *Ghostbreakers* (1967, TV), the hour-long show aired on NBC on 8 September 1967, the script having been originally intended as an episode of the respected anthology series *The Dick Powell Show* (1961–1963, TV), which began its two-season, 60-episode run on NBC on 26 September 1961. Hosted by and occasionally starring the former Hollywood crooner (who also executive produced), the series, which was created by Richard Alan Simmons, featured such top line Hollywood talent as Henry Fonda, John Wayne, Mickey Rooney, David Niven, Charles Boyer, Joan Blondell, Milton Berle, Ronald Reagan, Dana Andrews, Joan Fontaine and Steve McQueen, who appeared in a variety of well upholstered dramas of varying hues bearing such titles as *Ricochet* (1961, TV), *A Swiss Affair* (1961, TV) and *Thunder in a Forgotten Town* (1963, TV). However, *Ghostbreakers* was clearly something a little different from the usual offerings in that it featured a young parapsychology professor (Kerwin Mathews) and his assistant (Diana Van Der Vlis) who find themselves investigating a murder which has taken place in a supposedly haunted office building. Written by Peter Stone and Sherman Yellen (billed Mellin), and directed by Don Medford, the program co-starred Norman Fell, Kevin McCarthy, Richard Anderson and Margaret Hamilton, and had a score by legend-in-the-making John Williams. However, when it failed to be picked up as a series, any further cases for the professor and his assistant quickly disappeared into the ether, like Powell himself, who'd passed away back in 1963 (note that Williams' dynamic theme tune for the show is available to listen to on YouTube).

Comedy was meanwhile to the fore again in the sitcom *The Ghost and Mrs. Muir* (1968–1970, TV), though the results were rather more anodyne than either *The Addams Family* (1964–1966, TV) or *The Munsters* (1964–1966, TV). The show hailed from the 1947 film of the same name, itself based upon the 1945 novel by R.A. Dick, in which a young widow (Gene Tierney) discovers that the seaside cottage that she and her young daughter (Natalie Wood) are leasing is haunted by its former owner, a salty sea captain (Rex Harrison) with whom she falls in love. The film, which was directed by Joseph L. Mankiewicz, was set in 1900, while the TV series was brought forward to the sixties, with Hope Lange now in the role of the widowed Mrs. Muir, who is accompanied to Gull Cottage by her two young kids Candice and Jonathan (Kellie Flannagan and Harlen Carraher), and their devoted maid Martha (Reta Shaw), where she encounters the ghostly Captain Daniel Gregg (Edward Mulhare) who, while initially irked by their presence, grows to become fond of Mrs. Muir and her family. Developed for television by Jean Holloway and made by Twentieth Century–Fox (which had been behind the 1947 film), the half-hour show began its 50-episode run on NBC on 21 September 1968. Cancelled by the network after one season, it subsequently moved to ABC for its second and final season, which began on 18 September 1969. An inoffensive time filler, the series is ably enough performed (Lange won two consecutive Emmys for it), but one could hardly call it hilarious, despite the encouragement of a laugh track, while its whimsical aspects quickly wear thin, though it occasionally contains some neat trick effects (such as having the invisible captain walking down a flight of stairs, his progress noted by the imprints his shoes leave in the dust), and has a catchy theme tune care of Dave Grusin. It also featured a number of interesting guest stars, among them Kenneth Mars, Bill Bixby, Jonathan Harris, Shirley Booth, Richard Dreyfuss, Kathleen Freeman and the young Mark Lester, then riding the crest of success after playing the title role in the Oscar winning musical *Oliver!* (1968), who gets to perform a duet with Candice in a dream sequence (this in the 1969 episode titled *Puppy Love*).

Strange Journeys

Back in the UK, Hammer Films, known the world over for their luridly colored big screen gothic horrors, finally broke into television with the 17-part anthology series *Journey to the Unknown* (1968, TV), having previously failed with the aborted *Tales of Frankenstein* (1958, TV), of which only the pilot was filmed. Remembered for its eerie theme tune care of Harry Robinson and its opening credit sequence set amid the rides of a deserted amusement park, the series contained a mix of standalone psychological shockers, twist-in-the-tail thrillers and horror stories, the quality of which varied from excellent to the downright tedious. Provisionally known as *Fright Hour* and *Tales of the Unknown*, the show was made in conjunction with one of the company's American distributors of the period, Twentieth Century–Fox, for broadcast on the ABC network in the States and ITV in the UK. To oversee the shows, which were budgeted at a healthy $70,000 each, Fox sent over Joan Harrison and Norman Lloyd to executive produce, given their experience of working on *Alfred Hitchcock Presents* (1955–1962, TV) and *The Alfred Hitchcock Hour* (1962–1965, TV), leaving the day-to-day producing chores in the hands of Hammer's Anthony Hinds. To help give it audience appeal in the States, several American stars were also imported to headline many of the episodes, among them Roddy McDowall, Vera Miles, David Hedison, Patty Duke, Joseph Cotten, Stefanie Powers, Julie Harris and Chad Everett, while British stars involved included Tom Adams, Dennis Waterman, Nanette Newman, Barbara Jefford, Michael Gough, Kay Walsh and Bernard Lee.

Directors onboard included Don Chaffey, who'd made the popular dinosaur flick *One Million Years B.C.* (1966) for Hammer, and Roy Ward Baker, who'd helmed *Quatermass and the Pit* (1967) for them. Also involved were such upcoming names as Peter Sasdy, who'd go on to direct *Taste the Blood of Dracula* (1970) and *Hands of the Ripper* (1971) for the company, and Alan Gibson, who'd get to helm both *Dracula A.D. 1972* (1972) and *The Satanic Rites of Dracula* (1974). The stories emanated from such reliable sources as Richard Matheson, Charles Beaumont and Cornell Woolrich, while writers directly involved included Alfred Shaughnessy and Robert Bloch, with John Gould working as the story editor. The show's epic six-month filming schedule ran from 24 May 1968 to 27 November, by which time the first episode had been broadcast in the States on 26 September (the show premiered on the UK the following year on 23 June). This was *Eve* (1968, TV), a fairly penny plain story about a shop assistant (Dennis Waterman) who falls in love with a wax mannequin (Carol Lynley) who appears to come to life, and with whom he goes on the run when she is threatened with being melted down. The program was described as "an engrossing fantasy with subtle overtones" by the *New York Daily News* and got the series off to a reasonable start.

It was followed by such variable episodes as *Jane Brown's Body* (1968, TV), in which a young woman (Stefanie Powers) is brought back to life having committed suicide, and tries to recall why she came to kill herself; *Miss Belle* (1968, TV), in which a bitter spinster (Barbara Jefford) with a hatred

All about Eve. Dennis Waterman and Carol Lynley in an episode of Hammer's *Journey to the Unknown* (1968, TV) (ABC/ITV/Hammer/Twentieth Century–Fox Television).

of men dresses her seven-year-old nephew (Kim Burfield) as a girl by way of avenging an incident in her past; *One on an Island* (1968, TV), in which a young man (Brandon de Wilde) imagines himself a beautiful companion while stranded on a desert island; *Girl of My Dreams* (1968, TV), in which a seedy photographer (Michael Callan) exploits a young woman's predictions of the future for financial gain, only to fall foul of his own enterprise; *Somewhere in a Crowd* (1968, TV), in which a TV commentator (David Hedison) witnesses a series of disasters at which five "watchers" are always present; *Do Me a Favor and Kill Me* (1968, TV), in which a down and out actor (Joseph Cotten) asks a friend to kill him at an unspecified time so that his wife will benefit from the insurance pay out, but then changes his mind; *The Beckoning Fair One* (1968, TV), in which an American artist (Robert Lansing) preparing for his first London show is seemingly haunted by a beautiful woman whose portrait hangs in the house he is renting; *The Last Visitor* (1968, TV), in which a young woman (Patty Duke) taking a break at an off season seaside hotel is menaced by a shadowy figure who turns out to be the person she least expected it to be; *The Madison Equation* (1968, TV), in which an electronics expert (Allan Cuthbertson) attempts to kill his wife (Barbara Bel Geddes) via the giant computer they have designed together; and *The Killing Bottle* (1968, TV), in which a songwriter (Barry Evans) is invited to the country home of a potential backer, only to find his life in peril.

Of these, *Jane Brown's Body, One on an Island, Girl of My Dreams, Somewhere in a Crowd, The Beckoning Fair One* and *The Last Visitor* are quite reasonable TV fodder, while *Miss Belle, Do Me a Favor and Kill Me, The Madison Equation* and *The Killing Bottle* are pretty dull (to be frank, *Do Me a Favor and Kill Me* and *The Madison Equation* are downright awful). However, there were a handful of gems among the rhinestones, the first of which was *The Indian Spirit Guide* (1968, TV), which went out as episode three in the States (the UK ran the shows in a slightly different order). In it, a wealthy widow (Julie Harris) hires a private detective (Tom Adams) to help her find a genuine medium so as to be able to get in contact with her late husband, but having exposed a number of fakes so as to gain her trust, he makes plans to marry her for her money, only to fall foul of a real medium, whose Indian spirit guide shoots him dead with his arrows. Penned by Robert Bloch and directed with a sure hand by Roy Ward Baker, the episode generally moves with pace and has one or two neat surprises up its sleeve, among them the exposure of one fake medium, Mrs. Hubbard, who turns out to be a man, and the revelation that a mystic named Chardur is actually a Cockney con man. Featuring strong performances, particularly by character favorite Catherine Lacey as the genuine medium Miss Prinn, this is everything an anthology episode should be.

Other highlights in the series include *Paper Dolls* (1968, TV), in which an American exchange teacher (Michael Tolan) working in England finds himself part of a bizarre scenario involving four identical quadruplets who not only are in psychic contact with each other, but can also will others to obey their not always benign bidding; *Matatikas Is Coming* (1968, TV), in which an American crime journalist (Vera Miles) doing some research finds herself locked in a library whose caretaker murdered four women many years earlier, and who it seems has returned to claim another victim; *Poor Butterfly* (1968, TV), in which a commercial artist (Chad Everett) is invited to a country house costume party where he meets a beautiful girl, only to realize that he has somehow slipped back in time, and that many of the guests subsequently perished in a fire; and *Stranger in the Family* (1968, TV), in which a boy (Anthony Corlan) who has the power to make people obey his will is exploited by various parties interested in his abilities (this story by David Campton had previously done service as a 1965 episode of *Out of the Unknown* [1965–1971, TV]).

The show's highlight was undoubtedly *The New People* (1968, TV), which was used to launch the series in the UK. In it, a young couple, the Prentisses (Robert Reed and Jennifer Hilary), move into their dream house in an English village, where the social life appears to revolve around their charismatic neighbor Luther Ames (Patrick Allen), who keenly welcomes them into his circle. But all is not quite what it seems, and the couple eventually discover themselves to have been the victims of a deadly game of cat and mouse involving a group of Home Counties diabolists. Based upon a 1958 story by Charles Beaumont, the episode is filled with intriguing revelations and unexpected twists and turns, in which the audience, like the unfortunate Prentisses, is cleverly manipulated throughout the proceedings. As the sacrificial young couple, Robert Reed and Jennifer Hilary are perhaps a little on the bland side, leaving it to Patrick Allen to chew the scenery to great effect as the devious Luther ("I used to think he was a kind of snake charmer. He's not—he's just a snake," observes his wife Helen [Melissa Stribling] at one point). Looking magnificent as Mephistopheles during a fancy-dress party, he dominates the proceedings throughout, though others also leave their mark, among them Adrienne Corri as a kindly neighbor who likewise falls foul of Luther's machinations, and Milo O'Shea as the seemingly friendly Matt Dysal, who turns out to be Luther's ideas man. The real star of the piece, however, is director Peter Sasdy, whose visual flair helps to turn this into one of the most dynamic anthology episodes ever filmed. He opens the proceedings with the camera passing through the gaily chatting guests of a cocktail party, finally coming to rest on a body hanging from the ceiling (this proves to be the former owner of the house into which the Prentisses move). In fact, given the restraints of a TV schedule, his camera is surprisingly mobile throughout, while during the candlelit black mass climax, he provides some eye-catching tilt shots to add to the atmosphere. The concluding fade to black, in which the drugged husband at last registers the finality of the trick that has been played on himself and his wife, who has been sacrificed with a dagger before his unbelieving eyes, remains one of the most ruthlessly nihilistic endings ever put before a television audience.

Sadly, a second season of *Journey to the Unknown* failed to materialize given that it didn't perform up to expectations in the ratings in America, where it was up against the mighty *Hawaii Five-O* (1968–1980, TV) over on CBS. However, a number of episodes were subsequently packaged into two story TV movies. These were *Journey into Darkness* (1968, TVM), which featured *Paper Dolls* and *The New People*; *Journey to Midnight* (1968, TVM), which featured *Poor Butterfly* and *The Indian Spirit Guide*; *Journey to the Unknown* (1969, TVM), which featured *Matatikas Is Coming* and *The Last Visitor*; and *Journey to Murder* (1972, TVM), which featured *Do Me a Favor and Kill Me* and *The Killing Bottle*.

As the sixties drew to a close, viewers would have noticed that the standalone TV movie began to appear more regularly, to the point where it soon became a broadcasting staple. Feature-length plays and specials were no strangers to the airwaves, of course, but films specifically made for TV were quickly latched onto by broadcasters as a means of easily filling a 90-minute or two-hour timeslot, given that their budgets weren't substantially higher than a couple of filmed television episodes, especially if shot on the back lot or in nearby environs. Early examples included *The Killers* (1964, TVM), which was subsequently released theatrically owing to its violence, *See How They Run* (1964, TVM), *The Hanged Man* (1964, TVM), which was released theatrically in some territories, *The Borgia Stick* (1967, TVM), which was also released theatrically in some territories, and *Prescription: Murder* (1968, TVM), the latter of which acted as the pilot for the long running movie length detective series *Columbo* (1971–2003, TVM).

In fact, feature-length pilots in and of themselves also became something of a staple, allowing broadcasters to test the waters for potential series under the guise of a one-off, and *Fear No Evil* (1969, TVM), which aired on NBC on 3 March 1969, proved to be another of these. In it, Louis Jourdan starred as Dr. David Sorrell, a psychiatrist with an interest in the occult, which better allows him to assist those of his patients who find their lives blighted by the supernatural (one of his acquaintances describes him as a "doctor to the bedeviled," and it was under the title *Bedeviled* that the film went before the cameras). One such patient is Barbara Anholt (Lynda Day), whose fiancé, Paul Varney (Bradford Dillman), was killed in a car accident the day after he bought an antique mirror, in whose reflection Barbara now claims to see her dead boyfriend. Is she going crazy, or is she actually seeing images of her beloved from beyond the grave? And what has the demon Rakashi, in which Paul had a growing interest, got to do with matters?

Based upon a story by Guy Endore, the film was written and produced by Richard Alan Simmons for Universal, with direction in the capable hands of TV veteran Paul Wendkos, who treats the farfetched subject matter with sufficient gravity so as to avoid any unintentional chuckles, in which task he is aided and abetted by an atmospheric score by the ever-reliable Billy Goldenberg and straight-faced supporting performances from Marsha Hunt, Wilfrid Hyde-White and Carroll O'Connor. Someone at NBC was clearly keen on building a series around Sorrell and his various cases, to whit a second pilot was commissioned, given the ratings success of the first. Titled *Ritual of Evil* (1970, TVM), it was broadcast on NBC on 23 February the following year. This time, the writing and producing chores were in the hands of Robert Presnell, Jr., and David Levinson, respectively, and the story sees our hero (Jourdan again) investigating the apparent suicide of one of his patients, which leads him to a group of Devil worshippers (tagline: "Against the background of a supernatural cult, a psychiatrist tries to find the motive in a 'motiveless' suicide"). Handled with a little more visual panache than its predecessor thanks to the concerted efforts of director Robert Day and his photographer Lionel Lindon (who won an Emmy for his work), the film also benefits from another atmospheric score care of Billy Goldenberg (here rather grandly billed as William Goldenberg) and a return appearance by Wilfrid Hyde-White, plus guest shots by Anne Baxter, Diana Hyland and John McMartin. Again, it's a load of old nonsense, nevertheless put across with a certain degree of commitment by all concerned. Sadly, despite these concerted efforts, any plans for an ongoing series ended here.

By the late sixties, fantasy and horror had become such a staple on TV that even kids had their own shows devoted to it, among them the trippy *H.R. Pufnstuf* (1969–1970, TV), an elaborate pantomime which sees a young boy named Jimmy (Jack Wild) transported to a magical land known as Living Island where he is befriended by a dragon, H.R. Pufnstuf (voiced by Lennie Weinrib), who helps him combat the evil Witchiepoo (Billie Hayes), who has designs on a magical golden flute that Jimmy possesses. Created by Marty and Sid Krofft (who also produced), the 17 half-hour shows, all of which were directed by Hollingsworth Morse, began airing on NBC on 6 September 1969, and featured elaborate costumes, psychedelic sets (care of regular art director William Martin), songs and lots of silly jokes and shtick (accompanied by the inevitable laugh track), all of which proved to be a hit with its intended audience, so much so that it led to a spinoff movie, *Pufnstuf* (1970), also starring Wild and Hayes, and plenty of tie-in merchandise (comic books, pins, a game, etc.).

Scooby and the Gang

Even more popular, and a genuinely scary proposition for some younger viewers, was the much-loved cartoon series *Scooby-Doo, Where Are You!* (1969–1970, TV). The program was produced and directed William Hanna and Joseph Barbera, best known for their classic Tom and Jerry shorts, which they made for MGM, and which won a total of seven Oscars. After leaving MGM in 1957 following the closure of the animation department, the duo formed their own company, Hanna-Barbera, and went on to make such popular series as *The Ruff and Reddy Show* (1957–1960, TV), *The Huckleberry Hound Show* (1958–1962, TV), *The Yogi Bear Show* (1961–1962, TV), *Top Cat* (1961–1962, TV [UK title *Boss Cat*, as there was a brand of cat food called Top Cat available in Britain at the time]), *The Flintstones* (1960–1966, TV) and *The Jetsons* (1962–1963, TV), as well as such genre-centric shows as *Jonny Quest* (1964–1965, TV), in which a boy and his family use their scientific skills to combat a variety of monsters and villains, *Frankenstein Jr. and the Impossibles* (1966–1967, TV), which featured a segment about a boy named Buzz who constructs a giant flying robot he names Frankenstein Jr. (voiced by Ted Cassidy) to help fight crime, *Space Ghost* (1966–1968, TV), in which a superhero able to become invisible uses his powers to combat all manner of aliens and space monsters, among them giant ants and vampire men (this was later revived as a spoof talk show titled *Space Ghost Coast to Coast* [1993–2011, TV]), and *The Herculoids* (1967–1968, TV), in which King Zandor uses a team of monsters with special abilities, among them a laser ray dragon and a giant rock ape, to protect his planet from sinister invaders (other studios also got in on the act, among them Hal Seeger Productions, which presented *Milton the Monster* [1965–1966, TV], which followed the adventures of the world's most lovable monster, and *Batfink* [1966–1967, TV], in which a half-bat, half-cat creature goes about fighting evildoers).

In *Scooby-Doo*, the action centers on the adventures of four teenage sleuths, Fred, Velma, Daphne and Shaggy, who, accompanied by their cowardly Great Dane, Scooby-Doo, drive about in their Mystery Machine, solving cases involving monsters, ghosts and local legends, which usually turn out to be the work of a villain who is using the hoax as a cover for his crimes. The original show ran to just 25 episodes over two seasons but proved hugely successful and influential. It aired on Saturday mornings on CBS, and the first episode, *What a Night for a Knight* (1969, TV), went out on 13 September 1969, and sees the kids investigating the legend of the Black Knight, whose suit of armor comes to life during the full moon and roams the museum in which it is on display (it turns out to be the museum's crooked curator inside it, who is using the legend as a cover to forge copies of the artwork for financial gain). A lively introduction to the series, the episode has pretty much everything in place that would become familiar during its run, including chases (usually down the same endless corridor), mild scares (the kids always seem to be splitting up to explore dark places), corny gags (the show was the first Saturday morning cartoon to have a laugh track) and running jokes (such as the use of "Scooby snacks" to get the ever hungry dog to perform tasks he's not keen to, and Velma's perpetual ability to lose her glasses at the most inopportune moments, later to be accompanied her cry of "My glasses, my glasses!"). It also benefits from a psychedelic color palette, great sound effects, atmospheric music cues, a catchy theme tune (care of David Mook and Ben Raleigh) and some well cast vocals, among the original cast of performers being Frank Welker as Fred, Nicole Jaffe as Velma, Stefanianna Christophersen as Daphne, Casey Kasem as Shaggy and Don Messick as Scooby (Welker would still be playing Fred 50 years on). In fact, all that seems to be missing from this episode is the villain's parting exclamation of "And I would have gotten away with it, too, if it hadn't been for those meddling kids!"

Other highlights from season one include *A Clue for Scooby-Doo* (1969, TV), in which the kids run into a glowing deep-sea diver while investigating the disappearance of a number of boats; *Foul Play in Funland* (1969, TV), in which a robot runs amok in a deserted theme park which comes to life of its own accord; and *Scooby-Doo and a Mummy, Too* (1969, TV), in which the kids are menaced by an Egyptian mummy. Season two went on to include such episodes as *Nowhere to Hyde* (1970, TV), in which the gang discover the ghost of Mr. Hyde hiding out in the Mystery Machine; *Haunted House Hang-Up* (1970, TV), in which they encounter a headless ghost in a spooky mansion; *Who's Afraid of the Big Bad Werewolf?* (1970, TV), in which they investigate an abandoned mill in which the ghost of a werewolf is hiding; and *Don't Fool with a Phantom* (1970, TV), in which they investigate a wax museum where a strange figure has been scaring the patrons away.

Yikes! From left to right, Shaggy, Velma, Daphne, Freddy and Scooby make a hasty exit in the beloved *Scooby-Doo, Where Are You!* (1969–1970, TV) (CBS/Hanna-Barbera Productions/Taft Broadcasting).

This was by no means the end of Scooby and the gang, however, whose adventures have continued ever since in almost countless variations and follow ups, among them *The New Scooby-Doo Movies* (1972–1973, TV), *Scooby-Doo and Scrappy-Doo* (1979–1980, TV), *The New Scooby-Doo Mysteries* (1983–1984, TV), *The 13 Ghosts of Scooby-Doo* (1985–1986, TV), which featured the voice of Vincent Price as Vincent Van Ghoul, *Scooby-Doo and the Reluctant Werewolf* (1988, TVM), *What's New, Scooby-Doo?* (2002–2006, TV), *Shaggy and Scooby-Doo Get a Clue!* (2006–2008, TV), *Scooby-Doo! The Mystery Begins* (2009, TVM), *Scooby-Doo! Mystery Incorporated* (2010–2013, TV), *Lego Scooby-Doo* (2015, TV) and *Scooby-Doo and Guess Who?* (2019, TV). There have also been video games, such as *Scooby-Doo: Classic Creep Capers* (2000) and *Scooby-Doo! Mystery Mayhem* (2004), as well as two live action features, *Scooby-Doo* (2002) and *Scooby-Doo 2: Monsters Unleashed* (2004), and a cartoon feature, *Scoob!* (2020). However, all of them pale by comparison to the first two seasons of *Scooby-Doo, Where Are You!* which remain a model of their kind.

The show also inspired and influenced other cartoon shows, among them such Hanna-Barbera creations as *The Funky Phantom* (1971–1972, TV), in which a timid ghost and his cat, held captive in a grandfather clock since the American Revolution, team up with three teenagers and their dog to solve present day mysteries (the show was clearly inspired by Oscar Wilde's *The Canterville Ghost*); *Goober and the Ghost Chasers* (1973–1975, TV), in which a cowardly dog, which becomes invisible when frightened (go figure), accompanies three case solving teenagers on their adventures; and *Clue Club* (1976, TV), in which four teenagers investigate all manner of bizarre mysteries with assistance from their two pet bloodhounds. The company also put out a number of specials, among them *Casper the Friendly Ghost: He Ain't Scary, He's Our Brother* (1979, TV), in which the young ghost sets out to save Halloween, and

The Flintstones Meet Rockula and Frankenstone (1979, TV), in which the stone age couple and their friends the Rubbles win a trip to Rocksylvania. Hannah-Barbera's rival Filmation also got in on the act with *Sabrina and the Groovie Goolies* (1970–1971, TV, aka *Groovie Goolies*), in which a young witch finds herself involved with a rock band consisting of Dracula, the Frankenstein Monster and the Wolfman. A spinoff from *The Archie Comedy Hour* (1969–1970, TV), it subsequently morphed into *Sabrina the Teenage Witch* (1971–1974, TV), which itself has produced a number of follow-ups down the years, both animated and live action, among the latter *Sabrina the Teenage Witch* (1996–2003, TV), which notched up an incredible 163 half-hour episodes during its epic seven-season run during which the character was played by Melissa Joan Hart.

Although by no means a horror film, passing mention must be made of *The Immortal* (1969, TVM), the feature-length pilot for a brief series which went on to rack up just 15 episodes. In it, an ace test driver named Ben Richards (Christopher George) discovers that he has a special blood type which makes him immune to disease and the ageing process, thus making him pretty much immortal, all of which brings him to the attention of an elderly millionaire businessman named Jordan Braddock (Barry Sullivan) who is recovering from injuries sustained in a plane crash, and who is subsequently revived and rejuvenated following a transfusion of Ben's blood, albeit for a short period. Having traced the donor and arranged for his kidnap, Braddock holds our hero hostage so as to be able to drain his blood whenever the need arises. Consequently, Ben escapes and goes on the run (during which his driving skills come in handy), only to be followed by Braddock's henchmen.

Based on the 1964 book *The Immortals* by James Gunn and produced at Paramount by Lou Morheim for broadcast on ABC, the film, which aired on 30 September 1969, was directed by Joseph Sargent, and also featured Ralph Bellamy as Braddock's doctor, Carol Lynley as Ben's girlfriend and Jessica Walter as Braddock's duplicitous wife. The subsequent series, which ran from 24 September 1970 to 14 January 1971, featured Ben in a variety of adventures and escapades, all the while on the run and in search of his brother, who may share the same family trait and whom Braddock is also trying to track down, for as Ben observes in the closing moments of the pilot, "Wherever he is he's got to be warned—warned that Braddock is looking for him, waiting to throw him in a cage and drain him dry." A fairly routine production combining mild thrills and even milder science fiction elements, the story ultimately didn't have much place to go as a weekly series, yet it seems to be fondly remembered by those who saw it on its first run, perhaps given its affinity to such similar man-on-the-run shows as *The Fugitive* (1963–1967, TV) and *The Invaders* (1967–1968, TV), the latter of which starred Roy Thinnes as an architect trying to evade aliens who wish to silence him.

No doubt influenced by the success of *Dark Shadows* (1966–1971, TV), another weekday gothic soap appeared on television during this period. This was the Canadian-made *Strange Paradise* (1969–1970, TV), which began its 195-episode run on CBC on 20 October 1969. This time the setting was a small Caribbean island, and the first story strand followed the plight of the wealthy Jean Paul Desmond (Colin Fox), who makes a pact with the Devil in a bid to bring back to life his beloved wife.

Created by Jerry Layton and Ian Martin for Krantz Films, the half-hour show was a cheap affair even by the standards of the time, but clearly had its followers (so much so that the show produced three of spinoff novels by Dorothy Daniels care of Paperback Library: *Strange Paradise* [1969], *Island of Evil* [1970] and *Raxl, Voodoo Priestess* [1970]). Also featuring Cosette Lee (as voodoo priestess Raxl) and Kurt Schiegl (as mute strongman Quito), the program had everything grist to its mill—snakes, skulls and voodoo dolls, plus lots of bongos on the soundtrack—though it must be said that the atmosphere wasn't particularly Caribbean as a consequence.

And Now the Gallery

Next, a familiar face returned to television in a familiar format. The face was that of Rod Serling, and the show was *Night Gallery* (1969–1973, TV), a follow-up of sorts to his earlier hit *The Twilight Zone* (1959–1964, TV), though here the emphasis was more on the macabre than science fiction. As before, the show was created and hosted by Serling

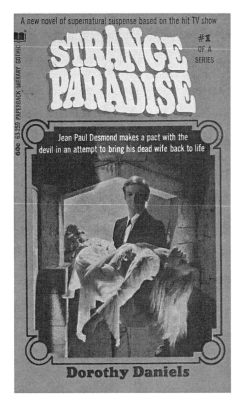

A new novel of supernatural suspense based on the hit TV show

STRANGE PARADISE

#1 OF A SERIES

Jean Paul Desmond makes a pact with the devil in an attempt to bring his dead wife back to life

Dorothy Daniels

Novel approach. The first of three novelizations based on the supernatural soap *Strange Paradise* (1969–1970, TV) (CBC/Krantz Films/Strange Paradise Company).

himself, who introduced each self-contained story via a picture in the titular art gallery, although this time the producing chores were primarily in the hands of Jack Laird, who also wrote many episodes, which meant that Serling didn't have quite the same creative (or quality) control he had previously enjoyed. Material was also sourced from the likes of Gene R. Kearney, Richard Matheson, H.P. Lovecraft, Robert Bloch and R. Chetwynd-Hayes, while directors included Jeannot Szwarc (who helmed 19 stories), John Badham (who also worked as an associate producer on the pilot), Don Taylor, Boris Sagal and Leonard Nimoy. As was the standard on most anthology shows of the period, the casts were peppered with visiting guest stars of varying degrees of fame, among them such names of the day as John Astin (who also directed three segments), Susan Strasberg, James Farentino, Stuart Whitman, Vincent Price, Tom Bosley, Leslie Nielsen, Laurence Harvey, Agnes Moorehead and Lindsay Wagner.

Made by Universal for broadcast on NBC, the show, which ran to 43 installments, actually launched with a movie length pilot, albeit featuring three stories penned by Serling ("Good evening, and welcome to a private showing of three paintings, displayed here for the first time; each is a collector's item in its own way—not because of any special artistic quality, but because each captures on a canvas, suspends in time and space, a frozen moment of a nightmare," he intones during his intro, which features the artwork of illustrator and portrait artist Jaroslav Gebr, whose work can also be found in such films as *Psycho* [1960] and *The Sting* [1973]). The first segment, *The Cemetery*, features Roddy McDowall as a young man who murders his uncle so that he can inherit his property, but is seemingly paid a visit one evening by his vengeful relative, whose journey from his nearby resting place is depicted in a painting in the hallway; the second story, *Eyes*, involves a ruthlessly self-centered blind woman (Joan Crawford) who blackmails a surgeon into operating on her so that she might see for the first time, albeit for a very short period (she has acquired the required corneas from a debt ridden gambler [Tom Bosley]), but, ironically, there is a blackout on the evening on which she takes off her bandages; while in the third, *The Escape Route*, a Nazi war criminal (Richard Kiley), hiding out in South America, becomes obsessed with a painting of a fisherman into which he finds himself drawn, but leaves it too late to escape there permanently.

The 98-minute movie (made to fill a two-hour timeslot) is something of a mixed bag. The third episode, directed by Barry Shear, is dreary stuff, all too obviously filmed on the back lot (in some shots, the old village set from the Universal horror films of the thirties and forties can be glimpsed in the background), while the first, helmed by Boris Sagal, is inordinately padded, though it does pick up a fair deal of tension and atmosphere once the uncle's corpse seemingly starts to wend its way towards the house in which his increasingly frantic nephew is cowering (spoiler alert: it's actually the old man's loyal butler [Ossie Davis] who is staging events for his own gain). It is the second episode which remains the most interesting, however, firstly because it stars Hollywood legend Joan Crawford in one of her better later performances, to which she brings her customary glamor and professionalism ("I want to see something: trees, concrete, buildings, grass, airplanes, *color!*" she rages at one point), and secondly because it was directed by the young Steven Spielberg (then just 22), who brings a fair deal of visual panache to the proceedings. His first work for television, its notable moments include an eye-catching shot through some chandelier baubles, a dizzying shot taken on a moving roundabout, the removal of the bandages from Crawford's eyes, achieved via a series of jump cuts towards her face, her subsequent scrambling about in the dark, and the fading of her sight just as the sun is rising.

The film was broadcast on 8 November 1969, and was generally well received, though episode one of the series proper didn't follow until 16 December 1970 (running to 20 January 1971), by which time the format had been downsized to 50 minutes (for a one-hour timeslot), and now featured two stories per installment (though episode two managed to cram three tales into its running time). The first program was comprised of *The Dead Man* (1970, TV), in which a doctor (Carl Betz) hypnotizes one of his patients into simulating various diseases for research purposes, and *The Housekeeper* (1970, TV), in which a devotee of the black arts (Larry Hagman) replaces the soul of his shrewish wife with that of a kindly housekeeper. As with the movie, however, the series was a somewhat variable affair, and it never quite managed to reach the heights of *The Twilight Zone*, having something of a bland corporate feel to it, although something of interest periodically turned up given the quality of the talent involved, among them Steven Spielberg, who returned to direct a second (albeit rather disappointing) story for the show. This was *Make Me Laugh* (1971, TV), which appeared in episode four, and which focuses on a failed comedian (Godfrey Cambridge) who wishes that he can make people laugh, only to regret his decision. Other stories of passing interest featured in season one were *The House* (1970, TV) from episode two, in which a woman (Joanna Pettet) comes across a house she has been dreaming about, and *The Doll* (1971, TV) from episode five, in which a Colonel (John Williams) finds himself at odds with his niece's evil doll (the story, by Algernon Blackwood, had already done service as a 1963 episode of *Tales of Mystery* [1961–1963, TV]).

For season two, which began on 15 September 1971, the story count varied from program to program, the first of which managed to shoehorn four stories into its running time. These were *The Boy Who Predicted Earthquakes* (1971, TV), *Miss Lovecraft Sent Me* (1971, TV), *The Hand of Borgus Weems* (1971, TV) and *Phantom of What Opera?* (1971, TV). Of these, the *Miss Lovecraft* story is perhaps the most interesting, given that it involves a vampire (a babysitter [Sue Lyons] goes to a castle to look after the child of a vampire [Joseph Campanella]). Other stories of passing interest include *The Merciful* (1971, TV) from episode two, which offers a variation on Edgar Allan Poe's much used *The Cask of Amontillado*; *Witches' Feast* (1971, TV) also from episode two, in which a coven of witches prepare a strange dish; *The Devil Is Not Mocked* (1971, TV) from episode six, in which Dracula (Francis Lederer, who'd already played the role in *The Return of Dracula* [1958]) regales his grandson with his wartime experiences against the Nazis; *A Matter of Semantics* (1971, TV) from episode eight, in which Dracula (Cesar Romero) visits a blood bank to make a withdrawal; *A Midnight Visit to the Neighborhood Blood Bank* (1971, TV) from episode nine, in which a young woman wakes to discover she is being visited by a vampire (Victor Buono); *Quoth the Raven* (1971, TV) from episode 12, in which Edgar Allan Poe (Marty Allen) suffers from writer's block; and *Last Rites for a Dead Druid* (1972, TV) from episode 18, in which an attorney (Bill Bixby) is tormented by a statue.

Season three, which began on 24 September 1972, now featured just one story per program (save for a couple of two-parters), and opened with *The Return of the Sorcerer* (1972, TV), in which a sorcerer (Vincent Price in his second segment for the series following *Class of '99* [1971, TV]) asks a language expert to help him translate an ancient text (this was one of two episodes made to fill a shorter half-hour slot, the other being *Whisper* [1973, TV]). This was followed by the likes of *Fright Night* (1972, TV), in which an author and his wife (Stuart Whitman and Barbara Anderson) inherit a house containing a trunk which they are told they must never open; *Smile, Please* (1972, TV), in which a photographer (Lindsay Wagner) has an encounter with a vampire (Cesare Danova); and *How to Cure the Common Vampire* (1973, TV), in which vampire hunters (Richard Deacon and Johnny Brown) debate the best way of killing a sleeping vampire. Following its cancellation, the show went into syndication, more often than not in a half-hour slot, for which many of the episodes were severely trimmed (to confuse matters, episodes from a later non–Serling series, *The Sixth Sense* [1972, TV], were also added into the mix, for which Serling recorded fresh intros).

In addition to feature-length pilots and one-offs, specific TV movie runs were also developed by several of the broadcasting companies, resulting in such ongoing strands as *ABC Movie of the Week*, which ran between 1969 and 1975 (usually on Tuesday evenings), and *The NBC Mystery Movie*, which ran between 1971 and 1977 (usually on Sunday evenings), the latter of which is remembered for its eerie title sequence featuring a lone figure making his way across a dramatically lit desert-scape with a flashlight, accompanied by the strains of a memorable Henry Mancini theme tune. The making of these movies turned into something of a cottage industry akin to the studio system of the thirties and forties, and a number of producers and production companies consequently found themselves busy providing feature-length content for the airwaves.

The first *ABC Movie of the Week* proved to be a standalone thriller, *Daughter of the Mind* (1969, TVM), and launched the strand in some style ("The movie of the week. Presenting the world premiere of an original motion picture produced especially for ABC. Tonight on the movie of the week…," grandly intones the link man introducing the 90-minute film). Made by Twentieth Century–Fox, it aired on 9 December 1969 and starred Don Murray as Dr. Alex Lauder, a doctor of parapsychology who is called in to investigate the case of Samuel Hale Constable (Ray Milland), a grieving professor of cybernetics who is led to believe that his recently deceased daughter Mary has returned from the grave so as to communicate with him ("Oh, daddy, I *hate* being dead"). However, his investigation reveals it to be an elaborate hoax perpetrated by enemy agents keen to prevent the professor from continuing with his work ("Daddy, they won't let me come any more if you don't stop doing those … those bad war things"). Or as General Augstadt (Frank Maxwell), who is also involved in the case, more bluntly puts it, "Oh, somebody's communicating with Professor Constable all right. Somebody from the other side all right. The other side in the Cold War."

Adapted by Luther Davis from the 1964 novel *The Hand of Mary Constable* by Paul Gallico, the film generates a good deal of atmosphere before things are eventually explained away, among its more effective sequences being the professor's first encounter with his daughter, whom he comes across on a lonely road as he returns from one of his many visits to the family tomb, and a séance, held in his wife's studio, during which the child not only appears but also leaves a wax cast of her arm. It soon becomes apparent that the professor is being manipulated by foreign agents, after which the film turns into an espionage thriller, while the final, somewhat farfetched explanations of how the ghostly effects were created have an air of *Scooby-Doo* about them (remote controlled tape recorders, a laser light projector capable of throwing a three-dimensional image, sleeper spies and the use of a double). Until then, however, this is a professionally made chiller, helmed with assurance by Walter Grauman (who also produced), and with the benefit of a strong supporting cast, among them Gene Tierney, Ed Asner, George Macready, John Carradine and Pamelyn Ferdin as the ghostly lookalike of Mary Constable. The atmospheric main title theme care of Robert Drasnin is also a major plus. However, if was intended that Alex Lauder was to go on to solve further cases in the form of a weekly series, it didn't come to pass. But there was plenty waiting in the wings to help compensate….

SECTION FOUR

The American TV Movie
Comes of Age (the 1970s)

Movie of the Week

In America in the seventies, the tele-movie truly came into its own. All genres were featured, resulting in comedies, thrillers, westerns and romances, although cop shows and medical dramas (or "disease of the week" as they came to be known) generally proved to be the most popular. Some of the movies were good, some bad, some just production line fillers, but there was usually something of interest popping up in the schedules, and they certainly proved to be a valuable training ground for a number of talents both in front of and behind the cameras. Horror naturally got a look in, too, and while the films were clearly never going to be as bloody or violent as their big screen counterparts, a number of them certainly delivered the goods when it came to chills and thrills, and have stayed in the minds of those who saw them on their first runs.

Having begun with *Daughter of the Mind* (1969, TVM), a horror film which technically turned into an espionage thriller midway through, ABC continued the trend in its *Movie of the Week* strand with a handful of other borderline cases, among them *How Awful About Allan* (1970, TVM), which aired on 22 September 1970. Adapted from his 1963 novel by Henry Farrell (best known for his 1960 novel *Whatever Happened to Baby Jane?* which had been successfully filmed in 1962), it sees a blind young man (Anthony Perkins) return home after a fire in which his father was killed to stay with his sister (Julie Harris), only to become convinced that a mysterious boarder is trying to kill him. More thriller than outright horror, it nevertheless ramps up the tension thanks to the exploitation of a number of horror film staples, including whispered voices, shadowy figures wandering around at night, thunderstorms and a last-minute revelation to help resolve matters (note that the story had already been filmed for German television as *Horror* [1969, TVM]).

Meanwhile, science fiction was more to the fore in *Night Slaves* (1970, TVM), which aired on 29 September 1970. In it, a young businessman (James Franciscus), recovering from a brain operation following a car crash, goes on vacation with his wife (Lee Grant) so as to recuperate. However, while staying in a small western township (for which read the back lot), he wakes to discover that the residents, along with his wife, are being herded onto trucks at night and driven away, only to reappear the

112

next day. Investigating matters, he discovers it to be the work of aliens, disguised as humans, who need the locals to help repair their spaceship, which has sustained internal damage while in flight (the plate in the husband's head prevents him from being controlled by them himself). Directed by Curtis Harrington and Ted Post, respectively, both films are efficiently made, have intriguing plots, and proved what *could* be achieved on a tight budget and schedule, even if *The New York Times* found *Allan* to have "neither a thrill nor a chill."

ABC's next venture into horror proper proved to be *The House That Would Not Die* (1970, TVM), which was broadcast on 27 October 1970. Based upon the 1968 novel *Ammie, Come Home* by Barbara Michaels, it was adapted for television by Henry Farrell, for whom this was turning into a busy period. In addition to Farrell, the tele-film had several other pluses going for it, in that it starred the legendary Hollywood actress Barbara Stanwyck, was directed by John Llewellyn Moxey (whose theatrical credits included *The City of the Dead* [1960, aka *Horror Hotel*]), and had a supporting cast that included Richard Egan, Michael Anderson, Jr., Doreen Lang and Kitty Winn (here billed as Katherine Winn, and soon to find fame in *The Exorcist* [1973]). Made at Paramount Studios care of Aaron Spelling Productions, it focuses on a remote house inherited by Ruth Bennett (Stanwyck), into which she moves with her niece Sara (Winn), but they soon come to realize that the place is haunted by two ghosts from the time of the American Revolution.

The story has everything grist to its mill, including slo-mo dream sequences, unearthly voices heard in the middle of the night, doors creaking open of their own accord, a séance during which another face appears over Sara's, possession (Sara is taken over by a troubled spirit and tries to strangle her aunt at one point), the discovery of an old scroll, the contents of which help to explain what has been going on (a 20-year-old girl disappeared from the house in 1780), the discovery a sealed room in the cellar in which a body is buried, and lots and lots of howling wind, both indoors and out. Indeed, it is this plethora of incident rather than any overt style that keeps one watching, yet for a 72-minute TV flick (made for a 90-minute slot), one can't accuse it of stinting on dramatic situations, even if they do take some swallowing.

Triple vision. Kitty Winn in an eye-catching promotional shot for *The House That Would Not Die* (1970, TVM) (ABC/Aaron Spelling Productions).

A slightly more gruesome prospect was *Only Way Out Is Dead* (1970, TVM, aka *The Man Who Wanted to Live Forever*), a buy-in made by Palomar and the Canadian Film Development Corporation, which aired on 20 November 1970. Pre-empting *Coma* (1978) by some years, it involves a heart surgeon (Stuart Whitman) who discovers that the remote research institute in which he is working isn't quite what it appears to be. Setting out to expose its enigmatic director, T.M. Trask (Burl Ives), he is helped by a fellow colleague (Sandy Dennis), with whom he learns that Trask has been benefiting from transplants himself for some time, his plan being to live forever, the various organs having been harvested from otherwise healthy patients. Naturally, Trask is keen to keep his secrets safe, and tries to prevent the couple from escaping, which they eventually do, resulting in a ski chase through the Canadian Rockies. Penned by Henry Denker and directed by John Trent, the film was released theatrically in some territories as *The Heart Farm* (tagline: "1,000 miles from civilization, but its terror reaches out to the world").

Another inherited house was meanwhile the focus of *Crowhaven Farm* (1970, TVM), the next horror film produced by Aaron Spelling Productions for the *ABC Movie of the Week* slot. This time, Maggie and Ben Porter (Hope Lange and Paul Burke), a young couple with marital problems, inherit a farm, into which they decide to move in the hope that a more easy-going rural life might help to sort out their issues, among them the inability to have a baby. However, it isn't long before supernatural forces start to make themselves felt, and Maggie gradually comes to realize that the area is in the thrall of a coven of witches. She also appears to be no stranger to the property ("I've been here before") and turns out to be the reincarnation of a young woman who, hundreds of years ago, broke a pact with the witches, who are now seeking revenge. "There are such things as witches. You know, in some other life they think I betrayed them," she confides to a friend, who naturally turns out to be one of them. As with *The House That Would Not Die*, the story is tricked out with plenty of incidents to keep one watching, including sobbing and mocking laughter in the night, thunder storms, a sacrificial ritual in a quarry, various visions (among them a "pressing" in which a young woman is crushed under a door on top of which rocks are laid), the discovery of teeth marks on the shoulder of a young girl (Cindy Eilbacher) the couple adopt, and lots of wind (a wind machine, it would seem, was a pre-requisite for such proceedings). The story also has echoes of *Rosemary's Baby* (1968), in that Maggie finally bears her own child, only for her husband to conclude she's had an affair with a neighbor, which leads him to shoot the guy, following which he goes on the run, ending up a victim of the coven himself.

Ably produced and directed by Walter Grauman (who'd made such a good job of *Daughter of the Mind*), the film moves along fast enough to prevent one from questioning its absurdities, and has a committed performance from leading lady Hope Lange, who, in the course of the action, finds herself confronting more perils than Pauline (Lange had previously starred in the spooky sit com *The Ghost and Mrs. Muir* [1968–1970, TV]). It also benefits from the presence of a number of guest stars, among them John Carradine as a creepy handyman and Milton Selzer as Maggie's doctor, both of whom prove to be members of the coven. Broadcast on 24 November 1970, for which it was trailed as "A chilling tale of vengeance from beyond the grave," the film proved to be a ratings hit, while the *LA Times* described it as "spooky, diverting."

The world of medicine was a frequent source for movie of the week subject matter, and two cases that made use of it teetered on the edge of the horrific and rate a passing mention. The first was *Dr. Cook's Garden* (1971, TVM), a euthanasia thriller in which a kindly rural doctor weeds out those in his township whom he deems either too ill to live, or whose lives he perceives as being detrimental to the community, but his lethal practices are discovered by a young doctor return-ing home after a long absence ("This is the happiest, healthiest town in the whole state!" argues the older doctor in his own defense). Based upon a 1967 play by Ira Levin, the film's major selling point was having the crooner Bing Crosby play the well-meaning doctor, whose God complex has turned him into a benign serial killer (*Variety* described Crosby's role as "an acting triumph"). Directed by Ted Post, it aired on 19 January 1971, and if its plotline seems a little farfetched, fast forward to the exploits of the real life British serial killer Dr. Harold Shipman (filmed as *Harold Shipman: Doctor Death* [2002, TVM]). The second film, *Escape* (1971, TVM), which aired on 6 April 1971, was more of a mishmash of genres. Directed by John Llewellyn Moxey, it follows the exploits of an escapologist (Christopher George) who becomes a spy, and whose first case sees him track down a mad doctor (John Vernon) who is experimenting with "synthesized life." Intended as the pilot for a series, it failed to be picked up as such by the network, perhaps because it was all just a little bit too silly (the film climaxes with a chase on a rollercoaster).

Rather more intriguing was *The Deadly Dream* (1971, TVM), which was broad-cast on 25 September 1971. In it, scientist Jim Hanley (Lloyd Bridges) finds his sleep continually disrupted by the same nightmare, in which he finds himself marked for murder by a tribunal for a crime he is convinced he has not committed. Finding it hard to discern fantasy from reality as a consequence, he becomes increasingly fraz-zled by the experience, believing his wife Laurel (Janet Leigh) and friends to some-how be in on the conspiracy. The sort of situation that might have made for a solid episode of *The Twilight Zone* (1959–1964, TV) is here ably enough tricked out to fea-ture length by writer Barry Oringer, and directed with reasonable pace and flair by Alf Kjellin, while the cast (also among them Leif Erickson, Don Stroud, Richard Jaeckel and Arlene Dahl) treat it all seriously enough so as to make it a more than adequate time filler, building as it does to a suitably downbeat ending for our unfor-tunate protagonist (commented *Variety*, "Leaves you guessing at the end as much as the beginning").

The supernatural then reared its head again on 2 October 1971 with *Sweet, Sweet Rachel* (1971, TVM), an ESP thriller in which Rachel Stanton (Stefanie Powers) wit-nesses her husband Paul (Rod McCary [billed McCarey]), who had been dabbling in psychic matters, jump to his death during what proves to be a deadly mind game with an unseen player. After receiving a series of recriminations ("I hear voices tell-ing me that I'm responsible for my husband's death"), she seeks the help of Dr. Lucas Darrow (Alex Dreier), a psychic investigator who uses his own abilities with ESP to try and track down the perpetrator and release Rachel from her unseen tormentor ("The unknown has frightened people since the beginning of time—the only cure is understanding it," he comforts her). Helped by his blind assistant Carey Johnson (Chris Robinson), who has a highly tuned sixth sense, the duo narrow the suspects down to Rachel's immediate relations, among them her cousin Nora (Brenda Scott), who not only was in love with her dead husband, but also appears to have been using the telephone to relay a number of disturbing trigger words to Rachel ("Eye, knife, raven, doll, coffin"), her aunt Lillian (Louise Latham), a medium who takes Rachel under her wing and uses her own powers to control her niece, and her seemingly benign uncle Arthur (Pat Hingle), who turns out to be the real perpetrator, his plan being to wrest away Rachel's fortune.

Clearly, with all the characters involved either displaying supernatural abilities or believing in them wholesale, one has to take a leap of faith with the plot of *Sweet, Sweet Rachel*, but if one accepts its premise at face value—that minds can be controlled and influenced over great distances—then this is a highly absorbing thriller, peppered with a number of exceptionally well staged sequences, among them the opening scene in which Paul is compelled to his death; a later scene in which Dr. Lucas, in the thrall of unseen forces, crashes his car, after which he tries to set it alight by dropping lit matches into the fuel tank; a brief scene in which a plaster bust of Rachel's husband appears to come to life and accuses her of killing him; and a sequence in a road tunnel in which the doctor has a vision of Rachel's recently deceased aunt, supposedly killed by Rachel but in fact, as "sensed" by the doctor's assistant, poisoned. Thanks to the work of director Sutton Roley and his cameraman James Crabe, these are filmed from a variety of eye catching angles, all of which add to the overall sense of unease that permeates the film, which is aided and abetted by a creepy score care of Laurence Rosenthal, a surprisingly well structured teleplay by Anthony Lawrence, and committed performances from its entire cast, notable among them Stefanie Powers, who generates genuine sympathy as the deceived Rachel, Louise Latham (best remembered for playing the prostitute mother in Hitchcock's *Marnie* [1964]) as her controlling aunt, and Alex Dreier as the concerned Dr. Darrow (and how refreshing it is to see an overweight middle-aged man take the lead here as opposed to a manufactured Hollywood pretty boy).

A genuinely absorbing and persuasive piece of genre television, *Sweet, Sweet Rachel* was broadcast on 2 October 1971, since when it has somehow managed to slip into comparative obscurity. As good as anything of a similar nature produced for the big screen during this period, it certainly deserves to be better known and appreciated than it presently is. Someone at ABC was clearly impressed by the movie at the time, however, as a TV show based upon its premise was subsequently ordered. Titled *The Sixth Sense* (1972, TV), it was created by *Sweet, Sweet Rachel*'s screenwriter Anthony Lawrence (who penned the pilot plus one further episode) and developed by its producer Stan Shpetner (who returned here in the same capacity). Direction was handled by the likes of Alf Kjellin (who directed the opening episode, plus two others), *Rachel*'s Sutton Roley (who handled three episodes), Richard Donner, John Badham, Daniel Haller and Robert Day, while guest stars included June Allyson, Will Geer, Joan Crawford, William Shatner, Paul Michael Glaser, Sandra Dee and Rachel herself, Stefanie Powers.

Running to 25 hour-long episodes over two seasons, the show followed the cases of Dr. Michael Rhodes (Gary Collins), a college professor who, with the help of his assistant Nancy Murphy (Catherine Ferrar), finds himself investigating a number of mysteries involving such supernatural phenomena as possession, out of body experiences, visitations and extra sensory perception. The first episode, *I Do Not Belong to the Human World* (1972, TV), was broadcast on 15 January 1972, and involves a young woman (Belinda Montgomery) who is having visions of her brother (Kip Niven), presumed to have been killed in Vietnam; she is also receiving messages in Chinese in "automatic writing." It transpires that her brother is in fact alive and being held in a prisoner of war camp, from which a friend of his has managed to escape, but whose actions are the reason why he is still being held captive. Rather more talkative and involved than *Sweet, Sweet Rachel*, and certainly more routinely handled, the episode was nevertheless a fair enough opener for the installments that followed, among them such titles as *The House That Cried Murder* (1972, TV), in which a young woman (Carol Lynley) has visions of murder connected to the works of Edgar Allan Poe; *Witch, Witch, Burning Bright* (1972, TV), in which a mother (Cloris Leachman) believes her daughter to be a witch; and *Face of Ice* (1972, TV), in which the only memory an amnesiac (Christine Belford) can recall is of a murder.

Season two, which began airing on 23 September 1972, kicked off with *Coffin, Coffin in the Sky* (1972, TV), in which an airline passenger (Jess Walton) suffers from a number of visions of impending death and destruction. This was followed by *Dear Joan: We're Going to Scare You to Death* (1972, TV), an extended (75-minute) story in which a woman (Joan Crawford) clashes with a group with supernatural powers who are out to scare her to death. In a somewhat odd interview between Gary Collins and Crawford at the conclusion of this particular episode (in which they awkwardly pretend to be themselves), an effusive Collins proclaims, "I think there's a lot to be learned yet about ESP, but I'll tell you one thing, I'm going to use mine to get you back on our show as soon as possible." Unfortunately, the installment proved to be Crawford's last role as an actress. Following the likes of *With Affection, Jack the Ripper* (1972, TV), *I Did Not Mean to Slay Thee* (1972, TV) and *Gallows in the Wind* (1972, TV), whose titles promised more than they delivered, the season concluded with *The Eyes That Wouldn't Die* (1972, TV), in which a blind woman (Kathleen Lloyd) suffers visions about the murder of the woman whose corneas have restored her sight. By this time, proceeding had become routine to the point that if one missed an episode, it didn't matter too much, but over its run, the show managed to provide a few minor chills and frissons for those prepared to wait for them. In fact on this front, it was considered good enough to have its episodes trimmed down to fill a half-hour slot by way of augmenting the syndication package for *Night Gallery* (1969–1973, TV), for which Rod Serling filmed new introductions. All very confusing for followers of both shows, especially as the original length versions of *The Sixth Sense* were considered lost for many years, though many of them have since emerged intact on YouTube.

Meanwhile, *ABC Movie of the Week* continued to provide the occasional genre offering (or a near enough variation thereof), the next being *A Taste of Evil* (1971, TVM), which aired on 12 October 1971 and reunited director John Llewellyn Moxey and leading lady Barbara Stanwyck, who had previously worked together on *The House That Would Not Die* (1970, TVM). A cheeky riff on Hammer's *Taste of Fear* (1961, aka *Scream of Fear*), penned by that film's writer and producer Jimmy Sangster (who by now had been working in Hollywood for a few years), it follows the tribulations of a young woman named Susan (Barbara Parkins), whose return home following a rape and a seven year recovery period in a Swiss clinic proves to be far from recuperative, given that it appears that someone is trying to drive her insane (breathing in the shadows, a body in her bath and a voice calling her name in the woods are among the various traumas she has to endure). That it all turns out to be a plot hatched by her mother Miriam (Stanwyck), working in cahoots with her loyal but dim-witted grounds man (Arthur O'Connell), in a bid to coerce Susan into shooting her stepfather (William Windom) so that she can wrest control of the estate her daughter inherited from her late father (rather than his leaving it to her), proves to be the not-too-surprising revelation mid-way through the piece. That Susan's stepfather then seemingly returns from the dead to avenge himself on his widow leads to further twists and turns (it ultimately transpires that Susan, her stepfather and a local doctor [Roddy McDowall] are responsible for turning the tables on the hate-filled Miriam). An old fashioned screamer complete with a thunderstorm climax and more contrivances than are feasible, the results certainly keep one watching if only to find out who is doing what to whom, though the proceedings fail to erase memories of the far more stylishly executed *Taste of Fear*, while the fact that the plot's motivation depends on the rape of a 13-year-old child (committed, it turns out, by the grounds man) simply beggars belief, especially given that this was meant for mainstream consumption.

A version of the Alberto Casella play *Death Takes a Holiday* followed next on 23 October 1971. Something of a TV staple in the fifties, the story had already appeared as installments of *Broadway Television Theatre* (1952–1954, TV), *Ponds Theater* (1953–1956, TV) and *Matinee Theater* (1955–1958, TV). In this version, Death (Monte Markham) takes human form and falls in love with a beautiful young woman named Peggy (Yvette Mimieux) while taking an Earthbound vacation from his duties, where he learns a little of man's desire to hold onto life for as long as possible. Unfortunately, despite a cast that also includes Melvyn Douglas as Peggy's increasingly suspicious father, Myrna Loy, Kerwin Mathews and Priscilla Pointer, this is a drearily talkative affair, flatly directed by David Butler and further hampered by its leading man's lack of charisma. As for its air of supernatural romance, it simply fails to take flight. That said, the *LA Times* found the film to be a "rare and elegant treat."

It was into crazy lady territory next with *Revenge!* (1971, TVM), in which a deranged mother (Shelley Winters) lures a businessman (Bradford Dillman) to her house having swapped briefcases with him, her intention being to imprison him in a cage in her cellar in revenge for seducing and impregnating her daughter, who subsequently killed herself. Unfortunately, she has captured the wrong man ("To avenge her daughter's loss of innocence, a woman imprisons an innocent man," ran the tagline). Having had no success with the police, the man's wife (Carol Eve Rossen) subsequently employs a medium (Stuart Whitman) to discover his whereabouts. That the wife seems to possess the powers of ESP (she senses which house her husband is being held in) and the medium proves to be a fake makes for an engaging twist in the proceedings, and the two subsequently join forces to stage a rescue, not realizing that time is running out for them, given that the madwoman intends to chop up her victim with an axe and dispose of the evidence in a trunk! Adapted by Joseph Stefano from the 1971 novel *There Was an Old Lady* by Elizabeth Davis, this incident packed little shocker, which aired on 6 November 1971, moves at a reasonable pace thanks to the efficient direction of TV veteran Jud Taylor. It also benefits from an atmospheric score care of Dominic Frontiere and solid, straight-faced performances from all concerned. And as always, the barnstorming Winters is good value for money as the increasingly unhinged Mrs. Hilton, who veers from polite hausfrau to poker-wielding maniac as the plot requires.

Another businessman meanwhile found himself in peril in *Duel* (1971, TV), which aired on 13 November 1971. The simple story of an account salesman (Dennis Weaver) on a trip though the desert back roads of California, during which he is menaced by the unseen driver of a fuel tanker, it managed to crank up the tension to almost unbearable levels, despite being set in broad daylight for its entirety. A triumphant example of what can be achieved on a comparatively small budget ($450,000) if the talent involved is inspired by the material, it was written with economy by Richard Matheson and directed with aplomb by the young Steven Spielberg who, since leaving his mark with a segment for the feature-length pilot for *Night Gallery* (1969–1973, TV), had been treading water helming episodes for such TV series as *The Name of the Game* (1968–1971, TV), *Marcus Welby, M.D.* (1969–1976, TV) and *Owen Marshall, Counselor at Law* (1971–1974, TV), though he had managed to prove his abilities again with *Murder by the Book* (1971, TVM), an early feature-length episode of the popular detective series *Columbo* (1971–2003, TVM). With *Duel*, however, he was finally able to let his talent fly, despite a punishingly tight schedule, presenting the road-bound action in a wide variety of stylishly conceived and executed shots, all of which are expertly captured by his cinematographer Jack A. Marta. With an excellent leading performance from Dennis Weaver as the cowed businessman, brilliant stunt work care of Carey Loftin (who plays the unseen driver) and an atmospheric score by Billy Goldenberg (who had already scored Spielberg's *Night Gallery* segment and his episodes for *The Name of the Game* and *Columbo*), the movie was a revelation (it went on to earn a Golden Globe nomination for best TV movie). In fact, following its air date, Spielberg and his team were quickly brought back to expand the 74-minute running time to 90 so that it could be released theatrically in foreign territories. And while one might be hard pressed to describe the film as an out and out horror movie (despite its various shock cuts and its unremitting suspense), there does appear to be an almost supernatural element to the proceedings, particularly in the closing moments as the gigantic truck goes over a cliff to meet its doom, accompanied by a slowed down dinosaur roar culled from *The Land Unknown* (1957), Spielberg having made the decision to treat the vehicle as a monster and not a machine (the same sound effect can be heard during the climax of *Jaws* [1975]).

The Devil reared his head again in *The Devil and Miss Sarah* (1971, TVM), a somewhat curious western in which the posse escorting an outlaw (Gene Barry) to justice comes to a sticky end at the hand of bandits, following which a homesteader and his wife (Janice Rule and James Drury) take over the responsibility. But it would appear that their captor, who has a gift for the gab, is in possession of satanic powers, which he uses to influence the wife to assist in his escape. Unfortunately, despite a good performance from Gene Barry and a supporting cast that includes Slim Pickens, Charles McGraw and Donald Moffat, the story is neither fish nor fowl, though the location work (the movie was shot in Utah) at least ensures that the proceedings have an authentic feel. Penned by Calvin Clements, directed by episode veteran Michael Caffey and produced by Stan Shpetner (the man responsible for *Sweet,*

Sweet Rachel [1971, TVM] and *The Sixth Sense* [1972, TV]), the film has been little revived since it first aired on 4 December 1971.

Kolchak Scores a Hit

There was no doubt about the content of ABC's next genre offering, however, which got the New Year off with a bang when it was broadcast on 11 January 1972. The film was *The Night Stalker* (1972, TVM), and it was a genuine shot in the arm to TV horror. Made on location in Las Vegas in just 12 days on a budget of $450,000, the story follows the exploits of Carl Kolchak (Darren McGavin), a smart talking newspaper reporter who has been assigned to look into the murder of a young woman whose bloodless body has been discovered in a trashcan by refuse workers. When other bodies start turning up in a similar state, and blood is stolen from a hospital, Kolchak believes he's onto something. As indeed he is: a vampire is terrorizing Vegas, and it appears that the authorities want to keep the case covered up ("We don't want to cause a panic; it's bad for police operations, it's bad for the people, and it's bad for business," argues the District Attorney [Kent Smith]). Kolchak's newspaper editor, Tony Vincenzo (Simon Oakland, best remembered for playing the psychiatrist at the end of *Psycho* [1960]) is also inclined to disbelieve Kolchak's conclusions that a vampire must be responsible for the killings. Thus the reporter sets out to track down the perpetrator himself. When the story finally breaks following a brawl at a hospital where the vampire has been stealing blood again, he is identified as being a Romanian named Janos Skorzeny (Barry Atwater), who is supposedly over 70 years old, and whose travels (including stopovers in Britain and Canada) have always been accompanied by unexplained killings.

Thanks to his various contacts, among them a coroner, a telephonist and a realtor (Elisha Cook, Jr.), Kolchak is able to keep one step ahead of the police, and finally tracks down the killer to his hideout in a rundown mansion on the outskirts of the city, where he discovers a fridge full of blood, an empty coffin and another victim tied up on a bed ("His own private blood bank"). When the vampire finally returns, Kolchak confronts him with a cross and, with the aid of a policeman who turns up on the scene, dispatches him by pulling down a window blind (it is dawn by this time) and impaling him with a stake, just as the Sheriff (Claude Akins) arrives to catch him in the act. As a consequence, the DA insists that Kolchak bury the story, otherwise he'll be arrested for murder, added to which he's also run out of town ("So all the loose ends had been gathered together and tied into a pretty knot right around the neck of guess who"). However, he has the last laugh by writing a book about the events, even though it would seem that all proof they ever occurred has been wiped from official records.

An engaging mix of detection and horror, *The Night Stalker* moves from A to B in a brisk and frequently exciting manner thanks to the efficient work of director John Llewellyn Moxey (whose genre credits for ABC were starting to stack up), and while not noticeably stylish in its camera angles, it benefits enormously from its on-the-spot location work which lends the proceedings a *cinema verité* vibe. The screenplay by Richard Matheson (which is based upon and unpublished story by Jeff Rice), is a brisk affair which keeps one fully engaged with its proceedings (among them a victim discovered on the freshly laid concrete of a storm drain without a trace of footprints by her body), all of which are relayed with economy and humor ("Well, it looks like Bela Lugosi's struck again," quips Kolchak upon the discovery of the fourth unfortunate victim, while elsewhere he makes reference to the legendary newspaper reporter and screenwriter Ben Hecht). Performance wise, everybody gives that little bit extra, given the quality of the script. As Kolchak, Darren McGavin is perfectly cast as the frayed around the edges reporter who is determined to get his story no matter what others may think of him, while strong support is provided by Simon Oakland as his irascible boss, Claude Akins as the sheriff and Carol Lynley as Kolchak's concerned girlfriend. As the vampire, Barry Atwater has little to do other than look menacing (he has no quips to exchange with our hero, given that his performance is entirely without dialogue), but he is undeniably a credible menace.

Smoothly produced by Dan Curtis and with a reasonably atmospheric score by his regular composer Robert Cobert (who cheekily lifts a few minor cues from his work on *Dark Shadows* [1966–1971, TV]), the film was one of several modern day vampire pictures made at the time, among them *Count Yorga, Vampire* (1970) and its sequel *The Return of Count Yorga* (1971), not to mention Curtis' own *House of Dark Shadows* (1970), compared to which it certainly holds its own. Indeed, the film seems to have been just what audiences craved, and it went on to claim a 54 percent share of viewers upon its original broadcast, making it the most watched TV movie up to that point. With success like that, it was only a matter of time before Kolchak would return to the airwaves to fight another monster.

The next genre offering from the movie of the week strand produced another one of its oddities, *The People* (1972, TVM), which was produced by Gerald G. Isenberg via Metromedia Producers Corporation and American Zoetrope, the latter founded by Francis Ford Coppola and George Lucas (Coppola executive produced the film with Charles W. Fries). In it, a young teacher (Kim Darby) is sent to work at a school in an isolated Californian valley where the inhabitants are secretive and emotionally distant—and with good reason. They are aliens from a dying planet in possession of paranormal powers (among them mind reading and levitation) who don't wish their existence to be known to outsiders who may be hostile to their presence on Earth. Based upon the 1955 story *Pottage* by Zenna Henderson (one of several to feature The People), the film co-stars William Shatner as a local doctor who is never called upon to treat any of the community given that they lead perfectly healthy lives, and Dan O'Herlihy as a dour elder with whom the young teacher stays. Photographed on pleasantly leafy locations by Edward Rosson and featuring a number of simple but well managed effects sequences, one of which sees a couple of children floating among the trees, the film begins in a mildly sinister manner before becoming a rather twee homily on the benefits of the community sharing their gifts with the rest of mankind. Written by James M. Miller and directed by John Korty, this is inoffensive, well-meaning stuff which does drag a little in places, yet nevertheless manages to produce some genuinely touching and unexpected moments.

Broadcast on 22 January 1972, it can best be described as a curio, especially given that it is usually overlooked in discussions of the career of its executive producer (note that Coppola's father Carmine [wrongly billed in the credits as Carmen] provided the score for the film).

With *The Screaming Woman* (1972, TVM), it was back to the realms of the lady-in-peril thriller, to which were added a few minor horror overtones. Based upon a story by Ray Bradbury (which had previously done service as a radio play in 1948), it stars Hollywood legend Olivia de Havilland as Laura Wynant, a wealthy woman who, while recovering from a breakdown, hears the muffled cries of a woman who, it transpires, has been buried alive where the smoke house used to stand on the grounds of her estate. Naturally, no one believes Laura's story, given that there is nothing left of the smoke house on the surface, while the basement was supposedly filled in with earth years earlier ("Either I'm insane or there really is a woman buried out there," she tells her attorney George Tresvant [Joseph Cotten]). The buried woman turns out to be the victim of a love spat with her philandering husband, but Laura's greedy relatives use the situation to try and wrest her estate from her so that they can build a development on it and make a fortune. Unfortunately, in trying to muster help to dig the woman out, Laura tries to enlist the help of a number of neighbors living on a nearby housing tract, among them the would-be-killer (Ed Nelson). Plainly but adequately directed by Jack Smight from a teleplay by Merwin Gerard, the film benefits chiefly from de Havilland's robust performance, as well as a solid supporting cast which, in addition to Cotten, also includes Walter Pidgeon, Charles Drake and Laraine Stephens, with Kay Stewart enduring great discomfort as the buried woman, whose final emergence from the soil is a genuinely disturbing moment. Also involved in the film, which was broadcast on 29 January 1972, were top Hollywood costume designer Edith Head, cinematographer Sam Leavitt and composer John Williams, who provided the main theme for the score, which otherwise was comprised of stock music by Jerry Goldsmith and Morton Stevens (the story was late remade as a 1986 episode of *The Ray Bradbury Theater* [1985–1992, TV], with a little girl [Drew Barrymore] now the source of everyone's disbelief).

Another thriller with horror overtones followed with *When Michael Calls* (1972, TVM), in which a woman named Helen Connelly (Elizabeth Ashley) starts to receive calls from her nephew Michael. But Michael has been dead for 15 years ("I'm dead, aren't I? I'm dead! I'm dead!"), and following the calls, a number of murders and attempted murders take place, and it would appear that Helen may well be next in line. Based upon the 1967 novel by John Farris (best known for his 1976 telekinesis shocker *The Fury* which was filmed by Brian de Palma in 1978), the movie was written by James Bridges and directed by Philip Leacock and features a supporting cast that includes Ben Gazzara as Helen's estranged husband, and the young Michael Douglas as Michael's surviving brother Craig, who (spoiler alert) turns out to be the unhinged mind behind the charade. A rather slow-moving affair with undeniably creepy moments, the film, which was shot in Canada care of Twentieth Century–Fox and Palomar, aired on 5 February 1972 (note that the opening and closing music is lifted from *Daughter of the Mind* [1969, TVM]).

A genre film of a rather more old-fashioned appeal followed next with the umpteenth version of Sir Arthur Conan Doyle's *The Hound of the Baskervilles* (1972, TVM), which was first published as a serial in *The Strand Magazine* in 1901 and 1902. By no means a success, the film was intended as the a pilot for a revolving series called *Great Detectives*, but low ratings and audience indifference saw only two other films made before the idea was dropped (these were *The Adventures of Nick Carter* [1972, TVM, aka *Nick Carter*], in which Robert Conrad starred as the famous private detective, and *A Very Missing Person* [1972, TVM, aka *Hildegarde Withers*], in which Eve Arden played the popular lady sleuth). Here, it is an inappropriately cast Stewart Granger who somewhat uncomfortably dons the deerstalker so as to investigate the case of a spectral hound which is seemingly roaming Dartmoor, but which turns out to be an all too real creation. Yet despite a strong cast that includes Bernard Fox (as Dr. Watson), Anthony Zerbe, Sally Ann Howes, William Shatner, Jane Merrow and John Williams, they are given little of substance to do in Robert E. Thompson's weak adaptation, and the film simply treads water for its 73-minute running time. It was broadcast on 9 February 1972, and the *LA Times* described the results as "laborious, talky, often poorly staged," which indeed they are, given the limited means with which director Barry Crane has to operate (the only atmosphere comes from a few matte paintings care of effects legend Albert Whitlock). Very clearly a back lot production, one can spot a number Universal's standing sets in the film (among them the old Frankenstein village set), as well as footage from other movies (a railway shot culled from *The Railway Children* [1970]), while the music score (supervised by Hal Mooney) features cues cribbed from other films owing to a strike by composers, most notably *Cape Fear* (1962) by Bernard Herrmann (note that versions of the story had already appeared on the small screen in Germany as *Der Hund von Baskerville* [1955, TVM] starring Wolf Ackva as Holmes; in Britain in 1968 as a two-parter for the series *Sherlock Holmes* [1964–1968, TV] starring Peter Cushing; in Italy as *L'ultimo dei Baskerville*, a three-part adaptation for the series *Sherlock Holmes* [1968, TV] starring Nando Gazzolo; and in France as a 1974 episode of the long running drama series *Au théatre ce soir* [1966–1990, TV] under the title *Le chien des Baskerville* [1974, TV], this time featuring Raymond Gérome as Holmes).

Another unsold pilot followed on 29 February 1972. This was *The Eyes of Charles Sand* (1972, TVM), but unlike the Holmes movie, this was a real doozy with genuine potential, and it remains a mystery why it didn't make the grade. In it, Peter Haskell stars as the title character who, upon the death of his uncle, inherits his ability to see people from beyond the grave. Having dreamed of his uncle's death, our hero is woken by a phone call from his aunt Alexandria (Joan Bennett) who tells him that his uncle really has died, and that he must come over to her home immediately, where she informs him of the Sand legacy and hands him the key to a book which explains things further: "To him who reads these words. The reason you have dreamed of my death is because you are the sole surviving son of the Sand family. As such you have inherited The Sight. At times you will feel it a gift, and at others, a curse." He also learns that he will retain his uncle's gift until his own death, and that "neither men of God nor men of science can help you now. You are alone."

Initially skeptical, as one would expect, the visions nevertheless begin almost immediately when Sand sees a spectral figure standing in front of a mausoleum while attending his uncle's funeral, at which he also spies a beautiful girl wandering among the headstones. Consequently, he seeks help from a psychiatrist friend (Adam West), who proves to be of little assistance, attributing his experiences to premonitions and hallucinations. But the visions persist. Meanwhile, Sand is visited in his apartment by the girl he saw at the cemetery. Called Emily Parkhurst (Sharon Farrell), she is seeking help regarding her brother Raymond, whom she believes to be dead, but whom her sister Katharine (Barbara Rush) and her brother-in-law Jeffrey (Bradford Dillman) insist is in London on business. Visiting the girl's palatial home the next day to look into matters, Sand discovers that Emily has become obsessed with a murder in her family's past, and is on the cusp of sanity, a predicament that, it transpires, her sister and brother-in-law are keen to exploit, given that they are behind the death of her brother (killed during an argument), and now wish her out of the way too. Consequently, Sand finds himself involved in saving Emily from their murderous machinations.

Although its supernatural elements become increasingly less central to the story, which turns into a fairly standard "driving someone insane" plot, *The Eyes of Charles Sand* is nevertheless a well engineered little shocker with several genuinely frightening moments, and while the script by *Baby Jane* author Henry Farrell and Stanford Whitmore (the former also providing the story) becomes a somewhat convoluted affair by its conclusion, involving as it does a fake brother and doctor among other staples, it is nevertheless well structured (even if we never do find out what coerces Emily into seeking the help of Charles in particular), and has better dialogue than most examples of its kind ("With The Sight comes a responsibility that will not be denied," Charles is informed by his aunt, who also tells him that "Some families pass on haemophilia, others blue eyes. It's fate"). The direction by Reza Badiyi, who spent most of his career working in the salt mines of episode TV, as well as designing the titles for such shows as *Hawaii Five-O* (1968–1980, TV), is certainly eye-catching, particularly in the opening dream sequence in which the coffin of Charles' uncle and the candle stands that surround it are captured from a variety of visually arresting angles. This sequence also contains two of the film's best jolts: the unexpected opening of the uncle's eyes (which are white blanks), and his sitting up in the coffin and pointing at Charles. The visions, when they come, are also well staged, including the appearance of the specter at the cemetery, which is presented via a number of jump cuts, and a later shot of Emily as she lies drowned in the pool of an ornate fountain. A shot in which a body falls from behind the collapsing wall of a handball court as Sand plays with his psychiatrist buddy also proves highly effective (it later transpires that Emily's brother is walled up in the basement of the family home).

Performance wise, Peter Haskell is a little bland as the hero, Adam West has little to do as his psychiatrist friend and Joan Bennett is her usual imperious self as Charles' aunt. However, as the unbalanced Emily, Sharon Farrell captures the girl's mood swings superbly, while as her sister Katharine, who proves to be the family's real psychotic, Barbara Rush truly lets it rip during the film's final chase sequence about the mansion, hunting down her sister with a knife as a thunderstorm starts to rage outside. Indeed, a shot in which she attempts to stab Emily through the gate of a departing elevator carries a genuine charge of madness to it; that she is waiting for her sister at the other end of the elevator's journey is the icing on the cake. One must also make mention of the film's suitably eerie score, cribbed primarily (owing to the previously mentioned composers' strike) from Henry Mancini's "wonky piano" score from *Wait Until Dark* (1967), for which permission was not sought, and for which the composer successfully sued (elements from Ron Grainer's soundtrack from *The Omega Man* [1971] are also featured).

It wasn't until much later in the year that ABC turned its attention to horror again with the broadcast of *Haunts of the Very Rich* (1972, TVM) on 20 September 1972, but the film was worth the wait. In it, a group of wealthy tourists, each of whom has apparently suffered a near fatal experience, seek respite at an exclusive resort, where circumstances eventually lead them to conclude that they may in fact be dead after all. Things start to take on a slightly sinister air almost immediately during the special charter flight to the Portals of Eden, which we join mid-journey, with the guests seemingly on some kind of mystery tour. One of their number, a disgruntled businessman (Ed Asner), seems to have joined the flight by mistake (he should be on his way to Dallas, he informs the other passengers), and becomes increasingly frustrated about the secrecy surrounding the group's final destination, especially given that the plane's windows have been painted out. The others, among them a honeymooning couple (Donna Mills and Tony Bill), a philanderer with a heart problem (Lloyd Bridges), a minister doing research on other religions (Robert Reed), an insecure woman with a craving for beauty treatments (Cloris Leachman) and a housewife recovering from a breakdown (Annette Larrier), are clearly happy to be along for the ride, but once settled into their hotel, presided over by the mysterious Seacrist (Moses Gunn), things gradually start to unravel. The first hint that things might not be what they seem is the discovery of a snake in the honeymoon couple's bed ("Well, I suppose every Eden has its serpent," observes the minister), and eventually it becomes clear to the guests that they will never be able to leave the world of high-end soft furnishings and muzak into which they have entered. A violent tropical storm, a power outage ("Everything's dead") and the odor of dead fish wafting in from the lake (electrocuted by lightning during the storm) ramp up the discomfort further, along with the desertion of the staff and the false hope of rescue care of the arrival in his private plane of a singer (Michael Lembeck) whose death we have already been told about.

Pretty much a *Twilight Zone* story writ large, this is a superior slice of macabre television, and it benefits from a well wrought and nicely paced script care of William Wood (based upon a story by T.K. Brown, with nods to Sutton Vane's 1923 play *Outward Bound*), solid but unflashy direction care of Paul Wendkos (whose feature films include the stylish occult thriller *The Mephisto Waltz* [1971]), and a handful of game performances from its starry cast, prime among them Moses Gunn, Lloyd Bridges, Cloris Leachman and Ed Asner, whose irascible businessman isn't above being racist towards the staff (in one eyebrow raising outburst he says to Seacrist, "What are you trying to pull, black man?" when he discovers a radio kept locked in a storage area). Shot at a villa in the Biscayne Bay area of Florida, with cinematographer Ben Colman making the most of the exotic exteriors, the film is notable for its pervading sense of dread and foreboding, and for its occasionally subtle touches (art director Eugene Lourié places all of the guests in opulent rooms, save for the businessman, whose accommodation has the appearance of a low rent motel ["I could be in Schenectady, for crying out loud"], and the minister, who is clearly accustomed to more humble surroundings), and while nothing innately shocking happens above and beyond the revelations and realizations of its guests, the results are certainly intriguing, and prove yet again what can be achieved on a low budget if the director and cast are in sympathy with the material. And it perhaps isn't assuming too much that the film had an influence on such later TV shows as *Fantasy Island* (1977–1984, TV) and *Lost* (2004–2010, TV).

The same month, lycanthropy raised its head with *Moon of the Wolf* (1972, TVM), which was broadcast on 26 September 1972. Perhaps because of the make-up requirements involved, Wolfman movies were a pretty rare beast on TV at the time. This one, based upon the 1967 novel by Leslie H. Whitten, follows the investigation into a number of murders in a Louisiana township, which the local sheriff (David Janssen) gradually comes to realize are the work of a werewolf. But who, in the small community he serves, is actually the beast on the prowl? With the mystery element to the fore, the movie is more of a detective piece than a full-on horror movie, with the investigation kick started by the discovery of the body of a young woman in the swamp, with fingers subsequently pointed at a number of potential suspects, among them the doctor who got her pregnant. On this count, things drag somewhat until around the halfway mark when the wolf (via subjective camera work and some heavy breathing on the soundtrack) goes on the prowl in the town, killing the sheriff's deputy and the brother of the murdered girl. However, when one of the town's wealthy residents (Bradford Dillman) suffers a fit after having smelled sulfur, used as a means of protection from werewolves by one of the locals, it isn't too long before the killer, who has been trying to keep his affliction at bay with medication, goes on the rampage in a hospital, after which he chases down his sister (Barbara Rush) around the family mansion.

Although it benefits from being shot entirely on location (in Clinton, Louisiana), this is an otherwise unremarkable addition to the werewolf canon, slackly directed by Daniel Petrie, and with a surfeit of tedious dialogue care of Alvin Sapinsley. Pretty dull for much of its length, it only comes into its own during the last 20 minutes or so when the werewolf, sporting a rather conventional make-up care of William and Tom Tuttle, finally gets to do his thing, but not even the seasoned cast, which also includes Geoffrey Lewis, John Beradino, Claudia McNeil and Royal Dano, can do much to enliven the rest.

It was back to lady-in-peril territory next with *The Victim* (1972, TVM), which aired on 14 November 1972, and though ostensibly a thriller, it uses one of the staple ingredients of horror movies, a raging thunder storm, to great effect in its story of Kate Wainwright (Elizabeth Montgomery), who travels up from the city to the remote house of her younger sister Susan (Jess Walton) having discovered that she is going to divorce her husband. However, when she arrives there, Susan has mysteriously disappeared, and no one, least of all the crotchety housekeeper Mrs. Hawkes (Eileen Heckart), seems to know what has become of her, given that her car is in the garage and her keys and purse are still in the house. Susan's husband Ben (George

Maharis) eventually turns up on the scene, having returned from an aborted business trip, by which time Kate has convinced herself that something bad has happened to Susan. And of course, it has.

Adapted from a 1947 short story *Night of the Storm* by McKnight Malmar, Merwin Gerard's teleplay has everything grist to its mill, including a prowler, cut phone lines, power outages and a body in the basement, to which Kate frequently has to go to close the inevitable banging window, not realizing that her sister's corpse has been dumped in a basket only a few feet away from her ("The phone is not the only thing that's dead in Susan's house," ran the tagline). The whodunit element is fairly obvious, given the size of the cast, and Gil Mellé's score could certainly have ramped up the atmosphere more than it does, but the various traumas Kate undergoes are well enough presented by director Herschel Daugherty, who has a nicely appointed set care of veteran art director Henry Bumstead in which to stage them, while Elizabeth Montgomery, whose first dramatic role this was since leaving the hit sitcom *Bewitched* (1964–1972, TV), makes for an appealing leading lady. "Something terrible has happened to Susan. I know it. I'm sure of it, Ben," she tells her brother-in-law at one point, not realizing she has confided in the wrong ally.

Things finally come to a climax when Kate attempts to make her escape using her sister's station wagon, only to discover that Susan's body has by now been moved into the back of it (as she drives out of the garage, the body rolls from under a blanket towards the camera in the film's best shock moment). As she attempts to drive away, the car slides in the mud and crushes Ben against a tree, at which Kate lets rip with a series of genuinely disturbing screams, her ordeal finally over, though a number of flash cuts back to the action as she is escorted from the house by the police, who have been called by Mrs. Hawkes, seem to indicate that she will be suffering after-effects for some time to come. Produced by William Frye at Universal and on location in Monterey, this is everything the efficient TV thriller should be (note that Malmar's story had already been presented for television five times by this point: three times for *Studio One* [1948–1958, TV] in 1948, 1949 and 1953, the first version of which marked the show's debut, as a 1959 installment of *The Unforeseen* [1958–1960, TV], and as a 1962 episode of *Thriller* [1960–1962, TV], the latter also directed by Herschel Daugherty).

Murder over the festive period was the subject of *Home for the Holidays* (1972, TVM), which aired on 28 November 1972, and was produced by Aaron Spelling and Leonard Goldberg via Spelling-Goldberg Productions and ABC Circle Films. In it, a wealthy old man, Benjamin Morgan (Walter Brennan), summons his estranged daughters Chris, Jo, Freddy and Alex (Sally Field, Jill Haworth, Jessica Walter and Eleanor Parker) home for the Christmas holidays, and tasks them with a particular job: that of murdering his second wife Elizabeth (Julie Harris), whom he suspects of trying to poison him. However, there is a killer with a pitchfork on the prowl at the old family homestead, and the sisters soon find their own lives in peril. Could their stepmother be trying to beat them at their own game, or is there someone else in the house with an agenda for murder? A rather slow starting affair that is housebound for a good deal of its running time, this is an old-fashioned Agatha Christie–style murder mystery gussied up with a with a few horror staples, among them a thunderstorm, a mad killer ("I want to be free of you all") and a twist revelation as to their identity. As written by Josef Stefano (best known for his screenplay for *Psycho* [1960]), this is an overly talkative melodrama that takes its time setting up the central situation (it isn't until around the 30-minute mark that the murders begin), and, like *The Victim* (1972, TVM), the final revelation isn't too much of a surprise given the limited number in the cast, yet with this particular line-up chomping away at the scenery there's usually something of interest going on, and though unimaginatively presented while indoors, director John Llewellyn Moxey at least manages to stage a reasonably thrilling chase through the woods, with the heroine of the piece (Fields) being pursued by the killer, who disguises their identity by wearing a yellow oilskin.

The Devil to Pay

The supernatural was back to the fore in *The Devil's Daughter* (1973, TVM), which kicked off the New Year in reasonable style on 9 January 1973. A foray into *Rosemary's Baby* country, it follows the plight of Diane Shaw (Belinda Montgomery), who, on her 21st birthday, discovers that the woman who adopted her (Shelley Winters) following her mother's death is involved with a Satanic cult, and that her father is in fact the Devil. Told that she is destined to marry the Demon of Endor ("The one with the glowing eyes"), she distances herself from the group and instead falls for an architect (Robert Foxworth), whom she subsequently agrees to marry. But at the ceremony, it is revealed that her beau is in fact the Demon after all, much to the delight of her cloven-hooved father, who, along with the rest of the coven, makes a late appearance at the proceedings.

Written by Colin Higgins (already famous for penning *Harold and Maude* [1971], and later to score major hits with *Foul Play* [1978] and *9 to 5* [1980], both of which he wrote and directed), this is a reasonably well plotted little shocker in which it is nevertheless clear from the start that things aren't going to end well for our heroine. Of note primarily as a vehicle for Shelley Winters, who lets rip with the melodramatics at several points as the duplicitous Lilith Malone, the film also benefits from a stronger supporting cast than usual, among them Joseph Cotten as the seemingly crippled Judge Weatherby, who it turns out is in fact Diane's father ("Arise, my daughter, and take thy father's hand"), Jonathan Frid as a mute butler, and Abe Vigoda as one of the cult's acolytes, plus the likes of Martha Scott, Lucille Benson and Diane Ladd (billed Lad in the credits). Helmed with reasonable dexterity by Jeannot Szwarc, the pay off at the wedding ceremony is certainly well staged, as the coven slips unnoticed into the pews behind Diane's back as she is saying her vows, after which her father reveals himself towering above the alter and her husband's eyes now glow with yellow flames! However, while *The New York Times* described the film as "one of the better made for TV movies," the *LA Times* averred that it "had about as much suspense as the Nixon-McGovern race."

With *The Wide World of Mystery* (1973–1976, TVM, aka *ABC Wide World of Mystery*), which began airing on 15 January 1973, ABC presented a run of 58 mysteries, thrillers and shockers, a handful of which were lifted from the British series

Thriller (1973–1976, TV), which notched up 43 episodes of its own (more about which at the appropriate place), many of which featured American as well as British actors. These episodes were augmented by American made originals during *Wide World*'s run, among them several horror subjects. Produced for a 90-minute late night slot beginning at 11:30 p.m., the series debuted with an installment of *Thriller* (episode four from the show's UK run). This was *An Echo of Theresa* (1973, TVM), which was re-titled *Anatomy of Terror*, and concerned an American in London who suffers from a number of strange experiences (the episode featured U.S. stars Paul Burke and Polly Bergen). The second and third episodes, which aired on 16 and 17 January 1973, were somewhat more tantalizing for horror fans however, being a two-part version of *Frankenstein* (1973, TVM) starring Robert Foxworth as Dr. Victor Frankenstein and Bo Svenson as the Monster. Directed by Glenn Jordan and written by Sam Hall from an adaptation by himself and Dan Curtis, the latter of whom also produced via Dan Curtis Productions, the movie, which was recorded on videotape at MGM, stands as one of the more faithful versions of Mary Shelley's 1818 novel, with the Monster, sporting a make-up care of Michael and Marvin G. Westmore, being presented as a sympathetic, child-like figure suffering as much from loneliness as from the hands of those who fear him. Unfortunately, despite the involvement of such Curtis regulars as art director Trevor Williams and composer Bob Cobert (whose score was derived from cues lifted from *Dark Shadows* [1966–1971, TV] and *The Strange Case of Dr. Jekyll and Mr. Hyde* [1968, TVM]), the program, which also featured Susan Strasberg, Robert Gentry and Curtis regular John Karlen, has not aged well, thanks primarily to its flat studio look, which certainly does it no favors in terms of atmosphere, and while it features lots of sparks and lightning during the creation sequence, is otherwise a somewhat underwhelming affair, though it did garner some surprisingly positive reviews, with the *LA Times* describing it as "quite a handsome show, with huge, foreboding sets and a splendid array of special effects," while *Variety* hailed it as "extraordinary entertainment."

Other episodes in the series with a fantastical or supernatural air to them included *A Little Bit Like Murder* (1973, TVM), in which evil spirits cause a woman to be overwhelmed with hatred for her family; *The Haunting of Rosalind* (1973, TVM), in which a family is haunted by the spirit of a woman thought to be the first wife of a man about to marry into their fold; *The House and the Brain* (1973, TVM), in which a woman finds herself imprisoned in a warlock's castle; *Suicide Club* (1973, TVM), an adaptation of the popular Robert Louis Stevenson story; *And the Bones Came Together* (1973, TVM), in a which a caretaker fired from his job in a graveyard uses supernatural forces to exact revenge; *The Satan Murders* (1974, TVM), in which a woman enters a pact with the Devil in order to do away with her husband; *Come Out, Come Out, Wherever You Are* (1974, TVM), in which two Americans on vacation in England find themselves subject to a number of mysterious happenings; *The Haunting of Penthouse D* (1974, TVM), in which a woman house-sitting an apartment for a friend is subjected to a number of strange disturbances; *The Cloning of Clifford Swimmer* (1974, TVM), in which a man has himself cloned so that he can escape his family; *The Werewolf of Woodstock* (1975, TVM), in which a farmer is transformed into a werewolf after being electrocuted while clearing the stage after the legendary 1969 rock concert; *Rock-a-Die Baby* (1975, TVM), in which members of a rock band start to die mysteriously following a premonition; *Too Easy to Kill* (1975, TVM), in which a nurse with a predilection for the occult is hired to look after an injured policeman on the trail of a cop killer; *Distant Early Warning* (1975, TVM), in which an Arctic research station is infiltrated by mind controlling aliens; and *Alien Lover* (1975, TVM), in which a teenager becomes romantically involved with an alien. Unfortunately, despite starring the likes of Farley Granger, Susan Sarandon, Laurence Luckinbill, Tyne Daly, Nina Foch, Sharon Farrell and Chris Sarandon, a good many of these episodes are now either lost or sitting in a vault in UCLA's Film and Television Archive. And if any of the surviving programs are anything to go by, this is probably the best place for them.

Having scored an unexpected hit with *The Night Stalker* (1971, TVM), it was perhaps inevitable that Darren McGavin's crusading reporter Carl Kolchak would return for another case involving the supernatural. Again penned by Richard Matheson, *The Night Strangler* (1973, TVM), which was broadcast on 16 January 1973, sees our hero relocated to Seattle, where he is reunited with his former editor Tony Vincenzo (Simon Oakland), and becomes involved in tracking down a corpse-like murderer with superhuman strength who goes on a killing spree every 21 years, emerging from the underground environs of Old Seattle, on which the modern city is built, strangling women and draining their blood by way of ensuring his immortality. "This is the story behind the most incredible series of murders to ever occur in the city of Seattle, Washington," Kolchak informs us in his opening narration, which subsequently sees him enter a twilight subterranean world of dusty streets and buildings ("It was like another world down there, a world of yesterday"), where he finally encounters the killer, one Dr. Richard Malcolm (Richard Anderson), a man of culture, whose reign of terror he finally brings to an end when he smashes the elixir of life that he has been working on in his laboratory. "If I don't take this final dosage now, the process will reverse itself," the doctor somewhat rashly informs our hero, after the destruction of which he reverts to his true age care of an excellent make-up by William Tuttle.

Directed with pace and flair in just 12 days by Dan Curtis, who had produced the previous film, Kolchak's investigation moves clearly and logically forward as he pieces together the puzzle ("How can

American werewolf. Tige Andrews (left) and Belinda Balaski in *The Werewolf of Woodstock* (1975, TVM), one of the many installments of *The Wide World of Mystery* (1973–1976, TVM, aka *ABC Wide World of Mystery*) (ABC/Dick Clark Productions).

he run like a track star, have superhuman strength and look like a stiff?" he ponders about the killer at one point, given that he leaves traces of rotting flesh on the throats of his victims). The narrative also provides opportunities for a number of nicely tuned cameos along the way, among them appearances by Wally Cox as a newspaper file clerk who uncovers the connection with the previous murders, Jo Ann Pflug as a fast talking belly dancer who finds herself helping Kolchak with the case, Margaret Hamilton as an anthropologist who informs the reporter of the components required for an elixir of life (among them human blood), Al Lewis as an old tramp who lives in the underground city, Scott Brady as the police captain with whom Kolchak has a number of run ins, and John Carradine as the increasingly frustrated newspaper publisher Llewellyn Crossbinder for whom he now works (named after John Llewellyn Moxey, perhaps, the director of *The Night Stalker*?).

Filmed on location in Seattle, as well as in the Bradbury Building in Los Angeles (where certain of the underground city scenes were shot), the film is a more light-hearted affair than its predecessor, with rather more banter between Kolchak and Vincenzo, whom the reporter describes as "City editor by profession, bilious grouch by disposition." That said, it doesn't skimp on the atmosphere, and provides a couple of well-timed jolts along the way, while the dialogue is fresh and peppy throughout (observes Vincenzo of Kolchak: "Looks like he just came from a road company performance of *The Front Page*"). A fast paced and incident packed movie, it proved to be another ratings winner for ABC. So much so that its running time was expanded from the original 74-minute broadcast length to 90 minutes so that it could be released theatrically overseas (note that the movie aired earlier the same evening as the first episode of *Frankenstein* [1973, TVM] that Curtis had produced for *The Wide World of Mystery* [1973–1976, TVM, aka *ABC Wide World of Mystery*], thus making it something of a showcase for him on ABC that night). Plans were subsequently put in motion for another case for Kolchak, whom we see heading for New York with Vincenzo at the climax of the film (after they have both been sacked from the newspaper). However, this third installment, *The Night Killers*, was actually to have been set on Honolulu, with our hero this time encountering UFOs and the replacement of government figures with replicants. Written by William F. Nolan from a story by Richard Matheson, it was eventually put aside in favor of a 20-episode TV series, *Kolchak: The Night Stalker* (1974–1975, TV), which sees Kolchak and Vincenzo relocate to Chicago (the unused script for the third film was eventually released as a novel titled *Kolchak the Night Stalker—Night Killers* in 2017, which was adapted by Chuck Miller).

On air from 13 September 1974, the series sadly lacked any involvement from Dan Curtis (Cy Chermak, known for his work as an executive producer on *Ironside* [1967–1975, TV], was now the producer), although compensations could be found in several of the new contributors, among them writers Jimmy Sangster, Robert Zemeckis and Bob Gale, while the directors included such reliable hands as Don Weis, Gordon Hessler and Vincent McEveety. The roster of guest stars meanwhile included Richard Kiel, Keenan Wynn, Tom Bosley, Erik Estrada, Pippa Scott, Henry Jones, Cathy Lee Crosby, Carolyn Jones, Tom Skerritt, Kathleen Freeman, Julie Adams, Dick Van Patten, Victor Jory, Jim Backus and William Daniels, while the show's technical personnel included supervising editor Richard Belding (who worked on all 20 episodes), art director Raymond Beal (who designed 19), stunt coordinator Paul Baxley (who also worked on 19), cinematographer Ronald W. Browne (who photographed 17) and composer Gil Mellé (who scored seven and also provided the theme tune).

The series started well with *The Ripper* (1974, TV), in which our hero finds himself pitted against a super-human killer who may well be the original Jack the Ripper. Following this he encountered a number of familiar monsters, among them *The Zombie* (1974, TV) and *The Werewolf* (1974, TV), as well as such lesser known entities as an evil spirit that incinerates its victims in *Firefall* (1974, TV), a demon with a penchant for human flesh in *Horror in the Heights* (1974, TV), and a deadly reptile which has been killing workers in a tunnel in *The Sentry* (1975, TV), which closed the series on 28 March, by which time our hero was running out of viable monsters to investigate. Among the better episodes were *The Spanish Moss Murders* (1974, TV), in which a moss-covered Cajun monster goes about killing people, and *Chopper* (1975, TV), in which a headless, sword-bearing biker avenges his death by beheading members of a rival gang (cue lots of motorbike stunts). However, there were occasional duds, such as *Mr. R.I.N.G.* (1975, TV), in which a prototype robot goes on the rampage, and *Demon in Lace* (1975, TV), in which a female demon uses her wiles to scare handsome college students to death. However, for many, the series' highlight was *The Vampire* (1974, TV), which sees Kolchak sent to LA to carry out an interview with a famous guru (Noel de Souza) only to find himself tracking down

a female vampire (Suzanne Charny), who was a victim Janos Skorzeny in *The Night Stalker* (1971, TVM), whom he dispatches with a giant burning cross! An important and influential genre series, *Kolchak* has since become a cult favorite around the world, and perhaps it was just as well that a second series didn't follow, which may well have diluted its impact and staying power with fans (note that although 26 episodes were commissioned, only 20 were shot; among the completed scripts that didn't go before the cameras were *Eve of Terror*, *The Get of Belial* and *The Executioners*; a reboot simply titled *Night Stalker* [2005–2006, TV] later followed, with Stuart Townsend now in the role of Kolchak).

Chills of a slightly different kind could be found in *A Cold Night's Death* (1973, TVM). In it, two scientists (Robert Culp and Eli Wallach) are sent via helicopter to the Tower Mountain Research

Not to be crossed with. Darren McGavin in action in *Kolchak: The Night Stalker* (1974–1975, TV) (ABC/Francy Productions/Universal Television).

Station, a remote, snowbound laboratory to discover what has become of their colleague, Dr. Vogel, who hasn't been in radio contact for five days, prior to which his communications had become increasingly sporadic and irrational. Fearing for his welfare, as well as that of the caged primates being used for the experiments, they head up to the institute, only to discover the place a wreck and their colleague frozen to death by the radio. With a new chimp with them for company, the duo settle down to their duties, but as time passes, they come to suspect that someone, or something, is in the base with them, sabotaging their work and putting their lives in jeopardy. But as one of them puts it, "There's nothing unnatural here, or supernatural, just you and me." So who or what is it? Or could it somehow be the monkeys?

Routinely written by Jarrold Freeman and rather plainly presented by director Christopher Knopf, who could have ramped up the atmosphere and suspense a little more, this is nevertheless an effectively claustrophobic two hander, with the two scientists inevitably suspecting each other's motives until the evidence that something is not quite right becomes overwhelming (such as the discovery of the body of the chimp they brought with them in a locked cupboard). With an unsettling electronic score by Gil Mellé and an increasing sense of mystery, this is clearly *Twilight Zone* territory, complete with a shuddery sting in its tail. Produced by Paul Junger Witt for ABC Circle Films, the film aired on 30 January 1973, since when it has undeservedly slipped into obscurity.

It was back to the studio floor for producer Dan Curtis and his team for *The Picture of Dorian Gray* (1973, TVM), which aired on 23 April 1973. The umpteenth version of the macabre Oscar Wilde saga about a handsome young socialite who retains his good looks while his portrait disintegrates the more sinful he becomes, the production is a faithful if slightly stifled take on the story, with a suitably epicene performance by Shane Briant as Gray, backed by a slightly miscast Nigel Davenport as Sir Harry Wotton. Adapted by John Tomerlin and directed by Glenn Jordan (who'd helmed *Frankenstein* for Curtis earlier the same year), the movie, which was made via Dan Curtis Productions, is slightly more atmospheric than most videotaped films of the period, but the sheer familiarity of the tale makes for a rather tedious viewing experience on the whole. Also featuring Charles Aidman as Basil Hallward and John Karlen as Alan Campbell, the film was designed by Curtis regular Trevor Williams and has a score by Bob Cobert, who yet again makes use of music from *Dark Shadows* (1966–1971, TV).

A superior lady-in-peril shocker involving an unexplained disappearance was the premise of *Dying Room Only* (1973, TVM), which was broadcast on 18 September 1973. Written by Richard Matheson from his own 1953 story and directed by Philip Leacock, it sees a woman (Cloris Leachman) stranded and in danger when she and her husband (Dabney Coleman) stop off at a seedy roadside diner in the desert, only for him to disappear without trace. The surly proprietor (Ross Martin) seems reluctant to help her, as does a drunken customer (Ned Beatty) and the receptionist (Louise Latham) at the motel next door, and when she calls the police, the local sheriff (Dana Elcar) is initially skeptical, which leaves our heroine to fend for herself and solve the mystery. Produced by Allen S. Epstein for Lorimar, this is an intriguing little puzzler, and while not a horror film per se, isn't without its thrilling moments in which the wife has to endure a number of unpleasant threats, among them murder, on which account it is included here for completeness (IMDb rates the film as a horror subject). Commented *The Village Voice* of the movie, "The acting (especially Miss Leachman's) was exceptionally good. The camera work was agile and the things the lens picked up were generally of interest."

Rather more routine was *Satan's School for Girls* (1973, TV), which went out on 19 September 1973 (tagline: "Evil is what they teach at Satan's School for Girls"). In it, a young woman named Elizabeth Sayers (Pamela Franklin) enrolls at a girls' school in Salem so as to better investigate why her sister Martha (Terry Lumley) was seemingly driven to leave the place in a panic and fly to her West Coast home, only to kill herself there. "My sister did not commit suicide, she had no reason to killer herself—she was happier than she's been for years," Elizabeth informs the police, who are naturally incredulous that something suspicious has been going on given that the girl was discovered inside a house locked from the inside. Once registered at the school, however, Elizabeth begins to realize that the 300-year-old institution isn't quite what it purports to be, especially when the suicides start to rack up ("They were murdered, or at least driven to do what they did," surmises our heroine). Also featuring Roy Thinnes as the school's art teacher, whom several of the girls have a crush on, Lloyd Bochner as its psychologist, Jo Van Fleet as its headmistress, and future *Charlie's Angels* stars Kate Jackson and Cheryl Ladd (billed as Cheryl Stop-

pelmoor) as fellow students, its script, by A.A. Ross, makes use of plenty of horror staples, including thunder storms, blackouts and much wandering about by lamplight in dark places, among them a secret room where eight women were hanged during the Salem witch trials. It eventually transpires that the art teacher is actually Satan himself, keen to recruit eight new acolytes to replace those who were killed centuries earlier, with Elizabeth now expected to sacrifice her mortal soul with seven others. Saving herself by starting a fire with an oil lamp, she escapes in the nick of time, leaving the other girls behind to go up in flames with their master. Pretty much a conveyor belt production with little in the way of style or thrills from director David Lowell Rich, the piece plays as a fairly run-of-the-mill Nancy Drew–style mystery with added supernatural elements, on which count it passes the time adequately enough, aided and abetted by a reasonably atmospheric score care

Evil is what they teach at Satan's School for Girls

Starring Roy Thinnes, Kate Jackson, Pamela Franklin, Jamie Smith Jackson, Jo Van Fleet and Lloyd Bochner
A World Premiere/Wednesday Movie of the Week
8:30pm

Killer curriculum. Promotional ad for *Satan's School for Girls* (1973, TVM) (ABC/Spelling-Goldberg Productions).

of Laurence Rosenthal (the film was remade for television in 2000, with Kate Jackson now having graduated to the role of the dean).

Much more fun was *Don't Be Afraid of the Dark* (1973, TVM), a creepy house thriller in which Sally Farnham and her husband Alex (Kim Darby and Jim Hutton) inherit a mansion from her grandmother, which turns out to be infested with small demon-like creatures which at first only the wife notices, and which only appear in the dark, leading her husband to suspect that she is losing her marbles ("Maybe you ought to see some kind of a doctor!"). Having escaped from behind a bricked-up fireplace in the old study ("Free, free, she set us free!"), the creatures run amok around the house, but where did they really come from? However, it isn't until their decorator (Pedro Armendariz, Jr.) has been killed and Sally has been dragged away by the demons into a hole leading deep into the Earth that Alex finally realizes that what his wife has been telling him is true.

Written by Nigel McKeand (who also provided the voices of the demons) and helmed with reasonable verve by actor-turned-director by John Newland (who'd played Victor Frankenstein in the *Tales of Tomorrow* [1951–1953, TV] version of *Frankenstein* back in 1952), the film, which was made by Lorimar Productions and broadcast on 10 October 1973, provides its fair share of fun, though it might have been more enjoyable had there been a little more knowing humor, as would be the case in the later theatrical feature *Gremlins* (1984), like the creatures in which, the monsters here cannot bear to be exposed to light (here the creatures cry "Fire!" as opposed to "Bright light, bright light!"). The film also features William Sylvester, William Demarest and Barbara Anderson, while the mini monsters are portrayed by Patty Maloney, Tamara De Treaux and Felix Silla (who'd played Cousin Itt in *The Addams Family* [1964–1966, TV]). Sporting make-ups care of Michael Hancock and Robert Sidell, the demons are shown running around large-scale sets (provided by production designer Ed Graves) so as to make them look smaller than they are, a fairly elaborate proposition for a TV movie of the week (note that the film was re-made in 2010 with bells and whistles and a $25 million budget, but the effect wasn't quite the same, despite it being produced and co-written by Guillermo del Toro, again proving the old adage that less is often better than more).

Shot on videotape and running to just 65 minutes, *The Invasion of Carol Enders* (1973, TVM), which aired on 5 November 1973, is a fairly familiar tale of possession, in which the title character (Meredith Baxter) and her fiancé Adam (Christopher Connelly) are the subject of an unprovoked attack, during her recovery from which Carol's psyche is seemingly invaded by the personality of a woman named Diana Bernard (Sally Kemp) who has died from injuries sustained in a suspicious car crash after having been brought to the same hospital as Carol ("Two beautiful women, two tragic accidents, or was it murder?" ponders the narration for the trailer). A whodunit with supernatural elements, with Carol/Diana now involved in tracking down her killer, the plot is actually a thinly disguised remake of *The Bride Possessed* (1959, TV), the debut episode of *One Step Beyond* (1959–1961, TV), in which a woman on her honeymoon finds herself possessed by the spirit of a woman killed in a suspicious car accident. *One Step*'s creator Merwin Gerard co-wrote the original 1959 teleplay with the show's regular writer Lawrence B. Marcus, though it is only Gerard, along with the writer of the new teleplay, Gene R. Kearney, who is credited here for the story, which was directed by Burt Brinckerhoff and an uncredited Dan Curtis, the latter of whom also produced the piece with Robert Singer via Dan Curtis Productions, hence the involvement of such Curtis regulars as composer Bob Cobert and actor John Karlen. Also featuring Charles Aidman, George DiCenzo and Sally Kemp, the program's hospital setting gives it the air of a daytime soap (with acting to match), and though it won't win any prizes for originality or production values, Curtis completists may well want to track it down for curiosity value if nothing more.

Although not a full on horror film *per se*, the thriller *Scream Pretty Peggy* (1973, TVM), which aired on 24 November 1973, rates a mention here given that it was co-written by Hammer legend Jimmy Sangster (along with Arthur Hoffe), directed by horror specialist Gordon Hessler (whose credits by this time already included the Vincent Price shockers *The Oblong Box* [1969], *Scream and Scream Again* [1970] and *Cry of the Banshee* [1970]) and starred Baby Jane herself, Bette Davis, as the elderly Mrs. Elliott, whose sculptor son Jeffrey (Ted Bessell) hires a pretty art student (Sian Barbara Allen) to work keeping house in their sprawling mansion, where dark deeds prove to be the order of the day (and night). Someone, it appears, is also living in the quarters above the garage. Could it be Jeffrey's sister Jennifer, supposedly away in Europe? But if so, why are the windows barred? When Mrs. Elliott, who is a secret drinker, tears a ligament in a fall, Peggy moves in to look after her, and sees a mysterious figure wandering around at night. Confronting Jeffrey over breakfast about it, she is told that it is indeed Jennifer, and that "she's hopelessly insane." Things then take on an even more sinister tone when the father of a girl who previously worked at the house turns up looking for his missing daughter. The real secret, however, is that it is Jeffery who is mad, murdering people and placing them inside his sculptures, among them his sister, who he now pretends to be. "He loved Jennifer. That's why he killed her," explains Mrs. Elliott, having shot her son just as he is about to stab Peggy. "He couldn't bear the thought she was going to leave him to be married. Afterwards, half of his mind became Jennifer. It was the only way he could hold on to her." With its borrowings from *Psycho* (1960) and Sangster's own *Taste of Fear* (1961), plus a dash of *Mystery of the Wax Museum* (1933), this is a fairly "routine shocker" with "trite dialogue and situations," as the *LA Times* had it, with the denouement carrying no real surprise. Yet despite this, all the elements, although familiar, still manage to keep one tuned in to see what happens next, and the film certainly has plenty of atmosphere, even if its heroine is somewhat irritating and Davis somewhat underused.

Creature Feature

Another celebrated horror writer, Robert Bloch, was meanwhile responsible for *The Cat Creature* (1973, TVM), which aired on 11 December 1973. Following the death of a wealthy Egyptologist, a solid gold amulet featuring a cat design is stolen from around the neck of a mummy locked away in his secret collection, after which a vengeful supernatural feline goes on the prowl, killing those who come into contact with the piece, among them an appraiser (Kent Smith), the thief himself (Keye Luke) and the owner of a store specializing in the occult (Gale Sondergaard). The detective in charge of the investigation (Stuart Whitman) invites a professor (David Hedison) from the nearby university to help with the case, and with the assistance of a fellow scholar (John Abbott) he discovers that the amulet was meant not for worship, "but to hold something captive." Rena Carter, a young assistant (Meredith Baxter) working at the occult shop, also becomes involved in the proceedings, but she isn't quite what she appears. As the professor informs her following further research, "That amulet is placed on the mummy's throat for the same reason a stake is driven through a vampire's heart: to keep it from rising and resuming an unnatural life, nourished by blood." And thus it proves to be that the girl is the mummy, a former priestess keen to retrieve the amulet so as to destroy it and gain immortality. However, when she attacks the professor in feline form, he manages to place the amulet, which has since been retrieved, around the cat's neck, causing it to at first transform back into the priestess and then the mummy, which is then torn to shreds by the many cats that have been amassing around the house in which she has been living.

Despite its somewhat involved storyline (the work of Bloch, the film's producer Douglas S. Cramer and his associate producer Wilford Lloyd Baumes), and a low budget that occasionally stymies director Curtis Harrington (the scenes in the occult shop are look rather cheap and drab), the film gets by primarily thanks to its stellar B-movie cast (also among them John Carradine), which at least makes up for the absurdity of it all. Performance wise, Sondergaard (best remembered for playing the title role in the Sherlock Holmes adventure *The Spider Woman* [1943]) steals the honors as the mysterious Hester Black, owner of the occult shop, who it turns out is not only a former fence, but a lesbian, given her overtures to Rena and her predecessor at the shop (the network specifically forbade Harrington from emphasizing this plot element in any way, yet it is certainly there for those who wish to pick up on it). An entertaining piece of arrant nonsense, the film doesn't deserve any awards for originality, yet it's surprising how many people recall it with affection (note that it was originally hoped that Diahann Carroll would play the title role, for which Baxter was subsequently cast).

Another creature was on the prowl in *Scream of the Wolf* (1974, TVM), which aired on 16 January 1974 ("Death comes out of the woods on four paws and returns on two feet," ran the tagline). In it, John Wetherby (Peter Graves), a former game hunter, now a successful writer, comes out of retirement to hunt down what appears at first to be a wolf, which has been attacking people (a businessman whose car has run out of gas, a local walking home), but as the killings continue (victims include a young couple and a cop), it becomes apparent that the creature may in fact be something rather more fantastic: could it be a rival hunter named Byron Douglas (Clint Walker), who was badly bitten by a wolf while in Canada, or maybe his hulking manservant Grant (Don Megowan, who'd played the Monster in *Tales of Frankenstein* [1958, TV])? Unfortunately, despite reuniting producer-director Dan Curtis and writer Richard Matheson, who worked from a 1969 David Case short story titled *The Hunter*, the results are somewhat pedestrian, and although the attack sequences are well enough staged, making use of subjective camerawork and lots of snarling on the soundtrack, like *Moon of the Wolf* (1972, TVM), the film only really comes to life in its last 20 minutes or so when the two hunters join forces to track the beast down. Unfortunately, the ending proves to be a con, in that it transpires that Douglas has been staging the killings himself with the aid of a specially trained dog for the thrill of the hunt (echoes of *The Most Dangerous Game* [1932, aka *Hounds of Zaroff*]), thus saving the make-up department the expense of a werewolf make-up. Hmm. Also featuring Jo Ann Pflug as Wetherby's girlfriend, the film overall proves to be something of a disappointment, leading us, as it does, down the wrong garden path to general frustration and disappointment.

At least *Killdozer* (1974, TVM), which aired on 2 February 1974, had the courage of its rather ludicrous convictions. Based upon a 1944 story by its screenwriter Theodore Sturgeon (who co-wrote the script with Ed MacKillop, working from an adaptation by the film's producer Herbert F. Solow), it follows the attempts by a construction crew working on an island 200 miles off the coast of Africa to survive attacks by a bulldozer which has taken on a murderous life of its own after being affected by a mysterious force emanating from a meteor ("Six men playing a deadly game of cat and mouse with a machine that wants to kill them," ran the tagline). On the island to build a base camp for a drilling outfit, the crew (among them Clint Walker, Neville Brand and Robert Urich) instead find themselves running for their lives, all the while growling and snarling at each other as they pit what wits they have against the relentless machine, its chimney stack angrily belching out acrid smoke and its two headlights flashing like demonic eyes. Of course, it's all completely ridiculous and doesn't bear any kind of scrutiny (the two remaining survivors eventually electrocute the machine, which dissipates the forces inside it), yet that said, the cast and crew are to be commended for at least making it with completely straight faces (despite such exchanges as "You can't kill a machine" which provokes the response, "Maybe we should appeal to its sense of decency and fair play"). Some of the attack scenes are passably well put over by director Jerry London, whose handling is otherwise rather routine, but whatever one might charitably claim for it, it certainly ain't *Duel* (1971, TVM). Yet its existence has lingered in the minds of many, and it seems to have inspired a sub-genre of similar movies, among them *The Car* (1977 [tag-line: "Is it a phantom, a demon, or the Devil himself?"]), *Christine* (1983 [tag-line: "How do you kill something that can't possibly be alive?"]), *Maximum Overdrive* (1986 [tagline: "Imagine your worst nightmare: trucks take over the world!"]) and *Trucks* (1997, TVM [tag-line: "U-turn, U-die!"]).

Maximum overdrive. Promotional ad for the enjoyably ludicrous *Killdozer* (1974, TVM) (ABC/Universal Television).

Also bordering on the fringes of lunacy was *Live Again, Die Again* (1974, TVM), which sees the revival of Caroline Carmichael (Donna Mills), a beautiful young woman who was cryogenically frozen 34 years earlier so that she might be brought back to life when medicine has progressed sufficiently to cure her of her ailments, key among them a fibrillating heart. Once back in the land of the living, however, she discovers that her husband Thomas (Walter Pidgeon) is an old timer clinging on to life, while her two children James and Marcia (Mike Farrell and Vera Miles) are older than she is. It would also appear that the "death" of her mother at an early age sent Marcia into a mental tailspin, and that she now wishes her back among the dead, while the family's devoted housekeeper Mrs. O'Neill (Geraldine Page) appears to be of the same opinion.

The story's cryonics angle is abandoned fairly early on, not long after Marcia has been defrosted—complete with full make-up, coiffed hair and polished nails—after which Joseph Stefano's screenplay, based upon David Sale's 1971 novel *Come to Mother*, concentrates more on the mysteries of who is doing what to whom and why, with Thomas expiring in his bed, James getting his brains bashed in and Caroline surviving a full-on attack by Mrs. O'Neill, with mother and alienated daughter finally reunited by the end credits ("Come to mother," beckons Caroline, and all seems to be forgiven). That Caroline returns to live in a vast mansion with gardens as immaculately manicured as her nails and gets to flounce around in a number of fetching outfits care of Universal's in-house costume designer Grady Hunt, gives the proceedings the air of a Joan Crawford movie from the 1940s (which, if the timeline is to be believed, is when Caroline was frozen), with the twists and revelations barely rising above the level of soap opera. That said, it all looks good thanks to Michael Margulies' soft focus photography, even if Richard A. Colla's direction piles on the cinematic effects a little too heavily during the final sequence (split screen shots, cross fades, freeze frames and various other devices are used to slightly confusing effect here). Still, the cast is good value for money (Page seems to be enjoying herself as the demented housekeeper), on which count alone audiences can't have been too disappointed with the results, which were aired on 16 February 1974.

Equally lunatic, albeit not quite so entertaining, is *Killer Bees* (1974, TVM), which went out on 26 February 1974, in which a prodigal son (Edward Albert) returns to the family vineyard with his fiancée Victoria (Kate Jackson), where she encounters his grandmother, the imperious matriarch Madame Maria von Bohlen (Gloria Swanson), who appears to have some kind of mystical hold over the bees that infest the place. "They came here with all of us from Africa. They understand the grapes and we understand each other," she explains to her guest, who is made to feel less than welcome. Indeed, interlopers of any kind, as we discover in the pre-credits sequence in which a trespasser is attacked and killed by a swarm of bees, are discouraged at every turn, and any deaths caused by them, among them that of a telephone line repair man, are hushed up by the family, whose hold on the nearby township which bears their name is absolute. However, when Madame dies from a heart condition, it is Victoria who assumes her place, having discovered the hive in the attic of the house, where Madame used to sit among the honeycombs.

Unfortunately, despite its rather ridiculous premise ("She controls the bees. They'll kill for her ... and die for her," ran the tagline), the screenplay by Joyce and John William Corrington is a singularly dull affair, bogged down with tedious chat about longstanding family traditions, while the bee attacks are perfunctorily handled, save for the final revelation in the attic, which is neatly put over by director Curtis Harrington who, like he was with *The Cat Creature* (1973, TVM), is otherwise hobbled by the film's meager budget and, in this case, some rather indifferent performances, save for that of silent movie queen Gloria Swanson, who chews the scenery as Madame, though her curious accent leaves a lot to be desired. Filmed on location in a wintry Napa Valley, the film was produced via the Robert Stigwood Organization by Ron Bernstein and Howard Rosenman, was designed by future director Joel Schumacher, and has a reasonably effective score by David Shire. Sadly, on most other counts, this was a missed opportunity, though it did seem to herald a brief sub-genre of similar movies, among them *The Savage Bees* (1976, TVM), *Terror Out of the Sky* (1978, TVM), *The Bees* (1978) and *The Swarm* (1978), prior to which there had also been *The Deadly Bees* (1966), none of which could remotely claim to be masterpieces.

Worth a brief mention at this point is *The Hanged Man* (1974, TVM), in which a gunslinger, James Devlin (Steve Forrest), miraculously survives being hanged—perhaps by divine intervention—and subsequently offers his services to a young widow (Sharon Acker), whose farm is under threat from a land grabber (Cameron Mitchell). Intended as a pilot for a series which failed to materialize, this old style western, which aired on 13 March 1974, generally plays down what mild supernatural element it possesses to offer a straightforward saga of action and revenge, with the bad guy falling to his death in a giant vat in a somewhat satanic looking mill at the climax. Written by Ken Trevey (from a concept by Andrew J. Fenady, who also produced via Bing Crosby Productions), the film was helmed by Michael Coffey, and co-starred Dean Jagger, Will Greer and Rafael Campos.

With *The Turn of the Screw* (1974, TVM), which aired on 15 April 1974, producer-director Dan Curtis, working as usual via Dan Curtis Productions, presented his take on the classic 1898 Henry James novella (originally published in serial form earlier the same year), which had already been adapted for TV in 1955, 1957, 1958 and 1959 (the latter a potted version of the 1954 Benjamin Britten opera), and been filmed definitively for the big screen by director Jack Clayton as *The Innocents* (1961). Here, Lynn Redgrave stars as Jane Cubberly, a Victorian governess who is sent to look after two seemingly sweet young children, Miles and Flora (Jasper Jacob and Eva Griffith), only to realize that they aren't quite so adorable as they at first appear. Haunted by the apparitions of her predecessor Miss Jessel (Kathryn Leigh Scott) and her lover Peter Quint (James Laurensen), Miss Cubberly's grip on reality gradually begins to crumble, much to the concern of the kindly housekeeper Mrs. Grose (Megs Jenkins, who'd played the same role in the 1961 film), who eventually takes away Flora, leaving Miss Cubberly to confront Miles about his challenging behavior. Although the exteriors were filmed on location in England, the movie's interiors were shot on videotape, which tends to kill the atmosphere, but otherwise this is a workmanlike adaptation of the story by William F. Nolan, benefiting primarily from Redgrave's performance as the increasingly unbalanced Miss Cubberly, whose delusions lead to the death of Miles during the film's well managed finale, in which, much to her shock, he appears to swap places in her arms with the ghostly Quint (note that this version of the story was slightly pre-empted by a French production,

Le tour d'écrou [1974, TVM], which was broadcast on TF1 on 25 February 1974 as part of the series *Nouvelles d'Henry James* [1974, TVM], with Suzanne Flon playing the role of the governess; other foreign language adaptations include a later Mexican three-parter, *Otra vuelta de tuera* [1981, TV], starring Angélica Aragon, which aired on Televisa).

Meanwhile, it was back to *Rosemary's Baby* territory next with *The Stranger Within* (1974, TVM), in which a pregnant woman (Barbara Eden) starts to behave out of character, much to the despair of her husband (George Grizzard), who not only has concerns for his wife's fidelity given that he has had a vasectomy, but also becomes the brunt of her irrational hostility and tardy housekeeping. She also develops bizarre dietary needs, among them a craving for raw food (octopus in particular), salt and lots and *lots* of hot coffee, and is able to absorb the contents of a book by simply flicking through it. Eventually, she comes to suspect that she is somehow being controlled by her unborn child. And she is. Under hypnosis she reveals that she was impregnated by an alien ray emanating from a spaceship while painting in the hills (!), and it turns out that she wasn't the only woman to be impregnated in such a fashion.... Based upon the 1953 short story *Trespass* by Richard Matheson, who also penned the screenplay, this is a modest, reasonably absorbing "alien within" scenario, given an extra fillip thanks to a surprisingly strong performance from its leading lady, then best known for playing the genie in the long running fantasy sitcom *I Dream of Jeannie* (1965–1970, TV). Otherwise, it is routinely presented by director by Lee Philips. Produced by Neil T. Maffeo for Lorimar, the film, which was broadcast on 1 October 1974, also starred David Doyle, Joyce Van Patten and Nehemiah Persoff, and came amid a number of similarly themed films, among them *It's Alive* (1974), *The Devil Within Her* (1974, aka *Chi sei?*) and *I Don't Want to Be Born* (1975).

Although by no means a horror film proper, *Bad Ronald* (1974, TVM) rates a brief mention here simply because it is so bizarre. In it, Scott Jacoby plays the title character, a nerdy 14-year-old who, following an accidental murder, is forced by his mother (Kim Hunter) to hide out in a secret room in their house, where he retreats into a fantasy world of his own creation. Remaining in residence after her death, he spends his time spying on the new family, and survives by stealing food from them when they are out ("The Wilby place is haunted ... by a ghost who isn't dead," ran the tagline). Adapted by Andrew Peter Marin from the 1973 novel by John Holbrook Vance and given a reasonable sense of claustrophobia by director Buzz Kulik, this is an uncomfortable little story of loneliness and voyeurism, and worth a look for Jacoby's increasingly disheveled and unhinged performance. Produced by Philip Capice for Lorimar, the film, which also starred Dabney Coleman and Pippa Scott, was broadcast on 23 October (it was later remade in France as *Méchant garcon* [1992]).

Another non horror, *Reflections of Murder* (1974, TVM), which aired on 24 November 1974, likewise rates a passing nod, given that it contains one of the great shock scenes of seventies TV. A remake of the classic French thriller *Les diaboliques* (1955), it follows the plans of the wife (Joan Hackett) and mistress (Tuesday Weld) of a much-disliked headmaster (Sam Waterston) to drug and drown him in a bathtub and then dump his body in the school's leaf covered outdoor swimming pool in the hope that, when discovered, it will be assumed that he fell in and drowned. But the body fails to surface, and evidence begins to suggest that the victim may still be alive, especially after the pool has been drained, revealing it to be empty (spoiler alert: the mistress and the headmaster are the real conspirators, having hatched the plot in a bid to shock his wife to death when he reappears, given that she has a weak heart, thus enabling him to inherit and then sell the school, which she owns). Adapted by Carol Sobieski from the 1952 novel *Celle qui n'était plus* (aka *The Woman Who Was No More*) by Pierre Boileau and Thomas Narcejac, and given an effective wintry ambience by director John Badham and his cinematographer Mario Tosi, the film's *raison d'etre* comes when the headmaster's body finally reappears in the bathtub and he begins to rise and walk towards his trembling wife, resulting in her demise. A genuinely creepy moment, it's certainly a hackle-raiser of the first order, and is the cherry on the cake of an already well staged thriller, which is capped off with a further twist when it is hinted that the wife may herself not be dead after all (the story was remade for TV as the Franco-Swiss *Les démoniaques* [1991, TVM] and *House of Secrets* [1993, TVM], and for the big screen as *Diabolique* [1996]).

Moving into 1975, the commitment to genre films continued with *Satan's Triangle* (1975, TVM), which was broadcast on 14 January 1975. In it, two coast guards, Haig and Pagnolini (Doug McClure and Michael Conrad), are sent to investigate a distress call 100 miles out at sea and come across a seemingly deserted boat within the bounds of what is known as Satan's Triangle, in which a number of craft have previously disappeared. At first it appears that all onboard are dead, among them a priest hanging upside down from the mast and a man who is literally floating in mid-air in one of the aft cabins! However, there proves to be one survivor, Eva (Kim Novak), who, following a failed rescue attempt in which the safety line breaks, remains onboard with Haig while Pagnolini flies off to get additional help, and it is while waiting for this to arrive that she proceeds to recall the incredible events that led up to the distress call being sent out.

This involved a fishing trip, during which the priest (Alejandro Rey) is spotted floating in the ocean on what appears to be the wing of a small plane. But as Eva notes of his arrival, "on the moment he came aboard a strange lightning started and the weather had suddenly changed." Shortly afterwards, most of the crew desert the boat in a motor launch, the captain (Ed Lauter) is killed while trying to get the engine started, the remaining crewmember disappears in a flash of lightning, Eva's boyfriend (Jim Davis) is discovered floating in the cabin, and the priest falls from the mast while trying to alert the coastguard with a flare gun, getting tangled in the rigging as he falls. That Haig is able to explain away all the events—even the floating man, who has been speared on a marlin being stored below—takes a little bit of swallowing, but it all seems just about feasible within the context of the story ("You know something, I don't think I believe in the Devil anymore," says a relieved Eva, who turns out to be a prostitute). However, when Eva and Haig are finally picked up, those left onboard the boat to investigate matters further discover that it isn't the priest who is hanging from the rigging, but Eva, the priest having somehow swapped places with her aboard the helicopter. Having pushed Haig out of the helicopter, the priest, who, it transpires is the Devil, next moves in on Pagnolini, who, rather than succumb to his will, crashes the helicopter into the ocean, where the priest's soul now enters Haig, who waits to be rescued by another ship.

The best way to describe *Satan's Triangle* is mumbo jumbo of the first order. That events are just about explained away and then turn out to be supernatural after all is a nice reversal of expectations thanks to the skill of writer William Read Woodfield, while the film has a genuine otherworldly ambience once on the boat thanks to the work of director Sutton Roley and cinematographer Leonard J. South, an industry veteran whose many credits include work as a camera operator on a number of Hitchcock films, among them *Vertigo* (1958) starring Kim Novak. This contribution is augmented by a satisfactorily eerie score care of Johnny Pate, which likewise helps to ramp up the atmosphere. As the swarthy-looking priest, Alejandro Rey certainly looks the part, and goes for broke with the scenery chewing when his identity is revealed, while Doug McClure makes for a reliably bland hero (as he always did). As for Kim Novak, she mostly seems catatonic, but then again, her character has been through a lot (note that the film's casting director was Joyce Selznick, the niece of *Gone with the Wind* [1939] producer David O. Selznick).

A Fetish for Horror

Director Dan Curtis returned next to the movie of the week slot with *Trilogy of Terror* (1975, TV), which aired on 4 March 1975. This starred Karen Black in four roles in three different stories, the first of which, *Julie*, sees her cast as a dowdy-looking lit teacher who is drugged and seduced on a whim by one her students, an unsavory young man called Chad Foster (Robert Burton, who at the time was briefly married to Black). Having taken photographs of her in several uncompromising positions, she agrees to have an affair with him under fear of blackmail. However, it turns out that it was in fact Julie who put the thought of seduction into Chad's mind ("Its kinda like the idea just jumped into my head"), just as she had done with several other unfortunate young men before him, all of whom ended up dead after she had become bored with them ("You've drugged me," he exclaims when he realizes the game is up, to which comes the flat reply, "No, dear, I've killed you"). In the second chapter, *Millicent and Therese*, the actress plays two sisters at war with each other, one straightlaced and the other a floozy. Their hate filled relationship eventually leads each to conspire to kill the other; however, when a body is discovered by their doctor (George Gaynes), it proves that there is only one of them after all ("Her name was Therese-Millicent Lorimor, the most advanced case of dual personality I have ever seen," he informs the paramedics). In the final chapter, *Amelia*, Black plays a young woman who finds herself trapped in her apartment at the mercy of a fetish that she has bought and which inexplicably comes to life. "Even your mother wouldn't love you," she says of the doll when she gets it out of its box. Having bitten her on the neck, Amelia then takes on some of its characteristics (frizzy hair and *very* sharp teeth), and invites her troublesome mother over for the evening, the fate of whom doesn't seem too promising ("I'll be waiting for you").

Written by William F. Nolan and based upon three short stories by Ray

Bradbury, there is nothing particularly outstanding about any of the episodes, although the third delivers a few good thrills once it gets going and the fetish is running amok around the apartment (at one stage, Amelia manages to throw it into her oven, pre-empting the microwave scene in *Gremlins* [1984] by several years). The middle episode is little more than a filler, without much going for it above and beyond its climactic twist, leaving it to the first episode to provide the most uncomfortable moments as the unethical Chad drugs Julie at a drive-in, having managed to convince her to go on a date with him to see an old vampire movie (the clips of which are cheekily taken from *The Night Stalker* [1971, TVM]). However, the date-rape scenario leaves an unpleasant taste, particularly in this age of # me too, even when it turns out that it is Julie who is the baddie after all. Indifferently directed by Curtis, save for some dynamic chase shots in the third episode, this is all rather disappointing as a whole, but the fetish itself seems to have haunted the minds of the generation who came across it when it first aired. And while the material she was given couldn't be described as great, the film at least acts as a solid showcase for Black, who deserved something a little better than this ("Karen Black is sensational in *Trilogy of Terror*, an electrifying experience—you won't believe your eyes," ran one newspaper ad).

Meanwhile, with *Song of the Succubus* (1975, TVM), which aired on 7 March 1975, a rock star finds himself haunted by the ghost of a Victorian musician. Featuring Kim Milford (who also provided the score), Brooke Adams and George Gaynes, the film was directed by Glenn Jordan, who had helmed *Frankenstein* (1973, TVM) and *The Picture of Dorian Gray* (1973, TVM) for producer Dan Curtis. Unfortunately, the movie, which was written by Robert Thom and executive produced by Howard Lipstone, has long been out of circulation, the only remaining copy being held in the Library of Congress, thus preventing any further evaluation.

Sadly, the film proved to be the last genre offering from the ABC strand, which came to an end the following month with a comedy-drama about computer dating titled *Promise Him Anything* (1975, TVM), though there was one last burst of glory with the pilot film for the detective series *Starsky and Hutch* (1975, TVM), which aired on 30 April 1975, and which led to a highly popular four-season run that managed to clock up 92 episodes, one of which (episode seven of season two), took on a supernatural element. This was *The Vampire* (1976, TV), which aired on 30 October 1976, just in time for Halloween, in which our heroes, played by Paul Michael Glaser and David Soul, respectively, track down a killer,

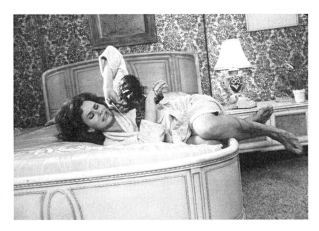

Hello, dolly. Karen Black fends off the killer fetish in *Trilogy of Terror* (1975, TVM) (ABC/ABC Circle Films/ Dan Curtis Productions).

René Nadasy (John Saxon), who, sporting fangs, is going about murdering dancers and sucking the blood from their bodies. But is he real or merely a psychopath?
The episode was penned by Michael Grais and Mark Victor, who would go on to
write *Poltergeist* (1982), while direction was in the hands of Bob Kelljan, whose feature credits at this stage included *Count Yorga, Vampire* (1970), *The Return of Count
Yorga* (1971) and *Scream Blacula Scream* (1973). David Soul would of course go on to
meet a rather more vicious vampire at the end of the decade in the superb *Salem's
Lot* (1979, TVM), more on which to come. Starsky and Hutch weren't the only TV
detectives to meet a horror icon in the seventies, however. In the final installment
of *McCloud* (1970–1977, TV), which aired on NBC on 17 April 1977, our hero (Dennis Weaver) investigates a killing that appears to be the work of a vampire, and subsequently encounters Loren Belasco (John Carradine), an old-time horror star who
sleeps in a coffin in a candlelit mansion and claims to be a descendant of Dracula.
Written by Glen A. Larson and directed by Bruce Kessler, the feature-length episode
was titled *McCloud Meets Dracula* (1977, TVM), and also featured Reggie Nalder
as Belasco's manservant, and contained a few brief clips from *House of Frankenstein* (1944) and *House of Dracula* (1945), which starred Carradine as Dracula. Elsewhere, *Fantasy Island* (1977–1984, TV) included an encounter with Jack the Ripper,
as played with relish Victor Buono, in a segment titled *With Affection, Jack the Ripper* (1980, TV), in which a writer (Linda Day George) researching a book about the
killer finds herself in a version of foggy old London.

Just because the *Movie of the Week* strand had come to a conclusion, it didn't
mean that ABC ceased to air original feature content in a variety of guises (such as
the *ABC Friday Night Movie*). Indeed, films of varying length (and quality) continued to pepper the schedules, among them the occasional genre offering. Or, as in
the case of *Brenda Starr* (1976, TVM), a movie with genre elements within it. Broadcast on 8 May 1976, the film was based upon the popular comic strip by Dale Messick, which first appeared in 1940, and follows the adventures of intrepid newspaper
reporter Brenda Starr (Jill St. John), who finds herself in Brazil, where she helps a
reclusive billionaire (Victor Buono) expose an extortion plot. Also featuring voodoo and supernatural occurrences, the script by George Kirgo (taken from a story
by himself and Ira Barmak) is something of a hotchpotch, which is perhaps why this
pilot for the character wasn't taken up as a series. Efficiently enough directed by Mel
Stuart, the film, which was produced by Bob Larson for David L. Wolper Productions, at least benefits from a lively score by Lalo Schifrin and a game performance
by St. John, who had longed to play the role. Yet for all her emancipation and self
assurance, she is nevertheless required succumb to the objectification of the camera, and at one point she sports an astonishingly brief bikini, which even at the time
must have raised an eyebrow or two ("What do you think, Hank? Too much south of
the border?" she asks her friend while modeling it).

Also something of a disappointment was *Death at Love House* (1976, TVM),
which aired on 3 September 1976. In it, Joel and Donna Gregory (Robert Wagner
and Kate Jackson), a husband and wife writing team, are working on a book about
an old time movie star named Lorna Love, who died back in 1935, and to better
assist their researches they make arrangements with the late star's studio to spend a

few days at her sprawling mansion, so as to better delve into her past, in which they are assisted by the housekeeper, Clara Josephs (Sylvia Sidney). They also encounter several of the star's contemporaries, among them her director Conan Carroll (John Carradine), and two fellow actresses, Denise Christian (Dorothy Lamour) and Marcella Geffenhart (Joan Blondell), each of whom proffers a wildly different opinion about Lorna, whom it transpires was obsessed by the black arts ("She destroyed everything she touched," Miss Christian informs them). However, while they are at the mansion, which also contains a shrine in the grounds in which Lorna's body lies in state, Donna sees a shrouded figure running about the gardens at night, while Joel becomes obsessed with a portrait of the star, which his late father had painted during an affair with the actress, and is soon imagining himself to be romancing her himself. So is Lorna really dead, or has her spirit somehow returned to haunt Joel, who is the spitting image of his father?

Clearly a trip into *Baby Jane* territory, this has everything one would expect from such a story, including a creepy mansion, a sepulchral housekeeper, thunderstorms on tap, mysterious figures wandering about at night, moments of peril for the leading lady (who finds herself locked in a gas filled bathroom at one point), and lots of references to old time Hollywood. Unfortunately, the lackluster teleplay by Jim Barnett makes too little of these familiar elements, most of which appear to have been included as a box ticking exercise ("It has everything going for it except a sensible script and intelligent dialogue," sniped critic Judith Crist of his efforts). As is the wont of such melodramas, there's naturally a twist in the tale, and here it transpires that (spoiler alert) Lorna didn't die quietly at home as was reported but was badly burned during a ritual performed by her mystic, Father Eternal Fire, and is alive and well in the guise of her housekeeper, whose clothes and mask Donna discovers. She also finds her husband in Lorna's boudoir being seduced by the aged actress, who seems convinced that Joel is in fact his father, her former lover. However, when Lorna's wig falls to reveal her true appearance, she hotfoots it to her shrine, where she sets fire to the place, hoping to take Joel, who has pursued her there, with her. But he is rescued at the last moment by Donna, thus leaving Lorna to go up in flames along with the wax figure of her that had been lying in state. "All she wanted was to be adored, to be worshipped forever," observes Joel the next day in a line almost as chintzy as the score by Laurence Rosenthal.

An overlong and rather fumbled effort which promises more than it delivers, this could have been a genuinely chilling little shocker, despite its absurdities, and is let down primarily by the disappointingly flat direction by E.W. Swackhamer, who too often mistakes musty nostalgia for genuine style and atmosphere, though the house and gardens in which the film is set certainly look the part (the movie was shot at Harold Lloyd's spectacular Greenacres Estate). The welcome inclusion of "special cameo appearances" by a handful of old-time players from the thirties is also an undeniable bonus, but they are unfortunately given rather too little to do during their brief scenes (Lamour is seen filming a cheesy coffee ad), while as the Gregorys, Wagner and Jackson aren't for a moment convincing either as a couple, or a couple of writers. Produced by Hal Sitowitz for Spelling Goldberg-Productions, this had the potential to be a minor classic, but instead all it leaves behind is a mild whiff of moth balls.

Another film that failed to live up its potential was *Look What's Happened to Rosemary's Baby* (1976, TVM), a catchpenny sequel to the big screen hit *Rosemary's Baby* (1968), in which a young woman (Mia Farrow) gradually comes to realize that the child she is about to give birth to is the son of Satan. In the sequel, which aired on 29 October 1976, Rosemary (here played by Patty Duke Astin) goes on the run with her young boy Adrian, but the coven of witches with whom they have been residing do not take this lightly and do everything in their power to retrieve the child. Divided into chapters (*The Book of Rosemary, The Book of Adrian, The Book of Andrew*), the film subsequently follows Adrian on his journey to manhood and the destiny that awaits him: the inheritance of Satan's powers.

Unfortunately, Anthony Wilson's follow-up script quickly resolves itself into a hotchpotch of incidents somewhat akin to *The Omen* (1976), with the adult Adrian (Stephen McHattie) going to the bad in various ways, his eyes shining red whenever crossed by anyone who would do him harm, among them a gang of bikers with whom he has a run in at one point. On the plus side, Ruth Gordon reprises her Oscar winning role as Minnie Castevet, Rosemary's busy body neighbor in the original, while Ray Milland takes over that of her Satanist husband Roman (Sidney Blackmer, who played the role in the first film having died in 1973). Sadly, as solid as the assembled cast is, among them Donna Mills as a psychiatrist who has a romance with Adrian, George Maharis as Rosemary's husband Guy, and Tina Louise as the prostitute who brings up Adrian after Rosemary has met an uncertain fate (she is driven off in a bus that proves to be devoid of both passengers and a driver!), there is little for them to get their teeth into dramatically, while the direction by Sam O'Steen (who had edited the Roman Polanski original) lacks both pace and visual flair. Thus it is left to Charles Bernstein's ominous score to provide what little atmosphere the film contains. Something of a disappointment all round, the movie concludes with Donna Mills' character giving birth to Rosemary's grandchild; thankfully, a second sequel failed to materialize (though a two-part TV mini-series starring Zoe Saldana, based upon the original Ira Levin novel, followed in 2014).

Monsters returned to the small screen next with *The Last Dinosaur* (1977, TVM), which was beamed into unsuspecting homes on 11 February 1977. An arrant piece of nonsense clearly aimed at ten-year-olds (one hopes), it follows the exploits of the improbably named Masten Thrust (Richard Boone), a billionaire big game hunter who fronts an expedition to a newly found lost world where he and his colleagues discover that dinosaurs do indeed still rule the Earth, among them a T-Rex, with which they have various encounters (tag line: "A lost world!! Ruled by the largest man-eating monster of all!!").

Produced by Rankin/Bass Productions (best known for their cartoons), the film was made in association with the Japanese company Tsuburaya Productions, whose team, led by Moriake Uematsu, was in charge of the effects, and while mostly a ludicrous and somewhat plodding affair, the proceedings are nevertheless roused to life when these cheesy effects take over. The T-Rex is clearly a man in a not entirely convincing rubber monster suit in the style of the old Toho Godzilla movies, while a Triceratops, with which it does battle at one point, is clearly *two* men in a not entirely convincing rubber monster suit. The film also features some rather immobile

Pterodactyls, a tribe of prehistoric cavemen and some monstrously over the top acting by a grumpy-looking (or possibly hung-over) Boone, who is joined on his adventure by Joan Van Ark, Steven Keats and Luther Rackley, the latter as Bunta, a towering Maasai tracker who at one point takes on the T-Rex with just a spear, which he successfully lobs into the monster's chest (Thrust also manages to catapult a small boulder at it at one stage, knocking it out in the process!). Unimaginatively directed by Alexander Grasshoff and Tsugunobu Kontai from a lackluster script by William Overgard, this could have provided much more tongue-in-cheek fun than it does. That said, while the monsters aren't in the league of those produced by the likes of Willis O'Brien and Ray Harryhausen, they are at the very least reasonably elaborate for what, after all, is a low-budget TV movie. As for the Bond-style title song, performed over the closing credits by Nancy Wilson (music by Maury Laws, lyrics by Jules Bass), prepare to cringe (note that the film's running time of 95 minutes was expanded to 106 minutes for its theatrical release in Japan and other territories).

Meanwhile, in *Good Against Evil* (1977, TVM), which was broadcast on 22 May 1977, an initially skeptical writer named Andy Stewart (Dack Rambo) discovers that his bride to be Jessica (Elyssa Davalos) has been "touched by Asteroth," as the priest who is to marry them informs him. However, when a number of deaths and strange events occur, among them the possession of the young daughter of a former girlfriend (Kim Cattrall), Andy joins forces with an exorcist named Father Kemschler (Dan O'Herlihy) to help restore order. Made as the pilot for a series that subsequently didn't happen, the film's credits sound promising, featuring as they do a screenplay by Jimmy Sangster, direction by Paul Wendkos and a score by Lalo Schifrin. Unfortunately, all involved are working below par in this instance, and the various borrowings from *Rosemary's Baby* (1968), *The Exorcist* (1973) and *The Omen* (1976) are all rather obvious. That said, Wendkos' visuals are occasionally striking (he makes use of a number of San Francisco locations previously used in *Vertigo* [1958]), and the supporting cast is not without interest, among them Lelia Goldoni as a malevolent nun and Richard Lynch as the leader of a cult who has promised Jessica to Satan (tagline: "She became Satan's plaything"). Unfortunately, the climactic scene of exorcism, although clearly modeled on sequences in *The Exorcist*, is not without its moments of unintentional humor, as furniture is all too clearly thrown across the room by off camera stagehands and, at one point, Father Kemschler is almost suffocated by a possessed pillow (no, really!). The best line comes early on, when Jessica's mother is in labor and cries, "This is not a hospital, this is not a hospital," as she realizes things aren't quite as they should be. Unfortunately, what follows fails to match it.

Horror supremo Dan Curtis was unfortunately far from being on top form with his next TV offering, *Curse of the Black Widow* (1977, TVM), which aired on 16 September 1977. The film certainly boasts a top-notch supporting cast, among them Vic Morrow, Sid Caesar, June Allyson, Max Gail, Roz Kelly, Jeff Corey and June Lockhart, who are unfortunately given too little to do in the pedestrian screenplay by Robert Blees (who also provided the story) and Earl Wallace, which follows the investigation by private detective Mark Higbie (Anthony Franciosa) into a series of bizarre murders perpetrated by a woman who has the ability to turn into a giant spider. But who could the deadly black widow be? All eyes are on twin sisters Leigh and Laura Lockridge (Donna Mills and Patty Duke Astin), the latter of whom turns out to be schizophrenic. Bitten by spiders as a baby, she now periodically transforms into the title creature, draining her mostly male (for a change) victims of blood and leaving their bodies encased in giant webs.

A disappointingly routine production in almost every way, the film is notable for its lack of style and atmosphere, even during the attack sequences, in which a lens featuring multiple images of the victims is used for the point of view shots. Indeed, Curtis's setups and the flat photography by Paul Lohmann have the look of episode television, while the effects (care of Roy L. Downey and his team) are strictly underwhelming when finally seen full on. The climax in which the spider goes up in flames when Higbie throws an oil lamp at it is also something of a disappointment, though there is a last minute twist, when it is revealed that Laura's daughter (played by Curtis's own daughter Tracy Curtis) could well have inherited her mother's inclinations (note that in the film, Leigh and Laura's surname is pronounced as Lockridge, but Astin is billed as Laura Lock*wood* in the opening credits).

Another onslaught care of Mother Nature was the focus of *It Happened at Lakewood Manor* (1977, TVM, aka *Panic at Lakewood Manor* and *Ants*), in which the owners and guests of a lakeside resort find their lives threatened by an army of poisonous ants after their nest has been disturbed by construction workers ("Pleasure seekers trapped by a deadly menace from the depths of the Earth," ran the tagline). Produced by Peter Nelson via Alan Landsburg Productions, the movie, which aired on 2 December 1977, was written by Guerdon Trueblood, who already had form with a similar threat, having penned *The Savage Bees* (1976, TVM) for Landsburg, with *Tarantulas: The Deadly Cargo* (1977, TVM) and *Terror Out of the Sky* (1978, TVM [more bees]) yet to come for him. Shot at Qualicum Beach in British Columbia, the movie follows the usual pattern for such fare, with the ants first attacking a couple of workmen before moving on to the hotel itself, which they take over floor by floor, forcing those inside to the upper levels where they are eventually rescued by helicopter and men in specialist survival suits bearing smoke canisters. A routine production in every way, from its concept to its un-ambitious handling care of director Robert Scheerer, this really is half-hearted stuff, bolstered by a far better cast than it deserves, among them Robert Foxworth, Lynda Day George, Bernie Casey, Suzanne Sommers, Steve Franken, Brian Dennehy and Hollywood veteran Myrna Loy, for whom this was definite comedown, though *Variety* wasn't too harsh in its judgment of the enterprise, commenting, "Telefilm moves smartly along and may leave some viewers scratching."

Rather more intriguing was *Night Cries* (1978, TVM), which aired on 29 January 1978, in which Susan Saint James stars as Jeannie Haskins, a young woman who is informed shortly after she has given birth to a baby daughter that her child has died. Tormented by vivid nightmares in which she hears her baby crying, she becomes convinced that her child is still alive, much to the concern of her husband (Michael Parks). However, with the help of a scientist (William Conrad) whose specialty is dreams, she eventually figures out what really happened to her baby, with whom she appears to have a psychic bond (it transpires that a disturbed nurse [Delores

Dorn], who has spent all her life caring for other people's babies, yet unable to have a child herself, has taken Jeannie's baby for her own). The teleplay by Richard Lang is a somewhat convoluted affair, albeit with a fairly conventional nick-of-time ending in which mother and child are finally reunited, yet the dream sequences are certainly vividly staged by director Brian Taggert and his cinematographer Charles Arnold, while James gives a strong performance as the disturbed mother who sticks to her guns, despite the incredulity surrounding her.

A far sillier prospect was *Cruise into Terror* (1978, TVM), which was broadcast on 3 February 1978, and about which there is little positive to say. In it, a group of passengers onboard a luxury pleasure cruise find themselves menaced by an evil spirit contained within a small gold sarcophagus that has been retrieved from the ocean floor (although not until the film is almost half over). An inane pot-boiler which is mostly dull chat in claustrophobic cabins and corridors, its screenplay by Michael Braverman is particularly unseaworthy, while Bruce Kessler's dull direction is strictly by the numbers, so much so that even the cast look bored, among them such familiar faces as Ray Milland, John Forsythe, Lee Meriwether, Dirk Benedict, Stella Stevens and Hugh O'Brian, none of whom are likely to have counted it as among their better experiences in front of a camera.

It was back to school again with *The Initiation of Sarah* (1978, TVM), which aired on 6 February 1978. In it, two sisters, Sarah and Patty Goodwin (Kay Lenz and Morgan Brittany), move to college together for the first time. However, when Patty proves to be more popular and is invited to join Alpha Nu Sigma, the best sorority house on the campus, her less glamorous sister Sarah, who it transpires is adopted (her mother disappeared and her father died), finds herself staying at the rather more downmarket Psi Epsilon Delta, where she falls under the influence of the house mother Mrs. Hunter (Shelley Winters), who already seems to know that Sarah possesses telekinetic abilities, which she helps her to make use of to avenge herself against the pranksters and bullies who make her life a misery during hell week. Then, at an initiation ceremony which takes place in a secret room before moving to the center of a candlelit maze conveniently situated in the back garden, Sarah is made the leader of her house and encouraged by Mrs. Hunter to use her powers against those who would destroy them, which she does via a mighty wind which wrecks the initiation ceremony taking place at Alpha Nu Sigma, turning its leader into a wizened old hag. However, when Mrs. Hunter wants to sacrifice one of her girls as part of the ceremony, Sarah rebels and sends the maze up in flames, killing both herself and Mrs. Hunter, who, it transpires, has killed before.

Unfortunately, despite a good cast that also includes Tony Bill, Tisa Farrow (sister of Mia) and Morgan Fairchild (who, controversially for the time, sports a wet tee-shirt at one point, having been thrown into a pond by Sarah), this really is tiresome stuff, in which even the highlights fail to raise a thrill, despite the promises of the film's promotional campaign ("An innocent co-ed, a secret sorority, its bizarre rites of womanhood.... Suddenly, a quiet college campus is plunged into an endless night of terror!"). Based upon a story by Tom Holland and Carol Saraceno, the teleplay by Saraceno, Don Ingalls and Kenette Gfeller owes a great debt to *Carrie* (1976), and even includes a scene in which Sarah is set up for a date with the college hunk

(Robert Hays), only to find herself pelted with eggs and mud when she appears at the door of the sorority house to meet him. Flatly directed by Robert Day and with little atmosphere to show for itself, the film is mostly concerned with the banal rivalries between the two sorority houses, and even Winters, who was known to enjoy chewing the scenery, has little to grasp onto here, even during the climactic initiation ceremony (note that the film was remade in 2006, with Fairchild returning as the mother of Sarah and Patty).

One of the loonier TV movies shown during this period was *The Power Within* (1979, TVM), which aired on 11 May 1979. In it, a stunt pilot (Art Hindle) is struck by lightning, and, thanks to the fact that his mother died of radiation poisoning following an atomic test, not only survives the incident, but finds himself able to discharge electricity from his body at will, all of which makes him of interest to the government (and counter agents), though the downside of his newly acquired super power is that he has to periodically regenerate his energy otherwise he will die. A somewhat farfetched concept given insufficient pizzazz by writer William Clark, the film also features David Hedison, Dick Sargent and Susan Howard, but the aerial stunts performed by Art Scholl and a rousing score by John Addison aside, it proved to be one of the lesser efforts from director John Llewellyn Moxey, and if a weekly series was hoped for, it failed to materialize ("No one involved distinguishes himself," sniped *Variety* of the results).

MTM Goes for the Jugular

Of far more interest to die hard genre fans would have been *Vampire* (1979, TVM), which, on the face of it, looked like something they could better sink their teeth into. Aired on 7 October 1979, it centers on the reappearance in modern day San Francisco of Anton Voytek (Richard Lynch), a centuries-old vampire who has not been seen for decades, but who emerges when his lair is disturbed by construction work on a new development for churches, schools and apartments, the shadow of a giant crucifix erected on the site having scorched the earth under which he lies. Befriending John Rawlins (Jason Miller), the architect responsible for the development, Voytek nevertheless finds himself at odds with the authorities when it transpires that his hoard of art treasures, worth millions, prove to have been plundered. Holding Rawlins and his wife (Kathryn Harrold) responsible for the betrayal, he vows to extract revenge. However, help is at hand in guise of Harry Kilcoyne (E.G. Marshall), a retired cop who helps Rawlins track down the vampire, who has placed a number of coffins across the city in places of safe haven.

There is no doubting that *Vampire* was intended a prestige event, given the pedigree of both the production company (Mary Tyler Moore's MTM Enterprises) and those involved. There are no aging second rank stars or cheesy guest spots here. Indeed, the cast would not have looked out of place in a big screen feature. As the charismatic vampire who has been terrorizing the city, Richard Lynch exudes the required old-world charm without laying it on too thick ("No Woman can resist him, no man can stand against him," ran the tagline), while Jason Miller brings the scowling angst he displayed to such effect as Father Karras in *The Exorcist* (1973) to the role of the architect, particularly after his wife has mysteriously disappeared. Meanwhile, E.G. Marshall lends an air of relaxed authority to the proceedings as the retired cop, determined on finally getting his man, while Jessica Walter adds touch of easy sophistication as Voytek's legal advisor, Nicole. The talent behind the camera is of an equally high caliber, among them executive producer Steven Bochco, who also co-wrote the script with Michael Kozoll, which thankfully steers clear of any overtly camp elements, composer Fred Karlin, whose cimbalom-led score adds a welcome middle-European air to the atmosphere, and director E.W. Swackhamer, who handles the proceedings in a steady, un-showy manner (an episode veteran, he had recently graduated to more distinctive enterprises, among them a well regarded three-part adaptation of the classic Dashiell Hammett crime novel *The Dain Curse* [1978, TVM], which had starred James Coburn).

But here's the rub: the result of all their labors is somewhat on the dull side, with rather too much serious-minded chat and, perhaps because the film aired at 8 p.m. on a Sunday evening, not enough action ("If you truly accept the existence of God, then you also have to accept the reality of evil," says Kilcoyne to Rawlins during one lengthy philosophical discussion). However, there are compensations, among them the sight of the sun-scorched cross on the earth of the building site, from under which Voytek later scrambles naked into the night air; his desperate run across the streets of the city as dawn is breaking, keen to find sanctuary after having been held in a police cell overnight; the staking of Rawlins' wife, who has been turned into one of the undead by Voytek; and the tracking down of his various coffins across San Francisco, culminating in Rawlins and Kilcoyne confronting the vampire in a candlelit crypt, by which time the sun has inevitably set. The ultimate let down is that (spoiler alert) the vampire escapes into the night at the end, his future fate presumably to have been dealt with in the ensuing television series which, in this case, failed to materialize, all of which makes for a frustrating ending, given the stately build up. Yet despite its faults, this remains for the most part a quality production, even if it does lack "a good scare" as *Variety* put it.

Rather more downmarket was *The Death of Ocean View Park* (1979, TVM), which went out on 19 October 1979 and made use of the fact that a real fairground, the Ocean View Amusement Park in Norfolk, Virginia, was set for demolition. In it, Sheila Brady (Diana Canova) has a number of dreams and visions about a disaster at an amusement park, which her husband Phil (James Stephens) puts down to the fact that she is three months pregnant. However, when a hurricane bursts a gas line just before the fourth of July and the accident goes undetected, it looks like her premonitions are about to come true ("A freak hurricane. A sudden rising tide. Thrill rides start by themselves and can't be stopped. A chain of mysterious events shatters a happy holiday celebration. And terror takes over a vast amusement park," ran the promotional copy). The premonition angle of the story is perhaps the least relevant element of this hokey disaster flick, save to offer brief glimpses of the devastation to come, so as to keep one tuned in for the fiery finale. Until then, the running time is tediously tricked out with various dramas involving the likes of Sam Jackson (Mike Connors) as the amusement park's jittery owner, and Tom Flood (Martin Landau) as his new partner, whose concerns for ride safety take a back seat to his hunger to make a profit. When the mayhem finally kicks off, it is adequately enough staged by director E.W. Swackhamer and his effects team, who certainly don't stint on the TNT. Written and produced by John Furia and Barry Oringer, the film was made via Furia/Oringer Productions and Hugh Hefner's Playboy Productions, through the latter of which the girly mag proprietor also financed Roman Polanski's *Macbeth* (1971) and several other mediocre TV movies. If, however, it's fairground thrills you seek, then *Rollercoaster* (1977) is the marginally better option.

A tired reboot of the popular series of supernatural film comedies from the thirties (not to mention the fifties TV series) came next with *Topper* (1979, TVM), with Jack Warden this time starring as the title character, a businessman who finds himself haunted by a recently deceased married couple, Marion and George Kerby (played by real life couple Kate Jackson and Andrew Stevens, who also executive produced), whose hope is to make it to heaven instead of wandering the Earth in limbo. However, until they get there, their ghostly hijinks make poor Topper's life a misery, especially as no one else can see them, least of all his increasingly frustrated wife Clara (Rue McClanahan). A flatly written, directed and performed romp, the movie, which aired on 9 November 1979, was intended as the launching pad for a new series. Unfortunately, few were amused by the couple's antics, and on this occasion the network didn't take the bait, despite Jackson's popularity in *Charlie's Angels* (1976–1981, TV), from which she had retired on 16 May the same year. She and Stevens divorced the following year on 4 January (note that this wasn't the only attempt to revive the character in the seventies; in 1973 Roddy McDowall had starred in a failed 30-minute pilot titled *Topper Returns* [1973, TV] in which his ghostly tormentors were played by Stefanie Powers and John Fink).

ABC's run of seventies genre movies finally came to an end with *An American Christmas Carol* (1979, TVM), an update of the Dickens classic which aired on 16 December 1979. Set in New England during the Depression, it sees an old miser named Benedict Slade (Henry Winkler) given an opportunity to mend his ways when visited by four ghosts on Christmas Eve. Clearly an attempt to prove that Winkler could do more than just play the Fonz in *Happy Days* (1974–1984, TV), the actor grasps the opportunity with both hands, and looks reasonably convincing in the old-age make-up provided by Greg Cannom and Rick Baker, thus allowing him to appear as his own age during the flashbacks. Unfortunately, the script by Jerome Coopersmith is rather pedestrian and the direction by Eric Till lacks flair, particularly during the visitation sequences, thus requiring a fair amount of Christmas spirit to see it to the end. Filmed in Ontario, the $2 million film also featured David Wayne, Chris Wiggins, Dorian Harewood and Susan Hogan.

It wasn't only ABC that produced horror films for showing on television in the seventies. Rival channels also dipped into the genre (and variations thereon), albeit not quite with the frequency with which ABC did. Over at NBC, the commitment was by no means as strong at first, but as the decade progressed, the station went on to broadcast a number of key works. One of the early examples was *Hauser's Memory* (1970, TVM), which was broadcast on 24 November 1970, and starred the ever-youthful David McCallum as Hillel Mondoro, a biochemist who is persuaded by the government to have the memories of a dying scientist chemically transferred into his own brain by way of safeguarding the missile defense secrets contained therein. Unfortunately, the scientist in question was a Nazi sympathizer, and Mondoro finds himself sought by various agencies interested in the secrets he now holds (tagline: "He stole another man's brain ... and became the most dangerous man on Earth!"). Produced by Jack Laird for Universal, the story, which was scripted by Adrian Spies, was yet another variation on Curt Siodmak's 1942 novel *Donovan's Brain*, already filmed as *The Lady and the Monster* (1944), *Donovan's Brain* (1953) and *The Brain* (1962), and was efficiently enough directed by TV veteran Boris Sagal, who'd already worked with McCallum on *The Man from U.N.C.L.E.* (1964–1968, TV) and *Mosquito Squadron* (1970). Also featuring Lilli Palmer, Leslie Nielsen and Susan Strasberg, the film, which was released theatrically in some territories, offers a reasonably engaging mix of science fiction, thrills and espionage, and though not quite a fully fledged horror film, deserves a mention here for its brain transference theme (variations on the premise include *Codename: Heraclitus* [1967, TVM], in which a man [Stanley Baker] brought back to life after dying on the operating table becomes a government spy given that he has lost his memory, and *The Ultimate Impostor* [1979, TVM], in which a secret agent [Joseph Hacker] whose memory has been wiped has his brain linked to a computer).

Another borderline case was *A Howling in the Woods* (1971, TV), which aired on 5 November 1971. More of a "town with a secret" saga (tagline: "What is the horrifying secret the whole town tried to hide?"), it nevertheless uses the trappings of the genre—the murder of a child, thunderstorms, a dog howling in the woods—to reasonably good effect. Based on the 1968 novel by Velda Johnston, it stars Barbara Eden as the lady in peril, Larry Hagman as her estranged husband, Vera Miles, who, despite initial appearances, turns out to be something of a wicked stepmother, and a young Tyne Daly. Filmed on location in Genoa, Nevada, by director Daniel Petrie, the results serve their purpose adequately enough, though at 96 minutes for a two-hour timeslot (as opposed to ABC's preferred 74 minutes for a 90-minute slot), the film does seem on the padded side.

If *The Mystery in Dracula's Castle* (1973, TVM), which aired on 7 and 14 January 1973 initially as a two-part

Brain drain. David McCallum is featured in the poster for the theatrical release of *Hauser's Memory* (1970, TVM). Note the misspelling of Lilli Palmer's name (NBC/Universal Television).

installment of *The Magical World of Disney* (1954–1997, TV, formerly *Disneyland*), sounded like it was going to be a scary adventure set in Dracula's castle, then kids tuning in were in for a disappointment. In it, a horror mad boy and his younger brother (Johnny Whittaker and Scott C. Kolden) are making a home movie about Dracula during their vacation and check out the nearby lighthouse as a location for the count's castle, not realizing that it's being used as a hideout by jewel thieves. Typically cheerful Disney fare of the period, it's harmless enough fun, though the climax in which the boys thwart the bad guys by throwing fireworks at them from atop the lighthouse seems a tad irresponsible (note that Dracula does actually make a brief appearance at the start of the film, albeit in a movie the boys are watching at their local theater).

Other films dealing with the supernatural (or sometimes just the suggestion of it) that were shown in the Disney series (either feature length or for an hour slot) included *The Ghost of Cypress Swamp* (1977, TVM), in which a boy (Jeff East) discovers a swamp to be inhabited by a man (Vic Morrow) thought to be long dead; *Halloween Hall o' Fame* (1977, TV), in which a night watchman (Jonathan Winters) working in a movie studio discovers a talking jack-o'-lantern (also Winters) hiding out in the prop store; *Child of Glass* (1978, TVM), in which a boy (Steve Shaw) helps the ghost of a Creole girl (Olivia Barash) solve a riddle that will allow her to rest in peace; *Shadow of Fear* (1979, TV), in which a boy (Ike Eisenmann) grieving over the death of his father learns that he is able to project his mind into that of an animal; *The Ghosts of Buxley Hall* (1980, TVM), in which three ghosts (Dick O'Neill, Louis Latham and Victor French) resolve to help a military academy through a financial crisis which has seen it merge with a girls' school; *A Disney Halloween* (1981, TV), a holiday special featuring clips from classic movies including *Snow White and the Seven Dwarfs* (1937) and *The Legend of Sleepy Hollow* (1949); *Mr. Boogedy* (1986, TV), in which a novelty salesman (Richard Masur) and his family move into a new home in Lucifer Falls only to find it haunted by a former occupant, Mr. Boogedy (Howard Witt), who is 300 years old; *Fuzzbucket* (1986, TV), in which an invisible goblin befriends a young boy (Chris Hebert); *Bigfoot* (1987, TVM), in which two kids (Adam Carl and Candace Cameron) vacationing in the mountains with their parents befriend a sasquatch and its mate; *Bride of Boogedy* (1987, TVM), in which the ghostly Mr. Boogedy (Howard Witt) returns to extract revenge on the Davis family and to find himself a mate; *Justin Case* (1988, TVM), in which the ghost of a private detective (George Carlin) enlists the help of a dancer (Molly Hagan) to help discover who killed him (written, directed and executive produced by Blake Edwards from a story by himself and his daughter Jennifer, this was a pilot for a series that didn't happen); a remake of *The Absent-Minded Professor* (1988, TVM), with Harry Anderson in the role of the professor who discovers an antigravity substance he names Flubber; and *The Absent-Minded Professor: Trading Places* (1989, TV), a sequel in which the professor agrees to swap jobs with his former roommate only to find himself using Flubber to prevent a weapons system demonstration. And the most horrific part of these movies? The introductions by Disney CEO Michael Eisner.

Meanwhile, back in the adult world, *Baffled!* (1973, TVM), which aired on 30 January 1973, starred Leonard Nimoy as Tom Kovack, a racing driver who, while taking part in the Pennsylvania 500 Mile Special, suffers the first in a series of premonitions in which he observes various strange and threatening events taking place in a English manor. Having seen him interviewed on television about his experience, Kovack is subsequently approached by Michelle Brent (Susan Hampshire), who has studied the occult and ESP, and together they travel to Wyndham Manor in Devon to try and solve the mystery of his visions. Produced and directed in the UK by Philip Leacock for Arena and ITC, the resultant film (which was released theatrically in some territories) suffers primarily from a particularly idiotic script by hack for hire Theodore Apstein, which takes almost lunatic pleasure in piling up red herrings and false trails for our hero and heroine to endure, before finally explaining things away as the machinations in a complex murder plot, the denouement of which takes some swallowing. That said, the proceedings benefit from some pleasant exterior work at Taplow Court (doubling for Wyndham Manor), which is attractively photographed by Ken Hodges, while the supporting cast is not to be sniffed at, among them Rachel Roberts as the landlady of the mysterious manor, and Vera Miles as film star Andrea Glenn, whose life its transpires is in peril from her husband, who hopes to gain control of her wealth (which he does by masquerading as a crippled old woman who tries to coerce her into killing herself!). If the film has the look and feel of an episode of ITC's *The Saint* (1962–1969, TV), it's perhaps because it was intended as the launch for a series which didn't happen (hence the setup for the next case at the end), which is a shame, as Nimoy and Hampshire make for a reasonably attractive team, even if he doesn't exactly convince as a top rank racing driver (the opening scenes on the racetrack, clearly filmed in the UK, feature some hilarious back projection shots).

Comedy was more to the fore with *Poor Devil* (1973, TVM), which aired on 14 February 1973. In it, song and dance man Sammy Davis, Jr., plays Sammy, a hapless resident of hell who is given a chance to redeem himself if he can secure the soul of a bungling department store accountant (Jack Klugman) for his master the Devil (Christopher Lee). Poorly conceived from the outset, the movie, which was made at Paramount, was intended as a pilot for a series which didn't happen, and with good reason, given the poor script by Earl Barret, Arne Sultan and Richard Baer (from a story by Barret and Sultan, who also executive produced) and the lackluster handling by director Robert Scheerer, which tends to leave the cast high and dry, among them guest stars Adam West and Gino Conforti. A snazzy score by Morton Stevens aside, this really is a devil to get through. Note that in a sign of the times, at one point, Adam West's character goes to a police station to report a robbery at the department store which he manages, to which end he tries to push in front of a woman who herself is in the middle of reporting a crime. "I was assaulted by a man in the park tonight," she informs the officer at the desk, to which comes West's response, "Congratulations." If that weren't bad enough, when told by the officer that she should not worry and that they will find the man responsible, she replies, "I hope so. I'd like to see him again."

Much better on all fronts was *The Norliss Tapes* (1973, TVM), which aired on 21 February 1973, and which found its producer-director Dan Curtis (working via Dan Curtis Productions) on top form, aided and abetted by a fast-moving script by William F. Nolan (originally titled *Demon*), itself based upon a story by Fred Mustard

Stewart. This follows the attempts by publisher Sanford T. Evans (Don Porter) to track down one of his authors, David Norliss (Roy Thinnes), who seems to have gone off the rails and done a bunk while working on a book exposing the supernatural, in which he intends to "go after the fake mediums, phony astrologers, the self-proclaimed seers and trick mystics." However, during his research, he finds his attitudes changing as he becomes increasingly involved in a case revolving round Ellen Sterns Cort (Angie Dickinson), the widow of an acclaimed sculptor who has apparently returned from the dead and is running amok around Carmel, draining the blood from his hapless victims, the details of which Norliss records on a number of cassette tapes, which Evans discovers when he calls by the author's deserted apartment. The publisher thus sits down and begins to listen to the incredible story, which we subsequently follow in flashback as Norliss and Cort's wife attempt to track down her late husband, who it transpires was involved with the occult, and foil his plan to make a sculpture of the demon Sargoth from clay and blood which, when brought to life, will grant him eternal life, to whit they must remove from the sculptor's finger the ring of Osiris, which is capable of granting restorative powers to its wearer.

An immediately involving collection of mysterious events and supernatural incidents, told with flair and economy within the framework of an investigation, itself relayed in flashback, this is a cleverly structured piece whose narrative flits about with speed and dexterity, punctuated with effective shock moments as the sculptor makes a number of surprise appearances, among them an attack on Norliss and Ellen and they search his studio, and his murder of Ellen's sister Marsha (Michelle Carey) at a nearby motel, where she discovers him lurking outside her window, through which he crashes to grab her (as she pulls back the drape, sensing that someone is there, she sees his grey face and yellow eyes staring back at her in what has to be one of TV's great shock cuts, though fans of Curtis may recall he pulled something similar in *Night of Dark Shadows* [1971]). Featuring everything grist to its mill, including thunderstorms, secret passages, crypts and a climactic conflagration, Curtis and his cinematographer Ben Colman ramp up the atmosphere by every means at their disposal, while the location work in Carmel and its environs, among them a couple of eye-catching aerial shots of the famed Seventeen Mile Drive, adds a welcome touch of scope to the story (commented *Variety* of the film, "The basic thrust, to scare, is what counts, and there Nolan, Curtis, Thinnes and company succeed," while *The Hollywood Reporter* described it as "a lot of fun, with a new twist on the old vampire story"). A creepy score by Curtis regular Bob Cobert also does its job effectively (note those trademark descending flutes, a holdover from his days on *Dark Shadows* [1966–1971, TV]).

As Norliss, Thinnes makes for a somewhat dour hero, but Dickinson is a more than attractive damsel in distress, screaming her lungs out with gusto on more than one occasion, while bit player and stuntman Nick Dimitri grabs his moment in the limelight, enthusiastically tearing up the scenery as the dead sculptor, whose final resting place, it should be noted, has a convenient sliding lid for easy escape into the night (his scariest moments are reprised during the end credits, just in case you were hiding behind the sofa). A good supporting cast also lends the proceedings a touch of class, among them Don Porter as Norliss' concerned publisher, Hurd Hatfield as a sniffy antiques dealer, keen on acquiring the ring of Osiris for himself, Claude Akins as the town's inevitably dubious sheriff, and Vonetta McGee as the mysterious Madame Jeckiel, who was responsible for introducing the sculptor to the occult and for giving him the ring. Sadly, despite its undoubted qualities, the movie failed to launch a series as intended, and the story ends with Evans still pondering the whereabouts of Norliss, who has already disappeared onto his next investigation. Nevertheless, it has since taken on cult status, and remains a highly enjoyable piece of genre entertainment which, despite the constraints of its budget, is told with efficiency and imagination.

One of the genre's best-known stories was again before the cameras in a new version of *Dr. Jekyll and Mr. Hyde* (1973, TVM), which aired on 7 March 1973. However, some bright spark had the idea of presenting the piece as a musical, with songs by none other than Lionel Bart, whose back catalogue included such hit shows as *Fings Ain't Wot They Used T'be* (1959), *Oliver!* (1960 [film 1968]), *Blitz!* (1962) and *Maggie May* (1964). Shot in England at Shepperton Studios on both videotape (interiors) and film (exteriors), the movie was written by Sherman Yellen and directed by David Winters (who turns out to have been the perhaps not so bright spark who conceived the idea). Winters, who also executive produced with Burt Rosen, had been responsible for a number of gaudy musical specials in the late sixties and early seventies, among them *Ann-Margret: From Hollywood with Love* (1969, TV), *Raquel* (1970, TV) and *The Special London Bridge Special* (1972, TV), the latter of which had guest starred Kirk Douglas, whom he somehow coerced into taking on the roles of Dr. Jekyll and his alter ego Mr. Hyde, despite the fact that the star, who'd famously played Vincent Van Gogh in *Lust for Life* (1956), proved to have the artist's ear for music (Douglas's production company, Bryna, was also involved in the making of the movie). A sturdy cast of British actors was subsequently assembled for the occasion, among them Stanley Holloway as Jekyll's loyal butler Poole, Susan Hampshire as Isabel, the young lady Jekyll is courting, Michael Redgrave as Isabel's father General Danvers, Susan George as Anne, the bar singer with whom Hyde becomes involved, and Donald Pleasence as the pickpocket Fred Smudge, whom Hyde uses to help him with his various schemes.

In this version, the good doctor is a Canadian neurologist living in London, where he is working on a drug to help the inmates of the local asylum, upon whom he wishes to try out his curative solution. "All they lack is the chemical balance that keeps the mind sane," he informs the institution's skeptical

Not dead yet. Nick Dimitri in a disturbing moment from *The Norliss Tapes* (1973, TVM) (NBC/ Dan Curtis Productions/Metromedia Producers Corporation).

governor, Mr. Hastings (Nicholas Smith). However, when permission is denied, Jekyll takes the potion himself, with the by now expected results, albeit this time accompanied by some indifferent songs, among them "Rules Were Made to Be Broken," "I Bought a Bicycle," "Our Time Together," "Two Fine Ladies" and "There Once Was a Lass Named Annie," none of which were destined to become standards, despite being pleasantly enough orchestrated by Irwin Kostal (note that Bart's work was bolstered by addi-

Name that tune. Kirk Douglas and Susan Hampshire are directed by David Winers (right) in a scene from the musical version of *Dr. Jekyll and Mr. Hyde* (1973, TVM) (NBC/Timex/Winters-Rosen Productions/Bryna).

tional music and lyrics by Mel Mandel and Norman Sacks, the latter billed as Sachs). Unfortunately, despite contributions from such established behind-the-scenes talent as Dick Bush (photography), Emma Porteous (costumes), Jack Shampan (art direction) and Eleanor Fazan (choreography), the film is a somewhat lackluster affair, despite Douglas's vigor during his scenes as Hyde, for which he sports a reasonable lip curling make-up care of Neville Smallwood. Otherwise, this is very much a curiosity piece. Not a *complete* car crash perhaps, but certainly a very nasty accident.

The True Story

Despite this misstep, 1973 proved to be a landmark year for NBC, given that it aired its most expensive and elaborate genre production yet, the two-part epic *Frankenstein: The True Story* (1973, TVM), which went out on 28 and 30 November 1973, with each installment filling a two-hour timeslot (though it will be recalled that it was beaten to the airwaves by Dan Curtis's videotaped two-parter of the same story earlier in the year over on ABC). The film was clearly intended as a prestige production, given that its teleplay was by the literary giant Christopher Isherwood and his partner Don Bachardy, while direction was in the hands of TV veteran turned movie director Jack Smight, whose small screen genre credits already included episodes of *The Twilight Zone* (1959–1964, TV) and *The Alfred Hitchcock Hour* (1962–1965, TV), and such one-offs as *The Screaming Woman* (1972, TVM).

Although it offers a fuller version of Mary Shelley's novel, the script is not without its own inventions, among them the character of the villainous Dr. Polidori (James Mason), presumably a stand in for Dr. Pretorious from *Bride of Frankenstein* (1935), but who in fact was based on a real life character, John William Polidori, a writer who not only knew Mary Shelley but was also the physician to Lord Byron, who seemingly nicknamed him Pollydolly, by which name the character is mock-ingly referred to in the film. In it, the young Dr. Victor Frankenstein (Leonard Whit-ing), grieving over the death of his younger brother William in a drowning accident, is spurred to expand his knowledge of medicine, no matter how unorthodox the means. "Why can't I raise life out of death? Out of my brother's corpse?" he asks his fiancée Elizabeth (Nicola Pagett). "That's how Satan tempted our Lord," she chides him, to which he replies, "If Satan could teach me how to make William alive again I'd gladly become his pupil."

Soon after, Frankenstein meets a fellow physician, Henri Clerval (David McCal-lum), whose interests mirror his own. In fact, Clerval has already been successfully experimenting with brining insects back to life, and with Frankenstein's assistance hopes to realize his plans for a much larger experiment, and following an accident at a nearby quarry which sees seven young men killed, they have the materials with which to build a man from scratch. However, when Clerval succumbs to the illness from which he has long been suffering, Frankenstein has no qualms about remov-ing his colleague's brain and making use of it ("No longer will our Adam have the brain of a peasant"). Then, using the rays of the sun to power the equipment Clerval has built, he successfully brings their creation to life. Yet unlike all previous screen versions of the story, in this instance the Creature (Michael Sarrazin) turns out to be a model of perfection. "You are beautiful," he informs the young man after he has emerged from his bandages. Inevitably, though, the beauty soon starts to corrupt around the edges, and upon seeing its true form, the Creature, after unsuccessfully trying to stab itself to death, jumps from a cliff into the sea below.

But it seems that the Creature is impervious to all attempts to do away with itself, and discovering itself still alive, finds momentary solace in the company of a blind hermit (Ralph Richardson). But things end in tragedy with the death of the hermit's daughter Agatha (Jane Seymour), whom the Creature now takes to Clerval's rival Dr. Polidori, whose secrets he stole, in the hope that he will restore her to life ("What poetic justice," preens Polidori on hearing the Creature speak with Clerval's voice while under hypnosis: "You stole my secrets, and now Frankenstein has stolen your brain"). Securing the services of Frankenstein to help him resurrect Agatha, whom he names Prima, Polidori insinuates the girl into the home of Frankenstein's fam-ily while Victor is away on honeymoon with Elizabeth, mesmerizing his adoptive mother into taking her in, his plan being to introduce her to society and marry her off to a wealthy suitor, whose money and power he intends to use for his own nefari-ous means ("Long live Polidori the invisible. May his plots thicken," toasts Victor at the ball). But the Creature has other ideas and gatecrashes the ball, and in the ensur-ing mêlée pulls Prima's head from her body in front of the shocked gathering. Deter-mined to get away from England and have their baby in America, the now pregnant Elizabeth urges her husband to sail there, but unbeknownst to them, both Polidori and the Creature are also onboard. Things finally reach a conclusion when the Crea-ture kills Polidori by hauling him into the rigging during a lightning storm and strangles Elizabeth, by which time the crew have abandoned the ship, and the Crea-ture has steered the vessel due north into the uncharted wastes of the Arctic, where he and Frankenstein finally meet their doom together under a collapsing iceberg.

Epic in both length and scope, one has to admire the respect with which all concerned handle the material here, the aim clearly being to recognize Shelley's work as the literary masterpiece it is, rather than the ghoulish horror comic it had become via its various big screen incarnations care of Universal, Hammer and others ("As the true Frankenstein story unravels—you're in for a shock!" ran the newspaper ads). Indeed, the saga, which was filmed at Pinewood Studios in England, is presented in almost Dickensian terms, with the various characters peopled by a roster of guest stars from the cream of British film and theatre, among them Michael Wilding as Frankenstein's adoptive father Sir Richard Fanschawe, John Gielgud as the Chief Constable investigating Prima's murder, Tom Baker as the Captain of the boat in which Frankenstein and Elizabeth make their failed escape to America, and Margaret Leighton as the ageing society heiress Francois DuVal, with further support provided by the likes of Agnes Moorehead, Clarissa Kaye (James Mason's wife), Peter Sallis, Yootha Joyce and Julian Barnes. Some of the UK's top technicians were also involved in the elaborate production, among them cinematographer Arthur Ibbetson, production designer Wilfrid Shingleton, editor Richard Marden and effects supervisor Roy Whybrow (whose team provides a highly convincing ambulatory severed arm), and if Jack Smight's direction isn't as visually sprightly as it might have been, one can't argue that producer Hunt Stromberg, Jr., was parsimonious with the finances.

For viewers expecting the usual simplified run through Shelley's otherwise complex narrative, the fact that the Creature begins its life as a thing of beauty, as opposed to the monster they had become used to, might well have appeared audacious, and in this respect Michael Sarrazin certainly fits the bill as the undeniably handsome result of Victor's experiment, giving a performance that is at times genuinely touching, and if there appears to be a homoerotic subtext in the relationship between creator and created, then Isherwood and Bachardy spell it out at one point by having Polidori observe of Frankenstein, "You loved your Creature so long as it was pretty, but when it lost its looks, hah, it was another matter." Indeed, the Creature's decaying features, created by an uncredited Roy Ashton, all but resemble the portrait in *The Picture of Dorian Gray*, which reflected the true appearance of its increasingly corrupt subject. Meanwhile, as both Agnes and Prima, Jane Seymour brings a welcome touch of elegance to the proceedings, and as Prima even gets to show off her dancing skills at the ball, in which she enchants the guests with a solo turn. She also manages to reveal her character's more sinister side when privately mocking Elizabeth, who at one point discovers her trying to strangle the family's pet cat. As Elizabeth, Nicola Pagett makes for a steely bride, providing strong support to Leonard Whiting's easily swayed Frankenstein, though the star turn is undeniably provided by James Mason as the devious Polidori, whose permanently gloved hands are revealed to be a stub and a withered claw. Reveling in the role, he clearly relishes delivering such lines as "Come on, I've no use for delicacy—particularly in monsters." However, not everyone was fond of the finished result. Carped the *Daily Express* when the film was shown in the UK: "I'd sooner see Boris Karloff with a bolt in his neck any day." There's just no pleasing some people.

Note that the film was released theatrically in some territories in an abridged

123-minute cut, while the original TV broadcast featured a
brief prologue in which Mason
visits Mary Shelley's grave
in a churchyard in St. John's
Wood (which is actually a
fake, given that her real grave
is in Dorset). The teleplay by
Isherwood and Bachardy was
subsequently novelized and
published by Avon and reveals
an unfilmed prologue akin to
Bride of Frankenstein (1935),
in which Mary Shelley starts
to tell her story to a gathering that includes her husband
Percy Shelley, Lord Byron and
John Polidori, and an epilogue

Head shot. From left to right, Dr. Polidori (James Mason)
looks on in disbelief as the Creature (Michael Sarrazin)
removes the head of Prima (Jane Seymour) in a surprisingly graphic scene from *Frankenstein: The True Story*
(1973, TVM) (NBC/MCA/Universal Television).

in which the Creature's body eventually thaws from the ice and stirs back to life in the
rays of the sun....

That old horror staple, the haunted house, was meanwhile the focus of *The
Strange and Deadly Occurrence* (1974, TVM), which aired on 24 September 1974.
In it, a tax lawyer (Robert Stack), his wife (Vera Miles) and daughter (Margaret
Willock) move into their dream home in the countryside, only to find themselves
disturbed by a number of unexplained events: the lights go out, the mother gets
locked in the sauna, the daughter is threatened by a sewing mannequin which moves
across her bedroom, and strange banging noises emanate from the walls. But all is
not quite what it seems, as it turns out that $700,000 is buried on the property from a
robbery that took place some years earlier, and someone is out to scare the family off
so that they can retrieve it. By this time, though, the film has delivered a few minor
scares, ably enough staged by director John Llewellyn Moxey, who was something
of an old hand at this kind of stuff by now. Otherwise, it's certainly nothing special,
and Sandor Stern's teleplay (based upon a story by himself and Lane Slate) is pretty
much by the numbers (viewers may well feel cheated by the explanation offered),
while the production values are down the line standard for the period.

Another borderline case clearly veering towards science fiction was *The Disappearance of Flight 412* (1974, TVM), which aired on 1 October 1974. In it, two fighter
jets disappear during a radar test, yet despite appearances that a UFO may somehow be involved, the air force proves keen to hush up the incident. Told in the style
of a docudrama, the story adds up to very little, though one can't deny that director Jud Taylor and his cast, among them Glenn Ford, Bradford Dillman and Kent
Smith, take things commendably seriously ("My men told their story as straight as
they could, based on what they saw," argues Ford's Colonel Pete Moore during the
subsequent investigation, to which comes the response "Or *thought* they saw"). Likewise, *Where Have All the People Gone* (1974, TVM [the onscreen title for which does

not carry a question mark]) was more sci-fi than full out horror, but is worth recalling in passing, given the horrific nature of its central premise, which sees a family returning from a mountain vacation only to discover that most of the population has been wiped out by a deadly virus, the result of solar radiation ("You can drive for miles, even in the city, and not find anybody," a fellow survivor informs them). With the victims disintegrating to dust, and animals turning on them, the film has an uncomfortable post-apocalyptic air to it thanks to the staging by director John Llewellyn Moxey, who uses the dusty back roads of the Santa Monica Mountains and its environs to eerie effect. Written by Lewis John Carlino and Sandor Stern, the film, which aired on 8 October 1974, was produced by Gerald I. Isenberg, and starred Peter Graves, Kathleen Quinlan and George O'Hanlon, Jr., as the hapless Anders family.

Horror of a more traditional style was to the fore in *The Dead Don't Die* (1975, TVM), in which an innocent man named Ralph Drake (Jerry Douglas) is sent to the chair for a murder he did not commit, just prior to which he encourages his brother Don (George Hamilton) to track down the real killer and clear his name. Set in 1934 and given the look and atmosphere of a gangster movie of the period, the film follows Don's attempts to get to the bottom of what really happened. However, when his dead brother turns up on the scene in Chicago, things take a decidedly sinister turn, especially after Don accidentally kills an antique shop proprietor (Reggie Nalder) during his investigations, only to have the corpse later attack him in a funeral home. Don is helped in his quest to clear his brother by a mysterious woman named Vera LaValle (Linda Cristal) and Jim Moss (Ray Milland), the owner of a rundown dance hall, in one of whose dance competitions Ralph had been taking part. But it seems that Moss is not content in reducing his contestants to shuffling zombies during his 20-day endurance marathons but has also been going the whole hog by actually raising the deceased via West Indian voodoo rituals, his plan being to take over the world with an army of the dead. "Each one has a key role in business, law enforcement, finance and government, and with them I can control the city and then the state," he informs Don (commented the film's tag line, "One man alone—against an army of the living dead! Can he stop the zombie-master who raises people from the grave to work his will?"). However, Moss eventually gets his comeuppance when he is killed by Ralph, who hangs him on a meat hook in a cold storage unit, where he has been keeping a number of corpses in readiness for the launch of his scheme.

Although written by genre favorite Robert Bloch and directed with reasonable flair by Curtis Harrington, the film's downfall is not so much its ludicrous plot, but its lack of pace. That said, the proceedings nevertheless contain several memorable sequences, among them the grim rituals surrounding Ralph's execution, a scene set during the concluding hours of a tortuous dance marathon (clearly inspired by similar scenes in *They Shoot Horses, Don't They?* [1969]), the moment the antiques dealer revives in his coffin and attempts to strangle Don (which is given additional impact thanks to the sepulchral appearance of Reggie Nalder), a sequence in which Vera goes up in flames, leaving behind a burning hand (a zombie herself, she goes up in smoke when Moss burns an effigy of her, having discovered that she has been blabbing to Don), and a graveyard scene in which Don digs down to his brother's coffin, only to discover it empty upon opening it. The film's atmosphere is also unde-niably authentic, thanks to the work of art director Robert Kinoshita and the use of some choice period vehicles (even the film's credits have a thirties air to them), while George Hamilton certainly looks the part as the crusading brother. The cast also benefits from appearances by a handful of names familiar from thirties movies (in addition to Milland, the film also features cameos from Joan Blondell and Wil-liam Benedict). However, despite its undeniable plusses, the film, which was broad-cast on 14 January 1975, doesn't quite achieve classic status, though it certainly earns top marks for effort, and for bringing zombies to the small screen, albeit as pawns in a plot that takes some swallowing, even for a low-budget TV movie.

As has been noted, TV had already tried its hand with some success at the sub-ject of invisibility in the fifties with the series *The Invisible Man* (1958–1960, TV). The seventies brought a new take on the H.G. Wells story with *The Invisible Man* (1975, TVM), in which writer-producer Steven Bochco, working from a story by him-self and Harve Bennett, updated the formula for more modern times. In it, David McCallum stars as Dr. Daniel Westin, whose experiments for the KLAE Corpora-tion see him discover the knack of turning objects invisible. Fearing that his find-ings will fall into the wrong hands, or be used for military purposes, he destroys his notes and makes himself invisible. Sporting a lifelike mask of himself made of a spe-cially applied liquid rubber, he sets to work to find a reversal process, aided and abet-ted by his wife, Dr. Kate Westin (Melinda Fee). Directed with reasonable efficiency by Robert Michael Lewis, this is a generally light-hearted, family-oriented version of the story, its best gimmick being Westin's removal of his mask and clothes as and when the need arises. The movie aired on 6 May 1975 and proved popular enough for Bochco and Bennett to develop it into a series, with Westin and his wife hiring themselves out as agents by way of funding his further research. The program, which began airing on 8 September 1975, contained reasonably good effects care of Johnny Borgese, yet lasted only 12 episodes, concluding on 26 January 1976 with an install-ment titled *An Attempt to Save Face*.

By way of saving face themselves, NBC subsequently reworked the show and launched it with its own feature-length pilot *Gemini Man* (1976, TVM), which aired on 10 May 1976, with the affable Ben Murphy now starring as Sam Casey, a navy diver who finds himself rendered invisible following an explosion while trying to retrieve an atomic powered laser disguised as a Russian satellite which has crashed into the ocean. Thanks to a special stabilizing device in the form of a million-dollar wristwatch, he is returned to normality, but by switching it off can become invisi-ble again for up to 15 minutes a day, thus allowing him to be used for special assign-ments; however, if he exceeds this timeslot, he will become invisible permanently. The pilot was written and produced by Leslie Stevens (who had penned three epi-sodes of *The Invisible Man*), directed by Alan J. Levi (who had himself helmed six), and executive produced by Harve Bennett via Harve Bennett Productions. The sub-sequent 11-part series, which was created by Stevens, Bennett and Bochco, began its run 23 September 1976 and, like the pilot, also co-starred Katherine Crawford and William Sylvester ("Forget bionics—no power matches the super-power to disap-pear!" ran the copy accompanying an ad for the show). Stunts and cheap effects were now to the fore, providing easy escapist fare aimed at younger audiences, with the best episode, *Minotaur* (1976, TV), involving a malevolent robot capable of destroying whole buildings with its laser gun (a TV movie titled *Riding with Death* [1976, TVM] was compiled from several episodes of the show).

Science fiction was more the focus again in *The UFO Incident* (1975, TVM), which aired on 20 October 1975. In it, James Earl Jones and Estelle Parsons star as Barney and Betty Hill who, while undergoing hypnosis, recall a half remembered encounter with aliens on a lonely road in the White Mountains of New Hampshire back in 1961 ("I saw the thing, I knew I saw the thing, but if my best friend told me he'd seen it I'd say he was crazy," argues the husband as they attempt to rediscover the site of their abduction). Unfortunately, although performed with reasonable conviction by its two leads, the film (based on an actual case history, via the 1966 book *The Interrupted Journey* by John G. Fuller, under which title the movie is also known) is a rather protracted and talkative affair, though the sequence in which the aliens examine the wife proves to be mildly unsettling.

The Bermuda Triangle, which had already been featured in ABC's *Satan's Triangle* (1975, TVM) earlier in the year, returned to the airwaves again on NBC on 6 November 1975 with *Beyond the Bermuda Triangle* (1975, TVM), albeit to somewhat lesser effect. This time, it's retired businessman Harry Ballinger (Fred MacMurray), whose company builds radars, who becomes involved in the search for a number of people who have gone missing in both boats and planes. Convinced that there is some sort of portal through which the craft are passing, he sets out to discover what has been happening in the notorious stretch of water, only to disappear himself, leaving behind his empty ship for the coastguard to discover. Sadly, a potentially intriguing situation is here sunk by an overabundance of soap opera situations on dry land featuring the likes of Sam Groom and TV movie staple Donna Mills, all of which are perfunctorily handled by director William A. Graham, who is somewhat stymied by Charles A. McDaniel's waterlogged script, which provides few noticeable thrills. Despite being shot on location in sunny Fort Lauderdale, this is a disappointingly dull affair care of Hugh Hefner's Playboy Productions, which would go on to make the previously mentioned *The Death of Ocean View Park* (1979, TVM).

Also lacking the necessary sting was *The Savage Bees* (1976, TVM), which aired on 22 November 1976. Written by Guerdon Trueblood and directed by Bruce Geller for Alan Landsburg Productions, the film sees a swarm of African killer bees on the loose during the Mardi Gras celebrations in New Orleans. Starring Ben Johnson as a local sheriff who is alerted to the impending situation when his dog is stung to death, the film also features Michael Parks, Gretchen Corbett and Horst Buchholz as a bee expert brought in to help resolve matters. Unfortunately, the narrative coasts along without generating too much excitement for most of its length, while the somewhat improbable ending sees the swarm attach itself to a bright red Volkswagen beetle which is then driven through the city to the Super Dome where the temperature is brought down low enough so as to kill off the bees (and naturally enough, the car breaks down on the way and has to be nudged to its destination by a police car). Amazingly, the movie was released theatrically in some territories, presumably to cash in on the impending arrival of *The Swarm* (1978), for which it carried the tag line, "They're coming this way … not to make honey, but to kill." Even more amazingly, it was followed by a sequel, *Terror Out of the Sky* (1978, TVM).

It was to *Beauty and the Beast* (1976, TVM), the perennial fairy tale by Jean-Marie Leprince de Beaumont, that NBC next turned its attention. For this new version, which was made via Palm Films, producer Hank Moonjean managed to secure the talents of the Oscar winning movie star George C. Scott to top line as the Beast, a cursed king who forces a merchant (Bernard Lee) who has stolen from him to make his daughter Belle (Trish Van Devere) come and live with him in his crumbling castle, by means of saving her father's life. Abhorred at first by his appearance, Belle gradually falls in love with the Beast ("I have come to care for you more than I have ever cared for any man," she tells him) and finally agrees to marry him, following which the curse is lifted from him and he transforms back to his former self.

Unfortunately, as written by Sherman Yellen, this is a somewhat twee adaptation of the story, with both Scott and his real-life wife Trish Van Devere, who plays Belle, clearly too old for their roles. Unadventurous direction by Fielder Cook, with whom Scott had previously worked on the fantasy *Mirror, Mirror Off the Wall* (1969, TVM), doesn't help matters, while the supporting cast, among them Virginia McKenna, Patricia Quinn and William Relton, are left to make bricks without straw. On the plus side, the film benefits from being shot on location in England (at Knebworth House, Salisbury Hall and Sudeley Castle), though like Fielder Cook's direction, the photography of Jack Hildyard and Paul Beeson is nothing special, save for a couple of aerial shots. A reasonably lush score by Ron Goodwin is, however, a bonus, while Scott's make-up, with its boar-like snout and teeth, is well enough executed by Del Acevedo and an uncredited John Chambers and Daniel C. Striepeke, who earned an Emmy nomination for their efforts, as did Scott for best actor and Albert Wolsky for the costumes (note that Chambers, best known for his Oscar winning make-up for *Planet of the Apes* [1968], used a similar make-up for one of the creatures in *The Island of Dr. Moreau* [1977]). Broadcast on 3 December 1976, the film has since been eclipsed by the 1991 Disney cartoon version and its 2017 live action remake, but remains a perfectly passable if unambitious rendering of the tale.

The public's fascination with such mythical creatures as Bigfoot and the Yeti continued with *Snowbeast* (1977, TVM), which aired on 28 April 1977. In it, a Colorado ski resort is menaced by a murderous creature with a penchant for killing tourists ("It's half-human. It's half-animal…. It's a cold-blooded killer!" ran the tag line). The story quickly resolves itself into a variation on *Jaws* (1975), with the resort's owner, Carrie Rill (Sylvia Sidney), insisting on keeping the place open so as to benefit from its 50th winter carnival, much to the chagrin of her grandson Tony (Robert Logan). "This wasn't an animal, and it wasn't human either," he informs her, following which he persuades his buddy Gar (Bo Svenson), a former Olympic ski champion, to help him track down the beast and destroy it.

Although featuring a reasonably strong cast (among them Yvette Mimieux and Clint Walker), this is an indifferently performed movie, in which the actors barely go through the motions, though given some of the dialogue provided by Joseph Stefano, one can't quite blame them ("He thinks because he's my grandson he can treat me as if I were his grandmother," comments Carrie at one point). That said, the attack scenes are handled reasonably well by director Herb Wallerstein (lots of subjective camera work, a handful of quick cutaways to the beast in question [played by Michael J. London], and several fades to red), though the film's chief asset proves to be is its snowy locale, which is captured to good effect by cinematographer Frank Stanley and his second unit cameraman Paul G. Ryan, who make the most of the glistening slopes during the ski and snowmobile sequences (the film was shot entirely on location at the Crested Butte Ski Resort in Colorado).

Evil powers meanwhile made themselves felt in *The Spell* (1977, TVM), which aired on 20 February 1977. In it, Rita (Susan Myers), an overweight schoolgirl bullied by her classmates, becomes possessed by supernatural forces, which she uses to avenge herself, much to the concern of her parents, played by Lee Grant and James Olson. However, it turns out that her mother has a few tricks up her own sleeve for dealing with her errant child. Unfortunately, despite its potential, the overall results (which also feature Helen Hunt and Lelia Goldoni) are somewhat tedious, and Lee Philips' dull script, which borrows liberally from *Carrie* (1976), is given little visual assistance by director Brian Taggert, though Gerald Fried's creepy score, which features synths and chanting, is certainly an asset. Its few highlights include a scene in which the skin of one unfortunate victim begins to smoke and smolder, and the climactic duel of wills between Rita and her mother, from whom it transpires she has inherited her power ("Where do you think you got it?" mamma asks her incredulous daughter after she has been thrown across the kitchen by a simple movement of the head from her mother).

Another form of possession was featured in *The Strange Possession of Mrs. Oliver* (1977, TVM), which aired on 28 February 1978. In it, Karen Black stars as staid housewife Miriam Oliver (26 but looking 40), who has been suffering from a series of nightmares in which she attends her own funeral. She also has a number of flashbacks in which fire and gasoline are a feature. Wanting more out of life than her dull existence, she is compelled to make herself over while out shopping (a body hugging red blouse, earrings and a blonde wig) and gradually takes on the personality of the more with-it Sandy, much to the chagrin of her businessman husband (George Hamilton), who is less than pleased with her new get-up ("What on earth?" he exclaims when he sees her all dolled up at home for the first time). However, when people start to recognize her as Sandy, Miriam begins to wonder if her alter ego had previously existed somehow, and so sets out to investigate matters, eventually discovering that Sandy *did* exist and disappeared five years earlier in order to break

Snow patrol. Michael J. London makes an appearance as the *Snowbeast* (1977, TVM) (NBC/Douglas Cramer Productions).

free from her brutal boyfriend Mark (Robert F. Lyons), taking on the persona of her close friend Miriam (Sunny Woods), who died in a car explosion after Mark tracks the girls down to where they are living, setting their car alight with gasoline ("She wanted to be someone else. But when she became Sandy her new friends wanted her dead!" ran the tagline).

As written by Richard Matheson (who also worked as the film's associate producer), this is an increasingly convoluted affair whose resolution takes some swallowing, but the ethereal atmosphere sustained by director Gordon Hessler and his photographer Frank Stanley, along with Black's performance as the progressively confused Miriam, make for a reasonably intriguing journey, even if the ultimate destination proves to be a twist too far. Inevitably, there are clues peppered along the way ("Are you telling me you're not yourself? Who are you then?" asks her husband at one point), but there are just too many coincidences and happenstances for comfort in order to make the overly contrived plot work. "I'm not Miriam. I'm not. Miriam was my best friend. I'm Sandy. Miriam died because of me, and I wanted so much for her to live again and I became her. But now I can let her go. I'm not Miriam, I'm Sandy. Now I know who I am, I know who I am," she explains to her husband when he turns up to rescue her after she has gone missing, and kudos to George Hamilton for keeping a straight face during this incredible piece of exposition which could well have been lifted straight out of a forties melodrama.

Having already given us three stories for the price of one with *Trilogy of Terror* (1975, TVM), producer-director Dan Curtis repeated the trick with *Dead of Night* (1977, TVM), which purloined its title from the 1945 Ealing classic (and an earlier failed Curtis pilot). A far better prospect than *Trilogy* thanks to improved scripts, handling and production values, the stories were "one of mystery, one of imagination and one of terror," as the opening voiceover has it. First up was *Second Chance*, in which Frank (Ed Begley, Jr.), a college senior who is also a car nut, restores a derelict Jordan Playboy only to find himself transported back to 1926 when he drives it one night, during which he prevents its original owner from crashing it and killing both himself and his girlfriend, who turn out to be the grandparents of a girl at school who he starts dating, but curiously can't remember having seen before. In the second, *No Such Thing as a Vampire* (already presented as an episode of the British series *Late Night Horror* [1968, TV]), the wife of a wealthy Victorian doctor (Patrick Macnee) is convinced that she is being attacked by a vampire each

Dead ringer. Karen Black is featured in this promotional artwork for *The Strange Possession of Mrs. Oliver* (1978, TVM) (NBC/The Shpetner Company).

night, but it proves to be an elaborate plot hatched by the good doctor to do away with her secret lover (Horst Buchholz), which he does by drugging him and placing him in a coffin with blood on his lips, which is enough to convince his loyal servant (Elisha Cook, Jr.) to stake him through the heart. Finally, in the third story, *Bobby*, a grieving mother (Joan Hackett) whose son (Lee Montgomery) has drowned contrives to bring him back from the dead via an occult ceremony, but when the child turns up during a thunderstorm, he proves to be less than angelic, and taunts her with a few home truths, among them the fact that he hated her and killed himself to get away from her ("Bobby hates you, mommy, so he sent me instead," he tells her, at which point he is revealed to be a demonic dwarf).

Intended as the launch for a TV series that didn't happen, this is nevertheless an enjoyable anthology, with punchy little scripts care of Richard Matheson which, for a change, don't dillydally about too much and get straight to the nub of each story in a brisk and efficient manner (the first episode was based upon a 1956 story by Jack Finney, the second on a 1959 story by Matheson himself, while the third was an original for television). Directed with some care by Curtis (again working through Dan Curtis Productions), the first well captures the twenties atmosphere during the time travel sequence, the second has a reasonable sense of pervading dread until the twist is revealed (keep an eye out for the old MGM back lot sets featured in some exterior shots), while the third ramps up the tension as Bobby forces his mother into playing hide and seek during a thunderstorm, during which Curtis delivers a few well timed thrills before the final revelation. Better looking than most TV movies thanks to the work of cinematographer Ric Waite, the film also benefits from solid contributions by such Curtis regulars as Bob Cobert (music), Dennis Virkler (editing), Paul Lohmann (additional photography) and Trevor Williams (art direction), while solid performances, best among them Hackett as the apparently devoted mother, help to put things across with a welcome degree of believability. Broadcast on 29 March 1977, the film deserves to be better known than it is, and certainly ranks among Curtis' better efforts of the period.

Elsewhere, in *The Possessed* (1977, TVM), which aired on 1 May 1977, the focus was an alcoholic priest (James Franciscus) who has lost his faith ("I believed in the bread and the wine"). Returned to life following an apparently fatal car accident on the understanding that he seek out evil and fight it by whatever means possible, he becomes an exorcist, and finds himself up against a demonic presence that has manifested itself in a girls' school in Salem, which is beset by a number of unexplained fires. Things come to a head when the biology teacher (Harrison Ford) goes up in flames and the headmistress (Joan Hackett) becomes possessed by a malevolent spirit, spitting out nails and red wine. In a final act of self sacrifice, the priest embraces her, goes up in flames and jumps into the school's swimming pool, igniting its entire surface in the process. However, when the conflagration dies down, the headmistress is saved, but the priest is nowhere to be seen…. In synopsis form, this all sounds very intriguing, but sadly John Secret Young's script is a particularly talkative affair, with only the scenes involving fire and possession bringing the proceedings to anything like life, despite the efforts of a cast that also includes Eugene Roche, Diana Scarwid, Ann Dusenberry, Dinah Manhoff and P.J. Soles. Flatly directed on location in Portland by TV veteran Jerry Thorpe, this could and should have been far better than it is.

It was off to Blighty again and Elstree Studios in leafy Borehamwood for another demonic encounter in *Spectre* (1977, TVM), which aired on 21 May 1977. In it, American criminologist William Sebastian (Robert Culp) flies to London to investigate a coven whose members include various members of the establishment. Unfortunately, despite the involvement of Gene Roddenberry as co-writer and producer, some top British technical talent (director Clive Donner, cinematographer Arthur Ibbetson, editor Peter Tanner) and a starry cast (among them Gig Young, Gordon Jackson, James Villiers, Jenny Runacre, Ann Bell, Majel Barrett [aka Mrs. Gene Roddenberry] and John Hurt, who turns into a somewhat unconvincing monster during the climax), the results are ineffably silly and somewhat tediously drawn out, with postcard views of London added into the mix to help justify the journey across the pond, among them the inevitable shots of Tower Bridge, Buckingham Palace, Nelson's Column and Big Ben, all conveniently passed during one improbable car journey. In fact it's only the eye-catching sets provided by art director Albert Witherick, among them Sebastian's apartment, the interior of an abbey and the subterranean lair of the worshippers (which collapses in spectacular fashion during the long-delayed climax) that prove to be memorable (note that a handful of topless shots were added to the film for its European theatrical release; a novelization by tie-in specialist Robert Weverka was published by Bantam in 1979).

A failed pilot titled *The Man with the Power* (1977, TVM) followed next on 24 May 1977. In it a schoolteacher named Eric Smith (Bob Neill) discovers that he possesses supernatural powers, which it transpires he has inherited from his father, who it is revealed was an alien from another world on a five-year mission to Earth. Mentored by agent Walter Bloom (Tim O'Connor), Eric is taught how to better use and control his telekinetic abilities, which he subsequently uses to guard and then rescue a beautiful Indian princess (Persis Khambatta) who is kidnapped during a state visit. Written by Allan Balter and directed by Nicholas Sgarro, the movie, which also features Vic Morrow and Roger Perry, is an ineffably silly affair, compromised by a lack of style and low-budget effects work, but for those with a liking for cheesy superhero flicks, it just about passes the time. Likewise, *Exo-Man* (1977, TVM), which was broadcast on 18 June 1977, offered proto super-heroics

It's not easy being green. Is that really John Hurt donning the monster suit in *Spectre* (1977, TVM)? (NBC/Twentieth Century–Fox Television/Norway Productions).

in the guise of Dr. Nicholas Conrad (David Ackroyd), who, after being paralyzed from the waist down following an attack by the mob, builds himself a creepy-looking bulletproof super suit that enables him to exact revenge. Written by Lionel E. Siegel and Henri Simoun (from a story by Simoun and Martin Caidin), and perfunctorily directed by Richard Irving (who also executive produced), the movie, which also features Kevin McCarthy, Harry Morgan and José Ferrer as crime boss Kermit Haas, takes its sweet time in getting going, yet clearly sets things up for further adventures, but like *The Man with the Power*, it failed to go to series, perhaps because it seemed somewhat anemic compared to the bionic exploits of *The Six Million Dollar Man* (1974–1978, TV), which was not only slicker and better produced, but also had better merchandising potential (note that the malfunction button inside Conrad's suit is misspelled "malfuntion").

Bringing In the Harvest

Rather more effective, if somewhat protracted, was the epic two-parter *The Dark Secret of Harvest Home* (1978, TVM), which was broadcast over two nights on 23 and 24 January 1978 as part of NBC's ongoing *Best Sellers* series, which had already seen such titles as *Captains and the Kings* (1976, TVM), *Once an Eagle* (1976, TVM) and *79 Park Avenue* (1977, TVM) adapted for the small screen in various formats. Based upon the 1973 novel *Harvest Home* by actor-turned-writer Thomas Tryon, it starred Mother Goddam herself Bette Davis as the seemingly benign Widow Fortune, the matriarch of the idyllic Connecticut township of Cornwall Coombe, to which the troubled Constantine family move from the city, having discovered the place after their car blew a tire during a drive in the countryside. Prior to their move, father Nick (David Ackroyd) had become disillusioned with his job in advertising and chucked it to become an artist, mother Beth (Joanna Miles) had been reliant on her psychiatrist as a result of her husband's drinking and philandering, while daughter Kate (Rosanna Arquette) suffered from asthma from the constant pollution. After falling in love with the place, they use money Beth has inherited following her father's death and purchase a property there, yet unlike most isolated communities, they are welcomed with open arms, and quickly find the quality of their lives improved no end thanks to the clean air and healthy country living.

Inevitably, the idyll is an illusion, with the first sign that things might not quite be what they seem occurring during the annual fair, at which a sheep is slaughtered and its blood is smeared on the face of the new Harvest Lord by one of the township's children, a perpetually scowling little girl called Missy Penrose (Tracey Gold) whom Nick, who has been somewhat disturbed by the event, describes as "a pre-pubescent pagan princess." His apparent sighting of a local ghost during a storm, and his discovery that a former Corn Maiden who subsequently went "against the ways" and was deemed responsible for a drought, might have been killed as a consequence, rouse Nick's concerns further. And with good cause, for when Worthy Pettinger (Michael O'Keefe), the reluctant Harvest Lord who has been harboring plans to leave the township curses the corn and the Widow, the townsfolk start to display their true colors. In fact, Nick's investigations reveal that not only had the former Corn Maiden been murdered, but that the local peddler (Rene Auberjonois) has had his tongue cut out and his lips sewn together by the Widow for speaking to the State Police, that Worthy is among the scarecrows burned at the annual bonfire, and that a local named Robert Dodd (Stephen Joyce) whom Nick has befriended was blinded for trying to discover the true meaning of the community's ways. Everything comes to a climax when Nick gatecrashes the women only Harvest Home ritual presided over by the Widow, during which Beth sexually succumbs to the former Harvest Lord before he is sacrificed by her with a scythe, his blood replenishing Mother Earth for the forthcoming year. As for Nick, we finally see him back at home, blinded like his friend for having dared to see something he should not.

Divided into 11 increasingly ominous chapter headings charting the seasonal events in the life of the community (among them *Ploughing Day, Choosing the Young Lord, The Day of Seasoning, Sheaving Tide, Husking Bee, Kindling Night* and *Harvest Home*), the story moves slowly but surely to its disturbing conclusion, dropping enough dark hints and revelations along the way to make sure that our interest is constantly piqued, despite the stately pace and the elongated running time (3 hours and 48 minutes on its original broadcast, although shorter versions have since appeared, among them a 118-minute video release). Ably if plainly helmed by Leo Penn (father of Sean, Chris and Michael), and given a reasonable pictorial sheen by photographers Charles Correll, Jim Dickson and Frank V. Phillips, who well capture the verdant landscape between themselves, the film plays like an extended version of *The Wicker Man* (1973), with Nick destined from the start to come to a sticky end thanks to his compulsive curiosity.

Developed for television by James and Jennifer Miller, and written by Jack Guss and Charles E. Israel, the adaptation at times is a little too slavishly faithful to the book, yet one can't deny that all involved are determined to do the material justice, prime among them Bette Davis as the redoubtable Widow Fortune, a role she had wanted to play since having read Tryon's book. By comparison, the remainder of the cast are passable if not outstanding in their roles, while the production values are solid throughout, with notable work being done by costume designer Bill Jobe, particularly during the ritual sequences. The film has since become something of a cult item, though not everyone who saw it first time round was impressed, among them critic Judith Crist, who described it as "dreary, attenuated and tasteless." Yet there is no doubting that this was a prestige production of its day, accorded a sufficient budget by producer Jack Laird for its makers to handle it with the reverence they clearly felt it deserved (note that the voice on the records which Robert Dodd is heard listening to was provided by Donald Pleasence).

After such a high watermark, things next took something of a nosedive with *The Ghost of Flight 401* (1978, TVM), in which the ghost of a flight engineer named Dom Cimoli (Ernest Borgnine) is seen on a number of planes making use of parts salvaged from the wreckage of the aircraft on which he was onboard when it crashed. Aired on 18 February 1978, the film was penned by Robert Malcolm Young, who based his teleplay on the 1976 bestseller by John G. Fuller, which chronicled the crash of the real Eastern Airlines flight 401 in the Florida Everglades in 1972, following which a number of passengers and flight crew claimed to have experienced sightings of the plane's captain and flight engineer. Unfortunately, what could have been an unsettling depiction of alleged events is stymied by dull direction care of Steven Hilliard Stern, which generally lacks atmosphere, save for a climactic "soul rescue" in which Cimoli is sent "toward the light" during a fire lit séance. Also starring Gary Lockwood, Tina Chen and a young Kim Basinger, the movie comes across as a rather tacky exploitation of an actual tragedy, though no more controversial than the fact that parts salvaged from the real wreck were re-used on other aircraft. At least the closing narration puts our minds at rest regarding this particularly ghoulish piece of cost saving: "Salvaged parts installed in other

Widow's weeds. Bette Davis as the Widow Fortune in *The Dark Secret of Harvest Home* (1978, TVM) (NBC/Universal Television).

L-1011's were ordered removed," we are comfortingly informed of subsequent practice (note that the disaster was also the subject of a more realistic telling in *Crash* [1978, TVM, aka *The Crash of Flight 401*], which aired on ABC later the same year on 19 October, and was based upon a second book, *Crash* by Bob and Sarah Elder, which was published in 1977).

Cloning was the subject to hand in *The Clone Master* (1978, TVM), which was broadcast on 14 September 1978. In it, Art Hindle plays Dr. Simon Shane, a biochemist who produces multiple versions of himself, each of whom is able to communicate with the other telepathically. However, once the experiment is completed, he finds his life in danger from the mysterious group that backed the project ("He created life… Now his own was in danger!" ran the tag line). Written by John D.F. Black (who also produced), this was intended as a pilot for a series which, on this occasion, didn't happen, the idea being that each episode would deal with the trials and tribulations of a different clone. Unfortunately, despite the concept and the Saturday serial atmosphere, Don Medford's direction lacks sufficient zest to carry it off, save for a few fleeting moments in the doc's eye-catching high tech lab (the work of art director Daniel Lomino), though Hindle seems to be having fun during the split screen sequences in which he gets to act opposite himself several times over ("I'm Simon Shane," he says in exasperation to one of the clones at one point, to which comes the reply, "So am I. So are we all"). Also featuring Robyn Douglass, Ed Lauter and Ralph Bellamy, the film has since slipped into obscurity.

If it was arrant nonsense that audiences craved, then they certainly got it with *Kiss Meets the Phantom of the Park* (1978, TVM), which aired on 28 October 1978.

In it, "super-hero rock band Kiss battles against powerful cybernetic creatures created by a brilliant, warped inventor," as one of the newspaper ads had it. Secreted at an amusement park at which the band are set to play, the scientist, Abner Devereaux (Anthony Zerbe), plans to unleash his creations upon an unsuspecting world during a concert they are to hold there, but the band members (The Demon [Gene Simmons], Star Child [Paul Stanley], Space Ace [Ace Frehley] and Cat Man [Peter Criss]) have other ideas, and use their superpowers to thwart the professor and his androids, among them an animatronic Frankenstein Monster as well evil robot Kiss clones. Written by Jan-Michael Sherman and Don Buday, the film was directed by Gordon Hessler, who had to overcome major problems with the recalcitrant band during filming, much of which took place at the Magic Mountain theme park in California, with the budget spiraling to a reported $2 million as a consequence. Nevertheless, the results, despite being an almost incomprehensible mess, were a ratings success thanks to the popularity of the band, which was riding high at the time, since when the film has attained cult status, albeit not necessarily for the right reasons (the performances by the four singers, when not doubled by stand-ins and stuntmen, are dire). Produced by Terry Morse, Jr., for Hannah-Barbera, the whole thing might have worked better as one of the studio's semi-animated Saturday morning cartoons, given the band's heavily made-up appearance, but it's certainly worth a look for the curious, if only to see how jaw-droppingly bad it truly is (the film was released theatrically in some territories in a different edit known as *Kiss in Attack of the Phantoms*).

Also less than stellar (albeit not quite so ludicrous) was *Stranger in Our House* (1978, TVM), which was based upon the 1976 novel *Summer of Fear* by Lois Duncan (under which title the film was also released theatrically in some territories). In it, Lee Purcell plays Julia Trent, whose mother and father, as well as their young maid, have been killed in an automobile accident, as a consequence of which she is invited to live with her aunt's family in California, who she hasn't seen since she was a child. However, her cousin Rachel (Linda Blair) comes to suspect that the initially shy Julia may not be all she appears to be and is increasingly led to believe that she may in fact be a practicing witch following a series of accidents and illnesses. Having proved herself right, Rachel sets out expose Julia, who everyone has taken to their hearts, discovering along the way that the girl claiming to be her cousin is in fact the maid who supposedly died in the auto crash, and who has now assumed Julia's identity, the real Julia having died with her parents.

Despite featuring the star of *The Exorcist* (1973), Linda Blair, and being helmed by horrormeister Wes Craven, whose genre films already included *The Last House on the Left* (1972) and *The Hills Have Eyes* (1977), the film, which aired on 31 October 1978 for Halloween, is criminally dull, with little to raise one's pulse rate, save for a well staged sequence in which Julia is attacked by Rachel's beloved horse Sundance, on whom she later extracts revenge, and a dark room sequence in which Rachel discovers that Julia doesn't appear in any of the photographs that have been taken of her. A climactic car chase in which Julia, her eyes now a demonic red, tries to run Rachel and her boyfriend off the road, is rather more perfunctorily presented, ending as it does with Julia driving over a cliff and dying in the subsequent explosion when swerving to avoid Rachel's mother, who is driving from the opposite direction. As for the twist ending in which Julia turns up at another family's house, this time as governess Susan Peterson, it really does scrape the barrel. Poorly performed by all concerned, this is bland stuff by any definition.

A modern-day adaptation of H.G. Wells' *The Time Machine* (1978, TVM) followed next on 5 November 1978, which was broadcast as one of a series of films under the umbrella title *Classics Illustrated* (it was preceded by *Last of the Mohicans* [1977, TV] and *Donner Pass: The Road to Survival* [1978, TVM]). Unfortunately, this poorly conceived and executed update failed to erase memories of the classic 1960 George Pal version starring Rod Taylor as the Victorian scientist who builds a time machine that takes him into the far future where he encounters the placid Eloi peo-

House guest. Promotional ad for *Stranger in Our House* (1978, TV), emphasizing Linda Blair's connection with *The Exorcist* (1973). Also featured (bottom, with glowing eyes) is Lee Purcell (NBC/Inter Planetary/Finnegan Associates).

ple and the monstrous Morlocks. Produced by James Simmons for Sunn Classic Pictures (best known for the TV series *The Life and Times of Grizzly Adams* [1977–1978, TV]), the remake stars lantern jawed John Beck as Neil Perry, a scientist working for a space agency who builds a machine that first transports him back to Puritan times before whisking him to the distant future, where he likewise encounters the Eloi and the Morlocks. Written by Wallace C. Bennett, the film was helmed by the improbably named Henning Schellerup, a Danish director and cinematographer whose usual métier was low-budget blaxploitation and porno flicks such as *Night Pleasures* (1976) and *Three Shades of Flesh* (1976), which he directed under the pseudonym of Hans Christian. Sadly, if this was his attempt to enter the mainstream, the results are decidedly flaccid, with any potential the reimagining might have had stymied by slack pacing, bland acting and cheap effects, though the Morlocks, with their glowing eyes, may unsettle younger viewers (note that Whit Bissell, who here plays Ralph Branly, also appeared in the 1960 version as Walter Kemp; as for Schellerup, after directing a rather better version of *The Legend of Sleepy Hollow* [1980, TVM] for the *Classics Illustrated* series starring Jeff Goldblum as Ichabod Crane, he went on to work as a second unit camera operator on Wes Craven's *A Nightmare on Elm Street* [1984] and a cinematographer on *Silent Night, Deadly Night* [1984]).

Director John Carpenter, who'd recently scored a box office hit with his horror classic *Halloween* (1978), made his TV debut with the woman-in-peril thriller *Someone's Watching Me!* (1978), which was broadcast on 29 November 1978 (it was actually made just before *Halloween*). In it, Leigh Michaels (Lauren Hutton), who's moved to Los Angeles, takes up a new job as a director of live television. However, her apartment is under surveillance by a voyeur in the building opposite, who not only has access to her flat, which has been bugged, but goes on to terrorize her with anonymous phone calls. Naturally, the police prove to be of no help when she reports the matter to them, leaving it to herself, her friend Sophie (Adrienne Barbeau) and her boyfriend Paul (David Birney) to discover the identity of the culprit and bring his reign of terror to an end ("She has everything to live for, but someone wants her dead," ran the promo). Originally to have been titled *High Rise*, and filmed in just 18 days, the film, which Carpenter also scripted, recalls Hitchcock's *Rear Window* (1954), and uses a number of techniques that would become familiar in his subsequent films, prime among them the use of gliding camerawork, point of view shots and unexpected shock cuts. Executive produced by Richard Kobritz (who would go on to produce *Christine* [1983] for Carpenter), the film was made via Warner Bros. Television, and genuinely ratchets up the tension during its key sequences, best among them a brief shot in which the intruder unexpectedly crosses behind the heroine. It certainly deserves to be better known than it is (note that Carpenter and Barbeau, whom he also featured in *The Fog* [1980] and *Escape from New York* [1981], went on to marry).

Sunn Classic Pictures was back in business again with an adaptation of Poe's *The Fall of the House of Usher* (1979, TVM) starring Martin Landau as Roderick Usher, Robert Hays as Jonathan Cresswell, Charlene Tilton as his wife Jennifer, and Ray Walston as the manservant Thaddeus. Written by Stephen Lord and directed by Sunn Classic regular James L. Conway (who also produced), this is a low-budget but reasonably lively *Dark Shadows*–style rendering of the familiar tale, which benefits from some unexpectedly dexterous camerawork by Paul Hipp, several eye-catching (if somewhat cardboard-looking) sets care of designer Paul Staheli and a full-blooded score by Bob Summers. Strewn with the expected cobwebs and shadows, the film isn't without its drawbacks (notably a miscast Hays), but those who tune in to mock may well find themselves finding it a surprisingly tolerable version of the story, with Landau making a perfectly adequate Roderick Usher, while Dimitra Arliss plays it with the pedal to the floor as his unhinged, flail-wielding sister Madeline (note that the film was briefly released theatrically in 1979 before eventually being shown on TV on 25 July 1982).

NBC's final genre production of the decade proved to be *Skinflint: A Country Christmas Carol* (1979, TVM), which aired on 18 December 1979. Yet another variation on Dickens' *A Christmas Carol*, it sees Hoyt Axton's miserly Cyrus Flint visited by four ghosts on Christmas Eve who help him to mend his ways. Produced and directed by Marc Daniels from a script by Mel Mandel, this modern-day country and western version of the story takes some swallowing, and the production values of this videotaped studio production aren't exactly standout, though the supporting cast occasionally deliver the goods, among them Tom T. Hall as Jacob Marley (here Burley) and Martha Raye as the Ghost of Christmas Past. Also onboard are Barbara Mandrell, the Statler Brothers, Mel Tillis and Dottie West, which should give a good indication of where it's coming from.

America's other major TV network, CBS, also dipped its toe into the horror genre on occasion, though like NBC, its commitment was somewhat erratic, yet as we shall see, it did produce the occasional classic, one of which still stands heads and shoulders above all else made during this period. The decade began on a mild note with *Sole Survivor* (1970, TVM), the company's very first television feature, which it made via its feature film division, Cinema Center Films (aka Cinema Center 100). Set in 1960, it involves the discovery by an oil surveying flight of a wrecked World War II bomber in the Libyan desert. A mission to recover and repatriate the bodies of the crew is led by Lieutenant Colonel Josef Gronk (William Shatner) and Major Michael Devlin (Vince Edwards), who are joined by the aircraft's sole survivor, its navigator Russell Hamner (Richard Basehart), who has since become a general in the 17-year interim. However, upon reaching the wreckage, the team can find no trace of the crew, whose ghosts have been haunting it ever since, and now plot a means of revealing Hamner to be a coward who bailed his post and left his fellow airmen to overfly their airbase by some 300 miles, eventually to bail out themselves over the desert, leaving the plane to fly on further before finally crashing ("Terrible secrets never die," ran the tagline). Following a number of clues to be found in the aircraft, the recovery team eventually discover the remains of the crew some considerable distance from the plane, and as each one is found, their ghosts finally vanish, save for one who, thanks to a discovered diary, they realize followed the plane's course into the desert in the hope of retrieving food and water from the wreckage for the others, only for him to die under its tail, where he had been sheltering from the sun, and where his body is finally discovered.

The teleplay by Guerdon Trueblood, with its echoes of the *Twilight Zone* episode *King Nine Will Not Return* (1960, TV), was actually based upon a real story, the disappearance of the B-24 Lady Be Good in 1943, whose wreckage was eventually discovered in 1958 (the crew weren't found until two years later). Filmed on location in the Mojave Desert (at the El Mirage Dry Lake), the film certainly benefits from the dusty landscape, whose eerie atmosphere is well captured by photographer James Crabe and further augmented by a discordant score by Paul Glass, while the interplay between the baseball loving airmen is not without its moments of humor ("You guys look like death warmed over," quips one of them to his comrades, to which comes the reply, "I got news for you!"). Also featuring Lou Antonio, Brad David and Patrick Wayne, the film, which was produced by Wally Burr, is very ably directed by Paul Stanley, and certainly deserves to be better known than it is.

It wouldn't be until later the following year that horror reared its head again film wise, this time with *Black Noon* (1971, TVM), which aired on 5 November 1971. Set in the old west, this overstretched curio sees the Rev. John Keyes (Roy Thinnes) and his sick wife Lorna (Lynn Loring) rescued from certain death in the desert by Caleb Hobbs (Ray Milland), who takes them back to the township of San Melas, where they are welcomed with open arms, particularly after the preacher cures a crippled local boy during one of his sermons. However, over the coming weeks, the Reverend finds himself succumbing to corruption in a variety of ways, from lusting after Hobbs' mute daughter Deliverance (Yvette Mimieux) to shooting a local bad man named Moon (Henry Silva), who turns up periodically to threaten the townsfolk and take his share from the local gold mine which they work. All the while, his wife seems to get sicker and sicker. But it all proves to be a ruse to keep the Reverend in San Melas, given that the boy wasn't crippled in the first place, and the bullets in the gun he shot the bad man with were blanks. Hobbs then reveals that he and the townsfolk are in fact diabolists hailing from Salem, and wish to sacrifice the preacher during an eclipse, hanging him upside down in the church they have built for him before setting it alight.

Rather too much of a slow burner, the teleplay by Andrew J. Fenady (who also produced via Andrew J. Fenady Productions and Screen Gems Television) takes its sweet time building up to the final revelation, during which interest waxes and wanes somewhat thanks to the lackluster pacing of director Bernard Kowalski. Thinnes, it must be said, also fails to generate much sympathy as the misled preacher, yet the dusty desert setting comes across well, and the climax itself is well enough staged, featuring as it does much flash cutting care of editor Dann Cahn. Having already served its purpose, the film then goes on to add a further modern-day twist as a family, whose car has broken down in the desert, is rescued by Hobbs and Deliverance, who are alive and well and looking exactly the same. And as Hobbs drives off, towing the family's car behind him, we see the sign depicting the border of San Melas reflected back in the truck's wing mirror as Nas Salem (though it should be noted that the letters aren't properly mirrored, given that they are all the correct way around when they shouldn't be).

Next, Steven Spielberg returned to the airwaves for the first time following his triumph with *Duel* (1971, TVM), and if his follow up, *Something Evil* (1972, TVM), which was broadcast on 21 January 1972, doesn't quite match it for either pace or impact, it still presented viewers with one of the better made creepy house thrillers of the period. Written by Robert Clouse, who would soon go on to direct the martial arts blockbuster *Enter the Dragon* (1973), it stars Darren McGavin and Sandy Dennis as Paul and Marjorie Worden, who relocate to the country, in this case a farmhouse in Pennsylvania, with their young son Stevie (Johnny Whitaker) and their toddler Laurie (played by sisters Debbie and Sandy Lempert). However, it isn't long before things start to go bump in the night—or rather cry in the night, given that Marjorie is woken by the sound of a baby crying, which seems to be coming from the barn. As the incidents increase, Marjorie turns to her husband for consolation, but being a harassed advertising executive who is making the lengthy commute to New York each day to oversee a new campaign, he inevitably pooh-poohs her worries. Luckily, help is at hand in the form their kindly neighbor, Harry Lincoln (Ralph Bellamy), a cookery writer who is more inclined to believe her given that he has an interest in the Devil and his various guises, and after reading several books he has given her, Marjorie paints a pentacle on the floor of the children's playroom. "If you believe there's a Devil, and believe the Devil's in your house, then for you it's true," Harry advises her. However, when it transpires that it is Stevie her son who is the Devil in disguise, it proves to be Marjorie's love for him that finally conquers the evil spirit that has possessed him.

Filmed on location in California at Disney's Golden Oak Ranch and at Studio City in Los Angeles (for the interiors), *Something Evil* is undeniably well staged for a low-budget TV movie, and Spielberg and his cameraman Bill Butler (who would go on to work with the director on *Jaws* [1975]) are always in the right place to capture the action to best effect, be it with a close-up, a tracking shot or a crane lift. There are also moments of visual invention, among them a quickly edited mini montage in which Marjorie threads four talismans she has made in her kiln, during which the director zooms out from a tight shot of the thread going through the hole each time to a wider shot of Marjorie's face. There's also a point of view shot from a torch as Marjorie explores the barn at night. The story even has a handful of unsettling moments, among them a long shot of a local farmer named Gerhmann (Jeff Corey) waving a headless chicken in a field, the blood from which is intended to ward off evil spirits, and Marjorie's discovery of a jar in the barn which contains a pulsating red light, and from which the cries are emanating (the jar later reappears in one of her kitchen cupboards, presumably put there by her son). Unfortunately, despite these pluses, the story as a whole just isn't strong enough to sustain the movie, and despite its brief running time (73 minutes), one's interest begins to wane before the finale, during which Marjorie hugs her son within the pentacle as a mighty wind rages through the playroom, wrecking everything around them.

Performance wise, Sandy Dennis comes off best as the increasingly fraught mother, while Ralph Bellamy adds a touch of class to the proceedings as the Wordens' kindly neighbor, who himself is attacked and subsequently hospitalized by an unseen force in his own home, no doubt a result of the advice given to Marjorie. As Paul, Darren McGavin is perfectly passable in a fairly thankless role as the indifferent husband, too caught up in his work to see what is unfolding around him, while Johnny Whitaker is a little too sweet natured to convince as Marjorie's possessed son Stevie (already known for playing Jody Patterson-Davis in the long running sitcom *Family Affair* [1966–1971, TV], he would go on to be a familiar face in a number of 70s movies, among them such Disney fare as *Napoleon and Samantha* [1972], *Snowball Express* [1972] and *The Mystery in Dracula's Castle* [1973, TVM]). Otherwise, this is an initially diverting but ultimately overextended shocker which might have worked better as a half-hour episode of an anthology series (note that Spielberg and future *Jaws* screenwriter Carl Gottlieb are featured briefly as party guests).

Meanwhile, in *She Waits* (1972, TVM), which aired on 28 January 1972, a young bride named Laura Wilson (Patty Duke) joins her new husband Mark (David McCallum) on a return trip to the family mansion he has not visited for some time, having been away working as a magazine correspondent in Tokyo. Mark's ill mother (Dorothy McGuire) is convinced that the house is haunted by his first wife, Elaine, who it seems he may have killed during an argument. In the following days, Laura becomes obsessed with Elaine, hearing her voice and sensing her presence, until things reach crisis point and Laura becomes possessed by Elaine's spirit, in which guise she reveals that it was her lover, Mark's friend David (James Callahan), who actually killed her. "She can possess your body. She can do it," Mark's mother had told Laura during a prior conversation about Elaine, all of which makes the family doctor (Lew Ayres) wonder if Laura was really possessed or whether it was a form of suggestion, leaving it for viewers to make up their own minds.

As penned by Art Wallace, this is a straightforward spooky house thriller with everything grist to its mill, from billowing curtains to turning doorknobs, not to mention a music box belonging to Elaine, the mournful tune from which Laura already seems to know, given that she is able to hum along with it. Unfortunately, despite assistance from a frequently dramatic score care of Morton Stevens (complete with organ riffs), the proceedings are scuppered by particularly unimaginative handling care of veteran director Delbert Mann (an Oscar winner for *Marty* [1955]), all of which makes for heavy going viewing (commented the *LA Times*, "You wait and wait for it to take hold but to no avail"). As for the cast, which also features Beulah Bondi as a family retainer, they don't seem particularly enthused by the material, least of all a glum faced McCallum, but who can blame them given the facile dialogue they have to mouth.

A childless middle-aged couple who have moved to a remote property in the country and are yearning for company was the basis for *Crawlspace* (1972, TV), which aired on 11 February 1972. Unfortunately, they choose the wrong candidate to fill the void in their lives. Adapted by Ernest Kinoy from the 1971 novel by Herbert Lieberman and directed by John Newland (and an uncredited Buzz Kulik), it sees Albert and Alice Graves (Arthur Kennedy and Teresa Wright) take under their wing Richard Atlee (Tom Happer), the young man who delivers the oil for their furnace. Having remained late to make a repair for them, Alice asks him to stay for dinner, during which they develop a rapport with him. Some days later, Albert discovers signs that someone has been in their cellar, and it isn't long after that he discovers that Richard, who has quit his job, has been living in the crawlspace under the house. Preferring not to involve the police, they start to leave food out for him, and eventually invite him upstairs to live with them, but he insists on sleeping in the crawlspace because he feels safer there. Things take the inevitable turn for the worse when the couple trust him to go town to get the groceries for them, where he has a run in with the locals, which is enough to send him over the edge, resulting in the trashing of the grocery store, whose surly clerk (Matthew Cowles) had refused to serve him. With Alice now growing wary of the boy, the couple eventually ask him to leave ("Well, you wanted him, you fussed over him, you mothered him, you took him to your bosom in some crazy menopausal fantasy," Albert tells her), but he refuses to go, and when the locals turn up to avenge themselves, he grabs the axe with which he has been using to chop logs and kills the clerk, following which things come to a dramatic conclusion in the cellar later that night.

A decidedly oddball melodrama in which things clearly don't bode well from the start, the motivations of the couple nevertheless take some swallowing given that Richard very clearly has mental health issues and is obviously going to be trouble. Yet if one is prepared to go with the flow, this is at times a creepy, claustrophobic little thriller, lacking any noticeable style, but well enough acted by the three principals, and reaching a fine frenzy with Richard's axe attack on the unfortunate clerk, which is accompanied by an explosion of percussion from Jerry Goldsmith's otherwise restrained score. It certainly doesn't win any awards for plausibility, but given its restrictions, both budgetary and in terms of action, it somehow maintains one's interest, even if only to find out how the situation will resolve itself.

Premonitions of something nasty set to happen in the near future was the subject of *Visions...* (1972, aka *Visions of Death*), which was broadcast on 10 October

1972. This time it's a college professor named Mark Lowell (Monte Markham) who is troubled with unsought thoughts involving the bombing of a building. But are the premonitions real, and if so, how will he convince the police, in the guise of the inevitably skeptical Lieutenant Keegan (a pre–Kojak Telly Savalas), to believe him? As written by Paul Playdon and directed by Lee H. Katzin, this is a generally well managed ticking time thriller, in which the race is on to catch the mad bomber before he is able to carry out his deeds, doubly so after the media gets hold of the story and the bomber becomes wise to the investigation. Slickly photographed in Denver, Colorado, by John A. Alonzo, this is clearly more of a thriller than a horror story, yet it nevertheless makes good use of its supernatural element, offering no pat explanations. Sadly, though ripe for a weekly follow-up, on this occasion no series was commissioned.

The supernatural was more to the fore in *Sandcastles* (1972, TVM), a somewhat soppy romance in which a young man named Michael (Jan-Michael Vincent) is killed in an auto accident, only to return from the dead to romance Jenna, a young violinist (Bonnie Bedelia) who stayed with him during his last moments following the crash. As they build sandcastles on the beach and sit in the moonlight together, he gradually recalls the name of the man responsible for his death, a drink driver with whom he'd hitched a ride, thus enabling Jenna to find justice for him, following which he disappears into the afterlife. Tosh of the highest order, accompanied by an incessant score of syrupy violins care of composer Paul Glass, this would have been hard to swallow in the forties, never mind the more hardnosed seventies. Written by James M. Miller and Stephen and Elinor Karpf, it's hard to believe that anyone thought this moon eyed nonsense might have been a flier, yet producer Gerald I. Isenberg and director Ted Post clearly did. Broadcast on 17 October 1972, the film was actually shot on videotape before being transferred to film in a bid to save costs, but given the loss of clarity, the process was dropped on further productions.

Gargoyles

A good, old-fashioned B-movie monster fest was on the cards next with *Gargoyles* (1972, TVM), which aired on 21 November 1972. In it, Cornel Wilde stars as Dr. Mercer Boley, a successful anthropologist who is joined in Mexico by his daughter Diana (Jennifer Salt) on a research trip for his latest book, *Five Thousand Years of Demonology*. Before they embark on their journey, they first stop by to visit Uncle Willie's Desert Museum, whose grizzled proprietor (Woody Chambliss) has written to the doctor about an amazing find he has discovered in the desert, which appears to be the skeleton of a winged, gargoyle-like creature, which he has stored in his barn. Initially incredulous, the doctor at first believes Willie has made it himself from animal bones, but the old man insists that it is genuine. "This is not a trick, this is not for them tourists, this is the real thing," he tells the doc, who soon changes his mind when the barn is attacked by clawed creatures who chase him and his daughter as they escape in their car with the skull, having left behind old Willie, who has been killed by a falling beam in the now burning barn.

Taking refuge in a motel, they next day take the police out to the scene of the attack, but the cops instead believe the culprits to be a local biker gang led by James Reeger (Scott Glenn). That night the gargoyles return to retrieve the skull from the motel, but one is hit by a car as they make their escape, and when they later return to retrieve the body, which the doctor has kept as evidence, they also kidnap Diana. The doc consequently enlists the help of the police and the bikers to help get her back, and they all head into the desert where they track down the gargoyles to their cave, where many eggs are awaiting to hatch and take over the world ("The end of your age, the beginning of mine," their leader informs the doctor). But in the fight that follows, many of the creatures are shot, and Reeger manages to set the eggs alight with some gasoline, sacrificing himself in order to do so, leaving only the gargoyle leader and an injured breeding mate to fly away into the night.

Shot on location in New Mexico, as well as in the Carlsbad Caverns, this is tongue in cheek nonsense of the silliest order (the eye-catching slime-green titles are perhaps a giveaway), but the early build up in the desert and at the barn is well managed by director B.W.L. Norton and his photographer Earl Rath, who make the most of the arid landscape, particularly during a well staged chase between the police and the bikers. And although it gradually turns into a routine save the damsel-in-distress scenario, the script by Stephen and Elinor Karpf is not without its clever touches, such as linking the gargoyles, which we learn appear every 500 years, with ancient myths and legends, as well as paintings, wood carvings and the statuary to be found on churches (images of which appear during a prologue compiled by Michael S. Clark), thus making them an ancient adversary to man. "Now my book will be not only about myths and legends, but reality," exclaims the doctor once convinced that they really do exist. However, having the leader, played by Bernie Casey (voiced by Vic Perrin), able to talk and read, ultimately dilutes the scare factor somewhat, as does the fact that the monsters, after such a nice build up, are then seen full body for much of the action, though one cannot deny that for a low-budget TV movie shot in just 18 days, the make-up effects and body suits designed by Stan Winston, Ellis Burman, Jr., and Ross Wheat are pretty effective, particularly those sported by Casey (Winston, Burman and make-up supervisor Del Armstrong won an Emmy for their efforts).

Performance wise, Wilde makes for a fairly dull lead, while Salt is required to do little more than scream while sporting a number of skimpy-looking tops, thus leaving it to character actress Grayson Hall to steal the movie with her few scenes as Mrs. Parks, the alcoholic owner of the Cactus Motel at which the doctor and his daughter stay (in an amusing touch, she is never seen without a glass, and even knows where the booze is stored when she visits the police station, filling her empty glass by taking a bottle out of the chief's top drawer). Produced by Rick Rosenberg and Bob Christiansen for Tomorrow Entertainment, one couldn't quite argue that *Gargoyles* is a classic, but as a nostalgic hark back to the desert-set monster flicks of the fifties, it is certainly great fun for the most part.

Horror of a slightly more traditional style could be found the following month in *The Horror at 37,000 Feet* (1973, TVM), which is basically a haunted house thriller set onboard a 747 bound to New York from London, peopled with a variety of clichéd characters one might find in a typical disaster movie of the period, among them a priest who has lost his faith (William Shatner), a movie star (Will Hutchins), a millionaire businessman (Buddy Ebsen), a doctor (Paul Winfield), a model (France Nuyen) and a little girl (Mia Bendixsen), not to mention an architect and his wife (Roy Thinnes and Jane Merrow) who are transporting back home a number of features taken from an ancient abbey, among them a sacrificial stone used by Druids in ancient times. Naturally, it isn't long before a strange presence makes itself felt onboard, resulting in a variety of phenomena, including sudden temperature drops, icy winds, dimming lights, strange voices speaking in Latin and faulty gauges on the flight deck, where the crew discover that strong jet streams are somehow preventing the aircraft from making progress. Moss in the bulkhead and a strange ooze also appear, while an investigation into the hold by the captain (Chuck Connors)

Pinch of salt. Jennifer Salt and friend in *Gargoyles* (1972, TVM) (CBS/Tomorrow Entertainment).

leads to the discovery of a frozen dog belonging to one of the passengers, a fate to which the flight engineer accompanying him also succumbs. However, when the priest reveals that a fire might keep the presence at bay until sunrise, given that it is the midsummer solstice and this is how the Druids kept demons at bay during their ceremonies, the passengers at last have a glimmer of hope as to how they might survive their ordeal, and the plane begins to climb in order to meet the new dawn.

Written by Ron Austin and Jim Buchanan from a story by V.X. Appleton, the movie, which is adequately if plainly directed by David Lowell Rich, is little more than a checklist of fairly standard things that go bump in the night, save for the novelty that here they take place at 37,000 feet. Yet there is just about enough going on to sustain interest in the proceedings, while the climax, during which the priest confronts a cowled figure which has manifested itself in the galley just before sunrise, sees the clergyman sucked out into the atmosphere when one of the cabin doors suddenly bursts open. As for the cast, also among them Lyn Loring (Mrs. Roy Thinnes at the time), Darleen Carr and Tammy Grimes (the latter as Mrs. Pinder, an Englishwoman who has been suing Thinnes' character over the removal of the stones), they perform their tasks adequately enough under the circumstances, and are even given the occasional good line to deliver. Says Shatner's priest during one theological discussion, "There's never been any shortage of idiot things to believe in, nor idiots to take them up," though the best goes to Will Hutchins' western movie star Steve Hol-comb (for which read hokum). When told what is down in the hold by Mrs. Pinder, he flatly asks her, "Hey, lady, you tryin' to tell me that a piece of rock's got something to do with killing the flight engineer?" which pretty much sums up the plot: pas-sengers on an aircraft are threatened by a killer rock, which doesn't sound quite so frightening in the cold light of day. Broadcast on 13 February 1973, the film was pro-duced by Anthony Wilson, whose tight budget sees that effects are pretty basic and kept to a minimum, with as much of the action as possible taking place within the confines of the aircraft (shot at the CBS Studio Center), which it does, save for the opening check-in sequences. Yet despite these restrictions, the film meets its remit by filling 73 minutes of airtime with a reasonable degree of diverting nonsense for those in the mood for such shameless shenanigans.

One of the genre's great characters returned to the small screen next in a new production of *Dracula* (1974, TVM, aka *Bram Stoker's Dracula*) care of TV's master of the macabre, Dan Curtis. Originally to have been broadcast on 12 October 1973, the film was postponed to 8 February 1974 following the resignation of Vice Presi-dent Spiro Agnew, which led to an unscheduled address to the nation by President Richard Nixon.

Like all previous adaptations of Bram Stoker's voluminous novel, the film, which was scripted by Curtis regular Richard Matheson, presents a simplified ver-sion of the storyline, and begins with the arrival in Transylvania of solicitor Jon-athan Harker (Murray Brown), who, on behalf of his client Count Dracula (Jack Palance), has brought details of a number of properties in England for his host to examine and from which to select a new home. Having left Harker locked in his cas-tle at the mercy of his three vampire "brides" (Sarah Douglas, Virginia Wetherell and Barbara Lindley), the Count travels to Whitby on the *Demeter* with a number of boxes containing soil from his home country, and once ensconced in his new abode, Carfax, begins a reign of terror in the nearby neighborhood, whose residents just happen to include Lucy Westenra (Fiona Lewis), the best friend of Harker's fian-cée Mina (Penelope Horner), who has come to stay with her. Having seen a photo in Harker's room picturing himself with Mina, Lucy and her own fiancé Arthur Hol-mwood (Simon Ward), the Count notes that Lucy bears an uncanny resemblance to his long dead wife, with whom he can be seen pictured in a painting dated 1175, and he determines to make her his new bride. However, when Lucy dies and becomes a vampire, she is dispatched with a wooden stake in her coffin by Dr. Van Helsing (Nigel Davenport), the physician who has been treating her for anemia. Thus, the Count now turns his attention to Mina, forcing her to drink his own blood ("Now she will be blood of my blood, kin of my kin"). But Van Helsing is able to use this to his advantage, and using hypnosis, is able to track Dracula through Mina, allowing himself, Holmwood and the girl to follow him back to Transylvania, where Van Hel-sing and Holmwood not only destroy the Count's three brides and Harker, who has himself become a vampire, but also Dracula himself.

Clearly intended as a quality production, Curtis, who also produced via Lat-glen, persuaded CBS to allow him to film on location in Yugoslavia, where Trakos-can Castle in Croatia stood in for Castle Dracula, and in England, where Oakley

Court stood in for Carfax (the latter was situated adjacent to Bray Studios, the former home of Hammer Productions, which had made use of the house in a number of its horror films, among them *The Mummy* [1959], *The Brides of Dracula* [1960] and *The Plague of the Zombies* [1966]). In addition to Palance, with whom Curtis had worked before on *The Strange Case of Dr. Jekyll and Mr. Hyde* (1968, TVM), the high profile cast, which also includes Pamela Brown as Lucy's mother, was augmented by a team of top British technicians, among them the Oscar-winning cinematographer Oswald Morris and costume designer Ruth Myers, as well as such Curtis diehards as art director Trevor Williams and composer Bob Cobert, and all appear to have been under instruction to take things very seriously indeed.

Consequently, the finished film, which was also released theatrically in a slightly bloodier version in some territories, is a somewhat humorless and overly sober affair, further hampered by an occasionally leaden pace and the miscasting of Palance in the title role, who is perhaps a little too full of face to play the Count (but then again, so was Lon Chaney, Jr., in *Son of Dracula* [1943]). He does nevertheless spit out his lines with venomous conviction when the occasion demands him to do so ("So, you play your wits against mine. Me, who commanded armies hundreds of years ago before you were born," he snarls at Van Helsing in his best moment). As Van Helsing, Nigel Davenport (who'd already appeared in *The Picture of Dorian Gray* [1973, TVM] for Curtis) plays things straight as an arrow, and is a little on the dull side, while as his accomplice, Simon Ward is somewhat wooden as Arthur Holmwood, as are both Fiona Lewis and Penelope Horner as Lucy and Mina, respectively (note that the entire cast pronounce the latter's name as "Mi*nn*a" rather than the usual "M*ee*na" for some reason). And despite the involvement of Oswald Morris, the film is also visually unadventurous for the most part, save for a couple of tilt shots (note that lighting paraphernalia can be spotted on the ceiling in the Westenra home just prior to the scene in which a wolf bursts through the window), while Bob Cobert's score doesn't rank among his best for the director. In fact compared with Curtis' first theatrical feature, *House of Dark Shadows* (1970), the big screen version of *Dark Shadows* (1966–1971, TV), the film seems somewhat stifled, while the lack of a disintegration scene after Dracula has been destroyed by both sunlight and a well aimed spear from Van Helsing, makes for a disappointing climax. Yet one can't fault Curtis' determination to treat the subject with care and respect, and it will certainly hold some interest for fans of the director.

Another of the genre's great stories, Gaston Leroux's *The Phantom of the Opera*, was meanwhile given the update treatment in *The Phantom of Hollywood* (1974, TVM), which was broadcast on 12 February 1974. However, instead of an opera house, it is the neglected back lot of Worldwide Studios that is here the domain of a mysterious figure, disguised as a medieval knight, who wanders about the place, killing those he deems responsible for its fall into disrepair, among them a couple of young vandals who have broken in for kicks, and two survey engineers who are involved in the preparations to sell off the land, given that the crumbling standing sets are now redundant in an age of location filming (comments the studio's head of publicity [Peter Haskell] during a tour of the lot, "There must be a hundred different staircases here, all going nowhere at the moment"). In a bid to halt the sale, the phantom kidnaps the studio president's daughter (Skye Aubrey) who, while held captive in his underground lair, discovers him to be a onetime actor named Karl Vonner (Jack Cassidy), whose career was destroyed when an explosive charge went off in his face, since when he has lived out his days in secret on the increasingly decrepit lot, thanks to the help of his brother Otto, the company's aged stills archivist.

Written by George Schenck from a story by himself and Robert Thom under the original title of *The Phantom of Lot 2*, the commendably straight-faced teleplay, which mercifully eschews camp, contains few new surprises of its own, the real coup here being that the film is set on the old MGM back lot (many of whose own props and costumes had been auctioned off in 1970), the dilapidated streets of which provide an abundance of buildings and alleyways for the phantom to skulk about in. In fact the film's best sequence comes early on, as the camera roves about the lot, alighting on specific buildings, among them a college campus and railroad station, which are then intercut with brief shots of them as they were in the films they appeared in, and the contrast between the sets as they are now and were then is saddening indeed, as is the fact that several of them are casually bulldozed for the cameras during the climax, during which the phantom finally falls to his death while goading the police in pursuit of him.

Thanks to the Emmy nominated make-up skills of William Tuttle (himself an MGM stalwart whose credits stretched all the way back to *Mark of the Vampire* [1935]), leading man Jack Cassidy is able to play both the elderly archivist Otto as well as his disfigured brother Karl, whose reign of terror reaches its height during a nostalgic back lot party, at which he cuts loose an overhead rig of speakers (in lieu of a chandelier) which crashes down and kills his brother, who has threatened to expose him. The film also features a number of old-time players in cameo roles, among them Jackie Coogan, John Ireland, Billy Halop, Kent Taylor and Regis Toomey, as well as Broderick Crawford as the police captain investigating the murders, and Rat Pack alumnus Peter Lawford as studio head Roger Cross. Helmed with reasonable panache by Gene Levitt, the film occasionally slows up during some of the dialogue scenes, while Leonard Rosenman's score is a little too discordant at times, yet the desolate back lot sequences are certainly effectively captured by cinematographer Gene Polito, who had already worked as an additional photographer on MGM's rose tinted nostalgia fest *That's Entertainment* (1974), which would be released in May the same year (note that though signage depicting the lot as belonging to Worldwide Studios is abundant throughout, the name Metro Goldwyn Mayer can be spotted over an archway in an aerial shot early on in the film).

Masked avenger. Jack Cassidy as *The Phantom of Hollywood* (1974, TVM) (CBS/MGM Television).

In 1977, CBS turned to comic

book characters for fresh inspiration, and the first to go before the cameras was Spider-Man, who was created by Stan Lee and Steve Ditko, and first published by Marvel in August 1962. The resultant film, *Spider-Man* (1977, TVM), starring Nicholas Hammond as the web slinging superhero, was aired on 14 September 1977, and led to a two-season run of adventures between 1978 and 1979 (an earlier cartoon series titled *Spider-Man* had run on ABC between 1967 and 1970). The second Marvel character to receive the live action treatment was the Hulk, who was created by Stan Lee and Jack Kirby, and first published in May 1962. The resultant movie, which was written and directed by Kenneth Johnson, was *The Incredible Hulk* (1977, TVM), which aired on 4 November 1977, and proved to be even more popular than Spidey's exploits. In it, Dr. David Banner (Bill Bixby), who has been exposed to a massive dose of gamma rays during his research, finds himself transforming into a raging green monster whenever angered (hence Banner's celebrated catchphrase: "Don't make me angry. You wouldn't like me when I'm angry").

The series that followed (1977–1982, TV) was a worldwide ratings success, and made a star of two-time Mr. Universe winner Lou Ferrigno, who appeared as Banner's muscle-bound alter ago, whose transformations and slow-motion rampages proved to be the highlight of each episode, and may well have caused a few nightmares for younger fans of the show, on which count it rates its brief mention here (three further TV movies followed the finish of the series, concluding with *The Death of the Incredible Hulk* [1990, TVM]). A third Marvel superhero, Dr. Strange, also got the TV movie treatment during this period. Created by Stan Lee and Steve Ditko, and first published by Marvel in July 1963, the film version, *Dr. Strange* (1978, TVM), which aired on 6 September 1978, sees our hero, a hospital psychiatrist (Peter Hooten), inherit the role of Sorcerer Supreme from the weary Thomas Lindmer (John Mills) in order to conquer his old adversary Morgan LeFey (Jessica Walter), who has been granted the ability to dominate men's souls by the Nameless One (David Hooks). Colorful comic-strip hokum with cheesy effects typical of the period, it was written, directed and executive produced by Philip DeGuere, and can best be described as a load of camp old nonsense, given momentary touches of class thanks to the presence of Mills and Walter, who may well have wondered what they had signed themselves up for. On this occasion, however, the pilot didn't go to series. Hanna-Barbera also produced an animated version of yet another Marvel superhero at this time, a Stan Lee-Jack Kirby creation called The Thing, who had first appeared in 1961. An impregnable rock-like monster whose true identity in this instance is a shy teenager named Benjy Grimm (voiced by Wayne Morton, with Joe Baker providing the voice of his alter ego), he appeared in just 13 episodes which aired in syndication from 8 September 1979 as a segment of the half-hour show *Fred and Barney Meet the Thing* (1979, TV), among his own adventures being *Bigfoot Meets the Thing*, *The Thing's the Play* (clever!) and *The Thing and the Captain's Ghost*.

Even camper than *Dr. Strange*, if that were possible, was the movie length TV special *Once Upon a Brothers Grimm* (1977, TVM), which aired on 23 November 1977, in which the celebrated fairytale writers, separated in the woods, find themselves involved in a number of their stories, among them *Little Red Riding Hood*, *The Frog Prince*, *Sleeping Beauty* and *Hansel and Gretel*, in the latter of which an evil witch (Chita Rivera), who lives in a gingerbread house, captures two children who she plans to fatten up. Mild stuff, of course, given its intended audience, but an undeniably colorful extravaganza thanks to the inventive work of art director Ken Johnson and costume designer Bill Hargate. A bright and breezy pantomime in the style of *The Wizard of Oz*, the production, which was written by Jean Holloway and directed by Norman

Strange days. Peter Hooten as *Dr. Strange* (1978, TVM) (CBS/Universal Television).

Campbell, was shot on tape at the Samuel Goldwyn Studios, and also benefits from a bouncy score by Mitch Leigh, and lots and lots of guest stars, among them Arte Johnson, Teri Garr, Ruth Buzzi, Clive Revill, Cleavon Little and Sorrell Booke, with the brothers themselves being played by Dean Jones and Paul Sand. By no means as sophisticated as the later Stephen Sondheim musical *Into the Woods* (which didn't appear until 1986), but perhaps a little more fun on the whole.

Nature was on the rampage again in *Tarantulas: The Deadly Cargo* (1977, TVM), which aired on 28 December 1977, which was produced by Paul Freeman for Alan Landsburg Productions (which had already given us *The Savage Bees* [1976, TVM] and *It Happened at Lakewood Manor* [1977, TVM, aka *Panic at Lakewood Manor* and *Ants*]). In it, a plane carrying coffee beans to the U.S. from Ecuador crashes near a Californian township. Unbeknownst to the locals, the aircraft is also carrying a horde of lethal tarantulas which subsequently escape and begin to attack the unwary inhabitants, who eventually combat them by employing a somewhat unusual method: the amplified sound of wasps, which is enough immobilize the critters so that they can be gathered up and drowned in buckets of alcohol! Flatly directed by Stuart Hagmann from a by-the-numbers script by John Groves and Guerdon Trueblood, this is artless nonsense with no sign of humor, though it's not above being laughable at times (particularly when, somewhat inevitably, there's a power failure during the gathering process). Featuring Claude Akins, Pat Hingle, Howard Hesseman and Tom Atkins, the results are hardly comparable to the later *Arachnophobia* (1990), or even *Kingdom of the Spiders* (1977), for that matter.

Slightly better, but not much, was *Deathmoon* (1978, TVM), in which Jason Palmer (Robert Foxworth), a workaholic executive who has been suffering from nightmares, decides to take a much-earned vacation in Hawaii where his grandfather worked as a missionary, only to find himself turning into a vicious werewolf during the full moon, having inherited the condition through the male line of the family, which was cursed by a voodoo clan many years earlier. One of TV's lesser werewolf sagas, this particular example suffers primarily from an interminable build-up, which is more a romantic travelogue than a horror movie, with George

Schenck's teleplay, based upon a story by himself and producer Jay Benson, taking the longest route possible towards the climax, when Palmer finally transforms before our eyes via a series of lapse dissolves into a reasonable if not outstanding make-up by Michael Westmore and Jack Dawn, following which he goes on the rampage, only to be tracked and shot dead by Rick Bladen (Joe Penny), the house detective of the resort at which he has been staying, who has been investigating the various slayings Palmer has perpetrated. Unimaginatively directed by Bruce Kessler, the film benefits from some eye-catching flash cutting care of editor Tony DiMarco during the various dream sequences, but is otherwise technically routine, despite its attractive backgrounds, which are rather plainly photographed by Jack Whitman (the movie was shot on the island of Kauai and at the Coco Palms Hotel). Broadcast on 21 May 1978, the film was made via EMI Television and Roger Gimbel Productions.

It was back to frightened lady territory again with *Are You in the House Alone?* (1978, TVM), which went out on 20 September 1978. In it, Kathleen Beller stars as Gail Osborne, a young student who finds herself plagued by threatening phone calls and notes ("I'm watching you…," reads one of them), only to be attacked and raped by the culprit in her living room when she inadvertently lets him into the house ("I really had you fooled, didn't I?"). And when she refuses to identify him to the police for fear of not being believed because she wasn't a virgin, he subsequently turns his attention to another student, which eventually prompts Gail into action. Adapted by Judith Parker from the 1976 novel by Richard Peck, the film is slackly directed by Walter Grauman, whose handling, despite the occasional use of subjective shots during the early stalking sequences, is disappointingly routine in most regards. It also takes an age to get going and becomes increasingly uncomfortable in its tactless use of rape as a plot device, even if it does lead to some rather clumsy debate about the subject. It at least benefits from a good supporting cast, among them Blythe Danner and Tony Bill as Gail's concerned parents, Scott Colomby as her boyfriend and the young Dennis Quaid as a fellow classmate. Ultimately, though, it leaves a sour taste in the mouth.

Sadly lacking a much-needed sense of fun, despite being promoted as "A Halloween Howler" in the press, was *Devil Dog the Hound of Hell* (1978, TVM), which aired on 31 October 1978. In it, an ideal suburban family take in a new puppy following the death of their previous dog, only to discover that as it grows, it is possessed by an evil spirit that exerts a destructive influence upon them all: the father (Richard Crenna) finds himself compelled to stick his hand into the lawnmower, the mother (Yvette Mimieux) becomes a sexpot, and the kids (Ike Eisenmann and Kim Richards) go to the bad. As for their poor maid (Tina Menard), she burns to death in her room (ran the tagline: "Mike and Betty. Just an average American couple. They have a house, a car, two kids, and one lovable dog—*possessed by the Devil*"). When mom and the kids turn to Devil worship in the attic, dad starts to look into the matter, and discovers that the dog is a barghest, a demon in the shape of a dog, and travels to Ecuador to consult with a shaman (Victor Jory) on how best to deal with the matter, and eventually destroys it in a battle of wills staged at the aerodynamics plant at which he works.

Hobbled by a poor script by Stephen and Elinor Karpf, and bland as butter direction by the usually reliable Curtis Harrington, this is utter poppycock from beginning to end, with little tension and few real surprises, the best sequence coming at the top of the show, in which a group of Satanists, led by the sultry Martine Beswick, buy a dog from a kennel, which they then breed with a hound from hell summoned during a candlelit ritual, following which they give away the offspring to unsuspecting families. Had it been more knowingly humorous, this all might have been mildly amusing, but the sunny California locations, the brightly lit interiors, the lackluster effects and the generally dull performances combine to make for a tedious experience that makes even the derided *Dracula's Dog* (1977, aka *Zoltan, Hound of Dracula*) look like high art by comparison (note that Richards and Eisenmann had previously appeared together in *Escape to Witch Mountain* [1975] and its sequel, *Return to Witch Mountain* [1978]).

Also lacking a sense of humor was *Terror Out of the Sky* (1978, TVM), which aired on 26 December 1978. A sequel to *The Savage Bees* (1976), not that one was needed, it delivers more of the same, with a swarm of African killer bees escaping from the National Bee Center, where they are being studied. This time, instead of a red Volkswagen beetle, they attach themselves to a yellow school bus full of boy scouts, and are eventually drawn off by a man hanging from a helicopter in a hazmat suit, who then dumps them in an abandoned missile test center. Like its predecessor (which had actually been broadcast by rival station NBC), it was made via Alan Landsburg Productions and written by Guerdon Trueblood, this time with assistance from Peter Nelson and Doris Silverton, but the three of them deal in nothing but disaster movie clichés, which are flatly put over by director Lee H. Katzin, whose cast includes Dan Haggerty, Efrem Zimbalist, Jr., Tovah Feldshuh (in a role played by Gretchen Corbett in the first film) and Ike Eisenmann as one of the unfortunate boy scouts. Commented *TV Guide* of the results, "As dopey as its special effects are amateurish."

The horrors of cloning were meanwhile the subject of *The Darker Side of Terror* (1979, TVM), which was broadcast on 3 April 1979. In it, the aging Professor Meredith (Ray Milland) clones his best student, Paul Corwin (Robert Forster), himself now a college professor, the only giveaway between the two being the clone's right eye, which periodically turns white. Having received a high-speed education from Corwin via computer, the clone, which it transpires has murderous impulses, inevitably escapes and is taken for the professor by one of his students who has a crush on him. However, when he murders her, it is the real Corwin who comes under suspicion for carrying out the crime. When the clone also murders Professor Meredith and another rival professor, and becomes involved with Corwin's unsuspecting wife Margaret (Adrienne Barbeau), he clearly has to do something about his predicament, and in the ensuing fight, one of the men is killed, but the question is, which one? Unfortunately, a potentially intriguing doppelganger scenario is here let down by unimaginative scripting by Al Ramrus and John Herman Shaner, while the staging by director Gus Trikonis fails to add any atmosphere of its own to the proceedings, particularly during the drab-looking lab sequences, which should have been the film's *raison d'etre*. As Corwin and his murderous clone, Forster is perfectly fine, while TV staple Milland is his usual crotchety self, but otherwise this is routine mad scientist fare, despite the modern-day trappings, and becomes something of a chore to sit through well before the end.

Deadly premonitions of things to come again cropped up as the focus of *Mind Over Murder* (1979, TVM), in which a pretty young model (Deborah Raffin) suffers a series of visions involving a sinister looking bald man (Andrew Prine) who turns out to have been responsible for a jet crash in which 83 people were killed. Helping the police to track down the man, she subsequently finds her life in jeopardy when her investigations lead her directly to him. Its premonition angle aside, this is basically little more than a lady-in-peril thriller, with situations typical of its genre, including plenty of wandering around down dark alleyways with the inevitable results, which was nevertheless enough to commend it to *Variety*, which commented, "It may seem improbable but it sure has its breathcatchers." Routinely directed by Ivan Nagy from a script by Robert Carrington, the film is an adequate time passer but little more, marred by the fact that the villain forces himself upon our heroine after he has kidnapped her ("What would you like to do first? Make love or die?"). Produced by Jay Benson via Paramount, the film, which aired on 23 October 1979, also features Bruce Davison, David Ackroyd and Robert Englund.

Up at the Marsten House

The commitment to horror at CBS may have yielded some patchy results, yet there's no doubting that the channel finished the decade on a high with the broadcast of *Salem's Lot* (1979, TVM). Warner Bros. originally acquired Stephen King's 1975 novel with the intention of turning it into a theatrical feature, to which end Stirling Silliphant, Larry Cohen and Robert Gretchell all attempted to adapt the author's 400-page opus into a two-hour movie. When none of them could overcome the problem of length, producer Richard Kobritz instead decided to turn the project into a two-part mini-series, with each episode tailored to fill a two-hour timeslot. To this end, Paul Monash—who had produced *Carrie* (1976), the highly successful version of King's first novel—was brought onboard to pen a new script, with Silliphant remaining as the show's executive producer. Tobe Hooper, whose credits already included the notorious horror film *The Texas Chainsaw Massacre* (1974), was meanwhile hired to direct.

Set in the township of Salem's Lot, Maine, the story revolves round a writer named Ben Mears (David Soul) who returns home following a prolonged absence, his plan being to write a book about the Marsten House, a supposedly haunted property on the edge of town which he dared to enter as a boy, and was convinced that he saw its former owner, Hubie Marsten, who was suspected of abducting children, "hanging by his neck." However, when Ben tries to rent the semi-derelict house, which has remained empty ever since, he is surprised to learn that it has already been taken by Richard Straker (James Mason), a suave antiques dealer who is about to open a shop in town with his partner, Kurt Barlow (Reggie Nalder), who has yet to appear. Taking a room at a nearby lodging house, from which he can see the Marsten House from his window as he writes, Ben starts to re-establish himself in the community, meeting up with his old drama teacher Jason Burke (Lew Ayres), and falling for a local girl, Susan Norton (Bonnie Bedelia), who is the daughter of the town's doctor (Ed Flanders). However, following the delivery of a large crate to the Marsten House, people in the vicinity start to disappear under mysterious circumstances, among them a youngster named Ralphie Glick (Ronnie Scribner), who had been rehearsing the school's annual play with his brother Danny (Brad Savage) at the home of another boy, Mark Petrie (Lance Kerwin), who has, like Ben before him, written the pageant. Naturally, the locals suspect that the newcomers are somehow behind the disappearances, particularly the town's police constable, Parkins Gillespie (Kenneth McMillan). But it soon becomes clear to Ben that they are in fact the work of a vampire, and as one begets another ("The vampires are creating vampires," he observes), he is helped by Jason, Susan and the doctor to end their spread and bring the reign of terror to an end.

TV's ultimate spooky house horror saga, *Salem's Lot* lives up to its potential in every conceivable manner, from its adaptation, which skillfully streamlines King's convoluted plot by excising any extraneous characters and situations, to Hooper's stylish and authoritative direction which, as well as delivering a number of perfectly timed shock moments, manages to imbue the proceedings with a palpable sense of dread. Indeed, the sight of little Ralphie Glick, floating outside the window of his brother's bedroom without any visible means of support, proves to be one of the movie's most unsettling moments (a masterfully handled effect, this was achieved by attaching actor Ronnie Scribner to the end of a Gimbel surrounded by mist and filming the scene in reverse). That Mark Petrie is a horror buff and amateur magician (his room is filled with posters and memorabilia) proves advantageous to the plot, especially when Danny Glick, himself now a vampire, comes floating to his own window, only to be repelled by a small cross that Mark snatches from a model graveyard he has made.

Other highlights include a number of genuine jolts, among them the death of realtor Larry Crockett (Fred Willard), who is attacked after being caught with his pants down at the home of his secretary Bonnie Sawyer (Julie Cobb) by her gun toting husband Cully (George Dzundza); an attack on gravedigger Mike Ryerson (Geoffrey Lewis) who, while filling in the grave of Danny Glick, is compelled to jump in and open the coffin, only to be greeted with a nasty surprise; and, best of all, the unexpected appearance

Soul mates. From left to right, David Soul and James Mason in a publicity shot for *Salem's Lot* (1979, TVM) (CBS/Warner Bros. Television).

of Kurt Barlow in Mark's kitchen, where he kills his parents by smashing their heads together. Elsewhere, there are creepy sequences aplenty, prime among them the transportation of the crate containing Barlow from the docks of Portland to the Marsten House, during which the box slowly moves from the back of the truck towards the driver's cabin.

The sight of Barlow, with his bald head, grey skin, yellow eyes and rat-like teeth, is truly hideous, and make-up artists Jack H. Young and Ben Lane seem to have been inspired more by Max Schreck's Graf Orlok in *Nosferatu* (1922) than any of the more romantic interpretations of Dracula down the years, and his every appearance proves to be a genuine threat to those unfortunate enough to cross his path. Like many monsters before him, the fact that Barlow never speaks makes him all the more menacing, and though his scenes are fleeting, Reggie Nalder makes a major impact as the character, who must surely rank as one of the small screen's most memorable genre creations. Any verbal threats are instead carried out by Richard Straker, whose superior air and mild sarcasm are artfully conveyed by the calm and measured performance of the elegantly suited James Mason, whose Hollywood pedigree lends a genuine touch of class to the proceedings. His quietly knowing delivery of the otherwise innocent line, "You'll enjoy Mr. Barlow—and he'll enjoy you," to Ben, is expertly put across, while his earlier unfolding of a package in the basement of the Marsten House, which proves to contain the body of Ralphie Glick, whom he has procured as an offering for his master, is an unsettling moment indeed, especially given the underlying implications of child abduction that go with it.

As the bookish Ben Mears, David Soul immediately wipes away any memories of the gun toting heroics of *Starsky and Hutch* (1975–1979, TV) to provide a more thoughtful and reserved man of action, while as the horror-obsessed Mark Petrie, Lance Kerwin proves equally effective as a younger if somewhat braver version of Ben, given his unafraid determination to destroy Barlow for killing his parents by boldly entering the Marsten House alone to carry out the deed. That he and Ben eventually team up to kill Barlow just as the sun is setting makes for a thrilling finale. As Ben's love interest, Bonnie Bedelia's Susan at first seems superfluous to the plot, yet later proves a useful ally to both Ben and Mark, while as her father, Ed Flanders adequately provides a voice of reason to Ben, only to come to a memorably sticky end in the Marsten House when Straker impales him on some decorative antlers. Effective cameos are also provided by Marie Windsor as Ben's landlady Eva Miller, Elisha Cook, Jr., as the town's drunkard Weasel Phillips, Lew Ayres as Ben's former teacher, and Clarissa Kaye (James Mason's wife) as the Glick boys' grieving mother, who herself becomes a vampire, attacking Ben in the hospital morgue, where he defends himself with a cross hastily made by taping together two tongue depressors.

The real hero of the $4 million production, however, is director Tobe Hooper, whose handling is both restrained and, given the restrictions of television, gore free, allowing the characters and narrative to develop in a measured pace that benefits from excellent location work (the township scenes were shot in Ferndale, California) and atmospheric studio work, most notably in the moldering Marsten House, whose sepulchral interiors include a hallway with a grand staircase, on which Straker proves to be mortal by succumbing to gunshots, and a dank cellar, both of which are imaginatively realized by production designer Mort Rabinowitz and his set decorator Jerry Adams. As for the exterior of the house, built over an existing property in Ferndale, it easily ranks alongside the mansions belonging to the Addams and Munster families as one of TV's spookiest. "Do you believe a thing can be inherently evil?" asks Ben of the property at one point, given its grim history of murder and suicide, before adding, "I think that an evil house attracts evil men." And looking at it, one is inclined to agree. Cameraman Jules Brenner meanwhile provides some impressive crane shots within Marsten House hallway, which add a touch of scope to the narrative, while the many night time sequences carry a genuine fear of what may be lurking in the shadows, all of which are augmented by a particularly atmospheric score by Harry Sukman, which, as well as providing a few "zingers" to accompany the shock moments, is by turns eerie and throat grabbing, particularly during the pounding main title sequence, during which it accompanies Gene Kraft's eye-catching graphics (Sukman and Kraft were both nominated for Emmys for their work, as were make-up men Young and Lane).

Broadcast on 17 and 24 November 1979, the film was an instant hit with horror fans, and has rightly become a classic over the years ("The ultimate in terror," ran the tagline). A theatrical version which trimmed the running time to 112 minutes was prepared for release in certain territories (this was also made available on VHS in 1987), and although this contains most of the major sequences, the truncated running time does bear an impact on the overall effect of the film, though one scene is stronger (in the TV version, when Cully Sawyer catches Larry Crockett in bed with his wife, he makes him hold the shotgun he is toting in front of the realtor's face, whereas in the theatrical cut, he makes him put the gun barrel into his mouth). The mini-series was followed by a particularly poor theatrical sequel, *A Return to Salem's Lot* (1987), which was directed by Larry Cohen (who also wrote the screenplay with James Dixon), and a passable but unnecessary two-part TV remake, *Salem's Lot* (2004, TVM), which was written by Peter Filardi and directed by Mikael Solomon, with Rob Lowe now in the role of Ben Mears, supported by Donald Sutherland as Richard Straker and Rutger Hauer as a rather more talkative Kurt Barlow. Yet despite a few slipshod moments of production, no doubt owing to the hasty shooting schedule (visible boom mics and set tops, some choppy editing and some narrative inconsistencies), the original remains the best—and certainly ranks among the most frightening horror films ever made, either for the large screen or the small (note that Ferndale was also used as a location for the movie *Outbreak* [1995], which coincidentally also features a brief appearance by Lance Kerwin).

Bespoke TV movies aside, American television also continued to provide weekly shows devoted to the horror genre, among them a number of hosted programs, such as *Fright Night* (1970–1981, TV), in which Sinister Seymour (Larry Vincent) presented all manner of low-budget sci-fi and horror movies on which he would pass sarcastic comments. Clearly influenced by *The Vampira Show* (1954–1955, TV), it aired in LA on KHJ-TV, and its later hosts included Moona Lisa (Lisa Clark) and Grimsley (Robert Foster). *Fright Night* was also the title of a similar show which aired between 1973 and 1987 on WOR-TV, Channel 9 in New York, where the initial emphasis was on Universal horror from the thirties before taking on more recent fare.

Occasional one-offs were also sometimes commissioned, among them *An Evening of Edgar Allan Poe* (1970, TV), a one-hour special in which horror star Vincent Price reads four of Poe's stories: *The Tell-Tale Heart*, *The Sphinx*, *The Cask of Amontillado* and *The Pit and the Pendulum*. Price was of course well known for his appearances in a number of popular Poe inspired films in the sixties, among them *House of Usher* (1960, aka *The Fall of the House of Usher*), *The Raven* (1963) and *The Masque of the Red Death* (1964), and AIP, which had been behind the films, now sponsored this one man show via their television arm, AIP-TV, on which it aired on 1 January 1970. Recorded at the Hollywood Video Center, the program was executive produced by Samuel Z. Arkoff and James H. Nicholson, and produced and directed by Ken Johnson, who also adapted the stories with David Welch. With each tale presented in a setting suitable to its narrative care of art director Henry C. Lickel, Price, aided and abetted by Mary Grant's costumes and Joseph DiBella's make-up, assumes four different characters to relate the tales in his inimitable style. However, while his film performances tended towards camp, there is no mistaking that he is passionately serious here, never more so than in the relating of *The Pit and the Pendulum*, in which he reaches a fine frenzy during its climactic moments. Augmented by an atmospheric score by Les Baxter (who'd scored many of Price's Poe films), this is a masterclass of timing and delivery, and the lighting and camerawork are surprisingly good for a videotaped production of the period, with careful use of well framed close-ups. As a showcase for his talents, Price certainly couldn't have wished for anything better.

The following year, a festive treat in the form of an animated version of *A Christmas Carol* (1971, TV) appeared just in time for the holidays on 21 December 1971. This was by no means the first cartoon presentation of the Dickens classic to hit the airwaves during the festive period, among them, as has already been noted, *Mr. Magoo's Christmas Carol* (1962, TV). As produced and directed by Richard Williams for ABC (via Richard Williams Productions), this 28-minute version is, however, undoubtedly the definitive animated adaptation of the timeless tale of a miser brought to his senses after being visited by ghosts from his past, present and future on Christmas Eve (at the time, Williams was best known for his inventive title sequences

Four for the price of one (a cut price Vincent?). The great Vincent Price is featured in this eye-catching promotional ad for *An Evening of Edgar Allan Poe* (1970, TV) (AIP-TV/Ken Johnson Productions).

for such films as *What's New Pussycat* [1965], *A Funny Thing Happened on the Way to the Forum* [1966] and *Casino Royale* [1967]). Narrated by Michael Redgrave, it presents the story in a series of brisk vignettes in the style of Victorian etchings and illustrations, through which the camera periodically swoops and dives with dazzling effect. Brilliantly designed by Richard Purdum and superbly realized by a clearly dedicated team of animators led by Ken Harris (whose credits numbered countless cartoons for Warner Bros., many of them directed by Chuck Jones, who here executive produces), it is as rich and satisfying as a flaming plum pudding, and contains one impressively detailed sequence after another, the most chilling of which is inevitably the miser's encounter with the cowled figure of Christmas Yet to Come ("Ghost of the future, I fear you more than any specter I have seen"). Featuring the vocal talents of Alastair Sim as Scrooge, it also benefits from a sterling supporting cast, among them Michael Hordern as Marley's ghost, Diana Quick as the Ghost of Christmas Past, Melvin Hayes as Bob Cratchit, Joan Sims as Mrs. Cratchit and Paul Whitsun-Jones as Fezziwig. A critical hit, the film was so highly regarded that it was released theatrically in 1972 and went on to win Williams a well deserved Oscar for best animated short (note that Alastair Sim had previously played the title role in the celebrated film *Scrooge* [1951], which also featured Michael Hordern as Jacob Marley, while Abe Levitow, who'd helmed the Magoo version, was involved in this production as a "guest artist").

As good as this version of the story is, yet another animated rendering followed seven years later, again on ABC, under the title *The Stingiest Man in Town* (1978, TV), which made excellent use of the vocal talents of Walter Matthau as the miserly Scrooge. Written by Romeo Muller, the 50-minute film, which aired on 23 December 1978, was produced and directed by Arthur Rankin, Jr., and Jules Bass via Rankin-Bass, and is notable for its surprisingly catchy score by Fred Spielman (music) and Janice Torre (book and lyrics), and while the animation is pretty basic compared to the Williams version, the supporting vocal cast, among them Tom Bosley, Theodore Bikel, Paul Frees and Robert Morse, ensure that the story is relayed in a lively manner.

Program wise, ongoing anthology series were usually thought of as a reliable bet by the three big broadcasters, and several appeared during the decade, among them *Ghost Story* (1972–1973, TV), a *Night Gallery* wannabe in which the host, Winston Essex (Sebastian Cabot), presents stories from his hotel, Mansfield House (actually the Hotel del Coronado in San Diego). First broadcast on NBC on 17 March 1972, the 23-episode run was developed by Richard Matheson, who also wrote the pilot, *The New House* (1972, TV), about a pregnant young wife (Barbara Parkins) who finds herself taunted by the spirit of a young woman who was hanged on the spot of her new home. This was produced by William Castle via Screen Gems and William Castle Productions, with Joel Rogosin producing the remaining 22 installments, which Castle executive produced. With episodes penned by Jimmy Sangster (who wrote five), Robert Bloch and Elizabeth M. Walter, and helmed by the likes of John Llewellyn Moxey, Richard Donner and Robert Day, the stories included the expected gamut of restless spirits and possessed houses, and featured such top line stars as Helen Hayes, Angie Dickinson, Stuart Whitman, Geraldine Page, John

Ireland, Tab Hunter, Melvyn Douglas, Carolyn Jones, Rip Torn and Karen Black. However, when the ratings didn't quite meet expectations, the show was re-titled *Circle of Fear* mid-season, and the host unceremoniously dropped. Like *Night Gallery*, the episodes were well enough made in the style of the time, but often felt overstretched in a one-hour timeslot, among them *The Summer House* (1972, TV), in which a married couple (Carolyn Jones and Steve Forrest) are affected by a malevolent force in their vacation home; *Elegy for a Vampire* (1972, TV), in which two college professors (Mike Farrell and Hal Linden) find themselves amid a number of co-ed murders that are attributed to a vampire; and *Dark Vengeance* (1973, TV), in which a construction worker (Martin Sheen) unearths a mysterious box.

The best episode was perhaps *Graveyard Shift* (1973, TV), in which Fred Colby (John Astin), a nighttime security guard who used to be an actor in horror films, finds himself haunted by the monstrous creatures he once appeared with at the soon-to-be demolished studio at which he works, among them the Claw, the Wolfman, Scarface, the Mummy and Dr. Death. "I don't know how, but all those characters we created in the old days, they've taken on lives of their own, and they inhabit that place, the old studio, and they want to live on, after it's destroyed" he informs his pregnant wife Linda (Patty Duke), who thinks they want to possess her unborn baby, and it is only by burning the reels of film in which they appear that Colby is finally able destroy them. Note that the show's executive producer William Castle, who had also produced and directed such big screen genre fare as *House on Haunted Hill* (1959) and *The Tingler* (1959) among others, has a small role as the studio's owner J.B. Filmore in this episode, and in a self-reflexive nod, he comments, "I knew what the public wanted: to be scared out of their wits." He can also be spotted briefly in the pilot episode.

Aimed at a much younger audience was *The ABC Saturday Superstar Movie* (1972–1974, TV, later *The New Saturday Superstar Movie*), a sort of junior *ABC Movie of the Week*, whose two-season run of 20 hour-long episodes began airing on ABC on 9 September 1972. Featuring established characters from live action shows, as well as pilots for new series, it showcased cartoons from such established animation houses as Hanna-Barbera, Filmation, DePatie-Freleng and Rankin-Bass, and opened with the fantasy adventure *The Brady Kids on Mysterious Island* (1972, TV), following which it went on to include such genre-centric installments as *Mad, Mad, Mad Monsters* (1972, TV), which sees all the old movie monsters (among them Dracula, the Invisible Man, the Mummy and the Wolf Man) gather to celebrate the midnight wedding of the Frankenstein Monster and his bride (which naturally takes place on Friday the 13th); *Nanny and the Professor* (1972, TV), in which the magical Nanny and her employer the Professor (voiced by Juliet Mills and Richard Long from the live action version) find themselves involved in a mystery surrounding a microdot; *The Banana Splits in Hocus Pocus Park* (1972, TV), which blends live action segments with animation in a story which sees the band rescue a young girl (Michelle Tobin) from a witch in a theme park; *Tabitha and Adam and the Clown Family* (1972, TV), in which Tabitha and Adam Stephens (the children of Samantha Stephens from *Bewitched* [1964–1972, TV]) help their cousins defeat a warlock known as Count Krumley; *Daffy Ducky and Porky Pig Meet the Groovie Goolies* (1972, TV), in which

Daffy and Porky encounter a number of monsters while in Hollywood to make a movie, among them the Mummy, Count "Tom" Dracula, Franklin "Frankie" Frankenstein and Wolfgang "Wolfie" Wolfman (with Richard Monda, Jeffrey Thomas and Ed Fournier playing Dracula, Wolfie and the Frankenstein Monster in the live action movie within the movie); *Lost in Space* (1973, TV), in which a space shuttle encounters a meteor storm that sends it through a space warp to an uncharted planet inhabited by evil, one-eyed robots known as Tyranos and large frog-like creatures called Throgs (the character of Dr. Zachary Smith was voiced by Jonathan Harris as per the live action series); *The Mini-Munsters* (1973, TV), in which the family of friendly monsters is visited by their relations from Transylvania (Al Lewis returned from the live action series to voice Grandpa Munster); and *Nanny and the Professor and the Phantom of the Circus* (1973, TV), in which Nanny and the Professor help to track down a phantom who is kidnapping the performers from a circus belonging to Nanny's Aunt Henrietta. The results were a pretty mixed bag, but there was usually something zany or colorful going on to keep the show's target audience glued between the ad breaks.

While we're tuned into kids' TV, we should perhaps take a moment to mention that The Count, one of the most popular characters on *Sesame Street* (1969–, TV), made his debut in 1972. First appearing in episode one of season four on 13 November 1972, the lavender colored vampire (full name Count von Count) has remained one of the show's mainstays ever since. Voiced by Jerry Nelson for 40 years until his death in 2012 (Matt Vogel took over in 2013), he is noted for his rich Bela Lugosi–like accent and his pleasure in counting anything and everything, which he climaxes with a satisfied laugh. His lady friend, Countess Natasha von Numeral (voiced by Fran Brill), first appeared on 5 January 1977. The show's many other creatures include the Cookie Monster, Oscar the Grouch and Grover, though it should be noted that their aim is to educate, not to frighten.

Although by no means a genre show, *The ABC Afternoon Playbreak* (1972, TVM, aka *ABC Matinee Today*), which began its three season, 17-episode run on ABC on 7 December 1972, occasionally dipped its toes into the supernatural, although stories involving custody battles and unexpected pregnancies were the usual territory of its 90-minute dramas, which featured such names as Diana Hyland, June Lockhart, Pat O'Brien, Juliet Mills, Michael Callan, Cathleen Nesbitt, David Hedison and Don Porter. Exceptions proved to be *The Gift of Terror* (1973, TVM), in which a young woman (Denise Alexander) begins to have premonitions about her friends dying, and *The Last Bride of Salem* (1974, TVM), in which a woman (Lois Nettleton) tries to protect her family from supernatural forces ("A 17th century curse… A cult of superstitious neighbors… And a diabolic threat to her family are waiting for… *The Last Bride of Salem*," ran the tagline for the latter). Routinely shot on tape (with filmed inserts), the series made for perfectly passable daytime viewing at the time, though it needs to be watched through rose tinted glasses today.

Monsters of a more benevolent kind could be found in the kids' show *Sigmund and the Sea Monsters* (1973–1975, TV), which began airing on NBC on 8 September 1973. Created by Si Rose and Sid and Marty Krofft (who also produced), it was an elaborate affair in the style of the Krofft's *H.R. Pufnstuf* (1969–1970, TV), which they had followed with the likes of *The Bugaloos* (1970–1971, TV), about a magical forest whose inhabitants include a rock band with bug wings, and *Lidsville* (1971–1972, TV), in which a boy finds himself in a land populated by hat people. The new show focused on the adventures of brothers Johnny and Scott Stuart (Johnny Whittaker and Scott C. Kolden) and their friend Sigmund Ooze (Billy Barty), a sea monster who has been thrown out of his home because, unlike his family (Big Daddy, Sweet Mamma and his brothers Blurp and Slurp), he doesn't like to scare people. Running to 29 episodes over two seasons, it also featured the likes of Mary Wickes as the boys' Aunt Zelda, Rip Taylor as Sheldon the Sea Genie and Joe Higgins as Sheriff Chuck Bevans, while guest performers included Pamelyn Ferdin, *H.R. Pufnstuf* star Jack Wild and the Wicked Witch of the West herself, Margaret Hamilton. Like most of the Krofft's output, it was all rather silly, even by Saturday morning standards, but one can't deny the enthusiasm with which it was put together (note that an unaired reboot pilot followed in 2017).

Prehistoric monsters were meanwhile the selling point of *Land of the Lost* (1974–1976, TV), a live action series care of animation studio Hanna-Barbera which began its three-season run, amounting to a healthy 43 episodes, on NBC on 7 September 1974. Produced by Marty and Sid Krofft, who also created the show with Allan Foshko, it follows the adventures of widowed ranger Will Marshall (Wesley Eure [billed simply as Wesley]) and his two kids Holly (Kathy Coleman) and Rick (Spencer Milligan) who, following an earthquake while on a routine rafting expedition, find themselves transported to a lost land (as the country and western-style theme tune informs us), where they have to survive encounters with all manner of weird creatures, among them dinosaurs, all the while trying to figure out a way back home. Cheesy nonsense interspersing studio footage with effects shots, it featured special make-up and costumes by Michael Westmore, among them those sported by an ape-like being known as Cha-Ka (Philip Paley) from the Pacuni tribe, whom the Marshalls befriend, and reasonable dinosaur effects designed by Wah Chang and executed by stop motion director Gene Warren (who was also an associate producer) and his team of animators (the nineties saw a reboot of the series [1991–1992, TV], again care of Sid & Marty Krofft, while 2009 saw a big screen version starring Will Ferrell, again produced by the Kroffts).

Interestingly, *Land of the Lost* first aired on the same Saturday morning as *Valley of the Dinosaurs* (1974, TV), a 16-part animated series also care of Hanna-Barbera in which the Butler family and their dog find their raft drawn into a whirlpool while exploring an uncharted river canyon in the Amazon, only to emerge in a valley where prehistoric creatures still roam. Befriended by a family of cave dwellers, they likewise survive various adventures while trying to figure out how to get home. Why two such similar shows were commissioned by the same studio and then aired on the same day seems somewhat curious, but for a weekly animated series, the overall quality is pretty good, and certainly better than some of the yackety-yak product Hanna-Barbera churned out in the seventies, given that in this case dad is a science teacher who insists on imparting his knowledge to his children.

Kids were also the intended audience for *The Ghost Busters* (1975, TV), a live-action comedy series for Saturday mornings care of animation studio Filmation, which aired on CBS from 6 September 1975. Running to 15 half-hour episodes, the show, which was written and created by Marc Richards, followed the bumbling adventures of Kong (Forrest Tucker), Spencer (Larry Storch) and their pet gorilla Tracy (Bob Burns) as they investigate various spooky situations, many of them involving such classic monsters as Dracula, the Mummy, the Werewolf, Dr. Jekyll and Mr. Hyde and Frankenstein and his Monster, all of them out to wreak havoc until thwarted by the team's Ghost De-Materializer. Slapstick nonsense in the style of The Three Stooges, its level of wit was fairly low, even compared to *Scooby-Doo*, and whoever thought Forrest Tucker had a funny bone in his body was sadly mistaken, yet it contained a few gems among the shenanigans ("Hey, whaddaya know about that, a baseball bat!" exclaims Spencer in one episode after opening a filing cabinet containing information about vampires, out of which flies a bat carrying a baseball). Featuring such episode titles as *Dr. Whatshisname* (1975, TV), *The Vampire's Apprentice* (1975, TV) and *Merlin the Magician* (1975, TV), the program was typical Saturday morning fodder, and certainly went down well with its intended audience, who no doubt enjoyed its cardboard sets (the same graveyard seemed to feature every week), silly sound effects and ancient puns, all of them accompanied by the prerequisite laugh track. Had they known what their kids were watching, parents may well have been less impressed (the series was followed by an animated sequel involving the sons of Spencer and Kong titled *Ghostbusters* [1986–1987, TV], also care of Filmation).

Also launching on 6 September 1975 care of Filmation, albeit on ABC, was *Fraidy Cat* (1975, TV), a cartoon series whose 18 six-minute episodes revolved round a cat who is on his ninth and final life. Unfortunately, whenever he says any number between one and eight, a feline ghost appears to help him, among them Tinker Elephunt "Cave One" Cat, Jasper "Six" Catdaver and Hep "Eight" Cat. However, should he say the number nine, he will find his life in peril from the malevolent Cloud Nine. Featuring the voices of Alan Oppenheimer (Fraidy Cat and Cloud Nine) and Lennie Weinrib (cats one to eight), the series sported such episode titles as *The Not So Nice Mice* (1975, TV), *A Scaredy Fraidy* (1975, TV) and *It's a Dog's Life* (1975, TV). By no means a classic, the animation is pretty basic here, and not even the laugh track can help the tired scripts.

Not too dissimilar to *The Ghost Busters* (1975, TV) was *Monster Squad* (1976, TV), another live action Saturday morning romp whose 13-episode run began on NBC on 11 September 1976. In it, a criminology student named Walter (Fred Grandy) works as a night watchman at a

Busted. From left to right, Larry Storch, Forrest Tucker and Bob Burns in a publicity shot for *The Ghost Busters* (1975, TV) (CBS/Filmation Associates).

wax museum, where he secretly builds a crime computer, whose oscillating vibrations bring to life the effigies of Dracula (Henry Polic II), the Wolfman (Buck Kartalian) and the Frankenstein Monster (Mike Lane) who are "now determined to make up for their past misbehaving" as Walter puts it in the opening credits, and become crime fighters, and as such take on such villains as Queen Bee, Mr. Mephisto, No Face, Ultra Witch and Lawrence of Moravia. The show was developed by Stanley Ralph Ross and created by Ray Allen, Harvey Bullock and William P. D'Angelo, who also produced, and again garish sets and corny gags were the order of the day, though the quality of the guest stars, among them Julie Newmar, Alice Ghostley, Jonathan Harris and Marty Allen, made it a slightly classier affair than *The Ghost Busters*. But only slightly. And if the program resembled a low rent variation on *Batman* (1966–1968, TV), that was perhaps because D'Angelo had worked as an associate producer on 118 of its 120 episodes, while Ross had written 27 of them and appeared in two as Barney "Ballpoint" Jackson.

A kids' show with slightly more serious intentions was the long running *ABC Weekend Specials* (1977–1995, TV), which began its epic 15-season run of 85 half-hour episodes on ABC on 29 January 1977. Made primarily by ABC Circle Films, although other production companies were involved (among them Ruby-Spears, Hanna-Barbera and Highgate Pictures), it aired on Saturday mornings at 11 a.m., and presented "children's novels for television" via a series of live action and animated "short story specials," as the opening credits have it. Originally hosted by Michael Young (later replacements included the ventriloquist Willie Tyler and his dummy Lester and the puppet character Cap'n O.G. Readmore), it launched with *Valentine's Second Chance* (1977, TV), a story about a safecracker (Ken Berry), and went on to include such genre-centric episodes as *The Haunted Trailer* (1977, TV), *The Girl with ESP* (1979, TV), *The Ghost of Thomas Kempe* (1979, TV), *Bunnicula, the Vampire Rabbit* (1980, TV), *Zack and the Magic Factory* (1981, TV), *The Haunted Mansion Mystery* (1983, TV), *The Secret World of Og* (1983, TV), *Henry Hamilton Graduate Ghost* (1984, TV), *The Adventures of a Two-Minute Werewolf* (1985, TV), *Cap'n O.G. Readmore Meets Dr. Jekyll and Mr. Hyde* (1986, TV), *The Monster Bed* (1989, TV) and *Commander Toad in Space* (1993, TV). Harmless if sometimes bland fun, each installment usually had a moral or educational element which the makers managed to sneak in under the wire, though it was never as serious as *ABC Afterschool Specials* (1972–1997, TV), which managed to deal with such subjects as bullying, alcoholism, drug use and even gonorrhea.

Meet the Hardy Boys

Another show aimed primarily at kids (it aired on Sundays at 7 p.m.) proved to be the next big series to have brushes (albeit rather tame ones) with the horror genre. This was *The Hardy Boys/Nancy Drew Mysteries* (1977–1979, TV), which began its three-season, 46-episode run on ABC on 30 January 1977. The show, which initially alternated between the adventures of teenage detectives Joe and Frank Hardy (Shaun Cassidy and Parker Stevenson) and spunky amateur sleuth Nancy Drew (Pamela Sue

Martin, later Janet Louise Johnson), was based on the popular novels by Franklin W. Dixon and Carolyn Keene, respectively, and was developed for television by the prolific Glen A. Larson, who also executive produced via Universal and Glen Larson Productions, following a suggestion from Joyce Heft Brotman and Arlene Sidaris that the books would be ideal for a weekly series (both went on to work as producers on the series). Directed by the likes of Joseph Pevney, Noel Black, Jack Arnold and Sidney Hayers, the show featured such guest stars as Stuart Whitman, Clive Revill, Pamela Franklin, Guy Stockwell, Rick Springfield, James Booth, Dorothy Malone, Leon Ames, Kim Cattrall, J.D. Cannon, Dennis Weaver, Jaclyn Smith, Robert Wagner, Victor Buono and Jamie Lee Curtis (who was among those who originally auditioned for the role of Nancy Drew).

Season one kicked off with a Hardy Boys case titled *The Mystery of the Haunted House* (1977, TV), in which they follow their father (Ed Gilbert), himself a private detective, on a case that leads them to a fog wreathed graveyard and a haunted house (the old Bates house from *Psycho* [1960]) which turns out to be a nightclub run by Richard Kiel dressed as the Frankenstein Monster. Written and directed by Larson himself (who also provided the theme tune, as he went on to do for many of his other shows), it all starts rather abruptly and very quickly turns into a live action version of *Scooby-Doo* (the boys even have their own Mystery Machine–style van in which they store their motorbikes), with much running about the back lot and the haunted house, the interior of which is nicely realized by art director Roy Steffensen, among its best touches being a stairway accessed through a coffin and a mirror maze that allows for a sequence that pays homage to the funhouse climax of *The Lady from Shanghai* (1947). It's all quite cheerful if somewhat straightforward, and one never doubts that the brothers will win the day and have everything neatly wrapped up by the finale. Still, it's harmless fun, and its perfectly coiffed young leads carry the proceedings well enough (the episode's best line goes to Kiel who, upon hearing that there has been some trouble out back, comments to one of his waitresses, "This could be bad for business. Listen, keep it under your hat, we don't want to scare anybody").

Episode two, *The Mystery of Pirate's Cove* (1977, TV), featured Drew's first adventure, in which she investigates a long-abandoned lighthouse which suddenly starts up again. Is it haunted, or has the new owner, a parapsychology professor (Monte Markham), got something to do with it? Of course he has, given that he's on the hunt for treasure, and he didn't want anyone to know about it. Things resolve themselves in the caves underneath the lighthouse where, after almost drowning because of the rising tide, Nancy discovers the pirate gold the professor has been looking for, but things aren't quite what they seem, as a final twist reveals him to be rather more devious than he appears to be (spoiler alert: in a rather complex resolution, it turns out he's laundering money from the hijacking of an airline!). Written by Larson and directed by E.W. Swackhamer, the episode is a little more serious in tone than the Hardy Boys installment, but Martin makes for a game heroine, who isn't above putting herself in danger to solve the case, and the supporting cast, among them Jean Rasey as Nancy's best friend George, William Schallert as her attorney father and George O'Hanlon, Jr., as his assistant Ned Nickerson (who has a crush on Nancy), are pleasant enough. The remainder of season one saw the Hardy Boys deal with such cases as *The Mystery of Witches' Hollow* (1977, TV), in which they become caught up in strange events surrounding an old local legend, while Nancy becomes involved in the staging of a play at a theatre supposedly haunted by a phantom in *A Haunting We Will Go* (1977, TV).

With the start of season two changes began to occur, with Nancy teaming up with the Hardy Boys for the opening two-part adventure, *The Hardy Boys and Nancy Drew Meet Dracula* (1977, TV), in which the Boys, while searching Europe for their missing father, attend a rock concert at Dracula's castle in Transylvania, and become involved with a police inspector (Lorne Greene) who may or may not be a vampire. The Hardy Boys next found themselves investigating a scam involving stolen artefacts in *The Mystery of King Tut's Tomb* (1977, TV), following which Nancy joined them again for another two-parter, *The Mystery of the Hollywood Phantom* (1977, TV), in which they become involved with a phantom-like figure while attending a detective convention (cue much running around the Universal back lot tour). The next four episodes belonged to the Boys, and though Martin returned on and off for a further three appearances as Nancy, it was gradually becoming clear that the series was being skewed towards the Boys, among their cases being *The House on Possessed Hill* (1978, TV), in which they help a girl (Melanie Griffith) accused of being a witch (the episode again featured the Bates house from *Psycho* [1960]). Consequently, Martin elected to leave the show, and was replaced by Janet Louise Johnson, who joined the Boys in the two-parter *Voodoo Doll* (1978, TV), in which they are threatened by a voodoo master (Julius Harris), and the following *Mystery on the Avalanche Express* (1978, TV). After another Hardy Boys escapade, Nancy joined them again in *Arson and Old Lace* (1978, TV), after which the Boys concluded the season by themselves in *Campus Terror* (1978, TV).

For season three, Nancy was dropped altogether, and the show was re-titled *The Hardy Boys*. The more fantastical elements were also pared back in favor of more realistic stories. However, midway through the season, the show was cancelled in a failed bid by ABC to improve their Sunday night ratings and ended with a motor cross adventure titled *Life on the Line* (1979, TV). Still, it had been fun while it lasted, and the show still has its admirers to this day (note that Pamela Sue Martin guest starred in the pilot for the 2019 reboot of *Nancy Drew* which starred Kennedy McMann in the title role; a reboot of *The Hardy Boys* followed in 2020 starring Alexander Elliot and Rohan Campbell as Joe and Frank; a movie version of *Nancy Drew* appeared in 2007 with Emma Roberts in the title role).

It was back to the anthology format next with *Tales of the Unexpected* (1977, aka *Quinn Martin's Tales of the Unexpected*) which ran to only eight episodes, despite being executive produced by the profligate Quinn Martin, whose hit shows included *The Fugitive* (1963–1967, TV), *The Invaders* (1967–1968, TV) and *The Streets of San Francisco* (1972–1977, TV). Narrated by William Conrad, who'd starred in *Cannon* (1971–1976, TV) for Martin, the hour-long show, which aired on NBC from 2 February 1977, featured the usual mix of sci-fi, horror and the farfetched, capped by a sting in the tail, and began with *The Final Chapter* (1977, TV), in which an investigative reporter (Roy Thinnes) goes undercover on Death Row, only to find that his contacts on the outside have disappeared. Other episodes included *The Mask of Adonis* (1977,

TV), about a film producer (Robert Foxworth) who hopes to undergo a rejuvenation procedure only to learn it comes at a price; *Devil Pack* (1977, TV), in which a farmer (Ronny Cox) battles a pack of dogs belonging to a Satanist; and *A Hand for Sonny Blue* (1977, TV), in which a baseball star (Ricky Nelson) who has undergone a hand transplant following an accident discovers that his new limb has a mind of its own. Yet despite fair production values, a reasonable line up of guest stars (Lloyd Bridges, Bill Bixby, Joanna Pettet, Ned Beatty, Gary Collins) and workmanlike direction care of Walter Grauman and Curtis Harrington (among others), the show just didn't click with audiences, perhaps because the material was familiar rather than surprising (note that the episode titled *Force of Evil* [1977, TV] ran to 96 minutes for a two-hour timeslot; in the UK the show was known as *Twist in the Tale*, and should not be confused with the slightly later British series *Tales of the Unexpected* [1979–1988, TV, aka *Roald Dahl's Tales of the Unexpected*]).

The Bermuda Triangle was a subject of particular fascination with the public in the seventies and had already been the focus of such TV movies as *Satan's Triangle* (1975, TVM) and *Beyond the Bermuda Triangle* (1975, TVM), as well as a documentary on the matter, *The Devil's Triangle* (1971, TVM), which was narrated by Vincent Price. Now came *The Fantastic Journey* (1977, TV), in which members of a scientific expedition encounter a luminous green cloud at sea and find themselves shipwrecked on an uncharted island somewhere in the Bermuda Triangle. Here, they slide through time portals and encounter travellers from other worlds and dimensions, all the while searching for the doorway that will lead them back to their own time. On air on NBC from 3 February 1977, the series was created by Bruce Lansbury (who also executive produced), produced by Leonard Katzman, and starred Carl Franklin as Dr. Fred Walters, Scott Thomas as Professor Paul Jordan (who disappears back to his own time after the feature-length pilot), Ike Eisenmann as his son Jordan, Roddy McDowall as Dr. Jonathan Willaway (who joined the cast in episode three) and Jared Martin as Varian, who hails from the 23rd century, and whose Sonic Energizer proves to be an invaluable device on their adventures, given that it can perform all manner of helpful tasks. A show very much of its period, it featured such guest stars as Joan Collins, Nicholas Hammond, Ian McShane, Cheryl Ladd, Leif Erickson, Mel Ferrer and John Saxon, and was directed by the likes of Andrew V. McLaglen, Vincent McEveety and Alf Kjellin. Unfortunately, the program, which ditched the Bermuda Triangle angle early on to concentrate on encounters with future races, struggled in the ratings, and was pulled after just ten episodes.

With *In Search of...* (1977–1982, TV), which began its syndicated run on 17 April 1977, television turned its attention to a documentary examination of "extraterrestrials, magic and witchcraft, missing persons, myths and monsters, lost civilizations, special phenomena" as the credits announced at the top of each show, which took in such wide-ranging topics as the disappearance of Amelia Earhart, the Jack the Ripper murders, the Amityville massacre, the myth of Bigfoot and the legend of the Loch Ness Monster, as well as the Salem witches, Vlad the Impaler and, of course, the Bermuda Triangle. Executive produced by Alan Landsburg (and others) and hosted by Leonard Nimoy, the original series racked up 144 half-hour episodes, and was inspired by the success of two earlier programs, *In Search of Ancient Astronauts*

(1973, TV), itself an edited version of the German documentary *Chariots of the Gods* (1970, aka *Erinnerungen an die Zukunft*), and *In Search of Ancient Mysteries* (1974, TV). Featuring witness interviews, re-enactments and supposedly real photographs and cine footage, the programs were often sensationalist and highly speculative, no doubt hence the disclaimer that "this series presents information based in part on theory and conjecture. The producer's purpose is to suggest some possible explanations, but not necessarily the only ones to the mysteries we will examine." It nevertheless proved popular, and its influence can be found in such similar series and one-offs as *The Occult: Mysteries of the Unknown* (1977, TV), in which Christopher Lee hosted a look at such topics as ESP, faith healing, astrology and superstition, *Arthur C. Clarke's Mysterious World* (1980, TV), *Ripley's Believe It or Not* (1982–1986, 2000–2003, 2019, TV [original pilot 1981]), *Sightings* (1991–1997, TV), *Ancient Mysteries* (1994–1998, TV) and *History's Mysteries* (1998–2011, TV), while *In Search of …* itself was revived in 2002, with Mitch Pileggi now hosting, and again in 2018, with Zachary Quinto.

A far less successful proposition proved to be *The World of Darkness* (1977, TV), a pilot for a new hour-long supernatural series which aired on CBS on 17 April 1977. In it, sportswriter Paul Taylor (Granville Van Dusen) suffers a near-death experience following a road accident, the consequence of which allows spirits from the afterlife to contact him to help someone they know. An intriguing enough premise, it was created and written by Art Wallace, was directed in Canada by Jerry London, and co-starred Beatrice Straight, Tovah Feldshuh and Gary Merrill. A second pilot, this time titled *The World Beyond* (1978, TV), appeared the following year on CBS on 21 January 1978, again written by Wallace, which sees our hero ("Condemned to fight a living nightmare," as the tagline has it) travel to Logan's Island in Maine (actually, Canada again), where he tackles a golem made of mud which can only be destroyed with salt. Directed by Noel Black, and also featuring JoBeth Williams and Barnard Hughes, the episode's highlight is a scene in which the monster loses its hand, which goes on to have a life of its own. Unfortunately, despite the show's potential, it failed to get picked up as a series.

As we have already noted, sitcoms occasionally ventured towards the supernatural, one of which, *A Year at the Top* (1977, TV), began its brief (very brief) run on CBS on 5 August 1977. Created by Heywood Kling and executive produced by Norman Lear, it presented a variation on the Faust legend, with two struggling musicians (Greg Evigan and Paul Shaffer) offered a year's worth of success by music promoter Frederick J. Hanover (Gabriel Dell) on the understanding that they sign their souls over to his father, who just happens to be the Devil. The pilot featured a guest spot from Hollywood legend Mickey Rooney, with support in the following five episodes provided by Nedra Volz, Julie Cobb and Priscilla Morrill, but audiences weren't interested in the lame premise, and the series was pulled. Evigan and Shaffer subsequently went on to better things, the former in *B.J. and the Bear* (1979–1981, TV) and the latter as the music director for talk show king David Letterman in thousands of episodes of *Late Night with Letterman* (1982–1993, TV) and the *Late Show with David Letterman* (1993–2015, TV).

Dracula meanwhile made another small screen appearance in *Cliffhangers*

(1979, TV), which began airing on NBC on 27 February 1979. A cleverly devised hour-long show that paid tribute to the movie serials of yesteryear, it was divided into three weekly segments running 20 minutes apiece (including ad breaks). These were *Stop Susan Williams*, which followed the exploits of an intrepid reporter (Susan Anton); *The Secret Empire*, a period piece set in 19th-century Wyoming in which a U.S. marshal (Geoffrey Scott) discovers a secret underground city inhabited by aliens; and *The Curse of Dracula*, in which the Count (Michael Nouri) hides in plain sight as a history teacher in South Bay College—night courses only—all the while trying to evade his Nemesis, Kurt Von Helsing (Stephen Johnson). "The excitement of the chase! The lure of the exotic! The shock of the unexpected!" ballyhooed the publicity for the show. Unfortunately, it aired opposite ABC's *Happy Days* (1974–1984, TV) and *Laverne and Shirley* (1976–1983, TV), at the time the nation's number one and two shows, respectively, and was cancelled after ten episodes. By this time the Dracula segment had concluded its story, but the other two were left dangling, with the Susan Williams element left with one episode to go and *The Secret Empire* with two (though foreign territories which had acquired the series did broadcast the last program, which included these installments). The full run of the Susan Williams episodes was subsequently edited down into a 96-minute TV movie titled *The Girl Who Saved the World* (1979, TVM), while the Dracula saga was edited into two tele-films, *Dracula '79* (1979, TVM) and *World of Dracula* (1979, TVM), thus leaving only the final two chapters of *The Secret Empire* unaired in the States.

For horror fans, the Dracula segment was of course the one that mattered. Featuring such chapter titles as *Lifeblood*, *Sepulchre of the Undead* and *Pleas for the Damned*, it begins with Von Helsing and his assistant Mary (Carol Baxter) destroying the 13th of 20 boxes of native soil that Dracula has brought with him to America ("Your grandfather would be proud of us," comments Mary). Having discovered that Dracula, who apparently hasn't seen daylight for 512 years, is now posing as a teacher, Mary enrolls in his evening class so as to help Von Helsing flush him out, urged on by the fact that Dracula killed her mother, who it is revealed he once loved ("In my lifetime I have known many women. I have loved only a few. I loved your mother," he informs her). However, when Dracula professes to wanting to possess Mary, she finds herself in a sticky situation. "There is a passion within me which I cannot control; a passion to live, to possess. I should like to possess *you*, Mary," at which she burns his hand with a small cross she has with her and attempts to escape, only to be cornered by three fellow students who turn out to be his acolytes. With Von Helsing unable to provide assistance owing to the fact that the car he had been following her in has a broken fuel line, things consequently don't look too good for our heroine ("Is this the end for Kurt Von Helsing? Is Mary marked for doom? For the surprising answers, don't miss *Blood Stream*, the next thrilling chapter of *The Curse of Dracula*," intones the narrator in mock dramatic fashion at the end of the episode).

Written and directed by Kenneth Johnson, who also developed and executive produced the program for Universal, the show clearly had its tongue in its cheek. Yet despite the knowing air of camp that pervades all three portions, Michael Nouri manages to play it reasonably straight as Dracula in his own segment, and even sports a Bela Lugosi–style Transylvanian accent, while Carol Baxter makes for a perfectly adequate damsel in distress. The story itself is paper thin, with the cliff-hanger situations conveniently resolved in the opening moments of the following week's episode, yet despite being fairly insubstantial in itself, the series was enjoyed by younger audiences if not the critics ("It's just not the same without the stale pop-corn and the sticky carpets," moaned *TV Guide*). And for executives to have pulled the rug from under it with just one episode to go seems more than a little mean spir-ited, given it was they who scheduled the show opposite two such popular sitcoms in the first place. But such is the world of commerce (the above ground sequences in *Secret of the Empire* were presented in "beautiful black and white" as the announcer has it, while, to give the show a sense of urgency, each serial began *in media res*, with *Stop Susan Williams* starting with chapter two, *The Secret Empire* with chapter three and *The Curse of Dracula* with chapter six, a misguided idea which must surely have confused some viewers).

A spooky house sitcom came next with *Highcliffe Manor* (1979, TV), which began airing on NBC on 12 April 1979. Created by Robert Blees and produced by Eugene Ross-Leming and Brad Buckner via Alan Landsburg Productions, it sees Helen Blacke (Shelley Fabares) inherit a creepy mansion which is home to her late husband's research institute, the Blacke Foundation, in which a variety of oddball characters, among them a number of mad doctors and scientists, are working to var-ious agendas, among them a plot to clone world leaders. A rather desperate parody of low-budget horror movies, the program (which was promoted as "A haunting new comedy") also featured Stephen McHattie as the womanizing Ian Glenville, Jenny O'Hara as the mysterious housekeeper Rebecca, Chris Marlowe as a low rent bionic man named Bram Shelley, complete with an Erector Set arm, Ernie Hudson as the valet Smythe, and Harold Sakata as the henchman Cheng. Despite a *Soap*-style nar-ration by Peter Lawford, the humor was all rather strained and obvious, with the laugh track working overtime. Unfortunately, audiences remained indifferent to the broad gags and performances, and only four of the six episodes recorded made it to the airwaves before the plug was unceremoniously pulled.

Lessons clearly weren't learned, and another spooky house comedy was attempted with *Struck by Light-ning* (1979, TV), which began air-ing over on CBS on 19 September 1979. This time it's a high school sci-ence teacher named Ted Stein (Jeffrey Kramer) who inherits a spooky old inn whose grouchy handyman, Frank (Jack Elam), turns out to be none other than the Frankenstein Mon-ster, Ted himself being a descendant of Dr. Frankenstein. As it transpires, the Monster needs a special serum to stay alive, and coaxes Ted into starting up

Vamping it. Michael Nouri as Dracula in *Cliff-hangers* (1979, TV) (NBC/Universal Television).

the lab again. Created by Arthur Fellows and Terry Keegan, who also produced via Fellows-Keegan and Paramount, and co-starring Millie Slavin, Bill Erwin and Richard Stahl, the program's chief asset was the boggle-eyed Elam (who played the role without the usual make-up), his deadpan delivery getting most of what laughs there were (recalling a dinner with Dracula, he comments, "I had a glass of red wine, he had a glass of the waiter," to which he adds, "Dracula was a jerk. He'll be a jerk till the day he dies, which is never"). Unfortunately, if a series along the lines of *The Addams Family* (1964–1966, TV) or *The Munsters* (1964–1966, TV) was intended, then its makers were in for a disappointment, for despite reasonable production values (including some good sets care of art director Arch Bacon), the show failed to click with audiences and was pulled after just three episodes, although other territories, such as the UK, aired the complete 11-episode run.

More madcap yocks were provided by *The Halloween That Almost Wasn't* (1979, TV, aka *The Night That Dracula Saved the World*), a half-hour special that aired on ABC on 28 October 1979. Written by Coleman Jacoby (from a concept by associate producer Bruno Caliandro) and directed by Bruce Bilson, it sees Dracula (Judd Hirsch) call his fellow monsters together, among them the Frankenstein Monster (John Schuck), the Mummy (Robert Fitch), the Werewolf (Jack Riley), Zabaar the Zombie (Josip Elic) and the Witch (Mariette Hartley), in a bid to save Halloween, which is under threat of cancellation because they are no longer deemed scary. "People are laughing at you instead of shrieking," the Count informs them, hence the tagline, "No more tricks? No more treats? No more Halloween? Not unless Dracula, Frankenstein, Wolfman, the Mummy, the Zombie and Igor can convince the Witch

The eyes have it. Jack Elam in a publicity shot for *Struck by Lightning* (1979, TV) (CBS/Fellow-Keegan Company/Paramount Television).

to fly over the moon." Featuring Henry Gibson as Dracula's loyal servant Igor, the program is a somewhat underwritten affair which never quite captures the madcap atmosphere it seeks, with only Hirsch as an amusing Lugosi-style Dracula and Hartley as the short-tempered Witch leaving a mark (the program ends with them disco dancing together, with Dracula in full John Travolta garb). On the whole, something of a missed opportunity, though younger audiences (under fives, perhaps) might be amused by the antics (the film later aired regularly on the Disney Channel between 1983 and 1996 during the Halloween season).

America wasn't the only nation producing genre programming in the seventies, and like the States, Canada also provided light-hearted genre programming for its younger audiences. While American kids enjoyed such live action fare as *The Ghost Busters* (1975, TV) and *Monster Squad* (1976, TV), Canadian kids got stuck into *The Hilarious House of Frightenstein* (1971, TV), which clocked up 130 one-hour-long episodes, all of which were recorded during a hectic nine-month period. Produced by the independent station CHCH-TV, the program was created by Rafael (Riff) Markowitz (who also produced and directed many of the episodes), and starred Billy Van as Count Frightenstein, the 13th son of Count Dracula, who has been exiled to Castle Frightenstein, which plays host to zany sketches and educational segments involving animals and science. Also onboard were Fishka Rais as Igor, Guy Big as Mini-Count, Julius Sumner Miller as the Professor and, most surprisingly, horror legend Vincent Price as the Narrator (who filmed close to 400 linking segments in just four days for a fee of $13,000). Other characters included the Wolfman, the Oracle and Grizelda the Ghastly Gourmet. Ramshackle low-budget shenanigans performed with manic energy, it was destined to become a cult favorite, especially with college students in America, where it aired in a late-night slot.

Meanwhile, with *Purple Playhouse* (1973, TV), the Canadian Broadcasting Company dipped its toes into the anthology format to produce a series of eight one-hour dramas which began airing on 25 February 1973, among them adaptations of *Sweeney Todd, the Demon Barber of Fleet Street* (1973, TV) starring Barry Morse as Todd, *The Corsican Brothers* (1973, TV) and *Ticket-of-Leave Man* (1973, TV). A potted version of *Dracula* (1973, TV) starring Norman Welsh as Dracula, Nehemiah Persoff as Van Helsing and Blair Brown as Mina was also included in the run. Adapted by Rod Coneybeare and directed by Jack Nixon-Browne, it was a fairly parsimonious studio production, yet managed to feature the scene in which the Count scales down the walls of his castle, much to the astonishment of Dan MacDonald's Jonathan Harker, who observes him do so from a turret window. CBC was also behind *Christmas Carol* (1978, TV, aka *Rich Little's Christmas Carol*), a 50-minute potted version of the Dickens perennial, which aired on the station on 17 December 1978. In it, impressionist Rich Little plays all the famous characters, albeit with a twist, given that Scrooge sounds like W.C. Fields ("I'm dreaming of a tight Christmas," he sings at one point), Jacob Marley sounds like Richard Nixon and Tiny Tim sounds like Truman Capote, etc. The script is pretty risible (the laugh track doesn't help) and Little's impersonations are rather variable, but the good ones are truly uncanny, among them his takes on Johnny Carson, Jimmy Stewart and James Mason. The same year, the Canadians also presented a straight version of the story simply titled *Scrooge* (1978, TVM), which it aired on 22 December 1978, this time with Warren Graves as Scrooge, supported by Ray Hunt, Drew Borland and Nicole Evans.

Down Under, the Australians tried their hand at an anthology series of their own with *The Evil Touch* (1973–1974, TV). Hosted by Anthony Quayle, it ran to 26 half-hour episodes from 16 September 1973, and featured a number of visiting American guest stars, among them Julie Harris, Susan Strasberg, Carol Lynley and Mildred Natwick (presumably to help secure an American sale), as well as such home-grown talent as Jack Thompson and Tony Bonner. Produced by Mende Browne (who also directed 15 episodes) and made via Amalgamated Pictures Australasia, its mix of mystery, drama and science fiction also included occasional forays into horror, among them the opening installment, *The Lake* (1973, TV), in which a husband (Robert Lansing) allows his wife (Anne Haddy) to drown during a boat-ing accident so that he can marry his secretary (Anna Bowdon), but it seems that the wife—whose ring he pulled from her finger as she went under, so that he could give it to his mistress—has come back to haunt him. No one can have been fooled by the implied American setting, and the budget was clearly low, while the twist, in which the husband himself now drowns having heard his wife call him to the lake, is somewhat watery, but the cast and crew at least deserve a mark for trying. Other stories included *A Game of Hearts* (1973, TV), in which a surgeon (Darren McGavin) removes a supposedly dead man's heart for transplantation purposes, only to have the victim return to take the doctor's own heart in vengeance; *Seeing Is Believing* (1973, TV), in which an actor (Robert Lansing) working on a horror film is con-fronted by a real monster; and *Kadaitcha County* (1974, TV), in which a missionary (Leif Erickson) becomes involved with an Aboriginal witch doctor who wishes to take his soul. As for our congenial host, he concluded each program with the same sign off: "So, until we meet next, this is Anthony Quayle reminding you that there is a touch of evil in all of us. Good night. Pleasant dreams."

More Tales from Europe

Over in Europe, the Spanish presented a five-part series involving Dracula titled *Otra vez Dracula* (1970, TV [*Dracula Again*]). In it, a theatre troupe put on a play that satirizes the Count, not realizing that the old boy is in residence in their basement, from whence he extracts his revenge. Featuring local star Narciso Ibanez Menta as Dracula and Selva Mayo and Betty Solis as his brides, the series, whose episodes ran a lengthy 90 minutes each, was written by Horacio S. Meyrialle and co-directed by Menta (who also produced) and Alberto Rinaldi (note that this was Menta's sec-ond brush with Dracula, having previously hosted a 90-minute Argentinean tele-vision drama titled *Hay que matar Dracula* [1968, TV], again directed by Alberto Rinaldi, with Gianni Lunadei as the Count and Pepe Novoa as Jonathan Harker, while he'd go on to play the Count again himself in the theatrical feature *La saga de los Dracula* [1973, aka *The Dracula Saga*]). Menta followed up *Otra vez Dracula* with *Robot!* (1970, TV), a 15-part science fiction/horror piece in which he played Professor Eric Strassberg, a mad scientist who has created a robot that the government wants, his price for which is being allowed to murder his adulterous wife (Silvia Legrand). The series, which was written by Osvaldo Dragun, was again directed by Menta and Alberto Rinaldi (as well as Raul Lecuna), with Menta producing four of the episodes.

Other Spanish series that made nods to the genre include *Teatro de misterio* (1970, TV [*Mystery Theatre*]), which presented a version of the haunted house com-edy *The Cat and the Canary* as *El gato y el canario* (1970, TV), and *Ficciones* (1971–1981, TV [*Fictions*]), which included an adaptation of Le Fanu's *Carmilla* (1973, TV)—which was also the subject of a 1976 TV movie from Venezuela—plus an adap-tation of Robert Louis Stevenson's *The Body Snatcher* as *El resurreccionista* (1974, TV). Also getting in on the act was *Los libros* (1974–1977, TV [*The Books*]), which presented a version of Stevenson's *The Suicide Club* as *El club de los suicidas* (1977,

TV), while *Palabras cruzadas* (1974–1977, TV [*Crossing Words*]) included an adaptation of Poe's *Murders in the Rue Morgue* as *Doble crimen en la calle Morgue* (1977, TV).

It was also during this period that Spain produced one of the most perfectly realized short films ever made for television, *La cabina* (1972, TV, aka *The Telephone Box*), an initially simple seeming but increasingly elaborate story about a hapless middle-aged man (José Luis Lopez Vazquez) who gets trapped inside a telephone booth. Directed with Hitchcockian panache by Anthony Mercero from a script by himself and José Luis Garci (taken from Mercero's own story), the 35-minute film, which first aired on Television Espanola on 13 December 1972, sees the man wave off his young son on the school bus before popping into a red, glass paneled phone booth to make a call. The booth, as we have seen, has just been installed by the phone company in the middle of a city square, and our protagonist proves to be its first customer. However, the phone doesn't work, and while he is attempting to make his call, the door slowly closes, trapping him inside, much to his increasing panic and consternation, especially so when his predicament begins to draw a crowd of curious onlookers, several of whom attempt to get him out. The police and the fire brigade eventually turn up on the scene to no avail, following which the men who installed the booth finally return, unscrew it from the ground and place it on their truck. The man subsequently finds himself being driven through the city, much to the amusement of various passersby, and then out into the suburbs and the countryside beyond on a seemingly endless journey which finally concludes when he is driven into a long tunnel that leads to a subterranean installation where more booths are being prepared for distribution. Here he is offloaded and placed in a vast storage facility full of similar booths, each of them occupied by a corpse....

As with all good filmmaking, the effect of the story lies in the detail, and here Mercero accrues many telling little moments as the trapped man, superbly played by Vazquez, finds himself the subject of scrutiny and even ridicule by the observing crowd, among them a bunch of taunting kids, a man carrying an ornate armchair which he subsequently offers to an elderly woman to sit upon, two men carrying a mirror in which he sees his anguish reflected back at him, and a baker's boy carrying a tray of pastries on his head, from which a fellow spectator surreptitiously steals a few samples. There is also comedy provided by a corpulent man who tries to help, but only succeeds in pulling off the booth's door handle, much to crowd's laughter. The subsequent journey through city and the countryside is also filled with incident, including the passing of another man who at first seems to be stuck in a booth but who subsequently manages to open the door much to the protagonist's exasperation, a momentary stop by a funeral in which the body is lying in state in a glass coffin, the passing of a school playground which reminds the man of his son, and the passing of another man on a truck who is likewise trapped in a booth and with whom he tries to communicate, only to later see that he has hanged himself on the cord of his own telephone during the nihilistic denouement, which is followed by a coda in which a new booth is placed in the square and its door pulled tantalizingly ajar ready for the next victim as the camera gently cranes away. And of course, we never do discover why the phone company is doing this. Sharply edited by Javier Moran and well framed by cinematographer Federico G. Larraya, this is the short story par excellence with a sting in its tail that is not easily forgotten, and it certainly deserves to be better known than it is outside Europe (note that Larraya and Vazquez had previously worked together on the comedy *Weekend* [1965], and that Vazquez went on to reprise his role in a 1998 ad for Retevision which sees him escape from a phone booth in the middle of a desert).

Other European countries that occasionally produced horror content during this period include France, whose contributions encompassed a handful of Gaston Leroux adaptations, among them his 1920 novel *Le coeur cambriolé* (1970, TVM [*The Burgled Heart*]), in which a young woman (Juliette Villard) falls under the mesmeric influence of a mysterious painter (Jean-Pierre Joris); *L'homme qui revient de loin* (1972, TV [*The Man Who Returns from Afar*]), a six-part version of his 1916 novel in which a businessman (Michel Vitold) disappears and returns as a ghost during a séance, claiming that he was murdered; and *La poupée sanglante* (1976, TV [*The Bloody Doll*]), a six-part adaptation of his 1923 novel, in which a watchmaker (Julien Verdier) creates a mechanical man into which he grafts the brain of a condemned murderer, who subsequently tracks down the real culprits responsible for the killings for which he stood accused (the story had previously been presented on TV in Argentina in 1962 as a 13-part series titled *El muneco maldita*).

France also aired a three-part version of Victor Hugo's 1869 novel *L'homme qui rit* (1971, TV, aka *The Man Who Laughs*), in which the son of a nobleman (Philippe Bouclet) is purposely disfigured so that he permanently bears a grotesque smile. Elsewhere, Czechoslovakia made another version of Karel Capek's *The Makropulos Affair* as *Vek Makropulos* (1970, TVM), as did Russia under the title *Stredstvo Makropulosa* (1979, TVM), while Poland produced a new half-hour version of Robert Louis Stevenson's *Markheim* (1972, TV) starring Jerzy Kamas in the title role, and a perfectly adequate half-hour version of Edgar Allan Poe's *The Cask of Amontillado* as *Beczka amontillado* (1972, TV), in which Henryk Boukolowski and Franciszek Pieczka play Montressor and Fortunato. Germany also chipped in with *H.P. Lovecraft: Schatten aus der Zeit* (1975, TV), which was based on Lovecraft's 1936 story *The Shadow Out of Time*, in which a professor (Anton Diffring) suffers a strange change of personality following a seizure. Hungary then went on to air a version of Capek's *R.U.R.* (1976, TVM), while the ever reliable Poe was meanwhile the subject of a four-part Italian series, *I racconti fantastici di Edgar Allan Poe* (1979, TV [*The Fantastic Tales of Edgar Allan Poe*]), whose episodes included *Notte in Casa Usher* (1979, TV), *Ligeia forever* (1979, TV), *Il delirio de William Wilson* (1979, TV) and *La caduta di Casa Usher* (1979, TV), all of which were directed by Daniele D'Anza.

In fact it was Italy that developed the greatest taste for genre programming in the seventies, thanks primarily to the popularity of such home grown thrillers and horror films as *L'uccello dalle piume di cristallo* (1970, aka *The Bird with the Crystal Plumage*), *Il gatto a nove code* (1971, aka *The Cat O'Nine Tails*), *Profundo rosso* (1975, aka *Deep Red*) and *Suspiria* (1977), all of which were directed by Dario Argento, who came to be dubbed the Italian Hitchcock. As a consequence of his fame, Argento became involved with television with the four-part anthology series *La porta sul buio* (1973, TV [*Door into Darkness*]), which he produced via Seda Spettacoli (through which he made his films at the time). He also introduced the series, which played on RAI from 4 September 1973, and wrote and directed two of its episodes: *Il tram* (1973, TV [*The Tram*]), in which a police inspector (Enzo Cerusico) investigates the murder of a woman on a crowded tram (this was taken from an unused story element originally intended for *L'uccello dalle piume di cristallo*), and *Testimone oculare* (1973, TV [*Eyewitness*]), in which a lady driver (Marilu Tolo) thinks she's run down a woman on a lonely country lane, but the victim seems to have been killed by other means (the program's direction is actually credited to Roberto Pariante, who'd worked as Argento's assistant director on three of his films as well as on the other episodes of *La porta sul buio*, but Argento took over the episode without credit when it was deemed Pariante's work wasn't up to standard).

The other two episodes are *Il vincino di casa* (1973, TV [*The Neighbor*]), which was written and directed by Luigi Cozzi, and concerns a young couple (Aldo Reggiani and Laura Belli) who have just moved into a new apartment with their baby, not realizing that their upstairs neighbor (Mimmo Palmara) has just murdered his wife (the episode features clips from *Abbott and Costello Meet Frankenstein* [1948] which the couple watch on their portable TV), and *La bombola* (1973, TV [*The Doll*]), written and directed by Mario Foglietti, in which a patient who has escaped from an asylum goes on a killing spree, but the perpetrator isn't who we are led to believe it is. Surprisingly, despite the Argento connection, the series was not deemed a success, and though undeniably more *giallo* than full on horror, it certainly warrants inclusion here given the undeniable thrills it generates, and the style with which the episodes are executed, most notably *Testimone oculare*, which contains a genuinely disturbing sequence in which the leading lady is terrorized by an intruder in her apartment.

Other Italian series from this period devoted to fantasy, thrills and horror include *E.S.P.* (1973, TV), a four-part *giallo* mystery that began on RAI from 27 May 1973, and *Racconti di fantascienza* (1979, TV [*Science Fiction Stories*]), a three-part anthology which began airing on Network 2 (now RAI 2) on 19 January 1979, and included readings by Alessandro Blasetti and Arnoldo Foa, as well as re-enactments of stories by the likes of Richard Matheson, Robert Scheckley, Charles Beaumont and Ray Bradbury, among the latter's work being versions of *La cristalide* (1979, TV), taken from his 1970 story *Chrysalis*, and *L'esame* (1979, TV), taken from his 1954 story *The Test*.

Elsewhere, with *Drammi gotici* (1978, TV [*Gothic Dramas*]), came a series of four separate hour-long stories, again from a variety of literary sources. Broadcast by RAI in July and August of 1978, they included *Kaiserstrasse* (1978, TV), which was based on material by Oliver Onions and Hanns Heinz Ewers, *Ma non e! un vampire?* (1978, TV [*But Is He a Vampire?*]), which was taken from a fable by Luigi Capuana, *La casa della streghe* (1978, TV [*The House of Witches*]), which was based on three works by H.P. Lovecraft, and *Diario di un pazzo* (1978, TV [*Diary of a Madman*]), which was based on an 1835 story by Nikolai Gogol. Created, written and directed by Giorgio Bandini and designed by Eugenio Guglielminetti (who also provided the costumes), the series featured Flavio Bucci as a student who is involved in each of the stories either an observer or a victim. Other actors involved included Micaela Pignatelli, Alessandro Haber, Osvaldo Salvi and Oreste Rizzini, though the main attraction for many would have been the atmospheric music provided the legendary Ennio Morricone.

While we are in foreign waters, we should also note in passing that, in addition to the Spanish series *Otra vez Dracula* (1970, TV), the old Count also appeared in a number of other European adaptations of the Stoker book during this period, best among them being *Hrabe Drakula* (1971, TVM), a surprisingly good black and white Czech version, financed and broadcast by Ceskoslovenska Televize, starring Ilja Racek as a bearded Dracula and Jan Schanilek as Harker. For a change, the blend of filmed exteriors and videotaped interiors work well together here (the early snowbound location sequences are excellent), and despite the brief running time (just 76 minutes), the script by Oldrich Zelezny and Anna Prochazkova hits all the salient points of the story, while the latter's assured direction includes one particularly nifty dissolve, which sees Dracula pass through a window, his cloak pulled through the glass behind him. An eerie score by Milos Holecek also adds to the frosty atmosphere.

West Germany also had a stab at the Stoker story, twice, with *Dracula* (1972, TVM), which starred Werner Vielhaber as Dracula, and *Dracula. Uber das Interesse an Vampiren* (1976, TVM [literal translation *Dracula—About the Interest in Vampires*]), for which IMDb does not list a cast, while Mary Shelley's most famous creation was the subject of the French TV film *Frankenstein: Une histoire d'amour* (1974, TVM, aka *Frankenstein: A Love Story*), a slightly glum looking affair in which the young doctor (Gérard Berner) revives a village idiot, killed during a fall from a mountain. Slightly further afield, the Argentinean anthology series *Las grandes novelas* (1970–1972, TV [*The Great Novels*]) presented versions of *Dr. Jekyll and Mr. Hyde* (as *El extrano caso del Doctor Jekyll y Mister Hyde* [1971, TV]), *The Picture of Dorian Gray* (as *El retrato de Dorian Gray* [1971, TV]), *The Queen of Spades* (as *La dama de pique* [1971, TV]) and *The House of the Seven Gables* (as *La casa de los siete tejados* [1972, TV]), the latter of which had already been featured in the Brazilian series *Grande Teatro Tupi* (1951–1964, TV) as *A Casa das Sete Torres* (1957, TV) and would go on to appear as an episode of *Novela* (1963–1968, TV) as *La casa de las siete buhardillas* (1972, TV). *Dr. Jekyll and Mr. Hyde* was also the subject of a Brazilian adaptation, *O Médico e o Monstro* (1972, TV). The Poles meanwhile had a go at *The Queen of Spades* as *Dama pikowa* (1972,

Czech mate. From left to right, Jan Schanilek and Ilja Racek in the obscure *Hrabe Drakula* (1971, TVM).

TV), while the Venezuelans tackled Stoker's vampire epic via the miniseries *Dracula* (1979, TV), with Héctor Mayerston in the role of the Count.

Meanwhile, back in Spain, another anthology series, the 14-part *El quinto jinete* (1975–1976, TV [*The Fifth Horseman*]), included surprisingly well mounted adaptations of Tolstoy's 1839 novella *The Family of the Vourdalak* (as *La familia Vourdalak* [1975, TV]), in which the family of a Serbian innkeeper suspect that he has become a vampire while away hunting for a Turkish outlaw (he has); Edgar Allan Poe's 1843 story *The Black Cat* (as *El gato negro* [1975, TV]), in which a man kills his wife and walls up the body, only to be betrayed by her cat; Robert Louis Stevenson's 1884 story *The Body Snatcher* (as *El ladron de cadavers* [1975, TV]), previously presented as a 1966 episode of *Mystery and Imagination* (1966–1970, TV), in which two body snatchers resort to murder to keep up supply to a surgeon; and Sheridan Le Fanu's 1870 story *Madam Crowl's Ghost* (as *El misterio de Madame Crowl* [1976, TV]), in which a young girl goes to live with her aunt, a housekeeper in a mansion, only to be haunted by the nightly cries of a child. Full of atmosphere and wry humor, the series benefits from strong production values and a sure hand from director José Antonio Paramo (who helmed all 14 episodes), though the use of music from *The Towering Inferno* (1974) in the *Vourdalak* episode may seem a little odd to those who know the score.

Despite all these valiant efforts, however, when it came to genre television, the truth of the matter is that there was only one country that could match America for both output and quality in the seventies, and that, as we shall discover in the next chapter, was Britain....

SECTION FIVE

Enter the Brits
(the 1970s)

The Doomsday People

Given their substantial financial resources, obtained primarily via advertising and sponsorship, American networks were able to spend reasonably healthy sums of money on their television output. In Britain, the country's two broadcasters, BBC and ITV, had to be a little more cautious, given that the BBC (which also operated BBC2) was financed by a fixed annual license fee, while ITV (which was made up of a number of regional affiliates) was funded by advertising which, though adequate, was far from extravagant compared to the U.S. Consequently, TV movies, which became a staple in the States in the seventies, were rarely produced in the UK. Instead, drama came in the form of series and one-off plays. This also applied to genre productions, which were mostly presented in a series format.

The first of these to emerge in the new decade was *Doomwatch* (1970–1972, TV), which made its debut on BBC1 on 9 February 1970, and followed the exploits of the Department of Measurement of Scientific Work, nicknamed Doomwatch, whose remit is to keep a watchful eye on the research sector, ensuring the safety of the environment from rogue companies and scientists, whose discoveries may have an adverse effect on mankind. Led by Dr. Spencer Quist (John Paul), a Nobel Prize winning physicist, he and his team, among them Dr. John Ridge (Simon Oates), Barbara Mason (Vivien Sherrard) and Tobias Wren (Robert Powell), find themselves confronted by all manner of dangers, from deadly sound waves to genetic mutations.

A canny hybrid of science fiction and prophetic science fact, the program, which went on to rack up 38 episodes over three seasons, was created by Kit Pedler and Gerry Davis (who together had created the Cybermen for *Doctor Who* [1963–1989, TV] in 1966), and began its run with *The Plastic Eaters* (1970, TV), in which the team investigate a manmade virus able to destroy plastic, resulting in the downing of a plane mid-flight. With environmental concerns the subject of increasing national debate, the show, which was produced by Terence Dudley, hit a nerve with the public, and was soon pulling in audiences of up to 13 million, making it the program of the moment thanks to plots involving such topical elements as heart transplants, the dumping of deadly chemicals, sentient computers, nuclear threat, pollution, hallucinogens, mass observation, government cover ups, unusual diseases, pesticides, chromosomes, toxic gases, extreme weather conditions, censorship and pandemics via such episodes as *Project Sahara* (1970, TV), *The Human Time Bomb* (1971, TV) and *The Killer Dolphins* (1972, TV).

The series' most famous installment came early on with episode four, *Tomorrow, the Rat* (1970, TV), in which the team is required to tackle a breed of hyper intelligent, flesh-eating rats that have managed to escape a laboratory. Written, directed and produced by Terence Dudley (who also appeared as an attack victim, as did his wife and son Stephen), the program effectively traded on the commonly held fear of rodents, and featured several frightening and unsettling moments, all of which was enough to prompt a plethora of complaints. The BBC's switchboard subsequently became jammed with calls from concerned viewers, while ques-

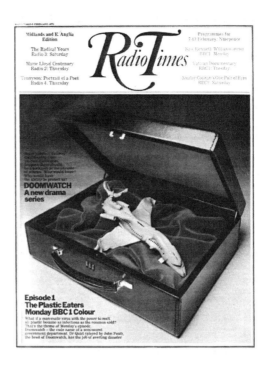

Fantastic plastic. *Doomwatch* (1970–1972, TV) makes the cover of the *Radio Times* (BBC/ Immediate Media Co.).

tions were even asked in Parliament following the ensuing furor in the press. However, the controversy resulted in even higher ratings, and though its production values were often Spartan and its effects crude, audiences were thrilled by the program's currency and its cleverly devised concepts, though its misogyny and poor attempts at humor have since dated it somewhat (note that, as per the policy of the day, some master tapes of the show were wiped by the BBC as a cost saving exercise, as a consequence of which some episodes no longer exist, while the series' final episode titled *Sex and Violence* [1972, TV] was withheld from broadcast owing to its subject matter, but has since been released on DVD; a low-budget film version produced via Tigon British was released in 1972 starring Ian Bannen, Judy Geeson and series regulars John Paul and Simon Oates; a TV movie titled *Doomwatch: Winter Angel* appeared in 1999, while a documentary titled *The Cult of Doomwatch* followed in 2006).

The Play's the Thing

In 1970, the BBC launched its long-running feature-length drama series *Play for Today* (1970–1984, TVM). A follow up to *The Wednesday Play* (1964–1970, TVM), which ended its lengthy run on 20 May 1970, the new series was launched on 15 October 1970 with *The Long Distance Piano Player* (1970, TVM), an innocuous comedy-drama about a man's attempt to break the record for nonstop piano playing. The focus of the series was new writing primarily in the category of social realism, and many acclaimed works followed, among them *Traitor* (1971, TVM), *Edna, the Inebriate Woman* (1971, TVM), *Kisses at Fifty* (1973, TVM), *Hard Labour* (1973, TVM), *84 Charing Cross Road* (1975, TVM), *Rumpole of the Bailey* (1975, TVM), *Nuts in May* (1976, TVM), *Bar Mitzvah Boy* (1976, TVM), *Spend Spend Spend* (1977, TVM), *Abigail's Party* (1977, TVM), *The Spongers* (1978, TVM) and *Blue Remembered Hills* (1979, TVM), which featured scripts by Mike Leigh, Jack Rosenthal, John Mortimer and Dennis Potter among others.

The series only occasionally dipped its toes into other specific genres during its incredible 306-episode run, the first time being during its premiere season with program nine, *Robin Redbreast* (1970, TVM), which was broadcast on 10 December 1970. In it, Norah Palmer (Anna Cropper), a BBC script editor who has just broken up with her boyfriend, leaves London and her friends behind and takes refuge in an isolated country cottage where, despite a warm enough welcome from the locals, she gradually comes to suspect that something sinister is going on. Having taken solace in the arms of Rob (Andy Bradford), the local gamekeeper, she soon discovers herself to be pregnant, and decides to return to the city for an abortion, but she changes her mind and returns to the cottage, only to find herself prevented from leaving the village or getting in touch with the outside world (her phone line is cut, her car won't start, and the local bus won't stop for her). Norah consequently begins to fear for her life, but it turns out that it is not she but Rob whom the villagers, led by the sinister historian Mr. Fisher (Bernard Hepton), are to sacrifice for the good of the land, given that he has been raised from birth for that sole purpose ("From his blood the crops will spring," Fisher explains to her). After this, Norah is left free to leave on the understanding that, in adulthood, her own child will one day suffer the same fate as Rob. And if she is in any doubt, as she is leaving, she briefly turns, only to see that the villagers have somehow transformed into pagan deities from a former era, with Fisher himself sporting antlers as Herne the Hunter.

With its references to *The Golden Bough*, Sir James George Frazer's 1890 study of magic and comparative religion, John Bowen's teleplay can clearly be seen as an early step into the same folk horror territory that *The Wicker Man* (1973) would explore a few years later, albeit with a little more panache. Here, restricted by budget, the events, most of which take place within the confines of Norah's cottage, are somewhat laboriously unfolded, leaving little room for the actors to make a mark with their somewhat caricatured roles (would-be sophisticates for Norah and her friends, yokel types for the country folk). The abrupt changes from video to film for the interiors and exteriors, respectively (a staple of the time), also tends to hobble any attempts at atmosphere, while the sets (care of Eileen Diss) give the impression of having been quickly built for the occasion. Nevertheless, despite these drawbacks, the basic nuts and bolts of the story are not without their intrigue, and the pebble-glassed Hepton makes for an unsettling figure as the all-knowing Mr. Fisher ("Study of religions is one of my many interests. I am a reading man, you know," he informs Norah as he explains to her what has been going on), while Freda Bamford's turn as Mrs. Vigo, the local charwoman, ably gives the impression of not quite being the ally Norah thinks she is. Unfortunately, Anna Cropper's performance as Norah sadly lacks any nuance or sympathy, while director James McTaggart only occasionally manages to elicit a *frisson* from the material, notably at the end, when one of the villagers makes his way into the cottage down the chimney in order to carry out the sacrificial ritual (note that though now only available in black and white, *Robin Redbreast* was first broadcast in color; unfortunately, a power outage that affected several regions in the UK meant that many viewers didn't see the end of the program, which prompted the BBC to repeat it on 25 February 1971).

The *Play for Today* strand took another step into pagan territory with *Penda's Fen* (1974, TVM), which was broadcast on 21 March 1974, since when it has gone on to acquire something of a cult reputation. Written by David Rudkin and directed by Alan Clarke, it follows the religious, political and sexual awakening of Stephen Franklin (Spencer Banks), the repressed son of a clergyman who, as he approaches the age of 18, is clearly reaching a moment of crisis in his life ("I am nothing pure. Nothing pure. My race is mixed, my sex is mixed, I am woman and man, light with darkness," he proclaims at one point). As well as being obsessed by the music of Edward Elgar ("The Dream of Gerontius" in particular), he is also beset by dreams and imaginings of demons and angels, and finds himself at odds with everything around him, even more so when told by his parents that he was adopted. Meanwhile, it seems that the government is conducting underground experiments in the area, resulting in the hideous injury of a local man....

Both portentous and pretentious, the film, which was produced by *Play for Today* regular David Rose, is verbose and somewhat indulgent, yet contains enough disturbing moments to keep one watching, among them an imagining Stephen suffers while concussed after a bicycle accident in which he hears an odd thudding sound, only to come across a scene in a country house garden in which a number of young people are happily having their hands cut off with a cleaver on a tree stump by what appears to be the squire. That Stephen is "marked down" to cherish the flame of the land he lives in by decree of King Penda himself seems to be the aim of the piece ("The flame is in your hands," he is informed by the deity after summoning him for protection), but the purposely obscure narrative, with its lengthy speeches and ponderings about land and religion, does itself no favors in its bid for intellectualism (even director Alan Clarke claimed to have been mystified by the story). Yet there were those who were impressed by Rudkin's bold concoction, among them Leonard Buckley, the critic for *The Times*, who proclaimed, "Make no mistake. We had a major work of television last night. Rudkin gave us something that had beauty, imagination and depth." There's undeniably something good, possibly even great, going on here, but it always seems just out of reach, never quite fully formed. That Spencer Banks is such an unappealing focus of the drama doesn't help matters either, yet despite all this, the program somehow stays in the mind, and the sunny countryside locations (among them the Malvern Hills) are attractively photographed by film cameraman Michael Williams.

If controversy was the aim of *Brimstone and Treacle* (1976, TVM), which was made some time later, then its firebrand author Dennis Potter finally met his match with the BBC's then director of programmes Alasdair Milne, who refused to broadcast it (the play didn't air until 25 August 1987). Set in the drab home of Tom and Amy Bates (Denholm Elliott and Patricia Lawrence), it focuses on their daily struggle to look after their severely disabled daughter Pattie (Michelle Newell), whose brain has been damaged after being hit by a car. However, things seemingly take a turn for the better when Tom literally bumps into Martin Taylor (Michael Kitchen), who claims to have known Pattie at college, and who insinuates himself into the household, not only

Heir apparent. Spencer Banks (left) and Geoffrey Staines in a moment from the weird and occasionally wonderful *Penda's Fen* (1974, TVM) (1974, TVM) (BBC).

becoming their lodger but a carer for Pattie. But he is not quite what he seems, and his motives, at first hidden by a sheen of charm, prove to have a devilish motive. Indeed, it may even be that he is in fact the Devil himself ("I must buy some mints to hide the smell of sulphur," he comments to himself at one point).

An ultra black domestic satire that takes pot shots at everything from religion to racism, its most provocative scene sees Martin rape the helpless Pattie. When he later attempts to molest her a second time, she begins to scream, finally shocked from her vegetative state and able at last to recall why she ran out before a car in the first place (she had discovered her father having sex with her best friend). By no means the author's best work, the program, which was produced by Potter regular Kenith Trodd and directed by Barry Davis, is somewhat clumsy in its relentless striving to be provocative, with any attempts at atmosphere nixed by flat studio lighting and multi-camera video recording for the interior sequences as per the standard of time (the exteriors were shot on film). A good performance by Elliott as the racist father is undoubtedly the play's main asset ("There'll always be an England? Hah, not with half the cities filled with colored men there won't," he complains at one point), though Kitchen, who would go on to become a film and television staple, particularly in the long running *Foyle's War* (2002–2015, TV), just doesn't convince as the devilish Martin (note that the play was rewritten for the stage in 1977; it was also filmed in 1982, with Denholm Elliott repeating his role as the father, with Joan Plowright now cast as the mother and Sting as Martin).

With *A Photograph* (1977, TVM), which aired on 22 March 1977, writer John Bowen was back in folk horror territory again with a story about a philandering, self obsessed newspaper columnist, Michael Otway (John Stride), who, out of the blue, is sent a photograph of two young women sat in front of a caravan, much to the chagrin of his long-suffering wife Gillian (Stephanie Turner). Both mystified and intrigued, given that there is no accompanying letter, they begin to investigate where it might have come from and who might have sent it, using the post mark as a clue, and blowing the image up so as to better see any details it might contain ("It's a doctored photograph. It's not two girls. It's the same girl, twice," notes Gillian of the enlargement). Encouraged by his wife, who is suffering from depression, Michael eventually decides to travel to Leamington, the area the letter was posted from, and by happenstance following a conversation in a pub, discovers the whereabouts of the caravan, which turns out to be occupied by an old woman, Mrs. Vigo (Freda Bamford), who has in her possession a small alabaster love heart with a chip in it ("Broken heart," she informs him), just like one Michael used to have. Leaving the photo with Mrs. Vigo so that she can make enquiries in the village about the girls, Michael makes his exit, having been invited to return the next day for tea. But once he has left, Mrs. Vigo sets the photo alight in front of her son, a young poacher (Eric Deacon), who has come to call. Returning home in the meantime, he is told by Gillian that it was she who sent the photo, but he dismisses her claim and returns to the caravan the next day, only to learn that the girls, whom Mrs. Vigo brands as evil, have since died. He also finds himself drugged and paralyzed by a glass of homemade wine she has given him during afternoon tea ("You rest there quiet, mister, until needed"), at which she is soon after joined by her son and (spoiler alert) Gillian, who, it transpires, is Mrs. Vigo's daughter, and at whose urging her brother strangles Michael to death with a rabbit snare. The play ends with Mrs. Vigo sharpening a knife, presumably to dismember Michael's body.

A very cleverly plotted piece which leads one up the garden path with precision, the play is unfortunately let down by an overabundance of dull marital scenes, most of which give the impression of having been concocted by way of padding out the running time. These, combined with flat studio direction care of John Glenister, generally make the program somewhat tedious to plough through, but the central premise and the final revelations in the caravan are expertly contrived, and one wishes they had been accompanied by better dialogue (not one of Bowen's strong points it would seem) and presented in a more cinematic manner (only the location sequences are recorded on film). As Michael, John Stride exudes an air of self-satisfied superiority as the doomed columnist, while Stephanie Turner is suitably mousy as his put upon wife, though it is Freda Bamford as the seemingly kind Mrs. Vigo, who may possibly be a witch, who stays in the mind ("Village folks says I put bat's blood in my medicine," she says as Michael unwittingly downs his glass of spiked wine, having inquired what is in it). For this climactic scene, if for little else, the play is worth persevering with, though how and why Gillian has kept her mother and brother's existence a secret from Michael doesn't bear too much scrutiny (note that Freda Bamford also played the role of Mrs. Vigo in Bowen's earlier *Robin Redbreast* [1970, TVM]).

The series' final brush with horror occurred with *Vampires* (1979, TVM), which aired on 9 January 1979, in which Stu and Davey, two young brothers obsessed with science fiction and horror, convince themselves that vampires really do exist, having been spooked by watching Hammer's *Dracula—Prince of Darkness* (1966) on late night TV with their friend Dingo. Stu proves to be particularly susceptible, and not only begins to suffer from nightmares as a consequence of seeing the movie, but becomes convinced that there are sinister influences at work all around him, particularly when one of his teachers suffers a heart attack. Could the mysterious man they have spotted in the local cemetery perhaps be the vampire responsible, they ponder, even though, unbeknownst to them, he is only the caretaker (John G. Heller). Though not officially a horror piece, rather more the imaginings of three impressionable boys, the play is similar in theme to *Whistle Down the Wind* (1961), in which three naive north country farm children believe that a man on the run hiding out in their barn is Jesus, and here, the action likewise benefits from similarly realistic settings (in this case the rough and ready streets of Liverpool) and a lack of sentimentality, though Dixie Williams' script and John Goldschmidt's direction do make use of several of the horror genre's devices to good effect, prompting the lads (played by real life brothers Peter and Paul Moran as Stu and Davey, and Tommy White as Dingo) to accept what they see at face value, encouraged in their beliefs by what they have seen on television. Says Stu of vampires, "They live in castles with big doors and bars on the windows and a faithful servant and a coach with no driver that takes you where you don't want to go," though the vampire they encounter turns out to be rather more mundane.

Meanwhile, *Play for Today*'s sister show, *BBC2 Playhouse* (1974–1983, TVM), which began its 106-episode run on 13 March 1974 with the apartheid drama *Sizwe Bansi Is Dead* (1974, TVM), also occasionally turned its hand to genre subjects, among them an adaptation of the 1971 Daphne Du Maurier story *The Breakthrough* (1975, TVM), which aired on 8 January 1975. In it Stephen Saunders (Simon Ward), a young electronics engineer who has been sent to work on a computer at Saxmere, a remote research laboratory in Cornwall belonging to the Ministry of Defence, becomes involved with Maclean (Brewster Mason), a scientist experimenting with hypnosis, ESP and controlled high frequency transmissions and response, his ultimate aim being to discover what actually happens at the moment of death and beyond, to which end he has enlisted a volunteer named Ken (Martin C. Thurley) who is dying of leukemia, and whose life spirit (which Maclean calls "force six") he wishes to capture electronically. Written by Clive Exton, the story offers a reasonably intriguing blend of cloak and dagger and highly speculative scientific mumbo jumbo, and climaxes with Ken's death and the capture of his soul. Ably enough directed by Graham Evans, who does rather better with the filmed location scenes (which were photographed in Covehithe and Orford Ness in Suffolk by Peter Sargent) than he does with the videotaped studio sequences, the play also features Clive Swift as the lab's doctor, and John Westbrook as the voice of the super-computer Charon One. Inevitably, the technology on display now seems prehistoric, but taken on face value, the story itself is not without its dramatic moments.

A genre story of a more traditional kind appeared the following week. This was *Mrs. Acland's Ghosts* (1975, TVM), which aired on 15 January 1975. In it, Mr. Mockler (John Bluthal), a middle-aged tailor, receives out of the blue a number of letters from a woman named Mrs. Acland (Sara Kestelman), whom he has never met before. Having chosen his name from the telephone directory, she goes on to relate her life story, from her childhood years to her present whereabouts in a mental institution, in which she was placed by her husband (Frank Middlemass) after having claimed that, while left alone in their large house while he was away on business, she gradually came to believe that she was being haunted by the spirits of her three dead siblings, George, Alice and Isobel, killed many years earlier in a car crash. Annoyed by the letters at first, Mockler initially dismisses them, but gradually gets drawn into Mrs. Acland's story, to the point that he senses the spirits himself and, subsequently, agrees to her pay her a visit, during which he comforts her by telling her that he believes her story, much to the chagrin of the institution's head doctor (James Grout).

A rather drawn-out piece, William Trevor's teleplay is a somewhat rambling and unfocussed affair that would have benefited from some pruning, while the helming by future Harry Potter director Mike Newell is somewhat unadventurous, particularly in the flatly lit studio sequences, which singularly fail to come to life, though the filmed inserts, among them a brief nighttime sequence in Mrs. Acland's garden and her eventual meeting with Mr. Mockler, help to balance things out a little. Passably well performed by Sara Kestelman as Mrs. Acland and John Bluthal as Mr. Mockler, this is otherwise something of a disappointment, given its potential, and more careful scripting and handling may well have produced something along the lines of M.R. James. Unfortunately, that is just not the case in this instance.

A more substantial stab at the genre appeared the following year with a six-part series of hour-long plays that went out under the umbrella title of *The Mind Beyond* (1976, TV), whose remit was to explore what lies beyond the world of normal, rational experience. Produced by Irene Shubik, who had produced *The Breakthrough* (1975, TVM) and *Mrs. Acland's Ghosts* (1975, TVM), the series, which has since fallen into obscurity, kicked off with *Meriel, the Ghost Girl* (1976, TV), which aired on 29 September 1976, and starred Donald Pleasance, who'd already appeared in two *BBC2 Playhouse* installments for Shubik: *The Joke* (1974, TVM) and *The Cafeteria* (1974, TVM). Here he plays George Livingston, a psychic investigator who attends a séance in order to debunk the proceedings for his latest book, only to be confounded when confronted with the manifestation of a seven-year-old girl who it is claimed to be Meriel, the dead daughter of one of the attendees, Mrs. Brown (Izabella Telezynska). Unable to explain away what he has seen, Livingston fails to reach a conclusion on his findings, preferring to leave them with a question mark hanging over them.

Unfortunately, as intriguing as this section of the drama is, it is followed by a second story strand in which an American private eye (John Bluthal), who is investigating the case following Livingston's death, comes to the conclusion that he made up the events so as to fraudulently bolster the falling sales of his books. This is then followed by a third strand in which an amateur sleuth (Janet Street-Porter) launches her own investigation, only to discover that the apparition was faked so as to con Mrs. Brown, a revelation that she decides to dismiss having seen documentary footage of a Finnish medium producing a woman from ectoplasm, which she prefers to believe was how Meriel was created. This is in turn is followed by a fourth strand, in which another expert, Dr. Delane (Charles Keating), offers reasons why those attending the séance should have wanted to see Meriel, and in what form.

As written by David Halliwell (best known for his 1965 play *Little Malcolm and His Struggle Against the Eunuchs*), this is an unnecessarily convoluted piece which perhaps should have satisfied itself solely with the opening segment dealing with Livingston's investigation, which is ably put over by the always reliable Pleasence. The rest is a mixed bag indeed, with each section being dealt with in a variety of mismatched styles by director Philip Saville, while the performances range from the awkward (Bluthal speaks with an unconvincing "Noo Yoik" accent) to the amateur (Street-Porter, better known these days as a journalist and television presenter, is clearly not an actress). Perhaps in wishing to establish the series' credentials, all concerned seem to have over-reached with their lofty ambitions, yet one can't deny the audacity of the piece, though what audiences made of the baffling confusion of styles and approaches on display can only be presumed.

This was followed by *Double Echo* (1976, TV), in which a couple take their autistic teenage daughter (Geraldine Cowper, best known for playing Rowan Morrison in *The Wicker Man* [1973]) to a see a Harley Street doctor (Jeremy Kemp) about her condition, only for him to discover that she is telepathic and has the ability to see into the future. Written by Brian Hayles and directed by Alan Bridges, this is low-budget television drama by any standards, with any interest in the script destroyed by relentless padding and a lethargic pace, further compounded by cheap looking sets and the usual flat studio look of the period. A little better was *The Love of a Good Woman* (1976, TV) by William Trevor (author of *Mrs. Acland's Ghosts* [1975, TVM]), in which an unhappy publican (William Lucas) murders his wife (Anna Massey) so as to marry his new love (Diana Bishop), only for him to find the child they have together begin to take on the qualities of his dead wife as she grows up. Benefiting from filmed location sequences and the performances of Lucas and Massey, this is at least a step up production wise, though it's certainly no classic. Another convoluted affair was *The Daedalus Equations* (1976, TV), in which Hans Daedalus (George Coulouris), a nuclear physicist who has defected to the UK from East Germany, dies while working on a project, only for a medium (Megs Jenkins) to appear on the scene, claiming that she has somehow accessed his equations. As much involved with espionage as the supernatural (it transpires that the medium used to work for the atomic energy authority and may have passed secrets on to Russian intelligence), Bruce Stewart's script is another story with too many elements for its own good (the medium in the end turns out to be a fake seeking publicity), but at least the cast, which also includes Michael Bryant and Peter Sallis, is a notch above the norm.

Perhaps the best of the plays is *Stones* (1976, TV) by Malcolm Christopher, in which Nicholas Reeve (Richard Pasco), an Oxford academic working on a book about Stonehenge and the Druids, becomes involved in preventing a ludicrous plan by Harvey Fenton-Jones (T.P. McKenna), the new Minister for Tourism, to move the ancient stones up to Hyde Park in London where tourists can better access them, replacing the originals on Salisbury Place with fiber glass replicas ("I suppose you could surround it with Loch Ness and replace the monster with an inflatable model," quips Reeve's friend Porton [John Wells] during the dinner at which the idea is floated). But will the powers inherent in the stones allow the desecration to take place? Featuring curious symbols found hidden in the spines of books and the disappearance of Reeve's young daughter (Rebecca Saire), who appears to be in tune with the stones, the story builds in the style of one of M.R. James's antiquarian mysteries, and not only benefits from strong location work, including scenes at Stonehenge itself, but a surprisingly witty and erudite script ("Too much claret, dear boy, not enough clarity," comments the Minister as Reeve pooh-poohs his plans).

That Fenton-Jones gets his comeuppance in a car crash neatly rounds out the story (though for budgetary reasons, this is represented by sound effects and a few scattered papers), and for once, the videotaped studio sequences work almost as well as the filmed inserts, thanks to the concerted efforts of director Graham Evans, who appears to have been particularly enthused by the project.

The final play in the series was *The Man with the Power* (1976, TV), in which a painter and decorator named Boysie (Willie Jonah) comes to realize that he possesses special powers, which take on the form of predictions, intuitions and the ability to heal, which bring him to the attention of a parapsychologist (Geoffrey Bayldon), much to the concern of his girlfriend (Vikki Richards), who believes him to have gone mad, which prompts him to leave her. Going on a voyage of self discovery, Boysie subsequently becomes a fairground fortune teller, has encounters with a number of eccentric types, among them his new landlady (Peggy Aitchison), whose failing eyesight he cures, and a tramp (Cyril Cusack) with insights of his own, before finally confronting the Devil (Rayner Bourton) who (controversially for the time) kisses him on the lips, presumably in a bid to corrupt him. The piece ends with the messiah-like Boysie and his now devoted landlady sat in the park, waiting for those who would follow him. A somewhat meandering piece of writing care of Evan Jones (whose big screen credits numbered a handful of films for director Joseph Losey), the story is a somewhat disjointed affair, made to seem more so thanks to the usual mix of filmed and videotaped sequences, though the scene in which Boysie has to "wrestle all night with the Devil" in his burning room is ably enough staged by director John Gorrie. An air of pretention otherwise hangs over the proceedings, and the final attempts at religious allegory are somewhat fumbled. But like *Meriel, the Ghost Girl*, one can't deny that the play has a certain ambition which it can't quite attain through a lack of budget and a sharper focus in the writing. After this, the experiment with the supernatural appeared to be over for the series, and such notable plays as *School Play* (1979, TVM), *Speed King* (1979, TVM), *Caught on a Train* (1980, TVM), *Grown-Ups* (1980, TVM) and *Going Gently* (1981, TVM) filled out the remainder of the lengthy run.

Festive Frissons

But we are jumping ahead of ourselves again here and must return now to 1971 and the launch of what proved to be arguably the best strand of genre television the BBC (or, for that matter, British television on the whole) ever produced: *A Ghost Story for Christmas* (1971–1978, 2005–2021, TV). The series' origins can be found in the previously discussed episode of *Omnibus* (1967–2003, TV) titled *Whistle and I'll Come to You* (1968, TV), the celebrated adaptation of M.R. James' short story *Oh, Whistle, and I'll Come to You, My Lad*, and would go on to become something of an institution over the following years, as much a part of a British TV Christmas in the seventies as the annual Morecambe and Wise special. In charge of the series was Lawrence Gordon Clarke, a director whose work for the corporation already included episodes of such documentaries as *The Human Side* (1964–1965, TV) and *Six Sides of a*

Square (1966, TV). Working as director, producer and adaptor, Clarke was responsible almost singlehandedly for bringing James' work to a more mainstream audience, and launched the series with a 45-minute presentation of the author's 1911 story *The Stalls of Barchester Cathedral* under the title of *The Stalls of Barchester* (1971, TV).

The story opens in 1932 with the scholar Dr. Black (Clive Swift) at work in the library of Barchester Cathedral, where he has been busy cataloguing its contents without much enthusiasm ("It was a disappointing collection, and what volumes of value I found were much fallen into decay," he observes in his narration). However, his interest is piqued when the librarian (Will Leighton) presents him with a long unopened box (by order of the Dean) which contains the papers of the venerable Archdeacon Haynes (Robert Hardy), which had been bequeathed by his sister Letitia (Thelma Barlow) in 1894. In them he discovers a diary recalling Haynes' arrival in Barchester as a junior deacon in 1872, and the increasingly disturbing events that occurred in the years thereafter, during which he becomes impatient for his superior, the aged Dr. Pulteney (Harold Bennett), to vacate his position so that he might inherit it. But as Dr. Black reads on, the old man "showed no willingness to relinquish his post." Until, that is, he conveniently falls down the stairs to his death at the age of 92, thus allowing Haynes to at last acquire the position he has long coveted.

The accident is attributed to a missing stair rod, and a servant girl, Jane Lee (Penny Service), is blamed, but it would seem the real explanation is rather more sinister, and guilt begins to consume the new Archdeacon. Observes Dr. Black, "Traces of uneasiness impinge, rather as though his waking hours had to be crammed with activity in order to keep the shadows at bay." Black also discovers what appears to be a blackmail letter from the maid, along with payments registered in the accounts to one J.L. The diary also begins to reveal Haynes' increasingly fragile state of mind, particularly during his sister's long absences with their cousin Henrietta in Brighton during the winter months ("The evenings, after I have worked as long as I can, are very trying," he notes, adding, "I get an uncomfortable impression when going to my room there is company of some kind").

His guilt also begins to take on physical manifestations, for while stroking a carved cat upon the armrest at his place in the cathedral's choir stalls, he momentarily seems to be stroking fur. Noticing the many other wooden carvings about the place, among them angels and the damned, Haynes begins to investigate their origins, learning from a local priest (Erik Chitty) that they were carved by John Austin (known locally as Austin the Twice-Born), who apparently had second sight, while the trees from which they came "were used at one time for much darker rites than those they now fulfil." As the days progress, the manifestations increase, and Haynes not only hears voices, but imagines he sees a cat about the house. "The hall and staircase seemed to be unusually full of what I can only call movement without sound," he observes of one evening's activities. Meanwhile, another of the carvings on his stall momentarily turns into a skull, while one night, a grey, skeletal hand alights on his shoulder. Things soon after reach a climax when Haynes encounters a cowled figure on the stairway, whose fingernails scratch his face, prompting him to fall to his death, breaking his neck in the process. As Black reads from correspondence of the time, his "features [were] almost unrecognisable." Deciding to examine the carvings in the cathedral stalls himself, Black finds that they have long since been replaced, and enquiries as to their whereabouts lead him to the local museum, whose curator (Ambrose Coghill) reveals that a note was discovered within one of them when it split in two, the contents of which, written by the man who did the carving in 1699, warn that anyone who touches it who has blood on his hands should beware "lest he be fetched away." As for the carved figures themselves, it transpires that they have since been burned, as they frightened the children of the old man who discovered the note.

The slightly flat ending aside, this is macabre television at its peak, providing chills that are both subtle and, as the story progresses, genuinely startling (the stroking of the fur, the skeletal hand on the shoulder and the final encounter on the stairway are frissons to be savored). The 1932 framing device was of Lawrence Gordon Clark's own devising, yet is perfectly in tune with the story it goes on to tell via the documents discovered in the long unopened box (to which the librarian conveniently has the key). Indeed, there is much to enjoy in the exchanges between Dr. Black and the librarian as they look for something—*anything*—of interest among the library's papers and manuscripts ("Some mute inglorious Milton, perhaps?" ponders the librarian). The fact that the increasingly aged Dr. Pulteney just won't vacate his position is also dealt with some humor, given the mention in conversation between Haynes and his sister of Methuselah, who lived 900 years ("I find it entirely credible," bemoans Haynes), Pulteney's reference in one of his sermons to Abraham, who lived 103 score years and 15, and the fact that the old boy manages to survive an infection in the town that has already seen off a number of people. That his birthdays are attended by fewer people of his generation is also nicely observed ("Long life, Dr. Pulteney," toasts Haynes at one sparse gathering, to which a colleague adds "And absent friends").

What raises all this above the norm is Clark's observational detail, not only of cathedral rites and rituals (sermons, evensong, etc.), but of Haynes' increasingly isolated and cloistered life, in which it always seems to be winter ("I find that I absolutely shrink from the dark season," he reveals), and his determination, as a confirmed rationalist, to remain level-headed, despite the fact that the world to which he has aspired is now falling apart ("I must be firm," he write in his diary on more than one occasion, prompting Black to observe, "The Archdeacon's diary provides the one outlet for all his troubles and fears, although I expect that much is concealed even from this"). But as has been strongly intimated, these are circumstances Haynes has brought upon himself ("What a pity that he couldn't wait for Dr. Pulteney to leave the stage gracefully," comments Dr. Black).

In the making of the program, Clark was assisted enormously by his cameraman John McGlashan who, working on 16mm film, perfectly captures the gloom of Haynes' home, as well as the shadows of the cathedral and its environs (Norwich Cathedral and its famous close), along with the slightly further flung location of the now overgrown grove where the wood for the carvings hailed from, and where the stump of a tree known as the Hanging Oak remains for Haynes to see ("Human bones were found between its roots when it was felled," the priest informs him). The use of sound is also expertly utilized, especially during Haynes' trying evenings, while the costumes (by Vera Coleman) and design (by Keith Harris) relay the period with care but undue fuss. Clark also peppers the proceedings with a few sly touches of black humor, such as the cracking of a boiled egg by Letitia at breakfast just after Dr. Pulteney has fallen to his death, and Haynes' observation of the cathedral's carvings: "There appears to be more conviction in the figures of the damned."

On the acting front, Robert Hardy is in his element as the quietly vainglorious and fatally ambitious Haynes, while able support is provided by Thelma Barlow as his prim sister, Harold Bennett as the aged Pulteney and Erik Chitty as the local priest, while Clive Swift enlivens the bookends with his turn as Dr. Black (note that all the aforementioned players went on to notable success in a variety of well-known dramas, soaps and sitcoms, thus making the watching of the film a curious experience nowadays, particularly for British audiences). Broadcast at 11:05 p.m. on BBC1 on Christmas Eve 1971 just before Midnight Mass of the Nativity (whose broadcast from Manchester's Roman Catholic Church of the Holy Name must have worked as a welcome restorative for shattered viewers), this must surely have been a Christmas present to relish for anyone who came across it at the time.

Clark and his cameraman were back again the following year (same date, time and channel) with *A Warning to the Curious* (1972, TV), based upon James' 1925 story, here updated to the Depression era of 1929. In Clark's 50-minute adaptation, a middle-aged clerk named Paxton (Peter Vaughan), who has recently been made unemployed, decides to indulge his passion for archaeology by visiting the small seaside town of Seaburg in Norfolk, where he hopes to discover the site of the last of three royal crowns buried in the area. "No foreign army would invade the kingdom of Anglia so long as at least one of them remained undisturbed," the opening narration informs us, going on to reveal that since their hiding, one has been plundered by thieves and another covered by the encroaching sea. Consequently, "only one crown now remains, lying somewhere in its royal burial ground."

Staying at a small hotel, Paxton begins to explore the area, encountering on his travels the local vicar (George Benson), who reveals that the story of the crowns is "still current folklore round here," to the point that the locals "take these traditions more seriously than their churchgoing." He also learns that one family in particular kept guard over the crowns down the generations, the last of them, one William Ager, having died from consumption in 1917. Says the vicar, "In times of war, the oldest male would watch to see that it remained unmolested. The last surviving member of the family took the duty upon himself during the four years of the Great War. It became an obsession with him, poor fellow. He haunted the spot night and day," to which he adds, "The secret lies buried with him, I should think." However, when Paxton searches out Ager's gravestone in an overgrown corner of the churchyard, he notices a lone figure watching him from a nearby field....

Having found a book on the subject in the local antiques shop, Paxton discovers it to have belonged to the Ager family, the frontice piece listing the names of five generations of the family, including that of William Ager (whose birth date, it should be noted, is given as 1885 in the book, with no death date provided, yet on his tombstone, which lacks a birth date, the death date given is 1917 at the age of 35, which doesn't quite add up). Having encountered another guest at the hotel, a regular visitor called Dr. Black (Clive Swift), Paxton asks if he has ever heard of the Ager family, to whit the doctor refers him to the hotel's boot man (David Cargill), who despite being a local, professes to never having heard of Ager, although having glimpsed the book that Paxton has purchased, which bears three crowns upon its cover, he appears to be hiding something. Coming across a young woman (Gilly Fraser) at a nearby cottage, Paxton learns that it used to be the home of Ager, and that, according to the locals she has spoken to, he used to "wait around in that little wood, over by the sand dunes," which is enough to prompt Paxton to prepare for a night dig, telling the boot man that he has to return to London on an urgent matter overnight so as to avert suspicion, on which pretext he gets a train to the next town.

Having dug in the dunes all night, Paxton manages to locate the third crown, yet while doing so clearly feels that he is somehow being watched, and even imagines himself being chased by the figure of Ager. Traveling back to the hotel by train, during which the guard at the station opens his carriage door to admit another passenger who fails to get in ("Oh, sorry, sir, thought I saw someone"), Paxton discovers the book he has bought has been slashed to bits by his razor, and hears a consumptive cough. Unnerved, he goes for a walk and encounters Dr. Black, who is painting on the shore, and tells him of his discovery, later showing him the crown in his room. "I used to dream of doing something big, to show people you didn't need a string of letters after your name to be recognized," he tells the doctor, adding, "An Anglo-Saxon crown—no one's ever discovered one before. And I found it." But when the doctor enquires what he is going to do with it, Paxton replies, "I'm going to put it back," and when asked why, he replies, "Ever since I've touched this thing I've never been alone.... If I return it there might be some hope."

Thus Paxton asks Dr. Black to accompany him in returning the crown, but before they leave, Paxton receives a visit from Ager in his room, during which the candle blows out and a figure is seen crouching on the floor by the light of his torch before it too is extinguished ("He was here, you see. He came to take it back," he tells the doctor, who has entered with the boot man, having heard Paxton's screams). But returning the crown to its burial site is far from the last of the story, for while walking on the sands the next day, Paxton is chased by Ager and hacked to death when they reach the burial site, much to the distress of Dr. Black, who has followed Paxton and observed events from a distance. Black leaves soon after on the train, but as he is sitting in the carriage waiting for it to depart, the porter opens the door for another passenger, who fails to get in ("Oh, sorry, sir, thought I saw someone"), thus leaving Black to an uncertain fate as the train pulls away.

With its desolate dunes and beaches, superbly captured by cameraman John McGlashan, *A Warning to the Curious* recalls similar scenes in *Whistle and I'll Come to You* ("You can't see where the beach ends or the sky begins," comments Dr. Black at one point), and like its predecessor, it makes much use of threatening lone figures in the landscape, whether real or imagined. "Now there's an extraordinary thing. I've put a figure on my shore to give it some perspective, and if you look, you'll see there's someone standing there, just where I put him," notices Dr. Black while painting. And like *Whistle*, its central character comes a-cropper for taking something he ought not to have, and although in this case he realizes the error of his actions, it's too late to save him. The film actually begins with another archaeologist (Julian Herington) digging for the crown, only to find himself hacked to death for his troubles by the real William Ager ("No digging here," he warns), after which the action moves forward 12 years with the arrival of Paxton, all of whom we see at first being his suitcase and the telltale shovel strapped to it. Like *Whistle*, hotel life proves somewhat alienating for our hero, with the boots man quickly catching on to his job situation, much to his discomfort. However, in Dr. Black, he at least finds an ally, albeit one whose own future is put in some doubt by the association.

As with *The Stalls of Barchester*, this is a film in which small details and telling gestures matter, and although a period piece, the drama isn't overwhelmed by twenties bric-a-brac, the main set, Paxton's hotel room, being sparsely decorated with only the essential items (bed, wardrobe, wash basin, etc.), allowing the various characters to carry the burden of the story, in which instance Peter Vaughan is excellent as the curious Paxton, forever looking over his shoulder, with ideal support provided by the returning Clive Swift as the kindly Dr. Black (whose final appearance in the series this would mark, following his character's uncertain end), David Cargill as the not always helpful boot man, George Benson as the local vicar and Roger Milner (billed Millner) as the proprietor of the antiques shop. Mention must also be made of bit player John Kearney, who strikes an unsettling aspect as the spectral William Ager (and top marks to costume designer Joyce Hammond for providing him with such a sinister looking cape and hat).

As with the previous film, sound effects are particularly well used, especially during Paxton's lonely (well, not quite so lonely) night dig, in which his efforts are accompanied by the sounds of crickets and a barely heard consumptive cough, as well as some disturbingly abstract music (for which no credit is given), while the dialogue of the secondary characters doesn't always auger well for Paxton ("I've seen an old tramp or something in the trees from time to time," comments the woman at the cottage). As before, Clark proves himself a master when it comes to the more thrilling sequences, among them Paxton's night dig, Ager's unexpected appearance in the hotel room, and the climactic chase through the woods, not to mention Ager's various appearances in the distance, best among them a brief scene in which Paxton encounters a farmer on his way back to the train after his dig; at first believing the farmer to be Ager, he warily passes him by, following which the farmer turns to see Paxton walk away, only to notice that he is now being pursued by a figure who wasn't there a moment earlier (note that although Clark is credited for writing and producing the film, he receives no credit for having directed it).

Given the success of the first two films, which were made under the aegis of the BBC's arts department, by the time Clark came to make his third Christmas ghost story, *Lost Hearts* (1973, TV), the corporation's larger drama department had become involved in their production. As a consequence, Rosemary Hill became the series' producer, while established writers were assigned the scripts, in this case Robin Wright (who'd recently completed a five-part adaptation of *Jane Eyre* [1973, TV] for the BBC), and though this meant that Clark didn't quite have the freedom he'd previously enjoyed, the films at least got a little more money, and became somewhat tighter in their telling, with the third installment, based upon James' 1895 story, running to a compact 35 minutes. However, it's unlikely that audiences tuning in at 11:35 p.m. on Christmas Day 1973 felt unduly cheated, as this remains another genre highlight.

This time the focus of the story is an 11-year-old orphan named Stephen (Simon Gipps-Kent) who has come to stay with his cousin twice removed, Peregrine Abney (Joseph O'Conor), an eccentric scholar whose homely cook, Mrs. Bunch (Susan Richards), describes him as "kindness itself." Indeed, it seems that Stephen is not the only child who has come under Mr. Abney's wing, as Mrs. Bunch goes on to explain to the inquisitive young lad. "He may be an old bachelor, but he's very partial to children. You're not the first little orphan he's given hearth and home, food and shelter," she tells him. But what Stephen doesn't know is that his cousin is actually an alchemist whose goal is to acquire immortality, to which end he has already murdered two children, a young girl and an Italian boy, whose ghosts Stephen sees about the house and gardens, and whose presence acts as a portent of what is to come. Stephen first sees the children waving to him from a field during the coach journey to his cousin's estate, following which they appear with increasing regularity, at one point waking him in the night, the Italian boy beckoning him on with a tune from the hurdy-gurdy he left behind when he disappeared, only for them to reveal that they've had their hearts torn from their rib cages, prompting Stephen to let out a piercing scream. This attracts the attention of Mrs. Bunch and Mr. Abney, who is keen to assure Stephen that it all must have been a dream ("No hearts, they had no hearts," cries the boy). In fact, Abney himself sees the children moments later and consequently burns the hurdy-gurdy the boy has been playing ("Some annoyance may be experienced from the psychic portion of the subjects," he notes in his journal).

Abney seems particularly excited about Stephen's upcoming twelfth birthday, which is to take place on Halloween, and for which he is keen for him to be fit and well ("Eat well, sleep well, we want you full of bounce for your birthday"). However, it is on this day that he plans to kill the boy ("The heart must be removed from the living subject, reduced to ashes over the sacred fire, and then mixed with a generous measure of fortified wine," he notes to himself), to which end he offers to tell the boy's "secret fortune" at midnight in his study, where he forces him to drink a glass of drugged port. "Your fortune is my fortune, Stephen, as was the girl's, as was the little Italian boy's. You complete the work of twenty years, Stephen," he tells him. But just as he is about to butcher the boy, the two ghostly children appear to the

Nailed it. Michelle Foster and Christopher Davis as ghostly children in *Lost Hearts* (1973, TV), from *A Ghost Story for Christmas* (1971–1978, 2005–2021, TV) (BBC).

sound of the hurdy-gurdy, and the Italian boy stabs Abney to death with the knife he is about to carry out his deadly deed. Things conclude with the old man's funeral, at which the vicar (Roger Milner) comments, "What precisely was the nature of his research I think it better for God-fearing mortals not to enquire," before going on to ponder whether "he was struck down by his own hand or by forces which in another age might well be attributable to the Devil, to Satan himself."

A fast moving and compact piece in which cameraman John McGlashan again distinguishes himself in both the interiors of Abney's country hall residence and the lush exteriors of the surrounding parkland (which includes a columned mausoleum), *Lost Hearts* (which had previously been presented for television as a 1966 episode of *Mystery and Imagination* [1966–1970, TV]) gets down to the business at hand pretty much immediately, with the first appearance of the ghosts coming within the first minute of the narrative, although it isn't until later that their deathly blue pallor or the long fingernails they sport become more apparent. Accompanied by the unsettling music of the hurdy-gurdy to which they gently sway as they walk, they are an increasingly disturbing presence, and make a stark contrast to the true villain of the piece, the Pickwickesque Abney, who is played with jovial vivacity by Joseph O'Conor, known to most as the kindly Mr. Brownlow in *Oliver!* (1968). As Stephen, Simon Gipps-Kent carries the burden of the plot on his young shoulders very well (he was actually 14 going on 15 at the time of filming), while Susan Richards as the cook and James Mellow as Abney's manservant Parkes bring their somewhat typical "downstairs" characters adequately to life, while Christopher Davis and Michelle Foster certainly leave their mark as the long nailed ghosts (quite literally at one point, leaving five long scratches on the wall by Stephen's bed, for which he gets the blame). That children are the victims of Abney's gruesome intentions makes the drama all the more disturbing here; that a slight air of pedophilia hangs over the piece as a consequence, whether intended or not, makes for an occasionally uncomfortable atmosphere, however.

Another compact tale, this time running 37 minutes, appeared the following Christmas on 23 December 1974 at 11:35 p.m. This was an adaptation of James' 1904 story *The Treasure of Abbot Thomas* (1974, TV), and like *A Warning to the Curious* (1972, TV), it involves the search for hidden treasure, although here it is scholarly detective work rather than good luck that leads to the discovery of a hoard of gold hidden by one Abbot Thomas in the 15th century. Those on its trail are the Rev. Justin Somerton (Michael Jayston), who is making a study of the period while a guest at the monastery where the abbot lived until his death in 1429, and his young friend, Peter, Lord Dattering (Paul Lavers), with whom he deciphers clues found in an old Latin text in the monastery's library ("You're treasure hunting!" exclaims Peter, despite his friend's claims to the contrary). Somerton describes the abbot as an alchemist ("Not a suitable occupation for a fifteenth century churchman," he avers) who has somewhat playfully left clues as to the whereabouts of his "mass of gold" which is secreted somewhere in the monastery. "Bartholomew, Jude, Simon and Mateusz will tell either you or your successors," the abbot is said to have replied to those who asked him of the treasure's whereabouts, and being a scholar himself, Peter recalls that all four can be found together "in the east window of Gravely Church—the church on the water," to which they hie, Peter with his camera and Somerton with his sketch book. Here, they discover further clues in the stained glass of the window. "He looks down from on high to see what is hidden," reads one, while the others mention "writing which no man knoweth" and a stone with "seven I's." Peter surmises the first of these to be a reference to the gargoyles on the monastery's tower, from the top of which they spy a hidden culvert. Somerton also notices a broad black band "on the edge of the cope" in one of the window's panels which, once scratched off, reveals a coded message which, when deciphered, reveals that "2,000 pieces of gold are deposited." Peter also notes that the abbot "set a guardian over the treasure."

Armed with all this information, Somerton at last sets forth one night to retrieve the gold, but having found the stone with seven I's and chiseled it open, he is greeted not only by a bag of coins, but also a vile sludge which pours out of the niche, while the manifestation of a monk-like figure runs its bony fingers across his face and through his hair. Bolting from the scene, he takes refuge in his rooms, where the strange sludge now oozes under his door. Finding his friend there after two days, Peter spies the bag containing the loot, which Somerton informs him is merely "pieces of lead, iron, bronze, various metals, all worthless," though a quick look inside reveals it to be full of gold. Like Paxton with the crown, Somerton urges Peter to put the bag back on his behalf, not being able to bring himself to go back to the culvert, his nerves being shattered by his experience. Later recovering at Peter's estate, Somerton is taking the air in a bath chair when Peter's mother notices the doctor walking towards them, and so they leave the reverend to be ministered to. However, it is not the doctor who approaches the now lone Somerton on the gravel path, but the figure of a monk....

Adapted by John Bowen, *Abbot Thomas* is easily one of the most engaging of the Christmas ghost stories, thanks to its treasure hunt theme and the various Holmesian clues and conundrums that the protagonists have to solve, in which their fluency in Latin proves to be of invaluable help. Bowen also adds elements of his own to the story, among them an amusing sequence in which Somerton is invited by Peter to a séance at his mother's ("Dear lad, I'm interested in all forms of the higher silliness. I should be delighted to come along"). It appears that Lady Dattering is having trouble accepting the fact that her husband has passed away, and is using the mediums, a married couple who have been staying with her, as a means of comfort. "Mama can't accept my father's death. I fear she finds me a most inadequate substitute," Peter informs the rev, who is clearly suspicious of the situation. "You would have been burned as witches in the period I am studying," he remarks to them over tea and slab cake, before going on to expose them as the charlatans they are, much to Lady Dattering's distress.

As always, there are portents of the dark things to come, which Somerton either ignores or fails to recognize to his eventual peril. The photograph of the stained-glass window contains a blemish which looks like a bird, while atop the tower, he is momentarily disorientated by what appears to be a black cloak ("Something seemed to come at me"). And of course, there is that warning of a guardian watching over the treasure, whose approach in the culvert while the reverend is chiseling away is marked by some unsettling hand-held point of view camerawork. His eventual appearance proves to be another well handled shock sequence care of Clark, who at first depicts the specter reflected in the water of the culvert before finally revealing his face, which is accompanied by a spine-tingling scream from Somerton and a maniacal laugh from the abbot. Other directorial flourishes include an eye-catching overhead shot at the séance depicting the touching hands of all those present, and the climactic high angle shot of the cowled figure approaching Somerton in his bath chair. Cameraman John McGlashan is meanwhile in his element, providing such pictorial highlights as the interiors of the monastery, with its lurking monks (shot at Wells Cathedral in Somerset), and the painterly image of the church on the water, which is good enough to be framed. As Somerton, Michael Jayston is perfectly cast as the reverend who is distracted from his learning by avarice, while Paul Lavers makes for a keen and helpful Lord Dattering. Good support is meanwhile provided by Frank Mills and Sheila Dunn as the fake mediums, last seen struggling away with their luggage after they have been unceremoniously evicted, and Virginia Balfour as Peter's emotionally susceptible mother. As for the spectral abbot himself, he is played by John Herrington. Tightly edited by Roger Waugh and featuring an atmospheric choral and percussion score by Geoffrey Burgon (the first to be specifically commissioned for the series), this all helps to turn *Abbot Thomas* into arguably the best of the Christmas ghost stories.

It was David Rudkin's "television version" of James' 1904 story *The Ash Tree* (1975, TV) that provided the next Christmas ghost story, which aired at 11:35 p.m. on 23 December 1975. Set in the mid–18th century, the 32-minute film opens with the arrival by horse of Sir Richard Fell (Edward Petherbridge) at the vast country seat he has inherited upon the death of his uncle ("He isn't pale enough for a lord," notes one serf to another as their new master passes by, to which comes the response, "He's been in Italy"). With his grand plans for the house (he intends to be a "pestilent innovator") and his pending marriage to the beautiful Lady Augusta (Lalla Ward), his future certainly looks rosy, but almost immediately upon setting foot in his new home, Sir Richard is beset by voices and visions seemingly pertaining to his great uncle Matthew ("In this dread matter we entreat thee"). It would also seem that something is ailing the livestock in the locality, prompting the shepherd to bring in the sheep at night, even though it's far from winter.

Sir Richard's plans include the expansion of the church to accommodate a new family pew, which involves the relocating of a grave, whose occupant, a young woman called Anne Mothersole, was hanged during his great uncle's time for being a witch. But when the grave is finally opened, its inhabitant is not in residence. The voices and visions meanwhile persist, in which Sir Richard envisions himself as his great uncle who, as county sheriff, oversaw the hanging of the young woman, which preyed much upon his mind, while curious sounds from the ash tree outside his bedroom window keep him awake at night, the source of which proves to be a number of scuttling creatures which can best be described as babies' heads with spiders' legs. Sir Richard also learns from the estate's long serving clergyman, Dr. Croome (Preston Lockwood), that his great uncle was apparently murdered, having been "found dead in his chair by his bed, dead and black, disordered, some poison, though no trace what, nor how—a popeish plot, they said," to which he adds that when he tried to close Sir Matthew's eyes, "there began in my hands such a violent smarting, for six weeks after my arms were so swollen—the women who laid him out the same."

Eventually, one night, the creatures emerge from the ash tree and prey upon Sir Richard in his bed, and when the housekeeper Mrs. Chiddock (Lucy Griffiths) enters his room and spots one of them scuttling out of the window, she throws her candle at the tree, which catches fire, revealing in its charred roots the next day the withered form of Anne Mothersole, who had placed a curse on Sir Matthew and the estate before being hanged ("Mine shall inherit, and no sweet babes"). Finally, upon her return from Paris where she has been buying her trousseau, Lady Augusta is led to her husband-to-be who lies dead in his bed, his skin black. And when she touches him, she recoils as if from a stinging shock.

In terms of plot, *The Ash Tree* is perhaps the least substantial of the James adaptations, and the one with the least quotable dialogue, yet thanks to John McGlashan's fine landscape photography, it is certainly among the most visually satisfying. That said, the tripping between times in which Sir Richard imagines himself to be Sir Matthew isn't always successfully achieved, though the flashbacks involving the torture and subsequent hanging of Anne Mothersole (Barbara Ewing) are not without their interest, having an air of *Witchfinder General* (1968) to them, albeit lacking that film's viciousness, with Clifford Kershaw's Witchfinder being no match for Vincent Price's Matthew Hopkins (the exposure of Ewing's breasts during her torture was something of a rarity at the time, though). Elsewhere, the spider-like creatures that emerge from the ash tree are most convincing thanks to the work of visual effects technician John Friedlander, whose experience as a puppet maker appears to have served him well. As Sir Richard, Edward Petherbridge certainly looks and acts the part of a country squire of the period, while Lalla Ward makes for an attractive Lady Augusta, even though she is given little to do ("You find me laying to rest the great unread," says Sir Richard to her while sorting out his predecessor's library when she first arrives, from which she nevertheless swipes a copy of *The Adventures of Tom Jones*, despite her initial shock at finding it there). As always with the Christmas ghost stories, there is solid work from the supporting cast, chief among them Preston Lockwood as Dr. Croome and, in particular, Lucy Griffiths as the housekeeper Mrs. Chiddock, who looks like she might have been born to the period. Likewise, costumes (Sue Cable), design (Allan Anson) and editing (Roger Waugh) are all up to par, while Clark's continued hold on the series is without question. On the whole, though, this does seem to be one of the more insubstantial of the adaptations.

Perhaps by way of ringing the changes, M.R. James was abandoned for the remainder of the series, despite the availability of many other suitable stories. Instead, with *The Signalman* (1976), which aired at 10:40 p.m. on 22 December 1976, Clark turned to Charles Dickens for his source material. Adapted by Andrew Davies from the author's 1866 short story, the 38-minute film sees a traveller (Bernard Lloyd) who is staying at a country inn encounter a lone railway signalman (Denholm Elliott) in a remote cutting at the edge of an ominous looking tunnel. "This must be a very lonesome spot to occupy I should think," observes the traveller of the location, having scrambled down a steep bank to reach it. The signalman seems somewhat disturbed by the traveller's arrival, however, and with good reason, for it appears that he is being haunted by an apparition whose appearances portend to accidents on the line, and he at first takes the traveller for the spectral figure ("You look at me as if you had some dread of me," says the traveller). The two get to talking, and the signalman invites the traveller up to his box for a cup of tea, where he reveals the simplicity but also the importance of his job ("So little to do, with so much depending on it"), as well as his concerns for safety on the line ("A tunnel collision's the worst to be feared. Your nightmares would go hard to equal it").

Invited to return the following night to continue their conversation, the signalman informs the traveller of a "memorable accident" that occurred in the tunnel some six hours after he first saw the specter waving to him at its mouth ("A remarkable coincidence, my friend, but no more than that," assures the traveller), while another appearance by it was followed by a bride (Carina Wyeth) falling to her death from a train. "The specter came back a week ago and has been there now and again by fits and starts," the signalman reveals, thus leading him to wonder what form the next accident might take ("These disturbing appearances—you can't be called upon to try to interpret them," says the traveller). However, when he next sees the specter waving to him by the tunnel, the signalman stays too long on the line, and is himself killed when a train bursts out of the tunnel (says the distraught train driver [Reginald Jessup], "He didn't seem to heed the whistle").

The most intimate of the Christmas ghost stories, this is pretty much a two hander for most of its length, with great reliance placed upon the performances of its two leading protagonists, on which count Bernard Lloyd and Denholm Elliott are very well matched as the mysterious traveller and the lonely signalman, about whom we learn very little, not even their names. "I have spent much of my life shut up within narrow limits. I've been confined, but now I am free," comments the traveller enigmatically early on, while the signalman reveals, "I was at one time, sir, a student of natural philosophy," but otherwise they remain ciphers, and it is to Lloyd and Elliott's credit that the characters are as believable and well fleshed out as they are, their intimate exchanges taking on a dramatic intensity which raises the level of foreboding to surprising heights within the confines of the claustrophobic signal box (shot on location at Highley), with its crackling fire and warning bells, the humming of one in particular seeming to herald the arrival of the specter, much to the signalman's evident consternation, prompting him to dramatically stop speaking midsentence at one point when he hears it.

This is by no means a one-set drama, though, and the scenes on the railway line itself, with its steep banks and yawning tunnel mouth (Bewdley Tunnel in Kidderminster), are full of frosty atmosphere, while the flashbacks to the crash in the tunnel, shot in hues of red, and the bride falling from the train, provide some moments of action (the tunnel sequence is said to be based upon the Clayton Tunnel crash of 1861). The appearances of the specter at the mouth of the tunnel are particularly unsettling, and the revelation of his white face with its closed eyes and gaping mouth is not easily forgotten. As always, Clark's grip on the proceedings is expert throughout, whether it be with the intimate interplay between the traveller and the signalman or the few open-air moments as the traveller walks in the countryside and first has his attention captured by the appearance of a distant train (the photography was now in the capable hands of David Whitson, John McGlashan having moved on to pastures new). The dialogue is also not without its merits, as per the signalman's comment that "I think the mind makes its own places, sir," and the traveller's observation of the wind making a "wild harp" of the telegraph wires. However, if it's shudders plain and simple that you seek, then *The Signalman* has them aplenty, and the revelation of the apparition's gawping white face truly is the stuff of nightmares (note that Denholm Elliott's surname is misspelled Elliot in the opening credits but is correctly spelled in the closing credits).

Having reached a high, the series next plunged to something of a low with *Stigma* (1977, TV), which aired on 28 December 1977 at 11 p.m. (though some sources claim the broadcast date was postponed to 29 December). The first story to be based upon newly commissioned material, in this case provided by the prolific Clive Exton, the 30-minute film was also the first to be set in the present. Set in and around a country cottage, it sees two workmen attempt to remove a large stone from the garden so as to make way for a new lawn. However, when the stone is partially lifted, a great wind is released from beneath it, and Katharine (Kate Binchy), the lady of the house, finds herself in its path, following which she begins to bleed from her abdomen with increasing profusion during the following hours, albeit without any signs of a wound. Discovered in a pool of blood in bed the next morning by her husband Peter (Peter Bowles), he rushes her to hospital with their doctor (Jon Laurimore). Meanwhile, back at the house, the workmen manage to lift the rock to reveal a skeleton underneath, surrounded by rusty knives. Comments Katharine and Peter's daughter Verity (Maxine Gordon), who has been observing, "It's the old religion—I read about it in a book. They used to bury them under stones. They thought they were witches," at which she begins to skin an onion she is holding, while down the road her mother expires in the doctor's car. And that is pretty much that.

A trite story which amounts to very little, the material would have better suited an anthology series along the lines of the later *Hammer House of Horror* (1980, TV), and gives the impression of having been hastily scribbled over a weekend to meet a deadline. Lacking the atmosphere of the period pieces, not to mention the subtle frissons, the film's bloody images as the mother attempts to clean herself in the white bathroom of the cottage are more likely to induce nausea rather than chills, and one feels for the poor actress having to deal with the never-ending flow of Kensington gore during the overly prolonged sequence, especially as she is required to go topless to do so. Given the thinly sketched

The stuff of nightmares. The ghostly presence reveals itself in *The Signalman* (1976, TV) from *A Ghost Story for Christmas* (1971–1978, 2005–2021, TV) (BBC).

characters, one feels little empathy for the mother's situation, and even an actor of the stature of Peter Bowles as her husband is hard pressed to provide anything more than a fraught expression as he attempts to deal with the situation. The daughter has even less to do, save for delivering the final "explanation" as to what has been going on.

Directed with a total lack of flair rather than his usual panache by Clark, the film opens with a red dot moving towards the camera as the credits flick by, only for it to then rather clumsily transform into a red Citroen 2CV as it carries Katharine and Verity to the cottage, passing by similar stones we later see in the garden, and while it is eventually revealed that the cottage is sited amid the stones of Aylesbury, rather too little is made of the fact, save for having Verity wander through them meaningfully as her mother attempts to stem the flow of blood in the bathroom. The sheer number of the stones is finally revealed via an impressive aerial shot during the end credits, but what all this is meant to imply is never really addressed, and the only scene that comes close to being thrilling is a sequence in which Peter gets up to investigate noises in the middle of the night (he hears singing and drums), but even this amounts to very little (an onion rolls on the floor in the kitchen and a knife appears to move). Rather plainly photographed by John Turner, the film, which also features Christopher Blake and John Judd as the workmen, is otherwise inconsequential stuff which can't have impressed too many viewers, though the *Daily Mail* found that it "worked on the imagination as well as the senses." Sadly, it proved to be Lawrence Gordon Clark's last Christmas ghost story, and following two episodes of the dramatic reconstruction series *Life at Stake* (1978, TV), he left the BBC for ITV, where he helmed several episodes of the popular historical drama *Flambards* (1978, TV) and a version of M.R. James' *Casting the Runes* (1979, TV), more of which anon.

Slightly better, but by no means a classic, was *The Ice House* (1979, TV), which brought the series to a disappointing end (more a whimper than a bang). Written by John Bowen and directed by Derek Lister (a theatre director whose television work at this point included several episodes of *Coronation Street* [1960–, TV] and a couple of half-hour plays for the *Second City Firsts* [1973–1978, TV] series), it takes as its setting a country house resort to which Paul (John Stride) has retreated following the breakup of his marriage. The place is run by an enigmatic brother and sister, Jessica and Clovis (Elizabeth Romilly and Geoffrey Burridge), and though peopled by unattached, elderly well off types, Paul appreciates the comforts it provides. But all is not quite what it seems, for the masseur, Bob (David Beames), is keen to get away ("I urgently require assistance to get away from here—I can't do it on my own," he pleads to Paul). And for a masseur, his hands are also exceptionally cold (he describes it as a case of "the cools").

Meanwhile, Jessica and Clovis introduce Paul to the ice house, situated in the garden, over which grows a vine on which has blossomed two curious trumpet shaped flowers that emit an exceptionally seductive scent ("They are brother and sister," explains Jessica). However, there is something sinister about the building, and later we witness Jessica and Clovis kiss under the vine, whose flowers appear to move in response. Paul subsequently visits the ice house at night and, using matches and a letter from his wife to light his way, discovers to his horror Bob the masseur preserved in a large, upstanding block of ice. But when he returns the next day with Jessica, all he finds is ice. When he becomes cold himself while in the sauna, Jessica and Clovis come to his aid. "We only want what is best. My brother and I do not approve of death, you see" she explains. "Dust to dust, ashes to ashes is what is said, but that is not true. Flesh does not return to dust or ashes, it putrefies, it returns to maggots, to stench and to slime. We do not find that at all pleasing. Therefore, we will not tolerate it," she continues, to which Clovis adds, "Ice preserves." Jessica and Clovis then accompany Paul down to the ice house, which he enters and closes the door.

Although just 35 minutes in length, *The Ice House*, which was broadcast at 11:35 p.m. on Christmas Day 1979, is a somewhat ponderous affair, and though attractively photographed by Nigel Walters, Bowen's teleplay amounts to very little, being too much smoke and mirrors, and not enough substance, providing no clues as to the siblings' real motives. Are they pod people, aliens, the walking dead? We never do find out. Nor do we discover the true power and influence of the vine, other than that, as a variety, it is not known at all, having been "brought from abroad" and has been there as long as the ice house itself. Nor do we discover the meaning of the two flower shaped holes that appear in Paul's bedroom window. Similarly, we find out little about Paul himself, save that he has split from his wife and does his best to help people get through life, to which Clovis responds, "If life is something merely to be got through, then the only agreeable aspect of it might be its end," to which Jessica adds, "Perhaps you should assist people to *end* their lives, not to get through them."

Despite its title, the story actually begins in the heat of the resort's sauna, but it is to the ice house that Paul eventually finds himself increasingly drawn, and it is clear from almost the start that things will not end well for him when he finally enters it. Yet the story is so enigmatic, and so full of meaningful glances, quirky incidents and vague insinuations that in the end one gives up the ghost of trying to interpret them, for in all likelihood they mean nothing at all, and are simply there to intrigue and to trick out the narrative which, though helped along by a sympathetic performance from John Stride as Paul and suitably mannered work from Elizabeth Romilly and Geoffrey Burridge as the incestuous siblings, ultimately melts away before our very eyes.

Thus came to an end one of the highlights of genre television. However, a reasonable run of repeats initially helped to keep it in the public's mind, though over the years these became somewhat sporadic. *The Stalls of Barchester* (1971, TV) was repeated again in August 1972 before disappearing for decades, while *A Warning to the Curious* (1972, TV) fared a little better, with repeats in May 1974 and December 1992. *Lost Hearts* (1973, TV) had only one rerun in June 1974 before it too disappeared, while *The Treasure of Abbott Thomas* (1974, TV) had to wait until December 1983 and December 1993 for a rerun. *The Ash Tree* (1975, TV) meanwhile disappeared altogether until the new millennium. Of all the films, *The Signalman* (1976, TV) did best, with repeats in May 1977, December 1982, December 1991, December 1997, December 1998, October 2000 and June 2002. *Stigma* (1977, TV) only warranted one in May 1978, and like *The Ash Tree* (1975, TV), *The Ice House* (1978) didn't warrant any at all, at least not until well into the new millennium. Thankfully, all are now available on DVD (as a complete collection care of the BFI) and appear with reasonable regularity on television.

In fact, thanks to their growing cult reputation, the series was resurrected in the noughties with a 40-minute adaptation of M.R. James' 1925 story *A View from a Hill* (2005, TV). Produced by Pier Wilkie for BBC4, on which it was aired on 23 December 2005, the film was written by Peter Harness and directed by Luke Watson, who, along with cinematographer Chris Goodger, perfectly capture the unsettling atmosphere of the earlier James stories helmed by Lawrence Gordon Clark. Set in the forties just after the war, it sees a young archaeologist, Dr. Fanshawe (Mark Letheren), visit an impoverished squire (Pip Torrens) to authenticate a collection of artefacts on behalf of the Fitzwilliam Museum, with a view to purchase. Among them is a pair of field glasses made by a local watchmaker named Baxter (Simon Linnell), whose interests it seems leaned towards the dark arts, and through the binoculars Fanshawe is able to see back in time and view a nearby abbey in all its glory, despite it now being in ruins. While exploring the area, he also finds himself spooked by a lurking presence in the woods when he stumbles across the site of a gibbet on what is known as Gallows Hill, whose hanged men now reappear to extract their revenge.

With its frosty landscapes in which stand threatening lone figures, and its well staged sequences in which the young doctor finds himself in all too real peril, this proved to be a welcome return to form for a classic series that had somehow lost its way, and benefits from strong performances from Mark Letheren as the working class archaeologist and a perfectly cast Pip Torrens as the sarcastic squire ("Actually, I'm a doctor," says Fanshawe after his qualifications as an archaeologist appear to have been called into doubt, to which comes the retort, "Have to get you to take a look at my feet"). The film also benefits from the presence of David Burke as the squire's put-upon manservant, the only remaining member of staff from the hall's former glory days. Incredibly, the film was scripted in September 2005 and shot in November, which is an amazingly tight turnaround given its broadcast date.

Equally effective is *Number 13* (2006, TV), which was aired on BBC4 on 22 December 2006, and for which Pier Wilkie now found himself in the director's chair. Adapted by Justin Hopper from James' 1904 story, the 40-minute film follows the visit of an academic, Professor Anderson (Greg Wise), to a cathedral town to authenticate some old papers found hidden in a hole in a wall in the cathedral's archive, which leads him to investigate a former bishop whose home was used for witchcraft involving a strange foreign gentleman named Nicholas Francken, who apparently vanished into thin air when fired at by the authorities. Curiously, the room numbers at the professor's hotel, which proves to be the bishop's former home, skip from 12, in which he is staying, to 14, and when he hears noises in the night, he assumes they are coming from the adjacent room, which is occupied by a drunken solicitor (Tom Burke). But this is not the case, and eventually leads to the discovery of the phantom room 13, whose ghostly inhabitant, who proves to be Francken himself, tries to pull him though its door.

With its socially awkward moments of hotel life (an uncomfortable meal with other guests) and its atmosphere of academia, the film recalls elements of both *Whistle and I'll Come to You* (1968, TV) and *The Stalls of Barchester* (1971, TV), and is all the better for it, and though the presence of the evil Francken is seen mostly as a shadow in the professor's room, his later manifestation in room 13 accompanied by the crackle of static is effectively put over, as is the discovery of the possessions of missing hotel guests under the floorboards of Anderson's room. Strong performances from Wise as the slightly vainglorious professor and Burke as the drunken solicitor also prove an advantage, as are turns by David Burke (Tom Burke's father) as the hotel's landlord, and Paul Freeman as the cathedral's frosty archivist.

Following a hiatus of three years, the series resumed again with a disappointing remake of *Whistle and I'll Come to You* (2010, TV), already discussed elsewhere, while three years after this came an adaptation of M.R. James' 1911 story *The Tractate Middoth* (2013, TV), which aired on BBC2 on 25 December 2013. Written and directed by Mark Gatiss, the 35-minute film sees a young librarian, William Garrett (Sacha Dhawan), asked by an elderly man named John Eldred (John Castle) to locate a book called *The Tractate Middoth*, which has hidden within its pages a will written by a vicar named Dr. Rant (David Ryall), the contents of which are to the benefit of Eldred's cousin Mary Simpson (Louise Jameson). It's Eldred's hope to find the book and destroy the will, given that an earlier one worked in his own favor, but he doesn't count on the reappearance of Rant, who now seeks revenge from beyond the grave, confronting him when he at last gets his hands on the book and is about to tear out the telltale page. Set in the fifties, the film benefits from a nicely sustained air of academia and the detective work by the eager young librarian who, by rather too great a coincidence, becomes involved with Mary Simpson and her daughter Anne (Charlie Clemmow) and their attempt to discover the whereabouts of the book when he goes to stay in their guest house to recover from his own encounter with the spectral Rant, who just happens to have donated the book to the library at which he works. Carefully paced and mounted, the film is a more than worthy addition to the Christmas ghost story canon, and though perhaps not quite a match for *A View from a Hill* (2005, TV) and *Number 13* (2006, TV) in terms of atmosphere, it certainly delivers the goods when it comes to Rant's appearances, which are presaged by the presence of floating dust and an unhealthy aroma. Indeed, his rotting face, complete with cobwebbed eyes, is one of the series' more disturbing images. The film's chief asset, however, is its supporting cast, among them such welcome players as Eleanor Bron, Una Stubbs and Roy Barraclough.

Gatiss, it seems, is now ensconced at the keeper of the flame regarding the Christmas ghost stories. Unfortunately, despite his talents as both a writer and director, the next installment proved to be a misjudgment on the scale of *Stigma* (1977, TV) and *The Ice House* (1978, TV). A new story titled *The Dead Room* (2018, TV), it was broadcast on BBC4 on 24 December 2018, and takes as its central character Aubrey Judd (Simon Callow), a curmudgeonly radio personality whose series *The Dead Room* has provided "mild disquiet to radio listeners since 1976." Despite his own lack of belief in the supernatural, while recording a story he finds himself plagued by flashbacks involving a young man named Paul (Joshua Oakes-Rogers), a former lover whom he allowed to drown in a reservoir many years earlier because he was being threatened with blackmail by him. Set almost entirely within the confines of the recording studio (the Beeb's Maida Vale Studios), the 30-minute film wears its low budget all too visibly on its sleeve, being pretty much a dialogue heavy two hander for much of its length, as Judd exchanges quips with his young producer Tara (Anjli Mohindra), and while some of the dialogue has a certain wit, it ultimately adds up to very little, concluding as it does with the inevitable reappearance of the drowned lover. That an unrecognizable Susan Penhaligon plays the studio's Foley artist in a wordless performance remains somewhat mystifying.

Lesson perhaps learned, it was back to M.R. James the following year with an adaptation of his 1911 story *Martin's Close* (2019, TV), though the film, which was again written and directed by Mark Gatiss (who also executive produced via Can Do productions) did little to make amends for the previous year's *faux pas*. Broadcast on BBC4 on 24 December 2019, it follows the trial in 1684 of a young nobleman named John Martin (Wilf Scolding) who has been accused of slitting the throat of Ann Clark (Jessica Temple), a simpleminded servant girl with whom he had been having a dalliance which subsequently ruined his marriage prospects with a young woman of good standing. However, it seems that Ann, whose body Martin hid in the reeds of a lake, has been seen by a handful of witnesses since her death. A curiously ineffective mix of courtroom drama, flashbacks to the events leading up to the crime, and a redundant to-camera narration by a present day history buff (Simon Williams) who relates the story while quaffing Madeira, the 30-minute film is, like its predecessor, fatally hamstrung by its obviously low budget, and visually, despite the period clothes and authentic settings (Queen Elizabeth's Hunting Lodge in Epping Forest), has the appearance of a cheaply shot daytime drama. As Dolben, the king's counsel prosecuting the case, Peter Capaldi provides a strong center to the proceedings, but a comedic turn by Elliot Levey as the notorious Judge Jeffreys is astonishingly misjudged in both writing and performance, and trivializes the drama. Even the appearances of the specter fail to produce a shudder this time round. The series has recovered from missteps before, and hopefully it will return to chill the Yuletide airwaves again in the future, preferably with the budget it deserves (Gatiss made amendments in 2021 with a solid version of *The Mezzotint*).

It's back to the early seventies now and a little mentioned series titled *The Frighteners* (1972–1973, TV), a half-hour anthology of 13 stand-alone stories with surprising plot developments ("Thirteen tales to chill the blood," ran the tagline). Made by London Weekend Television for broadcast on the ITV network, the program, which aired from 7 July 1972, benefited greatly from being shot on film, which adds to the atmosphere of the various mini dramas. However, despite being labeled a horror anthology by some sources, the program concerns itself primarily with twist in the tale scenarios, the best of them being *The Disappearing Man* (1972, TV), in which a mouse of a man (Victor Maddern), barely acknowledged by anyone, including his wife, decides to remedy the matter by doing something that will certainly make him the focus of attention (spoiler alert: he shoots a number of people on the underground). With scripts by Jacques Gillies, William Greatorex and Mike Hodges (who also directed an episode), the series also featured such actors as Tom Bell, Ian Hendry, Jennie Linden, Ian Holm and Michael Craig.

Dead of Night

Not quite in the same league as the Christmas ghost stories was *Dead of Night* (1972, TV), which began airing on 5 November 1972. An anthology series of seven 50-minute stories involving the supernatural (of which only three episodes presently survive owing to the purging of the BBC's tape library in the 1970s), it launched with *The Exorcism* (1972, TV), a folk horror piece in which guests at a Christmas dinner party in a remote country cottage find themselves subjected to a series of strange occurrences. The once derelict building has been bought by Edmund and his wife Rachel (Edward Petherbridge and Anna Cropper), an affluent couple who have had it fully renovated with all the latest mod cons, and have invited over their friends Dan and Margaret (Clive Swift and Sylvia Kay) to show off their achievements ("Well, if one is going to live in the country, even at weekends, one must provide for the creature comforts," comments Margaret as she inspects Rachel's state of the art kitchen). However, once the evening starts, odd things begin to happen: Rachel plays a piece of music on the Clavichord of which she has no memory, the power is cut, taking out everything including the phone, Edmund's wine tastes of blood, the food is poisoned, and Rachel sees the skeleton of a dead child on her bed.

Is it all a form of mass hysteria, they wonder? However, when it appears *absolutely* dark out of the windows and the front door won't open, nor even the windows break when hit with a hammer, it seems that they are the victims of something far more sinister ("Something has got us trapped," fears Rachel). Could it be the house itself? When a set of photos Edmund has taken of the cottage now show the building how it used to look 200 years ago, complete with "a fair-haired woman with a thin face and a shawl" in one of the windows, they seem to be onto something, and soon after the plaster begins to fall from the ceilings, the bookshelves from the walls, and Rachel begins to talk about events from long ago, about which she couldn't possibly have any knowledge. Speaking as Sara Jane Morbey, a widow at 26 with two children to support, she recalls how they starved to death in the cottage when work dried up in the area and there was no food to be had for those who could not afford it ("Let my words burn themselves into the fabric of these walls, so that the brickwork, beams and plaster shall remember the agony and injustice of those dying under this roof"). And when the four go upstairs to look at the room in which the woman and her children died, they find it as it was 200 years ago, with Sara and her children dead on a straw mattress in the corner. "Yes, I understand now. Now I understand," says Margaret, at which the power returns and things conclude with the police taking photographs of the cottage as a news broadcast in the background on world famine relates that "the rich counties are getting richer and the poor countries are getting poorer," before concluding that four people have been discovered dead in a remote cottage, apparently from starvation.

As written and directed by Don Taylor for producer Inness Lloyd (who worked on all seven programs), this is an undeniably intriguing supernatural drama given a fairly lavish treatment for a videotaped studio production of the time (the interiors of a full cottage were provided by designer Judy Steele). Yet despite its comparatively brief running time, it's a slow moving and often laboriously verbose piece by present day standards (Anna Cropper's climactic near ten minute speech as the starving Sara Jane goes on *forever*), while the performances of the four principals are of the weekly rep variety, complete RP accents, thus making it hard to warm to their predicament, though given that their characters are all self-regarding middle class bourgeois types, perhaps this is the idea, given the underlying social message Taylor seems keen to relay. The idea of the walls of the cottage having recorded Sara Jane's dying words is certainly a good one, as is that of the gradual removal of the modern-day creature comforts the characters have become accustomed to ("Our civilization hangs by a thread. You throw a few switches and we're back in the Dark Ages," observes Margaret after the power has been cut). However, the twist ending in which it transpires that all four have perished is a somewhat pat conclusion to the story, which might better have been served by an epiphany in which, like Scrooge, they realize the error of their ways. Ultimately, though, they are the hapless victims of a ghostly revenge who are unfortunate enough to be in the wrong place at the wrong time ("Someone, surely, must pay for our unjust deaths," says Rachel/Sara). Note that a 90-minute radio version of the play, also by Don Taylor, followed in 1992, starring Kenneth Haigh and Susan Fleetwood as Edmund and Rachel, supported by Norman Rodway and Sara Kestelman as Dan and Margaret.

Despite its flaws, *The Exorcism* proved to be the highlight of the series, of which *Bedtime* (1972, TV) by Hugh Whitemore, *Death Cancels All Debts* (1972, TV) by Peter Draper, *Smith* (1972, TV) by Dorothy Allison, and *Two in the Morning* (1972, TV) by Leo Lehman are presently missing, thus leaving only the second episode, *Return Flight* (1972, TV) by Robert Holmes, and the concluding installment, *A Woman Sobbing* (1972, TV) by John Bowen, available for viewing. Of these, *Return Flight* concerns itself with Captain Hamish Rolph (Peter Barkworth), a modern-day airline pilot who finds himself taking evasive action to avoid hitting a World War II Lancaster Bomber on a night flight from Hamburg to Luton, but it seems he was the only member of the crew to have seen it. Making the same flight the following night, his plane loses all communications and cashes in the countryside where once there was an airfield during World War II, which was home to two squadrons of Lancasters. A particularly tedious talk fest which also takes in Rolph's grief over his recently deceased wife (which may be the root of his ongoing hallucinations, which go on to include the voices of long dead pilots), things only come to life during the final moments when the plane comes down, and we cut from the studio to a brief filmed sequence featuring a full-scale plane in a field. Something of a chore to sit through otherwise, the play is flatly directed by Rodney Bennett, who fails to make much of the endlessly dull dialogue, which is notable only for a passing moment of now unacceptable racism from Rolph (remarking on his daughter's failure to come home for her mother's funeral, given that she works as a missionary in Africa, he observes, "They can't spend *every* day dunking blacks in the Upper Zambezi").

Far better, though not exactly good, is *A Woman Sobbing*, in which Jane Pullar (Anna Massey), a depressed and sexually frustrated housewife, continually hears the sobbing of a woman while in bed with her husband Frank (Ronald Hines), who cannot hear anything. The sounds emanate from the attic, where over the following days Jane not only hears sobbing, but also cries and moans, which appear to be coming from behind the walls, the plaster from which she smashes off in order to get to them. Having discussed the matter with his friend Sandy (Julian Holloway), Frank decides they should employ an *au pair* (Yokki Rhodes) to help Jane with the children and to provide company for her. Having put the girl in the now redecorated attic, the sobbing momentarily appears to stop, only for things to resume again, this time with a voice calling Jane's name in the garden, where she briefly sees a dead body on the gravel underneath the attic window, which then appears to open by itself. Having phoned a crisis line given that she feels everyone thinks she is mad, Jane decides to follow the suggestion that she try exorcism, and so enrolls the help of a priest (John Lee) to carry it out, despite his misgivings ("I don't want you to cast out devils, I want you to get rid of the ghost in the attic," she tells him). When he is unable to help, she buys a book on the subject so as to do the job herself, but when this fails, she volunteers to have herself committed to a psychiatric hospital, where she undergoes electrotherapy. Inevitably, it fails to work and, once back home, the sobbing returns, which prompts her to go to the attic, where the window opens for her, and she is compelled to jump out of it. But it appears that the spirit has still not been satisfied, as it now begins to cry for the new occupants of the house.

A mildly diverting story which would have been better suited to a half-hour slot, this again suffers from over padding and dull direction, this time care of Paul Ciappessoni, although one can't deny that Anna Massey gives a strong performance as the increasingly frightened and frustrated Jane. As with the other plays, though, the videotaped studio sequences lack the required atmosphere, thus robbing the piece of potential frissons. And again, racism raises its unnecessary head. In the scene in which Frank's friend suggests that he employ an *au pair* to help Jane, he replies, "Well, we used to have one, but you know what the French are. She was caught shoplifting in Oxford Street and we had to get rid of her." Frank also isn't above a little misogyny. When he offers to teach the *au pair* to drive, he qualifies himself by saying, "If a man can teach his wife to drive he can teach anyone!"

Dead of Night, which concluded on 17 December 1972, had originally been conceived as an eight-part series, but the final episode (also produced by Innes Lloyd) was presented as a standalone piece. This was *The Stone Tape* (1972, TVM), a 90-minute play by Nigel Kneale, which was broadcast on BBC2 at 9:25 p.m. on 25 December 1972 as part of the Christmas night celebrations. A ghost story which matches science against the supernatural, it focuses on a research team for Ryan Electrics who have taken up residence in Taskerlands, a renovated gothic mansion where they are working to discover a new recording medium in a bid to take away the market from the Japanese. "Just record me, say, the whole of Wagner's *Ring Cycle* inside a ball bearing, with instant playback, of course, and you can name your own royalties," says the team's leader, Peter Brock (Michael Bryant). But the renovations in one of the rooms have been abandoned by the builders, who claim it to be haunted. One of the team, a particularly sensitive programmer named Jill Greeley (Jane Asher), actually sees a ghost there, which turns out to be an under maid named Louisa Hanks who died there in 1890, and which appears to be trapped in a stone wall (or, rather, recorded on a stone tape), despite an attempt to exorcise it in 1892. "The ghost laying didn't take," says Roy Collinson (Iain Cuthbertson), who has been project managing the renovation, and who has been looking into the matter, having heard screams in the room. Having heard them himself during his own visit to the room prompts Brock to order the team to start their own investigation, not only to analyze the phenomenon, but to try and harness and control it ("Let's say it's a mass of data waiting for a correct interpretation—it's never been done before," he informs them). However, it seems that the ghost of the maid, which each person experiences in a different way, is only the most recent recording on the stone tape, and that it masks an older, far more malevolent force, to which Jill, like Louisa, eventually succumbs, becoming part of the recording herself as a consequence.

Originally titled *Breakthrough*, Kneale's script, which was commissioned by the BBC's head of drama Christopher Morahan, who had earlier directed his play *The Road* (1963, TV), takes the traditional story of a residual haunting and confronts it with the cold, hard face of modern science in a bid to explain and even manipulate the phenomena, and as such it contains many highly effective moments in which the boffins, led by the obsessive Brock, attempt and fail with deadly consequences to use the technology at their disposal to decipher the mystery of the recording (the sound effects for these sequences, provided by Desmond Briscoe and the BBC Radiophonic Workshop, are undeniably spine tingling). Inevitably, given its age, this technology now seems archaic, while the jargon spouted by the technicians is little more than gobbledygook, but the main players, Bryant, Asher and Cuthbertson, bring a sense of immediacy to the proceedings, which benefit from exterior sequences shot at the imposing Horsley Towers in Surrey, which began filming on 15 November 1972, just over a month prior to the program's broadcast (the building had already been used as a location in the film *Kaleidoscope* [1966]). Less effective are the videotaped scenes in the brightly lit research labs, which were recorded in the studio between 20 and 22 November (with additional work carried out on 4 December), though director Peter Sasdy does manage to create a good deal of atmosphere in the haunted room itself (an impressively sepulchral piece of design care of Richard Henry, complete with a flight of stone stairs that go nowhere), about which he swoops his camera as the action requires.

The efforts of all concerned paid off, and *The Stone Tape* attracted an audience of 2.6 million when broadcast, while press reaction was generally very favorable, with London's *Evening Standard* describing it as "one of the best plays of the genre ever written." Unfortunately, as with many programs of the period, some of its attitudes are now somewhat regrettable, among them references to the Japanese as Japs (accompanied by the inevitable "ah-so"), while an impersonation by one of the technicians sporting paper teeth while pulling his eyelids sideways is simply jaw dropping. Brock's misogyny is also a concern (at one point, he jokingly presses Jill's nipples, pretending they are buttons on a TV). These regrets aside, along with a rather lengthy running time and some unfunny banter between the scientists, who seem to do a lot of standing around, the program remains something of a landmark work, and one is surprised that it hasn't been remade, although John Carpenter's *Prince of Darkness* (1987), which he wrote using the pseudonym Martin Quatermass, covers vaguely similar territory (Kneale had penned *Halloween III: Season of the Witch* [1982] for Carpenter, but had his name removed from the credits following artistic differences). A radio version of the play was broadcast by the BBC in 2015; adapted by Matthew Graham and Peter Strickland, it contained a cameo by Jane Asher.

With *Leap in the Dark* (1973–1980, TV), which began airing on BBC2 on 9 January 1973, the BBC stuck with the anthology format for a further series of supernatural stories, though the remit for the first season was an exploration of myths, practices and phenomena via seven documentaries bearing such titles as *Pendulums and Hazel Twigs* (1973, TV), *Mind Over Matter* (1973, TV) and *Hauntings* (1973, TV). Directed by Colin Godman and introduced by Linda Blandford and Gordon Snell, the half-hour programs featured contributions from the likes of Professor John Taylor and Dr. Derek Anton-Stephens to add a little gravitas to the proceedings ("Extrasensory perception, parapsychology, the psi factor; whatever grand names it's called by, it still remains largely a matter of faith rather than established fact, and among scientists, the believers are still a tiny minority," explains Snell in his introduction to the first episode, which goes on to explore telepathy, precognition, astrology and even water divining). Seasons two and three, which were presented by Colin Wilson and ran to a total of ten episodes, went on to present docu-drama re-enactments of supposedly real-life occurrences in the style of *One Step Beyond* (1959–1961, TV), beginning with *The Rosenheim Poltergeist* (1975, TV). Other installments during these seasons included *The Vandy Case* (1975, TV), *The Ghost of Ardachie Lodge* (1977, TV) and *In the Mind's Eye* (1977, TV). By the time season four rolled out, however, the show had moved on to original dramas penned by the likes of Russell Hoban and Fay Weldon. This season, which ran to seven episodes, kicked off with *Jack Be Nimble* (1980, TV) and went on to include *The Living Grave* (1980, TV), *Come and Find Me* (1980, TV) and *To Kill a King* (1980, TV), and though clearly low-budget affairs, there was usually something of passing interest going on for those wishing to fill a half-hour before bedtime. Actors involved in this final season included such names as Keith Barron, Rula Lenska, Bernard Hepton, Peter Egan, Lesley Manville, Patricia Quinn, Hugh Burden, David Buck, Jacqueline Pearce, Lalla Ward, Jennie Linden and Brian Blessed.

A far slicker enterprise was *Thriller* (1973–1976, TVM), an anthology series which embraced all aspects of the thriller genre, from psychological shockers with bizarre murder plots to supernatural horror. Created by Brian Clemens and featuring starry casts from both sides of the Atlantic (to better aid sales to America), the show's six-season run of 43 episodes launched on ITV on 14 March 1973 with *Lady Killer* (1973, TVM), in which a shy American girl (Barbara Feldon) falls for and marries a charming Englishman (Robert Powell) while on vacation, only to come to suspect that his plans for her are far from romantic. Made to fill a 75-minute timeslot, the series, which was shot on both film (exteriors) and videotape (interiors), is notable for its eerie title sequence, which features location shots from the upcoming program photographed with a fisheye lens, accompanied by a discordant, Herrmannesque three note theme tune composed by Laurie Johnson, who had already worked with Clemens on the TV series *The Avengers* (1961–1969, TV) and the film *And Soon the Darkness* (1970).

The show's first brush with the supernatural came with the second episode,

Possession (1973, TVM), in which a couple, Ray and Penny Burns (John Carson and Joanna Dunham), buy High Pines, their dream house in the country. However, while repairs are being carried out on the pipe work, a body is discovered in the basement, which turns out to be that of a previous owner, who was brutally murdered 20 years earlier. When Penny begins to hear screams in the night and senses that the killer has returned to the house, they decide to hold a séance, during which the medium, Cecily Rafting (Hilary Hardiman), manages to channel the murder victim, Elizabeth Millington, who relives the events leading up to her death. Cecily then reveals that the spirit of the killer is still in the house somewhere ("He's still here—the question is where?"), and when Ray starts to behave strangely, it seems the couple has something to worry about. Indeed, it is not the house that is possessed of an evil spirit, but Ray himself, but in a final twist (spoiler alert) we learn that Ray was the killer all along, compelled to return to the scene of his crime to discover the whereabouts of his victim's money ("You aren't possessed. The only evil presence in this house is you. It was always you…. You didn't *become* the murderer, you always *were*," Penny informs him after she has put two and two together). A talkative and overly contrived episode, it suffers primarily from over length and unimaginative direction care of John Cooper, who is compelled to confine much of the action to the house (i.e., the studio), but at least John Carson manages to get a fair amount of mileage out of his role as the doting husband who turns out to be a killer.

Other episodes with supernatural elements that aired during season one include *Someone at the Top of the Stairs* (1973, TVM), in which two American girls (Donna Mills and Judy Carne) take a room in a friendly lodging house, only for it to transpire that all the other lodgers are dead, and being manipulated by Carter (David de Keyser), the mysterious man living on the top floor, who has found eternal life through the power of the black arts; *A Place to Die* (1973, TVM), in which a doctor and his wife (Bryan Marshall and Alexandra Hay) move to a country village, only to discover that the locals, although outwardly pleasant, are diabolists keen to revitalize the village by sacrificing the wife during a ritual on Lady Day; and *Spell of Evil* (1973, TVM), in which a businessman (Edward de Souza) uses the Modernmates marriage bureau to secure himself a new wife after his first dies, only to find himself married to a witch (Diane Cilento).

Horror continued to rear its head during the following seasons, and could also be found in *Kiss Me and Die* (1974, TVM), one of the more elaborate episodes (complete with lavish sets care of designer Michael Eve) in which Robert Stone (George Chakiris), an American detective searching for his missing brother in an English village, finds that his investigations lead him to the estate of Jonathan Lanceford (Anton Diffring), whose obsession with the works of Edgar Allan Poe see him brick up Robert in the dungeon when he falls in love with his jealously guarded niece Dominie (Jenny Agutter); *One Deadly Owner* (1974, TVM), in which a model (Donna Mills) buys a second hand Rolls-Royce ("One careful owner") only to discover that it is haunted; *Nurse Will Make It Better* (1975, TVM), in which a seemingly kind nurse (Diana Dors) who arrives at a country house to look after a paraplegic (who she punches out cold when she first meets her!) turns out to be a Devil worshipper who uses her powers to make her patient walk again, albeit with consequences

("I'm a collector—a collector of souls!"); *A Killer in Every Corner* (1975, TVM), in which a professor (Patrick Magee) experiments with mind control as a means of curing psychopaths of their urge to kill, but the students invited to take part in his study find their lives in danger when things don't go according to plan; *Won't Write Home, Mom—I'm Dead* (1975, TVM), in which a young American woman (Pamela Franklin) with psychic abilities searches an artistic commune in England for her fiancé, only to uncover murderous foul play and stolen identity; *Sleepwalker* (1976, TVM), in which a young woman (Darleen Carr) prone to sleepwalking witnesses a murder, but cannot fathom if it was real or one of the nightmares she has been suffering from; and *Dial a Deadly Number* (1976, TVM), in which a wealthy woman (Gemma Jones) suffering from nightmares involving murder seeks solace by calling a psychiatrist, but accidentally dials an unemployed actor (Gary Collins) who proves keen to exploit the situation.

With their incredible plots and hard-to-swallow twists and coincidences, the series was a somewhat formulaic affair, full of red herrings and unexpected revelations, all of which now date it somewhat, yet the guest stars and better than average studio handling made it a favorite at the time, and the canny inclusion of American names in the casts achieved the intended aim of an American network sale (to ABC), although in the States the episodes went out under the umbrella title of *The Wide World of Mystery* (1973–1976, TVM), in which they were augmented with original American programming, and for which the British title sequences were removed and replaced with new ones; some of the episodes were also re-titled (for example, *Nurse Will Make It Better* became *The Devil's Web*, while *Won't Write Home, Mom—I'm Dead* became *Terror from Within*). Yet whatever its drawbacks now seem to be, one cannot deny the stamina of its creator Brian Clemens, who not only penned most of the episodes, but provided the stories (or in one case, the novel [*The Crazy Kill*]) on which each installment was based, which is quite an achievement (the other writers occasionally involved in fleshing out these ideas were Terence Feely [who scripted nine episodes], Dennis Spooner [two], Terry Nation [one] and Luanshya Greer [one]). A collection of some of the stories, also by Clemens, was published in 1974 care of Fontana ("Blood-chilling stories of mystery and murder from the famous TV series," ran the front cover blurb).

The BBC launched another of its epic play runs on 19 July 1973 with *Centre Play* (1973–1977, TV), which went on to clock up a healthy 68 installments starring the likes of Edward Hardwicke, Michael Gambon, Dandy Nichols, Freddie Jones, Michael Gough and Mona Washbourne. Kicking off with *Places Where They Sing* (1973, TV) by Jonathan Hales and Simon Raven, the series seems to have veered towards the supernatural just once, with an adaptation by Hugh Whitemore of Edgar Allan Poe's 1839 short story *William Wilson* (1976, TV), about a young man (Norman Eshley) who is followed throughout his life by a doppelganger. This had already been the subject of a 1961 episode of *Great Ghost Tales* (1961, TV), as well as a segment in the feature film *Histoires extraordinaires* (1968). Unfortunately, the episode appears to have been wiped, and so further evaluation is not possible at present (directed by James Ormerod, it also featured Stephen Murray and Anthony Daniels).

More concerned with twists rather than shocks, though occasionally veering towards the supernatural, was *Orson Welles Great Mysteries* (1973–1974, TV [note that the onscreen title actually lacks the possessory apostrophe following Welles' name]). Clearly a prestige production given the caliber of talent involved, it featured stories by Agatha Christie, Charles Dickens, W. Somerset Maugham and Arthur Conan Doyle, and starred such names as Susannah York, Jack Cassidy, Peter Cushing, Eli Wallach, José Ferrer, Christopher Lee, Joan Collins and Harry Andrews, who were directed by the likes of Peter Sasdy, Alan Gibson and Peter Sykes. Welles himself introduced each of the 26 episodes, which began airing on ITV on 1 September 1973 with a period blackmail drama *Captain Rogers* (1973, TV) starring Donald Pleasence. Other episodes included *The Leather Funnel* (1973, TV), in which a young man (Simon Ward) fears that a leather funnel he has discovered may have been an instrument of torture; *The Monkey's Paw* (1973, TV), in which an

All's Welles. The great Orson Welles in a promotional shot for *Orson Welles Great Mysteries* (1973–1974, TV) (Anglia Television/ Twentieth Century–Fox Television).

army sergeant (Patrick Magee) back from India shows his friends a monkey's paw which is supposed to make wishes come true; and *The Furnished Room* (1974, TV), in which a man (Clarence Williams III) searching for a missing girl finds his investigations leading him to a supposedly haunted room in a boarding house. Produced by John Jacobs via Anglia Television and Twentieth Century–Fox Television, the program also benefited from a eerie theme tune care of composer John Barry, which accompanies a be-cloaked Welles as he skulks around a disused warehouse.

Country Matters

An anthology series of a more literary nature was *Wessex Tales* (1973, TV), another filmed drama series this time based upon stories by Thomas Hardy. Produced by Irene Shubik for the BBC, the six-part, 50-minute series, which aired on BBC2, was clearly a quality production that not only attracted top acting talent, including Ben Kingsley, John Hurt, Barbara Kellerman and Kenneth Haigh, but also respected directors, among them Mike Newell, Gavin Millar and Michael Tuchner, as well as such well regarded writers as David Mercer and Dennis Potter. Among the stories filmed were *A Tragedy of Two Ambitions* (1973, TV), taken from the 1894 collection *Life's Little Ironies*, in which tragedy follows when two brothers, keen to improve their lot, ignore moral values in order to do so, and *The Melancholy Hussar* (1973, TV), taken from the 1888 collection *Wessex Tales*, in which an English gentleman does badly by his fiancée when he decides to marry another woman.

The series launched on 7 November 1973 with *The Withered Arm* (1973, TV), in which John Lodge (Edward Hardwicke), a wealthy landlord, takes for his wife a shy but pretty young woman named Gertrude (Yvonne Antrobus), who finds adjusting to country life more difficult than she imagined. Upon visiting her husband's farms and cottages to better acquaint herself with the various tenants, she strikes up an uneasy friendship with a local milkmaid named Rhoda (Billie Whitelaw), not realizing that John is the father of her teenage son Jamie (William Relton), and that Rhoda, who is naturally jealous of Gertrude, has been left to struggle raising the child on her own. "How that poor boy stared at me," Gertrude observes as she and John pass him by on the road in their trap as he struggles along with a bail of firewood. Feeling sorry for the lad, she buys him a new pair of boots, and thus the friendship between the two women begins. However, when Gertrude comes to her in a dream, leering over her in a disturbing manner, Rhoda reaches out and grabs the gentlewoman's arm when she raises it to attack her, after which Gertrude develops a number of painful sores upon it ("It looks almost like finger marks," she informs Rhoda, adding, "My husband says it is as if some witch or the Devil himself had taken hold of me there and blasted the flesh").

As her arm become increasingly painful and begins to affect her marriage ("It seems to come more and more between us"), Gertrude persuades Rhoda to take her to nearby Egdon Heath to see Conjuror Trendle (Esmond Knight), a local mystic who informs her, "Medicine can't cure that. Tis the work of an enemy." With the help of Trendle, Gertrude identifies Rhoda as the source of her affliction, following which Rhoda and Jamie decide to leave their cottage, which soon lies derelict, just as Gertrude's arm becomes even more withered and painful. While her husband is away, she visits Trendle again for help, and he advises that if she is able to touch her limb upon the neck of a man who has just been hanged, then she will be cured. Thus she makes her way to the town of Casterbridge, where a hanging is to take place, and seeks out the hangman (Paul Hardwick), in whom she confides her story. Having been involved in such remedies before, he agrees to help her ("I like the look of the wound—tis truly as suitable for the cure as any as I ever saw," he tells her). However, when she is finally able to touch the corpse the next day when it is brought to the jailhouse cellar, she is shocked to see that the hanged man is Jamie, which prompts her to collapse in front of Rhoda, who has been joined by John to accompany the body. Upon Gertrude's death, John decides to sell his land and move away, but not before leaving instructions that if she wishes, Rhoda can return to her cottage, which he has arranged to be refurnished and made over to her, and the story ends with Rhoda heading back home, bowed and alone.

Adapted by Rhys Adrian and directed with quiet care by Desmond Davis, this is a thoughtfully paced period drama which establishes its characters and situations in a manner that is well suited to the measured tempo of the impoverished rural life it depicts, which appears never less than authentic thanks to the contributions of production designer Jeremy Davies and photographer Brian Tufano, who makes much of the bleak Dorset locations. As the careworn Rhoda, of whom a fellow milk-maid comments, "Some do say she is a witch," Billie Whitelaw gives a restrained performance, in which her character, much wronged, knows to keep her own counsel given her lowly standing in the community. Equally well cast are Edward Hardwicke as the wealthy landlord, who abandons Rhoda to her fate, only to realize the error of his ways after the various tragedies have unfolded ("She has suffered greatly," he finally acknowledges), and Yvonne Antrobus as the retiring Gertrude, whose increasing pain and anxiety is relayed in an almost palpable manner (the sores on her arm look particularly believable thanks to the efforts of make-up artist Shirley Channing-Williams), though it would seem that she is not quite so innocent as portrayed, given the hovering threat she poses to Rhoda in her dream. Strong support is meanwhile provided by William Relton as Rhoda's doomed son Jamie, Esmond Knight as the mystical Conjuror, and Paul Hardwick as the understanding hangman, each of whom looks perfectly at home in the environments they inhabit. An absorbing tale that carefully builds to a genuinely disturbing climax, this is an admirably well-presented piece of folk horror that certainly deserves to be better known than it is (note that Whitelaw, who was featured as Rhoda on the cover of the *Radio Times* to launch the series, was nominated for a BAFTA for her performance, while producer Irene Shubik was nominated for best drama series).

A wry, modern day, adult take on the children's bedtime story was meanwhile the concept behind *Bedtime Stories* (1974, TV), which had originally been intended as a sequel of sorts to *Dead of Night* (1972, TV), and like which was produced by Innes Lloyd. The six-part, 50-minute series, which began airing on BBC2 on 3 March 1974, attracted a number of high-profile writers, and kicked off with a new version of *Goldilocks and the Three Bears* (1974, TV) by Alan Plater, with Angharad Rees in the role of Miss Goldie, who finds herself involved with the Burr family (geddit?) on the Backwoods Estate. This was followed by *The Water Maiden* (1974, TV) by Andrew Davies, *Sleeping Beauty* (1974, TV) by Julian Bond, *Jack and the Beanstalk* (1974, TV) by Nigel Kneale, *Hansel and Gretel* (1974, TV) by Louis Marks (who also worked as the series' script editor), and *The Snow Queen* (1974, TV) by John Bowen (said to be the best episode). Also featuring Jeff Rawle, Lisa Harrow, Diana Quick, Adrienne Corri, Rosemary Leach, Peter Jeffrey, Gwen Watford, Lesley Anne-Down and Julian Holloway, the series was directed by the likes of Paul Ciappessoni, Kenneth Ives and Roger Jenkins, yet despite the major talent involved, it sadly appears to have been wiped.

Made by Granada for broadcast on the ITV network, the short-lived series *Haunted* (1974, TV), which was produced by Derek Granger, curiously ran to only two episodes, the first of which, *The Ferryman* (1974, TV), aired on 12 December 1974. Based upon a story by Kingsley Amis, it sees arrogant horror writer Sheridan Owen (Jeremy Brett), who has just scored a hit with his novel *The Ferryman*, take a short holiday in the country with his wife Alex (Natasha Parry) to help revitalize their struggling marriage. Caught in a violent thunderstorm, they take refuge in a hotel that coincidentally happens to be called The Ferryman's Rest ("Do you know, it's incredible, it's just how I imagined it," he says as they check in), but as their stay progresses, Owen, who avowedly does not believe in the supernatural himself, begins to sense that his book, about a ferryman who attacks a number of women before being killed, is starting to come true, even down to the names of the staff working at the otherwise deserted hotel. Believing that they are somehow caught in a time warp ("I think we have strayed into a world which parallels the one that I made up," he reasons), Owen becomes unsettled by the increasing number of coincidences that occur, including the fact that it is midsummer's night, which, in his book, is when the dead ferryman returns to claim a final victim, the hotel owner's daughter. However, when he is assured by the landlord (Geoffrey Chater) that his daughter is in London, Owen starts to relax … that is until the girl (Lesley Dunlop) unexpectedly turns up, which prompts him to head down to the river at midnight to destroy the ferryman with a crucifix should he appear.

A curious little story which doesn't quite hang together, it nevertheless benefits from Brett's performance as the self-centered Owen, who we first encounter watching himself being interviewed on television by a non too bright presenter, and then at a crowded promotional event, during both of which he becomes increasingly irritated ("You know, I don't think I can stand this a moment longer," he comments of the lavish party staged for the latter before making a run for it with his wife). But as events progress, he becomes increasingly unnerved, especially with the arrival of the landlord's daughter, whom he rescues from sleepwalking towards her potential doom before going on to encounter the ghostly ferryman himself. Well enough directed by John Irvin, and filmed entirely on location by cameraman David Wood, Julian Bond's rather clubfooted adaptation, which runs to 49 minutes for a one-hour timeslot, might have worked better as a half-hour piece, and suffers from a fair bit of padding and confusion, despite a promising start, while the fact that it doesn't entirely embrace the parallel world theory does the narrative's internal logic some considerable harm ("The barman's got the wrong surname, the manager's got the wrong Christian name and this pub's called The Ferryman's Rest, not the Ferryman," reasons Alex, to which Owen replies, "That was my original title"). Ultimately, something of a disappointment then, given its potential, but certainly not without compensations along the way.

Rather more straightforward was the second episode, *Poor Girl* (1974, TV), which aired on 30 December 1974. Based upon a 1955 story by Elizabeth Taylor (the authoress, best known for her 1971 novel *Mrs. Palfrey at the Claremont*, not the actress), it sees Florence Chasty (Lynne Miller), a pretty Edwardian governess from a working class background, leave home to take up her first position at a country house, where her sole charge, a precocious and willful nine-year-old boy named Hilary (Matthew Pollock), proves to be a handful in more ways than one. Looked down upon by the boy's haughty mother (Angela Thorne), and with lustful eyes by his father (Stuart Wilson), Florence inevitably feels alienated in her new surroundings, especially when strange forces in the guise of a curiously dressed young man and woman present themselves to her, which prove to be flash forwards to Hilary's life as an adult in the 1920s. With its echoes of Henry James' *The Turn of the Screw*, the program, with its convincing period detail care of designer Colin Grimes, carefully recreates the stifling atmosphere of an Edwardian country house, with its various routines and social strictures, while the supporting cast, particularly Angela Thorne and Stuart Wilson as Hilary's parents, are particularly well suited to their roles. Adapted by Robin Chapman and directed by Michael Apted, the episode was again photographed on location by David Wood. Mild stuff, certainly, but as an observational piece on Edwardian mores and manners, it captures the sights and sounds of an age gone by with a certain alacrity.

Scottish Television presented a new half-hour version of the Robert Louis Stevenson story *Markheim* (1974, TV), which aired on 24 December 1974. Adapted by Tom Wright and directed by Tina Wakerell, it starred Derek Jacobi in the title role and Julian Glover as the mysterious Stranger who coerces him to kill for money. The year was then rounded out with a new version of *The Canterville Ghost* (1974, TV), which was broadcast on ITV on 31 December 1974. This time it was David Niven playing the centuries old spook seeking release from an ancient curse. Adapted by Robin Miller and directed by Walter C. Miller, the hour-long program was produced by Timothy Burrill via HTV West and Buricia Productions, and also featured Maurice Evans, Lynne Frederick, Flora Robson, Isla Blair, Nicholas Jones and Elizabeth Tyrrell. However, while the program's exteriors were filmed on location at Berkeley Castle in Gloucestershire, its interiors were shot in a studio on videotape, thus robbing the piece of atmosphere, and despite Niven's presence, the proceedings frequently fall flat as a consequence (the program was broadcast in America on NBC the following year).

Worthy of a passing mention at this point is *Country Tales* (1975, TV), a half-forgotten half-hour anthology series care of the BBC (BBC Bristol), which began airing on BBC2 on 4 April 1975 with *The Harbourer* (1975, TV). Produced by John King and Robin Drake, the programs were shot on film, and presented six narrated dramatic stories with countryside settings as told by the likes of June Barry, Alan Dobie and Jack Watson, and acted out by such names as Tony Robinson, Rex Holdsworth and Michael Turner. Unfortunately, the series now appears to be lost (presumably wiped), but it did lead to a follow up, *Sea Tales* (1977, TV), a seven-parter this time featuring nautical tales narrated by Leo McKern and Gary Watson among others, and featuring such names as Harold Goodwin, Jane Lapotaire, Jack Watson and Sheila Keith. Produced by Roger Jenkins (again care of BBC Bristol), it launched on BBC2 on 12 May 1977 with *The Return* (1977, TV), and likewise appears to have sunk without trace.

However—and we're getting to the point now—it was followed by a third series, *West Country Tales* (1982–1983, TV), a two-season run of 14 episodes produced by John King (this time care of BBC Plymouth), whose narrators featured Jack Weston (clearly a favorite), Keith Barron and June Bishop, while actors involved included Nanette Newman, Wendy Richard and Anita Harris. The series, several episodes of which were based upon experiences contributed by viewers, launched on BBC2 on 25 January 1982 with *The Sabbatical* (1982, TV), and went on to include such spooky installments as *The Beast* (1982, TV), in which a man returns to Cornwall to visit a farmhouse from his youth where a creature (Milton Reid) appears to be menacing the present owners; *Miss Constantine* (1982, TV), in which an elderly woman (Wynna Evans) believes the rambling manor in which she lives alone has been invaded by strange figures; and *The Wit to Woo* (1983, TV), in which an Elizabethan woman seeks the advice of a witch (Jo Anderson) to help win back her erring husband. The equivalent of a ghost story at bedtime, there is very little here to raise the hackles, yet someone must have been watching, otherwise why would so many episodes have been commissioned? That they were cheaply produced schedule fillers probably helped. Of passing curiosity for those who remember them, a handful are presently available for viewing on YouTube.

While we're on this minor detour, and for the sake of completeness, let's also take a brief look at the documentary *The Ghost Hunters* (1975, TV), which aired on BBC1 on 4 December 1975. A serious investigation into the existence of ghosts and spirits, it was produced by Hugh Burnett, and provided interviews with people who had either tried to track down supernatural manifestations or had experienced things they could not explain, be it phantom footsteps or abnormal phenomena. Filmed on location, it included sequences in a supposedly haunted house, a theatre and a church (Borley Church in Essex). Sadly, like *Country Tales*, it appears to be no longer available. By no means the only television documentary about the supernatural, it was preceded by *The Dracula Business* (1974, TV), which aired on 6 August 1974 as part of the BBC's ongoing *Tuesday's Documentary* (1968–1973, TV) strand. In it, investigative reporter Daniel Farson, the great nephew of *Dracula* author Bram Stoker no less, interviews a number of people involved with the various commercial enterprises that have derived from the celebrated character, among them films and even a children's ice lolly, *Count Dracula's Secret*, filled with red jelly. To whit he travels to Whitby (where scenes in the book are set), Transylvania (from where the legend derives), and Highgate Cemetery (where he discusses premature burial), encountering along the way members of The Dracula Society, the editors at Lorrimer Publishing as they prepare a new book on vampire films, producer Michael Carreras, head of Hammer Films, who discusses the impact of Dracula on the British film industry, and actor Denholm Elliott, who portrayed Dracula in a 1968 episode of *Mystery and Imagination* (1966–1970, TV), and who reads a passage from the novel. Produced by Anthony de Lotbiniere, this is fascinating stuff, and will be of great archival interest to devotees of the subject.

Stoker was also featured in *The Need for Nightmare* (1974, TV), which aired on BBC1 on 15 December 1974 as an episode of the ongoing arts series *Omnibus* (1967–2003, TV). Written by Robert Muller and directed by Harley Cokeliss (billed Cokliss), it offers an examination of how nightmares inspired the great genre writers of the 19th century, and in addition to Stoker (played by Dominic Allan), features impersonations of such well known literary figures from the era as Edgar Allan Poe (Ben Kingsley), Robert Louis Stevenson (Laurence Carter) and Mary Shelley (Vickery Turner). Narrated by Michael Gough, the program also features Rosalyn Landor as Virginia Poe and Dave Prowse as "Shadow of the Monster" as he is billed.

Back to drama now with *Against the Crowd* (1975, TV), an anthology series of seven hour-long dramas produced by Nicholas Palmer via Associated Television for broadcast on ITV. Launched on 13 July 1975, the programs took as their focus characters who find themselves at variance with their communities. Featuring teleplays by the likes of Kingsley Amis, Fay Weldon and Hugo Charteris, they were directed by Don Leaver, Paul Annett and Piers Haggard among others, and featured such names as Kenneth Cranham, Don Warrington, Tessa Wyatt, Don Henderson, Edward Hardwicke, William Russell, Donald Sinden and Peter Vaughan in their casts. For our purposes, the most intriguing installment is episode three, *Murrain* (1975, TV) by Nigel Kneale, his first piece of writing for ITV following his departure from the BBC.

In it, a young country vet, Alan Crich (David Simeon), is called out to Beeley's Pig Farm where a number of the animals have been dying from an unknown murrain (an ancient term for an infectious animal disease). "All that good pig meat gone to waste. What now? Slaughter the lot?" asks the perturbed owner (Bernard Lee). But this isn't all that has been going on: the farm's water supply has dried up, a child in the village has become seriously ill and one of the farm laborers has acquired a limp. As far as the locals are concerned, the person responsible for all of this is the elderly Mrs. Clemson (Una Brandon-Jones), whom they believe to be a witch with a hatred for her neighbors, and whose cat they have cut in two and thrown over her wall by way of punishment. "You're trying to justify the persecution of some poor half-witted old biddy—and how do you do that? Kill her cat in the name of magic, and then go home and watch your color telly!" exclaims Crich when confronted with their irrational superstitions. Consequently, when asked by the farmer to tip a bag of grit over the old woman to dispel her powers, he instead visits her in a bid to help her, especially when he discovers that she is living in squalor, and that the local shop won't serve her ("They're trying to starve me out," she tells him). But when he attempts to buy her some groceries, the locals turn nasty, so he returns the next day with provisions bought in the nearby town. However, while delivering them, the locals turn up at her cottage to kill her, given that someone else in the village is now ill, but when they run up to her door, she raises her arms and appears to curse them, and Beeley drops dead in his tracks. "A massive coronary, I think. He was due for that," assumes Crich. "Yes!" hisses Mrs. Clemson, at which the story concludes as Beeley's body is carried away.

With its "is she or isn't she?" scenario, the play carefully builds towards its inevitable climax of confrontation, leaving Mrs. Clemson's final cry of "Yes" nicely open to interpretation, and while this may irritate some, one can't deny that the program sustains its growing air of unease with a certain skill, given its obvious low budget. Rather plainly directed by John Cooper as a consequence, the piece nevertheless benefits from its bleak country setting, all mud and bare trees, while the performances, despite some variably broad accents from the supporting cast, effectively relay the fear and ignorance of the villagers. Lee, as the bluff farmer, recalls his performance in *Whistle Down the Wind* (1961) and is miles from his M persona in the Bond films, while Simeon makes for a solid voice of reason, standing up to the increasingly aggressive bullying tactics he encounters. Meanwhile, as Mrs. Clemson, Una Brandon-Jones effectively rouses our sympathy at first, before gradually raising the suspicion that the locals may in fact be right about her, despite having provoked her wrath through their ill treatment of her. By no means Kneale's best piece of writing, this is a rather overstretched tale, a little too padded at times so as to fill its one-hour timeslot, yet as a minor piece of folk horror, one can't deny that is does draw one into its story quite nicely.

It's a quick return to the classroom now (so pay attention at the back), this time for an adaptation of M.R. James' 1911 short story *Mr. Humphreys and His Inheritance* (1976, TV), which was broadcast on 21 June 1976 as part of *ITV Schools* (1957–1993, TV). From 1957, both the BBC and ITV produced programs suitable for the curriculum during school hours, among them series devoted to reading, writing, science and music. Many of the ITV regions were involved in the making of these programs, and one of Yorkshire Television's contributions

Country matters. Una Brandon-Jones in *Murrain* (1975, TV), an episode from *Against the Crowd* (1975, TV) (ATV).

was a strand titled *Music Scene*, one installment of which showed how romance, comedy and suspense can be suggested in a film with different kinds of music, even if applied to the same scene, in this instance, that of a young woman walking down a corridor. "You can suggest many things through music," the narrator informs us, before going on to introduce to Philip Wilby, "a modern composer of film music," so we're informed, who gives a brief talk on how music can be used to emphasize certain points in a narrative.

The short film itself then follows, in which we learn that Mr. Humphreys (Geoffrey Russell), a clerk of modest means, has inherited a country mansion called Wilsthorpe Hall from an uncle he has never seen before. The mansion has extensive grounds, which include a maze, which we discover the uncle used to keep locked, as it had been designed by his grandfather, "A man of most curious beliefs," as he is told by Cooper (Peter Wheeler), the hall's manservant, who also informs Humphreys that the remains of his uncle's grandfather are not in the family vault. Intrigued, Humphreys decides to explore the maze, discovering at its center a plinth on which rests a curious globe, under which lies the inscription "Territory of Death." Making arrangements for the servants to tidy up the overgrown foliage, he sets out to make a plan of the maze to hang in the hall for visitors, but as he is working on it in his study one stuffy night, he begins to sense that something or someone other than the moths that have been plaguing him through the open window "had a mind to join him," as the narrator (Peter Clough) tells us, adding, "How unpleasant it would be if someone had slipped noiselessly over the sill and were crouching on the floor." However, his visitor comes not through the window, but through the plan he is working on. After he has penciled in a circle for the globe at the center of his drawing, it seems to take on a life of its own, first as an ink spot, then as a hole, which "seemed to go not only through the paper but through the table as well, and through the floor below that, down and still down." A putrid face then begins to form at the bottom of it, following which a being emerges before Humphreys, prompting him to scream. "Open the globe. Open the globe. The globe in the maze," he cries to Cooper who comes rushing to his aid. At which we cut to the next day as Cooper smashes open the globe, which he discovers to contain ashes. The story then concludes with the narrator informing us that the episode has left poor Humphreys' nerves in such disarray that "he cannot even now see a blot of ink on a page quite unmoved."

Produced and directed with some precision by Tony Scull (who presumably also penned the script, given that there is no writing credit), this is a surprisingly well mounted adaptation which surmounts its low budget to provide a nicely detailed miniature which becomes increasingly unsettling as it moves along, climaxing in the perfectly realized shock moment as the being emerges from the hole in Humphreys' plan (the brief effects sequence was provided by David Speed). Nicely photographed by Dick Dodd, and well performed by Geoffrey Russell as the unfortunate Mr. Humphreys, the piece is not unlike one of the BBC's Christmas ghost stories, and had it been shown in a late-night slot, it seems doubtful that viewers would have complained that they had been fed something intended for children, many of whom surely suffered from nightmares having seen it in class. As for Philip Wilby's music (the whole point of the exercise, after all), it's a perfectly adequate small-scale woodwind and percussion score in the atonal manner that serves its purpose well enough, though if further commissions were expected on the evidence of this contribution, they failed to materialize, and to this date it remains his only film score, though he has since become recognized for his compositions for brass bands, among them several complex test pieces for competition. As for producer-director Tony Scull, his only other credit appears to be for Yorkshire TV's *Junior Sunday Quiz* (1977–1979, TV). However, if only for this 17-minute gem, he deserves at least a footnote in genre history.

Having launched on 19 October 1965 with a production of John Osborne's *Luther* (1965, TVM), the long running *BBC Play of the Month* (1965–1983, TVM) strand, which went on to clock up 120 installments during its epic run, concerned itself primarily with the staging of well known theatrical plays suitable for Sunday evening consumption, among them *Death of a Salesman* (1966, TVM), *The Corn Is Green* (1968, TVM), *An Ideal Husband* (1969, TVM), *The Importance of Being Earnest* (1974, TVM), *French Without Tears* (1976, TVM), *Design for Living* (1979, TVM) and *Dangerous Corner* (1983, TVM). Plays with a genre leaning included George Bernard Shaw's *Don Juan in Hell* (1970, TVM), in which our hero (Christopher Plummer) argues with the Devil (Michael

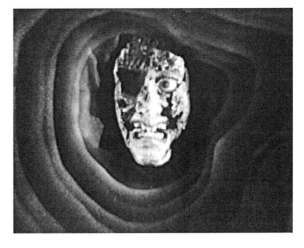

Face of fear. A startling moment from *Mr. Humphreys and His Inheritance* (1976, TV) (Yorkshire Television/Trident Television).

Hordern); yet another version of Paul M. Potter's adaptation of George L. Du Maurier's *Trilby* (1976, TVM), in which a young woman (Sinéad Cusack) falls under the influence of the hypnotist Svengali (Alan Badel); and J.B. Priestley's *déjà vu* drama *I Have Been Here Before* (1982, TVM), in which the mysterious Dr. Gortler (Herbert Lom) helps to change the lives of several fellow guests at a hotel following a precognitive dream, preventing an impending suicide in the process.

The series' most elaborate genre production was a new adaptation by John Osborne of Oscar Wilde's *The Picture of Dorian Gray* (1976, TVM), which aired on 19 September 1976. Directed by John Gorrie, the production, which starred Peter Firth as the corrupt Dorian, John Gielgud as Henry Wotton, Jeremy Brett as Basil Hallward and Judi Bowker and Sybil Vane, was notable primarily for emphasizing the novel's gay subtext more than most. Co-starring Nicholas Ball, Mark Dignam, Nicholas Clay and Gwen Ffrangcon-Davies, the videotaped play proved to be a critical hit at the time, with Gielgud coming in for particular praise for his delivery of some of Wilde's best epigrams ("There's no question, Basil, it's the best thing you've ever done," he says of Hallward's portrait, going on to add, "You'll have to send it to the Grosvenor. The Academy is too large and too vulgar. Whenever I've gone there, there have either been so many people that I've not been able to see the pictures, which was dreadful, or so many pictures that I've not been able to see the people, which was worse").

A Party with Barty

Nigel Kneale meanwhile continued his association with ITV (via ATV) with his six-part anthology series *Beasts* (1976, TV), which was produced by Nicholas Palmer, who had previously worked with the writer on *Murrain* (1975, TV), and who proposed that he might write a whole series for the company with a linked theme, in this case humanity's not always congenial relationship with the animal world. The result was a somewhat variable collection of hour-long videotaped dramas that nevertheless produced a couple of standout episodes that are still recalled with a shudder to this day by those who saw them first time round.

The series launched on 16 October 1976 with *Special Offer* (1976, TV), in which Noreen (Pauline Quirke), a painfully shy and much maligned checkout girl, unconsciously manifests a poltergeist at the Briteway supermarket in which she works as a means of avenging herself for the way she has been treated by the mean-spirited manager Mr. Grimley (Geoffrey Bateman) on whom she has a secret crush, but who in turn actually hates her guts ("I can't stand her," he informs a colleague; "She's a stupendous, giant-sized unrepeatable drag"). At first, Noreen's clumsiness is blamed when produce begins to fall from the shelves, but as the incidents continue, other members of staff come to believe that an animal of some kind has somehow got into the store—possibly Briteway Billy, the company's squirrel mascot, Grimley jokes—but as the cans inexplicably continue to fall off the shelves and packages of bacon are discovered chewed up in the fridge, the concerns of everyone begin to grow, to the point that Linda (Shirley Cheriton), a rattled co-worker whom Grimley has designs on, accuses Noreen of somehow making things happen ("I don't know how she does it, but she does it!" she screams). Eventually "Billy" runs rampant in the store, and the place is trashed before everyone's eyes, including those of Mr. Liversedge (Wensley Pithey) from head office, who is convinced that a poltergeist is responsible, believing it to be a manifestation of Noreen's suppressed sexual feelings which, in the final scene, kill Grimley in a hail of tin cans ("He loved me really. He took me by the hand," she says wistfully to Liversedge as the body is taken from the shop).

With its unglamorous setting (care of designer Roger Allan), in which the disinterested workers look even more disheveled than the mostly elderly female customers they are there to serve, the play perfectly captures the glum atmosphere of a low-budget chain market of the period, with its aisles of cheap own brand tins and cereals, its wire baskets and its rattling cash registers. Less padded than some of the later episodes, Kneale carefully observes the various personal dramas and petty grievances both on the shop floor and in the storerooms, all the while ramping up the tension as things take an increasingly supernatural turn, culminating in a number of spectacular effects sequences care of George Luenberger in which tins fly, washing up liquid squirts, milk bottles smash and cornflakes explode from their boxes. As the focus of all this, Pauline Quirke easily earns our sympathy as the shy and put-upon Noreen. At first as confused as everyone else as to what is going on, we can see that as the story progresses, she comes realize she has the ability to manipulate the strange force she has somehow conjured, and consciously starts to use it for own means, wreaking revenge with a knowing smile for her many humiliations at the hands of Geoffrey Bateman's increasingly rattled Grimley. All told, a surprisingly ambitious affair at times, especially given the technicalities involved in staging the various scenes of destruction, which are surprisingly well managed by director Richard Bramall given the restrictions of a videotaped studio production of the period.

The following episode, *During Barty's Party* (1976, TV), is perhaps the best-known installment, and is certainly the program that had the most impact at the time. A variation on Daphne Du Maurier's *The Birds*, is sees a middle-aged suburban couple, Angie and Roger Truscott (Elizabeth Sellars and Anthony Bate), find themselves under siege in their stockbroker belt home by a horde of rats which attempt to gnaw their way into the house. Having returned home from work, Roger finds his emotionally fragile wife in a state of hysteria which she can't quite explain, having woken from a nightmare during an afternoon nap ("It was as if something had been happening.... As if something had happened and I hadn't known about it"). An abandoned sports car just down the road is the first clue that something might be wrong, after which Angie tells Roger she's heard a rat under the floorboards. Their pet dog Buster also seems to have disappeared, and a work colleague who Roger telephones informs him that he heard about "rat migrations" on his car radio while driving home, all of which is enough to convince Angie that their lives are in peril, which is confirmed when they tune into an inane radio program called *Barty's Party*, which relays the news that hordes of rats are indeed on the move "*en famille*" as the deejay puts it. Following them about under the floorboards, the increasing number of rats appear to be stalking the couple. However, when Roger calls the police about the matter, he is pretty much dismissed, so when the water is cut off, Angela decides to ring the radio station and speak to Barty live on air about the situation. "We need help. Can you help us?" she implores, but she is cut off before she can give out their full address, soon after which the lights go out. Salvation momentarily seems to be at hand when their neighbors return home, only for them to be attacked before their very eyes ("All over them," gasps Roger), at which they run upstairs to escape the incoming rodents, only for Barty, who they can still hear on the portable radio, now suspect that Angela's call may actually have been a hoax.

Except for voices heard on the radio, telephone and through the window, this is a two hander that, save for a brief opening sequence involving the abandoned sports car, takes place entirely within the confines of the Truscott's home (primarily the garage, lounge, kitchen and hallway), with Sellars and Bate left to carry the increasingly frenzied action totally by themselves, which they do with theatrical aplomb (this could very easily have been a stage or radio play), with Roger patronizingly dismissive of his wife's hysteria at first until the proof becomes overwhelming, at which the tables gradually turn, and she becomes the proactive one and he the nervous wreck. Working on the supposition that what one *can't* see is more frightening than what one *can*, Kneale and director Don Taylor wisely shy away from actually showing the rats (which probably wouldn't have lived up to expectations anyway, given the budgetary restrictions). Instead, a variety of convincingly disconcerting sound effects care of sound director Roger Knight are used to ramp up the tension which, combined with the imagination of viewers and the general phobia for rats, makes for an often-unsettling experience. Not all the situations ring true. Indeed, credulity is somewhat stretched when Angela calls the radio show only to then have a lengthy on on-air discussion with the deejay about her plight. But one must remember that at the time, there were no 24-hour news stations (the Truscotts in any case don't seem to possess a television), which makes the couple seem even more isolated from the outside world. With its growing sense of claustrophobia and its genuinely nihilistic ending, this truly is the stuff to induce nightmares among the impressionable (note that among the voices heard during the program are Colin Bell as Barty, John Rhys-Davies as Roger's business associate, and Norman Mitchell as the policeman he speaks with).

Rather less successful was episode three, *Buddyboy* (1976, TV), in which Dave (Martin Shaw), the owner of an adult cinema club, looks into buying Finnyland, a dilapidated dolphinarium which he plans to turn into a nightclub-cum-cinema. The present owner, a shifty looking character called Hubbard (Wolfe Morris), seems rather keen to get rid of the property, leading Dave to speculate that he might be in debt, and possibly to the mob, but when he discovers a young girl named Lucy (Pamela Moiseiwitsch) lurking about the place, he learns that there may be a more sinister reason why the businessman wants to make a quick deal. Lucy, it transpires, used to work at the dolphinarium, and has been squatting there recently. She also reveals that the penny-pinching Hubbard may somehow have been responsible for the deaths of the five dolphins that used to entertain the crowds, and like Lucy, he seems somehow to be haunted by the memory of the creatures, and one in particular, their leader and the cleverest of them, Buddyboy, for whom he had developed a particular hatred. Dave eventually buys the dolphinarium, allowing Hubbard to go abroad, and Dave and Lucy, who are now romantically involved, to move into the businessman's lavish bachelor pad. However, after their first night there, during which Dave suggests he turn Lucy into an adult film star, he discovers her dead, drowned in the large bathtub. He is also disturbed to hear the noise of a dolphin squeaking and clicking overhead....

Set primarily in the run-down dolphinarium, whose pool doesn't look big enough to house one dolphin, never mind five, this is a particularly dreary little drama which ultimately amounts to very little. With no one likeable to root for, least of all Dave, who ultimately seems to be as bad a lot as Hubbard, the piece quickly becomes something of a chore to watch, the dialogue and situations being among Kneale's weakest. Character motivation and credibility is also stretched to its limits, particularly with the unkempt Lucy, who, despite her apparent affinity with the dolphins ("I'd go over and talk to them—they knew I was coming"), seems to have substantial mental health issues, which makes it all the more incredible that Dave should fall for her, particularly when he has far more attractive propositions in his employ at his cinema, one of whom, a busty usherette, he is introduced to by his manager Jimmy (Stuart McGugan). Wanting to get into adult films, she quickly undoes her top to reveal her charms. "Do you know how much they weigh?" Jimmy asks him after she has left the room. "Have you weighed them?" Dave enquires, to which comes the astonishing reply, "On her kitchen scales. I was round there the other night." By no means anyone's moment of glory, this tawdry little episode lacks finesse in both the writing and direction, the latter care of Don Taylor, who'd done such a creditable job on *During Barty's Party*. In fact the only genuine moment of amusement comes in the guise of the various posters advertising the dubious attractions playing at Dave's cinema club, among them *Rampant Virgins*, *Soft, Wet and Warm* and *Penelope Pulls It Off* (the latter an actual movie from 1975).

Slightly better, though equally drawn out, was *Baby* (1976, TV), in which a vet, Peter Gilkes (Simon MacCorkindale), and his pregnant wife Jo (Jane Wymark), have recently moved to the countryside so that he can take up his duties as a rural practitioner. To this end, they have bought and are having renovated an old cottage.

However, their cat Mud takes an instant dislike to the place and scarpers as soon as it is let out of its basket. Not long after, while knocking down one of the walls, Peter discovers a large, heavy jar hidden behind the brickwork ("For storing something?" ponders Jo, to which comes the reply, "In the *wall*?"). Curious, Peter breaks the seal, and inside they find the desiccated remains of a strange, clawed creature they can't quite identify ("A farmyard monster—a cross between two animals that ought to have known better," comments Peter, adding "I'm not

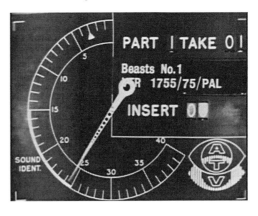

Transmission clock for Nigel Kneale's *Beasts* (1976, TV) (ATV).

sure it was actually born"). Jo hates the sight of the creature and attempts to burn it, after which Peter promises to take it to his surgery to perform an autopsy upon it, in the meantime leaving it, unbeknownst to his wife, locked in a cupboard in their unborn child's nursery.

Subsequently, Jo learns from Arthur (Mark Dignam), one of the laborers working on the cottage, that the previous owners, the Jacksons, had tried to breed dogs there, only for all the puppies to have died. It also seems that the fields surrounding the cottage are not in use, even for grazing, as doing so causes the cows to abort. Could a germ of some kind be responsible for this, or has a curse been put upon the place? Says Arthur of the jar, "It'd have purpose." "You mean bad purpose?" asks Jo, to which he replies, "Most like," adding, "In them days, they believed they could put harm on a person or a place…. On lands. It was often done." Not soon afterwards, Jo finds Mud dead, drowned in the woods, and is spooked by a strange shadow and noise. Following this Jo, who we learn has already suffered one miscarriage, starts to hear odd noises about the house, and catches a glimpse of a strange figure. Woken by the noises one night, she discovers the cupboard in the nursery to have been broken open from the inside. Going downstairs, she is horrified to come across what appears to be an old hag in the rocking chair, suckling what looks like a deformed pig, at which she collapses to the floor, clutching her abdomen….

At half the length, this would have been a reasonably nifty piece of folk horror, but yet again Kneale was forced to stretch out the story with a number of irrelevancies, among them Peter's relationship with Dick Plummery (T.P. McKenna), the local vet with whom he is working in partnership. A drunken scene between Peter, Dick and Dick's wife Dorothy (Shelagh Fraser), which is observed with increasing discomfort by Jo, is a particular strain to watch, given that those involved can't act drunk to save their lives. Indeed, the performances of all the main characters are strictly of the am-dram variety, save for that of Mark Dignam, who seems to relish his few moments as the sage Arthur, who appears to know more about the old country ways than he is letting on. As for the climax, although somewhat fumbled by director John Nelson, it certainly packs a wallop, even if the boggle-eyed old hag looks like a badly executed Muppet. As for the creature she is suckling, it is so briefly glimpsed that one can't really make head nor tail of it. As a companion piece to *Murrain*, however, one can't deny that *Baby* has its moments (note that though Dick is smashed on whisky, and barely able to stand, he is still happy to drive himself and his wife home; such was life in the seventies).

Next up was *What Big Eyes* (1976, TV), in which Bob Curry (Michael Kitchen), a keen young RSPCA officer, discovers that Leo Raymount (Patrick Magee), the owner of a small pet shop, has been carrying out experiments on the DNA of a number of timber wolves, which he has been procuring from a supplier of exotic animals (Bill Dean), his aim being to prove that lycanthropy actually exists, and that man derived from wolves some 50 million years ago. "It's the body not the brain that remembers," he explains to Bob of the cellular connection, going on to reveal that he has created what he calls the Grandma Vaccine. "Little Red Riding Hood. Don't you remember? Straight out of folklore. A case history. Don't you see, it wasn't the wolf that swallowed grandma, grandma *was* the wolf," he tells the incredulous Bob, revealing that he has been experimenting with the drug on himself ("There are side effects, of course, but they have to be borne").

Thus when Bob discovers a few days later that Raymount has taken delivery of another wolf, he hot foots it over to the shop, where he finds the animal crated up and howling in the back yard, which provokes the old man, now clearly ill and delirious from his experiments, to howl and growl in response. However, when he subsequently dies from septicemia, Raymount's devoted daughter Florence (Madge Ryan), who has been assisting him with his experiments, refuses to believe that he has passed away (and we are inclined to agree because Magee can't suppress his breathing). Reading his notes, Bob then discovers that just before he died, Raymount injected the wolf with a dose of his serum prepared with his own blood. Having put the wolf down, Bob later returns to pick up the animal's body, only to discover the pet shop and Raymount's laboratory have been ransacked by Florence. "You showed me. His work, rubbish, all of it rubbish," she exclaims, having finally realized why she could never understand her father's theories. "The reason I couldn't understand was that there was nothing *to* understand." But when she goes into the parlor to further berate her dead father (yes, the plot actually requires her to do this), she is shocked to see the sheet he is under start to move, while in the distance a wolf can be heard howling, but when Bob pulls back the sheet, he is still dead, and still his normal self. Yet in Florence's mind, he did turn into a werewolf. "Just for a moment, it was *true*," she convinces herself.

By far the weakest story in the series, this proves to be all build up and no climax, which must surely have disappointed viewers at the time keen to see Raymount turn into a werewolf, no matter how briefly. Unfortunately, in his bid to avoid the obvious, Kneale appears to have thrown the baby out with the bathwater, resulting in a series of dull scenes in which Raymount expounds his theories at great length to little ultimate purpose other than to prove how deluded he is. Routinely presented by director Donald McWhinnie, the program features a suitably over the top performance from the wild haired Magee as the nutty backstreet scientist, and one of restraint (until the final moments) from Madge Ryan as his devoted but much put upon and despised daughter ("The loyalty of a stupid person can be a very dulling commodity," says Raymount to Bob in what proves to be the script's best line), while as the idealistic RSPCA officer, Kitchen does his best with what is undeniably a very thinly sketched role. Otherwise, there is sadly little to muster one's enthusiasm here, save for the clever title.

The series concluded with *The Dummy* (1976, TV), a rather clumsy horror film spoof which goes behind the scenes on the making of the latest in a long line of movies featuring the Dummy, a bear-like monster with giant claws who is played by a wreck of an actor called Clyde Boyd (Bernard Horsfall), an alcoholic who is suffering not only from financial problems, but also from the loss of his wife to a fellow actor, Peter Wager (Simon Oates), who unexpectedly turns up on set, having been cast in a small part, much to Boyd's distress. Falling into a state of collapse, Boyd is talked round by his producer Bunny Nettleton (Clive Swift) and the film's director Sidney Stewart (Glyn Houston) to carry on filming, but goes on to kill an actor for real during the scene, following which he goes on the rampage in the studio, wrecking the set and sending the cast and crew running for their lives. The police are called to quell the situation and suggest that Wager bring Boyd's wife (Patricia Haines) to the studio to try and calm him down, but when he attacks her too, Wager grabs the shotgun he has brought with him and enters the studio, letting the creature have both barrels. However, Boyd is out of the costume by now, and strangles Wager to death with his own bare hands.

Supposedly a pastiche of Hammer films, several of which Kneale had worked on, the lumbering creature, which looks ludicrous in the extreme, is nothing like anything the fabled horror studio put before the cameras (the film's publicist, Mike Hickey [Ian Jacob Thompson], describes it to a visiting journalist as "a mixture of animal, vegetable, mineral, immortal, bulletproof, indestructible," adding somewhat patronizingly, "I mean, the customers don't really care"). That said, at least Hammer regular Thorley Walters turns up to enliven the proceedings as Sir Ramsey McFadden, a self-obsessed actor who is more keen to get off on his holiday than finish the picture. As the film's producer and director, Clive Swift and Glyn Houston do what they can with their two-dimensional characters, who don't appear to be based on any real-life counterparts, though as the smarmy Wager, Simon Oates at least manages to breathe a little life into his lines, commenting to Joan Eastgate (Lillias Walker), a journo doing a piece on the film, "I'm a great believer in women's lib. Liberating them from work, from their ghastly husbands and kids. Particularly husbands. I do what I can in that direction."

Unfortunately, as the emotionally unstable Clyde Boyd, Bernard Horsfall is a complete washout in a poorly written role whose mental collapse is little more than a device to get to the scenes of destruction, which are perfunctorily staged by director Don Leaver (who would go on to helm two episodes of *Hammer House of Horror* [1980, TV]). As for the improbably named Dummy itself, it's somewhat hard to swallow that such a ridiculous looking creature could possibly have sustained so many films (among them, so we're told, *Horror of the Dummy*, *Dummy and the Devil* and *Dread of the Dummy*), despite the publicist's claim that "he's very big with the Japs." The behind-the-scenes detail fails to convince either, which is quite a surprise given the number of sets Kneale must have visited during his career. The best moment comes when Boyd's wife slips in some stage gore while trying to escape from the Dummy, giving the false impression that she has been severely wounded, but otherwise this is a rather lazy piece which takes obvious pot shots at a target rich with possibilities, most of which it misses by a mile. Had it been written by a fan, rather than by someone with an axe to grind, things might have been different.

The BBC ended the year with a 100-minute videotaped studio production of *The Hunchback of Notre Dame* (1976, TVM), which aired on BBC2 on 30 December 1976 (it was shown in the U.S. on NBC on 18 July 1977). Written by Robert Muller and directed by Alan Cooke, it was one of the more faithful adaptations of the Victor Hugo novel, and featured Warren Clarke as a sympathetic Quasimodo, supported by Kenneth Haigh as Archdeacon Claude Frollo, Michelle Newell as Esmeralda and Christopher Gable as Pierre Gringoire. Clearly a prestige affair, it was given a Chaucerian air thanks to its mob of rhubarbing extras, particularly during the opening Feast of Fools sequence (and kudos to costume designer Maureen Winslade for dressing them all so convincingly). Surprisingly well staged given the confines of the studio, it was chiefly notable for its angular, abstract sets by Don Taylor, on which a good deal of money had clearly been spent by producer Cedric Messina, with the interiors of Notre Dame, complete with a giant rose window, being particularly eye-catching.

Teatime Terrors

A series that could well have been written by Nigel Kneale, but wasn't, was *Children of the Stones* (1977, TV), which was made for children's teatime television, but could equally have been broadcast in a more adult timeslot. Unlike America, where children's television programming consisted mainly of cartoons and sitcoms, the Brits tended toward slightly more educational fare and, music shows aside, favored magazine programs such as *Blue Peter* (1958–TV), *How* (1966–1981, TV) and *Magpie* (1968–1980, TV), documentaries like *Animal Magic* (1962–1983, TV), and the occasional literary adaptation, among them *Tom Brown's School Days* (1971, TV), *The Secret Garden* (1975, TV) and *Treasure Island* (1977, TV). From the early sixties, particularly following the advent of *Doctor Who* (1963–1989, TV), programs of a more fantastical nature began to appear with increasing regularity. Aside from the shows produced by Gerry Anderson (among them such favorites as *Fireball XL5* [1962–1963, TV], *Stingray* [1964–1965, TV], *Thunderbirds* [1964–1966, TV] and *Captain Scarlet and the Mysterons* [1967–1968, TV]), children's TV during this decade included such series as *Space Patrol* (1963–1968, TV), an elaborate Gerry Anderson–style puppet series in which Captain Dart and his crew patrol the solar system as peacekeepers; *Emerald Soup* (1963, TV), in which a group of children discover that secret radiation tests are being carried out at an installation near where they live; *The Lion, the Witch and the Wardrobe* (1967, TV), an adaptation of the ever popular 1950 book by C.S. Lewis about a fantasy land accessed through the back of a wardrobe (this was later remade as a feature-length television cartoon in 1979 and as a live action series in 1988); and *The Owl Service* (1969–1970, TV), in which three teenagers become involved with an ancient Welsh legend after deciphering a curious pattern on a set of dinner plates found in the attic of a manor house ("The most gripping, creepy serial we have seen on TV in a long time," commented *The Sun* of the latter).

The seventies brought even more diverse fare, including (deep breath, here we go) *Catweazle* (1970–1971, TV), in which an 11th-century wizard (Geoffrey Bayldon) finds himself transported through time to the present, where he is confounded by such modern day phenomena as electrickery and the telling bone; *Timeslip* (1970–1971, TV), in which two children (Spencer Banks and Cheryl Burfield) fall through a time hole and find themselves having adventures in both the past and the future; *Jamie* (1971, TV), in which a young boy (Garry Miller) discovers a time travelling magic carpet; *Man Dog* (1972, TV), in which two schoolgirls (Jane Anthony and Carol Hazell) befriend a man from the future whose mind has been transferred into the body of a pet dog (this program was notable at the time for the rarity of featuring a character in a wheelchair); *Pardon My Genie* (1972–1973, TV), in which an apprentice (Ellis Jones) working in an ironmonger's shop finds himself in posses-sion of a genie (Hugh Paddick [season one], Arthur White [season two]) who lives in a watering can; *Escape into Night* (1972, TV), in which the drawings of a girl (Vikki Chambers) come to life in her dreams, among them a strange house occupied by a sickly young boy (Steven Jones) who is under threat from a number of large stones with eyes (based upon the 1958 Catherine Storr novel *Marianne Dreams*, this was later filmed as *Paperhouse* [1988]); *Ace of Wands* (1972–1974, TV), which follows the adventures of Tarot (Michael MacKenzie), a mystery solving stage magician with telepathic abilities; *The Jensen Code* (1973, TV), in which a teenager (Dai Bradley) uncovers sinister events involving mind control while on an Outward Bound course; *Lizzie Dripping* (1973–1975, TV), in which a girl (Tina Heath) with a vivid imagi-nation forms a friendship with a witch (Sonia Dresdel) who only she can see; *The Tomorrow People* (1973–1979, TV), in which a group of teenagers (among them Nich-olas Young, Philip Gilbert and Elizabeth Adare) use their various powers (which include telepathy and the ability to transport themselves by "jaunting") to vanquish all manner of villains and aliens (memorable for its catchy synth theme tune by Dudley Simpson, the show was revived in 1992 and again in 2013); *Potty Time* (1973–1974, aka *Michael Bentine's Potty Time*, TV), in which host Michael Bentine presents absurdist puppet versions of classic books, among them *Dracula, Dr. Jekyll and Mr. Hyde* and *Frankenstein*, all of which were covered in the episode titled *Movie Mon-sters* (1973, TV), in which it is revealed that Count Dracula is not actually a vampire but an umpire, but *can* turn himself into a bat (a cricket bat); *Roberts Robots* (1973–1974, TV), which follows the adventures of Robert Sommerby (John Clive), an inven-tor who lives in a country house with his aunt (Doris Rogers) and a number of often malfunctioning androids; an adaptation of Philippa Pearce's 1958 novel *Tom's Mid-night Garden* (1974, TV), in which a young boy (Nicholas Bridge), who is staying with his aunt and uncle while his brother recovers from the measles, is transported to a back in time to a Victorian garden when a grandfather clock strikes 13 (the story had previously been presented in 1968 as part of the series *Merry-Go-Round* [1963–1983, TV] with Simon Turner as Tom); *The Changes* (1975, TV), in which a girl (Victoria Williams) tries to discover why a strange noise prompted mankind to sud-denly and violently turn its back on modern technology; *Sky* (1975, TV), in which a superhuman time traveller with piercing blue eyes (Marc Harrison) finds himself stranded on Earth, where he is helped by three teenagers; *Shadows* (1975–1978, TV), an anthology series of supernatural stories, among them *The Future Ghost* (in which a Victorian woman [Jane Wymark] staying at a guest house encounters a girl from the future), *Dark Encounter* (in which a man [Alex Scott] returns to the village he stayed in during the war and confronts an old fear), and *The Boy Merlin* (in which a boy [Ian Rowlands] is taught magic by his adoptive grandmother [Rachel Thomas], a Celtic witch [this episode was subsequently spun into a series in 1979]); *The Georgian House* (1976, TV), in which two teenagers (Spencer Banks and Adrienne Byrne) find themselves transported back in time to a Georgian house, in which they befriend a slave boy (Brinsley Forde) who possesses strange powers; *Rentaghost* (1976–1984, TV), in which a shop in South Ealing rents out ghosts to members of the public, among them a Victorian gentleman named Hubert Davenport (Michael Darbyshire) and a jester named Timothy Claypole (Michael Staniforth, who also wrote and sang the title song ["If your mansion house needs haunting just call Rentaghost" ran the lyrics]); *The Ghosts of Motley Hall* (1976–1978, TV), in which a stately home is haunted by a number of ghosts, among them Bodkin (Arthur English), The White Lady (Sheila Steafel) and Sir George Uproar (Freddie Jones), who are keen to keep the place for themselves, much to the chagrin of the estate agent Mr. Gudgin (Peter Sallis) who is trying to sell it; *The Feathered Serpent* (1976–1978, TV), in which a young Aztec boy (Richard Willis) clashes with a powerful high priest (Patrick Troughton) out to take control of the population (this particular series was notable for its surprisingly elaborate production design care of Patrick Downing and Jan Chaney, and its equally eye-catching costumes by Martin Baugh); *Nobody's House* (1976, TV), in which a family find that their new home is haunted by the ghost of a Victorian ragamuffin named Nobody (Kevin Moreton); an hour-long adaptation of Hans Christian Andersen's 1844 story *The Snow Queen* (1977, TV), in which the Devil makes a mirror that reflects only the bad in people, only for it to shatter, with one of the pieces finding its way into the eye of a boy (Joshua La Touzel) who is then abducted by the evil Snow Queen (Mercedes Burleigh); an adaptation of E. Nesbit's 1904 novel *The Phoenix and the Carpet* (1976–1977, TV), in which four Edwardian children (Jane Forster, Max Harris, Gary Russell and Tamzin Neville) discover an egg hidden in a rolled up carpet, which hatches into a talking phoenix and takes them on various adventures; *King of the Castle* (1977, TV), in which a bullied teenager (Philip DaCosta) living in a tower block finds himself transported to a creepy underground fantasy world via a malfunctioning elevator; *Raven* (1977, TV), in which a lad (Phil Daniels) just out of borstal is sent to assist an archaeologist involved with the excavation of some manmade caves beneath a stone circle, carvings in which are connected to the legend of King Arthur; *Come Back Lucy* (1978, TV), in which a bereaved girl (Emma Bakhle) is sent to live with her cousins, and meets the ghost of a Victorian child (Bernadette Winters) who wishes to take her back to her own time; *The Clifton House Mystery* (1978, TV), in which a concert pianist (Sebastian Breaks) and his family find themselves haunted by the spirit of a soldier when they move into an old house, and hire a ghost hunter (Peter Sallis) to exorcise it; *The Moon Stallion* (1978, TV), in which a blind Victorian girl (Diana Sutton) somehow connects with a mystical white stallion while accompanying her brother (David Pullan) and their archaeologist father (James Greene) to the site of a Celtic horse carved into a hillside; and *Worzel Gummidge* (1979–1981, TV), an adaptation of the Barbara Euphan Todd books (1936–1963) which follow the adventures of a scarecrow (Jon Pertwee) who has been given the gift of life by his maker (this was followed by *Worzel Gummidge Down Under* [1987–1989, TV] and a reboot in 2019 with Mackenzie Crook in the title role).

Which, somewhat circuitously, brings us back to *Children of the Stones* (1977, TV). Set in the quaint English village of Milbury, the seven-part series sees astrophysicist Adam Brake (Gareth Thomas) and his teenage son Matthew (Peter Demin) arrive for a three month stay to carry out research on the megalithic stone circle in the middle of which the village is situated. However, from the get-go, it would seem that their visit is going to be an eventful one, given that on the drive in they almost crash into what at first appears to be a giant stone in the middle of the road, but which turns out to be Mrs. Crabtree (Ruth Dunning), the lady who will be looking after them during their visit, and who has come to meet them. They soon after meet their landlord, the commanding Rafael Hendrick (Iain Cuthbertson), the lord of the manor, who calls by their cottage, and who expresses curiosity at a painting Matthew has brought with him, acquired a year earlier in a junk shop, and which appears to depict a pagan ceremony taking place within the stones of the very village in which

Shouting the odds. The great Freddie Jones in *The Ghosts of Motley Hall* (1976–1978, TV) (Granada Television).

they are staying, in the middle of which a powerful beam of light is shining. It also bears a curious Latin inscription, "Quod non est simulo de simalaque quod est," the translation of which reads, "I deny the existence of that which exists."

Making friends with Bob (Ian Donnelly), one of the local boys, Matthew explores the village by bike, all the while observed by a shabby looking poacher, Dai (Freddie Jones), who lives in a nearby cave known as The Sanctuary. However, when the boys narrowly avoid crashing into a truck, which seems to disappear at the last moment, Matthew begins to suspect that the village is perhaps not quite the idyllic place it seems, especially after meeting a young girl called Sandra (Katharine Levy), herself a newcomer, who warns him, "We've got to stick together," and experiencing his first day at school, at which the pupils are divided into two distinct groups, one of average intelligence (to which Sandra and Matthew belong) and one of almost supernatural ability who are able to work out the most complex mathematical problems set by their teacher (to which Bob belongs). That those children, and other inhabitants of the village, greet each other cheerfully with the term "Happy day" also singles them out as somehow different. "Sounds more like a password than a greeting, doesn't it?" observes Adam to Sandra's mother, Margaret (Veronica Strong), who is the new curator of the village museum, and with whom Adam forges a relationship. He also learns from her about the invisible ley lines that run through the village, which supposedly connect ancient sacred places, such as churches, mark stones, barrows (mound-covered graves) and stone circles. He also discovers that there are 53 stones in the village, which, curiously enough, matches the number of residents now that he and Matthew have arrived. However, when Margaret encourages Adam to touch one of the giant stones, he experiences a vision and is thrown back on the grass. And all of that in episode one.

As the series progresses, we learn that the stones are situated on a giant stone dish (as Adam's sonic readings reveal), that they all point in one precise direction, that the ley lines converge on Highfield House (which belongs to Hendrick), that the locals congregate at night to chant in a circle (as Matthew discovers), and that once resident in the village, people can't leave ("Nobody ever leaves the circle, not until the day of release" Dai informs Matthew). We also learn that newcomers eventually change ("Something seems to happen to them—I don't what is it, but something seems to happen," Sandra tells Matthew); the local church is deconsecrated and without a vicar; the stones themselves are highly magnetic, while some of them appear to have an almost human aspect to them; that Dai, who possesses a circular clay key bearing a serpent symbol (said to protect sacred hills and mazes) lives in fear of his life, and soon after dies and disappears; that Hendrick is an astronomer who discovered a supernova (now a black hole), towards which the stones point; that Matthew is able to "see" what others are doing when he touches something that belongs to them; and that the manor is full of digital clocks.

Things eventually come to a head when Margaret and Sandra are invited to dinner at the manor by Hendrick, who shows them to a room which contains a stone table and three stone chairs. Matthew is able to observe what is happening given that he has purloined Sandra's headscarf and uses it as a conduit. As the villagers gather outside to chant ("A hymn of celebration," says Hendrick), it is revealed that the table they are eating off is in fact an altar, that the stone circle is a temple, and that Hedrick is the high priest. At a specific time he recites an invocation and turns his chair away from the table, at which point the roof opens and a beam of immense power shoots from the table up to the sky, at which point Matthew loses contact ("Sandra seems to have stopped feeling," he says). Realizing that Margaret and Sandra have now changed, Matthew and Adam decide to pack and leave, but next morning before they go, Matthew breaks into the locked church, having seen Hendrick leave it bearing two large spools of tape, and discovers that the place is filled with computers. Caught in the act by Hendrick, he learns that he uses them to chart the stars with immaculate precision. However, when Matthew and Adam finally get in their car to drive out of the village, they find they can't leave the circle, and wake up at the manor house. "I think we missed the turning, the time turning, we failed to get through to our present," says Adam. He also asserts that Hedrick is a Magus, a "scholar-magician leading his people to beauty and truth," and believes that "we're in a *now* that's parallel to our own, a time shift that's caused by the energies received here in the circle." At which they realize they must either disconnect or reverse the power in order to escape, given that Hendrick is using energy from the ley lines to change people by purging them of sin and extracting from them the quality that makes them human, and beaming their psychic energy via the dish to the black hole, just as those in ancient times did to the supernova.

Deciding to beat Hendrick at his own game, Matthew and Adam alter his clocks (which they do with an oscillator), so that when Hendrick invites them to dinner to change them too, he does so at the wrong time. Consequently, when Adam and Matthew, who pretend to have been altered, join hands with the circle of chanting villagers outside the manor, the villagers return to their normal selves. Hendrick's protection also disappears, and when the beam appears at its appointed time, the stone table cracks into four and he takes on the appearance of an old man, while all the villagers, including Sandra and Margaret, are turned to stone. Next day, Dai reappears in The Sanctuary, where Adam and Matthew have been hiding out, but with a different personality. Indeed, all the villagers now seem back to normal, but with different personas. This time, Matthew and Adam are finally able to leave the village. "Did it happen, or didn't it?" asks Matthew as they stop to look back, and will it all happen again? "Time—perhaps that's circular too," ponders Adam, and as they drive away, a new version of Hendrick (now Sir Joshua Litton) motors into the village to purchase the manor, which is for sale. It would seem a repeat of events has already started....

Given that it was aimed at children, this is an often-complex saga of telepathy, paganism and enlightenment (a *Wicker Man* lite, if you will), yet at no time does the script by Jeremy Burnham and Trevor Ray talk down to its audience. If anything, it pulls them up to a higher level by the bootstraps and contains some surprisingly sophisticated exchanges. For example, says Hendrick at one point when Margaret and Sandra are running late for their dinner appointment at the mansion: "Women—delightful creatures, but punctuality is not among their virtues," to which Link (John Woodnutt) his manservant responds, "Yes, sir—there is much to be said for a celibate life." As with most series of this period, the interiors were shot on videotape in the studio, but thanks to slightly more atmospheric lighting than was the norm, this isn't too much of a distraction, given that the unfolding plot is so intriguing. Luckily, the majority of the action takes place outdoors and is shot on film (by Bob Edwards and Brian Morgan), making the very most of the sunny locations, prime among them the village of Aylesbury and its own remarkable circles and avenues of stone, which add considerable visual impact to the series (more so than they did in *Stigma* [1977, TV]). Augmented by fiberglass stones care of designer Ken Jones, they are an imposing sight indeed, particularly in the title sequence, in which they are shot from a variety of unsettling angles backlit by the sun, all the while accompanied by Sidney Sager's often disturbing choral score, which builds to a frenzied climax, following which we are treated to several spectacular aerial shots of the village.

Producer-director Peter Graham Scott meanwhile keeps the pace moving, even in the studio sequences (which, surprisingly for a kids' program, include scenes in the local pub), but it is during the exterior scenes, shot in the heat of the summer of '76, that he truly shines, capturing with finesse such events as a local morris dance with its sinister undertones, Adam and Matthew's examination of the stones, and the creepy night time gatherings outside the manor, which must have caused a few unsettled nights for younger viewers. The program also benefits from several good performances, among them Iain Cuthbertson's turn as Hendrick, who is clearly working to a hidden agenda, Freddie Jones as the grizzled old poacher Dai, Veronica Strong (who was married to writer Jeremy Burnham) as Sandra's mother Margaret, Ruth Dunning as the slightly creepy housekeeper Mrs. Crabtree, and Gareth Thomas as the scientist Adam Brake, who treats his son pretty much as an equal, particularly when working out calculus. Mercifully, the children, as played by Peter Demin (Matthew) and Katharine Levy (Sandra), aren't stage school types and appear reasonably natural for the most part. Executive produced by Patrick Dromgoole and made by HTV, the series was broadcast across the ITV network from 10 January 1977, yet despite its high quality and the considerable care with which it was made, it was never granted a repeat showing, yet seems to have seared itself into the minds of those lucky enough to have followed it during its one-time broadcast. Thankfully, it is now available on DVD.

If, however, it's the *scariest* thing broadcast on children's television that you seek, then look no further than *The Spirit of Dark and Lonely Water* (1973, TV, aka *Lonely Water*), a public safety film warning youngsters about the dangers of playing near water. Written and produced by Christine Hermon via Illustra Films for the Central Office of Information, it was directed by Jeff Grant in the style of a horror film, and sees a cowled figure appear by several bodies of water where children are playing in a variety of situations, not realizing the danger they are in. "I am the spirit of dark and lonely water, ready to trap the unwary, the show off, the fool, and this is the kind of place you'd expect to find me" begins the narration, spoken in whispered tones by Donald Pleasence over a shot of a misty, overgrown pond. It then goes on to observe a more ordinary seeming pool on a worksite in which a boy is trying to retrieve a football with a stick, guyed on by his friends ("The boy is showing off, the bank is slippery..."), a picturesque lake where a lone boy is hanging from a tree while fishing ("This branch is weak, rotten, it will never take his weight..."), and a dumping ground where a boy is swimming alone in an adjacent stretch of water, despite a "Danger No Swimming" sign ("Only a fool would ignore this, but there's one born every minute...").

As the spirit notes of this climactic situation, "under the water there are traps: old cars, bedsteads, weeds, hidden depths. It's the perfect place for an accident." Luckily, on this occasion, a couple of other kids just happen to be passing by (though the lad's cries for help are almost drowned out by a passing airplane). "Oi, look, there's someone in the woa-ah," says the boy in a thick Cockney accent. "Quick, get that big stick to get him out," suggests the girl. "Sensible children, I have no power over them," bemoans the spirit as the drowning boy is rescued, before adding a cautionary, "I'll be back, back, back, back, back...." Superbly shot from a variety of well framed angles and containing a couple of graceful dolly shots that wouldn't seem out of place in a feature, the film sees children either fall or get into difficulty as the shadowy figure impassively watches from the banks before turning away, the implication being that the victims have drowned. Sobering stuff, and genuinely chilling, this is a masterfully realized piece of storytelling which gets its message across with both power and economy. Indeed, the film runs just one minute and 28 seconds and contains only 19 shots, yet not a single frame is wasted. To say that this haunted a generation is something of an understatement.

Back in the world of grown-up television, *Supernatural* (1977, TV) saw the return of the anthology format with this series of 50-minute period dramas care of the BBC, the focus of which was The Club of the Damned, a secret society, membership to which is granted through the telling of tales of horror which, if they prove to be insufficiently chilling, cost the teller their life. Produced by Pieter Rogers and created by Robert Muller, who wrote seven of the eight episodes, the (mostly) studio bound series launched on BBC1 on 11 June 1977 with one of the weaker stories, *Ghost of Venice* (1977, TV), in which Adrian Gall (Robert Hardy), a retired Shakespearean actor on a return visit to Venice, is reunited with the ethereal Leonora

(Sinead Cusack), an old flame he thought dead. A somewhat slowly paced affair with rather lackluster direction care of Claude Whatham, and production design by Allan Anson that is more theatrical than realistic (or, to put it more bluntly, on the cheap side), it got the series off to a slightly creaky start. However, things got into their stride with the next two episodes, *Countess Ilona* (1977, TV) and *The Werewolf Reunion* (1977, TV), a two-parter in which a widowed countess (Billie Whitelaw) invites to her remote castle four former lovers (Ian Hendry, Charles Kay, John Fraser and Edward Hardwicke) to inform them that one of them, rather than her late husband, may be the father of her young son Bela (Stefan Gates). The men then start to die, seemingly at the hands of a werewolf. With wittier scripts, better production values care of designer Allan Anson and costumier Ken Morey, and firmer handling by director Simon Langton, the two installments also benefit from the presence of its starry cast, prime among them Whitelaw as the scheming countess (the actress was in a relationship with Robert Muller at the time, whom she later married). Also featuring Charles Keating, Sandor Eles and Molly Veness, the programs also contain some atmospheric forest location photography by David Whitson.

The series went on to include *Mr. Nightingale* (1977, TV), in which a staid Englishman (Jeremy Brett) on business in Hamburg finds his personality gradually being taken over by an evil doppelganger (via excellent character make-up by Toni Chapman); *Lady Sybil* (1977, TV), in which the elderly Lady Sybil Manners (Cathleen Nesbitt) appears to be being haunted by her late husband; *Viktoria* (1977, TV), in which a young girl (Genevieve West) becomes obsessed with a new doll, which she believes to be the reincarnation of her late mother (this episode was penned by Sue Lake, who also worked as a script associate on *Countess Ilona*); *Night of the Marionettes* (1977, TV), in which a literary critic (Gordon Jackson) on holiday in Switzerland with his family visits a puppet show with disturbing life-size marionettes; and *Dorabella* (1977, TV), which recounts how a young man (Jeremy Clyde) managed to escape from the clutches of a beautiful female vampire (Ania Marson) and her father (John Justin). Of these, *Night of the Marionettes* is easily the best, thanks to its creepy-looking puppets, a strong supporting performance from Vladek Sheybal as Herr Hubert, the puppet master, and some atmospheric location footage by cameraman Nigel Walters.

Sadly, despite strong supporting casts, among them such names as Denholm

Pull the string. Vladek Sheybal in *Night of the Marionettes* (1977, TV), the best episode of *Supernatural* (1977, TV) (BBC).

Elliott, Kathleen Byron, Lesley-Anne Down and John Osborne, the series failed to find a substantial enough audience to warrant a second season. Remembered for its unsettling title sequence in which imposing organ music (care of composer Paul Lewis) plays over images of gargoyles, the series is worth searching out for those able to transport themselves back to a time when narratives were taken at slower pace, and not everything was shocks and gore. Those who can't will inevitably be disappointed (a book by Robert Muller titled *Supernatural: Haunting Stories of Gothic Terror* was published by Fontana to accompany the series).

What Music They Make

Having proved itself capable of presenting genre programming of the highest quality with its Christmas ghost stories, the BBC next decided to tackle the granddaddy of horror literature, Bram Stoker's 1897 opus *Dracula* under the title *Count Dracula* (1977, TVM). The BBC's head of plays, the respected Gerald Savory, was charged with adapting the book, while the responsibility of directing such a large-scale enterprise was handed to the equally reliable Philip Saville, whose earlier credits included a now lost version of *Dr. Jekyll and Mr. Hyde* (1956, TV), as well as multiple episodes of *Armchair Theatre* (1956–1974, TV) and *Play for Today* (1970–1984, TVM). Intended as a definitive whistles and bells presentation of the story, Savory's epic teleplay offers a far fuller version of events either skipped over or deleted from most film adaptations, given the restrictions of running time, and thus we get more complete representations of such events as Harker's journey to Castle Dracula, his forced stay by the Count, his encounters with the Count's brides, his observation of the Count scaling down the castle walls, and his attempts to escape. The Count's subsequent arrival in England and his nighttime encounters with both Lucy and Mina are also more detailed, as is the eventual involvement of Van Helsing in the case, the tracking down of the Count's boxes of earth across London, and his final destruction back at Castle Dracula, where he has been pursued by Van Helsing, Dr. Seward, Harker, Mina and Lucy's lover Quincey P. Holmwood (whose presence in the story is often omitted entirely).

With a running time of two and a half hours, the film has the time and space to tell Stoker's tale with some degree of leisure, while at the same time offering a carefully structured version of the book, whose narrative is relayed from a variety of perspectives. All the familiar ingredients are check listed, and Savory makes sure that the Count gets to quote his most famous lines ("Listen to them, the children of the night, what music they make"), while Saville punctuates the proceedings with a number of eye-catching visual flourishes, among them the use of black and white footage (for Harker's train journey across Europe), negative imagery (when Dracula sees that Harker has cut himself while shaving) and even animation (one of Dracula's manifestations before Lucy). Casting is also key to the film's overall effect, and to this end Saville is well served by his leading man, the French matinee idol Louis Jourdan, who was in his mid-fifties at the time of filming, and whose courtly old world charm adds immeasurably to his performance, particularly during his initial exchanges with Harker, played by Bosco Holden, whose journey to and subsequent attempts to escape from Castle Dracula are among the more gripping elements of the early stages of the story. And while Dracula himself conforms to the more romantic interpretation of the role that films would have him be (the opening credits describe the production as "a gothic romance based on Bram Stoker's *Dracula*"), at least here he is shown to have hairy palms and pointed fingernails to counter his middle European savoir faire, which allows him to deliver such lines as "A house cannot be made habitable in a day, and after all, how few days go to make up a century," with the expected panache. Jourdan's also provides one of the more calculating interpretations of the role.

As Van Helsing, who doesn't appear until halfway through the action, Frank Finlay presents believable man of science who quickly grasps the situation when called upon by his friend Dr. Seward (Mark Burns) to examine Lucy, who by now is wearing a velvet choker to disguise the telltale signs that she has been attacked by a vampire, and is gradually turning into one herself (explains Van Helsing to Quincey, "She has already joined the ranks of the undead.... The Nosferatu, the walking dead, those who cannot die, who are cursed with immortality, who must go on age after age, adding new victims, multiplying the evils of the world"). And though Susan Penhaligon makes for a slightly simpering Lucy, she nevertheless has some strong moments, among them her apparent possession just before she dies, her appearance in the graveyard after she has risen as a vampire, and her dispatch at the hands of Quincey, who stakes her as Van Helsing reads the prayer for the dead, following which Van Helsing stuffs a garlic flower into her mouth before cutting off her head (the staking is surprisingly bloody for a television film, and is particularly well staged, while the stuffing of the garlic flower into Lucy's mouth can't have been a pleasant experience for Penhaligon).

As Mina, Judi Bowker perhaps has the better of the two female leads, getting to take succor from her undead lover as Harker, by now her husband, sleeps on unaware beside her in bed ("We shall cross land and sea together," the Count informs her as she drinks his blood from a self-inflicted wound on his chest). She also gets to accompany the men folk as they follow Dracula back to his homeland, where she and Van Helsing have a memorable encounter with the Count's three brides in the forest at night, from whom Van Helsing provides protection by scoring a circle round himself and Mina with a stick and sprinkling it with communion wafers. Admittedly, the supporting cast is something of a mixed bag, with Anna Queensberry somewhat vapid as Mrs. Westenra (the mother of Lucy and Mina), and Richard Barnes downright laughable at times as Quincey (his American accent has to be heard to be believed), though compensation can be found in Mark Burns' dependable Dr. Seward and, in particular, Jack Shepherd's Renfield, whose madhouse ramblings are given a more realistic interpretation here as he works his way up the insect chain, even if his connection with the Count, who visits him in his cell where he eventually kills him, is never fully explained ("Master, Master, are you coming soon?" he queries early on).

Other highlights in the production include the moment when Harker realizes he cannot see Dracula reflected in his shaving mirror, which the count disposes of by dropping it out of the window ("The trouble with mirrors is that they don't reflect quite enough, don't you think?"); Harker's attempts to write a letter home by using shorthand; the clever use of billowing cloth to represent the sea during Dracula's voyage to England; Lucy's first nocturnal wandering, during which she is seduced by the Count in a graveyard; the mist creeping across the lawn as the Count comes to pay a call on Mina (in fact all the smoke effects are excellent); and the final destruction of Dracula, who disintegrates in a powerful eruption of wind and smoke, leaving behind nothing but his clothes. As for the most disturbing moment, it is undoubtedly Dracula's delivery of a baby in a carpetbag for his three brides to feast upon (a similar scene can be found in the Czech adaptation, *Hrabe Drakula* [1971, TVM], although in that film only the bag is briefly shown, accompanied by the sound of an older child crying).

Other pluses include the location filming in such places as Whitby (where the Westenras have their summer home), Highgate Cemetery (for Lucy's first appearance as a full-blown vampire), and Alnwick Castle in Northumberland (which stands in for Castle Dracula). Mention must also be made of the simple but atmospheric score by Kenyon Emrys-Roberts, which uses percussion and a Theremin to creepy effect. Less impressive is the video recording of the interiors, for though the Castle Dracula sequences are carefully lit with an eye for atmosphere, the other sets have that flat look of the period, with much flare on the lens. The BBC's familiar sound effects library is also made rather free use of. Still, there are compensations in the dialogue, among them Dracula's invitation to Harker to step into his home ("Come freely, go safely"), Van Helsing's description of the Count ("My books tell me that he was an extraordinary man. A soldier, a cunning statesman. No branch of study was too difficult for him, and the power of his brain has survived his death"), Dracula's comeback when Van Helsing holds up a cross to him and chants a quick prayer ("Yes, yes, it always sounds more convincing in Latin, doesn't it, Professor"), his description of the cross ("An instrument of torture and humiliation") and, best of all, his pithy comment to Harker during their final face to face ("We must survive, all of us. The blood of a human being for me, a cooked bird for you. What is the difference?").

Broadcast in its entirety on BBC2 on 22 December 1977 from 9:30 p.m. (with a break at the halfway point at

Out for the count. Louis Jourdan in a publicity shot for *Count Dracula* (1977, TVM) (BBC).

10:40 p.m. for the late news and weather), the film was subsequently repeated twice in 1979 (first in January on BBC2 and then again in December on BBC1), both times as a three-parter shown on consecutive nights, and then again in 1993 (on BBC2) as a two-parter, which is perhaps the best way to enjoy it (the DVD is released in this format). Critical reaction was generally strong, with *The Guardian* describing it as "a nice plushy production with much galloping off in all directions," while *The Times* heralded, "Bram Stoker's original tale is back with us—and with what panache." Undeniably a little slow in patches now, and inevitably dated by its mix of film and videotaping, this nevertheless remains one of the key adaptations of the Stoker book, and is certainly television's best representation of it to date.

The BBC also aired another classic story during this particular festive season in the guise of a new version of *A Christmas Carol* (1977, TV), which was broadcast at 6:30 p.m. on 24 December 1977. This time Michael Hordern starred as the miserly Ebenezer Scrooge (the actor had previously played Jacob Marley in the fifties film version, *Scrooge* [1951], and the 1971 animated version, in both cases opposite Alastair Sim's Scrooge). Dramatized by Elaine Morgan and directed by the prolific Moira Armstrong, it also featured John Le Mesurier as Jacob Marley, Patricia Quinn as the Ghost of Christmas Past, Bernard Lee as the Ghost of Christmas Present, Michael Mulcaster as the Ghost of Christmas Future, Clive Merrison as Bob Cratchit, Zoe Wanamaker as Belle and Christopher Biggins as Topper. Running to just 58 minutes for an hour-long timeslot, it is more notable for its acting than its production values, which are typical of a videotaped studio piece of the time, with Hordern in fine fettle as the cowering Scrooge.

An early evening anthology series is our next port of call. Titled *Armchair Thriller* (1978–1981, TV), it began its 55-episode run on the ITV network on 21 February 1978, and presented a number of unrelated stories which ran to several half-hour episodes each (either four or six). Devised by Andrew Brown (who also occasionally produced) and made primarily in the studio (i.e.: on videotape) by Thames Television (who introduced the program with a moonlit version of their famous London skyline logo), it mostly concerned itself with espionage and kidnappings (as per the first story, *Rachel in Danger* [1978, TV]), but occasionally stepped towards the slightly more fantastical, as with the six-parter *Quiet as a Nun* (1978, TV), an adaptation by Julia Jones of Antonia Fraser's 1977 novel, the first to feature the reporter Jemima Shore (Maria Aitken), who returns to her old convent school to investigate the mysterious death of one of the nuns, who it seems starved herself to death in a locked room.

The story is chiefly remembered for featuring the legend of a faceless specter known as the Black Nun, who is said to be a portent of death, and whom Jemima memorably encounters in a spooky tower at the end of episode three. However, the *Scooby-Doo* denouement eventually reveals that things aren't quite what they seem, but it doesn't matter, as this well managed shock moment appears to have scarred a generation (our intrepid reporter eventually got her own series, *Jemima Shore Investigates* [1983, TV], in which she was now played by Patricia Hodge). As for the show's remaining episodes, which peaked with an audience of 17 million, they returned to the more usual mix of murder and mystery, but thanks to this one shocking image, plus the series' creepy opening credits sequence, which sees the shadow of a man approach and sit down in a white chair and splay his hands menacingly over the armrests accompanied by an atmospheric theme by Roxy Music's Andy Kay, it appears to have remained in the subconscious of a good many people (note that the series played in America on PBS under the title *Mystery*, which was hosted by Vincent Price, and sported a new animated title sequence by Edward Gorey and Derek Lamb).

Likewise, *Scorpion Tales* (1978, TV), another anthology show that aired on ITV, occasionally tilted towards the apparent supernatural. Produced by David Reid via ATV, the hour-long series began its six-episode run on 29 April 1978, and like *Armchair Thriller*, primarily concerned itself with stories involving murder and intrigue. However, we got a slightly more unusual story with *The Great Albert* (1978, TV), about a young boy (Max Harris) who comes across a 16th-century book of spells, which he uses to resolve the issues between his two feuding parents, who have made his life a misery, but things takes an unexpected turn when his mother's lover murders his father. Meanwhile, with *The Ghost in the Pale Blue Dress* (1978, TV), a business executive (Tony Britton) discovers that his son's fiancée bears an uncanny resemblance to his late wife. However, given the more realistic nature of the series as a whole, the stories in this case have a logical explanation. Memorable primarily for its title sequence by Alastair MacMunro, which features two fighting scorpions, and a driving theme tune by Cyril Ornadel, the mostly studio bound show top lined such names as Trevor Howard, Anthony Bate, Patrick Allen and Jack Shepherd.

Thrills of a more supernatural flavor could be found in the half-hour anthology show *Classics Dark and Dangerous* (1977–1978, TV), which had a somewhat checkered history. A British-Canadian co-production between HTV and the Ontario Educational Communications Authority, it was made via Highgate Associates Limited and featured stories involving mystery, horror and science fiction. It began with *The Ugly Little Boy* (1977, TV), an adaptation of the 1958 Isaac Asimov story (originally published as *Lastborn*) about a nurse (Kate Reid) who becomes attached to a Neanderthal boy (Guy Big) who has been brought to the present day via a time travel experiment. This was then followed by adaptations of D.H. Lawrence's 1926 story *The Rocking Horse Winner* (1977, TV), about a boy (Nigel Rhodes) who is able to predict race winners while riding his rocking horse, much to the delight of his uncle (Kenneth More), only for things end tragically; Robert Bloch's 1937 story *The Mannikin* (1977, TV), in which a singer (Ronee Blakley) finds herself possessed by the spirit of a demon; L.P. Hartley's 1924 story *The Island* (1978, TV), in which a soldier (John Hurt) on leave from the front during World War I travels to a remote island to visit a former lover; Arthur Conan Doyle's 1892 story *The Adventure of Silver Blaze*, presented as *Silver Blaze* (1977, TV), in which Sherlock Holmes (Christopher Plummer) and his friend Dr. Watson (Thorley Walters) investigate the disappearance of a famous racehorse; and E.F. Benson's 1923 story *Mrs. Amworth* (1978, TV), in which a lady vampire (Glynis Johns) descends upon an unsuspecting English village.

The programs were aired somewhat haphazardly in the UK, with *Silver Blaze* eventually appearing as an installment of *The Sunday Drama* (1977–1978, TV), while *Mrs. Amworth* went out on its own in a late-night slot. The three most fantastical episodes were also presented in an anthology film (via Highgate Pictures) titled *Three Dangerous Ladies* (1977), which is comprised of *The Mannikin*, *The Island* and *Mrs. Amworth*. Of these, *The Mannikin* is a fair possession drama helped by a good performance by Ronee Blakley as a singer who has been hearing strange voices and suffering back pain, more so since the death of her much-despised mother, who as a child had made her take part in séances against her will. In the most memorable scene, a creature emerges from her back during a ceremony performed by her mother's close friend and confidante (Pol Pelletier), and subsequently kills the doctor (Keir Dullea) who has been treating her. Equally watchable is *The Island*, in which the former lover of a married woman visits her on her island, where he is confronted by her husband (Charles Gray) who appears to have murdered her, but according to the butler (Graham Crowden [mistakenly billed as Craham Crowden in the film version's credits]), he couldn't have, given that he is away in South America. Both are adequately handled by Don Thompson and Robert Fuest, respectively, and though perfectly passable, neither is truly out of the ordinary, unlike *Mrs. Amworth* which, in its own small way, is an absolute gem.

Mrs. Amworth Pays a Visit

Concisely adapted by Hugh Whitemore, the story sees a small English village charmed by the arrival of the vivacious Mrs. Amworth (Glynis Johns), whose sunny disposition seems to have done much to cheer the local populace. "This place was half dead before you arrived," she is informed by Major Pearsall (Ronald Russell) at a garden party she has thrown for the locals. Indeed, everyone seems happy to know her. However, she is not the only new arrival in the village, which has been infested with gnats, the bites from which cause anemia in the victims, among them David (Pip Miller) who is visiting his uncle Benson (Derek Francis) while his parents are away in Spain. The local doctor (Rex Holdsworth) is baffled by the strange virus, which is claiming more and more victims, and blood specialists are called in from London to investigate. In fact it appears the only person who is immune is Mrs. Amworth herself. Letting slip that her ancestors hailed from the village, among them one Elizabeth Chaston, Benson's friend Urcombe (John Phillips), who has an interest in the occult, begins to look into the matter, and discovers that in the 1640s the village was likewise beset by "a strange disease of the blood" which the locals put down to witchcraft. Could this present outbreak somehow be connected to the earlier one? Indeed it could, as Mrs. Amworth and her ancestor Elizabeth Chaston are both one and the same. Consequently, Urcombe decides to confront Mrs. Amworth, and attempts to cast her away when she comes to call on him one day. Unfortunately, in backing away from him in confusion, she steps into the road and is killed by a car. Could she really have been a vampire after all? The proof finally comes when she later returns from the grave to pay the ailing David a late-night visit in his sick bed, after which Urcombe and Benson take matters into their own hands and head for the cemetery, where they exhume Elizabeth Chaston's coffin and Urcombe plunges his pickaxe into her heart, thus bringing her reign of terror to an end.

The short film par excellence, *Mrs. Amworth* moves with dexterity through its narrative, yet never seems rushed, despite its brief running time, and even takes time to detail the social intricacies of a garden party, during which Mrs. Amworth mingles amiably among her various guests in a particularly well managed two-minute take. It also observes the intimacies of a quiet game of cards, during which Mrs. Amworth reveals her heritage, and the gradually increasing concern of Urcombe and Benson, which finally provokes them to take action, despite the unreality of the situation. "You knew all along, didn't you?" Benson asks his friend after they have carried out their wild work, to which comes the reply, "Yes, but who would've believed me?" However, there is a final twist, for as they walk home down the road, they are passed by a car from which the sound of singing emanates not unlike that of Mrs. Amworth, who was prone to hum *Greensleeves* wherever she went.

Other highlights include an early scene in which Urcombe follows Mrs. Amworth to the cemetery where he observes her place flowers on the grave of Elizabeth Chaston (1603–1644), only for them to wither as he walks away; Mrs. Amworth's various nocturnal prowlings about the village, which are presented in slow motion to give her an ethereal quality, which is further enhanced by her flowing white dress; the appearance at Urcombe's window of a spectral hand; Benson's discovery of Mrs. Amworth preying on David; her dawn return to her grave, complete with a descent into the earth; and her final exhumation and destruction, which is given an extra fillip thanks to the inclusion of a shot taken on high from the nearby church tower. Handled with both style and restraint by director Alvin Rakoff (a Canadian who spent much of his career in the UK), the film benefits enormously from its sunny English village setting and its location shot interiors, which are superbly captured by cameraman Bob Edwards. Mention must also be made of the tight editing by Alex Kirby, who still manages to let the story breathe, and of the atmospheric score by Arlon Ober and Harry Manfredini, which uses both synths and orchestra to great effect. Performance-wise, Glynis Johns is delightful as the initially endearing Mrs. Amworth, who seems unable to drive her car without causing mayhem around her, yet when her true nature is revealed, this takes on an undeniably sinister aspect, while sterling support is provided by Derek Francis, John Phillips and Pip Miller, who between them prove that there are no small roles, despite the comparative brevity of their screen time. Leagues ahead of anything Amicus was churning out at this time with their big screen horror compendiums, *Mrs. Amworth* is that rare thing indeed: the perfectly realized short film.

Elsewhere, the detective Sexton Blake returned to the small screen with *Sexton Blake and the Demon God* (1978, TV). Created in 1893 by Harry Blythe (writing as Hal Meredeth), the character went on to appear in numerous cartoon strips, novels and films, among the latter *Sexton Blake and the Hooded Terror* (1938). He'd actually made his small screen debut in the late sixties in the long running series *Sexton Blake* (1967–1971, TV), in which he was portrayed by Laurence Payne through 50 half-hour episodes. Broadcast on ITV from 25 September 1967, his many adventures occasionally involved a minor brush with the fantastic, as with the opening story, *The Find the Lady Affair* (1967, TV), which begins with a thief disguised as a mummy emerging from a sarcophagus to help rob the Palazzo Medici, and *The Invicta Ray*

(1968, TV), in which the villain, Mr. Mist (Denis Goacher), is able to make himself invisible. Jeremy Clyde subsequently took on the role of Blake for *Sexton Blake and the Demon God*, which was produced by Barry Letts for the BBC, who broadcast it in their Sunday afternoon tea-time slot from 10 September 1978. Written by Simon Raven and directed by Roger Tucker, the six-part series saw Blake become involved in a plot revolving round the theft of the mummy of Tu Fu Edas from the British Museum and the determination of the evil Hubba Pasha (Derek Francis) to sacrifice the beautiful Zigiana (Jacquey Chappell). Unfortunately, as tantalizing as all this sounds, the series is currently unavailable for further assessment, though given the hour of its broadcast, one can't imagine that it contained anything too horrifying (the series was subsequently novelized by John Garforth as a tie-in published by Mirror Books).

With *Late Night Story* (1978–1979, TV), it was the turn of adults to have a bedtime story read to them in what could best be described as *Jackanory* (1965–1996, TV) for grownups. Produced by Tony Harrison for the BBC and running to just ten 15-minute episodes over two seasons, the first five, which began airing on 23 December 1978, were read by Tom Baker, and concerned themselves with macabre episodes from childhood, the first of which was *The Photograph* (1978, TV) by Nigel Kneale (taken from his 1949 collection *Tomato Cain and Other Stories*). The others were *The Emissary* (1978, TV) by Ray Bradbury, *Nursery Tea* (1978, TV) by Mary Danby, *The End of the Party* (1978, TV) by Graham Greene and *Srendi Vashtar* (1978, TV) by Saki (real name Hector Hugh Munro). In the second season, it was the turn of John Mills to read the stories, which this time were all penned by Len Deighton and concerned themselves with the war.

Stories of a more adult nature were also the basis of the long running *Tales of the Unexpected* (1979–1988, TV, initially *Roald Dahl's Tales of the Unexpected*), an anthology show that proved to be a ratings hit in Britain, despite the sometimes variable quality of both the handling and the stories themselves, whose twists weren't always entirely unexpected (and in some cases were even something of a damp squib). Described as "30 minute time bombs," by *TV Guide*, it began its nine-season run on the ITV network on 24 March

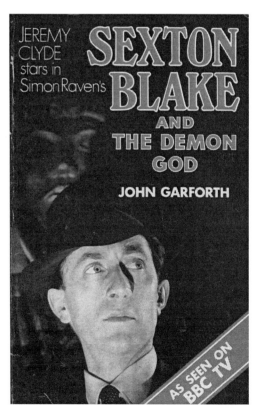

Jeremy Clyde is featured on the cover of John Garforth's 1978 novelization of *Sexton Blake and the Demon God* (1978, TV) (BBC/TBS/Mirror Books).

1979, and went on to notch up 112 episodes. Like the earlier 'Way Out (1961, TV), it was originally hosted by Roald Dahl (who did his introductions sitting by a fireside), and at first featured his stories exclusively. A close cousin to *Alfred Hitchcock Presents* (1955–1962, TV), it even contained remakes of stories already filmed for the Master's series (among them *Lamb to the Slaughter, Poison* and *Mrs. Bixby and the Colonel's Coat*), as well as stories previously featured in other shows (such as *Parson's Pleasure, Mrs. Bixby and the Colonel's Coat* [again] and *Taste,* all which had done service on *Thirty Minute Theatre* [1965–1973, TV]). Produced by John Rosenberg under the watchful eye of executive producer John Woolf, the series was made via Anglia Television, and was undoubtedly a prestige production of its time, attracting many quality names to its casts, among them John Gielgud, George Peppard, Joan Collins, Samantha Eggar, Michael Gambon, Topol, Peter Cushing, Don Johnson, John Mills, Nigel Havers, Wendy Hiller, Telly Savalas, Janet Leigh, Joseph Cotten, Susan Strasberg, Denholm Elliott, Robert Morley, Gloria Grahame and Julie Harris to name a few, while directors involved included Herbert Wise, Alan Gibson, Gordon Hessler, Christopher Miles, Claude Whatham, Michael Tuchner, Peter Duffell, Philip Leacock, Leo Penn, Norman Lloyd and Wendy Toye (who helmed a remake of her celebrated short *The Stranger Left No Card* [1952] under the title *Stranger in Town* [1982, TV]).

The series, which featured location filming as far afield as Jamaica and California, as well as videotaped interiors recorded at Anglia's Norwich studios, launched with *The Man from the South* (1979, TV), which had already appeared on *Cameo Theatre* (1950–1955, TV) and *Alfred Hitchcock Presents* (1955–1962, TV), and which Dahl introduced by commenting, "I ought to warn you if you haven't read any of my stories that you may be a little disturbed by some of the things that happen in them." And like the Hitchcock series, amid the tales of murder, mystery and intrigue, it very occasionally leaned toward the more horrific and fantastical, as with *William and Mary* (1979, TV), which had already been featured as episodes for both 'Way Out (1961, TV) and *Late Night Horror* (1968, TV), in which a professor (Jimmy Mac) volunteers to have his brain preserved after death, only for his wife (Elaine Stritch), who has grown to despise his frugal and controlling ways, to have the last laugh. Other stories in a similar vein included *The Landlady* (1979, TV), previously presented as an episode of *Alfred Hitchcock Presents* (1955–1962, TV), in which the kindly proprietress (Siobhan McKenna) of a small hotel kills and then preserves her guests; *Royal Jelly* (1980, TV), in which a beekeeper (Timothy West) becomes addicted to the royal jelly produced from his hives, with disconcerting side effects for both himself and his newborn baby; and *The Sound Machine* (1981, TV), previously seen as an installment of *CBS Television Workshop* (1952, TV), in which an inventor (Harry Andrews) creates a machine capable of recording even the slightest of sounds, including those made by flowers when they are cut ("I heard them shrieking," he tells a neighbor who has been cutting roses in her garden). However, rather than individual stories, most of which could best be described as time fillers, the series is primarily remembered for its catchy, carnivalesque theme tune by Ron Grainer and its low rent Maurice Binder–style title sequence, complete with colored flames, a spinning roulette wheel, tarot cards and a silhouetted dancing girl.

M.R. James' 1911 story *Casting the Runes*, which had previously been filmed as *Night of the Demon* (1957, aka *Curse of the Demon*) and presented as a 1968 episode of *Mystery and Imagination* (1966–1970, TV), returned to television again in 1979 as an episode of the long running *ITV Playhouse* (1967–1982, TV), which clocked up an incredible 250 episodes during its seemingly endless run. Created by David Nobbs, the series presented comedies and dramas of varying length, and featured new writing by the likes of Alun Owen, Jack Rosenthal and Dennis Potter, as well as adaptations of established works by Terence Rattigan, George Bernard Shaw and Oscar Wilde, whose celebrated 1892 play *Lady Windemere's Fan* (1967, TV) launched the series on 25 September 1967.

In this new version of the James' story by Clive Exton, which was made via Yorkshire TV and transmitted on 24 April 1979, television producer Prudence Dunning (Jan Francis), who has just broadcast a program denigrating the "gallimaufry of mumbo jumbo" surrounding the supernatural, finds herself on the receiving end of the ire of the

THE MAJOR NEW TELEVISION SERIES

ROALD DAHL'S Tales of the Unexpected

Paperback hero. Roald Dahl appears on the cover of this collection of his stories published to tie in with the series *Tales of the Unexpected* (1979–1988, TV) (Copyright: Anglia Television).

"self-styled Abbott of Lufford," an imposing American occultist named Karswell (Iain Cuthbertson), who, ten years earlier, had used diabolical means to see off one John Harrington (Christopher Good) for providing a scathing report to a publishing house denigrating his book *A History of Witchcraft*, in which the demonologist advocates, "Vice is the only true virtue, lust is the only true modesty, indecency the only true decorum and evil the only true good." Having slipped the unfortunate victim a slip of paper bearing runic symbols during a concert, which we later learn blew into a fire, Harrington was subsequently found dead, with almost every bone in his body broken, as Prudence is informed by his brother Henry (Edward Petherbridge), a sculptor who she tracks down after having found a curious message about the death somehow imposed on a tele-cine copy of her program ("One month allowed. In memoriam John Harrington 1937–1968," it reads).

Having herself discovered a similar piece of paper in a book she has borrowed from the Brotherton Library, which Karswell has surreptitiously slipped between its pages, she now begins to fear for her life, but having learned from Karswell's own book that the spell can be broken by passing back the runes, she attempts to turn the tables. "Once you know how it works, you can put the curse back on the sender by giving the piece of paper back to them," she tells her boss (Bernard Gallagher), in whom she has confided, and with whose help she contrives to return the runes before it is too late, first by disguising herself and meeting Karswell at his home, which fails, and later at the airport as he is flying off to Venezuela, which she finally does by passing over the paper in his ticket at the flight desk.

On the whole, this is a generally disappointing take on the story, whose patchwork mix of filmed (location) and videotaped (studio) sequences actively work against it, as does the noticeably low budget. The piece starts well enough with the death of John Harrington in a snow-covered field, pursued by a barely glimpsed figure of demonic aspect, after which it settles down into a fairly routine nick of time thriller, in which Prudence schemes to return the runes. There are a few mildly effective moments along the way, among them Pru's discovery of a giant spider under her bed clothes (mitigated by some cheap special effects which amount to little more than a few rubbery legs), and her face-to-face encounter with Karswell at his home, in which he clearly has the advantage. The final swap at the airport is also nicely handled. However, given that the director was Lawrence Gordon Clark, who had done such sterling work for the BBC's *A Ghost Story for Christmas* (1971–1978, 2005–2021, TV) strand, the film lacks both immediacy and atmosphere, and even at just 47 minutes in length (for a one-hour timeslot) seems overstretched. That it also under uses the Karswell character reduces both the threat and the conflict (in any case, Iain Cuthbertson's decidedly odd accent doesn't help matters), while Jan Francis makes for a fairly watery heroine. Even the supporting players somehow lack vitality, save for a very brief turn by Christine Buckley as Karswell's housekeeper Mrs. Pierce, who we later learn from a local has apparently been dead for nearly three years. Good marks for Peter Jackson's location photography, particularly during the wintry opening sequence (Jackson had already worked with Clark on several episodes of *Flambards* [1979, TV], and would do so again on the glossy *Romance on the Orient Express* [1985, TVM]), but as much as one wants to rate the program as a lost treasure, it doesn't quite make the mark, though as a typical production of its time, it is otherwise perfectly adequate. Finally, a brief word for all of the unfortunate passengers killed along with Karswell when his plane mysteriously goes down in the Bristol Channel. Revenge, it seems, has consequences of its own.

Department 7, a secret government organization created to investigate and experiment in paranormal phenomena, was the focus of *The Omega Factor* (1979, TV), a ten-part series which sees journalist Tom Crane (James Hazeldine), who is fascinated by the occult, persuaded to join their ranks thanks to his own dormant supernatural abilities, on the understanding that he can use the department's resources to exact revenge on a powerful, Karswell-like Satanist named Edward Drexel (Cyril Luckham), whom a fellow occultist describes as "the man that Crowley wouldn't meet, just in case," and who was responsible for the death of his wife in a car crash. He also finds himself investigating Omega, an organization whose agenda appears to be to take over the world via mind control. Created by Jack Gerson and produced by George Gallaccio via BBC Scotland, the series, which was shot on videotape, began airing on 13 June 1979, and also starred John Carlisle as the department's head Dr. Roy Martindale, and Louise Jameson as fellow colleague Dr. Anne Reynolds. A rather slow moving and humorless affair with a surfeit of chat in flatly lit sets, with Hazeldine looking dour throughout (as well he might), the series was a typical studio production of its period, and its 50-minute episodes are now something of a chore to endure, despite storylines involving séances, witches, poltergeists and hallucinations.

Rather more enjoyable, thanks to better writing and some lucky casting, was *Sapphire and Steel* (1979–1982, TV), an equally low-budget enterprise that nevertheless managed to overcome its shortcomings to provide an engaging and entertaining blend of science fiction, mystery and mild horror, plus a nod to the time and place writings of J.B. Priestley. In it, Joanna Lumley and David McCallum star as the title characters, interdimensional operatives whose mission is to secure the continuing flow of time and prevent evil forces from penetrating any weaknesses, in which task they are occasionally aided and abetted by Lead (Val Pringle) and Silver (David Collings). Created by Peter Hammond, who also penned many of the scripts (with additional contributions by Anthony Read and Don Houghton), the series was produced by Shaun O'Riordan, who also directed 24 of the 34 episodes, and the four-season run of half-hour programs proved to be an early evening hit when broadcast twice a week (Tuesdays and Thursdays) on the ITV network from 10 July 1979.

Divided into assignments lasting several episodes each (ranging between four and eight), *Assignment One* (1979, TV) sees the duo investigate the disappearance of a boy's parents after singing nursery rhymes to his younger sister while putting her to bed, at which point all the clocks in the house stopped. However, rather than the police, it is the mysterious Sapphire and Steel who turn up to investigate the disappearance, which is somehow connected to the time when the house was built, its foundation stone (which bears the inscription "Jed Mace 2 February 1736"), the nursery rhyme "Ring a Ring o' Roses," and three sinister pools of light. A complex, studio bound story which takes its time in establishing the characters and situations, it set the tone for what was to follow, yet for audiences who could adjust to its pace, it proved to be riveting stuff. The dramatic theme tune by Cyril Ornadel and the opening titles set against a moving starscape

Cool customers. Joanna Lumley and David McCallum feature in this ad for the *Sapphire and Steel* ice lolly (ITC/Lyons Maid).

featuring animated graphics of Gold, Lead, Copper, Jet, Diamond, Radium, Sapphire, Silver and Steel were also a bonus ("Sapphire and Steel have been assigned," intones the narrator at the end of the sequence).

Assignment Two (1979, TV) proved to be one of the show's most memorable stories, and featured a haunted railway station which is being used as a recruiting ground for the dead, who are controlled by a living darkness (note that this story was interrupted by a long running strike after just three episodes, which were subsequently repeated when the series finally went back on air almost three months later). *Assignment Three* (1981, TV), which contained some filmed sequences, involved the investigation of an apartment block on top of which is situated an invisible time capsule from 1,500 years in the future, while *Assignment Four* (1981, TV) focused on a pawn shop haunted by children from old photographs in the thrall of a man with no face. *Assignment Five* (1981, TV) sees the duo gatecrash a party at a country house with a 1930s theme, only to find themselves investigating a number of Agatha Christie–style murders, while the final story, *Assignment Six* (1982, TV), finds them at a gas station where time initially seems to be stuck at 8:54 p.m., and where they are visited by people from other periods, including 1925, 1948 and 1957. The series ends with our heroes trapped in the building, floating through space forever. Popular with both adults and younger audiences, the program was featured on a number of magazine covers, including *TV Times* and *Look-In* (which also ran a picture strip featuring the characters), had a paperback novelization of the first series published by Star Books in 1979 by Peter Hammond, and its own annual published by World International in 1980 featuring such stories as *Rogue Robot* and *Chamber of Horrors*. The ultimate accolade, however, was that the show had a Lyons Maid ice-lolly named after it, all for the princely sum of 10p ("Cool blue raspberry ice on a real stainless steel stick!" ran the colorful ad, which also urged kids to "Buy one now… Before time runs out!!").

An Old Master

Just as the decade had ended on a highpoint in America with *Salem's Lot* (1979, TVM), so it did in the UK with *Schalcken the Painter* (1979, TVM). A pet project for its writer-director Leslie Megahey, it was based upon the 1839 story *Strange Event in the Life of Schalken* [sic] *the Painter* by Sheridan Le Fanu. Megahy originally offered the idea to the BBC in 1976. However, when the Head of Music and Arts suggested it as a possible entry for the corporation's Christmas ghost story strand, which was the province of director Lawrence Gordon Clark, he elected to hold onto it, given that he wanted to helm it himself. Providence eventually smiled upon him when he was offered the job of overseeing the BBC's respected arts series *Omnibus* (1967–2003, TV), whose mix of music programs and documentaries had already seen the broadcast of such docu-dramas as Ken Russell's *Dante's Inferno* (1967, TVM), which opens with the recovery of a book of poems from the grave of Elizabeth Siddal, as well as an adaptation of M.R. James' *Whistle and I'll Come to You* (1968, TV), which had effectively launched the annual ghost story. On the understanding that being able to make a couple of his own films was part of the deal, Megahey signed on as series editor for *Omnibus*, and in the process secured additional funding for *Schalcken* from the German company R.M. (Reiner Moritz) Productions, which allowed him a certain artistic freedom from the Beeb's watchful eye, given that the project was now a co-production. As he had already made documentaries for the BBC on such figures as Gauguin and Rodin, Megahey was able to legitimately pitch *Schalcken* as a dramatized arts lecture, given that it was based upon the life of a real painter, albeit one that takes a disturbing turn. To this end, the film opens with the caption "This fictional story is based on the real paintings of Godfried Schalcken (1643–1706)," following which the narrator (Charles Gray) proffers a brief biographical history of the artist and his work, finally alighting on a picture of a young woman holding candle in the chamber of an "antique religious building." But the picture has more to reveal than a first glance might suggest, at which we segue into the story.

Set in Leiden in 1665, it begins with Schalcken (Jeremy Clyde) learning his craft as a student at the home of the curmudgeonly Gerrit Dou (Maurice Denham), whose niece Rose Velderkaust (Cheryl Kennedy) he falls for during his studies ("In short, Godfried Schalcken was in love … as much as any Dutchman *can* be," the narrator casually informs us). However, when a mysterious figure named Vanderhausen of Rotterdam (John Justin) appears one evening when Schalcken is working late, requesting to meet Dou the following night on "A matter of some weight," it transpires that the nobleman wishes to marry Rose, having seen her in the Church of St. Lawrence, to which end he offers the old man a dowry of gold coins. Given the irresistible value of the dowry, and that his niece is a chattel to dispose of as he pleases, as was the custom of the time, Dou agrees to the marriage ("The unfortunate girl was simply the object of a contract," we are told), and, unbeknownst to her, Rose is introduced to her future husband at a dinner soon after ("Trick yourself out handsomely, now," her uncle advises her). Unfortunately, Rose is less than impressed by the wealthy gentleman caller and, like him, doesn't touch her food, albeit for a different reason. "What a terrible creature. I could never look on that face again for all the wealth of the states," she informs her uncle after Vanderhausen has left, only to learn that her fate has already been sealed (intones the narrator, "I have no sentimental scenes to describe, no exquisite details of the cruelty of a guardian, no agonies or transports of lovers. The record I have to make is one of heartlessness, nothing more. The contract was signed and settlements made even more splendid that Dou ever dreamed of"). Like Rose, Schalcken is equally aghast, and vows to buy back the contract when he is wealthy enough to do so ("I'll buy it back double," he tells Rose), but as the days following the wedding pass, he finds that the impulse of love instead gives way to that of ambition.

After the marriage ceremony, Vanderhausen and his bride disappear, and nothing is heard from them during the following months, to the point that Dou, worried, sends Schalcken to Rotterdam to seek them out, but despite his best efforts, the young painter is unable to track the couple down, and instead ends up consoling himself with a visit to a brothel. Upon his return to Leiden, life returns to normal, and as the years pass, Schalcken's reputation grows to outstrip that of the now aged and infirm Dou, who continues to keep close company with his former pupil through sheer loneliness. Consequently, both are together in Dou's home examining the accounts, when Rose unexpectedly arrives one night in a state of hysteria and dishevelment, craving wine and food and a minister of God ("The dead and the living can never be one," she moans as Schalcken takes her upstairs to the safety of a bedroom). She begs not to be left alone, but in getting a light as she requests for fear of the dark, he is forced to leave her momentarily, at which point the bedroom door slams shut, following which there is a piercing scream, and Rose again is gone.

By now in his late thirties, Schalcken marries Francoise van Dimen de Breda (Amanda Carlson), a girl from a rich merchant's family, and settles into a life of domesticity, and such is his fame that he is even able to imperiously turn down portrait commissions, save one from a particularly wealthy gentleman (Anthony Sharp), who persuades him to paint his daughter at play with her beloved doll (money, it seems, is the master of art as well as that of the heart). It is following the death of Dou and Schalcken's attending of his funeral at the Church of St. Lawrence that the story reaches its conclusion. As the narrator informs us, "Some impulse stronger than mere curiosity led him to the door of the church vaults," inside which, much to his astonishment, he encounters Rose, who beckons him to follow her. However, what at first appears to be a benign encounter turns to horror when she pulls back a drape to reveal the spectral Vanderhausen sitting up in what appears to be a bed. Seemingly rooted to the spot and unable to escape the scene, Schalcken looks on in horror as Rose removes her nightshift and, naked, mounts her husband in carnal bliss. Waking on the floor of the now empty vault, Schalcken discovers the bed to be a tomb bearing the inscription "United with his beloved wife." At this we cut to the painting we had seen earlier, that of a young damsel in a crypt (the picture was actually created for the film by artist Paul Martin in the style of Schalcken, as was that of the portrait of the young girl and her doll). Behind the girl, a young man is drawing his sword, while in the shadows lurks "some form," as we had been earlier told. Intones the narrator, "To this day, Schalcken was convinced of the reality of the vision he had witnessed, and he left behind this picture as testimony to it," following which he concludes, "And apart from the story I have told you, which was passed down through the mouths of my father and his father's father, there is no other record of this mysterious romance in the life of Schalcken the painter."

"Turn from the light," Schalcken instructs a model as he sets a scene for his canvas in the pre-credits sequence of this immaculately presented anecdote, and it is the revelation of that which lies half out of sight, lurking in the shadows, that provides the various frissons in this perfectly realized blend of fact, fiction and nightmare. With its ravishing period settings care of production designer Anna Ridley (whose best work this proved to be), its impeccably detailed costumes by Christine Rawlins and its Vermeer-like lighting by film cameraman John Hooper (a Megahey regular), *Schalcken* is as much enjoyable for its historically authentic appearance as it is for the scholarly telling of its macabre story, which begins in the form of an arts lecture before gradually drawing us into its chilling tale of avarice, betrayal and revenge. With its minimal dialogue ("Still life drawing, one hour, begin," Dou belligerently instructs his students), much is left to the narrator to instill, and it is to this end that the casting of Charles Gray was a masterstroke, his mellifluous, delightfully blasé tones adding immeasurably to the piece (though it should be noted that both Vincent Price and Peter Cushing were considered for this key off camera role), and it is from him that we learn that "the mantle of romance does hang a little ungracefully upon the form of Godfried Schalcken," that he would grow to become "a boorish man of great ambition, foul temper and few manners," and that his later work "seems to have it roots in some private world of dreams, perhaps never otherwise expressed."

Megahey's control of the film is accomplished throughout, particularly with regard to the scrupulous formality of the framing and composition, in which he was inspired by director Walerian Borowczyk's film *Blanche* (1971) and such works as Vermeer's *Art of Painting*, elements from which are lovingly and painstakingly reproduced. Among the many highlights are the early scenes in which the students are seen sketching the studies Dou sets for them; the arrival of the spectral Vanderhausen, who is first revealed, via a slight camera dolly, to be standing in the gloom behind Schalcken as he paints; the dinner at which Rose is introduced to Vanderhausen, whose alarmingly pallid appearance we finally get to see in close-up (the meal's various courses include a far from appetizing serving of oysters, mussels and salmon that is worthy of a pictorial study itself); and the final vision in the crypt, as Vanderhausen sits up in his bed and Rose mounts him, the horror of which Schalcken is unable to escape, his legs seemingly held to the floor by an invisible force. The film also benefits from being punctuated by a number of sly touches that add immeasurably to the overall ambience, among them a blink-and-you'll-miss-it self portrait-style cameo appearance by Rembrandt (Charles Stewart), and a Val Lewton-esque moment as Schalcken, while looking for Rose in Rotterdam, unexpectedly backs into a carriage horse whose snort gives him (and us) an unexpected fright. Sound is also well used throughout, from the scratching of quills and the heavy chink of money to the unsettling creak of floorboards which precede each appearance of the spectral Vanderhausen, while the editing of Paul Humfress (who also worked as Megahey's script associate), though sharp and clean, never forces the pace, instead embracing the carefully modulated telling of the story.

Tales from the crypt. John Justin as the spectral Vanderhausen in *Schalcken the Painter* (1979, TVM) (BBC/RM Productions).

As the irascible and avaricious Dou, Maurice Denham, who inhabits his costumes as though born to them, undoubtedly gives the best performance, which varies from the vague to the dismissive, depending with whom his character is interacting (note that Arthur Lowe was considered for the role). A slightly blanker canvas is Jeremy Clyde as Schalcken, whose heart grows harder as the story progresses, while Cheryl Kennedy is pretty as a picture as the unfortunate Rose. By contrast, John Justin is a hideous sight indeed as the spectral Vanderhausen thanks to Jean Steward's death's head make-up, and the creak of the floorboards heralding each of his appearances carries a definite chill of anticipation. All the supporting roles are well cast for the quality of their faces, most notably Victor Dear as Dou's manservant, Ann Tirard as the brothel's madam, and Val Penny as Schalcken's most frequent model, taken from the streets, bathed and dressed in finery for his compositions, among them Lesbia holding a scale bearing her pet sparrow which proves heavier than the jewels with which it is balanced. Broadcast at 10:55 p.m. on BBC1 on 23 December 1979, *Schalcken the Painter* was a more than suitable one-off replacement for the annual Christmas ghost story, which had concluded its run the previous year, and to which it is a more than worthy companion piece, given its artistic and literary ambitions.

SECTION SIX

New Realms
(the 1980s)

Hammer Has Risen from the Grave

Having ended the seventies on something of a high on both sides of the Atlantic, TV horror continued to be a staple in the schedules, even if it didn't always quite reach the heights of its glory days during the previous two decades, though this didn't mean that quality genre programming wasn't still being made. The first series of real note to be produced in the new decade came care of the legendary British horror studio Hammer, whose previous ventures into television had already produced the one-off *Tales of Frankenstein* (1958, TV) and the 17-part series *Journey to the Unknown* (1968, TV). The company's last theatrical feature had been a remake of *The Lady Vanishes* (1979), following which it had been declared insolvent. However, producers Roy Skeggs and Brian Lawrence were able to resurrect the name via their own company Cinema Arts International, having licensed it from ICI, the idea being to pay off the company's debts through the international sales of a new 13-part anthology series titled *Hammer House of Horror* (1980, TV, originally to have been *The House of Hammer*), which began airing on the ITV network on 13 September 1980.

Running to 50 minutes per episode for a one-hour timeslot, the shows offered a tried and tested mix of witchcraft, lycanthropy and possession, and made sure to make use of such familiar Hammer faces as Peter Cushing, John Carson, Philip Latham, Robert Urquhart and Barbara Ewing, as well as such recognized behind-the-scenes talent as directors Don Sharp, Alan Gibson, Robert Young and Peter Sasdy, composer James Bernard and writer Anthony Hinds (working under his usual pen name of John Elder). To finance the series Roy Skeggs (who produced) and Brian Lawrence (who executive produced with David Reid) approached Lew Grade, who provided financing through ITC Entertainment, as did Jack Gill via Chips Productions ("Jack Gill Presents," ran the opening credit). As a cost saving measure, the series, which was shot entirely on 35mm, was filmed in and around the environs of Hampden House in Buckinghamshire, which also acted as the show's production base, and also provided the backdrop for its memorable title sequence, in which a lone figure can be seen lurking on the battlements and peering through a leaded window to the strains of Roger Webb's memorable theme tune (for which the composer didn't even rate a credit).

The series, for which a two-week filming schedule was allotted to each episode, began well with *Witching Time* (1980, TV), in which film composer David Winter (Jon Finch) is visited by Lucinda Jessop (Patricia Quinn), a buxom 17th-century witch who used live in the farmhouse which he now occupies. Increasingly possessive of him ("I've put my mark on you forever and ever, amen"), she proceeds to make his life a misery, much to the consternation David's wife Mary (Prunella Gee), who finds herself in mortal combat with Lucinda, whom she finally dispatches with the aid of a bucket of water during the fiery climax ("Water—so *that's* what you can't take! I should have known!"). Written by Anthony Read (who also worked the series' story editor) and directed with reasonable zest by Don Leaver (who played the lone figure in the show's title sequence), the program benefits from a solid score care of Hammer stalwart James Bernard and good performances from its well chosen cast, particularly Quinn as the mischievous witch, who isn't above disrobing to achieve her aims ("Is that the body of a ghost?" she asks David at one point, having grabbed his hand and placed it upon her breast). Commented the *Daily Mail* of the opener, "With its canny mixture of sex and the supernatural, Hammer may have hit the nail on the head."

The second episode, *The Thirteenth Reunion* (1980, TV), is equally good, and sees Ruth Cairns (Julia Foster), a crusading lady journalist, investigate a weight loss program at the Chesterton Clinic, where she discovers dubious things going on, among them an illicit association with the local undertakers to provide bodies for the monthly dinner parties attended by survivors of a plane crash in the Atlas Mountains, who had to resort to cannibalism before eventually being found and rescued. Inadvertently gate crashing the 13th of these reunions, Ruth consequently finds herself on the receiving end of a meat cleaver wielded by the clinic's PE instructor (James Cosmo), who proves to be in on things ("I was on that plane as well," he informs her). Macabre fun directed with flair by Peter Sasdy from an amusing teleplay by Jeremy Burnham, the program's chief asset is its strong cast of supporting players, among them Dinah Sheridan as Ruth's editor, Warren Clarke as a fellow guest at the clinic with whom she has a brief romance, and whose body she later identifies from her phone number, which she had written on the back of his hand, and Richard Pearson as Sir Humphrey Chesterton, the jovial host of the dinner party, whose guests include a down-to-earth Bolton woman played with flat-voweled aplomb by Barbara Keogh.

Even better was *Rude Awakening* (1980, TV), in which a seedy estate agent, Norman Shenley (Denholm Elliott), finds himself caught up in a series of *Dead of Night*-style nightmares from which he seemingly cannot awaken, and which climax with him, under the impression that he is still dreaming, confessing to the police that his frumpy wife (Pat Heywood) lies dead at home. "I suppose I should have been surprised that she was found so quickly, but I'm not. It seems there's no sense of time in dreams," he says, adding, "But I'll tell you one thing—do you know, it was all in color!" With a highly engaging central performance from the always reliable Elliott, who becomes increasingly confused as things spiral out of his control, the story features a number of wild scenarios, including sequences in a stately home, during one of which his wife's body falls out of the dumb waiter, the demolition of a building in which he and his secretary enter by mistake, and an operation scene in which he finds himself undergoing brain surgery. Written with tongue-in-cheek fun by Gerald Savory and directed with flair by Peter Sasdy, the episode's supporting cast also seem to be having fun, among them James Laurenson, who appears in a variety of roles, including a tramp, a butler and a surgeon, Lucy Gutteridge as Shenley's secretary Lolly, and Eleanor Summerfield as the rather grand Lady Strudwick, whom he encounters during one of his visits to Lower Moat Manor ("I can't help you, Mr. Shenley," she says to him when things again take a turn for the macabre, adding, "You see, I'm dead—aren't you?").

The series unfortunately took a dive here, and the following episodes were something of a mixed bag, suffering from half baked ideas and padding, among them *Growing Pains* (1980, TV), in which a couple (Gary Bond and Barbara Kellerman) adopt a morbid child (Matthew Blakstad) following the death of their own boy; *The House That Bled to Death* (1980, TV), in which a young couple (Nicholas Ball and Rachel Davies) collude with an estate agent (Milton Johns) to make it appear that their house is haunted so that a bestselling *Amityville*-style book can be written about it (the episode is best remembered for a pipe gushing out blood during a children's birthday party); *Charlie Boy* (1980, TV), in which a young man (Leigh Lawson) inherits a voodoo doll from his late uncle, which leads to a number of strange deaths; and *The Silent Scream* (1980, TV), in which an ex-con (Brian Cox) goes to work for an eccentric pet shop owner (Peter Cushing) who has a menagerie of wild animals in his basement which he is training to live in zoos without cages by way of using deadly electronic beams instead of bars.

Things improved somewhat with *Children of the Full Moon* (1980, TV), in which a couple (Christopher Cazenove and Celia Gregory) who have crashed their car while on a delayed honeymoon take refuge with a West Country matriarch (Diana Dors) with a strange brood of children whose father, the local woodcutter (Jacob Witkin), turns out to be a werewolf (this episode is best remembered for the unexpected shock appearance of the werewolf at the couple's bedroom window). The series then took a tumble for the worse again with *Carpathian Eagle* (1980, TV), in which an authoress (Suzanne Danielle) becomes obsessed with a serial killer she is researching, to the point that she carries on her bloody legacy (among her victims being a very young Pierce Brosnan), but picked up again with *Guardian of the Abyss* (1980, TV), a story about an antiques dealer (Ray Lonnen) who becomes involved with Satanism in the Home Counties after his friend (Barbara Ewing) buys a "scrying glass" at an auction house. With a better script than usual by David Fisher and stylish direction care of Don Sharp, this showed what really could be achieved in genre television if the elements were right. Again, a good supporting cast certainly helps matters here, among the Rosalyn Landor as a damsel in distress who proves not to be quite so in distress, John Carson as the leader of the Devil worshipping Choronzon Society, and Paul Darrow as a fellow antiques dealer keen to have the strange mirror for himself.

The series then plumbed new depths with *Visitor from the Grave* (1980, TV), in which an apparently devoted husband (Simon MacCorkindale) attempts to drive his wealthy American wife (Kathryn Leigh Scott) to suicide so that he can get his hands on her money, only for her return as a ghost to extract revenge. Penned by former Hammer producer Anthony Hinds (writing as John Elder), the episode recalls the studio's "mini Hitchcocks" of the sixties, but is put over in such a slapdash manner that its incompetence quickly becomes contemptuous (when the husband says of the wife's money, "I couldn't care less about it," his true intentions immediately become apparent). Much better was *The Two Faces of Evil* (1980, TV), in which a family vacation turns into a nightmare when, after giving a sinister hitchhiker a lift, they are involved in a car crash. Unfortunately, having recovered from their injuries, the wife (Anna Calder-Marshall) ends up taking home from the hospital an evil

Daddy's home. Jacob Witkin appears to have been cutting down something other than trees in *Children of the Full Moon* (1980, TV) from *Hammer House of Horror* (1980, TV) (ITC/ACC/Hammer Film Productions/Cinema Arts International Productions/Chips Productions).

doppelganger who looks just like her husband (Gary Raymond). With a well devised story care of writer Ranald Graham and some surprisingly stylish moments of direction care of Alan Gibson (who even makes use of the famous track and reverse zoom shot used in *Vertigo* [1958] and *Jaws* [1975] at one point), this is undoubtedly one of the series' strongest episodes, with a well-staged car crash and some genuinely disturbing moments thereafter involving the evil doppelganger, whose discolored teeth and pointed fingernail are not easily forgotten. Sadly, the show came to something of a disappointing conclusion with *The Mask of Satan* (1980, TV), in which a paranoid mortuary attendant (Peter McEnery) becomes obsessed with the number nine, which he begins to see everywhere, and convinces himself that evil forces are attempting to take over his life, as indeed they are. With a padded script by Don Shaw and flat direction care of Don Leaver, this was certainly a less than stellar way to end things.

The hope had been that a second series would follow, and indeed plans were already afoot for filming to resume in January 1981, but these were scuttled when financial support from ITC dried up following the box office failure of *Raise the Titanic* (1980). Instead, Roy Skeggs and Brian Lawrence turned their sights to America and Twentieth Century–Fox in particular, which had not only distributed many of Hammer's films in the U.S. but had also bankrolled *Journey to the Unknown* (1968, TV). On the understanding that the emphasis would be on suspense rather than horror, Fox committed $4 million to the new series, which would go by the title *Hammer House of Mystery and Suspense* (1984, TVM), whose 13 episodes, likewise shot on 35mm, would this time run to 75 minutes for a 90-minute timeslot. Again, several members of Hammer's old guard were onboard, among them directors John Hough, Peter Sasdy and Val Guest, and actors Stephanie Beacham, Patrick Mower and Isla Blair, while the Hollywood connection ensured that a number of American stars were signed to the series to give it appeal in the States, among them Dirk Benedict, David Carradine, Mary Crosby, Carol Lynley, Dean Stockwell, Shirley Knight and Peter Graves, the latter of whom also filmed introductions for the American market, where the show was known as *Fox Mystery Theater*. Other British actors involved included Susan George, David McCallum, Oliver Tobias, Jenny Seagrove, Nicholas Clay and Peter Wyngarde.

Despite the emphasis on thrills and mystery, the series, which Skeggs again produced and Lawrence executive produced, did occasionally involve more fantastical storylines, among them the opening episode, *Mark of the Devil* (1984, TVM), which aired on ITV on 5 September 1984. In it, a corrupt London based American businessman (Dirk Benedict) in need of money to pay off a mobster murders a Chinese tattooist and sometime witchdoctor (Burk Kwouk) for his money, only for a tattoo to grow on his body depicting his various crimes, the result of being pricked by the Chinaman's knife during their fight over the stash. Flatly directed by Val Guest from a poor script by the usually reliable by Brian Clemens, this was arrant nonsense of the tallest order, and might have passed muster as a half-hour episode of *Tales of the Unexpected* (1979–1988, TV), but at this length is tedious beyond endurance. Similarly scuppered by over length was *A Distant Scream* (1984, TVM), in which a prisoner (David Carradine) accused of murdering his lover (Stephanie Beacham) during a holiday in Cornwall many years earlier revisits the events in his mind so as to find out who really committed the crime, inserting himself into the action as his older self in order to do so, much to the shock of his lover and the hotel staff, who believe they are seeing a ghost of some kind. Unfortunately, although well enough handled by director John Hough, who makes good use of the bleak cliff top settings and the constantly crashing waves below, the teleplay by Martin Worth (previously filmed as an episode of *Out of the Unknown* [1965–1971, TV] titled *The Last Witness* [1971, TV]) is rather too convoluted for its own good, and is further compromised by some slushy Mills & Boon-style dialogue exchanges between the two lovers.

Other episodes that leant towards the supernatural included *In Possession* (1984, TVM), in which a couple (Christopher Cazenove and Carol Lynley) about to leave their home for a life new life in Botswana share what appear to be a series of flashbacks in which an old man plans to murder his wife, only for them to realize that they are witnessing events involving their flat's future tenants; *Black Carrion* (1984, TVM), in which a journalist (Leigh Lawson) is sent to track down the Verne Brothers (Allan Love and Julian Littman), a popular singing duo from the sixties who disappeared without trace, only to discover a bizarre plot involving a "ghost" village and the corpse of one of the brothers; and *The Corvini Inheritance* (1984, TVM), in which an auction house security expert (David McCallum), who has been stalking his neighbor (Jan Francis), is charged with overseeing the arrival of a priceless collection of gems from Italy, the necklace of which is said to change color if its wearer is guilty of infidelity. Sadly, dull scripting, lackluster direction and over length combined with indifferent performances make all of them something of a chore to sit through.

Rather better was *And the Wall Came Tumbling Down* (1984, TVM), in which a young Londoner (Brian Deacon) finds his life being influenced by a former incarnation, that of a 17th-century Satanist who betrayed his coven to the authorities, and who was bricked up in an alcove in the de-sanctified church in which they worshipped as a consequence, along with the coven's enigmatic leader (Peter Wyngarde), who plans to return in a new age to wreak revenge on the world. With the action switching between the past and the present, this is a reasonably intriguing installment, with the added twist that the coven's leader has been reincarnated as an army general intent on unleashing a nuclear holocaust. With a solid script by Dennis Spooner and assured handling care of director Paul Arnett, it manages to fill out its running time without the appearance of the padding that blighted so many of the other episodes. A true test of endurance was the series' penultimate episode, *Child's Play* (1984, TVM), a ridiculous science fiction piece in which a young couple (Nicholas Clay and Mary Crosby) and their daughter (Debbie Chasan) find themselves inexplicably trapped in their house. However, it transpires that the family are in fact miniature robot dolls, and that the house they live in has been placed in a heating duct by the mischievous brother of its owner ("Mummy—Rudy hid my house in that heating duct and it scraped all the sides. And he didn't even turn the dolls off"). Silly beyond belief, it proved to be the final film of its well-regarded director Val Guest, who certainly deserved better a better swan song.

Thankfully, the series went out on a comparatively high note with *Tennis Court* (1984, TVM), a rather silly story about a haunted tennis court which was nevertheless given some visual panache thanks to the work of director Cyril Frankel and his cameraman Frank Watts, who make good use of a number of eye-catching tilted shots during the more dramatic moments. Written by Andrew Sinclair from a story by Michael Hastings, it sees Maggie Dowl and her husband Harry (Hannah Gordon and Jonathan Newth) move into a large country house given to them by Maggie's mother (Isla Blair), and it quickly becomes apparent that the indoor tennis court is haunted by a malevolent spirit which not only possesses the players but also displays increasingly violent signs of paranormal activity. The explanation involves Maggie's real father (Peter Graves), the local priest, who was unable to pull his friend from a burning aircraft during the war. The man, who Maggie assumed was her father, didn't die, as Maggie believed, and is still being cared for in a home, where he has built up such resentment that it is now manifesting itself in the tennis court where the two friends used to play with Maggie's mother. Roy Skeggs had originally hoped to make the story as a theatrical feature under the rather more explanatory title *The Haunted Tennis Court*, but it makes for a fine climax to a series that was, at best, a very hit and miss affair.

Over on the BBC, it was a *Jackanory*-style series aimed at older children titled *Spine Chillers* (1980, TV) that launched the corporation's commitment to genre TV in the eighties. Running to 20 episodes, the ten-minute programs, which opened with a stylishly animated black and white sequence set in a gloomy hallway, presented a selection of stories of fear and imagination, among them *The Red Room* by H.G. Wells, *The Mezzotint* by M.R. James, *A Sin of Omission* by R. Chetwynd-Hayes and *The Hounds of Fate* by Saki. Produced by Angela Beeching, they began airing on 17 November 1980 on BBC1 in a 17:25 slot, and were expertly told by Freddie Jones, Jonathan Pryce, John Woodvine and Michael Bryant, who took on five episodes each. However, given their dark nature, they inevitably resulted in complaints from concerned parents worried that their children might suffer sleepless nights as a consequence of tuning in, having been alerted to the program's content firsthand while waiting for the evening news to begin at 17:40 ("Not for the nervous!" warned the listing in the *Radio Times*).

The Beeb's first major genre production of the decade for adults proved to be a new feature-length adaptation of Robert Louis Stevenson's *Dr. Jekyll and Mr. Hyde* (1980, TVM), which appeared on BBC2 on 20 November 1980 (its first U.S. showing followed a couple of months later on 6 January 1981). This time it's David Hemmings who stars as the respectable Victorian scientist who concocts a drug to split the twin sides of human nature so that he can be left "to do the good works to which I have dedicated my life," as he puts it, only to find his character becoming increasingly dominated by his evil alter ego. A videotaped studio production with filmed inserts, the talent involved clearly marked it out as a prestige production, but with a running time just five minutes short of two hours, it becomes something of a chore, given the familiarity of the material, no doubt hence the occasional diversion from the original story care of adaptor Gerald Savory, which sees the middle-aged Jekyll transform into a handsome young gadabout gradually corrupted by the seamier offerings of London's night scene, the first of which is an uncomfortable encounter with a 14-year-old flower seller (Anna Faye) who is down on her luck ("Well, Mary, now you take off all your clothes and I'll tell you what I'm going to do to you"), which he follows with similar experiences with a maid (Toyah Wilcox) and a rent boy (Ashley Knight). Produced by Jonathan Powell in conjunction with Time-Life and the Australian Broadcasting Commission, the drama was directed in a somewhat somnambulant fashion by Alastair Reid and accompanied by an irritating synth score written and performed by Dave Greeslade, with supporting turns provided by Lisa Harrow, Clive Swift, Ian Bannen, Roland Curram, Gretchen Franklin, Ben Arris, Terry Downes, Desmond Llewelyn and Diana Dors. Yet despite its pedigree and a strong performance by Hemmings, it's undoubtedly on the dull side.

Frissons of a more genteel nature could be found in *Miss Morison's Ghosts* (1981, TVM). Produced by John Rosenberg via Anglia Television for broadcast on the ITV network, it was based upon the 1911 memoir *An Adventure* by Charlotte Anne Moberly and Eleanor Jourdain, writing as Elizabeth Morison and Frances Lamont, in which they claim to have seen Marie Antoinette (Anna Korwin) and others, as well as a cottage and pavilion from the same period, while strolling through the grounds of Versailles in 1901, an event that came to be known as the Moberly-Jourdain incident ("This story is based on actual events that began in Oxford in 1901," the opening caption informs us). "Who do you suppose they were, those people?" asks Miss Morison once they have returned to their hotel rooms, to which her companion replies, "I thought perhaps there was to be a fancy dress parade or *tableaux vivant*." However, when Miss Morison urges Miss Lamont to return to the gardens to find evidence of their sightings, she can find no trace of what they have seen, and the gardens themselves appear to be completely different than those they had wandered through ("It seems to me quite clear that on the day we saw those strange people, we were either mistaken as to the route we took, or we followed paths which it is no longer possible to follow, though how or why this can be I do not know," she writes to Miss Morison, who has by now returned to Oxford).

Written by Ian Curteis and directed by John Bruce, the film stars Wendy Hiller as Miss Morrison, the principal of St. Gilbert's College, and Hannah Gordon as Miss Lamont, who has just been appointed vice principal, and who has agreed to accompany her superior on a trip to Paris to cement their working relationship. Although it benefits from location work in both Oxford and Versailles, this is a rather talkative and slow moving affair which, with a running time of one hour and 40 minutes for a two-hour timeslot, proves to be too much of a good thing by its conclusion, but it is pleasantly enough photographed by Richard Crafter, and Hiller and Gordon (perfectly attired by costume designer Annie McGugan) spark well off each other, particularly when their relationship becomes more strained during the subsequent fallout the case engenders. Able support is meanwhile provided by Bosco Holder as the Rev. Oliver Hodgson, the college's visiting chaplain who makes his own trip to Versailles to investigate the matter, and Vivian Pickles as Dr. Celia Hadley, the research officer for the Society of Psychical Research (note that many of the film's production personnel worked for its executive producer John Woolf on the series *Tales of the Unexpected* [1979–1988, TV], on which Hiller had also guested).

A rather more oddball affair was *Unfair Exchanges* (1985, TVM), which aired on BBC2 on 20 January 1985 as part of the strand *Screen Two* (1985–2002, TVM) following a showing at the London Film Festival on 29 November 1984. In it, Julie Walters plays Mavis Potter, a single mum who finds herself subjected to a number of strange phone calls, the first of them from her ex, Ronnie (Robert Kingswell), who later claims he never made the call. But odd things continue to happen with Mavis's phone, leading her to wonder if there is some kind of conspiracy going on with the phone system ("The telephone network: is it a brain?" ponders a newspaper headline). However, things take a dark turn when she discovers that one of her neighbors, thought to have been away, has in fact been burnt to a crisp while on the telephone, which prompts her to escape to the home of her widowed father (Joe Black), but the calls follow her there, and now take the form of maniacal laughter. Having informed the phone company, they decide to monitor the line, and when the prankster calls again, she is shocked when they break into the call to tell her, "Get out of the house immediately, that laugh's coming from the extension!" but when she returns inside with an axe for protection, the house is empty save for her sleeping son (George Lapham). That she ends up having a conversation with herself on the phone proves to be the unnerving climax, which pushes her over the edge and sends her out into the night to snip off all the phone receivers in the neighborhood call boxes and break into the local exchange to rip out the wiring system.

Written by Ken Campbell from an idea by Ion Will, the film is almost determinedly quirky in its ideas and plotting, which proves to be both intriguing and frustrating in equal measure, particularly in scenes where background noise and other distractions are used to further obfuscate matters, yet despite its smoke and mirrors approach, presumably employed to disguise the fact that under close inspection the plot doesn't really hang together, the piece has many excellent sequences, and the central conceit that the phone system has somehow become sentient and is taking over the world is certainly a good one if one can swallow it, given the archaic technology of the period. The film is also chock full of interesting characters and cameos, among them Mavis's ex, who is now gay and living with another man in Brighton, a dwarf (David Rappaport) who lives in the flat downstairs from her and with whom she has an affair, her dad, who spends most of his time stripping all the paper and plasterwork from the walls of his house, and a songwriter (Ken Campbell) who has written a pop song called *I Ring Therefore I Am*, and who has various theories about the phone system ("It's got access to all the computer knowledge of the world; no one knows exactly what the world telephone network is, only *it* knows," he explains at one point). Produced by Kenith Trodd and directed with an eye for the wry touch by Gavin Millar, this is a curious little drama which doesn't offer any real conclusions, yet proves to be extremely watchable nevertheless, thanks to Walters' performance and the various tics of Campbell's teleplay, which provides much incidental amusement along the way.

Other films in the *Screen Two* series with a genre leaning include *Northanger Abbey* (1987, TVM), an adaptation of Jane Austen's 1803 novel (published posthumously in 1817) in which a young woman (Katharine Schlesinger) with a vivid imagination and a passion for gothic novels comes to suspect that an abbey at which she has been invited to stay holds a dark secret; *The Lorelei* (1990, TVM), in which a lonely teacher (Amanda Redman) has a frightening encounter in a Welsh boarding house; *Truly Madly Deeply* (1992, TVM), which had been released theatrically in 1990, in which a grieving woman (Juliet Stevenson) is haunted by her late husband (Alan Rickman); *Genghis Cohn* (1994, TVM), which had been released theatrically in 1993, in which a former SS officer (Robert Lindsay) is haunted by the ghost of a Jewish comedian (Anthony Sher) who he murdered during the war; *The Reflecting Skin* (1994, TVM), which had been released theatrically in 1990, in which a young boy (Jeremy Cooper) in fifties mid-west America believes that a local widow (Lindsay Duncan) is a vampire; and *Midnight Movie* (1994, TVM), in which events in an English mansion, rented by an American producer (Brian Dennehy) and his wife (Louise Germaine), come to resemble the plot of a horror movie shot there many years earlier.

Another BBC series, *Theatre Night* (1985–1990, TVM), which featured television versions of such stage classics as *Lady Windemere's Fan* (1985, TVM), *The Birthday Party* (1987, TVM) and *All My Sons* (1990, TVM), also presented a new version of Robert Ardrey's *Thunder Rock* (1985, TVM), which aired on BBC2 on 6 October 1985. This time Charles Dance stars as Charleston, the young man who takes a job at a remote lighthouse to escape impending war, only to discover that the place is haunted. Also starring Anna Massey, Kathleen Byron, David de Keyser, Barry Morse and Graham Crowden, it was directed by the prolific Mike Vardy. The series also featured a version of Franz Kaka's *The Metamorphosis* (1989, TVM), which aired on 21 May 1989. Written by Steven Berkoff from his own stage adaptation, it starred Tim Roth as Gregor Samsa, the young man who wakes to find that he has turned into a giant insect. The cast also featured Berkoff himself as Samsa's father, supported by Saskia Reeves, Gary Olsen and Linda Marlow, who worked under the direction of another television warhorse, Jim Goddard.

Genre shows also continued to be popular schedule fillers in America in the eighties, though not all were successes. One such case was *Tales of the Haunted* (1981, TV), which debuted on CBS on 12 July 1981. Written by Louis M. Heyward and directed by Gordon Hessler (who'd previously worked together on several features, among them *The Oblong Box* [1969] and *Murders in the Rue Morgue* [1971]), it was intended as a late night alternative, and stars Jack Palance as a man who finds himself and his children staying at a spooky old house after their car has broken down, only to discover the place to be rammed with antiques, over which he becomes covetous, much to the chagrin of the two old ladies who live there (Helen Hughes and Frances Hyland), who turn out not to be so vulnerable as they appear (they are in fact witches). Shot on videotape in Canada and looking *very* cheap, five hour-long installments were made, any of which make *Dark Shadows* look like high art, and one can fully understand why it failed to go any further than this. Hosted by Christopher Lee, the show was subsequently edited down into a TV movie, *Evil Stalks This House* (1981, TVM), which is none the better for being shorter. Another failure was *Comedy of Horrors* (1981, TV), a series whose pilot aired on CBS on 28 July 1981. Written and produced by Harry Colomby and John Boni for MTM, the half-hour program was directed by Bill Persky and starred Kip Niven, Vincent Schiavelli and Deborah Harmon, with Patrick Macnee onboard as host. In it, yet another family find themselves menaced, this time while staying at a remote inn during a storm, among the threats being an axe wielding maniac. Featuring humor in the style of *Airplane!* (1980), it wasn't deemed a goer.

A show that did run to series was *Darkroom* (1981–1982, TV), which began showing on ABC on 27 November 1981. Hosted by James Coburn and starring such names as David Carradine, Billy Crystal, June Lockhart, Brian Dennehy, Signe Hasso and Ronny Cox, the hour-long series, which offered a mix of fantasy, science fiction and horror, featured two, sometimes three stories per episode, and opened with *Closed Circuit* (1981, TV), in which an ageing news reporter (Robert Webber) learns that he is going to be replaced by a computer simulation of himself, and *Stay Tuned, We'll Be Right Back* (1981, TV), in which a man (Lawrence Pressman) discovers that his crystal radio is in contact with the Nazi U-boat that sank his father's ship during the war. The segments that leant more towards horror included *The Bogeyman Will Get You* (1981, TV) by Robert Bloch, in which a girl (Helen Hunt) comes to believe that an old acquaintance (Randy Powell) is a vampire; *Needlepoint* (1981, TV), in which an old woman (Esther Rolle) uses voodoo to avenge herself on a pimp (Lawrence Hilton-Jacobs) who took advantage of her granddaughter; *Catnip* (1981, TV), another Robert Bloch story, this time about a man (Cyril O'Reilly) who accidentally kills an old woman (Jocelyn Brando) who was a witch, and whose cat now begins to stalk him; and *Lost in Translation* (1982, TV), in which an archaeologist (Andrew Prine) discovers that an ancient Egyptian scroll contains a spell that grants him power over his enemies. Perhaps because the stories, although professionally enough presented, were nothing out of the ordinary, the show, which was directed by the likes of Rick Rosenthal, Curtis Harrington and Jeffrey Bloom (who also worked as the executive story editor), ran to just one season of seven episodes, yet it remains memorable for its opening sequence in which a camera glides through the rooms of an empty house to the strains of an eerie piano and synth theme by David Shire, over which Coburn's basso tones beckon viewers "into the terror that awaits you in the darkroom."

In the UK, children's television continued to be a home for genre programming, among them the six-part half-hour series *The Haunting of Cassie Palmer* (1982, TV), which began airing on the ITV network on 26 February 1982. Based upon the 1980 novel by Vivien Alcock, it sees the title character (Helen Probyn), the daughter of a fake medium (Elizabeth Spriggs), discover that she has genuine powers herself in this regard, to which end she inadvertently summons a spirit known as Deverill (Geoffrey Rose), whom she isn't sure is entirely benevolent. Dramatized by Alfred Shaughnessy and directed by Dorothea Brooking, the series was shot on film and may well have unsettled younger viewers, given its subject matter and its atmospheric graveyard scenes, where the sepulchral Deverill makes his presence felt. In America, the program aired on Nickelodeon under the umbrella title of *The Third Eye* (1983–1984, TV), which also broadcast a handful of other half-hour genre shows from Britain's ITV network, among them the afore-mentioned *Children of the Stones* (1977, TV), along with *Into the Labyrinth* (1981–1982, TV), which clocked up 21 episodes over three seasons, during which a group of children find themselves involved in a feud between a sorcerer (Ron Moody) and a witch (Pamela Salem), and *The Witches and the Grinnygog* (1983, TV), a six-part adaptation of the 1981 book by Dorothy Edwards, in which a family is visited by three witches from the Middle Ages (Anna Wing, Patricia Hayes and Eva Griffith) after coming into possession of an odd looking statue called the Grinnygog. Also part of the *Third Eye* package was *Under the Mountain* (1981, TV), an eight-part adaptation of the 1979 novel by Maurice Gee, in which twins Rachel and Theo (Kirsty Wilkinson and Lance Warren) are called upon to help an alien known as Mr. Jones (Roy Leywood) while vacationing in Auckland, where the series was made via Television New Zealand (a film version followed in 2009, also shot in New Zealand).

Other children's series produced during this period include the ten-part *Dark Towers* (1981, TV). Written by Andrew Davies, it was made as part of the BBC's educational strand *Look and Read* (1967–2004, TV), and sees a young girl (Juliet Waley) and her dog enter the overgrown grounds of an imposing old house named Dark Towers, where she encounters its impoverished owner Lord Dark (David Collings) and his son Edward (Gary Russell), and is told by a friendly ghost (also Collings) that the house is in danger (an earlier series in the strand also seems to be remembered by some as being particularly unsettling; this was *The Boy from Space* [1971, TV], in which a brother and sister [Stephen Garlick and Sylvestra Le Touzel] help an alien boy they name Peep-Peep [Colin Mayes] avoid the clutches of the evil Thin Man [John Woodnutt]). A series that appears to have fallen through the cracks is *Shadow of the Stone* (1987, TV), a six-parter which aired on Scottish Television from 26 July 1987, in which a girl encounters an ancestor who was burned as a witch. Written by Catherine Lucy Czerkawska and directed by kids show regular Leonard White, it starred Elizabeth Finlay as both the girl and the witch, and featured an early appearance by Alan Cumming. One of the most popular programs, however, proved to be *Wonders in Letterland* (1985, TV), the first in a long series of escapades featuring a witch called T. Bag (Elizabeth Estensen, later Georgina Hale) and her young tea boy, T. Shirt (John Hasler), from whose magical brew she obtains her powers. Created by Lee Pressman and launching on ITV on 4 April 1985, the ten-part, 20-minute series was originally intended as an educational piece, but instead went on to feature increasingly fantastical adventure plots, among the follow ups being such series and one-offs as *T. Bag Strikes Again* (1986, TV), *T. Bag's Christmas Cracker* (1988, TV), *T. Bag's Christmas Carol* (1989, TV), *T. Bag and the Rings of Olympus* (1991, TV), which also featured a vampire called Count Igor Von Fledermause (Gavin Richards), *T. Bag and the Sunstones of Montezuma* (1992, TV) and *Take Off with T. Bag* (1992, TV), in which broad comedy and simple effects were to the fore. Magical mayhem was also the focus of *The Worst Witch* (1986, TVM), an adaptation of the popular 1974 Jill Murphy book which sees a young girl, Mildred Hubble (Fairuza Balk), attend an academy for young witches, where she encounters such characters as Miss Hardbroom (Diana Rigg) and the Grand Wizard (Tim Curry). The book had already been featured on the long-running *Jackanory* (1965–1996, TV) in 1978 and would (along with its sequels) form the basis of a later series, also titled *The Worst Witch* (1998–2001, TV), which ran up 40 episodes and starred Georgina Sherrington as Mildred. This was followed by a reboot (2017–2020, TV), which clocked up 53 episodes, and in which Mildred was now played by Bella Ramsay.

Rather more frivolous was the American show *The Powers of Matthew Star* (1982–1983, TV), an hour-long fantasy adventure series which began on NBC on 17 September 1982. In it, teen heartthrob Peter Barton starred as the title character, a super powered high school student who is in fact an alien prince hiding out on Earth. Accompanied by his guardian (Louis Gossett, Jr.) who is posing as the school's science teacher, the pair subsequently find their abilities being called upon by the government. Created by Steve E. De Souza, the series, silly as it was, nevertheless managed to clock up a healthy 22 episodes during its single-season run. It wasn't the only oddball superhero show to go before the cameras during this period though, among the others being *Automan* (1983–1984, TV), which began on ABC on 15 December 1983, in which a computer generated being (Chuck Wagner) and his creator (Desi Arnaz, Jr.) become crime fighters, and *Manimal* (1984, TV), which began airing on NBC on 4 June 1983, in which a college professor (Simon MacCorkindale) uses his special powers to turn into any animal he wishes to help fight crime. Like *Matthew Star*, they both ran to just a single season (13 and eight episodes, respectively), but we are starting to stray from path again with their inclusion here (*Variety* described the latter as "the kind of series that gives television a bad name").

Doctor Who star Tom Baker next took on the mantle of Sherlock Holmes in a new four-part adaptation of *The Hound of the Baskervilles* (1982, TV), whose half-hour episodes began airing in the UK in an early Sunday evening slot on BBC1 on 3 October 1982. Adapted by Alexander Baron and directed by Peter Duguid, the series also starred Terence Rigby as Dr. Watson, Will Knightley (father of Keira) as Dr. Mortimer and Nicholas Woodeson as Sir Henry Baskerville. A rather serious production, its interiors were shot on videotape in the studio, which tends to flatten the atmosphere, with much of episode one taking place at 221b Baker Street, thus giving the proceedings the air of a filmed play, and though Baker has a fair stab at

Holmes, the series sadly lacks pace and ultimately becomes something of a chore to sit through long before he dispatches the hound with a well aimed round of bullets (in fact the story had been rather more successfully filmed for television the year before as a Russian two-parter titled *Priklyucheniya Sherloka Kholmsa i doktora Vatsona: Sobaka Baskerviley* [1981, aka *The Adventures of Sherlock Holmes and Dr. Watson: The Hound of the Baskervilles*, TV], in which Holmes was played by Vasiliy Livanov).

Another anthology show that only managed a short run was the British *Shades of Darkness* (1983–1986, TV), whose nine hour-long episodes began airing on ITV on 27 May 1983 (season one contained seven episodes, while a belated follow up in 1986 managed only two). Produced by June Wydham-Davies and featuring mostly period stories by Elizabeth Bowen, L.P. Hartley and Agatha Christie, the series was directed by the likes of Gordon Flemyng, Simon Langton and Wyndham-Davies herself, and starred such names as Francesca Annis, Eileen Atkins, Jeremy Kemp, Robert Hardy, Jeanne Moreau and a young Hugh Grant. Season one opened with *The Lady's Maid's Bell* (1983, TV), which was based upon the 1902 story by Edith Wharton, and sees a lady's maid (Joanna David), recently recovered from a bout of typhoid, go to work at a large hall where she is haunted by the presence of her predecessor (June Brown), who died after 20 years of devoted service, and who it seems wishes to relay something to her. Mild stuff which ultimately amounts to very little (the ending is a shade too ambiguous), it is nevertheless nicely put over by director John Glenister, who well conveys the atmosphere of an Edwardian country house, both upstairs and down, with Joanna David perfectly cast as the pallid lady's maid, as is June Brown as her sepulchral predecessor.

This was followed by *The Intercessor* (1983, TV), based upon the 1911 May Sinclair story, in which a writer (John Duttine) takes a room at an isolated farm so as to work on a book, only to be haunted by the ghost of a young girl; *Feet Foremost* (1983, TV), based upon the 1948 L.P. Hartley story (updated to the present), in which a property tycoon (Jeremy Kemp) buys an old manor which proves to be haunted by a young woman (this had already been filmed as a 1968 episode of *Mystery and Imagination* [1966–1970, TV]); *Afterward* (1983, TV), based upon the 1910 novel by Edith Wharton, in which an American couple (Michael Shannon and Kate Harper) retire to a remote manor house in England only for the husband to be spirited away by a ghost that can only be remembered in retrospect; *The Maze* (1983, TV), based upon the 1953 story by C.H.B. Kitchin, in which a woman (Francesca Annis) returns to her childhood home with her husband and daughter (James Bolam and Sky Macaskill) only to find her daughter drawn to the garden maze where a tragedy once took place; *Seaton's Aunt* (1983, TV), based upon the 1923 story by Walter de la Mare, in which a boy (Adam Lal) tries to convince his friend (Joshua De La Mere) that his aunt (Mary Morris) is in league with the Devil; and *Bewitched* (1983, TV), based upon the 1926 Edith Wharton story, in which a minister (Alfred Burke) looks into the bewitchment of a local farmer (Alfred Lynch) by the ghost of a dead village girl. Season two meanwhile featured *The Demon Lover* (1986, TV), based upon the 1945 Elizabeth Bowen story, in which a woman (Dorothy Tutin) living through World War II discovers a letter from her lover who died in the previous war, only for her memories of him to become all too real; and *The Last Séance* (1986, TV), based upon the 1926 story (aka *The Woman Who Stole a Ghost*) by Agatha Christie, in which a medium (Norma West) is persuaded into performing one final séance before retiring. Unfortunately, despite the qualities of the series, it was perhaps a little too vapid at times to leave a lasting impression on audiences, despite the concerted efforts of all concerned, yet for those with time and patience, it is certainly not without its rewards.

Back in the States and clocking up rather more episodes was *The Hitchhiker* (1983–1991, TV, aka *Deadly Nightmares*), a half-hour anthology show that went on to rack up an incredible 85 episodes during its six-season run, which began on HBO on 23 November 1983. Created by Riff Markowitz, Lewis Chesler and Richard Rothstein, it featured twist-in-the-tale stories upon which a mysterious wanderer would pass comment. The first season, which was made via Corazon Productions, was a short one, amounting to just three episodes, and launched with *Shattered Vows* (1983, TV), in which a man (Bruce Greenwood) has an affair with his wife's stepdaughter (Alesia Shirley), with whom he plans to bump off his missus with the aid of a statuette given to him by his grandmother. This was followed by *When Morning Comes* (1983, TV), a thriller about a womanizing music producer (August Schellenberg) who discovers a beautiful girl (Pamela Bowman) taking refuge in his hunting cabin, and *Split Decision* (1983, TV), in which a realtor (Jackson Davies) tries to persuade twin sisters (Judy and Audrey Landers) to sell their house. All three episodes were directed by Ivan Nagy and featured Nicholas Campbell as the mysterious wanderer.

Quintina Productions then took over for the following three seasons (amounting to 36 episodes), while La Cinq and Atlantique joined Quintina for the remaining two seasons (which amounted to 47 episodes), for all of which Page Fletcher now assumed the role of the hitchhiker (note that Fletcher reshot Campbell's intros for the first three episodes when the show went into syndication). Directors who worked on the series included Mai Zetterling, Carl Schenkel, Philip Noyce, David Wickes, Paul Verhoeven, Mike Hodges and Roger Vadim, while the casts featured Margot Kidder, Susan Anspach, Stephen McHattie, Robert Vaughn, Brad Davis, Klaus Kinski, Tom Skerritt, Elizabeth Ashley, Harry Hamlin, Paul Le Mat, Virginia Madsen, Jeremy Clyde, Joe Dallesandro, Gary Busey, David Soul, Zach Galligan, Lauren Hutton, Geraldine Page, Rae Dawn Chong, Elliott Gould and Jerry Orbach. Shot in both Canada and France (once La Cinq and Atlantique were onboard), the series occasionally included stories with a supernatural element, among them *The Curse* (1986, TV), which involved black magic, *Last Scene* (1986, TV), which was about the making of a horror movie, and *New Blood* (1991, TV), which featured vampirism. Although adequately made and performed, the show was fairly routine in most respects, which is perhaps why it hasn't acquired classic status, yet at the time it served its purpose.

Venturing into the Darkside

An anthology series that *was* cult viewing for a period, despite being somewhat variable, was *Tales from the Darkside* (1983–1988, TV), which clocked up a hefty 90 episodes during its four-season run. Created by director George A. Romero on the back of his successful multi story horror film *Creepshow* (1982, TV), the half-hour series more fully embraced horror and the supernatural than did *The Hitchhiker*. Executive produced by Romero and Richard P. Rubinstein via Laurel Entertainment (which had been behind *Creepshow*) and Tribune Entertainment (which syndicated the run), it launched on 29 October 1983 with a one-off pilot that went out under the title of *Trick or Treat* (1883, TV), in which a Scrooge-like money lender (Barnard Hughes), to whom many in his town are in debt, each year rigs his house for Halloween and hides within it a number of IOUs, the discovery of which will cancel the debt of the parents whose child finds them, but such are the shocks and surprises he arranges, he always manages to frighten off the kids. However, the tables are finally turned on the old miser when a witch (Frances Chaney) comes to call and gives him a taste of his own medicine. Written by George Romero and Franco Amurri, and directed by Bob Balaban, the story moves at a fair clip and features an amusing performance by Hughes and some excellent character make-up for the witch care of Ed French and Timothy D'Arcy, all of which was enough help take the show to series.

This began airing the following year on 30 September 1984 with a so-so episode titled *The New Man* (1984, TV), in which a recovering alcoholic (Vic Tayback) is visited by his young son Jerry (Chris Herbert), and soon finds himself falling back into his old ways, because he doesn't *have* a son called Jerry. A real disappointment on which to launch a series, things nevertheless improved as the weeks went by, as stories by Stephen King, Clive Barker, Robert Bloch and Harlan Ellison made it to the airwaves. Like most shows of its ilk, it featured plenty of name guest stars, among them Danny Aiello, Patrick Macnee, Debbie Harry, Ronee Blakley, Joe Turkel, Tippi Hedren, Divine, Jean Marsh, Christian Slater, Susan Strasberg, Brent Spiner, Bruce Davison and Dick Miller, while directors included Tom Savini, Jodie Foster and Armand Mastroianni. Each episode opened with a voice over care of Paul Sparer who, speaking over idyllic shots of lush countryside, warns, "Man lives in the sunlit world of what he believes to be reality, *but* there is, unseen by most, an underworld—a place that is just as real, but not as brightly lit ... a dark side," at which the image flips and takes on a negative hue, leading us into that week's story. Once it settled down, season one went on to include such well remembered installments as *Inside the Closet* (1984, TV), in which a grad student (Roberta Weiss) suspects that a strange creature is living in the room she is renting (the creature was provided by make-up supremo Tom Savini, who also directed); *A Case of the Stubborns* (1984, TV), in which a recently deceased grandfather (Eddie Bracken) refuses to accept that he is dead, much to the concern of his family, especially when he starts to rot; and *Madness Room* (1985, TV), in which a wealthy couple (Stuart Whitman and Therese Pare) discover the existence of an extra room in their home with the assistance of a Ouija board.

Season two's highlights included *Halloween Candy* (1985, TV), in which a nasty old man (Roy Poole) gets him comeuppance at the hands of a goblin for taunting kids at Halloween (this again featured another creature make-up care of its director Tom Savini); *Monsters in My Room* (1985, TV), in which a young boy (Seth Green) discovers that monsters are living in his bedroom, much to the annoyance of his disbelieving stepfather (Greg Mullavey); and *Strange Love* (1986, TV), in which a doctor (Patrick Kilpatrick) finds that his latest patients (Harsh Nayyar and Marcia Cross) are in fact vampires. Season three's better episodes included *The Circus* (1986, TV), in which a newspaperman (Kevin O'Connor) who takes pride in debunking fakes and charlatans comes face to face with some real monsters (a vampire and a werewolf) while investigating the circus of Dr. Nis (William Hickey); *Seasons of Belief* (1986, TV), in which a father (E.G. Marshall) tells his kids a scare story at Christmas about a creature known as the Grither which supposedly gets one step closer

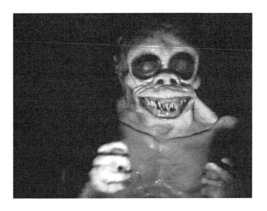

Closet space. Something nasty lurks *Inside the Closet* (1984, TV), an episode of *Tales from the Darkside* (1983–1988, TV) (Laurel Entertainment Inc./Tribune Entertainment/ CBS Television Distribution).

each times its name is mentioned; and *My Ghostwriter—The Vampire* (1987, TV), in which a hack horror writer (Jeff Conaway) is given the opportunity to write the life story of a real vampire (Roy Dotrice), while season four's better installments included *The Yattering and Jack* (1987, TV), in which a salesman (Anthony Carbone) receives a visit from a diminutive horned demon who wants to take his soul; *The Cutty Black Sow* (1988, TV), in which a young boy (Huckleberry Fox) vows to protect the soul of his dying great-grandmother (Paula Trueman) from a Celtic monster; and *Family Reunion* (1988, TV), in which a father (Stephen McHattie) does his best to protect his son (Daniel Terrence Kelly) who turns into a werewolf during the full moon (effects again care of its director Tom Savini). Although an undeniably hit and miss affair, the series has remained popular in syndication down the years, and even led to a feature-length spinoff, *Tales from the Darkside: The Movie* (1990), a better than expected three story compendium film featuring Debbie Harry, Christian Slater and William Hickey, all of whom appeared in episodes of the series (there was also a video compilation movie featuring five stories from the series that went out under the title *Stephen King's Golden Tales* [1985]).

Back in the UK, the BBC turned its attention to H.G. Wells' *The Invisible Man* (1984, TV), which it presented as a six-part half-hour series which began airing on BBC1 on 4 September 1984 with an episode titled *The Strange Man's Arrival* (1984, TV). Here, it is Pip Donaghy who plays Griffin, the scientist who has discovered a means of making himself invisible, but when this becomes permanent, he has to race to find a cure before his mental facilities deteriorate. Adapted by James Andrew Hall and helmed by Brian Lighthill, it also featured David Gwillim, Lila Kaye, Esmond Knight, Michael Sheard, Roy Holder and Frank Middlemass, and was pretty faithful to the source material. It also benefited from reasonably solid period production values care of designer Don Giles and some atmospheric music by Stephen Deutsch, but was otherwise regarded as being rather too slow moving (which it undoubtedly is), while the videotaped interiors compare badly to the photographed location work in Somerset. As for the effects, which were provided by John Brace and Dave Jervis, they are pretty much par for the period, and include a scene (in episode five) in which Griffin imbibes the potion he's been working on and gradually fades before our eyes, appearing as a skeleton just before he completely disappears. Surprisingly, the show was never repeated, and didn't emerge again until 2005 when it was released on DVD.

It was back to territory similar to *The Fantastic Journey* (1977, TV) with the American series *Otherworld* (1985, TV), which began its brief run on CBS on 26 January 1985. In the hour-long show, which was created by Roderick Taylor, the Sterling family (Sam Groom, Gretchen Corbett, Tony O'Dell, Jonna Lee and Brandon Crane [who was replaced after two episodes by Chris Hebert]) find themselves transported to the two-mooned world of Thel while on a tour of the Great Pyramid of Giza during an alignment of six planets that hasn't taken place for over 10,000 years. Here they have to adapt to an entirely new way of life, all the while outrunning a zone trooper named Kroll (Jonathan Banks) whose access crystal they have taken following a confrontation with him while travelling through the planet's various provinces, which is strictly illegal ("The family's only hope for survival is each other!" ran the tagline). A reasonably engaging adventure series with surprisingly good production values and better dialogue than one might expect, it sadly only ran to eight episodes, the last of which ended with the family taking to the air in a balloon, Professor Marvel–style, in the hope of discovering their freedom.

Very similar to *Tales from the Darkside* (1983–1988, TV) in both concept and execution was *The Ray Bradbury Theater* (1985–1992, TV), which managed to run up 65 half-hour episodes during its six-season run, the first two seasons of which aired on HBO before moving to the USA Network in 1988. Filmed in Canada, New Zealand and England, and made via Alberta Filmworks, Atlantis Films and Granada Television, the series was developed for TV by Mark Massari, and was based upon Bradbury's hefty back catalogue of cherished novels and short stories, which the author not only executive produced, but also introduced himself each week from his writing den. Directed by the likes of Paul Lynch (who helmed the opener), Lee Tamahori and Anne Wheeler, the show featured a better crop of guest stars than most of its ilk, among them Peter O'Toole, Patrick Macnee, James Coco, William Shatner, John Kerr, Leslie Nielsen, Louise Fletcher, Denholm Elliott, Alan Bates, Carol Kane, Michael J. Pollard, Donald Pleasence, Susannah York, Drew Barrymore, Tyne Daly and Jeff Goldblum. The series piloted with *Marionettes, Inc.* (1985, TV) on 21 May 1985, in which an unhappy computer salesman (James Coco) is offered the chance to have himself replaced by an exact replica both at home and work, thus allowing himself the freedom he craves, though inevitably the plan doesn't go entirely to his liking (the story had already been presented as an episode of *Historias para no domir* [1966–1968, TV] under the title *El doble*).

The show began its official run somewhat tentatively the following year with just five further episodes, starting on 5 January 1986 with *The Playground* (1986, TV), a story about a father (William Shatner) still traumatized by the bullying he received as a child, and though the series tended to lean towards science fiction, fantasy and twist-in-the-tale thrillers, it did delve into more chilling fare in two of the remaining four episodes of season one. These were *The Crowd* (1985, TV), in which a man (Nick Mancuso) involved in an auto accident discovers that the same crowd of people keeps turning up at different accident sites (spoiler alert: they're all dead, being victims of accidents themselves), and *Banshee* (1986, TV), in which a writer (Charles Martin Smith) encounters a banshee (Jennifer Dale) while in Ireland. Season two, which ran a more substantial 12 episodes, more fully embraced horror with the likes of *Gotcha* (1988, TV), in which a man (Saul Rubinek) meets a woman (Kate Lynch) at a party with whom he falls in love, but comes to regret it when she suggests they play a game called "gotcha" during which she seems to disappear; *On the Orient, North* (1988, TV), in which a nurse (Magali Noel) meets a dying ghost (Ian Bannen) while journeying on the Orient Express; and *And So Died Riabouchinska* (1988, TV), in which a dummy belonging to a famous ventriloquist (Alan Bates) has rather more to say about a murder than he is comfortable with (this was previously filmed as a 1957 episode of *Alfred Hitchcock Presents* [1955–1962, TV]).

Season three included *The Haunting of the New* (1989, TV), in which a socialite (Susannah York) has her mansion rebuilt after a fire only to find that the new place won't let her back in, plus a new version of *Boys! Raise Giant Mushrooms in Your Cellar!* (1989, TV), an oddball alien invasion story that had already been filmed as a 1959 episode of *Alfred Hitchcock Presents* (1955–1962, TV [as *Special Delivery*]) and a 1966 episode of *Historias para no domir* (1966–1968, TV [as a two-parter titled *La bodega*]). Season four meanwhile included *Exorcism* (1990, TV), in which a ladies' guild president (Sally Kellerman) is thought to be a witch by her rival (Jayne Eastwood), while season five featured *The Jar* (1992, TV), in which a farmer (Paul Le Mat) buys a jar containing a strange specimen at a fair, but his wife determines to prove that it is a fake much to his chagrin (this had previously been filmed as a 1964 episode of *The Alfred Hitchcock Hour* [1962–1965, TV] and a 1986 episode of the re-booted *Alfred Hitchcock Presents* [1985–1989, TV]). Finally, season six contained *The Dead Man* (1992, TV), in which a lonely manicurist (Louise Fletcher) falls in love with a small-town eccentric (Frank Whitten) who claims that he is dead. Yet, despite the big name guest stars, the series was a rather hot and cold affair, and not all the stories translated well to the small screen, even though Bradbury wrote all of the teleplays himself, but like all series of this kind, there are undoubtedly plums to be had in the pudding (note that some of Bradbury's stories also featured in the reboot of *The Twilight Zone* [1985–1989, TV] during this period).

The Spielberg Touch

Running pretty much concurrent with the Ray Bradbury series (as well as the reboot of *The Twilight Zone*) was *Amazing Stories* (1985–1987, TV), a mega budget half-hour anthology show created and developed for television by Joshua Brand, John Falsey and, most importantly, cinema wunderkind Steven Spielberg, who also executive produced with Frank Marshall and Kathleen Kennedy. Given his global dominance at the box office during this period, Spielberg was in the enviable position of being able to secure a deal for 45 episodes straight up via Universal

Television, with whom he made the series in conjunction with his own production company Amblin Entertainment (Spielberg's hits for Universal alone included *Jaws* [1975] and *E.T.* [1982], which gave him incredible standing within the company). To this end he was able to secure top talent for the series, both in front of and behind the cameras. Indeed, the show's impressive roll call of directors included Martin Scorsese, Robert Zemeckis, Irvin Kershner, Clint Eastwood, Joe Dante, Peter Hyams and Tobe Hooper, as well as Spielberg himself, who helmed two episodes (and also contributed to many of the storylines), while the starry cast of guest artists included such top rank names as Kevin Costner, Harvey Keitel, Charlie Sheen, Charles Durning, Gregory Hines, Patrick Swayze, Mary Stuart Masterson, John Lithgow, Christopher Lloyd and Bob Balaban (who also directed an episode), as well as such old timers as Sid Caesar, Eddie Bracken, Royal Dano, Evelyn Keyes, Ian Wolfe and Eve Arden. The series also attracted a number of Hollywood's top composers, among them John Williams (who also provided the series' dynamic title theme), Jerry Goldsmith, James Horner, Georges Delerue, John Addison, Bruce Broughton, Alan Silvestri, Danny Elfman, Leonard Rosenman and Billy Goldenberg (the latter of whom had worked with Spielberg during his early television years).

Presenting a mix of fantasy, mystery, science fiction, horror and even comedy, the two-season run kicked off with *Ghost Train* (1985, TV), which aired on NBC on 25 September 1985. Scripted by Frank Deese from a story by Spielberg himself, who also directed, it starred Roberts Blossom as Opa Clyde Globe, an old man who, as a child, was responsible for a derailment that killed many people when he fell asleep on the rails while listening for the train that would take him to visit his grandfather. Visiting his grandson (Lukas Haas) in his old home town, he is convinced that the train will soon return, crashing through the newly built house of his son Fenton (Scott Paulin) and daughter-in-law Joleen (Gail Edwards), which just happens to be built on the land where the railway used to run ("This is where the Highball Express ran off its tracks," he tells his incredulous grandson). This time, however, it's his belief that the "ghost" train will take him along with it. Naturally, his son and daughter-in-law are incredulous, until, that is, the train turns up at the appointed time and drives right through their living room to pick up the old man ("There's a train in my house," observes Joleen flatly, as well she might).

A sentimental story somewhat typical of Spielberg's output at the time (so much so that the train's ghostly passengers and crew bear no outward malice towards the old man for being responsible for their deaths all those years earlier!), it is well enough staged and performed (particularly by Blossom), and benefits from the *coup de theatre* of having a life-size mock-up of an old-style steam train drive through the center of the Globe's home, which is impressively put over by Spielberg, aided and abetted by his production designer Rick Carter and his favored cinematographer of the time Allen Daviau. Yet this water cooler moment aside, the episode, although perfectly passable, is otherwise nothing out of the ordinary, despite its notably high production values, and without the inclusion of a heartfelt score by John Williams, it would have even less dramatic substance than it appears to carry (commented *Variety*, "Nothing new ... too much of it felt like scenes spliced together from *E.T.*, *Close Encounters of the Third Kind*, *Poltergeist* and other Spielberg films").

Yet despite this slightly underwhelming opener, it was a cert that the show would go on to provide a number of high-water marks once it settled into its run, which indeed it did, given its incredible talent pool. Among these was one of the first season's more horror-centric episodes, *Mummy Daddy* (1985, TV), in which a hapless actor (Tom Harrison) playing a mummy in a horror movie gets mistaken for the real thing by a bunch of rednecks as he attempts to get to the hospital in costume after his pregnant wife goes into early labor, only for a real marauding mummy, Ra Amin Ka (Michael Zand), the relic of a travelling gypsy carnival from the turn of the century, to become involved in his plight. Well conceived and executed by writer Earl Pomerantz (working from a story by Spielberg) and director William Dear, the episode effectively trades on a number of established horror movie tropes including a swamp setting, a blind hermit and torch-wielding villagers, and contains some genuinely hilarious moments along the way, with Harrison wringing every moment of comic shtick possible from the various situations his character finds himself in (the excellent mummy make-ups were provided by Greg Cannom).

Other horror-themed installments from season one include *The Amazing Falsworth* (1985, TV), in which a nightclub psychic (Gregory Hines) has a run-in with a serial killer (Richard Masur); *The Sitter* (1986, TV), in which a Jamaican babysitter (Mabel King) uses voodoo to control two unruly brothers in her charge (Seth Green and Joshua Rudoy); *Boo!* (1986, TV), in which two much married ghosts (Eddie Bracken and Evelyn Keyes) are prompted into action when a porn director and his wife (Robert Picardo and Wendy Schaal) move into their house; *Mirror, Mirror* (1986, TV), in which a successful horror novelist (Sam Waterston), who dismisses the supernatural in real life, finds himself haunted by a strange figure in his bathroom mirror; *Hell Toupee* (1986, TV [geddit?]), in which an attorney (Tony Kienitz) finds himself defending an accountant (E. Hampton Beagle) who was compelled to murder three lawyers after acquiring a new toupee; and *Grandpa's Ghost* (1986, TV), in which an old man (Ian Wolfe) who died in his sleep returns to his apartment to hang out with his wife (Herta Ware), much to her delight (this episode recalled *A Case of the Stubborns* [1984, TV] from *Tales from the Darkside* [1983–1988, TV], though it doesn't share any writing credits). Season two went on to include *Welcome to My Nightmare* (1986, TV), in which a teenager (David Hollander) obsessed with horror films finds himself "living" through scenes from *Psycho* (1960); *Go to the Head of the Class* (1986, TV), in which a teenage horror buff (Scott Coffey) helps a classmate (Mary Stuart Masterson) use black magic on a despised professor (Christopher Lloyd); and *The Eternal Mind* (1986, TV), in which a dying scientist (Jeffrey Jones) transfers his mind to a computer so as to survive death (this has echoes of the much-filmed Roald Dahl story *William and Mary*).

Clearly intended as a prestige production, the success or failure of *Amazing Stories* ultimately depended on the quality of its stories, and like most anthology shows, many of them just weren't amazing enough, and no amount of production gloss could disguise this fact, despite all the lofty ambitions and good intentions (writing in *People* magazine, critic Jeff Jarvis described the series as "one of the worst disappointments I've ever had watching TV"). Nevertheless, despite its poor batting average, a handful of the episodes managed to hold their own against the competition of the time, and three of them were even packaged together to form a theatrical feature, *Amazing Stories* (1986), which played in certain foreign territories (the film led with *The Mission* [1985, TV], Spielberg's second episode as a director, in which a World War II gunner [Kevin Costner] uses his abilities as a cartoonist to escape from a deadly situation; this was followed by *Mummy Daddy* [1985, TV] and *Go to the Head of the Class* [1986, TV], the latter of which was directed by Robert Zemeckis from a teleplay by Bob Gale, Tom McLoughlin and Mick Garris, the latter of whom also worked as the series' story editor). The series was redeveloped for TV by Adam Horowitz and Edward Kitsis in 2020, with Spielberg back onboard as an executive producer, but the results were again something of a mixed blessing, and only five episodes were made, perhaps indicating that its moment had passed. Note that season one of the original series contained an episode that was shot entirely in black and white; this was the World War II story *No Day at the Beach* (1986, TV). Season two meanwhile featured an episode that was fully animated; this was *Family Dog* (1987, TV), which was written and directed by Brad Bird, who went on to direct *The Incredibles* (2004) and its sequel (2018), and led to a ten-part series of its own in 1993.

An oddball mix of comedy and the supernatural was the format of *Shadow Chasers* (1985–1986, TV), which made its debut on ABC on 14 November 1985. The hour-long show starred Trevor Eve as Dr. Jonathan McKenzie, an anthropology professor who finds himself teamed with a tabloid reporter, Edgar "Benny" Benedek (Dennis Dugan), with whom he investigates a number of cases involving the paranormal. Unfortunately, the series was scheduled opposite *The Cosby Show* (1984–1992, TV) and *Family Ties* (1982 1989, TV), and did particularly poorly in the ratings as a consequence, and was pulled after only nine of its 14 episodes were shown (though the rest aired elsewhere). The two-part pilot, which was written by its creators Kenneth Johnson and Brian Grazer, sees our duo encounter Billy (Bobby Fite), a boy whose recently deceased father was an occultist who claimed to have derived his powers from a Salem witch, and whose supernatural abilities he seems to have inherited. Neither funny enough nor scary enough (or endearing enough), the series, which featured guest shots from the likes of Nina Foch, Hermione Baddeley, Avery Schreiber and Grace Zabriskie, subsequently fell between two stools, with Eve and Duggan also failing to gel as a team. *Scooby-Doo* it certainly wasn't.

Over in the UK, *Classic Ghost Stories* (1986, TV) presented "five chilling tales for dark winter nights," as the *Radio Times* listing billed them. Perhaps best enjoyed with a large glass of port, all five were by M.R. James, and were spread over the Christmas period, beginning on BBC2 on 25 December 1986 with *The Mezzotint*, which was followed by *The Ash Tree*, *Wailing Well*, *Oh, Whistle, and I'll Come to You, My Lad* and *The Rose Garden* on 26, 28, 29 and 30 December, respectively. Narrated by Robert Powell and running just 15 minutes in length each, the programs, which were produced by Angela Beeching and written and directed by David Bell, were presented from within the confines of a slightly musty looking study (care of designer Austin Ruddy) that can't have been too unlike James' own room at King's College, all of which adds to the atmosphere of the proceedings (the concept was revived in 2000 with *Ghost Stories for Christmas* [2000, TV], a four-part half-hour series in which Christopher Lee, in the guise of M.R. James, narrated *The Stalls of Barchester*, *The Ash Tree*, *Number 13* and *A Warning to the Curious*).

Animation remained a major part of the American schedules during the decade, especially on Saturday mornings, but there were fewer genre shows as there had been in the seventies, one of the exceptions being *The Real Ghostbusters* (1986–1991, TV), which managed to clock up an astonishing 140 half-hour episodes during its seven-season run. It was based on the phenomenally successful live action movie *Ghostbusters* (1984), in which Bill Murray, Dan Aykroyd and Harold Ramis starred as Dr. Peter Venkman, Dr. Raymond Stantz and Dr. Egon Spengler, a group of parapsychology professors who set up a ghost removal business and go about the business of ridding Manhattan of a number of spirits before finally saving the world from the ancient Hittite god Gozer. In the TV series, the trio (voiced by Lorenzo Music [later Dave Coulier], Frank Welker and Maurice LaMarche, respectively) now go about their ghost busting duties assisted by the Slimer, one of the unruly spirits they had encountered in the movie. Made by DIC Entertainment, the show, which was executive produced by Michael C. Gross and Joe Medjuk, debuted on ABC on 13 September 1986 with *Ghosts R Us* (1986, TV), and went on to feature such playfully titled episodes as *The Boogieman Cometh* (1986, TV), *Adventures in Slime and Space* (1987, TV), *The Old College Spirit* (1987, TV), *A Fright at the Opera* (1987, TV), *Ghost Fight at the O.K. Corral* (1987, TV), *Poultrygeist* (1989, TV), *My Left Fang* (1990, TV) and *20,000 Leagues Under the Street* (1991, TV). The show was presumably titled *The Real Ghostbusters* to differentiate it from *Ghostbusters* (1986–1987, TV), Filmation's cartoon sequel to their earlier live action series *The Ghost Busters* (1975, TV), whose own 65-episode run had debuted five days earlier on 8 September 1986. Yet another series also ran parallel with *The Real Ghostbusters*. This was *Slimer! And the Real Ghostbusters* (1988–1990, TV), which clocked up 33 of its own episodes during its single-season run, while *The Real Ghostbusters* was itself later followed by a sequel, *Extreme Ghostbusters* (1997, TV), which ran to 40 episodes.

Meanwhile, with *Unsolved Mysteries* (1987–2010, TV), we were back in the same territory as *In Search of...* (1977–1982, TV) and its ilk. Running to 620 hour-long episodes over an epic 16-season run, the series, which was created by John Cosgrove and Terry Dunn Meurer, explored all manner of mysteries and supernatural events, from missing persons stories and unsolved murder cases to UFO sightings, which it did via re-enactments and witness interviews. The pilot, which aired on NBC on 20 January 1987, was hosted by Raymond Burr, and was followed by a number of specials throughout the same year and early 1988, which were hosted by Karl Malden and Robert Stack. The series itself started on 5 October 1988, with Stack now the regular host (he went on to notch up 292 episodes). The first installment featured an unexplained UFO sighting, while the following episodes dealt with the likes of Bigfoot, reincarnation, the Bermuda Triangle, ghosts, crop circles, the Mary Celeste, psychics and vampire kids, as well as more mundane murders and mysteries (note that the show ran on NBC between 1987 and 1997, after which it moved to CBS between 1997 and 1999, then on to Lifetime between 2001 and 2002, and Spike between 2008 and 2010 [during which time it was hosted by Dennis Farina, who logged 174 episodes]; it was later revived by Netflix in 2020). The show's creepy theme tune was by Gary Malkin and Michael Boyd.

European fairytales aimed primarily at children, though also appealing to discerning adult audiences, were the source for the anthology series *The Storyteller* (1987–1988, TV), whose half-hour episodes, which were narrated by John Hurt, began airing on NBC on 31 January 1987. Created by Muppet Master Jim Henson, and developed for television by Anthony Minghella, who wrote each of the scripts, the nine-part series, which was filmed at Elstree Studios in the UK, included such tales as *Fearnot* (1987, TV), in which a young man (Reece Dinsdale) goes on a quest to discover true fear; *The Soldier and Death* (1987, TV), in which a kindly soldier (Bob Peck) manages to capture a group of devils with a magical sack he has been given; and *The Three Ravens* (1987, TV), in which a witch (Miranda Richardson) places a curse on the three sons of a widowed king. With their charming mix of puppetry and live action, backed by top notch production values typical of the Henson stable, the show was directed by the likes of Steve Barron, Charles Sturridge and Henson himself, and featured many top-name guest stars, among them Joely Richardson, Jonathan Pryce, Sean Bean, James Wilby and Gemma Jones. A popular success across the globe, it led to a spin off series, *The Storyteller: Greek Myths* (1991, TV), in which the role of the storyteller was this time assumed by Michael Gambon, and whose four episodes included *Perseus and the Gorgon* (1991, TV) starring Jeremy Gilley and Frances Barber as the title characters.

Perhaps because of the elaborate make-up requirements, which came at a certain cost, TV's forays into lycanthropy were initially on the rare side, but finally a series devoted to the subject appeared under the title *Werewolf* (1987–1988, TV), which began its 29-episode run on the Fox Network on 11 July 1987 ("There are those who believe … and those who will," ran the tagline). Created by the appropriately named Frank Lupo, the half-hour series, which launched with a 90-minute pilot (for a two-hour timeslot) penned by Lupo, follows the adventures of graduate student Eric Cord (John J. York), who finds himself turning into a werewolf after being attacked by his friend Ted (Raphael Sbarge), who has been responsible for a series of murders, and who was himself infected by one Captain Janos Skorzeny (Chuck Connors) while working on his fishing boat. On the run for killing Ted, it seems that Eric's only chance of freeing himself from the curse is to kill Skorzeny, the bearer of the original bloodline, but matters are further complicated when Skorenzy kidnaps Eric's girlfriend Kelly (Michelle Johnson), who is Ted's sister; he also finds himself being pursued for skipping bail by a bounty hunter named Alamo Joe (Lance LeGault), who knows his secret, and whose arsenal includes silver bullets.

The pilot, directed with reasonable alacrity by actor-turned-director David Hemmings, sets up the central conceit with a fair degree of economy, and while it has an undeniable eighties vibe, thanks to its rock soundtrack and its synth score by Sylvester Levay, one can see that a certain degree of effort has gone into the telling of the story, which makes use of a number of stylistic touches typical of the genre, including subjective camera work and atmospheric back lighting, not to mention the inevitable thunder storm for the sake of atmosphere. As the unfortunate Eric, John J. York makes for a personable lead, and is supported by good work by Raphael

Sbarge as his hapless friend Ted ("Nothing can cure me, except dying," he tells Eric), Chuck Connors as the villainous Skorzeny ("Do you think your instincts are any match for mine?" he informs Eric, who has tracked him down to his boat), and Lance LeGault as the scenery chewing bounty hunter Alamo Joe ("When the world isn't the same as our minds believe, then we are in a nightmare, and nothing is worse than a nightmare, except one you can't wake up from," he informs us via his narration at the top and tail of the film).

Shadow play. Promotional ad for *Werewolf* (1987–1988, TV) (Fox Network/TriStar Television).

Given that there had been a glut of werewolf movies in the eighties, each of them featuring state of the art effects work, a lot was riding on the show's make-up effects, which thankfully weren't skimped on, given that they were designed by the great Rick Baker, whose landmark work in this field had already taken in *An American Werewolf in London* (1981), which had won him the first of his seven Oscars. His designs, along with the transformation sequences, were subsequently executed by future Oscar winner Greg Cannom, whose experience at this time included contributions to *The Howling* (1981), on which he'd worked with Rob Bottin and Baker (in fact some of the werewolf heads look like they might have been borrowed from *The Howling*).

In the series that followed, Eric hits the road, primarily to track down Skorzeny, all the while keeping one step ahead of the pursuing Alamo Joe, encountering along the way a variety of characters, including other werewolves, in a set-up that isn't too far removed from *The Incredible Hulk* (1977–1982, TV), with Eric often righting a wrong while in the guise of his alter ego. Of these episodes, Hemmings helmed another seven, while other directors involved included Sidney Hayers, Larry Shaw and another actor-turned-director James Darren, who, like Hemmings, also helmed eight. Inevitably, as the season wore on, the stories became a little more formulaic, among them *Running with the Pack* (1987, TV), in which Eric helps to protect a Mom and Pop diner from a gang of bikers, *Blood on the Tracks* (1987, TV), in which he takes a job on the railroad, and the climactic episode, *Amazing Grace* (1988, TV), in which he becomes a custodian at a mental institution so as to care for an old woman (Billie Bird) who has been committed after seeing Eric as a werewolf. Still, there was always the make-up effects to compensate for any narrative shortcomings (note that the name Janos Skorzeny is a direct reference to the vampire in *The Night Stalker* [1972, TVM]).

A familiar and much filmed story was taken to popular new heights with the TV series *Beauty and the Beast* (1987–1990, TV), an updating of the evergreen Jeanne-Marie Leprince de Beaumont fairytale, this time set in modern-day New York. In it, Catherine Chandler (Linda Hamilton), a go-getting Assistant DA, discovers a labyrinthine world under the city where she encounters Vincent (Ron Perlman), a lion-like beast of a man with whom she falls in love. Created by Ron Koslow (who also executive produced), the series debuted on CBS on 25 September 1987 with *Once Upon a Time in the City of New York* (1987, TV), which was penned by Koslow and directed by Richard Franklin, and sees Catherine rescued by Vincent after being attacked. Thanks to the chemistry of the two stars, and the effectiveness of the beast's appearance care of make-up legend Rick Baker, the show proved to be a hit. Also with Roy Dotrice, Jay Acovone and Renn Woods, and featuring such guest stars as Richard Roundtree, Edward Albert, Joseph Campanella and Tony Plana, the show ran to 55 hour-long episodes over three seasons, with Hamilton being replaced by Jo Anderson in the third when she decided to leave because she was pregnant (her character was killed off as a consequence, leading to an investigation by Anderson's criminal profiler Diana Bennett), though the results weren't quite so effective following her departure (note that a reboot created by Sherri Cooper-Landsman, Jennifer Levin and Ron Koslow [who again executive produced] starring Kristin Kreuk and Jay Ryan appeared between 2012 and 2016, itself running to 70 episodes over four seasons; further film versions included the 1991 animated Disney film and its 2017 live action remake; there had also been a 35-minute British version of the story in 1982 starring Lysette Anthony and Andrew Forbes in the title roles).

It was back to the anthology format next with *Friday the 13th: The Series* (1987–1990, TV [originally to have been *The 13th Hour*]), whose hour-long episodes began airing in first run syndication on 28 September 1987. Inspired by the successful film franchise featuring the hockey masked killer Jason Voorhees, the series was created by Larry B. Williams and Frank Mancuso, Jr., the latter of whom had been involved with several of the films in various producing roles, and who here took on the capacity of executive producer. However, rather than chronicling the further exploits of Jason, which would quickly have exhausted itself, the series instead takes as its focus an antiques store, whose owner, Lewis Vendredi (R.G. Armstrong), has made a pact with the Devil to sell cursed antiques to unsuspecting customers. But when he breaks the pact and is killed, the store passes to his niece, Micki Foster (Louise Robey) and her cousin Ryan Dallion (John D. LeMay), and together they make it their mission to track down the antiques via Vendredi's records so as to prevent their owners from coming to any harm, in which task they aided and abetted by Jack Marshak (Chris Wiggins), a former stage magician who is also an expert in the occult. But not all of the owners are willing to give up their possessions, particularly those who have discovered their magical properties.

Made in Toronto via Variety Artists Productions in association with Paramount Television on a budget of approximately $500,000 per episode, this simple premise went on to notch up 72 episodes over a three-season run, the first two of which proved to be something of a ratings winner before things began to run out of steam. "Introducing a show so good, it's scary," ran the promotional copy for the series' premier episode, *The Inheritance* (1987, TV), which was directed by William Fruet, who went on to helm a total of ten installments. Other directors involved included Timothy Bond, Armand Mastroianni, Tom McLoughlin (who'd helmed *Friday the 13th Part VI: Jason Lives* [1986]) and, perhaps most surprisingly, David Cronenberg, who directed an episode titled *Faith Healer* (1988, TV), which involves a cursed glove that has fallen into the hands of a fake faith healer (Miguel Fernandes).

On a lighter note, and running up 72 episodes over three seasons, was *Monsters* (1988–1990, TV), a half-hour show created Mitchell Galin and Richard P. Rubinstein, the latter of whom also executive produced. A follow-up of sorts to *Tales from the Darkside* (1983–1988, TV), it sees a family of monsters tune in to watch their favorite TV show, a horror anthology featuring cautionary tales involving a different creature each week, among them vampires (*The Vampire Hunter* [1988, TV]), zombies (*My Zombie Lover* [1988, TV]), trolls (*Fool's Gold* [1989, TV]), witches (*La Strega* [1989, TV]), demons (*The Demons* [1989, TV]), mutant babies (*Small Blessings* [1990, TV]), werewolves (*Werewolf of Hollywood* [1991, TV]) and aliens (*The Space Eaters* [1991, TV]). There was even a variation on *A Christmas Carol* with *A New Woman* (1990, TV) starring Linda Thorson in the Scrooge role, with the visiting ghosts replaced by zombies. Directors involved included Debra Hill, Greg Cannom, Michael Brandon and Bruce Feirstein, who worked from scripts and stories by the likes of Robert Bloch, Edithe Swenson and David Odell. Guest stars were a somewhat eclectic bunch, among them Linda Blair, Jeff Conaway, Glynis Barber, Meat Loaf, Adrienne Barbeau, Eddie Deezen, Frank Gorshin, Darren McGavin, Imogene Coca, Steve Buscemi, Eddie Bracken, Clifton James, Troy Donahue and Carol Lynley. However, for horror fans, the most notable credit would have been that of make-up supremo Dick Smith, who was credited as the series' special effects make-up consultant. Like *Tales from the Darkside*, the show was made via Laurel Entertainment and Tribune Entertainment, and veered towards comedy rather than out and out horror, the result being that the series, which launched on first run syndication on 22 October 1988, was more often silly than chilling, yet it nevertheless found an enthusiastic audience among its intended demographic.

Rather more serious was *War of the Worlds* (1988, TV), a 44-part series

Unlucky for some. Promotional ad for *Friday the 13th: The Series* (1987–1990, TV) (Variety Artists International/Lexicon Productions/Hometown Films/Paramount Television/Triumph).

derived from the 1898 novel by H.G. Wells (first serialized in 1897), in which mankind finds itself under threat from Martians who have been in hibernation following defeat during an earlier invasion in the 1950s. Created for television by Greg Strangis (who also executive produced with his father Sam Strangis and Frank Mancuso, Jr.), it was a sequel to the Oscar winning 1953 film produced by George Pal and directed by Byron Haskin, in which an invasion was halted when the aliens succumbed to common bacteria. This having been eradicated by radiation, the aliens (now said to be from a planet called Mor-Tax) emerge from hibernation after "many orbits around their sun," as one of them puts it, following a terrorist attack on the installation where their bodies are, it must be said, somewhat haphazardly stored, and given their abilities to take over human bodies, begin to insinuate themselves into society, their bid being to take over mankind by stealth ("In 1953, aliens started taking over the world; today they are taking over our bodies," intones the opening narration). However, a dedicated group, among them Dr. Harrison Blackwood (Jared Martin), Colonel Paul Ironhorse (Richard Chaves), computer programmer Norton Drake (Philip Akin) and microbiologist Suzanne McCullough (Lynda Mason Green), combine their talents to try and eradicate the invaders once and for all, but the task proves to be far from straightforward given that it isn't clear who among their allies is really an enemy.

Made in Ontario via Hometown Films and Paramount Television, the two-season series, which began airing in first run syndication on 7 October 1988, was helmed by the likes of Colin Chilvers (who directed the two-part opener *The Resurrection* [1988, TV]), William Fruet and George Bloomfield, and featured such guest stars as Ann Robinson (who'd appeared in the 1953 film), John Vernon, Patrick Macnee and John Colicos. It all seems quite cheesy now, and there was a notable fall off in quality during season two, for which the format was revised and key members of the cast from season one were killed off, but the special effects and prosthetics (by Marianne Klein, Andrew Kenworthy and Bill Sturgeon) and some of the action sequences helped to keep audiences glued during its early stages. The story has since been remade for the big screen as a 2005 blockbuster directed by Steven Spielberg, while 2019 brought a 16-part Anglo-French television version set in contemporary France created by Howard Overman and starring Gabriel Byrne, Elizabeth McGovern and Léa Drucker.

Ready for Freddy

Just as *Friday the 13th: The Series* (1987–1990, TV) had been inspired by a movie franchise, so too was *Freddy's Nightmares* (1988–1990, TV), another hour-long anthology show, which began airing in first run syndication on 9 October 1988. The series was created by Wes Craven, the writer-director behind the phenomenally successful *A Nightmare on Elm Street* (1984), in which the spirit of a badly scarred, razor gloved child killer, Freddy Krueger, returns to haunt the dreams of the kids whose parents were responsible for his burning to death. The film led to a number of sequels of varying effect and quality, through which the wisecracking and increasingly cartoonish Krueger, played by Robert Englund, became something of a cultural icon. Hence it made sense to have him host his own show, in which he would introduce stories (often two per episode) revolving around the dark deeds of the inhabitants of his hometown, Springwood ("A brand new hour of twisted tales with Freddy Krueger as your guide," exclaimed the promotional ad).

Executive produced by Robert Shaye (who'd produced the films) and produced by Gilbert Adler, the show was made via New Line Cinema and Lorimar Telepictures, and debuted with *No More Mr. Nice Guy* (1988, TV), which tells the back story of how Freddy came to be. This was then followed by stories of murder and mayhem reveling in such titles as *Do Dreams Bleed?* (1988, TV), *The Art of Death* (1989, TV), *Safe Sex* (1989, TV), *Lucky Stiff* (1989, TV), *Prime Cut* (1990, TV) and *Dust to Dust* (1990, TV), in which Freddy himself was occasionally involved (as he was with *Sister's Keeper* [1988, TV], which was a follow up to *No More Mr. Nice Guy*). Directed by the likes of Tobe Hooper (who helmed the opener), Mick Garris, Tom McLoughlin and Englund himself (who made two), the series featured such guest stars as Mary Crosby, Jeff Conaway, George Lazenby, Dick Miller, Walter Gotell, Sharon Farrell, Timothy Bottoms and a pre-fame Brad Pitt. With Englund in full flow and sporting his famed pizza face make-up care of David B. Miller and Kevin Yagher (both of whom had worked on the films and did 22 episodes each), the series offered a

fair mix of shocks and laughs, clearly aimed at teenagers and twentysomethings, who no doubt appreciated the "little bedtime treat" promised in the ads, which also offered to take them "to destinations unknown, where the only thing real is the pounding of your heart."

It was the UK's turn to venture into genre animation next with *Count Duckula* (1988–1993, TV), a half-hour show which managed to notch up 65 episodes during its four-season run, which began on the ITV network on 6 February 1988. The show was made by Cosgrove Hall, who'd been behind the highly popular secret agent spoof *Danger Mouse* (1981–1992, TV [reboot 2015–2019, TV]), in which the character had appeared as a recurring villain. In the spin off (likewise made in association with Thames Television and Nickelodeon), we follow the adventures and mishaps of the vegetarian vampire duck, his nanny and his butler Igor ("He won't bite beast or man 'cause he's

Ready for Freddy. Promotional ad for *Freddy's Nightmares* (1988–1990, TV) (New Line Cinema/Lorimar Telepictures/Stone Television).

a vegetarian," run the lyrics to the theme tune). Featuring the voices of David Jason, Brian Trueman and Jock May as Count Duckula, Nanny and Igor, respectively, and with Barry Clayton providing the narration, the series provided much madcap fun which, like its predecessor, appealed to youngsters and indulgent adults alike via such episodes as *No Sax Please: We're Egyptian* (1988, TV), in which the count hopes to track down a mystic saxophone that gives its owner power over life and death, and *The Vampire Strikes Back* (1988, TV), in which he hopes to become a superhero like his idol Tremendous Terrance. The award for best episode title, however, goes to *The Return of the Curse of the Secret of the Mummys Tomb Meets Frankenduckulas Monster and the Wolfman and the Intergalactic Cabbage......* (1990, TV), despite its lack of apostrophes. Note that Count Duckula was not related to Quacula, another vampire duck who appeared in season one of the Filmation series *The New Adventures of Mighty Mouse and Heckle & Jeckle* (1979–1982, TV), which began airing in America on CBS on 8 September 1979. Making his debut in *Star Boars* (1979, TV), the character went on to appear in a total of 16 segments, among them *Monster Mash* (1979, TV), *Haunted House* (1979, TV) and *The Fantastic 2½* (1979, TV), after which he was dropped from the line-up.

The decade's penultimate anthology series was *Tales from the Crypt* (1989–1996, TV), another long runner that accumulated 93 half-hour episodes (though some ran longer) during its substantial seven-season run on HBO, where it made its debut on 10 June 1989. Created by Steven Dodd, the series was based upon the popular E.C. comic books of the fifties, which were loved by kids and hated by parents and teachers, and each episode, which presented a standalone story, was introduced by the skeletal Crypt Keeper (voiced by John Kassir), who quickly became an audience favorite thanks to his pun-filled lead-ins and wrap-ups. Like *Amazing Stories* (1985–1987, TV), this was something of a prestige production given the talent involved, yet unlike its predecessor, it had a far darker sense of fun and didn't place itself on a pedestal. It also featured more violence, adult language and nudity. Made by HBO and Tales from the Crypt Holdings, the series was executive produced by such heavy hitters as Robert Zemeckis, Richard Donner, Joel Silver, Walter Hill and David Giler, and attracted such directors as Russell Mulcahy, Tom Holland, Stephen Hopkins, William Friedkin, Mary Lambert, Kevin Yagher (who also directed the Crypt Keeper segments), Tobe Hooper, John Frankenheimer, Tom Mankiewicz, Mick Garris and Freddie Francis (Zemeckis, Donner and Hill themselves helmed three installments each, with Hill taking the opener, while actors Arnold Schwarzenegger, Tom Hanks, Kyle MacLachlan and Michael J. Fox were also given the opportunity to direct an episode).

The roll call of writers involved was also impressive, among them Frank Darabont, Jeffrey Boam, Bob Gale, Scott Nimerfro and Brian Helgeland, with a number of the episodes derived from stories by fabled E.C. publisher William M. Gaines. Contributors to the show's music meanwhile included such respected talents as Danny Elfman (who provided the quirky theme tune), Alan Silvestri, Michael Kamen, Ry Cooder, Brad Fiedel, Bruce Broughton, Cliff Eidelman, James Horner, David Newman and Jay Ferguson. The cast list was likewise top notch, and included such genuine star guests as Kirk Douglas, Malcolm McDowell, Whoopi Goldberg, Tim

Roth, Don Rickles, Joe Pesci, Christopher Reeve, Tim Curry, Demi Moore, Patricia Arquette, Timothy Dalton, Margot Kidder, Donald O'Connor, Roger Daltry, Natasha Richardson, Bob Hoskins, David Hemmings, Dan Aykroyd, Sam Waterston and Brad Pitt.

The show launched with *The Man Who Was Death* (1989, TV), in which Niles Talbot (William Sadler), a state executioner, loses his job when the death penalty is abolished, yet continues his work as a vigilante, tracking down and electrocuting criminals who have, in his eyes, managed to slip through the justice system. However, when the penalty is reinstated and he is caught for his crimes, he finds himself sentenced to a taste of his own medicine ("Hang on to your hats, kiddies, this one's a real shocker," the Crypt Keeper informs us during his intro). This was a curious episode with which to launch a new show perhaps, given that it features no star names to entice audiences, while the subject matter is undoubtedly on the grim side, yet the teleplay, penned by Robert Reneau and director Walter Hill, is taut and to the point ("I guess this ain't the kind of work they give you a gold watch for, is it?" says Talbot on learning that he has lost his job), while Sadler gives a good account of himself as the self appointed executioner, addressing many of his thoughts direct to camera.

The second story, *And All Through the House* (1989, TV), in which a woman (Mary Ellen Trainor) murders her husband (Marshall Bell) on Christmas Eve, only to have her plans foiled by an escaped mental patient dressed as Santa Claus (Larry Drake), had already been filmed as a segment for the 1972 Amicus compendium *Tales from the Crypt* (1972), with Joan Collins in the role of the murderous wife,

Dressed to impress. The Cryptkeeper in all his glory during one of his intros for *Tales from the Crypt* (1989–1996, TV) (HBO/Tales from the Crypt Holdings).

and though a fair take on the story (this time the director was Robert Zemeckis, back then it was Freddie Francis), the earlier version is actually better staged. Other episodes in season one, which ran to only six installments, included *Dig That Cat… He's Real Gone* (1989, TV), in which a vagrant (Joe Pantoliano) is given nine lives by a scientist (Gustav Vintas) who has injected him with cells from a cat, and *Collection Completed* (1989, TV), in which a sales manager (M. Emmett Walsh), forced into early retirement, takes up taxidermy, which he carries out on his wife's many pets, prompting her to avenge herself and her beloved animals. Having established its credentials, season two went on to feature 18 episodes, while season three and four contained 14, season five 13, season six 15 and season seven 13, the latter climaxing with a cartoon version of *The*

Three Little Pigs titled *The Third Pig* (1996, TV). Other more or less self-explanatory titles from the previous seasons included *The Thing from the Grave* (1990, TV), *The Ventriloquist's Dummy* (1990, TV), *Abra Cadaver* (1991, TV), *The Reluctant Vampire* (1991, TV), *Split Personality* (1992, TV), *Werewolf Concerto* (1992, TV), *Creep Course* (1993, TV), *Only Skin Deep* (1994, TV) and *Report from the Grave* (1996, TV).

The series proved to be highly successful with younger audiences, and led to a Saturday morning cartoon spinoff, *Tales from the Cryptkeeper* (1993–1999, TV), which clocked up 39 episodes during its three-season run, which began airing on ABC on 18 September 1993 (it moved to CBS for its belated third season), and for which John Kassir again provided the voice of the title character (episode titles included *Pleasant Screams* [1993, TV], *Hyde and Go Shriek* [1993, TV], *All the Gory Details* [1994, TV] and *Monsters Ate My Homework* [1999, TV]). There were also two theatrical features, *Tales from the Crypt: Demon Knight* (1995), which proved to be a reasonable box office success, and *Bordello of Blood* (1996, aka *Tales from the Crypt Presents: Bordello of Blood*), which wasn't, as by now the novelty had worn off. But for a moment there, the Crypt Keeper certainly gave Freddy and Jason a run for their money (note that three episodes from the series, *Yellow* [1991, TV], *Showdown* [1992, TV] and *King of the Road* [1992, TV], were originally intended for a spinoff series, but were instead broadcast as part of *Tales from the Crypt*, even though they weren't horror stories as such; they were also packaged as a TV movie titled *Two-Fisted Tales* [1992, TVM], which aired on the Fox Network 18 January 1992).

The decade's final anthology series proved to be the disappointing *Nightmare Classics* (1989, TV), a short-lived show which began its four-part run on Showtime on 12 August 1989 (six episodes had originally been the plan). Created by actress Shelley Duvall, who also executive produced via Think Entertainment, it was a follow-up to her two previous series, *Faerie Tale Theatre* (1982–1987, TV), which had included a version of *Beauty and the Beast* (1988, TV) starring Susan Sarandon and Klaus Kinski in the title roles, and *Tall Tales and Legends* (1985–1988, TV), which had included a presentation of *The Legend of Sleepy Hollow* (1985, TV) starring Ed Begley, Jr., as Ichabod Crane. This time the accent was on more adult themes, and the hour-long series began with an indifferent adaptation of Henry James' *The Turn of the Screw* (1989, TV), starring Amy Irving as the haunted governess and David Hemmings as the uncle of her charges, Miles and Flora, here played by Balthazar Getty and Irina Cashen. Directed by Graeme Clifford from a script by James M. Miller, it lacked both atmosphere and surprise. Not much better was an adaptation of Sheridan Le Fanu's *Carmilla* (1989, TV), in which writer Jonathan Furst had the temerity to change the setting to a plantation just before the American Civil War. Directed by Gabrielle Beaumont, it featured a somewhat miscast Meg Tilly as the vampiric title character, though fair support was provided by Roy Dotrice and Roddy McDowall. An adaptation by J. Michael Straczynski of Robert Stevenson's *The Strange Case of Dr. Jekyll and Mr. Hyde* (1989, TV) followed, with Anthony Andrews taking on the dual role under the direction of Michael Lindsay-Hogg, with whom he'd worked with such success on the series *Brideshead Revisited* (1981, TV), albeit to rather less compelling effect here. Support this time was provided by Laura Dern, Nicholas Guest and Rue McClanahan. The series concluded with *The Eyes of the Panther*

(1989, TV), an adaptation by Art Wallace of the 1897 Ambrose Bierce frontier story, in which a hermit, Jenner Brading (C. Thomas Howell), recalls how many years earlier he had fallen in love with a woman who seemingly had the ability to turn into a panther, the result of her mother having been frightened by a black panther while pregnant. Directed by Noel Black, it was a slightly muddled affair that, rather like the rest of the series, failed to make the most of the material to hand.

TV movies with a genre theme were a little rarer in the eighties than they had been in the seventies, but quite a few still made it to the airwaves in America, the first notable one of the decade being an update of the Frankenstein story, *Doctor Franken* (1980, TVM), which was broadcast by NBC on 13 January 1980. In it, dedicated Manhattan surgeon Dr. Arno Franken (Robert Vaughn) uses his skills to rebuild the body of a John Doe patient (Robert Perault) in the basement of his brownstone, to which end he makes use of parts retrieved from other bodies. Also featuring David Selby, Teri Garr, Cynthia Harris and Josef Sommer, the film, which was a little gorier than most TV movies of the period, was written by Lee Thomas, whose script was put over with a comparatively straight face by directors Marvin J. Chomsky and Jeff Lieberman, the latter of whom also provided the story with Thomas.

Dracula also hit the airwaves again in January 1980 in *The Passion of Dracula* (1980, TVM), which was shown as an installment of *Broadway on Showtime* (1979–1981, TVM), a series of six Broadway productions broadcast on Showtime, among the others being *Bullshot Crummond* (1979, TVM) and *The Robber Bridegroom* (1980, TVM). Written by Bob Hall and David Richmond, with Hall also directing, it was a variation on the original Stoker story, and was first performed at the Cherry Lane Theatre in New York on 28 September 1977, pre-empting a Broadway revival of the 1924 play of *Dracula* by Hamilton Deane (revised in 1927 by John L. Balderston), which opened at the Martin Beck Theatre the following month on 20 October 1977 with Frank Langella in the title role (Langella went on to appear in the lavish 1979 film version). In this production, which was described by the *New York Daily News* as "a genuine old fashioned horror thriller," it is Christopher Bernau who plays Dracula, supported by Malachi Throne (as Van Helsing), Elliot Vileen (as Renfield), Gordon Chater (as Dr. Seward) and Julia MacKenzie (as Wilhelmina Murray) in a story which, set in 1911, sees a number of village girls die under mysterious circumstances, with the finger of suspicion pointing towards the recently arrived Count Dracula.

One of the sillier genre films to air during this period was *The Aliens Are Coming* (1980, TVM), which was broadcast on NBC on 2 March 1980. Executive produced by Quinn Martin, and intended as the pilot for a series, it sees aliens land near the Hoover Dam, whose hydro energy they wish to harness, to which end they take over the mind and body of Russ Garner (Max Gail), a local man who works there. Shot on location at the dam itself, the movie, which has a similar premise to Martin's hit series *The Invaders* (1967–1968, TV), was written by Robert W. Lenski and directed by Harvey Hart, and co-stars Tom Mason, Eric Braeden, Caroline McWilliams and Ed Harris. Unfortunately, the familiarity of the premise and the rather foolish appearance of the robotic aliens scuppers proceedings at an early stage, all of which makes for a rather tedious 100 minutes, though the scene in which Garner is taken over while partaking of a midnight snack in his kitchen is effectively put over.

Tut, Tut

The year's first big-budget affair proved to be *The Curse of King Tut's Tomb* (1980, TVM), which was broadcast on NBC on 8 May 1980. An Anglo-American co-production between Harlech Television and Columbia, it presents a pulpy account of the expedition to the Valley of the Kings by Howard Carter (Robin Ellis), his discovery of the tomb of King Tutankhamen in 1922, and the often strange events that followed, among them the deaths of a number of the expedition members in mysterious circumstances ("Death will come swiftly to those who disturb the eternal sleep of the king," warns a gold seal discovered during the dig). Nicely shot on location in Egypt and England by cinematographer Bob Edwards, this could best be described as hokum of the first order, which makes it all the more surprising that such a top notch cast was persuaded to take part, among them Eva Marie Saint, Harry Andrews, Wendy Hiller, Barbara Murray, Tom Baker, Faith Brook, Patricia Routledge, Angharad Rees, Paul Schofield (who narrates) and Raymond Burr (who, as an Arab villain, looks particularly ridiculous in an ill-fitting turban and a non–PC make-up that makes him look like he's been basted in Bisto). Written by Herb Meadow from the 1972 book *Behind the Mask of Tutankhamen* by Barry Wynne, and directed with a surprisingly straight face by Philip Leacock, this was clearly intended as a prestige production, but is fairly absurd in most respects, on which count it provides its fair share of undemanding fun (the film was broadcast in the UK on ITV on 31 August 1980).

The Devil in the guise of Richard Kiley proved to be the highlight of *Angel on My Shoulder* (1980, TVM), which aired on ABC on 11 May 1980. A remake of the 1946 film, it sees a gangster (Peter Strauss), executed in the forties, sent back to Earth by Old Nick in 1980 on the understanding that he corrupt Marcus Harriman, an honest DA whom he resembles, but he uses the opportunity to avenge himself against his old partner (Seymour Cassel) who betrayed him, before finally being invited up to heaven by the Stranger (Murray Matheson). Also featuring Barbara Hershey, Janis Paige and Scott Colomby, this is a mildly amusing romp with predictable situations which are flatly handled by director John Berry and rather broadly played by Strauss as the wise-talking gangster. That said, it's well worth a look for the early sequence in hell, all fire and brimstone amid a cavern of arches and walkways, which is superbly realized by art director Tom John. As for the rest, *Variety* found that it "just trudges blindly onwards."

Equally routine was *Revenge of the Stepford Wives* (1980, TVM), which aired on NBC on 12 October 1980. In it, a television reporter (Sharon Gless) arrives in Stepford to make a program about the town's seemingly perfect way of life (it has the lowest crime and divorce rates in the country), in which task she is helped by one of the local women (Julie Kavner), but her investigations lead to some disturbing revelations ("The women of Stepford are … polite, refined and murderers," ran the tagline). The film was a sequel to the popular theatrical feature *The Stepford Wives* (1975), itself based upon the 1972 bestseller by Ira Levin, in which it is revealed that the town's men folk have replaced their wives with androids. However, this follow up, which is little more than a rehash of the first film, fails to add anything new to the story, save for the fact that the wives are now controlled by pills. It passes the time adequately enough (*Variety* described it as "uneven horror meller"), and Gless and Kavner make for a pleasant double act, but it somehow lacks atmosphere, despite being helmed by cult director Robert Fuest (*And Soon the Darkness* [1970], *The Abominable Dr. Phibes* [1971], *The Devil's Rain* [1975], etc.). TV executives clearly thought there was mileage in the setup, and it was later followed by *The Stepford Children* (1987, TVM) and *The Stepford Husbands* (1996, TVM), as well as a theatrical remake of the original (2004) starring Nicole Kidman.

A horror/thriller hybrid appeared next in the guise of *The Babysitter* (1980, TVM), which aired on ABC on 28 November 1980, in which a family is threatened by a psychotic live-in babysitter (Stephanie Zimbalist). Of the results, which were directed by Peter Medak, *Variety* noted, "Only lesson to be learned from the slow-paced vidpic is to demand references before hiring live-in help." Another horror/thriller hybrid could also be found with *Nightkill* (1980, TVM), which aired on NBC on 18 December 1980. In it, the lover (James Franciscus) of a wealthy woman (Jaclyn Smith) poisons her husband (Mike Connors) in front of her, but when a police detective (Robert Mitchum) arrives to look for the husband, and the lover instead turns up in the ice chest where the body had been hidden, things start to get convoluted. Is the husband still alive (he appears to be), but if not, who is stalking the wife? An old-fashioned lady-in-peril shocker with a few good plot twists care of John Case (story) and Joane Gil (screenwriter), this is slickly enough handled by director Ted Post, with Mitchum a welcome presence as the cop who isn't quite what he seems.

A house with a mind of its own was meanwhile the premise behind *This House Possessed* (1981, TVM), which aired on ABC on 6 February 1981. In it, a rock star (Parker Stevenson) who has suffered a nervous breakdown takes refuge in a house in the country, only for his nurse (Lisa Eilbacher) to find that the building has a strange hold over her ("Something terrifying is falling in love with Sheila," ran the tagline). Routinely handled by director William Wiard, it's a rather slow-moving piece climaxing with dark revelations and the inevitable conflagration, but it at least benefits from an atmospheric score care of the reliable Billy Goldenberg.

Then it off was to Antarctica for *The Intruder Within* (1981, TVM), which aired on ABC on 20 February 1981. In it, workers on an oil platform inadvertently bring to the surface a prehistoric creature which attacks and kills one of the men, while another is adversely affected after pricking his finger on one of several egg-like rocks that were also retrieved, which the science officer (Joseph Bottoms) hatches in his lab with the expected results. Flatly directed by Peter Carter, this is a somewhat drawn out *Alien* (1979) rip-off with rather too much dull chat in the rig's various under-lit quarters, yet it features a reasonably good monster suit care of creature designers James Cummins and Henry Golas for the climactic run around, during which the monster is finally blown away in an explosion, only for things to end with the suggestion that, as the surviving crew are sailed away to safety, there may be another egg onboard on the rig ("Not without holes," commented *Variety*).

This was followed by yet another horror/thriller hybrid, *No Place to Hide* (1981, TVM), which aired on CBS on 4 March 1981, in which a young woman (Kathleen

Beller) fears that she is being stalked by a mysterious man in black (she is). Although directed by John Llewellyn Moxey from a script by Jimmy Sangster (from an unpublished story by Harriet Steinberg), it was nothing out of the ordinary, though *Variety* was slightly more enthusiastic this time, commenting, "Vidpic offers some good jumps for viewers, and maybe that'll do for now."

College had been a favorite setting for films featuring witchcraft and Satanism in the seventies, and the eighties continued the trend with *Midnight Offerings* (1981, TVM), which aired on ABC on 27 February 1981. In it, a student (Melissa Sue Anderson) uses witchcraft to achieve her aims, only to find her powers challenged by a new girl (Mary Beth McDonough) with whom she does battle. Directed in a fairly straightforward manner by Rod Holcomb, the film isn't without its livelier moments, among them a fight in the college woodwork shop, in which the two witches use the various tools to hand to attack each other, and a fiery climax in which the new girl is almost sacrificed on a bonfire, only to be saved by the intervention of her rival's mother (Cathryn Damon), who also proves to be a witch. Typical TV fare, it was nevertheless dismissed by *Variety*, which commented, "Witchcraft brings on polite, glassy stares; so do vidpics with such limited dimensions."

Judson Scott next starred as the improbably named Bennu of the Golden Light in *The Phoenix* (1981, TVM), which aired on ABC on 26 April 1981. An extraterrestrial god who returns to life after being discovered entombed in an ancient Peruvian sarcophagus, his character has to learn to survive in the modern world, in which task he is helped by an amulet with magical properties. Arrant nonsense played completely straight, it nevertheless led to a short-lived series the following year (also starring Scott), but it only managed to muster four episodes before being pulled (a further four installments went unaired). Rather better was *Dark Night of the Scarecrow* (1981, TVM), which aired on CBS on 24 October 1981, in which Bubba (Larry Drake), an innocent backward man hiding in a field disguised as a scarecrow, is wrongly murdered by members of a farming community for a supposedly harming a little girl, who he actually saved from a dog attack, only to seemingly return from the grave to exact revenge. Directed with reasonable flair by Frank De Felitta and containing plenty of atmosphere during its nighttime sequences, it also featured Jocelyn Brando as the dead man's mother and Charles Durning (in excellent form) as the crazed postman who instigated of the crime, and who isn't above murder to cover his tracks.

It was then clearly the beginning of the silly season with the two-part movie *Goliath Awaits* (1981, TVM), which aired in syndication on 16 and 17 November 1981. In it a team of oceanographers (among them Mark Harmon) discover a community of survivors living in air pockets onboard a liner that was sunk during World War II, since when they have developed into a Utopian society led by the third engineer (Christopher Lee). With sequences filmed onboard the *Queen Mary* (previously used in *The Poseidon Adventure* [1972]), the movie also features Emma Samms (memorably spotted at one of the cabin windows), Eddie Albert, John Carradine, Jean Marsh, John Ratzenberger, Alex Cord and Robert Forster, all of whom are to be commended for keeping their faces straight while performing such nonsense.

Over in the UK, the BBC broadcast a genuine television epic with *Artemis 81*

(1981, TVM), a three-hour, five-minute-long saga written by David Rukin in which Gideon Harlax (Hywel Bennett), a paranormal novelist, becomes involved in a battle for the future of mankind, in which good is represented by Helith (Sting), an alien angel, and bad by his brother Asrael (Roland Curram). Produced by David Rose and directed by Alastair Reid, the film, which aired on 29 December 1981, also featured Anthony Steel, Dan O'Herlihy, Ingrid Pitt, Margaret Whiting, Sylvia Coleridge and a young Daniel Day-Lewis. And, like Rudkin's *Penda's Fen* (1974, TVM), it is full of fascinating ideas, not all of which work, and some of which border on the pretentious. It's also something of an endurance test, given its elephantine running time, yet has many rewarding passages along its wending way for those willing to commit to it.

A killer working his way through the cast of a soap was the theme for *Fantasies* (1982, TVM, aka *The Studio Murders*), which was broadcast on ABC on 18 January 1982. Not exactly stalk and slash, it sees the show's creator (Suzanne Pleshette) keen to catch the perpetrator, given that the crimes are playing havoc with the show's storylines, all of which makes for a reasonably diverting murder mystery, helped along by its cast, which also includes Robert Vaughn, Barry Newman and Patrick O'Neal, along with "five of you favorite daytime stars," as the ads had it, among them names from *All My Children* (1970–2011, TV) and *Ryan's Hope* (1975–1989, TV).

It was then back to the classics with *The Hunchback of Notre Dame* (1982, TVM), which aired on CBS on 4 February 1982. Adapted by John Gay and directed by Michael Tuchner, it was a fairly lavish version of the oft-filmed Victor Hugo novel, with a starry cast led by Anthony Hopkins as the deformed bell ringer Quasimodo, Lesley-Anne Down as Esmeralda and Derek Jacobi as Frollo, supported by Robert Powell, David Suchet, Tim Pigott-Smith, Nigel Hawthorne, Roland Culver, John Gielgud, Rosalie Crutchley, David Kelly, Pam St. Clement and June Brown. Filmed at Pinewood Studios in England, the film was produced by Norman Rosemont, who had something of a predilection for remaking literary classics for the small screen, among them *The Count of Monte-Cristo* (1975, TVM), *The Man in the Iron Mask* (1977, TVM), *Les Miserables* (1978, TVM) and *A Tale of Two Cities* (1980, TVM). His take on *Hunchback* is neither better nor worse than his other productions, though the scale of the exterior set (a muddy square in front of Notre Dame) doesn't exactly convey the vast metropolis of Paris, and Hopkins (sporting a so-so make-up care of Nick Maley) doesn't always seem comfortable as Quasimodo, and ultimately fails to eschew memories of Charles Laughton in the 1939 version, or even Lon Chaney in the 1923 silent. Otherwise, it's a perfectly passable if uninspired rendition of the story.

Elsewhere, *Mysterious Two* (1982, TVM), which aired on NBC on 31 May 1982, sees two aliens (John Forsyth and Priscilla Pointer), who may in fact simply be leaders of a cult, search out people to join them on their travels through the universe ("They promised a better life … but at a frightening price!" ran the tagline). Written and directed by Gary Sherman, best known for the cannibal shocker *Death Line* (1972, aka *Raw Meat*), it presents a curious mix of *Close Encounters* (1977) and religious mania, and while not a success as a whole is not without its intriguing moments, among them an address to a mass gathering keen to believe in what they are seeing and being told. The threatening phone call was meanwhile the subject of

Hotline (1982, TVM), which was broadcast on CBS on 16 October 1982, in which a crisis center operator (Lynda Carter) finds herself menaced by a mysterious caller with murderous intent ("The surprise ending is only a scream away," ran the tagline). An unremarkable lady-in-peril thriller, flatly directed by Jerry Jameson, it suffers from a surfeit of padding before the psycho finally turns up in person to attack our heroine.

Bloodsucking was back on the agenda with *I, Desire* (1982, TVM), which aired on ABC on 15 November 1982. In it, David Naughton, fresh from his success in *An American Werewolf in London* (1981), plays David Balsiger, a law student working as an aide at a coroner's office, where a number of bodies start showing up drained of blood, which is also being purloined from the nearby hospital where his girlfriend (Marilyn Jones) works as a nurse. Could the crimes somehow be connected, and what has a strange young priest (Brad Dourif) who keeps turning up got to do with all? The perpetrator proves to be Mona (Barbara Stock), a beautiful vampire who lures her victims by pretending to be a prostitute. She has also inveigled her way into the hospital as a volunteer, and it's in this guise that she entices David to her apartment, where she attempts to put the bite on him, only to end up falling to her death from her balcony. However, our hero's woes aren't quite over yet, for the priest, who has been trailing Mona and has since been vamped by her, now attacks David, who manages to stake him with a branch from an ornate tree in her apartment. But with two bodies on his hands, how is David going to make the police believe that he has been defending himself against vampires? A reasonably involving story with a slight twist on the material, this is all well enough handled by veteran director John Llewellyn Moxey. Visual flourishes are fairy minimal, among them a shot of a shiny red coffin filled with earth discovered by the police in a secret room in Mona's apartment, but the scenes of nighttime sleaze on the streets L.A. have a certain documentary realism. As for the cast, Naughton and Dourif are on good form in their respective roles, and Stock certainly looks a picture as the sexy vampire, though her death in a mere fall (albeit from a certain height) proves to be a little anti-climactic. An atmospheric score by Don Peake certainly helps.

Elsewhere, with *Don't Go to Sleep* (1982, TVM), which aired on ABC on 10 December 1982, a young girl (Robin Ignico) starts seeing the ghost of her older sister who died a year earlier, much to the upset of her parents (Dennis Weaver and Valerie Harper) and her brother (Oliver Robins), but is it really a ghost or is she possessed by the spirit of her dead sister ("Mary thinks there is something alive under her bed. Mary is right," ran the tantalizing tagline)? Although presented in a fairly straightforward manner by director Richard Lang, this is a reasonably absorbing shocker thanks primarily to the efforts of its cast, which also includes Robert Webber and Ruth Gordon, though few of them survive till the conclusion, which manages to pack in one final twist before the fadeout. With *Cry for the Strangers* (1982, TVM), which was based on a 1979 book by John Saul, and which went out on CBS the following day on 11 December 1982, a psychiatrist and his wife (Patrick Duffy and Cindy Pickett) move to a picturesque coastal town to get away from it all, but a mysterious death occurs each time a storm rolls in, and they begin to wonder if an old Indian legend is behind it all. Packed with thunderstorms and mysterious goings on in the dead of night, it's all ratcheted up by a moody score by John Cacavas, though one loses count how many times director Peter Medak cuts to shots of rolling clouds for dramatic effect. As for the denouement, it's pure *Scooby-Doo*. Much more fun was *Mazes and Monsters* (1982, TVM), which aired on CBS on 28 December 1982. In it, four college friends (Chris Makepeace, Wendy Crewson, David Wysocki and the young Tom Hanks) decide to play a *Dungeons and Dragon*s-style role playing game in a nearby cavern, but one of them (Hanks) starts finding it difficult to distinguish fantasy from reality ("Players in a dangerous game—risking their hearts, their minds, their lives!" ran the tagline). Taken from the cautionary 1981 novel by Rona Jaffe, this is engagingly put over by director Steven H. Stern, and given extra appeal by its young cast, who are ably supported such established names as Vera Miles, Murray Hamilton, Susan Strasberg, Anne Francis and Lloyd Bochner.

The Music of the Night

Another old warhorse came to American television next with a new version of Gaston Leroux's *The Phantom of the Opera* (1983, TVM), which aired on CBS on 29 January 1983. The story had already been filmed for the cinema a number of times by this point, notably in 1925 with Lon Chaney as the Phantom, in 1943 with Claude Rains, and 1962 with Herbert Lom, with the earliest version dating back to 1916 with Nils Olaf Chrisander in the title role (as previously noted, there had also been a nine-part TV version made in Spain in 1960 starring Narciso Ibanez Menta). For this version it was Maximilian Schell who donned the mask of the Phantom, an opera house conductor out to avenge the suicide of his wife (Jane Seymour) after her career has been ruined by the building's owner (Jeremy Kemp), whose advances she had rejected. Deformed by sulphuric acid during a fight with a critic (Philip Stone) who was bribed to write a bad review of his wife's performance, the Phantom continues his revenge from the opera house cellars, and later becomes involved with a young singer (also Seymour) who resembles his wife, and whose career he takes an interest in. Adapted by Herman Yellen and directed by Robert Markowitz, this is a reasonably lively presentation of familiar elements, among them a masked ball secretly attended by the Phantom, his eventual unmasking in his candlelit lair, and a climactic slo-mo chandelier drop during which he meets his doom. Featuring supporting performances by Michael York, Diana Quick and Paul Brooke, this is an undeniably a plush version of the story by TV standards, nicely photographed in Budapest by Larry Pizer, and though by no means definitive, it certainly keeps one watching, and Schell (sporting an excellent make-up care of Stan Winston) provides a solid performance as the brooding Phantom.

On a lighter note, *The Invisible Woman* (1983, TVM), which aired on NBC on 13 February 1983, presented a comedic version (complete with laugh track) of the old story in which this time a cub reporter (Alexa Hamilton) accidentally becomes invisible after mopping up a spilled potion mixed by a chimpanzee belonging to her scientist uncle (Bob Denver). The special effects aren't too bad, but the intended series failed to materialize.

A young boy (Charlie Fields) possessed by a demon was the subject of *The Demon Murder Case* (1983, TVM), which aired on NBC on 6 March 1983. However, when the demon moves into his older brother (Kevin Bacon) and he kills someone, he finds himself in the dock for murder. Featuring several well staged possession sequences care of director William Hale, including a pretty good levitation scene, this is a fair knockoff of *The Exorcist* (1973), with an interesting supporting cast that includes Cloris Leachman, Andy Griffith, Ken Kercheval, Richard Masur, Joyce Van Patten and Harvey Fierstein (who provided the voice of the demon), though the court case element stretches credulity and seems out of place with the rest of the story, even though based on an actual trial (the Arte Cheyenne Johnson "Devil Made Me Do It" case) which used demonic possession as a defense.

A school was again the setting for *Deadly Lessons* (1983, TV), a fairly conventional murder mystery that went out on ABC on 7 March 1983. In it, students at an exclusive school are being killed, much to the consternation of the aloof headmistress (Donna Reed). The old war horse *Svengali* (1983, TVM), taken from George L. Du Maurier's *Trilby*, reared its head again on CBS on 9 March 1983, albeit in an uneasy update, with Peter O'Toole this time playing the charismatic voice coach who is determined to make a rock singer (Jodie Foster) into a star. The story doesn't quite work in modern dress, prompting *Variety* to comment, "Never comes away with anything deep, despite posh packaging," which included a score by John Barry. Meanwhile, another lady (Lauren Hutton) found herself in peril in *The Cradle Will Fall* (1983, TVM), this time from a doctor (James Farentino) in pursuit of a youth serum. Taken from the 1980 novel by Mary Higgins Clark, it aired on CBS on 24 May 1983.

Yet another version of *The Hound of the Baskervilles* (1983, TVM) appeared on HBO on 3 November 1983. This time it's Ian Richardson's Sherlock Holmes who heads for Dartmoor in pursuit of the titular spectral hound, accompanied by Donald Churchill as Dr. Watson. Filmed in England at Shepperton Studios and on location in Devon, the film, which also features Denholm Elliott, Glynis Barber, Brian Blessed, Martin Shaw, Ronald Lacey and Eleanor Bron, often benefits from the atmospheric photography of Ronnie Taylor, particularly during the fog wreathed moorland sequences, which are undoubtedly the highlight, though Richardson is

"...and please, don't let me kill again."

THE DEMON MURDER CASE

starring
EDDIE ALBERT • ANDY GRIFFITH • KEVIN BACON • CLORIS LEACHMAN
Parental Discretion Advised

WORLD PREMIERE   3.40   9 PM

The Devil made me do it. Promotional ad featuring Charlie Shields for *The Demon Murder Case* (1983, TVM) (NBC/Dick Clark Productions/Len Steckler Productions).

arguably a little too aloof in the role of Holmes (note that earlier in the year, the Australians had made a surprisingly passable animated version of the story under the title *Sherlock Holmes and the Baskerville Curse* [1983, TVM], with a well cast Peter O'Toole providing the voice of Holmes; a further version of the story also appeared in 1988 as a feature-length episode in the ongoing series of much admired Holmes adaptations starring Jeremy Brett [1984–1994, TV], which also tackled Doyle's 1924 story *The Adventure of the Sussex Vampire* as *The Last Vampyre* [1993, TVM]).

Notably more steamy was *The Haunting Passion* (1983, TVM), which aired on NBC on 24 October 1983, in which a former football player and his wife (Gerald McRaney and Jane Seymour) move to a remote new home where she begins to have erotic dreams involving a mysterious lover who eventually turns up in real life. The year was then rounded out with *Prototype* (1983, TV), which aired on CBS on 7 December 1983. In it, a team of scientists develop an android named Michael (David Morse) who can pass for human, but when the government want to turn him into a soldier, he goes on the run with the team leader (Christopher Plummer). Unfortunately, despite the presence of Morse and Plummer, "the adventure lacks substance," as *Variety* put it.

A little more traditional was *Invitation to Hell* (1984, TVM), in which a computer scientist named Matt Winslow (Robert Urich) and his family move to a new community for his job, where they are expected the join the Steaming Springs Country Club. However, when his wife and kids join without him, Matt learns that they have been replaced by non-human doppelgangers, and has to enter the club's inner sanctum, a gateway to hell, to retrieve them. A reasonably good-looking affair thanks to the input of director Wes Craven and his cinematographer Dean Cundey, the film, which aired on ABC on 24 May 1984, is otherwise fairly predictable, but made tolerable by its cast, which also includes Susan Lucci as the club's duplicitous director, Joanna Cassidy as Matt's wife, and Barret Oliver and Soleil Moon Frye as their kids. Kevin McCarthy and Michael Berryman were also onboard in supporting roles.

Another version (not that one was *really* needed) of *A Christmas Carol* (1984, TVM) appeared next on CBS on 17 December 1984, and although perfectly adequate in most respects, the sheer familiarity of the story makes this adaptation, which was shot in England, a little tiresome to sit through, with George C. Scott not quite sitting right in the role of Ebenezer Scrooge, and Clive Donner's flat direction adding little mood to the proceedings, though there are compensations in the well upholstered cast, among them Angela Pleasence, Edward Woodward and Michael Carter as the Ghosts of Christmas Past, Present and Yet to Come, respectively (with the latter's appearance accompanied by a disconcerting sound effect that sounds like a rusty gate opening). Joining them were Frank Finlay (as Jacob Marley), David Warner (Bob Cratchit), Susannah York (Mrs. Cratchit), Roger Rees (Fred Holywell) and Nigel Davenport (Silas Scrooge), plus such familiar faces as Timothy Bateson, Michael Gough, Joanne Whalley, Liz Smith and Spencer Banks (this was by no means the last TV version of the story to appear, among them such variations as *Scrooge's Rock 'n' Roll Christmas* [1984, TV], which sees Jack Elam's Scrooge presented with Christmas songs sung by a number of modern day performers, including

The Association, The Raiders and Three Dog Night; *Blackadder's Christmas Carol* [1988, TV], a reverse of the story in which Rowan Atkinson's goodly Ebenezer Blackadder resorts to become more dastardly after discovering how treacherous his ancestors were; *Ms. Scrooge* [1997, TVM], a distaff version starring Cicely Tyson as Ebenita Scrooge; *Ebenezer* [1998, TVM], a western version starring Jack Palance; and *Karroll's Christmas* [2004, TVM], a modern take in which a writer of greeting cards [Tom Everett Scott] is mistakenly visited by four ghosts who have gone to the wrong address!).

The same month, the Brits had another stab at *Frankenstein* (1984, TVM), which aired on ITV on 27 December 1984. An Anglo-American co-production, the 73-minute movie (for a 90-minute slot) was a reasonably starry affair, and featured Robert Powell as Victor Frankenstein, David Warner as the Creature, Carrie Fisher as Elizabeth and John Gielgud as the blind hermit De Lacey. Written by Victor Gialanella and directed by James Ormerod, it was a rather hesitant production, shot on a mix of videotape (studio) and film (location), the latter including scenes at Ripley Castle in Yorkshire (Yorkshire Television was one of the production companies involved). A somewhat tedious affair, it takes itself a little too seriously, and somehow lacks the required spark to bring it all to life, though David Warner engenders a certain sympathy as the Creature, whose disfigurements are this time the result of burns received during the creation process.

A disappointing version of *The Bad Seed* (1985, TVM) came to the small screen on ABC on 7 February 1985. In it, a mother (Blair Brown) comes to believe that her seemingly angelic young daughter (Carrie Wells) is in fact psychotic and capable of murder when she doesn't get her way. The story had already seen life as a 1954 book by William March, a 1954 Broadway play by Maxwell Anderson and a 1956 film starring Nancy Kelly and Patty McCormack as the mother and daughter (there'd also been a Turkish film based on the material titled *Kotu tohum* [1963]). This version has the benefit of a strong supporting cast, among them Lynn Redgrave, David Carradine and David Ogden Stiers, but is otherwise flatly directed by Paul Wendkos, with blandly over lit interiors typical of the period, and unlike the 1956 film, one just doesn't believe that the child is capable of committing the crimes (another TV remake followed in 2018).

Somewhat better was *Deadly*

Bah humbug! George C. Scott looks suitably grumpy in this publicity shot for *A Christmas Carol* (1984, TVM) (CBS/Entertainment Partners Ltd./Enterprises).

Messages (1985, TVM), which was broadcast on ABC on 21 February 1985. In it, a young woman (Kathleen Beller) witnesses a murder following the discovery of a Ouija board in her apartment closet and finds herself being stalked by the killer. She also receives a message through the board informing her that she will be next, all of which leads to a complex identity plot involving a trip to a mental hospital, where the truth of what has been happening to her finally starts to be revealed. With a cleverly plotted script by Bill Bleich, a gutsy performance from its leading lady, who is well supported by Michael Brandon as her boyfriend and Dennis Franz as a disbelieving cop, plus some well staged jolts care of director Jack Bender, this is something of a gem, and reaches its climax in the grounds of a lonely motel during an atmospheric windstorm. And though it ultimately downplays its supernatural element, there's still a nice payoff at the end, when the owners of the motel (Charles Tyner and Barbara Collentine), who have discovered that our heroine has left her Ouija board behind, begin to play with it, only for a knock to come at their door. "Is anybody there? Is anybody there?" asks the husband, at which the wooden pointer moves by itself to the word "yes." Nice.

Rather more ludicrous was *Covenant* (1985, TVM), a *Dallas*-style soap which went out on NBC on 5 August 1985. In it, a wealthy family, which has made a pact with evil and built its banking empire with Nazi gold, uses its supernatural powers to finance death, terrorism and destruction all over the world, all the while being pursued by an order known as The Judges, led by Zachariah (Barry Morse), who wish to destroy them. That such names as José Ferrer, Bradford Dillman, Judy Parfitt and Michelle Phillips could some-how have been coerced into appearing in this diabolical nonsense is perhaps the most astonishing thing about this misguided and misconceived claptrap which, not surprisingly, didn't make it to series. Complete with *Omen*-esque music care of Charles Bernstein, it was directed with neither flair nor humor by the prolific Walter Grauman, its only moments of interest taking place in the subterranean vault of the family's bank, the focus of which is an eye-catching burning hell mouth care of production designer Fred Harpman, whose film credits included *Damien: Omen II* (1978). Commented *Variety* of the resultant mess, "It sails smartly along till it sinks of its own silliness."

Writer Bill Bleich and director Jack Bender were together again for *The Midnight Hour* (1985, TVM), in which a group of high school kids break

Negative reaction. Promotional ad for *Deadly Messages* (1985, TVM) (ABC/Columbia Pictures Television).

into their smalltown Witchcraft Museum on Halloween and steal a trunk containing a scroll, the reading of which prompts a mass rising of the dead in the local cemetery, who are at first mistaken for fellow revelers. An enjoyable romp whose tone is set with the opening shot (a street sign bearing the name Elm St.), it benefits from a personable cast, among them Lee Montgomery, LeVar Burton and Shari Belafonte-Harper, who are supported by such old timers as Kevin McCarthy and Dick Van Patten, and a good selection of ghoulish make-ups care of Steve LaPorte, whose work here would stand him in good stead for his Oscar winning stint on *Beetlejuice* (1988). There's even time for a "Thriller"-like dance number, "Get Dead." It wasn't enough to impress *Variety*, though, which described the film, which aired on ABC on 1 November 1985, as "A deadly dull Halloween party," a quote that somehow became "It's a deadly.... Halloween party," on the cover of the video release (note that Macauley Culkin made his screen debut in the film as an uncredited Halloween kid).

An hour-long version of *The Canterville Ghost* (1985, TV) appeared on PBS in 1985, with Richard Kiley now cast as the playful ghost Sir Simon. Directed by William F. Claxton and based upon a script by B.W. Sandefur (itself taken from a story by Joseph Maurer and Bradley Wigor), it was filmed at the Greystone Park and Mansion in Beverley Hills (a familiar location from numerous films) and also featured Shelley Fabares, Barry Van Dyke, Mary Wickes and Jenny Beck. A fair degree away from the Wilde original, it was nevertheless declared "memorable" by *Entertainment Weekly*, which awarded it an A rating.

Jack the Ripper returned to the small screen again in *Terror at London Bridge* (1985, TVM, aka *Bridge Across Time*), which aired on NBC on 22 November 1985. A rather fanciful conceit, it sees the notorious killer (Paul Rossilli), who drowned in the River Thames in 1888 after being shot during a police chase, reappear in modern day Lake Havasu City in Arizona, his spirit having been transported there via one of the stones in London Bridge, which has been taken piece by piece to America and reassembled as a visitor attraction. Naturally, it isn't too long before the murders start up again, and a young cop (David Hasselhoff) becomes convinced that Jack is up to his old tricks again. Written by William F. Nolan and directed by E.W. Swackhamer on location on and around the bridge itself, it's all very silly of course, but done with a surprising amount of conviction, with an appealing performance from the fresh-faced Hasselhoff and a full-blooded score care of Lalo Schifrin.

It was back to *Dark Shadows* territory with *Dark Mansions* (1986, TVM), in which Shellane Victor (Linda Purl), an assistant book editor hired by a Seattle matriarch, Margaret Drake (Joan Fontaine), to pen her family's biography, discovers that she bears an uncanny resemblance to Yvette, the dead wife of Margaret's son Jason (Michael York), who died in a tragic cliff fall. A glossy but sudsy hybrid of *Dynasty* (1981–1989, TV) and *Rebecca* (1940), it was produced by the production team responsible for the former (Aaron Spelling, E. Duke Vincent and Douglas S. Cramer), and headlined the star of the latter (Fontaine), who was supported by Dan O'Herlihy, Melissa Sue Anderson, Nicollette Sheridan and Lois Chiles. Unfortunately, the mix of shoulder pads, cliff top revelations and ghostly laughter failed to make it to series, with the film, which aired on ABC on 23 August 1986, ending on something of an abrupt note (reads the concluding scroll, "Shellane Victor finished the Drake Family memoirs, and married Jason Drake. One week later, her body was found on the rocks at the bottom of the Bluffs … in the same spot where Yvette died").

Yet *another* version of *The Canterville Ghost* (1986, TVM) starring John Gielgud as Simon de Canterville was syndicated in America on 15 October 1986. A U.S./UK co-production between Columbia Pictures Television and HTV (the latter of which had been behind the 1974 David Niven version), it was filmed on location in Britain at Eastnor Castle in Hertfordshire under the direction of Paul Bogart. Also featured were Ted Wass, Lila Kaye, George Baker, Brian Oulton, Deddie Davies and Harold Innocent, though it was "the droll, charming Gielgud," as *Variety* described him, who inevitably stole the show, bringing a welcome touch a Shakespearean gravitas to his performance. An atmospheric score by Howard Blake was also an asset.

A 60-minute potted version of *Frankenstein* (1986, TVM) care of The Children's Theater Company & School of Minneapolis appeared on CBS on 28 November 1986. A U.S./Canadian co-production, it was written by Malcolm Marmorstein from a play by Thomas W. Olson and presented the story in terms suitable for younger audiences. A videotaped studio production, it starred Carl Beck as Victor Frankenstein and Chris Sarandon as the Creature, sporting a non too convincing pull-on mask in lieu of a more elaborate make-up, yet the scene in which he comes to life and, clearly distraught, lurches after an abhorred Frankenstein may well have been a little too scary for smaller viewers.

Lynda Carter was back under threat again in *Stillwatch* (1987, TVM), which was broadcast on CBS on 10 February 1987. Taken from a 1984 novel by Mary Higgins Clark, it sees her play a television journalist who moves into her childhood home in Washington so as to do a profile on a lady senator (Angie Dickinson), and while there she is helped by a psychic neighbor (Louise Latham) to help face her tragic past in which her father apparently murdered her mother and then tried to kill her. It's a rather complex affair in which politics and a labyrinthine back story don't quite mix with the psychic element, but Carter (who was also one of the executive producers) and Dickinson are good value, and the supporting cast, among them Stuart Whitman, Don Murray and Barry Primus, is a notch above the norm.

Rather less good was *Bates Motel* (1987, TVM), a spinoff from the *Psycho* franchise in which Alex West (Bud Cort), Norman Bates' former roommate at the mental asylum, inherits the Bates Motel when he dies, and makes plans to renovate it and reopen, but it appears that the place is haunted ("Norman Bates may be gone, but his mother lives on," ran the tagline). Written, directed and executive produced by Richard Rothstein, the movie co-stars Moses Gunn, Lori Petty, Jason Bateman and Gregg Henry, with Kurt Paul making a brief appearance as Norman during the introductory black and white flashback. Unfortunately, without the film's original star, Anthony Perkins, audiences just weren't interested, and the film was greeted with indifference when it aired on NBC on 5 July 1987, thus sinking plans for a proposed series ("If you ever need a room, come on by," says Alex straight to camera at the end).

Over in the UK, the BBC's long running drama series *Screenplay* (1986–1993, TV), which notched up 87 episodes of varying length during its eight-season run, featured a new piece by David Rudkin, who also directed for the first and last time.

Titled *White Lady* (1987, TVM), it was broadcast on BBC2 on 26 August 1987, and presents a country idyll in which a father (Cornelius Garrett), working close to poverty to rebuild a dilapidated farmhouse, is periodically visited by his two young daughters (Jessica Martin and Sophie Thompson), who live elsewhere with their mother. But not all is well in the countryside, whose fields and orchards are being poisoned by pesticides which, according to data presented throughout the film, have already entered the food chain and are having an adverse effect on mankind. To this end the White Lady (Meg Wynn Owen), to whom a number of harvest festival offerings have been made in a nearby wood, manifests herself to spirit away the girls, leaving in their stead two changelings to return to their father. With a running time of just 45 minutes, this lacks the usual complexity of Rudkin's work. In

Free shower caps in all rooms. Bud Cort and Lori Petty in a publicity shot for *Bates Motel* (1987, TVM). Is that mother peeking through the net curtains? (NBC/Universal Television.)

fact little of real consequence happens until the belated arrival of the ethereal title character who, although appearing benign, clearly has sinister motives. As for Rudkin's own agenda, the ecological message is relentlessly hammered home in a far from subtle manner, though this was perhaps the point (in addition to the data, we are also shown a number of shots of monkeys who appear to be the worse for having been experimented upon), while the piece concludes with the revelation that the harvest offerings of fruit and vegetables, beautifully presented on what appear to be white clothed tables, are actually atop barrels of poisonous chemicals ("Each time you have eaten, I have kissed you," the White Lady informs the girls, adding, "All children are mine now"). Still, the countryside photography by John Kenway is often arresting, and while not quite a full-on folk horror piece, the eventual appearance of the White Lady at least gives the slowly paced production a dramatic point on which to conclude. In fact the most shocking thing about it is that, over 30 years on, its environmental concerns are as relevant as they have ever been, if not more so (the only other play with a genre leaning in the *Screenplay* series appears to be *The Spirit of Man* [1989, TVM], in which a group of people use a number of means in the pursuit of faith, God and the Devil [this was divided into three sections: "A Hand Witch of the Second Stage," "From Sleep and Shadow" and "The Night of the Simhat Torah"]; note that the actress credited as Sophie Thompson in *White Lady* is not the better known Sophie Thompson, who clearly would have been too old to be playing a young child here, despite IMDb's claim to the contrary).

Meanwhile, back in the States, *Haunted by Her Past* (1987, TVM, aka *Secret Passions*), which aired on NBC on 5 October 1987, sees Karen Beckett (Susan Lucci), already troubled by strange dreams, confronted by a malevolent spirit in an antique mirror while staying at an *olde worlde* country hotel with her husband Eric (John James). Claiming to be her ancestor, the spirit (Finola Hughes), who went to the gallows for killing her lover when he refused to marry her when she was with child, encourages Karen to follow suit by killing her husband, a spell that can only be broken by the destruction of the mirror. One of the sillier movies of this type, this is a rather foolish story, complete with cheesy period flashbacks as narrated by the old innkeeper (Douglas Seale), all of which would be laughable if it weren't so earnest. Amazingly, the cast manage to keep their faces straight throughout.

A community with something to hide was the oft-used plotline for *Bay Coven* (1987, TVM, aka *Bay Cove*), which was broadcast by NBC on 25 October 1987. In it, a young couple, Jerry and Linda Lebon (Tim Matheson and Pamela Sue Martin), move to a picturesque island town, only for her to become convinced that they are living amid a coven of witches who are 300 years old. And not only *are* they, but her husband (spoiler alert) turns out to be one of them ("Welcome to a town where everyone is friendly ... except when the moon is full—that's when all hell breaks loose!" ran the promotional tagline). Despite a slow start and the familiarity of its story, the structure of which seems to have been lifted from *Rosemary's Baby* (1968), which is alluded to early on by Linda's doomed friend Slater (Woody Harrelson), the proceedings are quite slickly presented by director Carl Schenkel, while the climax in which the witches are destroyed in an exploding church is certainly spectacular. Also featuring James B. Sikking, Susan Ruttan, Jeff Conaway, Inga Swenson and Barbara Billingsley, this is definitely a few marks up on most TV genre movies from this period.

Something of a classy affair by virtue of those involved was *Mister Corbett's Ghost* (1987, TVM). Set on New Year's Eve 1767, it sees apprentice Benjamin Partridge (Mark Farmer) kept working late by the town apothecary Mr. Corbett (Paul Scofield). Sent on a last-minute errand to deliver some medicine, the irritated lad wishes his cruel employer dead, only for this to be granted by the man in receipt of the

By the light of the silvery moon. Pamela Sue Martin is featured in this promotional ad for *Bay Coven* (1987, TVM) (NBC/The Guber-Peters Company/Phoenix Entertainment Group/Jerlor Productions Inc.).

delivery, who turns out to be the Soul Collector (John Huston). But young Ben soon regrets his wish, as a consequence of which he is not only haunted by his boss, but also accused of his murder. An Anglo-American co-production, this atmospheric hour-long anecdote was adapted by Gerald Wilson from a 1969 story by Leon Garfield and directed by Danny Huston on location in Britain in the village of Chiddingstone in Kent. Also featuring Burgess Meredith, Alexei Sayle, David Parfitt and Jools Holland, it aired in the UK on ITV on 31 December 1987.

A police procedural with a difference was the feature of *Something Is Out There* (1988, TVM), a two-part movie (each running approximately 96 minutes for a two-hour slot) that aired on NBC on 8 and 9 May 1988. Written by Frank Lupo (who also executive produced with John Ashley) and directed by Richard A. Colla, it follows the investigation by a cop (Joe Cortese) into a series of murders whose victims have had their organs removed. However, the perpetrator turns out not to be a run-of-the-mill serial killer, but a shape-shifting alien who has escaped from a prison ship, and he is helped to track it down by the ship's medical officer (Maryam d'Abo), whose various superhuman abilities prove to be an invaluable asset in doing so. Unfortunately, despite a reasonably healthy budget of $7.5 million, effects care of John Dykstra, and an interesting insect-like alien designed by make-up supremo Rick Baker (which is kept a little too much in the dark), the results are rather dull and overstretched, and are only slightly redeemed by an explosive climax to part two, but it's a long time coming. Perhaps surprisingly, it was followed by a short-lived series (1988–1989, TV), also starring Cortese and d'Abo, which began airing on 21 October 1988, three episodes of which were also helmed by Colla, but the plug was pulled after just eight installments.

Raising Caine

It was to the UK next for one of the decade's quality genre productions, *Jack the Ripper* (1988, TVM), another two-part movie (both again running approximately 96 minutes for a two-hour timeslot) in which we follow the investigation led by Chief Inspector Frederick Abberline (Michael Caine) and his assistant Sergeant George Godley (Lewis Collins) into a series of brutal murders in London's East End in 1888, whose mysterious perpetrator came to be dubbed Jack the Ripper, and whose grisly activities were the bafflement of Scotland Yard. With a solution supposedly based on secret Home Office files, this was clearly a classy affair made to mark the hundredth anniversary of the Whitechapel Murders, with top notch production values care of designer John Blezard and a first rate cast that also included Jane Seymour, Susan George, Ray McAnally, Harry Andrews, Michael Gothard, Gary Love and Armand Assante (the latter as stage actor Richard Mansfield, whose performance in *Dr. Jekyll and Mr. Hyde* sees him transform from Jekyll to Hyde via some excellent, if improbable, make-up effects care of Aaron and Maralyn Sherman). The playing may be a little over the top at times, but Caine and Collins spark well off each other, and the teleplay by Derek Marlowe and producer-director David Wickes is generally well structured in the style of a whodunit, so as to provide something thrilling just before each commercial break. An Anglo-American co-production between Euston Films (for Thames Television) and Lorimar (for CBS), it first aired in Britain on ITV on 11 and 18 October (pulling in some 14 million viewers for the first installment), and in the U.S. on CBS on 21 October. Note that production actually began with Barry Foster and Brian Capron in the roles of Abberline and Godley, with interiors being shot on videotape. When CBS became interested in the project, the original cast was paid off, and Caine was hired for a $1 million fee, as a consequence of which the budget was upped to $11 million and the photography switched entirely to film, with principal scenes taking place at Pinewood Studios as well as on location in Greenwich, which provided the backdrop for the bustling street scenes, which are magnificently lensed by industry veteran Alan Hume to the accompaniment of John Cameron's heraldic music Note that David Wickes had previously directed two episodes of the six-part series *Jack the Ripper* (1973, TV, aka *The Whitechapel Murders*), which offered a re-examination of the Ripper files starring Stratford Johns and Frank Windsor as Charles Barlow and John Watt, the Detective Chief Superintendents they played in the long running police drama *Z Cars* (1962–1978, TV), which began airing on BBC1 on 13 July 1973, while 31 August 1988 (a month or so before the Caine film aired) saw the broadcast

Not a lot of people know that. Michael Caine on the set of *Jack the Ripper* (1988, TVM) (CBS/Euston Films/Lorimar Telepictures/ Hill-O'Connor Television).

of *The Secret Identity of Jack the Ripper* (1988, TVM), an Anglo-American documentary on the subject hosted by Peter Ustinov, in which a number of crime specialists examine the case, moments from which were also re-enacted.

Rather more of an endurance test was *From the Dead of Night* (1989, TVM), another two-parter, the first of which was broadcast on NBC on 27 February 1989. In it, a fashion designer (Lindsay Wagner) falls into a swimming pool and has a near death experience, following which strange forces in the guise of the walking dead are keen for her to return to the great beyond. Directed by Paul Wendkos and adapted by William Bleich from the 1980 novel *Walkers* by Gary Brandner, the material is undeniably overstretched, though the supporting cast, among them Bruce Boxleitner, Diahann Carroll, Robert Prosky and Merritt Butrick, help to guy things along, and Wagner's near-death experience in which she floats through a tunnel of smoke and lasers is well enough handled (the *Hollywood Reporter* found the film to be "Genuinely spooky entertainment").

Hokum was to the fore again with *Amityville Horror: The Evil Escapes* (1989, TVM, aka *Amityville 4: The Evil Escapes*), a TV follow on to the first three theatrical features about a haunted house in Long Island (these were *The Amityville Horror* [1979], *Amityville II: The Possession* [1982] and *Amityville 3-D* [1983]). Adapted from the 1988 book by John G. Jones, and broadcast on NBC on 12 May 1989, the film was written and directed by Sandor Stern (who penned the first film) and sees the malignant forces of the Amityville house transmigrate into an ornate lamp which, following a yard sale, ends up in a house in California where it causes mayhem with a new family. If one can accept the rather ludicrous premise of a lamp being possessed by an evil spirit (particularly such an odd looking one), then the film presents its fair share of nonsense as various people succumb to its deadly powers (which include the turning on of household appliances at the least opportune moments, among them the disposal unit), to which end the cast (among them Patty Duke, Norman Lloyd and Jane Wyatt) can be commended for taking it all so seriously (a second TV film, *Amityville: The Horror Returns*, was proposed by NBC, but was never made; instead a number of direct to video sequels followed, among them *The Amityville Curse* [1990], *Amityville: It's About Time* [1992], *Amityville: A New Generation* [1993] and *Amityville Dollhouse* [1996], while 2005 saw a theatrical reboot of the original film, which was itself followed by *Amityville: The Awakening* [2017] and several other low-budget cash-ins exploiting the Amityville moniker).

The old driving someone insane plot was meanwhile resurrected yet again for *The Haunting of Sarah Hardy* (1989, TVM), in which the title character (Sela Ward), who had witnessed the suicide of her mother as a child, finds herself being troubled by voices from the past in the large house in which she and her new husband (Michael Woods) live, all of which is enough to drive her to drown herself. Or does she, given that her body is never recovered? An involved story of cross and double cross taken from the 1983 novel *The Crossing* by Jim Flanagan, this bland production, which aired on the USA Network on 31 May 1989, was directed and executive produced by Jerry London, and is routine in every way, with only guest star Polly Bergen leaving a mark as the family retainer Emily Stepford (commented the *LA Times*, "Every twist and turn of the story is predictable by a mile"). Elsewhere, with *Nick Knight* (1989, TVM, aka *Midnight Cop*), which aired on CBS on 20 August 1989, we follow an investigation led by Detective Nick Knight (Rick Springfield) into a series of murders in which the victims' bodies are discovered to be drained of blood, which proves to be of particular interest to our hero, given that he is himself a vampire who only works the night shift, but is keen to find a cure that will finally allow him to see the light of day for the first time in 200 years. A mildly diverting case in the *Kolchak* tradition, it was intended as a pilot for a new series, but this failed to materialize until five years later as *Forever Knight* (1992–1996, TV), by which time the leading man was Geraint Wyn Davies (about which more in the next chapter).

Location filming in Mexico City helped to add a little distinction to the horror comedy *Nightlife* (1989, TVM), which aired on the USA Network on 23 August 1989. In it, Maryam d'Abo plays Angelique, a beautiful vampire whose perfectly preserved body is discovered during a dig to retrieve mummified remains. However, her former lover, the bloodthirsty Vlad (Ben Cross), is hot on her heels, but she wants no part of him. Luckily, help is a hand in the guise of a young American doctor (Keith Szarabajka) who falls for Angelique's charms and provides her with a supply of blood so she doesn't have to kill. A reasonably amusing romp whose acting is a little broad and whose humor is a little forced, it nevertheless looks good, and a fight between Vlad and the doctor in a vaulted corridor as the sun begins to stream through its portholes is well staged by director Daniel Taplitz. Camille Saviola also leaves a mark as Angelique's sassy maid Rosa (as has already been noted, Cross would go on to play vampire Barnabas Collins in the reboot of *Dark Shadows* [1991, TV]).

A series spun from the hit movie *Alien Nation* (1988) began airing on the Fox Network on 25 September 1989, which was preceded by a feature-length pilot on 18 September. In the original film, aliens arrive on Earth in 1988, and by 1991 have integrated themselves into society, resulting in one of the newcomers (Mandy Patinkin) being teamed up with a veteran cop (James Caan) with whom he investigates the alien underworld. The pilot film offers more of the same, with the cop and his alien partner (now played by Gary Graham and Eric Pierpoint) out to investigate a drugs conspiracy in the alien subculture. Written and directed by Kenneth Johnson, who also created and executive produced the series, it set up the format for the weekly show, which ran to 21 episodes during its single-season run. Notable for its alien make-ups care of Rick Stratton and his team, and its themes of racism and discrimination, the series was sadly pulled before it truly got into its stride. However, it was followed by a number of feature-length sequels. These were *Alien Nation: Dark Horizon* (1994, TVM), *Alien Nation: Body and Soul* (1995, TVM), *Alien Nation: The Enemy Within* (1996, TVM), *Alien Nation: Millennium* (1996, TVM) and *Alien Nation: The Udara Legacy* (1997, TVM), all of which were directed by Johnson.

It was out to the wilds next for *High Desert Kill* (1989, TVM), which aired on the USA Network on 1 November 1989. In it a hunting party (Anthony Geary, Micah Grant and Marc Singer) find themselves subjected to strange forces, and their usual hunting ground devoid of all game when they arrive for their annual jaunt. Where have all the animals gone, and what is prompting the men to act in such a strange manner ("In the badlands of New Mexico it waits for them…" ran the tagline)? Also featuring Chuck Connors as a grizzled professional hunter, and Lori Birdsong and Deborah Ann Mansy as two campers the men encounter along the way, the film benefits chiefly from its eerie setting, though the revelation that they are being manipulated by an alien for experimental purposes makes for a rather hokey resolution (commented *Entertainment Weekly* of the initially intriguing situation, "plot suggests *Deliverance* and *Predator* poured into a blender").

Over in the UK again, ITV presented a version of Susan Hill's 1983 Edwardian ghost story *The Woman in Black* (1989, TVM), which aired on 24 December 1989. Already the subject of a successful stage adaptation by Stephen Mallatratt first performed in 1987 (and still running in London's West End to this day), the TV version was written by Nigel Kneale and directed by Herbert Wise, and sees junior solicitor Arthur Kidd (Adrian Rawlins) sent to Eel Marsh House, a remote property at the end of a causeway that is cut off from land at high tide, his task being to sort out the effects and documents of a recently deceased client, the reclusive Mrs. Drablow (Pauline Moran), and put the house up for sale. However, Mrs. Drablow's spirit returns to haunt those who would meddle in her affairs, and young Arthur has a number of terrifying encounters with her as a consequence, the most memorable of which has her hovering over him in bed and letting out a terrifying shriek (those who have seen the film usually refer to this as "that" scene). Nicely shot in atmospheric, fog-wreathed locations, including Maldon in Essex, the film, which also features Bernard Hepton, David Ryall and John Cater, has sequences in the style of the BBC's Christmas ghost stories, and is all the better for its overall restraint, which makes each of the apparition's visitations all the more effective, including a final appearance stood in the middle of a lake (the film was followed by two BBC radio adaptations in 1993 and 2004, and a 2012 theatrical feature, the success of which led to a sequel, *The Woman in Black: Angel of Death* [2014]).

Animation wise, Hanna-Barbera Productions still led the way with genre related cartoons, and began the eighties with *Drak Pack* (1980, TV), which began airing on CBS on 6 September 1980. In it, the great, great nephew of a reformed and retired Count Dracula (known as Big D) leads a group of young superheroes whose aim is to make amends for the mayhem caused by their ancestors, and to tackle the nefarious schemes of the evil Dr. Dred and his cohorts, to which end they transform into benign versions of Dracula, the Wolfman and the Frankenstein Monster ("From the monsters of the past comes a new generation dedicated to reversing the evil image of their forefathers," the opening voice over informs us). Running to 16 episodes, the half-hour show featured the voices of Jerry Dexter (Drak, Jr.), Alan Oppenheimer (Dracula), William Callaway (Frankie/Howler), Hans Conreid (Dr. Dred) and Julie McWhirter (Vampira). One of the studio's more lunatic concepts, it was another in a long line of *Scooby-Doo* wannabes, yet it is colorfully designed and executed in typical Hanna-Barbera style and provides a certain amount of easygoing fun.

Other animated shows from the period that involved superheroes combating evil include *Space Stars* (1981, TV) and *Thundarr the Barbarian* (1981–1982, TV), both of which were produced by Hanna-Barbera, *Blackstar* (1981–1982, TV), which was produced by Filmation, and *Silverhawks* (1986, TV), which was produced by Rankin/Bass, while *Heathcliff* (1980, TV, aka *The Heathcliff and Dingbat Show*), which was produced by Filmways, featured a segment titled *Dingbat and the Creeps*, which revolved round the adventures of a vampire dog, a skeleton and a jack-o'-lantern.

Gearing up for action. The team from *Drak Pack* (1980, TV) (Hanna-Barbera Productions/Taft Entertainment Television/Worldvision Enterprises/Warner Bros. Television).

Meanwhile, the Geffen Film Company and Tim Burton Incorporated produced *Beetlejuice* (1989–1991, TV), an animated series based on the popular 1988 live action feature film of the same name, which began airing on ABC on 9 September 1989. Running to 94 episodes over four seasons (the fourth of which transferred to Fox), the series was executive produced by David Geffen and the film's director Tim Burton (who developed it for television), and it followed the madcap adventures of a ghostly conman (Stephen Ouimette) and his 12-year-old friend Lydia Deetz (Alyson Court). Wild and wacky, and featuring a catchy theme tune by Danny Elfman (adapted from his film score), it had more visual flair than most cartoons of the period (note that Burton had already dabbled with TV by this point with a stylized 36-minute version of *Hansel and Gretel* [1983, TV] which he designed and directed; featuring a mix of live action and puppetry, it had aired on the Disney Channel on 31 October 1983).

Overseas, the Russians produced a reasonably plush version Pushkin's *The Queen of Spades* under its original title *Pikovaya dama* (1982, TVM), in which the story, told in six chapters, was narrated by Alla Demidova and performed by such local names as Viktor Proskurin, Innokentiy Smoktunovskiy and Irina Dymchenko under the direction of Igor Maslennikov, while the following year the South Africans presented a 63-minute version of *The Canterville Ghost* (1983, TV). Written and directed by Ralph Mogridge, it starred James Irwin as Simon de Canterville. The Hungarians presented a musical version of the same story later in the decade as *A cantervillei kísértet—zénes jaték* (1987, TVM) starring Erzsi Galambos in the title role, which aired as an episode of *Zenés szinha* (1970–1998, TV, aka *Musical TV Theater*). This in turn was followed two years later by a Czech version titled *Strasidlo cantervilleské* (1989, TVM) starring Jiri Bartoska as the spook. The Hungarians also aired a new version of Karel Capek's *The Makropulos Affair* as *A Makropulosz-ugy* (1988, TVM).

Animation-wise, the Australians got in on the act with a series of animated classics care of Burbank Studios Australia, among them adaptations of *Oliver Twist* (1982, TV), *The Old Curiosity Shop* (1984, TV) and *Ivanhoe* (1986, TV), whose running times varied from 46 to 75 minutes. The series also included lively presentations of *A Christmas Carol* (1982, TV), *Sherlock Holmes and the Baskerville Curse* (1983, TV), *Dr. Jekyll and Mr. Hyde* (1986, TV), *The Hunchback of Notre Dame* (1986, TV) and *The Odyssey* (1987, TV). In similar style in Ireland, Emerald City Productions also had a go with *Charles Dickens' Ghost Stories* (1987, TV), *The Phantom of the Opera* (1988, TV), which is notable for its stylish backgrounds, and still another version of *The Canterville Ghost* (1990, TV), which had been preceded by an animated American version in 1988, which was written and produced by Dick Orkin, who also provided the voice of Sir Simon. Japan also produced a couple of good-looking variations on two old staples, with *Yami no teio kyuketsuki Dorakyura* (1980, TVM, aka *Dracula, Tomb of Dracula* and *Dracula—Sovereign of the Damned*), which was based on the Marvel comic *The Tomb of Dracula* and sees Dracula as the head of a Satanic cult, with whom one of its followers he fathers a child. This was followed by *Kyofu densetsu: Kaiki! Furanhenshutain* (1981, TVM, aka *Monster of Frankenstein*), which was likewise based on a Marvel comic, *The Monster of Frankenstein* (later *The Frankenstein Monster*) and sees the newly created Monster escape the confines of

Frankenstein's turret top lab and go on the rampage in a surprisingly violent take on the story. The long running Brazilian series *Turma di Monica* (1982–, TV, aka *Monica and Friends* [pilot 1976]) also stepped into genre territory with a handful of its many seven minute episodes, among them *O Vampiro* (1986, TV [*The Vampire*]), *Chico Bento em: O Monstro de Lagoa* (1986, TV [*Chuck Billy In: The Monster from the Lagoon*]), *A Gruto do Diabo* (1986, TV [*The Devil's Grotto*]), *O Bicho-papao* (1987, TV [*The Boogeyman*]) and *Frank em Ser Crianca* (1997, TV [literal translation: *Frank in: Being Child*]), in which the Frankenstein Monster asks his creator where he came from.

Further Tales from Europe

In Europe, Poland presented an atmospheric adaptation of Le Fanu's *Carmilla* (1980, TVM), which starred Izabela Trojanowska as the vampiric title character under the direction of Janusz Kondratiuk. Eight years later, the story was adapted by the French as *Carmilla: Le coeur pétrifié* (1988, TVM), in which the title role was this time played by Emmanuelle Meyssignac in a production co-written and directed by Paul Planchon. The French also tackled the works of Edgar Allan Poe with the six-part series *Histoires extraordinaires* (1981, TV), which began airing on FR3 on 7 February 1981. A reasonably prestigious affair whose directors included Claude Chabrol, Maurice Ronet and Juan Luis Bunuel (the son of Luis Bunuel), it featured adaptations of *Ligeia* (1981, TV) and a rather more realistic interpretation than usual of *The Fall of the House of Usher* as *La chute de la maison Usher* (1981, TV), the latter starring Mathieu Carriere as Sir Roderick Usher. They also had a stab Kafka's *The Metamorphosis* as *La métamorphose* (1983, TV), which aired on TF1 on 5 June 1983, with Sami Frey playing Gregor Samsa, the young man who wakes to discover that he has turned into an insect, while the following year they presented the Dickens favorite *A Christmas Carol* as *Christmas Carol* (1984, TVM), which aired on TF1 on 25 December 1984. Written and directed by Pierre Boutron, it starred Michel Bouquet as the miserly Scrooge, and featured Pierre Clémenti, Georges Wilson and Lisette Malidor as the ghosts of Christmas Past, Present and Yet to Come, respectively. The country also presented a new version of Gaston Leroux's *Le coeur cambriolé* (1986, TVM), which aired on FR2 on 20 June 1986, with Katherine Erhardy starring as the young woman who falls under the influence of a mysterious painter (Arthur Denberg). The Czechs meanwhile presented a version of H.G. Wells' *The Story of the Inexperienced Ghost* as *Nezkuseny duch* (1987, TV).

Elsewhere, the Austrian series *Teta* (1987, aka *Frankenstein's Aunt*), presented an affectionate send up of the Frankenstein story, with Viveca Lindfors starring as Hannah von Frankenstein (Hanna in the credits for the English version), who arrives at the castle of her nephew Henry (Bolek Polivka), where she sets out to restore the family name and to bring to heel the various supernatural residents, among them the dim witted Monster, here named Albert (Gerhard Karzel), a werewolf named Talbot (Flavio Bucci), a water creature called Alois (Eddie Constantine) and Count Dracula himself (Ferdy Mayne, who had previously played Count von

Krolock in Polanski's *The Fearless Vampire Killers* [1967, aka *Dance of the Vampires*]). Also featuring Jacques Herlin as Igor and Mercedes Sampietro as Elisabeth Bathory, the seven-part, hour-long series, which first began airing in West Germany on 1 February 1987, was based upon the 1978 novel *Frankensteins faster* (*Frankenstein's Aunt*), a homage to the old Universal classics by the Swedish author Allan Rune Pettersson. A mildly amusing romp with reasonably good production values, including location filming, its best asset is the presence of Lindfors and Mayne, who bring a little dignity to the otherwise broadly played shenanigans, of which a half-hour serving would have been more than enough (in fact the series was also available as a 13-part series running 25 minutes per episode).

Over the border, the neighboring Italians continued to produce their own anthology series with *Il fascino dell'insolito* (1980–1982, TV [*The Charm of the Unusual*]), which began its three season, 14-episode run on RAI on 12 January 1980 (season one was in black and white, the remainder in color). Featuring both period and modern day stories by the likes of Ray Bradbury, M.R. James, Richard Matheson, Truman Capote, H.P. Lovecraft and Philip K. Dick, it launched with *La mezzatinta* (1980, TV), a version of M.R. James' *The Mezzotint*, about an engraving that changes appearance each time it is looked at, and went on to include *La stanza numero 13* (1980, TV), an adaptation of James' *Number 13*, about a haunted hotel room, *Veglia al morto* (1980, TV), a version of Ambrose Bierce's 1889 story *A Watcher by the Dead*, in which a corpse appears to return to life, and *La cosa sulla soglia* (1982, TV), an adaptation of H.P. Lovecraft's 1937 story *The Thing on the Doorstep*, in which a man finds himself changing bodies with a wizard he has killed and walled up in a cellar. Noted for their eye-catching opening titles, based upon a series of celebrated artworks, the series, which was made to fill an hour-long timeslot (though some episodes were longer), was primarily shot on video, and was on the whole stylistically unremarkable, though it occasionally pushed the boat out, as with *Vampirismus* (1982, TV), an adaptation of the 1821 E.T.A. Hoffman novel about a count (Antonio Salines) whose wife suffers from attacks of vampirism. Written and directed by Giulio Questi, this episode's chief asset was its surprisingly lavish period decor care of Antonio Capuano and its costumes by Elena Mannini. Lovecraft's 1929 story *The Silver Key* was also adapted by the Italians as a one-off during this period as *La chiave d'argento* (1982, TVM), in which one of the author's recurring characters, Randolph Carter (Jobst Grapow), becomes obsessed by his dreams. Written and directed by Ciriaco Tiso, it was a mostly rather talkative version of the story.

Meanwhile, another anthology series, *I giochi del diavolo—storie fantastiche dell'ottocento* (1981, TV [*The Devil's Games—Fantastic Nineteenth Century Stories*]), took as its theme the corruption of a number of 19th-century characters via stories by Robert Louis Stevenson, E.T.A. Hoffman, H.G. Wells and Henry James. Produced by Franca Franco on a mix of film and video, and featuring such names as Gabriel Ferzetti, Veronica Lario and William Berger, the six-episode run began airing on RAI on 20 May 1981, and was helmed by the likes of Marcello Aliprandi and Giulio Questi. With running times varying between an hour and 90 minutes, the series launched with *L'uomo della sabbia* (1981, TV), a version of E.T.A. Hoffman's 1816 story *The Sandman*, about a young man's gradual descent into madness, and went on to include and *Il diavolo nella bottiglia* (1981, TV), a version of Robert Louis Stevenson's *The Bottle Imp*, and *Il sogno dell'altro* (1981, TV), an adaptation of H.G. Wells' 1896 piece *The Story of the Late Mr. Elvesham*, in which an unexpected inheritance proves to have dire consequences.

For fans, though, the highlight was no doubt *La Venere d'Ille* (1981, TV), an adaptation of the 1837 story by Prosper Mérimée about a statue of Venus that appears to come to life. Helmed by horror maestro Mario Bava and his son Lamberto (the latter of whom also penned the adaptation with Cesare Garboli), it starred *giallo* queen Daria Nicolodi, who had previously worked with Bava on *Shock* (1977), and proved to be the cult director's last work. In it a statue is discovered by workmen in the roots of a tree they are digging up on an estate, and the landowner, Alfonso De Peyrehorade (Fausto Di Bella), brings in an antiques expert (Marc Porel) to examine it, only for him to notice that it bears a resemblance to De Peyrehorade's daughter-in-law (Nicolodi, who never looked more beautiful than here), with whom he falls in love. Shot on film, and with Bava's mobile camerawork and eye-catching framing well in evidence, and accompanied by a swooning score by Ubaldo Continiello, it proves to be a charming swansong to a celebrated career that included such influential big screen genre classics as *La maschera del demonio* (1960, aka *Black Sunday*), *I tre volti della paura* (1963, aka *Black Sabbath*) and *Sei donne per l'assassino* (1964, aka *Blood and Black Lace*), of which the former was re-imagined to variable effect for TV by Lamberto Bava in 1990 (aka *The Mask of Satan*).

Lamberto Bava subsequently went on to become a successful director of horror films in his own right, and had a hit with *Demoni* (1985, aka *Demons*), which was produced and co-written by Dario Argento. He also continued to work in television, first with *La casa con la scala nel buio* (1983, TV, aka *A Blade in the Dark*), a four-part *giallo* whose half-hour episodes revolved around a composer (Andrea Occhipinti) who finds himself being stalked by a killer whist staying in a Tuscan villa to write the music for a horror film. When the series proved to be too gory for the small screen, Bava edited the episodes together to form a theatrical feature. He also found himself directing six episodes of the 15-part series *Turno di note* (1987–1988, TV [*Night Shift*]), the other nine of which were helmed by Luigi Cozzi. Produced by Dario Argento via ADC Produzione TV and running on RAI 2 from 2 October 1987 as a segment on the series *Giallo* (1987–1988, TV), a crime series created by Enzo Tortora, each episode ran to just 16 minutes and invited viewers to solve a series of murder mysteries involving one of three cabbies (Matteo Gazzolo, Antonella Vitale and Franco Cerri) and their customers. Also featuring Lea Martino as their radio operator, the program had guest spots from David Brandon, Asia Argento, Corinne Cléry and Daria Nicolodi, and concluded with *Il taxi fantasma* (1988, TV [*The Ghost Taxi*]), about a phantom taxi that had been seen in several of the previous installments (rather cheekily, the episode cribs music cues from such films as *Psycho* [1960], *Star Wars* [1977] and *Close Encounters of the Third Kind* [1977] for its soundtrack). Other titles in the series of mini films included *E' di moda la morte* (1987, TV [*Death Is in Fashion*]), *L'impronta dell'assassino* (1987, TV [*The Footprint of the Killer*]) and *Via delle Streghe* (1988, TV [*Street of the Witches*]).

Argento himself was also responsible for nine three-minute mini *gialli* that formed part of the same package under the title *Gli incubi di Dario Argento* (1987, TV [*The Nightmares of Dario Argento*]), which he wrote, produced, directed and hosted. These preceded the *Turno di note* segments and kicked off with *La finestra sul cortile* (1987, TV [*The Window on the Court*]), in which a young man who has been watching Hitchcock's *Rear Window* (1954) on TV finds himself involved in a nightmarish variation on the story. These then went on to include *Il verme* (1987, TV [*The Worm*]), in which a worm begins to emerge from a young woman's eye, which she then proceeds to stab with a knife; *Nostalgia punk* (1987, TV), in which a young woman whose water has been poisoned by an aggrieved fortune teller ends up pulling out her guts (this episode came in for particular criticism); and *La strega* (1987, TV [*The Witch*]), in which a severed head is passed round in the dark during a children's party game.

Bava next found himself directing four 90-minute films for the series *Brivido giallo* (1989, TVM [*Yellow Thrill*]), which began airing on the Canale 5 cable channel on 8 August 1989. These were *Una note nel cimitero* (1989, TVM, aka *Graveyard Shift*), in which five young shoplifters (Gregory Lech Thaddeus, Lea Martino, Karl Zinny, Beatrice Ring and Gianmarco Tognazzi) take refuge at a remote tavern when their van breaks down, and accept a challenge to stay in a cursed crypt all night for the promise of a fabulous reward, only to find themselves fending off zombies; *Per sempre* (1989, TVM, aka *Until Death*), in which a woman and her lover (Gioia Scola and David Brandon) murder her husband, only for the crime to come back and haunt them (the plot appears to have been purloined from James M. Cain's 1934 novel *The Postman Always Rings Twice*, which had been filmed in 1946 and 1981); *La casa dell'orco* (1989, TVM, aka *The Ogre* and *Demons 3: The Ogre*), in which a lady horror novelist (Virginia Bryant) moves to a remote Italian villa with her husband and son (Paolo Malco and Patrizio Vinci) to finish her latest book, only to be plagued by memories of a childhood incident involving an ogre; and *A cena con il vampiro* (1989, TVM, aka *Dinner with a Vampire*), in which an ancient vampire (George Hilton), awakened from his crypt, becomes a film director (!) and invites four auditioning actors (Patrizia Pellegrino, Riccardo Rossi, Yvonne Scio and Valeria Milillo) to his castle for dinner in the hope that they can be convinced to kill him, as he has grown weary of his existence. Clearly low-budget affairs, all four are carried off with reasonable panache by Bava, given his limited resources, and provide a certain amount of undemanding fun if expectations aren't set too high, with *Dinner with a Vampire* perhaps the best of them thanks to Hilton's performance as the gentlemanly vampire, though Daniele Aldrovandi's supposedly humorous turn as his Marty Feldman-esque hunchbacked servant takes some swallowing (note that the series was originally intended to have five films; all four were shown at film festivals [Sitges], released theatrically [in West Germany and Japan] or on video [West Germany and the UK] before being broadcast in Italy; Daniele Aldrovandi had already played a character named Marty Feldmann [sic] in Fellini's *Ginger e Fred* [1986, aka *Ginger and Fred*]).

Lamberto Bava wasn't the only horror film director working in Italian TV during this period. Lucio Fulci, whose features included such highly regarded works as *Una lucertola con la pelle di donna* (1971, aka *A Lizard in a Woman's Skin*),

Non si sevizia un paperino (1972, aka *Don't Torture a Duckling*) and *...E tu vivrai nel terrore! L'aldila* (1980, aka *The Beyond*), also found himself working for the small screen as his career wound down, first with the comedy series *Un umo da ridere* (1980, TV [*A Man to Laugh At*]), and then with the tele films *Il fantasma di Sodoma* (1988, TVM, aka *Sodoma's Ghost*), in which a group of teenagers (among them Claus Aliot and Sebastian Harrison) break into a remote villa and are terrorized by the ghosts of Nazi soldiers killed there during an orgy (yes, that really is the plot); *La dolce casa degli orrori* (1989, TVM, aka *The Sweet House of Horrors*), in which a couple (Lubka Cibulova and Pascal Persiano) who have been brutally murdered by a housebreaker return as ghosts to avenge themselves and to cast a watchful eye over their two children; and *La casa nel tempo* (1989, TVM, aka *The House of Clocks*), in which three hoodlums (Keith Van Hoven, Peter Hintz and Karina Huff) kill an old couple (Paolo Paoloni and Bettine Milne) while robbing their villa, only for them to return to avenge themselves when the clocks in their home turn back time. All three films are pretty low rent compared to Fulci's better efforts, with the first featuring a surprising number of topless shots for a TV movie during its opening sequence (which, incredibly, also includes a shot of a naked woman on a snooker table, between whose legs one of the Nazis pots the brown just as the bombs hit!), while the second has a surprisingly gory death in which the female victim has her face bashed in by the killer.

The latter two films were actually made as installments of a four-part series titled *Le case maledette* (1989, TVM [*The Cursed Houses*]), whose other two films were directed by fellow horror maestro Umberto Lenzi, whose own big screen career included such cult favorites as *Sette orchidee macchiate di rosso* (1972, aka *Seven Blood-Stained Orchids*), *Spasmo* (1974) and *Gatti rossi in un labirinto di vetro* (1975, aka *Eyeball*). These were *La casa del sortilegio* (1989, TVM, aka *The House of Witchcraft*), in which a man (Andy J. Forest) who has had a nightmare about a villa where a witch (Maria Clementina Cumani Quasimodo) boils a likeness of his head in her kitchen is taken to the very same place by his wife (Sonia Petrovna) for a vacation, only for them to be confronted with murder and mayhem, and *La casa delle anime erranti* (1989, TVM, aka *The House of Lost Souls*), in which a group of geologists (among them Joseph Alan Johnson and Matteo Gazzolo) take refuge in a rundown hotel only to discover it to be haunted by the malevolent spirits of those who were murdered there 20 years earlier, and whose decapitated heads have been walled up in the basement. A few marks up on the Fulci films in both style and content, the former features a number of surprisingly violent deaths, one of which involves a pair of garden shears, while in the latter a young boy is decapitated by a washing machine (yes, really). These films were preceded by Lenzi's first TV horror outing, *Le porte dell'inferno* (1989, TVM, aka *The Hell's Gate*), in which a group of scientists (among them Barbara Cupisti and Giacomo Rossi Stuart) enter a cavern to rescue a colleague (Gaetano Russo) who has been undergoing an isolation test and has begun to hallucinate, only to find themselves succumbing to strange forces in the form of ghostly monks whose graveyard they discover. Another low-budget production, this has little going for it save for a few atmospheric shots of the caves and passages, which the scientists spend much of the running time exploring, and a few moments of gore that are mild beer compared to those to be found in Lenzi's most notorious films, *Mangiati vivi!* (1980, aka *Eaten Alive*) and *Cannibal ferox* (1981).

If the seventies had produced many of television's greatest genre films and series, the eighties generally saw a tailing off in quality, despite the occasional gem. Yet compared to the nineties, the decade didn't fare too badly, even if it did bring the first golden age of small screen horror to something of a close, though the end of the following decade, as we shall see in the concluding section, ushered in a new golden era which took genre television to entirely new levels.

SECTION SEVEN

The End of an Era
(the 1990s)

The Anthology Lives On

TV's first golden age of horror may have come to an end, but there's no denying that the nineties saw something of an explosion in genre content across the airwaves. Like the eighties, there were undoubtedly gems to be found among the rhinestones, along with a couple of milestones, but an increase in quantity didn't always make for an increase in quality, and many series recycled familiar themes to often disappointing effect. As has already been noted, a handful of revivals of old favorites appeared during the decade, among them *Dark Shadows* (1991, TV), *The Addams Family* (1992–1993, TV) and *The Outer Limits* (1995–2002, TV). Anthology shows also continued to be popular with producers, as did series inspired by movies.

The first anthology show of the decade proved to be *Chillers* (1990, TV, aka *Mistress of Suspense* and *Les cadavres exquis de Patricia Highsmith*), an Anglo-French co-production which initially began showing in France on FR 3 on 14 April 1990. Introduced by Anthony Perkins and based upon the work of novelist Patricia Highsmith, it ran to 12 hour-long episodes, and was directed by the likes of Samuel Fuller, Mai Zetterling and Damian Harris, and featured such names as Paul Rhys, Tuesday Weld, Ian McShane, Nicol Williamson, Ian Richardson, Ian Holm, Maryam d'Abo, Anna Massey, Bill Nighy and Murray Melvin. Something of a mixed bag in the style of *Tales of the Unexpected* (1979–1988, TV), its episodes included *The Cat Brought It In* (1990, TV [taken from *Something the Cat Dragged In*]), in which a weekend at the country home of Michael Herbert (Edward Fox) takes a dark turn when the family cat returns with two human fingers in its mouth, and *The Day of Reckoning* (1990, TV), in which a young man (Cris Campion) begins to suffer from strange nightmares while working on his uncle's automated chicken farm (note that as well as appearing in a handful of TV horror films in the nineties, of which we shall get to presently, Anthony Perkins also appeared in a failed sitcom pilot titled *The Ghost Writer* [1990, TV], in which he played a writer who is haunted by the corpse of his first wife).

A slightly different kettle of fish to the usual anthology show was the half-hour British series *Without Walls* (1990–1996, TV), whose eclectic mix of biographies, documentaries, reenactments and critiques began airing on Channel 4 on 3 October

349

1990. Among its 58 episodes were occasional dramas, such as Steven Berkoff's adaptation of Edgar Allan Poe's *The Tell-Tale Heart*, which aired on 10 December 1991. The actor had previously performed the piece as part of a one-man stage show titled *One Man*, which also featured a play titled *Dog* about a foul mouthed football supporter and his pet. Here, the star is supported by Tony Bluto, Peter Brennan and Neil Caplan in a tight presentation of the familiar story which was produced and directed by John Carlaw, but really it's Berkoff's show all the way, and though larger than life (okay, over the top), one can't take one's eyes off him (the actor returned to the material a number of years later with the theatrical feature *Steven Berkoff's Tell Tale Heart* [2019], which he co-wrote with its director, Stephen Cookson).

Other anthology shows that aired in the States during the nineties include *Are You Afraid of the Dark?* (1990–2000, TV), in which the teenage members of The Midnight Society tell each other ghost stories around a campfire. Created by D.J. McHale and Ned Kandel, and aimed at a younger audience, it was a simple but effective concept that managed to rack up 91 half-hour episodes over seven seasons on Nickelodeon from 31 October 1990 (a three-part revival followed in 2019). An all-night diner was meanwhile the setting for *Nightmare Café* (1992, TV), an hour-long anthology series that was created by Wes Craven (who also executive produced) and Thomas Baum (who produced) and developed by Peter Spears and Craven's son Jonathan. In it, Robert Englund stars as Blackie, the owner of the café in question, whose new cook and waitress (Jack Coleman and Lindsay Frost) both died on the same night and have been given a second chance working for him, helping unsuspecting customers turn their lives around. "Of course, anything can happen to those who wander in. Their worst nightmares or their forbidden dreams," notes Blackie in the opening narration, at which cue that week's customer. Unfortunately, the series, which debuted on NBC on 29 January 1992, only ran to six episodes owing to a writers' strike, though this may have been a blessing given the review in *Variety*, which described it as, "Poorly conceived, badly acted and inanely written." Rather better was the British series *Chiller* (1995, TV), a five-parter that began airing on the ITV network on 9 March 1995. Its hour-long stories revolved round séances (*Prophecy* [1995, TV]), the debunking of the paranormal (*The Man Who Didn't Believe in Ghosts* [1995, TV]) and child sacrifice (*Number Six* [1995, TV]), and featured such names as Nigel Havers, John Simm, Phyllis Logan, Rosemary Leach, Peter Egan and Martin Clunes. Its contributing writers included Anthony Horowitz and Stephen Gallagher, while directors involved included the respected Lawrence Gordon Clark (of *A Ghost Story for Christmas* fame), who produced and directed two episodes, and produced a third.

A British anthology series simply titled *Ghosts* (1995, TV) began airing on BBC1 on 21 January 1995. Written by Stephen Volk, Monique Charlesworth and Terry Johnson (among others) and starring the likes of Tim Pigott-Smith, David Hayman, Julia McKenzie, Cheryl Campbell and Sylvia Syms, its six 50-minute episodes presented stories involving the supernatural, among them *I'll Be Watching You* (1995, TV), in which a prisoner (Derrick O'Connor) has an out of body experience that allows him to watch over his wife (Anita Dobson) whom he suspects of having an affair with his brother (David Hayman); *Three Miles Up* (1995, TV), in which two brothers (Douglas Henshall and Dan Mullane) holidaying on a narrow boat are haunted by memories of their past; and *The Chemistry Lesson* (1995, TV), in which a lovelorn schoolteacher (Alan Cumming) uses ancient means to attract a fellow colleague (Samantha Bond). Unfortunately, despite the talent involved, the results on this occasion proved to be rather lackluster.

The works of Edgar Allan Poe were the source of *Tales of Mystery and Imagination* (1995, aka *Edgar Allan Poe's Tales of Mystery and Imagination*), a 13-part half-hour series which included 11 stories (one was a two-parter) and a biographical portrait, in which Poe was played by James Ryan. Above and beyond Poe, the series' main attraction was that it was hosted by Christopher Lee, who introduced each of the installments, all of which were dramatized by Hugh Whysall, who also directed five of them. A British-America-Canadian co-production, it was filmed in Croatia and Johannesburg, and featured such names as Susan George, Freddie Jones, Catherine Schell, Patrick Ryecart and Moray Watson. Among the tales on offer were *The Fall of the House of Usher* (1995, TV), which kicked off proceedings, *The Oval Portrait* (1995, TV), *Berenice* (1995, TV), *The Black Cat* (1995, TV) and a two-part adaptation of *The Masque of the Red Death* (1995, TV), in which Lee also starred as Prince Prospero. Unfortunately, the series suffered from noticeably poor production values, which resulted in its failure to secure a transmission at the time, though it has since been made available on the Horror Channel and DVD (IMDb claims that the series aired in the UK from 7 September 1995, but does not list a channel).

Kids got another anthology series of their own with *Goosebumps* (1995–1998, TV), an American-Canadian co-production which began airing on Fox Kids on 27 October 1995. Based upon the popular series of books by R.L. Stine which began in 1992 with *Welcome to the Deadhouse*, it presented spooky stories involving ghosts, zombies and haunted houses, and opened with a two-parter titled *The Haunted Mask* (1995, TV), in which a schoolgirl (Kathryn Long) buys a Halloween mask only to find that it won't come off. Other stories included *The Girl Who Cried Monster* (1995, TV), in which a girl (Deborah Scorsone) who enjoys scaring people with tales of monsters finally gets to see one herself; *Vampire Breath* (1996, TV), in which a brother and sister (Zack Lipovsky and Meredith Henderson) discover a cave full of vampires beneath their house; and *The Haunted House Game* (1997, TV), in which two friends (Jonathan Hall and Laura Vanderwoort) find themselves transported into a game they have found while exploring an old mansion. An engaging series put over with a certain panache, it ran to 74 episodes over four seasons, and was perhaps best appreciated by its young audience for not patronizing them (two feature films later followed: *Goosebumps* [2015] and *Goosebumps 2: Haunted Halloween* [2018]).

A spinoff from *Tales from the Crypt* (1989–1996, TV) came next under the title *Perversions of Science* (1997, TV), which began airing on HBO on 7 June 1997. Hosted by a CGI female robot named Chrome (voiced by Maureen Teefy), several of its stories emanated from the EC comics *Weird Science* and *Weird Fantasy*. The show's directors included Russell Mulcahy, Walter Hill and Tobe Hooper, while actors involved included Keith Carradine, who starred in the opener, *Dream of Doom* (1997, TV), about a man who finds that he cannot wake from his dreams, and Kevin Pollak, who headlined *Boxed In* (1997, TV), in which he plays a weary space pilot returning from a years-long mission ("Space, the final frontier. My ass!"), only to discover that his fiancé has been fitted with an electronic chastity belt by her father (William Shatner, who also directed). As with *Tales from the Crypt*, the executive producers were Richard Donner, David Giler, Walter Hill, Joel Silver and Robert Zemeckis, but lighting failed to strike twice, and only ten half-hours were made, about which the best thing was the dynamic title sequence, in which the camera, accompanied by a typically zany theme care of Danny Elfman, zooms into a piece of popcorn to discover a whole new universe within.

A rather more modest affair was *Ghost Stories* (1997–1998, TV), which began airing on The Family Channel on 28 September 1997. As narrated by Rip Torn ("Come with me into the very cradle of darkness"), this half-hour show offered a mix of fantasy, horror and mystery, and kicked off with *Back Ward* (1997, TV), in which a hospital administrator (Marcy McGuigan) attempts to turn around the fortunes of an old mental institution, only to find herself haunted by scenes of mistreatment from its distant past. The series then went on to include *Wake in Fear* (1997, TV), in which an intern (Kris Bratton) suffers from dreams about those who will die the next day during their operations; *It's Only a Movie* (1998, TV), in which a horror fan (Kevin Sussman) finds that he is the intended victim when he gets a small role in a horror movie that turns out to be all too real; and *Parting Shot* (1998, TV), in which a paparazzo (Maya Israel) who has managed to photograph a dead celebrity finds herself being haunted by him. Clearly a low-budget affair, the series lacked the stars and directorial talent to lift it above the routine, yet it managed to notch up a healthy 44 episodes during its single-season run, so someone must have been watching.

Kids were again the focus of *A Twist in the Tale* (1999, TV, aka *William Shatner's A Twist in the Tale*), whose 15 hour-long episodes began airing in syndication in the U.S. on 6 February 1999. Shot in Wellington, New Zealand, the U.S./NZ co-production sees host William Shatner narrate a variety of stories involving children set in the past, present and future, ranging from straightforward adventures to something more fantastical, among the latter *Darkness Visible* (1999, TV), *A Ghost of Our Own* (1999, TV) and *The Skeleton in the Cupboard* (1999, TV). Like *Are Your Afraid of the Dark?* (1990–2000, TV), there's nothing too scary here, but Shatner makes for a genial host and the stories are well enough put over, best among them being *Bertie* (1999, TV), in which a playful young ghost (Sam Husson) who has only recently completed his training helps a family stave off their financial problems by appearing at a banquet to which tickets have been sold.

The decade's run of anthology shows was finally capped off with *Shockers* (1999–2000, TV), which began its six-episode run on Britain's Channel 4 on 19 October 1999. Featuring writing by Stephen Volk, Joe Ahearne and Chris Bucknall (among others), it began with *Déjà Vu* (1999, TV), in which a mother (Kerry Fox) appears to relive the car accident in which her young son was killed. The other installments included *The Visitor* (1999, TV), in which three flat mates inadvertently let a killer (Daniel Craig) into their home, and *Parents' Night* (2000, TV), in which a mother (Aisling O'Sullivan) avenges the death of her son who was bullied at school. Unfortunately, as with *Ghosts* (1995, TV), the results are strictly average, despite the talent involved.

As has been mentioned, the nineties also saw a number of shows inspired by movies, among them *Swamp Thing* (1990–1993, TV), which began airing on the USA Network on 27 July 1990. The series was inspired by the 1982 film of the same name and its sequel, *The Return of Swamp Thing* (1989), both of which were based on a DC Comics character who first appeared in 1972 in adventures initially written by Len Wein and drawn by Berni Wrightson. In the half-hour show, which was developed by Joseph Stefano, Dick Durock plays the title character (whom he'd played in both movies), a former research scientist named Alec Holland who has mutated into a creature formed of sludge and plant life, having dived into the swamp after being doused with chemicals and set on fire during a break-in at his lab. Now super powerful, he uses his abilities to fight evil, among his foes being the villainous Dr. Anton Arcane (Mark Lindsay Chapman). Arrant nonsense with somewhat variable production values (and acting), the most incredible thing about the series (aside from the make-up effects) is that it ran to 72 episodes over three seasons (note that a pilot for a cartoon version aired on 31 October the same year on Fox, with Len Carlson providing Swampy's voice, but only four further episodes followed in 1991, while in 2019 a live action reboot starring Derek Mears appeared, but ran only one season on DC Universe).

Other genre series that took their inspiration from the movies in the nineties included *Poltergeist: The Legacy* (1996–1999, TV), *Buffy the Vampire Slayer* (1997–2003, TV) and *The Hunger* (1997–2000, TV). The first of these took its title from the 1982 film, but otherwise bore no resemblance to its story of paranormal activity in suburbia. Created by Richard Barton Lewis (who also executive produced), it focuses on The Legacy, a centuries old secret society whose mission is to fight evil, which they do from their mansion on an island in San Francisco Bay, in which they have accumulated all manner of artefacts and knowledge to help them do so. Among the team are Dr. Derek Rayne (Derek de Lint), a scholar with the power of precognition, Alexandra Moreau (Robbi Chong), a researcher with extra sensory perception, and Nick Boyle (Martin Cummins), a former navy SEAL with an expertise in weaponry and tactics, skills which they use to tackle all manner of supernatural phenomena, from ghosts to witchcraft, thus allowing for a different story each week. Running to 87 episodes over four seasons, the hour-long show debuted on 21 April 1996 on Showtime with a feature-length story titled *The Fifth Sepulcher* (1996, TVM), which revolved round a chest containing five fallen angels (the show moved to the Sci-Fi Channel for its final season; Gary Sherman, who had helmed *Poltergeist III* [1988], worked as a co-executive producer on season two and also directed an episode, *Let Sleeping Demons Lie* [1997, TV]).

One of the decade's tent pole shows was undoubtedly *Buffy the Vampire Slayer* (1997–2003, TV), which was based on the 1992 film. Created by Joss Whedon (who also executive produced and occasionally directed), the series follows the adventures of 16-year-old high school student and cheerleader Buffy Summers (Sarah Michelle Gellar), who discovers that she is a slayer, and that it is her destiny to fight vampires, in which task she receives guidance from her Watcher, Rupert Giles (Anthony Head), and help from her school friends Willow (Alyson Hannigan), who becomes a witch, Oz (Seth Green), who just happens to be a werewolf, and Xander (Nicholas

Brendon), the joker in the pack whose humor provides the show with much of its comic relief. Romance is also present in the guise of Angel (David Boreanaz), a vampire who has been cursed with remorse for his past sins. Clocking up an incredible 145 episodes over seven seasons, the hour-long show (running time 43 minutes) began airing on the WB Television Network on 10 March 1997 (it moved to UPN for its final two seasons) and quickly became something of a pop culture phenomenon (a spinoff series, *Angel* [1999–2004, TV] featuring the Boreanaz character went on to notch up 111 episodes of its own across five seasons).

Elsewhere, *The Hunger* (1997–2000, TV), which was based on the erotic 1983 vampire film, proved to be more of a traditional half-hour anthology show, whose 44 episode-run over two seasons was hosted by Terence Stamp, who fronted the first season, and David Bowie (who'd starred in the film) taking over for the second. Created by Jeff Fazio (who also executive produced), and airing on Showtime from 20 July 1997, the stories focused on the hunger for power, sex, life, longevity, money and blood (as the opening titles inform us), and often featured supernatural elements, among them ghosts, vampires, mutant babies, a cursed dress and a Golem. Helmed by the likes of Tony Scott (who'd directed the film), Russell Mulcahy and Jake Scott, the series featured such guest stars as Karen Black, Jason Scott Lee, Margot Kidder, Balthazar Getty, Eric Roberts, Jennifer Beals and Brad Dourif, and were notable for their reasonably glossy look and for featuring more nudity and soft-core sexual content than similar programs.

Horror themed cartoons also proliferated during the decade, which began with *Gravedale High* (1990–1991, TV), in which the only human at a high school is the teacher Max Schneider (voiced by Rick Moranis), all the pupils being monsters of one variety or another, among them vampires, werewolves and mummies. Created by David Kirschner, and running on NBC from 8 September 1990, this lively 13-part Hanna-Barbera production benefited from an excellent voice cast that, in addition to Moranis, also included Shari Belafonte, Ricki Lake, Tim Curry, Jonathan Winters, Georgia Brown, Brock Peters and Frank Welker.

Other animated series that appeared during the nineties include the aforementioned *Tales from the Cryptkeeper* (1993–1999, TV) and *Extreme Ghost Busters* (1997, TV), along with *Gargoyles* (1994–1996, TV), whose 65 episodes revolve round the adventures of a group of ancient night creatures who have pledged to protect New York from evil (this was followed by a 13-part sequel, *Gargoyles: The Goliath Chronicles* [1996–1997, TV]); *Monster Force* (1994, TV), whose 13 episodes follow a team of monster hunters as they track down the likes of Dracula, the Wolfman and the Creature from the Black Lagoon; *Aaahh!!! Real Monsters* (1994–1997, TV), whose 52 episodes follow the adventures of three young monsters who are learning how to scare people; *Ripley's Believe It or Not* (1998–1999, TV), whose 26 episodes chronicle the adventures of a trio who search out unexplained mysteries and phenomena; *Archie's Weird Mysteries* (1999–2000, TV), whose 40 episodes follow the adventures of popular comic strip character Archie Andrews and his friends as they investigate aliens and monsters which they then write about in their school newspaper; and *Courage the Cowardly Dog* (1999–2002, TV), whose 52 episodes see a cowardly dog protect his owners' farm from all manner of interlopers, including the supernatural kind.

A number of Japanese cartoons also explored the supernatural during this period, among them *Jigoku sensei Nube* (1996, TV, aka *Hell Teacher Nube*), in which a teacher uses his abilities as an exorcist to help protect his pupils; *Kyuketsuki Miyu* (1997, TV, aka *Vampire Princess Miyu*), in which a vampire girl does battle with a race of demons known as the Shinma; *Kenpu Denki Berserk* (1997–1998, TV, aka *Berserk*), in which a young swordsman joins the Band of the Hawk, whose enemies include Nosferatu Zodd; *Devilman Lady* (1998–1999, TV, aka *Devil Lady*), in which a supermodel with an inner devil joins a secret government agency to fight demons; *Petto shoppu obu horazu* (1999, TV, aka *Pet Shop of Horrors*), in which the proprietor of a pet shop sells unusual animals which come with a contract which, if broken, leads to tragic consequences; *Betterman* (1999, TV), in which humanity finds itself in peril from a deadly virus; *Buru Jenda* (1999–2000, TV, aka *Blue Gender*), in which a man awakens from a cryogenically induced sleep to discover that the Earth has been invaded by alien bugs; and *Gregory Horror Show* (1999–2006, TV), which takes place in Gregory House, a creepy hotel run by a mouse.

Other foreign series that dealt with horror include *O Fantasma da Opera* (1991, TV), a Brazilian update of *The Phantom of the Opera* that ran to a stonking 37 episodes; *The Zee Horror Show* (1993–2001, TV), an Indian anthology series which managed to notch up 364 installments during its run; *Riget* (1994–1997, TV, aka *The Kingdom*), a Danish series set in a haunted hospital that was notable for the involvement of writer-director Lars von Trier (the series was also released as a theatrical feature in 1994 and was later turned into an American series titled *Kingdom Hospital* [2004, TV] which was developed by Stephen King); *Aahat* (1995–2015, TV), another Indian anthology series that accumulated an incredible 543 episodes during its 20-year run; *Eko eko azaraku* (1997, TV, aka *Eko Eko Azarak: The Series*), a Japanese show in which a school girl uses her satanic powers to fight demons (this was a follow up to two films, *Eko eko azaraku* [1995, aka *Eko Eko Azarak: Wizard of Darkness*] and *Eko eko azaraku II* [1996, aka *Eko Eko Azarak II: Birth of the Wizard*], and was in turn followed by a further five films and a second series, *Eko eko azaraku—manako* [2004, TV, aka *Eko Eko Azarak: Eye*]); *Chock* (1997, TV), a Swedish anthology series hosted by local favorite Ernst-Hugo Jaregard; *Anveshitha* (1997–1999, TV), an Indian supernatural drama involving black magic and the paranormal; *Woh* (1998, TV), an Indian version of Stephen King's 1986 novel *It*, which had already been filmed for American television in 1990 (more on which to come); and an 11-part Argentinean version of *Dracula* (1999, TV) set in both ancient and modern times, with Carlos Calvo as the title character.

Meanwhile, over in the UK, movie star Albert Finney took to the airwaves with *The Green Man* (1990, TV), a three-part ghost story based upon the 1969 novel by Kingsley Amis, which began showing on BBC1 on 28 October 1990. In it he plays a hedonistic country publican who regales the guests of his *olde worlde* establishment, The Green Man, with stories about the ghosts that supposedly haunt the place, only to find the stories rather more real than he imagined them to be. Unfortunately, despite the presence of Finney and such supporting players as Michael Hordern, Nickolas Grace, Nicky Henson, Linda Marlowe, Josie Lawrence and Michael Culver as the spectral Dr. Thomas Underhill, this is an overlong and rather clubfooted series that lacks the required atmosphere and subtlety to make it as effective as it could and should have been, its scarier moments being directed with all the finesse of a sledge-hammer by Elijah Moshinsky, who should perhaps have glanced at a couple of the BBC's Christmas ghost stories before embarking on the enterprise.

Duped by Auntie

Also in the UK, *Ghostwatch* (1992, TVM), which aired on BBC1 on 31 October 1992, amazingly managed to convince an astonishing number of gullible viewers that its investigation into the supernatural was real, given that the 90-minute program (prerecorded but presented as live) was done in the style of a typical documentary broadcast, and featured such established presenters as Michael Parkinson, Sarah Greene and Mike Smith. Like Orson Welles' famous radio broadcast of *The War of the Worlds* in 1938, the results caused a national outcry (the Beeb's switchboard received some 30,000 calls) and the program hasn't been repeated terrestrially in the UK since (though it has been made available on DVD). Written by Stephen Volk (who'd originally conceived the piece as a six-part series) and directed by Lesley Manning, it sees a camera crew visit what is deemed to be the most haunted house in Britain, where a malevolent presence makes its presence felt, and all hell breaks loose as a consequence. Yet despite some unconvincing performances and the fact that it was presented as an episode of the ongoing *Screen One* (1985–2002, TVM) series, audiences swallowed the hoax whole, perhaps because it was broadcast by such a trusted source as the BBC, hence the subsequent outcry. However, the program's lingering effect eventually led to such similar series as *Most Haunted* (2002–2019, TV), which notched up an incredible 381 episodes during its lengthy run of paranormal investigations, and made celebrities of its presenters Yvette Fielding and Derek Acorah (the only other film with a genre leaning presented as part of *Screen One* appears to be *Frankenstein's Baby* [1990, TVM], in which a man [Nigel Planer], keen to start a family, becomes pregnant after receiving treatment from Dr. Eva Frankenstein [Yvonne Bryceland]).

Ongoing series with a genre angle were proving to be increasingly popular with audiences during the nineties, particularly with younger demographics, though not all of them turned out to be classics. One of the decade's earliest was *Dracula: The Series* (1990–1991, TV), whose 21 half-hour episodes began airing in syndication on 29 September 1990. An update of the old legend developed by Glenn Davis and William Laurin (who also produced and wrote many of the episodes), it sees Dracula reincarnated in the guise of a billionaire industrialist called Alexander Lucard (Geordie Johnson), who finds himself being pursued by vampire hunter Gustav Helsing (Bernard Behrens) and his two young nephews Chris and Max (Joe Roncetti and Jacob Tierney), who are staying with their uncle in Europe while their mother (Lynne Cormack) is away on business. Filmed in Luxembourg, which adds immeasurably to the atmosphere, this is a surprisingly well-made show aimed at older children, with some good effects work, including Dracula's transformation into a horde of animated bats, to which end it is unexpectedly creepy at times, and may well have been the source of a few nightmares (A. Lucard is of course Dracula spelled backwards).

Another series that fully embraced the supernatural was *She-Wolf of London* (1990–1991, TV), which began airing in syndication on 9 October 1990. An American-British (Welsh) co-production between Universal and Harlech Television, it was created by Mick Garris and Tom McLoughlin, and follows the adventures in London of an American student (Kate Hodge) who is bitten by a werewolf and subsequently teams up with her mythology professor (Neil Dickson) to investigate the supernatural, which sees them tackle a succubus, a cursed bookstore, a warlock and a law firm run by vampires. A rather middling series, it suffered the indignity of having its finance pulled by HTV midway through filming, and so returned to the U.S. for its final six episodes, for which it was re-titled *Love and Curses*. It nevertheless remains of

Dressed to kill. Geordie Johnson as the title character in *Dracula: The Series* (1990–1991, TV) (Blair Entertainment/Cinexus-Famous Players/Homescreen Entertainment/RHI Entertainment).

passing note for its make-up effects by Christopher Tucker, who worked on 11 of the series' 21 hour-long episodes (Tucker already had form with the genre, having provided the effects for *The Company of Wolves* [1984]).

An explosion at The Shop, a secret lab run by the army, was the catalyst for *Golden Years* (1991, TV), a limited series care of Stephen King running to just seven half-hour episodes, which began airing on CBS on 16 July 1991. Described by King as "a novel for television" given that it originated in notes for a book, it sees 70-year-old janitor Harlan Williams (Keith Szarabajka) injured in an explosion at the facility, the result of which sees him gradually grow younger, all of which proves to be of interest to the military, who set out to capture him when he and his wife Gina (Frances Sternhagen) go on the run with a sympathetic agent (Felicity Huffman). King penned the first five installments himself, while Josef Anderson wrote the final two (working from King's outline), which were helmed by Allen Coulter (three episodes), Michael Gornick (two), Kenneth Fink (one) and Stephen Tolkin (one). It's all perfectly watchable though not exactly inspired (it lacks both visual panache and the pace of a serial), with Szarabajka overdoing the old fart stuff in the early episodes, but Huffman and the always welcome Sternhagen provide good support in a cast that also includes Ed Lauter, Bill Raymond and even King himself, who has a brief cameo in episode five as an impatient bus driver, while the theme tune was provided by David Bowie ("Run for the shadows in these golden years," go the lyrics). King had intended the short run to be followed by a regular series, hence the slightly abrupt ending (spoiler alert: Harlan and Gina disappear in a curious green glow), but CBS weren't interested in either this or a four hour follow up, so that was the end of that.

Rather more fun was another kids' series *Eerie, Indiana* (1991–1992, TV), whose 19 half-hour episodes began showing on NBC on 15 September 1991. Created by Jose

Rivera and Karl Schaefer, it follows the adventures of teenager Marshall Teller (Omri Katz) who, along with his friend Simon (Justin Shenkarow), spend much of their time investigating the strange goings on in their home town (population 16,661), which turns out to be "the center of weirdness for the entire planet," given that its residents include Elvis (Steve Peri) and a family who manage to stave off the ageing process by using a form of Tupperware known as ForeverWare.

Newsround. Omri Katz in *Eerie, Indiana* (1991–1992, TV) (NBC/Cosgrove-Meurer Productions/Hearst Entertainment Productions/Unreality).

Directed by the likes of Joe Dante, Bob Balaban and Ken Kwapis, this is an undeniably engaging show that benefits from quirky, in-jokey scripts (which *The Hollywood Reporter* acknowledged for their "smart, sharp insights"), and a supporting cast that includes such seasoned players as John Astin, Henry Gibson, Dick Miller, Julius Harris, John Standing and Belinda Balaski. The series was later followed by a spinoff titled *Eerie, Indiana: The Other Dimension* [1998, TV], which ran to 15 episodes.

One of the decade's early long runners proved to be *Forever Knight* (1992–1996, TV), which ran to 70 episodes over three seasons, beginning on CBS on 5 May 1992. A Canadian-West German co-production, its premise hailed from a TV movie *Nick Knight* (1989, TVM, aka *Midnight Cop*), in which a vampire cop (Rick Springfield) working the night shift finds himself investigating a case involving another vampire. The pilot failed to go to series, but the idea was revived five years later with Geraint Wyn Davies now in the role of Detective Nick Knight, a 13th-century vampire turned 20th-century cop who works the night beat in Toronto as a means of redeeming himself ("When the sun goes down, so does the crime rate," ran the promotional tag line). The first two episodes covered the same plotline as the earlier TV movie, following which our hero went on to tackle all manner of criminals and killers, both real and supernatural. Created by Barney Cohen and James D. Parriott (who provided the story for the original film, which the latter scripted), this was a high concept affair that embraced its central idea to generally good effect if one was prepared to go along with it, and many viewers were, turning it into a minor cult, so much so that when it was cancelled in the midst of its third season, fan protest resulted in a U-turn, thus enabling the series to carry on and reach a proper finale (note that some nude scenes, shot for German television, didn't make it into the U.S. broadcasts).

The X Factor

The decade's true game changer, however, proved to be *The X Files* (1993–2003, TV), which not only grew in popularity as its nine seasons progressed, but became something of a global phenomenon in the process, resulting in all manner of merchandise, including video games, trading cards and an official magazine. Created by Chris Carter (who also executive produced and directed a handful of episodes), it follows the case files of Fox Mulder (David Duchovny) and Dana Scully (Gillian Anderson), two FBI agents whose remit is to investigate all manner of paranormal activity, including UFO sightings, sentient computers, psychic predictions, the power to heal, humanoid organisms, Devil worshippers, telekinesis, religious cults and alien conspiracy theories (tagline: "The truth is out there"). Accompanied by a memorable whistle effect theme tune by Mark Snow (who also scored every episode), and featuring memorable supporting performances from its roster of guest stars (particularly Brad Dourif as a death row psychic in *Beyond the Sea* [1994, TV] and an Emmy winning turn by Peter Boyle as a grumpy seer able to predict how people will die in *Clyde Bruckman's Final Repose* [1996, TV]), the hour-long series was noted for the chemistry of its two leads and the intelligence of its scripts, which prompted *The Independent* to describe it as "one of the greatest cult shows in modern television." A further two seasons followed in 2016 and 2018, bringing the total episode count to 217. There were also two theatrical features, *The X Files* (1998) and *The X Files: I Want to Believe* (2008), and a spinoff series, *The Lone Gunmen* (2001, TV). The show also inspired a number of similarly themed series, either directly or indirectly, among them *Dark Skies* (1996–1997, TV), *Supernatural* (2005–2020, TV) and *Fringe* (2008–2013, TV).

The corrupt face of law enforcement was the focus of *American Gothic* (1995–1996, TV), whose 22 hour-long episodes began showing on CBS on 22 September 1995. In it, the charismatic Sheriff Lucas Buck (Gary Cole) holds sway over the seemingly peaceful township of Trinity ("In my town the American dream is still a reality," he informs us). However, he does this by way of the demonic powers he possesses, which not only allow him to manipulate the locals, but to escape detection for his evil ways, which include murder and rape, the result of the latter being a son, Caleb (Lucas Black), whose mother kills herself after giving birth to him, and whose husband he coerces into committing suicide. He also murders Caleb's sister Merlyn (Sarah Paulson) so as to be able to claim the child for his own, but a new doctor to the town (Jake Weber) slowly begins to uncover the truth, while the ghost of Merlyn prevents the growing boy from being corrupted by the sins of his biological father. Created by actor Shaun Cassidy (of *Hardy Boys* fame) and executive produced by Sam Raimi, this was a surprisingly dark and full-blooded slice of modern day gothic horror whose chief asset was undeniably Gary Cole's turn as the sinister sheriff, a dyed-in-the-wool villain one could truly love to hate (when challenged by his deputy [Nick Searcy] as to whether he has a conscience or not, he simply replies, "Conscience is just the fear of getting caught"). Sadly, CBS didn't know how to handle the show, which it not only shunted about the schedules, but often showed out of sequence, though it has since taken on cult status, and is now at least available to enjoy as intended on DVD.

Over in the UK, the kids' teatime show *Julia Jekyll and Harriet Hyde* (1995–1998, TV) managed to rack up 53 15-minute episodes over its three-season run on the BBC, beginning on 29 September 1995. In it, schoolgirl Julia Jekyll (Olivia Hallinan) concocts an elixir for a science project, only to have it interfered with by the school's bullies, the Blister Sisters (Tiffany Griffith and Karen Salt), a consequence of which she transforms into the hairy Harriet Hyde (John Asquith inside the monster suit) when she takes a sip of it. A mildly amusing romp clearly aimed at ten-year-olds, its best performance comes from Simon Green as the school's long haired "with it" head teacher Memphis Rocket, who gets all the best lines, among his various exclamations being "Procol Harum!"

Vampires returned to the airwaves again with *Kindred: The Embraced* (1996, TV), which began its eight-episode run on the Fox Network on 2 April 1996. The hour-long show was created by John Leekley (who also executive produced with Aaron Spelling and E. Duke Vincent) and hailed from the role playing game *Vampire: The Masquerade* by Mark Rein-Hagen, and follows an investigation by San Francisco police detective Frank Kohanek (C. Thomas Howell) into the activities of a powerful mobster, Julian Luna (Mark Frankel), who is actually the leader of five not entirely harmonious vampire clans known as The Kindred, whose members are able to disguise themselves as humans so as to be able to live and work in society, and who must abide by a strict set of rules or face an abrupt end to their existence. Unbeknownst to him, Frank's girlfriend Alexandra (Kate Vernon) is also a vampire, as well as being Luna's ex, a relationship for which she pays the ultimate cost (spoiler alert: she's toast by the end of the pilot). Unfortunately, the disparate elements of police procedural, soap opera, mobster melodramatics and vampirism didn't make for entirely comfortable bedfellows, and the series itself was curtailed by the studio mid-season before it could settle into its stride.

Sadly, the four-part British series *Cold Lazarus* (1996, TV), which began airing on Channel 4 on 26 May, proved to be the last work of its celebrated author, Dennis Potter. Set in the 24th century, it follows an experiment by Dr. Emma Porlock (Frances de la Tour) to access the memory of a cryogenically frozen 374-year-old head belonging to a writer named Daniel Feeld (Albert Finney), whose past she is able to project via virtual reality displays (Feeld had previously featured in another Potter series, *Karaoke* [1996, TV], again played by Finney). But as the experiment continues, it gradually becomes clear that Feeld's mind is actually conscious of his situation. One of the writer's lesser works, it presents the usual dystopian view of the future, and is hampered by verbose, often unspeakable dialogue, foolish technology and a tedious central conceit (*Donovan's Brain* was far more fun). It also goes on forever, and save for a good score by Christopher Gunning and a solid supporting cast (among them Ciaran Hinds, Diane Ladd, Richard E. Grant, Ian McDiarmid and Roy Hudd), is something of an ordeal to get through.

A series of children's books by Betsy Haynes and Daniel Weiss were meanwhile the source of another kids' show, *Bone Chillers* (1996, TV), which began airing on ABC on 7 September 1996. Created by Adam Rifkin, who also directed a number of episodes (along with Christopher Coppola, nephew of Francis Ford, and Richard Elfman, brother of Danny), it centers on a group of school kids who encounter all manner of supernatural events while attending the spooky Edgar Allan Poe High School, among them a mummy, a Frankenturkey (don't ask) and the ghost of Edgar Allan Poe himself. Filmed in a variety of mock processes (among them Insect-O-Scope, Arachnicolor, Tree-D, Neander-Cam, Ectoplasmarama and Howl-O-View), the half-hour series features Linda Cardellini, Saadia Persad, Esteban Powell and John Patrick White as the kids, plus Arthur Burghardt as the evil principal Percival Pussman and Charles Fleischer as the oddball caretaker Arnie. Energetically performed and surprisingly witty, it provides a good deal of colorful fun in the *Goosebumps* manner. Sadly, only 13 episodes were made, among them *Teacher Creature* (1996, TV), in which a substitute teacher (Stuart Pankin) turns into a giant frog, *Gorilla My Dreams* (1996, TV), in which a gorilla escapes from the canteen's walk-in freezer, and *Root of All Evil* (1996, TV), which sees the school overtaken by giant plants.

Fact versus fiction was the concept behind the anthology series *Beyond Belief: Fact or Fiction* (1997–2002, TV), which presented five separate stories during each hour-long episode, leaving it to viewers to decide if each story was true or simply made up for the benefit of entertainment (the answer was revealed at the end of the program). Created by Lynn Lehmann, the show, which clocked up 45 episodes during its four-season run, began airing on the Fox Network on 25 May 1997, and was hosted by James Brolin during season one, with Jonathan Frakes taking over thereafter. Unlike most anthology series, the stories, plainly but adequately presented, were not star driven, and featured unfamiliar actors so as to make the events portrayed appear all the more realistic, to which end it managed to provide a few minor frissons as a consequence (the series opened with *The Apparition*, which sees a woman [Toni Kalem] haunted by a ghostly figure in her hallway mirror, and was apparently true, so we're told). And if a particular story was dull or didn't work, at least there'd be another along after the commercial break to make up for it.

The Color Purple

A highly original modern day take on the vampire myth came next care of writer-director Joe Ahearne with *Ultra Violet* (1998, TV), a short form series whose six hour-long episodes ran in the UK on Channel 4 from 15 September 1998. In it, Detective Sergeant Michael Colefield (Jack Davenport) becomes involved with an elite squad whose mission is to track down and destroy vampires in present day London after discovering that his best friend (Stephen Moyer) has become a victim of the cult on the eve of his wedding. Armed with garlic-tinged tear gas and special guns that fire graphite bullets, the modern-day inquisitors, who are working with full government backing and the blessing of the Vatican, are out to protect mankind from a bleak future. "Do you know where your loved ones are going to be in fifty years time? Battery farms. Believe me, our free range days are over," the unit's leader Father Pearse J. Harman (Philip Quast) flatly informs the initially skeptical Colefield during a visit to a special ultra violet containment unit where the ashes of destroyed vampires are stored, given that they have the ability to regenerate. "It's a prison, not a cemetery," explains the squad's lead assassin, Vaughan Rice (Idris Elba). However, thanks to cars with tinted windows that allow them to drive around during the day, and their inability to be recorded on CCTV or bugging devices, the vampires appear to have the upper hand, but the squad is determined to vanquish the deadly scourge at almost any cost.

Presented as an investigative cop drama whose criminals just happen to be vampires (though they are never referred to as such), this is a slick and frequently very clever variation on an old formula, spanked into vibrant new life thanks to smart writing that vigorously reworks established mythology to engrossing dramatic effect, further helped by strong performances, particularly from Elba as the scowling assassin, Susannah Harker as Angela March, the unit's cool headed medical advisor who has suffered personal loss at the hands of the vampires, and Corin Redgrave, who makes a late appearance as a sardonic vampire. Filmed across London, which is captured in all its nineties glory, this is genre television at its very best; serious, focused, but not without moments of wry wit, and dealing with issues that many straight dramatic series would be envious of (ethics, morality, mortality, even pedophilia). Yet the series is barely remembered today, while far lesser shows from the period have taken on unearned cult status, which is a crying shame given its quality and inventiveness (note that a pilot for an American version was filmed in 2000 starring Madchen Amick and Spence Decker, with Idris Elba again appearing as Vaughan Rice; written by Chip Johannessen and directed by Mark Piznarski, it was deemed so poor it quite rightly wasn't picked up).

Creator Chris Carter gave his own series *The X Files* (1993–2003, TV) a run for its money with *Millennium* (1996–1999, TV), a particularly dark hour-long investigative series which began its 67-episode, three-season run on the Fox Network on October 25, 1996. In it, Lance Henriksen stars as Frank Black, a former FBI profiler who goes to work for the Millennium Group, an organization that specializes in the investigation of serial killers, the working of whose minds he has a particular affinity for reading ("I see what the killer sees," he reveals). Also featuring Megan Gallagher as Black's wife Catherine, and Terry O'Quinn as Peter Watts, a member of the Group with whom he often works, the show, which was filmed in Vancouver, also embraced supernatural elements, but unlike *The X Files*, its style was far more disturbing given the nature of its storylines (commented *The New York Times* of the series, "*Millennium* explores the darkness—and embraces it"). Benefiting from a strong performance by Henriksen and some of the better writing to be found in genre television of the period, it quickly developed a cult following, and though a drop in viewers saw its eventual cancellation during season three, the original pilot pulled in over 17 million viewers, no doubt thanks to the recognition factor of its creator (note that Henriksen appeared as Frank Black in a 1999 episode of *The X Files* titled *Millennium*, which effectively brought his story arc to a conclusion, given that it was left dangling following the series' cancellation).

The British animation studio Cosgrove Hall was back in action with the children's series *Wyrd Sisters* (1997, TV), a six-part, half-hour show that was based upon the eighth novel in Terry Pratchett's *Discworld* series. This was actually Cosgrove Hall's third Pratchett adaptation following *Welcome to the Discworld* (1996, TV), an eight-minute cartoon based upon the author's 1991 book *Reaper Man*, and the seven-part series *Soul World* (1997, TV), based upon his 1994 book of the same title, both of which featured the voice of Christopher Lee as Death, a role he reprises here. The focus of the story is three witches, Granny Weatherwax (Annette Crosbie), Nanny Ogg (June Whitfield) and Magrat Garlick (Jane Horrocks), who find themselves the guardian of a royal baby, whose father was murdered by his cousin, to which end they hand the child to a band of travelling players in the hope that he will grow to manhood and return to defeat his murderous relative. Broadcast on Channel 4 on 18 May 1997, the series (which was also available as a feature and a two-parter) is simply but sometimes charmingly animated, though its chief asset is undoubtedly its voice cast, also among them Eleanor Bron, Les Dennis, Jimmy Hibbert and Ron Rackstraw.

The female of the species proved to be more deadly than male in *Charmed* (1998–2006, TV), in which three sisters, Piper, Phoebe and Prue Halliwell (Holly Marie Combs, Alyssa Milano and Shannen Doherty), use the forces of witchcraft to fight a variety of evildoers, among them warlocks and demons. Created by Constance M. Burge, the series debuted on The WB Television Network on 7 October 1998, and went on to amass an incredible 179 episodes during its eight season run, beginning with the amusingly titled *Something Wicca This Way Comes* (1998, TV), in which the sisters are reunited following the death of their grandmother, and learn of the powers they were destined to possess after Phoebe recites an incantation from a book of spells she has discovered. Described by *Entertainment Weekly* as "*Charlie's Angels* with a Ouija board," this was a pro-feminist blend of fantasy and drama in which three confident and self asserted girls kick ass and win the day, albeit dressed in a manner that won't alienate male viewers, particularly teenage ones (note that Lori Rom played Phoebe in the un-aired pilot [available on YouTube], which tells the same story as *Something Wicca This Way Comes*; when Prue was killed in the season three finale, she was replaced Rose McGowan as the girls' half-sister Paige Matthews; a successful re-boot followed in 2018).

Satan showed his face on television again in *Brimstone* (1998–1999, TV), a 13-part series created by Ethan Reiff and Cyrus Voris in which a cop named Ezkiel Stone (Peter Horton), who has been killed in the line of duty, is sent to hell given that he had previously murdered the man responsible for raping wife. However, 15 years later he is sent back to the land of the living by the Devil (John Glover) in order to retrieve 113 escaped souls on the understanding that he will be given a second chance at life if he retrieves them. Another dark series occasionally leavened with humor, this benefited from strong writing, the chemistry between Stone and Glover, and the effects, which see the escaped souls returned to hell after receiving injuries to their eyes (the windows to the soul), which prompt them to disappear in a blaze of light. Sadly, the show, which aired on the Fox Network from 23 October 1998, was pulled mid-season, with an additional six episodes still to go before the cameras, synopses and titles for which had already been produced.

A trip to *The Lost World* (1999–2002, TV) care of Sir Arthur Conan Doyle proved to be a popular destination for many in the last year of the decade. The author's 1912 adventure story about an expedition led by Professor Challenger that finds itself stranded on a plateau in the Amazon basin where dinosaurs still roam had already been the subject of several films, among them a popular 1925 silent starring Wallace Beery as Challenger, which featured stop motion effects care of the legendary Willis H. O'Brien, a 1960 CinemaScope version in DeLuxe color starring Claude Rains as Challenger, with effects this time in the form of lizards with glued on horns and fins, and a low-budget 1992 adaptation starring John Rhys-Davies as the Professor, during the making of which a sequel titled *Return to the Lost World* (1992) was simultaneously shot. The big screen successes of Steven Spielberg's *Jurassic Park* (1993) and its sequel *The Lost World: Jurassic Park* (1997), which were based upon best sellers by Michael Crichton (published in 1990 and 1995, respectively), had meanwhile provoked a worldwide fascination with dinosaurs, particularly in children, and this new series was a way of latching on to this interest.

Set in the early years of the 20th century, it follows much the same story as the book, with an expedition led by Professor Challenger (Peter McCauley) finding itself in peril after their hot air balloon crash lands on a plateau whose inhabitants include dinosaurs and a race of lizard men. But assistance is at hand in the form of Veronica Layton (Jennifer O'Dell), a nubile young woman who has become jungle savvy after another research group that included her parents disappeared 11 years earlier. The series piloted on TNT on 3 April 1999 with a two-parter directed Richard Franklin which set up the plot (the episodes were titled *The Journey Begins* [1990, TV] and *Stranded* [1990, TV], and were later joined to create a TV movie which aired on New Line Television on 6 November 1999). With appetites suitably whetted, the first season proper then began on Pay Per View via Direct TV on 2 October 1999 with *More Than Human* (1999, TV), in which the expedition finds itself held hostage by the lizard men. Running to three seasons and 66 episodes in total (with seasons two and three broadcast in syndication), the serial-style show also featured Rachel Blakely, William Snow, David Orth and Michael Sinelnikoff, though the real stars were undoubtedly the CGI dinosaurs, which actually weren't too bad for a weekly TV show (note that a fourth season was planned, which was to have included appearances by Conan Doyle's two most famous characters, Sherlock Holmes and Professor Moriarty; later versions of the story include a 1998 film starring Patrick Bergin as Challenger, a two-part 2001 TV movie featuring Bob Hoskins as the Professor, and a 21st-century update, *King of the Lost World* [2005], which had Bruce Boxleitner as Lieutenant Challenger).

While there was something of an explosion of genre content in series form, TV movies were thinner on the ground in the nineties, yet a couple of goodies found their way to the airwaves, despite an overall drop in quality. Having scored a hit with the two-parter *Jack the Ripper* (1988, TVM), Michael Caine and his director David Wickes returned to the small screen with *Jekyll & Hyde* (1990, TVM), the umpteenth version of the Robert Louis Stevenson story, which Wickes also wrote and executive produced in London. Like its predecessor, this was a quality production with a top notch cast that also included Cheryl Ladd, Joss Ackland, Ronald Pickup, Lionel Jeffries and Diane Keen, and though Caine was slightly miscast in the dual role, one couldn't deny that the production, which aired in the UK on the ITV network on 6 January 1990 and in the States on ABC on 21 January 1990, was a reasonably plush affair boasting some effective transformation scenes care of make-up effects artists Stuart Conran, Mark Jones and Chris Lyons.

Not quite so effective was *Daughter of Darkness* (1990, TVM), in which a young woman (Mia Sara) travels to Europe to discover the identity of her father (Anthony Perkins), only to find that he is a vampire. Directed in Hungary by Stuart Gordon (best known for such gore fests as *Re-Animator* [1985] and *From Beyond* [1986]), the film, which aired on CBS on 26 January 1990, was a fairly routine vampire saga with Perkins in full Bela Lugosi mode ("Don't even wonder how goofy his accent is here," commented the *Chicago Tribune*). Still, the locations and Colin Towns' music help to add a little atmosphere to the otherwise predictable proceedings.

A lavish $10 million, two movie adaptation of Gaston Leroux's *The Phantom of the Opera* (1990, TVM) proved to be one of the year's genre highlights. Broadcast on NBC on 18 and 19 March 1990, and acclaimed by *People* magazine for "far surpassing the previous TV version with Maximilian Schell and Jane Seymour in 1983," it was directed by Oscar winner Tony Richardson and written by Arthur Kopit, who based his teleplay on *Phantom*, a then-unproduced play he had been working on prior to the advent of the blockbuster 1986 Andrew Lloyd Webber stage musical (Kopit's play, with music and lyrics by Maury Yeston, was eventually staged in 1991, making it the third musical based on the material, the first being a version by Ken Hill in 1976). Filmed in Paris at the famous opera house, it stars Charles Dance as a slightly more benign (but still murderous) Phantom, who takes under his wing the young singer Christine Daeé (Teri Polo), whom he helps to groom for stardom. But when her debut is sabotaged by another singer (Andréa Ferréol), he drops the theatre's chandelier onto the audience when they boo her, following which he abducts her and takes her to his lair below the opera house. At times playing like a serial (the first film climaxes with the chandelier drop), this is a lengthy and rather leisurely paced production, given the familiarity of the story, yet it benefits from solid production values and a strong supporting cast that includes Ian Richardson, Jean-Pierre Cassel, Adam Storke and Burt Lancaster, who top lines as opera house manager Gérard Carriere, who turns out to be the Phantom's father (note that in this version, during the mask reveal, the Phantom keeps his back to the camera; a fourth musical version of the story, with songs by Lawrence Rosen and Paul Schierhorn, was recorded for TV in 1991, with David Staller in the role of the Phantom; a concert version of the Lloyd Webber musical, which had already been filmed for cinema release in 2004 with Gerard Butler in the title role, was broadcast in the UK from the Royal Albert Hall in 2011 to mark the show's 25th anniversary, with Ramin Karimloo playing the Phantom).

A town under threat from a car whose unseen driver kidnaps and abuses young girls was the premise of *Wheels of Terror* (1990, TVM), which aired on the USA Network on 11 July 1990. In it, Joanna Cassidy stars as the town's newly hired school bus driver, whose own daughter (Marcie Leeds) has been kidnapped by the prowling vehicle, prompting her to give chase. The teleplay by Alan B. McElroy is a somewhat tactless affair, given the age of the victims, and once Cassidy gives chase the movie clearly enters *Duel* territory, but the action is well enough handled by director Christopher Cain (despite an overreliance on slow motion), and includes an effective scene in which the car drives off a ridge and kills a motorcycle cop who is having trouble believing our heroine's story, and a climax in which it goes over the edge of a quarry and lands in a conveniently placed explosives dump (McElroy clearly has a passion for car based horror as he went on to pen *Under the Car* [1992] and *Wrong Turn* [2003, plus 2020 reboot]).

Anthony Perkins popped up again, this time in a guest spot as a professor in *I'm Dangerous Tonight* (1990, TVM), in which a cursed red cocktail dress, fashioned from an ancient Aztec cloak, turns a college student (Madchen Amick) into a killer. Written by Bruce Lansbury and Philip John Taylor from a 1937 story by Cornell Woolrich, the film was directed by Tobe Hooper and was broadcast on the USA Network on 8 August 1990. Unfortunately, it failed to impress, prompting *Entertainment Weekly* to describe it as "sanitized horror movie piffle, with Anthony Perkins in a cameo role as—get this—a normal person."

Perkins was far less normal in his third TV movie outing of 1990, for which he revived his most famous role, serial killer Norman Bates, for the sequel/prequel *Psycho IV: The Beginning* (1990, TVM), which aired on Showtime on 10 November 1990 (tagline: "Before the terror can end, see how it all began"). Written by Joseph Stefano, who'd penned the screenplay for the Hitchcock original, it sees an apparently rehabilitated Bates, now married to a psychiatrist (Donna Mitchell) who is expecting his child, call into a radio talk show dealing with the subject of matricide, which allows him to recall his early life with his mother (Olivia Hussey), leading up to his murder of her and her brutish lover (Thomas Schuster) with poisoned ice tea. He also expresses concern that he may go insane again, and that his unborn child might inherit his mindset. Featuring Henry Thomas as the young Norman Bates, C.C.H. Pounder as the radio host and Warren Frost as her guest speaker Dr. Leo Richmond, who just happens to be Norman's former psychologist, the film climaxes with a final runaround in the Bates house, for which a facsimile was built at Universal's Orlando theme park, where the movie was made (it was the first film to be shot on the new lot). Directed with reasonable flair and restraint by Mick Garris, and performed with a sly wink by Perkins, it proved to be a perfectly acceptable conclusion to the franchise.

It

Amazingly, not since *Salem's Lot* (1979, TVM) 11 years earlier had there been a major adaptation of one of one of Stephen King's novels for television, perhaps because so many of them were turning up in theatres around this time, albeit to variable effect. This situation was remedied with a $12 million two movie presentation of his 1986 novel *It* (1990, TVM), which was broadcast on ABC on 18 and 20 November 1990. In it, Tim Curry stars as Pennywise, an evil demon who lures children to their deaths by posing as a clown whose habitat is the drains and sewers of Derry, Maine. In the first episode, set in 1960, a bunch of young outcasts find their lives in danger from the evil clown, and bravely set out to destroy him, while in the second installment we cut to the present, and the by now adult children find themselves confronting the reawakened demon, which this time reveals its true form, that of a giant spider. Directed by Tommy Lee Wallace, who also co-wrote the teleplay with Lawrence D. Cohen (who had successfully adapted King's *Carrie* [1976] for the big screen), the two-parter also starred Jonathan Brandis, Brandon Crane, Adam Faraizl, Seth Green, Ben Heller, Emily Perkins and Marlon Taylor as the kids, and Richard Thomas, John Ritter, Dennis Christopher, Harry Anderson, Richard Masur, Annette O'Toole and Tim Reid as their adult selves, with additional support provided by Olivia Hussey, Jarred Blancard, Sheila Moore and Frank C. Turner.

The film is certainly not without its creepy sequences, among them the opener in which young Georgie Denbrough (Tony Dakota) has a fatal encounter with Pennywise while trying to retrieve a paper boat that has sailed down a street drain, while others include a scene in which Pennywise emerges from a shower plughole to terrorize one of the boys, and a lengthy sequence in the drain system as the kids set out to track down the killer clown, during which the camera moves through the various pipes and crawlspaces to eye-catching effect. In fact the film is generally regarded as one of the better TV adaptations of the author's work, and was something of a ratings hit, with *The Oregonian* describing it as "the best horror show ever made for network television," though not everyone was convinced, with *The Record* commenting, "After a while, even the scary stuff starts to seem silly." Admittedly, the film does now seem dated and padded in spots, and the sight of such young kids

being menaced by Pennywise doesn't always make for comfortable viewing. That said, its best moments certainly stick in the mind, and the sight of Curry as the smiling Pennywise seems to have scarred a generation (a two-part big screen remake starring Bill Skarsgård as Pennywise followed in 2017 and 2019).

With *Murderous Vision* (1991, TVM), a cop (Bruce Boxleitner) finds himself on the trail of a serial killer, in which task he is helped by a woman (Laura Johnson) who claims to have psychic powers ("The mind of a killer through the eyes of a psychic," ran the tag line). A fairly routine procedural thriller distinguished only by the fact that the killer removes and preserves his victims' faces, it was directed in straightforward style by Gary Sherman (who also executive produced with Ross Albert) and aired on the USA Network on 20 February 1991.

The investigation by a catholic priest (Anthony John Denison) into two virgin births, one purportedly the child of God, the other the spawn of

Killer smile. Tim Curry is featured in this promotional poster for *It* (1990, TVM) (ABC/Warner Bros. Television/Lorimar Television/Green-Epstein Productions/Konigsberg-Sanitsky Company).

the Devil, was the concept behind *Child of Darkness, Child of Light* (1991, TVM), which was based upon the 1980 novel *Virgin* by James Patterson. "Two virgin mothers, both so pure and good, one carrying the seed of hope, the other carrying the seed of despair," a letter informs the cleric, but which is which? A devilish conundrum, this was clearly a step into territory already explored by *The Omen* (1976), from which it borrows a number of elements (mysterious deaths, a dog attack and a sinister housekeeper, etc.), to which it adds a few neat twists of its own along the way. Ably enough directed by Marina Sargenti, and with plenty going on to keep audiences intrigued, the film, which co-stars Brad Davis, Claudette Nevins, Viveca Lindfors and, very briefly, a young Brendan Fraser, aired on the USA Network on 1 May 1991 ("A holy miracle, an unholy terror," ran the tagline).

A family plagued by a demon in their new duplex was the subject of *The Haunted* (1991, TVM), which aired on the Fox Network on 6 May 1991. The film was supposedly based on true events that were subsequently chronicled in the 1986 book *The Haunted: One Family's Nightmare* by newspaper writer Robert Curran, paranormal investigators Ed and Lorraine Warren, and two of the victims, husband and wife Janet and Jack Smurl (who are played by Sally Kirkland and Jeffrey DeMunn), and sees the couple and their children, along with the husband's parents (Louise Latham and George D. Wallace), who have moved into the adjacent unit, subjected to various disturbances (shadows, voices, strange noises, etc.), which is enough for them to call in a pair of demonologists (Stephen Markle and Diane Baker) to help them deal with the matter ("No one believes in ghosts ... until they have no choice," ran the tagline). Soberly directed by Robert Mandel, this is a rather drab looking variation on *The Amityville Horror* (1979), whose best moment sees the wife floating above her bed. Otherwise, it's a rather tedious accumulation of incidents familiar from countless similar movies.

Thoughts and prayers. An intense looking Tony Denison in *Child of Darkness, Child of Light* (1991, TVM) (USA Network/G.C. Group/ Wilshire Court Productions).

A 1974 short story by horror-meister Stephen King was the source of *Sometimes They Come Back* (1991, TVM), which had originally been optioned as a segment for the theatrical feature *Cat's Eye* (1985). Executive produced by Dino de Laurentiis and co-produced by Milton Subotsky, both of whom had been involved with *Cat's Eye*, it sees high school teacher Jim Norman (Tim Matheson) return to his hometown to take up a new post, only to be haunted by the teenage bullies who murdered his brother some 27 years earlier, who themselves were killed in a railroad accident. A typical smalltown story from King, it is nevertheless smoothly handled by director Tom McLoughlin, and benefits from a convincing performance by Matheson, who is ably supported by Brooke Adams as his wife Sally. The film, which aired on CBS on 7 May 1991, was also released theatrically in some territories, and was followed by two video sequels: *Sometimes They Come Back... Again* (1996) and *Sometimes They Come Back... for More* (1998).

It was back to the forties for *Cast a Deadly Spell* (1991, TVM), in which a detective, Harry Philip Lovecraft (Fred Ward), is assigned the task of recovering a stolen grimoire belonging to the wealthy Amos Hackshaw (David Warner), whose pages contain the means by which to take over the world. A hit and miss Philip Marlowe spoof set in a time when everybody has the ability to use magic, and zombies and gremlins are an everyday sight, the various ingredients of this comedy noir monster flick don't quite gel, and the result is a somewhat patchy ride, despite a reasonably convincing period look care of production designer Jon Bunker and an engaging performance from Ward as the suitably world weary tec ("Imagine *Who Framed Roger Rabbit* with witches and zombies instead of toons," commented *USA Today*). Produced by Gale Anne Hurd and helmed by future Bond director Martin Campbell, the $6 million movie also starred Julianne Moore and Clancy Brown, and made its debut on HBO on 7 September 1991, and was deemed successful enough to warrant a sequel, *Witch Hunt* (1994, TVM), in which Lovecraft (now played by Dennis Hopper) investigates a murder in fifties Hollywood. Like its predecessor, it was written by Joseph Dougherty and again produced by Gale Anne Hurd, though this time the directorial reins were somewhat surprisingly in the hands of Paul Schrader. It aired on HBO on 10 December 1994.

A third sequel to *The Omen* (1976) titled *Omen IV: The Awakening* (1991, TVM) appeared on the Fox Network on 20 May 1991, though instead of following the continuing saga of Antichrist Damien Thorn, as had *Damien: Omen II* (1978) and *The Final Conflict* (1981), the focus this time is a baby girl who is adopted by Karen and Gene York (Michael Woods and Faye Grant), a childless congressman and his attorney wife. However, as the child (Asia Viera) grows up, it becomes apparent that her personality is becoming increasingly sociopathic, and with good reason, for it transpires that she is actually the daughter of Damien Thorn, and has been carrying within her the embryo of her twin brother, which the family doctor (Madison Mason), who is a Satanist, has transplanted into Karen, who subsequently gives birth to the next Antichrist. Unfortunately, although it contains the same elements as its predecessors (ominous music and plenty unusual deaths for those who get too close to discovering the little girl's lineage, among them a decapitation and a fatal blow from a wrecking ball), it's clearly a watered down affair, rather flatly directed in Vancouver by Jorge Montesi and Dominique Othenin-Girard from a teleplay by Brian Taggert, taken from a story by himself and producer Harvey Bernhard, who had worked on the movies. Commented *Variety* of the film, which was released theatrically in some territories, "Its structure is so convoluted that it's sheer hell to follow," while the *LA Times* described it as "witless, visually dull and slow-moving," as indeed it mostly is (note that Jonathan Sheffer's score, which is the best thing about the movie, was augmented by cues from Jerry Goldsmith's work for the film series; a 1995 pilot for a spinoff series titled *The Omen*, about a demonic entity that possesses people, failed to be picked up, despite being executive produced by the original film's director Richard Donner; a theatrical reboot of the 1976 film followed in 2006, which in turn was followed by a ten-part TV series, *Damien* [2016, TV], in which Bradley James played the title character).

It was into *Poltergeist* (1982) territory next with *Grave Secrets: The Legacy of Hilltop Drive* (1992, TV), in which a family (Patty Duke, David Selby, Kiersten Warren and Kelly Rowan) move into their dream house in a new development, where they become increasingly disturbed by supernatural phenomena, their investigations into which lead them to discover that their home has been built over an old graveyard. Based upon supposedly true events related in the 1991 book *The Black Hope Horror: The True Story of a Haunting* by John Bruce Shoemaker, Ben Williams and Jean Williams, the formula script care of producer Gregory Goodell features plenty of situations typical of such fare, which are routinely presented in by-the-numbers TV style by director John Patterson. Pretty mild beer, with little to disturb even younger viewers, the movie aired on CBS on 3 March 1992.

Another movie franchise came to the small screen with *Stepfather III* (1992, TVM, aka *Stepfather 3: Father's Day*), a sequel to *The Stepfather* (1987) and *The Stepfather II* (1989), in which Terry O'Quinn played a seemingly affable stepfather who murders one surrogate family before moving onto the next. In this third installment, which aired on HBO on 4 June 1992, the killer escapes from the asylum to carry on his murderous activities with a new family, having altered his appearance with plastic surgery, thus allowing a new actor, Robert Wightman, to assume the title role. A routine cash-in on two otherwise reasonably engaging shockers, this third helping from the same bowl sadly has little to recommend it, save for the killer's climactic demise in a garden shredder (ouch), and it was quickly dismissed by the critics, with *Variety* noting its "indifferent production values" and *Entertainment Weekly* labeling it "a poorly scripted, all-too-familiar chiller" (the film was released theatrically in some territories; the original film was also remade in 2009).

Reprieve at least could be found in another quality production from writer-director-executive producer David Wickes in the guise of a new version of *Frankenstein* (1992, TVM, aka *Frankenstein: The Real Story*), not that one was particularly needed, with Patrick Bergin here starring as Dr. Victor Frankenstein and Randy Quaid as the Monster, sporting make-up by future Oscar winner Mark Coulier and his team ("Tonight he will be unleashed," ran the tagline). Shown in the UK on ITV on 29 December 1992 and in the U.S. on TNT on 14 June 1993, the film was based in Britain and shot in Poland, with a supporting cast that includes John Mills, Lambert Wilson and Vernon Dobtcheff. A reasonably faithful telling of the story, it follows Frankenstein's attempts to reproduce life via a cloning machine, which results in a shared bond between creator and created (when the Monster suffers pain, so does the doctor). Fairly gruesome at times (notably an aborted attempt to create a mate for the Monster), it has solid enough production values and committed performances, though ultimately the sheer familiarity of the material works against it.

Writer-director Julie Taymor, whose skills in the art of puppetry made an international stage success of *The Lion King* (first performed in 1997), displays her considerable talents with *Fool's Fire* (1992, TVM), an hour-long adaptation of Edgar Allan Poe's 1849 story *Hop-Frog*, in which a diminutive court jester (Michael J. Anderson) avenges himself against the king for having humiliated a fellow performer, the equally diminutive Trippetta (Mireille Mossé), which he does by suggesting that the court dress as orangutans for a masquerade, at which he chains them up and sets them alight. A somewhat dark story (it's certainly not intended for children, given some of the language), its mix of live actors, large scale puppets and exaggerated art direction (care of G.W. Mercier) and costumes (Taymor) all make for a visually arresting experience, which is put across with both imagination and flair, all topped by an inventive score by Taymor's partner, Elliot Goldenthal, who would go on to win an Oscar for his work on her live action film *Frida* (2002). Made as an episode of *American Playhouse* (1980–1994, TV), the program aired on PBS on 25 March 1992, and is certainly worth seeking out for its sheer curiosity value alone. This wasn't the only puppet version of Poe to appear in the nineties, however, with *Joe's Marionette Theatre* (1995–1996, TV) presenting adaptations of *The Raven* (1996, TV) and *The Tell-Tale Heart* (1996, TV), as well as versions of *Rumpelstiltskin* (1995, TV), *The Headless Horseman* (1995, TV), *A Christmas Carol* (1995, TV) and *Beauty and the Beast* (1996, TV), all of which were written and directed by Joe Pinkerton. *The Tell-Tale Heart* was also featured in the Tiny Toons Halloween special *Tiny Toons' Night Ghoulery* (1995, TV) and as a 1999 live action short starring Jeff Ricketts.

A two movie length adaptation of Stephen King's 1987 novel *The Tommyknockers* (1993, TVM), in which the inhabitants of the small town of Haven discover an alien spaceship buried in the nearby woods, proved to be something of a disappointment given its potential, thanks to a frenzied filming schedule in New Zealand which saw the original director, Lewis Teague, replaced by John Power, whose most recent work had been *Charles and Diana: Unhappily Ever After* (1992, TVM). Written and co-produced by Lawrence D. Cohen (whose previous King adaptations included *Carrie* [1976] and *It* [1990, TVM]), it sees the townsfolk unduly influenced by the uncovering of the spacecraft, with several of them inventing strange gadgets from household objects, which emit a green glow when active ("You can't run. You can't hide. You can only become … one of them," ran the tagline). Starring Jimmy Smits, Marg Helgenberger, Joanna Cassidy, Robert Carradine, E.G. Marshall and Traci Lords, the $12 million production aired on ABC on 9 and 10 May 1993, but was generally regarded as a letdown, with *Variety* describing it as "hokey whoop-de-doo." Despite a few eerie moments, among them a climactic close encounter with the revived aliens, it certainly doesn't warrant its epic running time (the original video release of the film saw this cut down from three hours to two).

Another big name in horror, John Carpenter, was involved in the anthology film *Body Bags* (1993, TVM), two of whose three segments he helmed, with Tobe Hooper taking over the reins for the other. The stories were originally intended as part of a new half hour anthology series in the style of *Tales from the Crypt* (1989–1996, TV), but Showtime, which was backing the project, instead decided to package them as a single film. Carpenter (who also executive produced and co-scored with

Jim Lang) helmed the first two segments, *Gas Station*, in which a girl (Alex Datcher) working the night shift at a lonely gas station is threatened by a serial killer (Robert Carradine), and *Hair*, in which a man (Stacy Keach) who undergoes a miracle hair transplant finds that he has been infested by alien parasites, while Hooper took on the third, *Eye*, in which a baseball player (Mark Hamill) who has lost an eye in a car crash receives a transplant from a dead killer, only to take on his personality. Featuring a variety of cameos from the likes of Wes Craven, Sam Raimi, David Naughton, Twiggy, Sheena Easton, David Warner, Debbie Harry, Roger Corman and John Agar, the stories were introduced by Carpenter as a coroner (sporting make-up care of Rick Baker), with Hooper and Tom Arnold turning up as a couple of morgue attendants at the very end to perform an autopsy on him, given that he is actually a John Doe. Written by Billy Brown and Dan Angel, the film, which aired on Showtime on 8 August 1993, provides its fair share of undemanding fun, as well as a couple of well-timed jolts in typical Carpenter style in the opening segment ("Zip yourself in tight!" ran the tagline).

In complete contrast was *Ghost Mom* (1993, TVM, aka *Bury Me in Niagara*), which aired on the Fox Network on 1 November 1993. An American-Canadian co-production filmed in Toronto, it was an old style oddball comedy about a mom (Jean Stapleton) who returns from the grave to help her surgeon son (Geraint Wyn Davies) track down a stone with magical properties, all the while outwitting a deadly Japanese gang who are also after it. Directed and co-written by *Second City TV* alumni and former McKenzie brother Dave Thomas, this was never going to win any awards, but Stapleton, for whom the role was written, is clearly having fun as the ghostly mom ("She's meddlesome, worrisome, annoying and dead," ran the tagline). Also airing the same night, albeit on NBC, was another remake of *Les diaboliques* (1955) under the title *House of Secrets* (1993, TVM), in which the wife (Melissa Gilbert) and lover (Kate Vernon) of an abusive doctor (Bruce Boxleitner) form a plan to murder him, but the tables are turned when he appears to return from the dead (spoiler alert: the doctor and his lover are in it together so as to frighten to death the wife—who has a weak heart—for her money). A rather bland affair with none of the impact of the French original, nor the earlier TV version *Reflections of Murder* (1974, TVM) for that matter, it simply goes through the motions, playing out like a high-end soap opera, this time in a luxury sanatorium rather than a wintry school. Even the bathtub revival scene is rather unimaginatively staged by director Mimi Leder, and the only new thing the teleplay by Andrew Laskos brings to the table is a character named Evangeline (Cicely Tyson) who uses her powers in the black arts to summon the dead wife to appear in the doctor's dreams, making him believe that she herself has returned from the dead.

Meanwhile, Stephen King continued his invasion of the airwaves with *The Stand* (1994, TVM), an epic four movie version of his 1978 book which aired on ABC on 8, 9, 11 and 12 May 1994. Adapted by King (who also executive produced), the film sees most of the world wiped out by a deadly plague ("The end of the world is just the beginning," ran the tagline), with the survivors splitting into two factions, the good led by Mother Abigail Freemantle (Ruby Dee) and the bad led by the evil Randall Flagg (Jamey Sheridan). Directed by Mick Garris (who also appeared) and also featuring Gary Sinise, Molly Ringwald, Rob Lowe, Ossie Davis, Ray Walston and King himself, the $26 million production proved to be popular with fans, who couldn't have asked for a more faithful interpretation of the book, though as *The New York Times* noted, "once the story settles early on into its schematic oppositions of good versus evil ... monotony begins to seep through the superstructure," all of which makes for an ultimately exhausting experience (a reboot running to nine hour-long episodes followed in 2020, with Whoopi Goldberg and Alexander Skarsgård in the Freemantle and Flagg roles).

Rather more old-fashioned was *The Haunting of Seacliff Inn* (1994, TVM), which aired on the USA Network on 22 September 1994. In it, a couple (William R. Moses and Ally Sheedy) buy a large Victorian house overlooking the sea with the intention of turning it into a hotel, only to discover that the place is haunted. Directed by Walter Klenhard (who also co-wrote the script), this really is familiar stuff, prompting *Variety* to comment, "Tech credits are good but the story's not there," about which there is little else to add, save that the house itself looks amazing and steals the show.

Yet another Stephen King adaptation appeared the following year with *The Langoliers* (1995, TVM), a two-movie affair which aired on ABC on 14 and 15 May 1995. Taken from a novella featured in the 1990 collection *Four Past Midnight*, it was adapted and directed by Tom Holland. In it, a number of passengers inexplicably disappear from an aircraft midflight, with only those who were asleep remaining (luckily among them a deadheading pilot). When the plane finally lands at an airport, the place appears to be completely lifeless and powerless. Even worse, weird creatures are approaching from the horizon, eating everything in their path. Filmed on location at Bangor International Airport, it starred Patricia Wettig, David Morse, Dean Stockwell, Bronson Pinchot and Mark Lindsay Chapman, with small roles also going to King and Holland (both of whom had previously appeared in *The Stand* [1994, TVM]). A rather slow and protracted affair full of tediously staged chat, the cheap looking production takes forever for the chomping title creatures to appear (they don't turn up until well into the second chapter), and when they do, they look like they've strayed in from a badly animated arcade game. Poor as they are, however, they were distracting enough for the reviewer in *Entertainment Weekly* to comment, "I'd rather watch them than a Susan Lucci TV movie any day," which is fair enough.

Corman Quickies

Another titan of terror, the prolific film producer Roger Corman, was meanwhile approached by Showtime to make a series of low-budget science fiction and horror films for the network, among them a handful of remakes. Presented under the umbrella title of *Roger Corman Presents* (1995–1997, TVM), the films, all of them around the 90-minute mark, were clearly low-budget rush jobs of very variable quality, yet several well known names found themselves involved, though not necessarily to the betterment of their careers, among them Barbara Carrera, Don Stroud, Adrienne Barbeau, Clint Howard, Rick Rossovich, Parker Stevenson, Mason Adams,

Beverly Garland (who must've known what she was getting into given that she'd worked for Corman in the fifties), William Katt, Darleen Carr, a young Will Ferrell and an even younger Mila Kunis.

The series kicked off on 11 July 1995 with *Suspect Device* (1995, TVM), in which a government analyst (C. Thomas Howell) survives an attack on his workplace only to discover that he is in fact an ass kicking cyborg fitted with a nuclear device. It then went on to include *The Alien Within* (1995, TVM, aka *Unknown Origin*), in which the crew of a deep sea mining platform (among them Roddy McDowall) find themselves under threat from a long dormant parasite (the film featured shots cribbed from the Corman-produced *Lords of the Deep* [1989]); *Sawbones* (1995, TVM), in which a failed medical student (Adam Baldwin) captures patients on whom he can operate; *Virtual Seduction* (1995, TVM), in which a man (Jeff Fahey) mourning the murder of his girlfriend rediscovers her within a virtual reality game; *Burial of the Rats* (1995, TVM, aka *Bram Stoker's Burial of the Rats*), in which the young Bram Stoker (Kevin Alber) finds himself kidnapped by a female cult with an ability to control rats; *Not Like Us* (1995, TVM), in which two humanoid aliens (Joanna Pacula and Peter Onorati) invade a small township and carry out experiments on the locals; *Black Scorpion* (1995, TVM), which follows the exploits of a female crime fighter known as the Black Scorpion (Joan Severance); *The Wasp Woman* (1995, TVM, aka *Forbidden Beauty*), a remake of the 1959 film in which the owner of a cosmetics company (Jennifer Rubin) personally trials a new youth serum made from wasp hormones with predictable results (the original film was directed by Corman himself); *Not of This Earth* (1995, TVM), a remake of the 1957 film in which an alien (Michael York) visits Earth in a bid to find a cure for his dying race (Corman had directed the original and had already executive produced a theatrical remake in 1988); *A Bucket of Blood* (1995, TVM, aka *The Death Artist* and *Dark Secrets*), a remake of the 1959 film in which a busboy turned artist (Anthony Michael Hall) uses real bodies as the basis for his sculptures (Corman had directed the original film); *Hellfire* (1995, TVM, aka *Blood Song*), in which a novice composer (Ben Cross) hired to complete an unfinished symphony finds himself succumbing to the murderous impulses that inspired the original composer; *Piranha* (1995, TVM), a remake of the 1978 film (which had been executive produced by Corman) in which a private investigator (Alexandra Paul) working on a missing person case inadvertently releases a hybrid species of piranha from an abandoned army facility into a river, downstream of which lies a resort (the film rather cheekily recycled its predecessor's effects); *Terminal Virus* (1995, TVM, aka *The Last Chance*), in which a scientist (Bryan Genesse) has created a vaccine to combat a virus that has turned the population celibate; and *Where Evil Lies* (1995, TVM), a thriller in which two exotic dancers (Nikki Fritz and Melissa Park) find themselves kidnapped by slave traders.

Commented *The New York Times* of the films, "The human brain cannot tolerate a steady diet of high class entertainment. This is a proven scientific fact, and it is the reason that Roger Corman is still around after 40 years of cranking out low budget shockers." Amazingly, a second season was called for, which comprised of *Spectre* (1996, TVM, aka *House of the Damned* and *Escape to Nowhere*), in which a couple (Greg Evigan and Alexandra Paul) move to Ireland to the wife's ancestral home, only to discover that her forbears were practitioners of black magic; *Inhumanoid* (1996, aka *Circuit Breaker*), in which space travelers (among them Corbin Bernsen) come across a spaceship whose crew has been killed by a murderous android; *Alien Avengers* (1996, aka *Welcome to Planet Earth*), in which a cheerful couple (George Wendt and Shanna Reed) are in fact murderous aliens; *Shadow of a Scream* (1996, TVM, aka *The Unspeakable* and *Criminal Pursuit*), a thriller about a female cop (Athena Massey) who has to go deep undercover to capture a suspect; *Subliminal Seduction* (1996, TVM), in which a videogame programmer (Ian Ziering) finds himself working for a company that uses mind controlling software; *Last Exit to Earth* (1996, TVM), in which a group of women from the future (among them Kim Greist) are sent back in time to kidnap men for breeding purposes; *Humanoids from the Deep* (1996, TVM), a remake of the 1980 film (which Corman executive produced), in which a doctor (Emma Samms) responsible for the creation of humanoid amphibians for the army sees them escape and go on a spree of murder and rape in a fishing township (the film features carnival footage from the first version); *Death Game* (1996, aka *Mortal Challenge*), in which a detective (Timothy Bottoms) finds himself being hunted by a half-human half-machine killer while searching for a missing girl in New Los Angeles in the not too distant future; *Vampirella* (1996, TVM), in which the popular comic book character (Talisa Soto) travels to Earth from the planet Drakulon to seek Vlad (Roger Daltry), the vampire who killed her father (the comic's creator, Forrest J. Ackerman, appears briefly in the film); *Scene of the Crime* (1996, aka *Ladykiller*), in which a cop (Ben Gazzara) tracks down a serial killer nicknamed The Piggy Bank Murderer; *When the Bullet Hits the Bone* (1996, TVM), in which an emergency room doctor (Jeff Wincott) takes on a drugs dealer; *Marquis de Sade* (1996, aka *Dark Prince: Intimate Tales of Marquis de Sade*), in which a young woman's search for her missing sister leads her to the notorious marquis (Nick Mancuso); *Black Scorpion II: Aftershock* (1997, TVM), which features more crime fighting adventures of the leather-clad vigilante (Joan Severance); *Alien Avengers II* (1997, TVM, aka *Aliens Among Us* and *Welcome to Planet Earth II*), in which an alien vigilante and his wife (George Wendt and Julie Brown [replacing Shanna Reed]) rid Earth of criminals; *Spacejacked* (1997, TVM), in which a space cruiser is hijacked by a computer expert (Corbin Bersen) out to rob its wealthy passengers; and, finally, *The Haunted Sea* (1997, TVM), in which a sea captain (James Brolin) and his crew come across a drifting ship containing Aztec treasure, only for one of the crew (Duane Whitaker) to turn into a murderous reptile-like creature when he tries to steal a piece of it.

A new version of Henry James' *The Turn of the Screw* appeared under the title *The Haunting of Helen Walker* (1995, TVM), which aired on CBS on 3 December 1995. Executive produced by the prolific Norman Rosemont, it was clearly a prestige production, given that it was adapted by Hugh Whitemore, and had a supporting cast that included Diana Rigg, Michael Gough and Paul Rhys. This time it's Valerie Bertinelli who stars as the Victorian governess who is sent to the remote estate of Bly to look after two young children, Miles and Flora (Aled Roberts and Florence Hoath), only to become convinced that her charges are being corrupted by the spirits of their late governess Miss Jessel (Elizabeth Morton) and her lover, the valet Peter

Quint (Christopher Guard). Shot on location in England, primarily at Englefield House in Berkshire, it looks reasonably good thanks to the work of cinematographer Tony Imi, but inevitably pales beside *The Innocents* (1961), while the familiarity of the story ultimately works against it, despite director Tom McLoughlin's attempts to add a few frissons with the various manifestations.

An old favorite, Oscar Wilde's *The Canterville Ghost* (1996, TVM), got its umpteenth makeover in a version starring Patrick Stewart as the ghostly Sir Simon, which aired on ABC on 27 January 1996. Filmed in England at Knebworth House in Hertfordshire, the familiar story was adapted and produced by Robert Benedetti and directed by Syd Macartney, and also featured Neve Campbell, Joan Sims, Cherie Lunghi, Leslie Phillips and Donald Sinden. Pleasantly photographed and scored by Denis Lewiston and Ernest Troost, respectively (the latter of whom won an Emmy for his efforts), it's ably enough performed by its cast (in particular by the older Brits), but otherwise adds nothing particularly new to the telling. The following year saw two further versions of the story: a British adaptation which aired on ITV starring Ian Richardson as Sir Simon, supported by Celia Imrie, Rik Mayall, Pauline Quirke, Sarah-Jane Potts, Edna Doré and Donald Sinden again (albeit in a different role), and a 45-minute Austrian adaptation titled *Das Gespenst von Confettiville* (1997, TV). Richardson's performance aside, the British version is unremarkable in most respects, though it impressed the *Daily Mail*, which described it as "a sumptuous production."

Another fifties classic came to the small screen next, and although generally listed as a TV movie (as it is on IMDb and Wiki), *It Came from Outer Space II* (1996, TVM) actually made its debut on video, first in Norway on 7 February 1996, followed by releases in the UK, Japan and Greece during the following months. Though touted as a sequel to the 1953 movie, in which an Arizona community is invaded by aliens who can take on human form, it is in fact more of a remake, with a photographer (Brian Kerwin) this time trying to convince a township's residents that they are being taken over by aliens capable of looking like those they have abducted. Directed by Roger Duchowny (who also produced with Tony Dow via Duchowny Dow Films), the movie was shot in Arkansas, but in this case, lightning failed to strike twice.

This wasn't the only movie to warrant a sequel in 1996. The anthology film *Trilogy of Terror II* (1996, TVM) served up more of the same as its 1975 predecessor care of director Dan Curtis (working as usual via Dan Curtis Productions). This time it's Lysette Anthony rather than Karen Black who is featured in each of the segments, which include *The Graveyard Rats*, adapted by William F. Nolan and Dan Curtis from a 1936 short story by William Kuttner, in which a wife has to retrieve information from the coffin of the husband (Matt Clark) she murdered with her lover (Geraint Wyn Davies) in order to inherit; *Bobby* by Richard Matheson, in which a grieving mother conjures back her drowned son (Blake Heron), but instead brings back a demon (this was actually a remake of a story already seen in the Curtis anthology *Dead of Night* [1977, TVM]); and *He Who Kills*, also by Matheson, which is a sequel to *Amelia*, the killer doll sequence from the first film, in which a lady doctor is given the figure to examine following the first case only to find herself in mortal peril. A belated rehash of familiar scenarios, the movie, which aired on the USA Network on 30 October 1996 just in time for Halloween, is a reasonably slick affair, and while not exactly original, is a perfectly adequate time filler if nothing more.

Yet another haunted house was the setting for *Buried Secrets* (1996, TVM), which sees a young girl (Tiffani-Amber Thiessen) move to a new home with her mother (Melinda Cullen), where she keeps seeing the ghost of a girl her age, and thus sets out to discover what became of her ("Sometimes, there are good reasons to be afraid of the dark," ran the tagline). Also featuring Tim Matheson and Channon Roe, the film, which aired on NBC on 4 November 1996, lacks any particular visual flair from director Michael Toshiyuki Ono, while John Leekley's script adds nothing particularly new to this overworked sub-genre in which dark secrets from the past return to affect those in the present. Revelatory dreams were meanwhile the subject of *A Nightmare Come True* (1997, TVM), which aired on CBS on 12 February 1997. In it, a young nurse (Katy Boyer) moves back in with her parents following a fire, only to realize that her father (Gerald McRaney) is abusing her mother (Shelley Fabares), who soon after disappears, having supposedly packed and left. However, a series of dreams leads the girl to discover what really happened to her mother, despite appearances that she might have been killed by her lover (Joel Bissonnette). A straight-forward murder mystery with a slight paranormal twist leading to a final revelation in the basement, this is routine TV fodder by most standards, flatly directed by Christopher Leitch, though some may find it of passing interest for an early supporting performance by star-to-be Jeremy Renner.

With *The Hunchback* (1997, TVM, aka *The Hunchback of Notre Dame*), which aired on TNT on 16 March 1997, audiences were treated to yet another interpretation of Victor Hugo's novel *The Hunchback of Notre Dame*, this time with Mandy Patinkin in the role of Quasimodo (sporting an excellent make-up by Sacha Carter and David White), supported by Richard Harris as Frollo and Salma Hayek as Esmeralda. Adapted by John Fasano and directed by Peter Medak, the movie, which also featured Jim Dale, Nigel Terry, Vernon Dobtcheff and Nickolas Grace, was a co-production between America, Canada, Hungary and the Czech Republic, and was shot on location in Budapest. It's all perfectly adequate, with an

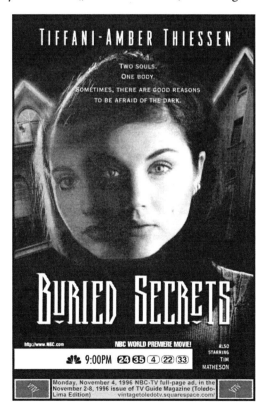

Body double. Tiffani-Amber Thiessen is featured in this promotional ad for *Buried Secrets* (1996, TVM) (NBC/Scripps Howard Entertainment/Michele Brustin Productions).

undeniably heartfelt performance from Patinkin as the deformed bell ringer, but like the remakes of *The Phantom of the Opera* and *The Turn of the Screw*, the familiarity of the material ultimately works against it (the previous year the French had presented a ballet version of the story as *Notre-Dame de Paris* [1996, TVM], with Nicholas Le Riche in the role of Quasimodo, while the following year they broadcast a musical version of the story under the same title, [1998, TVM], with Garou [sic] in the role of Quasimodo; in American, the character was even the subject of a 1996 episode of the long running series *Biography* [1987–, TV]).

King of the Airwaves

A three-movie adaptation of Stephen King's 1977 novel *The Shining* (1997, TVM) came to ABC on 27 and 28 April and 1 May 1997. The author had made his feelings known about Stanley Kubrick's highly regarded 1980 big screen version, which veered rather too much from the book's narrative for his liking, and so this new presentation of the story, adapted by King himself and directed by Mick Garris, was a means of making amends for its various transgressions. Unfortunately, for anyone who has seen the Kubrick film, this new version, despite being more faithful to the original, not only feels superfluous, but is ultimately something of a chore to sit through, despite its good intentions. In it, John Torrance (Steven Webber), his wife Winifred (Rebecca de Mornay) and their son Danny (Courtland Mead) take up residence as winter caretakers of the remote Overlook Hotel, only for the father, a recovering alcoholic, to be haunted by the ghosts of its former guests and employees, which prompts his mental health to take a dramatic turn for the worse. One can't deny that the three films have been made with a reasonable degree of care by normal TV standards, but it's all too drawn out, and the more ludicrous elements of the story, wisely cut in the Kubrick version, have here been reinstated to the general detriment of things, among them a sequence in which John is pursued in the snow by a number of topiary animals which move when he is not directly looking at them. The setting, although more claustrophobic than its predecessor, is also rather drab-looking, while the scares seem more obviously engineered. With exteriors filmed at The Stanley Hotel in Colorado (which had been the inspiration for the book), the $25 million production certainly pleased the purists and even some of the critics, with *Variety* praising it for its "edge-of-your-seat creepiness." It also garnered solid viewing figures, with the first installment pulling in a respectable 19.8 million. Yet there were dissenting voices, the most critical of which came from *The Washington Post*, which warned, "avoid like the plague, because it is the plague."

Another anthology, this time featuring just two stories, albeit by Stephen King and Clive Barker, aired on the Fox Network on 13 May 1997. This was *Quicksilver Highway* (1997, TVM), in which the proprietor of a touring fairground sideshow, Aaron Quiksilver (Christopher Lloyd), has a penchant for relating horror stories to those he encounters, the first of which, *Chattery Teeth*, was based upon a 1992 story by King. In it, a businessman (Raphael Sbarge) finds himself protected from the criminal intentions of a hitchhiker by a pair of chattering teeth he has picked up at a roadside convenience store. This was followed by *The Body Politic*, which was based on a 1984 Barker story, and sees the hands of a surgeon (Matt Frewer) take on a murderous life of their own, but its transpires he's not the only one so afflicted. The film was written and directed by Mick Garris (who also produced with Ron Mitchell), who originally intended the *Chattery Teeth* episode as the pilot for a new anthology series, but Fox preferred the idea of a two-part movie instead, the results of which are reasonably slick and entertaining in the *Twilight Zone* manner, albeit nothing too out of the ordinary (note that the film's video release reversed the order of the stories; John McTiernan, who worked as an executive producer on the film, was originally intended to direct; Clive Barker makes a brief appearance in his segment).

It was into *Duel/Killdozer/Christine* territory next with the Canadian-shot *Trucks* (1997, TVM), which aired on the USA Network on 29 October 1997. Based on a 1973 short story by Stephen King, who had already written and directed a big screen version of the piece under the title *Maximum Overdrive* (1986), it sees a dusty small town truck stop come under attack from a variety of vehicles which have inexplicably come to life and are attempting to kill all and sundry in the vicinity. With the writing and directing chores this time in the hands of Brian Taggert and Chris Thomson, respectively, the results are even more ludicrous than its big-budget predecessor ("The film is all premise and no plot," griped *TV Guide*), leaving its cast, among them Timothy Busfield, Brenda Bakke and Aidan Devine, little to do other than run round in circles as they attempt to outsmart and outrun the various gas guzzlers. The stunts themselves are well enough presented, but otherwise the proceedings rarely slip into top gear.

Yet another King story, this time a short one from 1988, provided the basis for *The Night Flier* (1997, TVM), an American-Italian co-production in which a bad-tempered tabloid reporter (Miguel Ferrer) tracks a serial killer, Dwight Renfield (Michael H. Moss), who turns out to be a vampire who uses a small plane to fly to different airfields in the pursuit of fresh victims. Adapted by Jack O'Donnell (who also co-produced) and the film's director Mark Pavia (who'd impressed King with his zombie short *Drag* [1993]), the $1 million film, which was shot in Wilmington, is a surprisingly engaging investigative thriller with a supernatural element, handled with some panache by Pavia, and featuring a strong performance from Ferrer as the journo. It also benefits from some excellent make-up effects care of Howard Berger, Robert Kurtzman and Gregory Nicotero (the vampire, when he is finally shown, is a doozy), while the script is nice and tight compared to many of the over bloated multi film adaptations of King's work that had been clogging up the schedules in the nineties, and was admired by *Variety* for its "clever commentary on bloodthirsty tabloid journalists." The film aired on HBO on 7 November 1997, prior to which it had received a theatrical release in Italy on 30 April; a U.S. theatrical release followed on 6 February 1998.

A new version of the Jack the Ripper legend simply titled *The Ripper* (1997, TV) helped to round out the year when broadcast on the premium cable network Starz on 6 December 1997. Set in 1888 London, it starred Patrick Bergin as Inspector Jim Hansen, who finds himself investigating a number of vicious murders perpetrated by a killer who appears to possess particular skills when it comes to dissecting his victims ("He carved a trail of horror into the heart of the city," ran the tagline). Written by Robert Rodat and directed by Janet Meyers, it also featured Michael York, Samuel West and Adam Couper, as well as Gabrielle Anwar as a former prostitute with whom Hansen falls in love and whom his boss wishes to use as bait to catch the killer. Although not quite in the same league as the 1988 Michael Caine two-parter, this is an otherwise perfectly adequate take on the case, though Bergin's Cockney accent takes some swallowing.

More routine was *Alien Abduction: Incident in Lake County* (1998, TVM, aka *Alien Abduction: The McPherson Tape*), which was a remake by writer-director Dean Alioto of an earlier video he'd made titled *UFO Abduction* (1989, aka *The McPherson Tape*), which appears to be one of the earliest "found footage" films to have been produced. Although obviously faked, the original movie, shot very cheaply on a home camera, nevertheless managed to convince a number of gullible viewers that it was real at the time. In this reboot of the material, which aired on UPN on 20 January 1998, a boy (Kristian Ayre) manages to capture footage of aliens following a blackout, only for them to follow him home, all of which he films. Like the first version, this is very much a smoke and mirrors affair, with plenty of shaky cam to add to the effect, or rather disguise its shortcomings, though some may enjoy the sheer hokeyness of it all, even if, second time round, they're not prepared to believe that the truth is out there.

Equally unremarkable, albeit for different reasons, was *I've Been Waiting for You* (1998, TVM), in which a teenage girl (Sarah Chalke) with an interest in the occult finds herself likened to a witch by her new classmates when she moves to a New England township, but it seems there might be some truth to their bullying after all. Based upon the 1997 novel *Gallows Hill* by Lois Duncan, best known for her 1973 book *I Know What You Did Last Summer* (which had been successfully filmed the previous year), the movie, which aired on NBC on 22 March 1998, is a typical teen horror concoction of high school angst and the supernatural which unfortunately got lost amid the other examples of its kind that could be found during this period. Indeed, the handling by director Christopher Leitch gives it the air of a TV episode writ large, but Chalke at least makes for a personable heroine. It was leagues ahead of *Dream House* (1998, TVM), however, in which a couple (Timothy Busfield and Lisa Jakub) and their kids (Dan Petronijevic and Jennifer Dale) move into a futuristic home in which all the gadgets are controlled by a supercomputer called Helen (voiced by Pam Hyatt), which subsequently tries to kill them with the various devices to hand. Despite featuring a precursor of Alexa, which provides a few minor moments of amusement, this would-be high-tech thriller, which was broadcast on UPN on 13 April 1998, now seems as dated as a VHS top loader.

The so-called Demon Barber of Fleet Street lathered up for another appearance in *The Tale of Sweeney Todd* (1998, TVM), which aired on Showtime on 19 April 1998 following an early screening at the Hampton International Film Festival in October 1997. A slightly disappointing version of the familiar story given the talent involved, it stars Ben Kingsley as the murderous throat slitter himself, Joanna Lumley as Mrs. Lovett, who makes meat pies from his victims, and Campbell Scott as Ben Carlyle, an American tracking down a missing jeweler who turns out to have been a casualty of the barber's razor. Shot in Dublin by Oscar winning director John Schlesinger, this isn't one of his more stylish productions (the *LA Times* felt it fell flat "because of an ill-conceived script and directorial miscalculation"), yet it tells its tale in reasonably convincing period surroundings (care of designer Malcolm Thornton) which emphasize the muck and poverty of its 19th-century setting (note that PBS had previously broadcast *Sweeney Todd: The Demon Barber of Fleet Street* [1982, TVM] on 12 September 1982, which was a recording of the national tour of Stephen Sondheim's acclaimed 1979 musical version of the story starring George Hearn as Todd and Angela Lansbury as Nellie Lovett; this in turn was filmed in 2007 by Tim Burton starring Johnny Depp and Helena Bonham Carter in the roles).

Another fifties favorite, *I Married a Monster from Outer Space* (1958), was meanwhile given the remake treatment with *I Married a Monster* (1998, TVM), which aired on UPN on 8 October 1998, In it, a suburban bride (Susan Walters) gradually comes to realize that her husband (Richard Burji) isn't all that he used to be, given that he has been taken over by an alien whose craft has landed nearby. One of TV's better remakes, it is sincerely put over by director Nancy Malone, albeit with the occasional sly wink. The effects aren't too bad either (the alien's spaceship even includes touch screens, which it manipulates with its three fingers). Also quite passable is *Lost Souls* (1998, TVM), a co-production between the U.S., Canada and Luxembourg (where the film was shot, although set in the States). First aired on UPN on 12 November 1998, it sees a family move into a new home in the country, in which the young son (Nicolas Deigman) discovers an old electrical device in the basement, through which his autistic sister (Laura Harling) communicates with the ghosts of two children, whose killer is still very much alive and free and living in the area. Also starring John Savage and Barbara Sukowa, this is an old-fashioned ghost story with a nick of time climax set in a nearby cave, during which the true identity of the murderer is finally revealed. It may be a little ponderous at times, but it whiles away the time inoffensively enough (the film was actually one of six titles that went out under the umbrella title *Nightworld*).

Stephen King's final teleplay of the decade was an original three movie story *Storm of the Century* (1999, TVM), which aired on ABC on 14, 15 and 18 February 1999, and which came with a hefty $35 price tag. Set in 1989 on a small island off the coast of Maine, it sees a powerful blizzard sweep into the local township, bringing with it a malevolent stranger, Andre Linoge (Colm Feore), who appears to know dark secrets about each of the inhabitants, whose minds he is able to control, inflicting hallucinations and suicidal thoughts into the populace. But help is at hand in the guise of the local constable, Mike Anderson (Tim Daly), who takes on Linoge (an anagram of Legion), who it is revealed is a supernatural being thousands of years old who, now nearing the end of his existence, wishes to pass on his abilities to one of the town's children. Ably enough directed by Craig R. Baxley, and with all the twists and revelations one would expect from King, this is a generally absorbing horror drama, though with a running time in excess of four hours it verges on wearing out its welcome towards the end. Still, Feore leaves his mark as Linoge, whose persona comes across like a demonic version of Anthony Hopkins' Hannibal Lecter in

The Silence of the Lambs (1991), and the old age make-ups he sports at various points, care of Steve Johnson's XFX, are truly top drawer.

The terrors of the deep were the subject of *Shark Attack* (1999, TVM), a co-production between the U.S., Israel and South Africa (where it was shot). If intended as a TV movie (which both IMDb and Wiki list it as), it instead made its American debut on DVD on 9 November 1999 following a brief theatrical release in Thailand on 28 May 1999, and is included here for the sake of completeness. In it, a marine biologist (Casper Van Dien) travels to the African port of Amanzi to look into a series of shark attacks in the area, among the victims being his friend (Cordell McQueen), whose sister (Jennifer McShane) joins him in his investigations, which reveal that the attacks aren't quite what they seem. The sequences featuring the sharks are well enough shot and edited, but the script by Scott Devine and William Hooke spends too much time on dry land. It was followed by two video sequels: *Shark Attack 2* (2000) and *Shark Attack 3: Megalodon* (2002), which make *Jaws: The Revenge* (1987) look like a masterpiece by comparison.

At least the decade ended on a comparative high with new productions of two old war horses. The first was another version of the Charles Dickens favorite *A Christmas Carol* (1999, TV), which aired on TNT on 5 December 1999. This time it's Patrick Stewart who stars as the miserly Scrooge, who is visited on Christmas Eve by four ghosts (Bernard Lloyd, Joel Grey, Desmond Barrit and Tim Potter) who compel him to mend his ways. Adapted by Peter Barnes and directed with a sure hand by David Jones, this is a slightly more realistic looking version than most, given that it doesn't hold back on showing the era's poverty in a truer light. Shot in England at Ealing Studios and on location at Kirby Hall in Northamptonshire, it also stars Richard E. Grant, Saskia Reeves, Dominic West, Trevor Peacock, Liz Smith and Kenny Doughty, though it's Stewart's performance that holds it all together, prompting *Variety* to comment that he was "such a perfect piece of casting that it will be hard to imagine anyone else as the sour ol' tightwad in years to come."

The second film was a further take on Henry James' *The Turn of the Screw* (1999, TVM), which aired in the UK on ITV (Meridian) on 26 December 1999 (it was shown in American on PBS on 27 February 2000). Also shot in England, it sees Jodhi May star as the Victorian governess who comes to suspect that her young charges (Joe Sowerbutts and Grace Robinson) are being corrupted by the spirits of their former governess (Caroline Pegg) and her lover (Jason Salkey). Adapted by Nick Dear and directed by Ben Bolt, it also starred Colin Firth and Pam Ferris, and, like *A Christmas Carol*, was a more realistic presentation of the story, nicely photographed on location by David Odd in and around Brympton House in Somerset, which adds a good deal of atmosphere to the oft-told tale.

Finally, we end with a quick step back to the feature-length documentary *Universal Horror* (1998, TVM), which aired on TCM on 8 October 1998. In it, film historian Kevin Brownlow examines the legacy of the classic Universal horror movies (along with films from other studios), among them such long standing favorites *Dracula* (1931), *Frankenstein* (1931) and *The Mummy* (1932), whose production histories and subsequent impact are explored via clips and interviews with such industry veterans as Fay Wray, Turhan Bey, Gloria Stuart, Lupita Tovar, Carla Laemmle, Curt

Siodmak and Ray Bradbury, as well as Sara Karloff (daughter of Boris). With a narration by Kenneth Branagh and a score by Hammer's James Bernard, this informative nostalgia fest is one of television's best examinations of the big screen horror movie, among the many others being *Hammer: The Studio That Dripped Blood!* (1987, TV), *The Real Frankenstein: The Untold Story* (1995, TV), *The Fear of God: 25 Years of* The Exorcist (1998, TVM), *A History of Horror with Mark Gatiss* (2010, TV) and *Eli Roth's History of Horror* (2018–2021, TV). Now if only someone would make a documentary about TV's equally rich history of horror....

Epilogue:
A New Era
(the 2000s and 2010s)

If the 20th century had ended on a slightly deflated note, then the new millennium saw the dawning of a *new* golden age in small screen horror, with genre programming mushrooming exponentially over the following two decades, during which science fiction, fantasy and horror subjects became a staple of both film and television. Series featuring vampires, zombies and supernatural phenomena were soon dominating the airwaves, proving highly successful across the globe, and worthy of a book length study in their own right. There were even channels specifically devoted to genre content.

As always, anthology series proved to be a popular way of filling the schedules by producers, and a number of new shows hit the airwaves during the first decade of the 21st century, among them *Urban Gothic* (2001–2002, TV), *Dark Realm* (2001, TV), *Night Visions* (2001–2002, TV), *The Nightmare Room* (2001–2002, TV), *Freaky* (2003, TV), *Masters of Horror* (2005–2007, TV), *Nightmares and Dreamscapes: From the Stories of Stephen King* (2006, TV), *Fear Itself* (2008–2009, TV) and *Point of No Return* (2009–2013, TV). There were also shows that revolved round more traditional horror subjects, such as *Wolf Lake* (2001–2002, TV), which featured werewolves, while vampires got to bare their fangs (and sometimes quite a bit more) in *Vampire High* (2001–2002, TV), *Salem's Lot* (2004, TV), *Dracula* (2006, TV, aka *Bram Stoker's Dracula's Curse*), *Blade: The Series* (2006, TV), *Moonlight* (2007–2008, TV), *Blood Ties* (2007, TV), *The Lair* (2007–2009, TV), *True Blood* (2008–2014, TV), *The Vampire Diaries* (2009–2017, TV) and *I Heart Vampires* (2009–2010, TV). Monsters also got a look in with *Tremors* (2003, TV), and the two-parter *Frankenstein* (2004, TVM), while cartoon shows included *Grim & Evil* (2001–2007, TV, aka *The Grim Adventures of Billy & Mandy*), *Evil Con Carne* (2001–2004, TV), *Phantom Investigators* (2002, TV), *Martin Mystery* (2003–2005, TV), *Danny Phantom* (2004–2007, TV) *Monster Allergy* (2005–2009, TV) and *Mary Shelley's Frankenhole* (2010–2012, TV). As for horror themed anime series from Japan, they were legion. Shows of a more humorous nature included *Dr. Terrible's House of Horrible* (2001, TV), *Dead Like Me* (2003–2004, TV), *Garth Marenghi's Darkplace* (2004, TV) and *Psychoville* (2009–2011, TV), while investigative "factual" series included *Most Haunted* (2002–2019,

TV), *Unexplained Mysteries* (2003–2004, TV), *A Haunting* (2005–2007, 2012–, TV), *The Haunted* (2009–2011, TV) and *Misteryo* (2009–2011, TV).

Some of the decade's biggest hitters, however, could be found among such ongoing series as *The Others* (2000, TV), *Dark Angel* (2000–2002, TV), *The Chronicle* (2001–2002, TV), *Witchblade* (2001–2002, TV), *Strange* (2002, TV), *The Dead Zone* (2002–2007, TV), *Glory Days* (2002, TV), *Haunted* (2002, TV), *Carnivale* (2003–2005, TV), *The Collector* (2004–2006, TV), *Hex* (2004–2005, TV), *Lost* (2004–2010, TV), *Supernatural* (2005–2020, TV), *Surface* (2005–2006, TV), *Invasion* (2005–2006, TV), *Afterlife* (2005–2006, TV), *Night Stalker* (2005–2006, TV), *Dante's Cove* (2005–2007, TV [unaired pilot 2004]), *Coma* (2006, TV), *Dexter* (2006–2013, 2021, TV), *The Dresden Files* (2007–2008, TV), *The Fairies of Liaozhai* (2007, TV), *Being Human* (2008–2013, TV), *New Amsterdam* (2008, TV), *Apparitions* (2008, TV), *Fringe* (2008–2013, TV), *E.S.P.* (2008, TV), *Maligno* (2008, TV), *Crooked House* (2008, TV), *Florinda* (2009, TV), *Harper's Island* (2009, TV), *Demons* (2009, TV) and *The Gates* (2010, TV).

If the first decade of the millennium had seen an explosion of genre content, then the second saw a tidal wave. As before, anthology series were something of a cornerstone, among them *R.L. Stine's The Haunting Hour* (2010–2014, TV), *Femme Fatales* (2011–2012, TV), *6 passi nel giallo* (2012, TV [*6 Steps in Yellow*]), *Deadtime Stories* (2012–2013, TV), *The Hotel Barclay* (2013–2016, TV), *Slasher* (2016–2019, TV), *Channel Zero* (2016–2018, TV), *The Terror* (2018–2019, TV), *The Fantasmagori* (2017, TV), *Creeped Out* (2017–2019, TV), *Saaya* (2018, TV), *The Purge* (2018–2019, TV), *Into the Dark* (2018–, TV), *The Twilight Zone* (2019–2020, TV [reboot]), *Creepshow* (2019–, TV), *Amazing Stories* (2020, TV [reboot]) and *50 States of Fright* (2020, TV). Comedy also had its turn with *Spirited* (2010–2011, TV), *Death Valley* (2011, TV), *Strange Calls* (2011, TV), *Holliston* (2012–2018, TV), *The Haunted Hathaways* (2013–2015, TV), *Inside No. 9* (2014–, TV), *Scream Queens* (2015–2016, TV), *BrainDead* [sic] (2016, TV), *Stan Against Evil* (2016–2018, TV), *Ghosted* (2017–2018, TV) and *Dimension 404* (2017, TV), while investigative "factual" shows included *The Unexplained* (2011–2012, TV), *Unsealed Alien Files* (2012–2015, TV), *In Search of Aliens* (2014, TV) and *Monsters Among Us* (2015, TV). Cartoons also delved into the genre again with *Supernatural: The Animation* (2011, TV), *Gravity Falls* (2012–2016, TV), *Trollhunters* (2016–2018, TV), *Bunnicula* (2016–2018, TV), *Castlevania* (2017–2020, TV), *Hotel Transylvania* (2017–2020, TV), *Vampirina* (2017–2020, TV), *Legend Quest* (2017, TV) and *Jurassic World: Camp Cretaceous* (2020–2022, TV).

Of the more traditional characters, werewolves had their time in the limelight with *Teen Wolf* (2011–2017, TV), *Hemlock Grove* (2013–2015, TV), *Bitten* (2014–2016, TV) and *The Order* (2019–2020, TV), while vampires were the focus of *My Babysitter's a Vampire* (2011–2012, TV), *The Originals* (2013–2018, TV), *Dracula* (2013–2014, TV), *Van Helsing* (2016–2021, TV), *A Discovery of Witches* (2018–2022, TV), *Legacies* (2018–2022, TV), *What We Do in the Shadows* (2019–, TV) and *Dracula* (2020, TV). There was also *The Frankenstein Chronicles* (2015–2017, TV). It was the zombie that proved most popular, however, primarily with *The Walking Dead* (2010–2022, TV), along with the likes of *Zombie Roadkill* (2010, TV), *iZombie* [sic] (2015–2019, TV), *Les Revenants* (2012–2015, TV, aka *The Returned*), *Z Nation* (2014–2018, TV), *The*

Returned (2015, TV [U.S. version of *Les Revenants*]), *Fear of the Walking Dead* (2015–, TV), *Ash vs. Evil Dead* (2015–2018, TV) and *Santa Clarita Diet* (2017–2019, TV).

Yet again, it was with the ongoing format that some of the most popular shows could be found, and the millennium's second decade produced an almost countless number of shows with which fans could sate their thirst for horror. Among them were (deep breath again) *Happy Town* (2010, TV), *Haven* (2010–2015, TV), *Lost Girl* (2010–2015, TV), *Being Human* (2011–2014, TV [U.S. version]), *Becoming Human* (2011, TV), *American Horror Story* (2011–, TV), *The Secret Circle* (2011–2012, TV), *Grimm* (2011–2017, TV), *Black Mirror* (2011–2019, TV), *The River* (2012, TV), *The Secret of Crickley Hall* (2012, TV), *Ripper Street* (2012–2016, TV), *666 Park Avenue* (2013, TV), *Da Vinci's Demons* (2013–2015, TV), *Witches of East End* (2013–2014, TV), *Darknet* (2013–2013, TV), *In the Flesh* (2013–2014, TV), *Bates Motel* (2013–2017, TV), *Hannibal* (2013–2015, TV), *Sleepy Hollow* (2013–2017, TV), *Ravenswood* (2013–2014, TV), *Spooksville* (2013–2014, TV), *From Dusk Till Dawn: The Series* (2014–2016, TV), *Helix* (2014–2015, TV), *Salem* (2014–2017, TV), *Penny Dreadful* (2014–2016, TV), *The Strain* (2014–2017, TV), *The Leftovers* (2014–2017, TV), *Forever* (2014–2015, TV), *Constantine* (2014–2015, TV), *Intruders* (2014, TV), *Heartless* (2014–2015, TV), *The Whispers* (2015, TV), *Fortitude* (2015, TV), *South of Hell* (2015, TV), *Wayward Pines* (2015–2016, TV), *Midwinter of the Spirit* (2015, TV), *Scream: The TV Series* (2015–2019, TV), *Shadowhunters: The Mortal Instruments* (2016–2019, TV), *Lucifer* (2016–2021, TV), *Damien* (2016, TV), *Houdini and Doyle* (2016, TV), *Second Chance* (2016, TV), *Wynonna Earp* (2016–2021, TV), *Wolf Creek* (2016–2017, TV), *Outcast* (2016–2017, TV), *Preacher* (2016–2019, TV), *Shockers* (2016, TV), *American Gothic* (2016, TV), *Dead of Summer* (2016, TV), *The Living and the Dead* (2016, TV), *Stranger Things* (2016–, TV), *Crow's Blood* (2016, TV), *The Exorcist* (2016–2017, TV), *Aftermath* (2016, TV), *Crazyhead* (2016, TV), *American Gods* (2017–2021, TV), *Midnight, Texas* (2017–2019, TV), *The Mist* (2017, TV), *The Gifted* (2017–2019, TV), *Blood Drive* (2017, TV), *Mindhunter* (2017–2019, TV), *Transferts* (2017, TV), *Electric Dreams* (2017–2018, TV), *Mr. Mercedes*

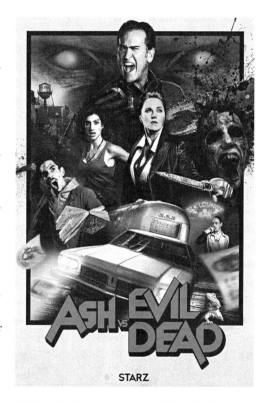

Night Gallery was never like this! Bruce Campbell tops this publicity shot for *Ash vs. Evil Dead* (2015–2018, TV), any episode of which probably contains more gore than was seen in the previous fifty years of genre television combined. Also featured are (left to right) Ray Santiago, Dana DeLorenzo, Lucy Lawless and (bottom) Ted Raimi (Starz/ Renaissance Pictures).

(2017–2019, TV), *Afterlife* (2017, TV), *Light as a Feather* (2018–2019, TV), *The Woman in White* (2018, TV), *The Haunting of Hill House* (2018, TV), *Castle Rock* (2018–2019, TV), *Chilling Adventures of Sabrina* (2018–2020, TV), *The Passage* (2019, TV), *Ghosts* (2019–, TV), *Good Omens* (2019, TV), *NOS4A2* (2019–2020, TV), *Swamp Thing* (2019, TV [reboot]), *Carnival Row* (2019, TV), *Servant* (2019–, TV), *The Witcher* (2019–, TV), *The Outsider* (2020, TV), *Locke & Key* (2020, TV [pilot 2011]), *October Faction* (2020, TV), *I Am Not Okay with This* (2020, TV), *Warrior Nun* (2020, TV), *Cursed* (2020, TV), *Motherland: Fort Salem* (2020, TV, aka *Fort Salem*), *Hungry Ghosts* (2020, TV), *Lovecraft Country* (2020, TV), *The Third Day* (2020, TV), *The Haunting of Bly Manor* (2020, TV), *30 Monedas* (2020–2021, TV, aka *30 Coins*) and *American Horror Stories* (2021, TV).

What distinguishes a good many of these series is not only the quality of the writing, but also the improved production values, the cinema quality cinematography, the casts (it's no longer deemed shameful for film stars to be associated with television) and the imagination of the concepts. Violence, sexual content and language are also now more noticeably adult. Truly, a new golden age is presently in full swing. Though it must be said, despite all that they have going for them, several of the series lack a vital element that marked the first golden age as special, and makes audiences return to these old shows and TV movies time and time again, just as they return to the classic output of Universal and Hammer. And that ingredient is pure and simple—*charm*.

Don't forget to switch off before you go to bed.

Bibliography

Books

Awalt, Steven. *Steven Spielberg and Duel: The Making of a Film Career.* Lanham, Maryland: Rowman & Littlefield, 2014.

Evans, Jeff. *The Penguin TV Companion.* Glasgow: Penguin, 2001.

Halliwell, Leslie, with Philip Purser. *Halliwell's Television Companion.* Chichester: Grafton, 1986.

Jones, Alan. *Profondo Argento: The Man, the Myths & the Magic.* Godalming: FAB Press, 2004.

Kerekes, David, ed. *Creeping Flesh: The Horror Fantasy Film Book.* Manchester: Headpress/Critical Vision, 2003.

_____, ed. *Creeping Flesh: The Fantasy Film Book, Vol. 2.* Manchester: Headpress/Critical Vision, 2005.

Maxford, Howard. *The A–Z of Hitchcock.* London: B.T. Batsford, 2002.

_____. *Hammer Complete: The Films, the Personnel, the Company.* Jefferson, North Carolina: McFarland, 2019.

Murray, Andy. *Into the Unknown: The Fantastic Life of Nigel Kneale.* Manchester: Headpress, 2006.

Rigby, Jonathan. *Christopher Lee: The Authorised Screen History.* Richmond: Reynolds & Hearn, 2001.

_____. *Euro Gothic: Classics of Continental Horror Cinema.* Cambridge: Signum Books, 2016.

Sherman, Fraser A. *Cyborgs, Santa Claus and Satan: Science Fiction, Fantasy and Horror Films Made for Television.* Jefferson, North Carolina: McFarland, 2000.

Smith, John G. *The Poe Cinema: A Critical Filmography.* Jefferson, North Carolina: McFarland, 1998 (2003 paperback referenced).

Viner, Brian. *Nice to See It, to See It, Nice: The 1970s in Front of the Telly.* Reading: Simon & Schuster, 2009.

Newspaper/Periodicals

Billboard
Chicago Tribune
The Daily Express
The Daily Mail
The Daily Mirror
Entertainment Weekly
The Evening News
The Evening Standard
The Guardian
The Hollywood Reporter
The Independent
The LA Times
Look-In
New Statesman
New York Daily News
The New York Times
The New Yorker
The Oregonian
People
Radio Times
The Record
The Sun
Sydney Morning Herald
The Times
TV Guide
TV Times
USA Today
Variety
The Village Voice
The Washington Post

Websites

BBC Genome Project (*Radio Times*, 1923–2009)
IMDb

Index

Numbers in **_bold italics_** indicate. pages with illustrations

A come Andromeda 70
A for Andromeda 69
Aaahh!!! Real Monsters 354
Aahat 355
Abbott and Costello Meet Frankenstein 86, 213
The ABC Afternoon Playbreak 198
ABC Afterschool Specials 201
ABC Friday Night Movie 145
ABC Matinee Today 198
ABC Movie of the Week 4, 111, 112, 117, 145
The ABC Saturday Superstar Movie 197
ABC Stage 67 18
ABC Weekend Specials 201
ABC Wide World of Mystery ***130***, 231
Abigail's Party 218
The Abominable Dr. Phibes 324
The Abominable Snowman 23, 74
The Abominable Snowmen 73
Abra Cadaver 321
The Absent-Minded Professor 155
The Absent-Minded Professor: Trading Places 155
The Accused 32
Ace of Wands 267
Across the Threshold 45
Actors Studio 13
The Addams Family 75, 76, ***76***, 78, 99
The Addams Family Goes to School 76
Addams Family Reunion 76
Addams Family Values 76
An Adventure 297
The Adventure of Silver Blaze 278
The Adventure of the Sussex Vampire 330
Adventures in Slime and Space 312

The Adventures of a Two-Minute Werewolf 201
The Adventures of Ichabod and Mr. Toad 47
The Adventures of Nick Carter 123
The Adventures of Sherlock Holmes and Dr. Watson: The Hound of the Baskervilles 303
The Adventures of Spin and Marty 47
The Adventures of Tom Jones 235
The Advisor's Mystery Theater 41
Afterlife 385
Aftermath 386
Afterward 303
Against the Crowd 255
Ahududu 64
Airplane! 300
The Alcoa Hour 26
Alcoa Presents One Step Beyond 50
The Alfred Hitchcock Hour 45, 46, 100, 159, 308
Alfred Hitchcock Presents 22, 43, ***44***, 46, 48, 54, 58, 62, 91, 100, 282, 308
Alice in Wonderland 98
Alien 324
Alien Abduction: Incident in Lake County 380
Alien Abduction: The McPherson Tape 380
Alien Avengers 375
Alien Avengers II 375
Alien Lover 130
Alien Nation 340
Alien Nation: Body and Soul 340
Alien Nation: Dark Horizon 340
Alien Nation: Millennium 340
Alien Nation: The Enemy Within 340

Alien Nation: The Udara Legacy 340
The Alien Within 374
Aliens Among Us 375
The Aliens Are Coming 322
All Hallows Eve 27
All My Children 326
All My Sons 299
All the Gory Details 321
An Almanac of Liberty 21
The Amazing Falsworth 310
Amazing Grace 314
Amazing Stories 308, 311, 319, 385
Amelia 143, 376
An American Christmas Carol 153
American Gods 386
American Gothic 359, 386
American Horror Stories 387
American Horror Story 386
American Playhouse 371
An American Werewolf in London 314
Amityville: A New Generation 339
The Amityville Curse 339
Amityville: Dollhouse 339
The Amityville Horror 339
Amityville Horror: The Evil Escapes 339
Amityville: It's About Time 339
Amityville: The Awakening 339
Amityville: The Horror Returns 339
Amityville 3-D 339
Amityville II: The Possession 339
Ammie, Come Home 113
The Anatomist 7, 24
Anatomy of Terror 129
Ancient Mysteries 205
Ancient Sorceries 67
And All Through the House 320
And So Died Riabouchinska 44, 308
And Soon the Darkness 324

And the Bones Came Together
    129
*And the Wall Came Tumbling
    Down* 295
And When the Sky Was Opened
    56
The Andromeda Breakthrough
    70
Angel 354
Angel on My Shoulder 323
L'angoisse 17
Animal Magic 266
Ann-Margret: From Hollywood
    158
Anne of the Thousand Days 95
Ants 149, 188
Anveshitha 355
The Apparition 361
Apparitions 385
Arachnophobia 188
The Archangel Harrigan 26
The Archie Comedy Hour 107
Archie's Weird Mysteries 354
Are You Afraid of the Dark?
    350, 352
Are You in the House Alone?
    189
Armchair Theatre 15, 19, 274
Armchair Thriller 277, 278
Arrow to the Heart 35
Arsenic and Old Lace 64
Arson and Old Lace 203
The Art of Death 318
Art of Painting 289
Artemis 81 325
*Arthur C. Clarke's Mysterious
    World* 205
El asfalto 91
The Ash Tree 234, 235, 239, 311,
    312
Ash vs. Evil Dead 382, **382**
Assignment Five 286
Assignment Four 286
Assignment One 285
Assignment Six 286
Assignment Three 286
Assignment Two 286
Asylum 63
Attack of the Monster Plants 74
An Attempt to Save Face 164
Atto di accusa 40
Audrey Rose 31
Automan 302
The Avengers 65, 66, 247
The Avenging of Anne Leete 46
Avventure di mare et di costa 89

Baby 262, 263
The Babysitter 324
Back to the Future 55
Back Ward 352
Bad Ronald 141
The Bad Seed 332
Baffled! 155

The Ballad of Peckham Rye 68
*The Banana Splits in Hocus
    Pocus Park* 197
Banquo's Chair 45
Banshee 308
Bar Mitzvah Boy 218
*Barnabas Collins and the Gypsy
    Witch* 94
The Baron 67
The Bat 22, 60
Bates Motel 334, **335**, 386
Batfink 105
Bay Cove 336
Bay Coven 2, 336, **336**
BBC Play of the Month 67, 258
BBC Sunday-Night Play 18
BBC Sunday-Night Theatre 23,
    35, 64
BBC2 Playhouse 222
The Beast 254
The Beast with Five Fingers 25
Beasts 2, 259, **262**
Beauty and the Beast 48, 166,
    315, 321, 371
The Beckoning Fair One 101
The Beckoning Shadow 85
Becoming Human 386
Beczka amontillado 212
Bedeviled 103
Bedtime Stories 252
The Bees 140
Beetlejuice 333, 342
*Behind the Mask of
    Tutankhamen* 323
Being Human 385, 386
The Bells of Hell 97
Berenice 351
Berkeley Square 16, 20, 23
Berserk 355
The Bespoke Overcoat 33
The Best of Broadway 64
Best Sellers 171
Betterman 355
Beware This Woman 12
Bewitched 78, 127, 197, 303
The Bewitchin' Pool 58
Beyond 42
The Beyond 347
Beyond Belief 25
Beyond Belief: Fact or Fiction
    361
Beyond the Bermuda Triangle
    165, 204
Beyond the Sea 359
Beyond the Sea of Death 46
Biblioteca di Studio Uno 90
O Bicho-papao 343
Bicie serca 14
Bigfoot 155
Bigfoot Meets the Thing 187
Das Bildnis des Dorian Gray 19
Billy the Kid Versus Dracula 46
*The Bird with the Crystal
    Plumage* 212

The Birds 22
The Birthday Party 299
Bitten 385
B.J. and the Bear 205
*The Black Bonspiel of Wullie
    MacCrimmon* 69
Black Carrion 295
The Black Cat 61, 215, 351
The Black Hand 54
*The Black Hope Horror: The
    True Story of a Haunting* 370
Black Mirror 386
Black Noon 177
Black Sabbath 345
Black Scorpion 374
Black Scorpion: Aftershock 375
Black Sunday 345
Blackadder's Christmas Carol
    331
Blackbeard's Ghost 47
Blackstar 341
A Blade in the Dark 345
Blade: The Series 384
Blanche 289
The Blessington Method 45
Blithe Spirit 8, 27, **27**
Blitz! 158
Blood and Black Lace 345
Blood Drive 386
Blood from the Mummy's Tomb
    88
Blood on the Tracks 314
Blood Song 374
Blood Stream 206
Blood Ties 384
Blue Gender 355
Blue Peter 266
Blue Remembered Hills 218
Bluebeard 40
Blunder 30
The Boarding School 91
Bobby 169, 376
La bodega 91
Body Bags 371
The Body Politic 379
The Body Snatcher 84, 210, 215
The Body Snatchers 42
The Bogeyman Will Get You
    300
La bombola 213
Bone Chillers 360
Boo! 310
The Boogieman Cometh 312
The Book of Adrian 147
The Book of Andrew 147
The Book of Rosemary 147
Bootsie and Snudge 33
Bordello of Blood 321
The Borgia Stick 103
*The Boris Karloff Mystery
    Playhouse* 61
Boris Karloff Presents 60
Boris Karloff's Thriller 60
Born Again 25

Boss Cat 104

Boston Blackie 49

The Bottle Imp 12, 16, 22, 25, 48, 89, 345

Boxed In 351

The Boy from Space 301

The Boy Merlin 267

The Boy Who Predicted Earthquakes 110

Boys! Raise Giant Mushrooms in Your Cellar! 91, 308

The Brady Kids on Mysterious Island 197

The Brain 154

BrainDead 385

Bram Stoker's Burial of the Rats 374

Bram Stoker's Dracula 1, 184

Bram Stoker's Dracula's Curse 384

Breaking Point 49

Breakthrough 246

The Breakthrough 222, 223

Brenda Starr 145

Bride of Boogedy 155

Bride of Frankenstein 9, 86, 159, 162

Bride of the Gorilla 54

The Bride Possessed 50, 51, 135

The Brides of Dracula 185

Brideshead Revisited 321

Bridge Across Time 333

Brimstone 363

Brimstone and Treacle 219

Britt Ponset's Christmas Carol 26

Brivido giallo 346

Broadway on Showtime 322

Broadway Television Theatre 22, 47, 118

A Bucket of Blood 374

Buddyboy 261

Buffy the Vampire Slayer 353

The Bugaloos 199

Bullshot Crummond 322

Bunnicula 385

Bunnicula, the Vampire Rabbit 201

Burial of the Rats 374

Buried Secrets 377, **377**

Buru Jenda 355

Bury Me in Niagara 372

La cabina 3, 4, 211

The Cabinet of Dr. Caligari 1

Les cadavres exquis de Patricia Highsmith 349

La caduta di Casa Usher 212

Caesar and Me 58

The Cafeteria 223

Cameo Theatre 282

The Camp on Blood Island 52

Campus Terror 203

The Canary Sedan 44

Canon Alberic's Scrapbook 23

Cannibal ferox 348

Cannon 203

The Canterville Ghost 13, 17, 19, 23, 26, 46, 89, 106, 254, 333, 334, 342, 376

A cantervillei kisértet—zénes jaték 342

Cape Fear 123

Cap'n O.G. Readmore Meets Dr. Jekyll and Mr. Hyde 201

Captain Midnight 41

Captain Nice 78

Captain Scarlet and the Mysterons 266

Captain Rogers 250

Captain Video and His Video Rangers 29

Captains and the Kings 171

The Captain's Guests 50

The Car 138

Carmilla 85, 210, 321, 343

Carmilla: Le coeur pétrifié 343

Carnival Row 387

Carnivale 385

Carol for Another Christmas 79, 80

Carpathian Eagle 293

Carrie 150, 167, 191, 366, 371

The Carroll Formula 27

Carry On 80

Carry On Christmas 80

A Casa das Sete Torres 214

La casa de las siete buhardillas 214

La casa de los siete tejados 214

La casa del sortilegio 347

La casa delle anime erranti 347

Le casa nel tempo 347

Le case maledette 347

The Case of Mr. Pelham 9

The Case of the Lively Ghost 61

A Case of the Stubborns 305, 310

Casino Royale 41

A Cask of Amontillado 14

The Cask of Amontillado 14, 15, 46, 89, 110, 195

El caso de Senor Valdemar 92

Casper the Friendly Ghost: He Ain't Scary, He's Our Brother 106

La casa con la scala nel buio 345

La casa della streghe 213

La casa dell'orco 346

Cast a Deadly Spell 369

The Castaway 32

Casting the Runes 2, 85, 238

Castle Rock 387

Castlevania 385

Cat Amongst the Pigeons 66

The Cat and the Canary 28, 60, 210

The Cat Brought It In 349

Cat Calls 39

The Cat Creature 2, 136, 140

The Cat O'Nine Tails 212

Cat People 1, 55

Catnip 300

Cat's Eye 368

Catweazle 266

Caught on a Train 225

CBS Television Workshop 32, 282

Celle qui n'était plus 142

The Cemetery 109

A cena con il vampiro 346

Centre Play 249

Chamber of Horrors 286

The Champions 66

Chandu the Magician 13

The Changes 267

Channel Zero 385

The Charge Is Murder 40

Chariots of the Gods 205

Charles and Diana: Unhappily Ever After 371

Charles Dickens' Ghost Stories 342

Charlie Boy 293

Charlie's Angels 3, 134, 153

Charly 26

Charmed 363

Chattery Teeth 378, 379

The Cheaters 62

The Chemistry Lesson 351

Chevron Theatre 25

The Chevy Mystery Show 60

Chi sei? 141

La chiave d'argento 344

Chico Bento em: O Monstro de Lagoa 343

Le chien des Baskerville 123

Child of Darkness, Child of Light 368, **368**

Child of Glass 155

Children of the Full Moon 293

Children of the Stones 266, 268, 301

Children of the Sun 18

Child's Play 296

Chiller 350

Chillers 349

Chilling Adventures of Sabrina 387

Chinatown 72

Chock 355

Choosing the Young Lord 172

Chopper 132

The Chopper 83

Christine 138, 176, 379

Christmas Carol 209, 343

A Christmas Carol 11, 16, 21, 25, 26, 79, 176, 277, 316, 330, 342, 343

The Chronicle 385

Chrysalis 213

La chute de la maison Usher 343

Cinderella 28

Cinderella '53 21

Cindy's Fella 28

Circle of Fear 197

Circuit Breaker 375

The Circus 306

The Cisco Kid 49

The City of the Dead 113

Class of '99 110

Classic Ghost Stories 311

Classics Dark and Dangerous 278

Classics Illustrated 175

Cliffhangers 205, *207*

The Clifton House Mystery 268

Climax! 41, 42, 54

The Cloak 33

The Clone Master 173

The Cloning of Clifford Swimmer 129

Close Encounters of the Third Kind 345

The Closed Cabinet 63

Closed Circuit 300

El club de los suicidas 210

Clue Club 106

A Clue for Scooby-Doo 105

Clyde Bruckman's Final Repose 359

The Cocoon 31

Codename: Heraclitus 154

Le coeur cambriolé 212, 343

Le coeur révélateur 14

Coffin, Coffin in the Sky 117

El cohete 91

Cold Hands, Warm Heart 72

Cold Lazarus 360

A Cold Night's Death 4, 132

Collection Completed 320

The Collector 385

Colonel March of Scotland Yard 61

Columbia Workshop 32

Columbo 103, 119

Coma 113, 385

Come and Find Me 247

Come Back Lucy 268

Come Death 67

Come into My Cellar 91

Come Out, Come Out, Wherever You Are 129

Come to Mother 139

Comedy Matinee 23

Comedy of Horrors 300

Commander Toad in Space 201

The Company of Wolves 357

Condemned in Crystal 54

A Connecticut Yankee in the Court of King Arthur 21

Conrad Nagel Theater 26

Constantine 386

The Convenient Monster 66

Coracao delator 14

O Cordcunda de Notre Dame 20

Corky and White Shadow 47

The Corn Is Green 258

Coronation Street 238

The Corpse Can't Play 96

Corridor of Mirrors 40

The Corsican Brothers 209

The Corvini Inheritance 295

La cosa sulla soglia 344

Cosmic Monsters 39

Count Dracula 4, 274, **276**

Count Duckula 318

The Count of Monte-Cristo 326

Count Yorga, Vampire 212, 145

Countess Ilona 273

Countdown at Woomera 24

Country Tales 254, 255

Courage the Cowardly Dog 354

Covenant 332

The Cradle Will Fall 329

Crash 173

The Crash of Flight 401 173

The Crawling Eye 39

Crawlspace 180

The Crazy Kill 249

Crazyhead 386

The Creature 23

Creature from the Black Lagoon 42

Creep Course 321

Creeped Out 385

Creepshow 305, 385

Criminal Pursuit 375

La cristalide 213

The Critical Point 23

The Croaker 68

Crooked House 385

The Crosby Show 311

The Cross and the Arrow 68

The Crossing 339

The Crowd 308

Crowhaven Farm 4, 114

Crow's Blood 386

Cruise Into Terror 150

Cry for the Strangers 327

Cry of Silence 72

Cry of the Banshee 136

The Crystal Egg 30

Cuentos para mayors 19

El cuervo 91

La culpa 92

The Cult of Doomwatch 217

El cumpleanos 91

The Curse 304

The Curse of Dracula 206

The Curse of Frankenstein 34, 51, 86

The Curse of King Tut's Tomb 323

Curse of the Black Widow 148

Curse of the Demon 2, 85, 283

Curse of the Mummy 88

Curse of the Mushroom People 48

The Curse of the Pharaohs 41

Cursed 387

Curtain Call 61

The Cutty Black Sow 306

The Cybernauts 66

Da Vinci's Demons 386

The Daedalus Equations 224

Daffy Duck and Porky Pig Meet the Groovie Goolies 197

The Dain Curse 152

Daleks—Invasion Earth 2150 A.D. 73

Dallas 332

A Dama de Espadas 18

La dama de los tres naipes 92

La dama de pique 214

Dama pikowa 214

Damien 370, 386

Damien: Omen II 332, 369

Dance of the Vampires 1, 344

Danger 22

Danger Mouse 318

Dangerous Corner 258

Daniel Webster and the Sea Serpent 47

Danny Phantom 384

Dante's Cove 385

Dante's Inferno 286

Dario di un pazzo 213

Dark Angel 385

The Dark Angel 86

Dark Encounter 267

Dark Image 12

Dark Mansions 333

Dark Night of the Scarecrow 325

Dark of the Moon 21

Dark Prince: Intimate Tales of the Marquis de Sade 375

Dark Realm 384

The Dark Secret of Harvest Home 2, 171, **173**

Dark Secrets 374

Dark Shadows 1, 2, 92, **93**, 94, 95, 96, 107, 121, 129, 133, 157, 176, 185, 300, 333, 340, 349

The Dark Side of the Earth 55

Dark Skies 359

The Dark Star 68

Dark Towers 301

Dark Vengeance 197

The Darker Side of Terror 190

A Darkness at Blaisedon 96

Darkness Visible 352

Darknet 386

Darkroom 300

Daughter of Darkness 364

Daughter of the Mind 4, 111, 112, 114, 122

The Day of Reckoning 349

The Day of Seasoning 172

The Dead Don't Die 163
Dead Level 39
Dead Like Me 384
The Dead Man 308
Dead Man's Coat 11
Dead of Night 96, 168, 243, 245, 252, 376
Dead of Summer 386
The Dead Part of the House 50
The Dead Room 241
The Dead Zone 385
Deadly Amphibians 74
The Deadly Bees 140
The Deadly Dream 115
Deadly Lessons 329
Deadly Messages 2, 331, **332**
Deadly Nightmares 304
Deadtime Stories 385
Dear Joan: We're Going to Scare You to Death 117
The Death Artist 374
Death at Love House 145
Death Cancels All Debts 244
Death Game 375
Death Has Many Faces 49
Death in Inner Space 61
Death Line 326
Death of a Salesman 258
The Death of Ocean View Park 152, 165
The Death of the Incredible Hulk 187
Death Ship 57
Death Switch 82
Death Takes a Holiday 26, 47, 118
Death Valley 385
Deathday 83
Deathmoon 188
Deep Red 212
Déjà Vu 352
Il delirio de William Wilson 212
Demon 156
Demon in Lace 132
The Demon Lover 303
The Demon Murder Case 329, **329**
Demoni 345
Les démoniaques 142
Demons 345, 385
The Demons 316
Demons 3: The Ogre 346
Department S 67
Design for Living 258
Design for Loving 44
Destination Nightmare 61
Detective 75
The Devil and Daniel Webster 47
The Devil and Miss Sarah 119
Devil Dog the Hound of Hell 189
The Devil in the Dark 74
The Devil Is Not Mocked 110
Devil Lady 355

Devil Pack 204
The Devil Rides Out 1
The Devil to Pay 25
The Devil Within Her 141
Devilman Lady 355
The Devil's Daughter 4, 128
The Devil's Messenger 54
The Devil's Piper 85
The Devil's Rain 324
The Devil's Ticket 63
The Devil's Triangle 204
The Devil's Web 249
Dexter 385
Diabolique 142
Les diaboliques 141, 372
Dial a Deadly Number 249
Il diavolo nella bottiglia 85, 345
The Dick Powell Show 99
Dig Me Later, Vampira 40
Dig That Cat… He's Real Gone 320
The Dimension Discovered 38
Dimension 404 385
Dingbat and the Creeps 341
Dinner with a Vampire 346
The Disappearance of Flight 412 162
The Disappearing Man 242
A Discovery of Witches 385
Discworld 362
A Disney Halloween 155
Disneyland 47, 155
Distant Early Warning 130
A Distant Scream 295
Do Dreams Bleed? 318
Do Me a Favor and Kill Me 101, 103
El doble 91, 307
Doble crimen en la calle Morgue 211
Doc Martin 37
Dr. Cook's Garden 114
Doctor Franken 322
Dr. Heidegger's Experiment 12, 92
Dr. Jekyll and Mr. Hyde 42, 92, 158, **159**, 274, 297, 337, 342
Dr. Strange 187, **188**
Dr. Terrible's House of Horrible 384
Dr. Terror's House of Horrors 1
Dr. Whatshisname 200
Doctor Who 4, 6, 73, **74**, 216, 266, 302
Dr. Who and the Daleks 73
Doctors 99
La dolce casa degli orrori 347
The Doll 67, 110, 213
Don Juan in Hell 67
Don Quixote 32
Donner Pass: The Road to Survival 175
Donovan's Brain 21, 68, 154, 360

Don't Be Afraid of the Dark 4, 135
Don't Fool with a Phantom 106
Don't Go to Sleep 327
Don't Look Now 12
Don't Torture a Duckling 347
Doomwatch 216, **217**
Doomwatch: Winter Angel 216
Dorabella 273
Dorian Gray 19
Il dottor Jeckill e mister Hide 90
Double Echo 224
Double Shock 41
The Doubtful Doctor 45
Douglas Fairbanks, Jr. Presents 32, 33
The Dow Hour of Great Mysteries 60
Dracula 1, 9, 16, 34, 46, 51, 86, 82, 92, 184, 209, 214, 215, 255, 267, 274, 275, 322, 342, 355, 382, 384, 385
Dracula A.D. 1972 100
The Dracula Business 255
Dracula—Prince of Darkness 221
The Dracula Saga 210
Dracula—Sovereign of the Damned 342
Dracula: The Series 356, **357**
Dracula. Uber das Interesse an Vampiren 214
Dracula's Dog 190
Drag 379
Drak Pack 341, **341**
Drama '61 60
Drammi gotichi 213
Dread of the Dummy 265
The Dream 27
Dream Cottage 67
Dream House 380
The Dream Monster 74
Dream of Doom 351
The Dresden Files 385
Duch z Canterville 18
Duel 119, 138, 178, 365, 379
Duet for Two Hands 47
The Dummy 57, 264
Dummy and the Devil 265
During Barty's Party 260, 262
Dust to Dust 318
The Dybbuk 67
Dying Room Only 133
Dynasty 333

E' di moda la morte 345
…E tu vivrai nel terrore! L'aldila 347
The Eagle's Nest 66
Eaten Alive 348
Ebenezer 331
An Echo of Theresa 129
Edgar Allan Poe's Tales of Mystery and Imagination 351

Edge of Terror 49
Edna, the Inebriate Woman 218
Eerie, Indiana 357, **358**
Eerie, Indiana: The Other Dimension 358
Egyptian Sorcery 67
84 Charing Cross Road 218
Eko Eko Azarak: Eye 355
Eko Eko Azarak: The Series 355
Eko Eko Azarak II: Birth of the Wizard 355
Eko Eko Azarak: Wizard of Darkness 355
Eko eko azaraku 355
Eko eko azaraku—manako 355
Eko eko azaraku II 355
Electric Dreams 386
Elegy for a Vampire 197
Eli Roth's History of Horror 383
Emerald Soup 266
The Emissary 281
The Enchanted Cottage 22
Encounter 18
The End of the Party 281
Enter the Dragon 178
The Entity 31
Epilogue to Capricorn 39
Erinnerungen an die Zukunft 205
L'esame 213
Escape 115
Escape from New York 176
Escape into Night 267
The Escape Route 109
Escape to Nowhere 374
Escape to Witch Mountain 190
E.S.P. 385
La espera 91
Espirito Travesso 27
E.T. 309
The Eternal Mind 310
Ett fat amontillado 89
Eve 100, **101**
Eve of Terror 132
Even Scarier 59
An Evening of Edgar Allan Poe 195, **195**
Evil Con Carne 384
The Evil of Frankenstein 86
Evil Stalks This House 300
The Evil Touch 209
The Evil Within 32
The Executioners 132
Exo-Man 170
Exorcism 308
The Exorcism 243, 244
The Exorcist 19, 113, 148, 152, 174, **175**, 329, 386
El experiment del doctor Heideger 92
Experiment in Evil 90
El extrano caso del Doctor Jekyll y Mister Hyde 214

El extrano secreto de Shalken, el pintor 92
Extreme Ghostbusters 312
Eye 372
Eye of the Beholder 56
Eyeball 347
The Eyeglasses 25
Eyes 109
The Eyes of Charles Sand 2, 4, 123
The Eyes of the Panther 321
The Eyes That Wouldn't Die 117

The Face in the Tombstone Mirror 52
Face of Ice 117
The Face of the Tiger 70
The Facts in the Case of M. Valdemar 14, 91
Faerie Tale Theatre 321
The Fairies of Liaozhai 385
Faith healer 316
The Fall of the House of Usher 12, 14, 15, 84, 176, 195, 343
False Face 69
La familia Vourdalak 215
Family Affair 179
Family Dog 311
The Family of the Vourdalak 215
Family Reunion 306
Family Ties 311
The Famous Adventures of Mr. Magoo 81
Fantasies 326
O Fantasma da Opera 355
El fantasma de Canterville 18
O Fantasma de Canterville 17, 18
El fantasma de opera 90
Il fantasma di Sodoma 347
The Fantasmagori 385
The Fantastic Journey 204, 307
The Fantastic 2½ 319
Fantasy Island 3, 126
Le fantome de Canterville 18
Farewell My Lovely 41
Farewell Performance 25
Il fascino dell'insolito 344
The Fatal Flower 32
Faust '57 17
The Fear 58
Fear Itself 384
Fear No Evil 103
The Fear of God: 25 Years of The Exorcist 383
Fear of the Walking Dead 386
The Fearful One 22
The Fearless Vampire Killers 1, 344
Fearnot 313
The Feathered Serpent 268
Feet Foremost 86, 303

Femme Fatales 385
The Ferryman 252
The Fetish 17
Ficciones 210
Fiddler on the Roof 89
The Fifth Sepulcher 353
El fin empezo ayer 92
The Final Chapter 203
The Final Conflict 369
The Find the Lady Affair 280
La finestra sul cortile 346
Fings Ain't Wot They Used T'be 158
Fireball XL5 266
Firefall 132
Fireside Theatre 6, 13, 15
First Blood 39
First Night 71
First Person Singular 11
The Five Doctors 73
Flambards 238, 284
The Flintstones 105
The Flintstones Meet Rockula and Frankenstone 107
Florinda 385
Flowers for Algernon 26
Flowers of Evil 64
The Flying Dragon 85
The Flying Saucers 17
Fog 66
The Fog 176
Folio 20
Fool's Fire 371
Fool's Gold 316
Forbidden Beauty 374
Force of Evil 204
Ford Star Jubilee 27
The Ford Theatre Hour 61, 64
Forever Knight 339, 358
The Formula 38
Fort Salem 387
Fortitude 386
Forward Base 66
The Fossil Men 74
Foul Play 128
Foul Play in Funland 105
Four O'Clock 48
Four Past Midnight 373
Four Star Playhouse 24, 25
Fox Mystery Theater 295
Foyle's War 220
Fraidy Cat 200
Frank em Ser Crianca 343
Frankenstein 1, 9, 30, **31**, 46, 52, 61, 83, 87, 92, 129, 131, 133, 144, 267, 331, 334, 370, 382, 384
Frankenstein: A Love Story 214
Frankenstein Jr. and the Impossibles 105
Frankenstein Meets the Wolf Man 385
The Frankenstein Monster 342
Frankenstein: The Real Story 370

Frankenstein: The True Story 4, 159, **162**
Frankenstein: Une histoire d'amour 214
Frankenstein's Aunt 343, 344
Frankenstein's Baby 356
Frankensteins faster 344
Freaky 384
Fred and Barney Meet the Thing 187
Freddy 92
Freddy's Nightmares 317
French Without Tears 258
Frida 371
Friday the 13th Part VI: Jason Lives 316
Friday the 13th: The Series 315, 317
A Fright at the Opera 312
Fright Hour 100
Fright Night 110
The Frighteners 242
Fringe 359
The Frog Prince 187
From Beyond 365
From Dusk Till Dawn: The Series 3 86
From Sleep and Shadow 335
From the Dead of Night 338
From Venus with Love 66
The Front Page 131
The Fugitive 107, 203
Funeral March of a Marionette 43
The Funky Phantom 106
A Funny Thing Happened on the Way to the Forum 196
The Furnished Room 250
The Fury 122
The Future Ghost 267
Fuzzbucket 155

The Galaxy Being 72
Die Galerie der groken Detektive 15
Gallows Hill 380
Gallows Humor 82
Gallows in the Wind 117
The Gallows Tree 32
Game of Hearts 210
Gargoyles 2, 4, 181, 182, **183**, 354
Gargoyles: The Goliath Chronicles 354
Gas Station 372
Gaslight Theatre 88
The Gates 385
Il gato a nove code 212
El gato negro 215
El gato y el canario 210
Gatti rossi in un labirinto di vetro 347
Gemini Man 164
General Electric Theater 25, 61, 68

General Hospital 95
General Motors Presents 18
Genghis Cohn 299
The Genie 33
The Gentleman from America 44
The Georgian House 267
Germelshausen 13
Das Gespenst von Canterville 17, 18
Das Gespenst von Confettiville 376
Get Dead 333
The Get of Belial 132
The Ghost and Mr. Chicken 77
The Ghost and Mrs. Muir 99
The Ghost Busters 199, 200, **200**, 201, 209, 312
Ghost Fight at the O.K. Corral 312
The Ghost Hunters 255
Ghost in Space 74
The Ghost in the Pale Blue Dress 278
The Ghost Is Your Heart 22
Ghost Mail 40
Ghost Male 40
Ghost Mom 372
The Ghost of Ardachie Lodge 247
The Ghost of Cypress Swamp 155
The Ghost of Flight 401 172
The Ghost of Frankenstein 30
The Ghost of Greenwich Village 16
A Ghost of Our Own 352
The Ghost of Sierra de Cobre 3, 4
The Ghost of Thomas Kempe 201
Ghost of Venice 272
Ghost Rider 1
Ghost Stories 352
Ghost Story 13, 19, 196
A Ghost Story for Christmas 2, 4, 98, **231**, 284, 350
Ghost Train 309
The Ghost Train 6
The Ghost Writer 349
Ghostbreakers 99
Ghostbusters 200, 313
Ghosted 385
Ghosts 350, 352, 387
The Ghosts of Buxley Hall 155
The Ghosts of Motley Hall 268
Ghosts R Us 312
Ghostwatch 356
Giallo 345
Gibel sensatsii 6
The Gift 51
A Gift of Murder 54
The Gift of Terror 198
The Gifted 386
Ginger and Fred 346

Ginger e Fred 346
I giochi del diavolo—storie fantastiche dell'ottocento 344
The Girl in the Glacier 54
Girl of My Dreams 101
The Girl on a Swing 96
The Girl Who Cried Monster 351
The Girl Who Saved the World 206
The Girl with ESP 201
The Girl with Something Extra 78
The Glass Eye 44
Glory Days 385
Gluck und Glas 89
Gnaws 66
Go to the Head of the Class 311
God Grante That She Lye Stille 63
Going Gently 225
The Gold Bug 15
The Golden Bough 218
Golden Showcase 19
Golden Years 357
Goldilocks and the Three Bears 352
Goliath Awaits 325
Gone with the Wind 143
Goober and the Ghost Chasers 106
Good Against Evil 148
Good Evening, Mr. Hyde 42
Good Omens 387
Goodbye Tomorrow 33
Goodyear Playhouse 24
Goosebumps 351, 361
Goosebumps 2 351
Gorilla My Dreams 361
Gotcha 308
Gramercy Ghost 16, 22, 46
Gran teatro 23, 64
Grande Teatro Tupi 64
Las grandes novelas 214
Grandpa's Ghost 310
Grave Secrets: The Legacy of Hilltop Drive 370
Gravedale High 354
The Graveyard Rats 376
Graveyard Shift 197
Gravity Falls 385
The Great Albert 278
Great Detectives 123
Great Expectations 19
The Great Gabbo 20
Great Ghost Tales 69, 85, 249
Great Stories of Mystery and Imagination 88
The Greatest Monster of Them All 45
The Green Man 355
Gregory Horror Show 355
Gremlins 135

The Grim Adventures of Billy & Mandy 384
Grim & Evil 384
The Grim Reaper 63
Grimm 386
Groovie Goolies 107
Growing Pains 293
Grown-Ups 225
A Gruto do Diabo 343
Guardian of the Abyss 293
The Gulf Playhouse 11

Hallmark Hall of Fame 20, 64
Hallmark Television Playhouse 64
Halloween 175
Halloween Candy 305
Halloween Hall o' Fame 155
The Halloween That Almost Wasn't 208
Halloween III: Season of the Witch 246
Halloween with the New Addams Family 76
Hamlet 8, 9
Hammer House of Horror 2, 237, 265, 291, **294**
Hammer House of Mystery and Suspense 2, 294
Hammer: The Studio That Dripped Blood 383
A Hand for Sonny Blue 204
The Hand of Borgus Weems 110
The Hand of Mary Constable 111
A Hand Witch of the Second Stage 335
Hands of Destiny 17
Hands of Murder 17
Hands of Mystery 17
Hands of the Ripper 100
The Hanged Man 103, 140
Hannibal 386
Hansel and Gretel 187, 252, 342
Happy Birthday 33
Happy Days 153
Happy Town 386
The Harbourer 254
Hard Labour 218
The Hardy Boys 203, 359
The Hardy Boys and Nancy Drew Meet Dracula 203
The Hardy Boys/Nancy Drew Mysteries 201
The Hardy Boys: The Mystery of the Applegate Treasure 47
The Hardy Boys: The Mystery of the Ghost Farm 47
Harold and Maude 128
Harold Shipman: Doctor Death 115
Harper's Island 385
Harvest Home 171, 172
Haunted 78, 96, 352, 385

The Haunted 49, 385
Haunted by Her Past 336
The Haunted Hathaways 385
Haunted House 319
The Haunted House 22
The Haunted House Game 351
Haunted House Hang-Up 106
The Haunted Mansion Mystery 201
The Haunted Mask 351
The Haunted: One Family's Nightmare 368
The Haunted Post Office 20
The Haunted Sea 375
The Haunted Tennis Court 296
The Haunted Trailer 201
A Haunting 385
The Haunting of Bly Manor 387
The Haunting Cassie Palmer 301
The Haunting of Helen Walker 375
The Haunting of Hill House 387
The Haunting of Penthouse D 129
The Haunting of Rosalind 129
The Haunting of Sarah Hardy 339
The Haunting of Seacliff Inn 373
The Haunting of the New 308
The Haunting Passion 330
A Haunting We Will Go 203
Hauntings 247
Haunts of the Very Rich 2, 125
Hauser's Memory 153, **154**
Haven 386
Hawaii Five-O 103, 124
Hay-Fork and Bill-Hook 62
Hay que matar Dracula 210
He Who Kills 376
The Headless Horseman 371
The Heart Farm 114
Heartbeat 13
Heartless 386
The Heat Monster 74
Heathcliff 341
The Heathcliff and Dingbat Show 341
The Heiress 22
Helix 386
Hell Teacher Nube 355
Hell Toupee 310
Hellfire 374
The Hell's Gate 347
Hemlock Grove 385
Henry Hamilton Graduate Ghost 201
The Herculoids 105
Here Come the Munsters 78
Hex 385
The Hex 16
High Desert Kill 340
High Rise 176
High Tor 21, 27

Highcliffe Manor 207
Highway Patrol 49
Hildegarde Withers 123
The Hilarious House of Frightenstein 209
The Hills Have Eyes 174
The Hiroshima Ghost 17
Histoires extraordinaires 249
Historias para la noche 91
Historias para no dormir 90, 91, 92, 307, 308
A History of Horror with Mark Gatiss 383
History's Mysteries 205
The Hitch-Hiker 56
The Hitchhiker 304, 305
Hjertet de sladrede 14
Holliston 385
El hombre y la bestia 90
Home for the Holidays 127
L'homme qui revient de loin 212
L'homme qui rit 212
Hop-Frog 371
Hora once 92
The Horn Blows at Midnight 20
Horror 112
Horror at 37,000 Feet 182
Horror Hotel 113
Horror in the Heights 132
Horror of the Dummy 265
The Hotel Barclay 385
Hotel Transylvania 385
Houdini and Doyle 386
The Hound of the Baskervilles 123, 302, 303, 329
The Hounds of Fate 296
Hounds of Zaroff 138
Hour of Mystery 16, 47
The House and the Brain 129
The House of Clocks 347
House of Dark Shadows 94, 95, 185
House of Dracula 46, 145
House of Frankenstein 46, 86, 145
The House of Lost Souls 347
House of Secrets 372
House of the Damned 374
The House of the Seven Gables 16, 17, 21, 49, 214
House of Usher 1
The House of Witchcraft 347
The House of Witches 213
The House on Dragon's Rock 66
House on Haunted Hill 197
The House on Possessed Hill 203
The House That Bled to Death 293
The House That Cried Murder 117
The House That Dripped Blood 64
The House That Screamed 91

The House That Would Not Die 113
The Housekeeper 109
How 266
How Awful About Allan 112
How to Cure the Common Vampire 110
The Howling 314
A Howling in the Woods 154
The Howling Man 56
H.P. Lovecraft: Schatten aus der Zeit 212
H.R. Pufnstuf 104, 198, 199
Hrabe Drakula 214, **214**, 276
The Huckleberry Hound Show 104
Human Interest Story 45
The Human Side 225
The Human Time Bomb 217
Humanoids from the Deep 375
The Hunchback 377
The Hunchback of Notre Dame 19, 20, 65, 326, 342, 377
Der Hund von Baskerville 123
The Hunger 353
Hungry Ghosts 387
The Hungry Glass 62
The Hunter 137
A Husband Disappears 25
Husking Bee 172
Hyde and Go Shriek 321

I Am Not Okay with This 387
I, Desire 327
I Do Not Belong to the Human World 116
I Don't Want to Be Born 141
I Dream of Jeannie 78, 141
I Have Been Here Before 10, 89, 259
I Heart Vampires 384
I Know What You Did Last Summer 380
I Like It Here 96
I Love Lucy 11, 43
I Married a Monster 381
I Married a Monster from Outer Space 381
I, Tobor 29
I Walked with a Zombie 1
Ice from Space 31
The Ice House 238, 239, 241
An Ideal Husband 258
I'll Be Watching You 350
I'm Dangerous Tonight 366
The Immortal 107
The Immortals 107
Imp on a Cobweb Leash 25
The Importance of Being Earnest 18, 258
L'impronta dell'assassino 345
In His Image 57
In Possession 295
In Praise of Pip 57

In Search of... 204, 312
In Search of Aliens 385
In Search of Ancient Astronauts 204
In Search of Ancient Mysteries 205
In the Flesh 386
In the Mind's Eye 247
The Incredible Hulk 187, 314
The Incredible Shrinking Man 53
The Incredible World of Horace Ford 21
The Incredibles 311
Gli incubi di Dario Argento 346
The Indian Spirit Guide 101
Indiana Jones and the Last Crusade 85
Inexperienced Ghost 13
The Inheritance 315
Inhumanoid 375
The Initiation of Sarah 150
The Inner Light 21
Inner Sanctum 39
Inner Sanctum Mystery 39
The Innocent Bystanders 62
The Innocents 140, 376
The Insect Play 7, 23
Inside No. 9 385
Inside the Closet 305
The Intercessor 303
The Interrupted Journey 165
Interview with the Vampire: The Vampire Chronicles 1
Into the Dark 385
Into the Labyrinth 301
Into the Woods 188
The Intruder Within 324
Intruders 386
The Invader 30
The Invaders 18, 107, 203, 322
Invaders from the Fifth Dimension 74
Invasion 385
The Invasion of Carol Enders 51, 135
The Invicta Ray 280
The Invisible Enemy 73
The Invisible Man 47, 51, **52**, 164, 306
The Invisible Woman 328
The Invisibles 72
Invitation to Hell 330
Ironside 131
Is There Another Civilization? 53
The Island 278, 279
The Island of Dr. Moreau 166
Island of Evil 108
Island of the Damned 93
It 366, **367**
It Came from Outer Space 42
It Came from Outer Space II 376

It Crawled Out of the Woodwork 72
It Happened at Lakewood Manor 149, 188
It's a Dog's Life 200
It's a Good Life 59
It's Alive 141
It's Only a Movie 352
ITV Play of the Week 24, 64, 67
ITV Playhouse 283
ITV Television Playhouse 23
Ivanhoe 342
I've Been Waiting for You 380
iZombie 385

Jack and the Beanstalk 252
Jack Be Nimble 247
Jack the Ripper 61, 63, 338, **338**, 364
Jackanory 281, 296, 302
Jamie 266
Jane Brown's Body 101
Jane Eyre 19, 93, 230
The Jar 46, 308
Jaws 119, 166, 178, 179, 294
The Jazz Age 23
Jekyll & Hyde 364
Jemima Shore Investigates 277
The Jensen Code 267
Jet Jackson, Flying Commando 41
The Jetsons 105
The Jewel of Seven Stars 88
Jigoku sensei Nube 355
Joe's Marionette Theatre 371
Johnny Blue 33
The Joke 223
Jonny Quest 105
The Journey Begins 364
Journey Into Darkness 103
Journey Into Terror 73, **74**
Journey to Midnight 103
Journey to Murder 103
A Journey to the Center of the Earth 82
Journey to the Unknown 53, 100, **101**, 103, 294
The Jovial Ghost 33
Julia Jekyll and Harriet Hyde 359
Julie 143
The Jungle 57
Junior Sunday Quiz 258
The Junkman 92
Jurassic Park 364
Jurassic World: Camp Cretaceous 385
Justin Case 155

Kadaitcha County 210
Kaleidoscope 246
Karaoke 360
Karroll's Christmas 331
Kenpu Denki Berserk 355

Kentervilski duh 18
Kick the Can 59
Killdozer 138, **138**, 379
Killer Bees 139
The Killer Dolphins 217
A Killer in Every Corner 249
Killer Tree 43
The Killers 103
The Killing Bottle 103
Kindling Night 172
Kindred: The Embraced 360
King Nine Will Not Return 56, 177
King of the Castle 268
King of the Lost World 364
King of the Road 321
King of the Zombies 40
The Kingdom 355
Kingdom Hospital 355
Kingdom of the Spiders 188
Kiss in Attack of the Phantoms 174
Kiss Me and Die 248
Kiss Meets the Phantom of the Park 173
The Kiss of Blood 97
The Kiss of the Vampire 1
Kisses at Fifty 218
Kolchak 132
Kolchak: The Night Stalker 131
Kolchak the Night Stalker— Night Killers 131
Kotu tohum 331
Kraft Suspense Theatre 17
Kraft Television Theatre 16
Kyofu densetsu: Kaki! Furanhenshutain 342
Kyuketsuki Miyu 355

El ladron de cadavers 215
The Lady and the Monster 154
The Lady from Shanghai 202
Lady Killer 247
Lady Sybil 273
The Lady Vanishes 291
Lady Windemere's Fan 283, 299
Ladykiller 375
The Lady's Maid's Bell 303
The Lair 384
The Lake 209
Lamb to the Slaughter 282
Land of the Giants 53
Land of the Lost 199
The Land Unknown 119
The Landlady 45, 282
The Langoliers 373
The Last Bride of Salem 198
The Last Chance 374
The Last Dinosaur 147
Last Exit to Earth 375
The Last House on the Left 174
The Last Man on Earth 30
The Last Mystery 70
The Last of the Clintons 5

The Last of the Cybernauts 66
Last of the Mohicans 175
Last Rites for a Dead Druid 110
Last Scene 304
The Last Séance 304
The Last Vampyre 330
The Last Visitor 101
The Last Witness 295
Lastborn 278
Late Night Horror 96, 168, 282
Late Night Story 281
Late Night with Letterman 205
Late Show with David Letterman 205
The Lateness of the Hour 57
Laura 55
Laverne and Shirley 206
Leap in the Dark 247
The Leather Funnel 250
The Leftovers 386
Legacies 385
Legend of Crater Mountain 42
Legend of Death 82
The Legend of Sleepy Hollow 47, 48, 155, 321
Legend Quest 385
The Leopard Lady 11
Los libros 210
Lidsville 199
The Life and Times of Grizzly Adams 175
Life at Stake 238
Life of Vernon Hathaway 27
The Life Work of Juan Diaz 46
Lifeblood 206
Life's Little Ironies 250
Ligeia 90, 343
Ligeia forever 212
Lights Out 2, 11, 15, 28
The Lion King 371
The Lion, the Witch and the Wardrobe 266
The List of Adrian Messenger 63
The Listener 85
A Little Bit Like Murder 129
Little Lost Robot 68
Little Malcolm and His Struggle Against the Eunuchs 223
Little Red Riding Hood 187
Little Shop of Horrors 32
Live Again, Die Again 138
The Living and the Dead 386
Living Doll 57
The Living Grave 247
A Lizard in a Woman's Skin 346
Lizard's Leg and Owlet's Wing 65
Lizzie Dripping 267
El lobo 91
The Lobster Man 74
Locke & Key 387
The Lodger 55
London After Midnight 62
The Lone Gunmen 359

The Lone Ranger 11
Lonely Water 4, 272
Long Distance Cal l 57
The Long Distance Piano Player 217
The Long Goodbye 41
Look and Read 301
Look What's Happened to Rosemary's Baby 147
Lords of the Deep 374
The Lorelei 299
Loss of Feeling 6
Lost 126
Lost Girl 386
Lost Hearts 230, **231**, 232, 239
Lost in Space 74
Lost in Translation 300
Lost Souls 381
The Lost Stradivarius 83
The Lost Will of Dr. Rant 11
The Lost World 363
The Lost World: Jurassic Park 364
The Lottery 13
Love and Curses 357
The Love of a Good Woman 224
Love Story 70
Lovecraft Country 387
Una lucertola con la pelle di donna 346
Lucifer 386
Lucky Stiff 318
Lust for Life 158
Luther 258
Lux Video Theatre 22, 41, 54

Ma non e! un vampire? 213
Macbeth 9, 153
The Machine Calls It Murder 60
The Macropulos Secret 24
Mad, Mad, Mad Monsters 197
Madam Crowl's Ghost 215
The Madison Equation 101
Madness Room 305
Maggie May 158
The Magic Egg 26
The Magic Shop 45
The Magical World of Disney 47, 155
Magoo Meets Frankenstein 81
Magpie 266
Make Me Laugh 110
The Makropulos Affair 24
The Makropoulos Incident 24
A Makropulosz-ugy 342
Maligno 385
Man and Superman 67
Man-Beast 74
Man Dog 266
Man-Eater of Surrey Green 66
The Man from the South 45, 282
The Man from U.N.C.L.E. 154
The Man in Half Moon Street 16, 46, 47

The Man in the Iron Mask 326
The Man Who Could Cheat Death 16, 48
The Man Who Didn't Believe in Ghosts 350
The Man Who Finally Died 39
The Man Who Haunted Himself 44
The Man Who Heard Everything 33
The Man Who Knew Tomorrow 26
The Man Who Laughs 212
The Man Who Sold His Shadow 26
The Man Who Vanished 17
The Man Who Walked Out on Himself 24
The Man Who Wanted to Live Forever 113
The Man Who Was Death 320
The Man with the Power 170
Man with Two Shadows 66
Manana puede ser verdad 90
Mangiati vivi! 348
Manimal 302
The Mannikin 278, 279
Marcus Welby, M.D. 119
Mardi Gras 13
Marianne Dreams 267
The Marionette Mystery 13
Marionettes, Inc. 307
Mark of the Devil 295
Mark of the Vampire 186
Markheim 26, 212, 254
Marnie 116
Marquis de Sade 375
The Martian Eyes 12
Martin Mystery 384
Martin's Close 242
Marty 47
Mary Poppins 20, 47
Mary, Queen of Scots 95
Mary Rose 23
Mary Shelley's Frankenstein 1
La maschera del demonio 345
The Mask of Adonis 203
The Mask of Satan 294, 345
The Masque of the Red Death 1, 12, 351
Master Zacharius 49
Masters of Horror 384
Masterworks of Terror 14, 90
Matango 48
Matatikas Is Coming 102
Matinee Theater 13, 15, 16, 17, 20, 2446, 188
A Matter of Semantics 110
Maximum Overdrive 138, 379
The Maze 303
Mazes and Monsters 328
McCloud 145
McCloud Meets Dracula 145
McCreary Moves In 39

The McPherson Tape 380
Méchant garcon 141
O Médico e o Monstro 214
The Medium 20
The Melancholy Hussar 251
Memento 30
Men into Space 53
The Menfish 74
The Mephisto Waltz 125
The Merciful 110
Meriel, the Ghost Girl 223, 225
Merlin the Magician 200
Merry-Go-Round 267
The Message 70
La métamorphose 343
La metamorfosis 92
The Metamorphosis 92, 299, 343
Le mezzatinta 344
The Mezzotint 24, 242, 296, 311, 344
Michael Bentine's Potty Time 267
The Mickey Mouse Club 47
Mickey's Gala Premier 7
Midnight Cop 339, 358
The Midnight Hour 332
Midnight Movie 299
Midnight Offerings 325
Midnight, Texas 386
A Midnight Visit to the Neighborhood Blood Bank 110
A Midsummer Night's Dream 5
Midwinter of the Spirit 386
Millennium 362
Millicent and Therese 143
The Milton Berle Show 14
Milton the Monster 105
The Mind Beyond 223
The Mind of Ann Pilgrim 39
Mind Over Matter 247
Mind Over Murder 191
Mindhunter 386
The Mini-Munsters 198
Minotaur 82
The Miracle Worker 28
Mirror, Mirror 310
Mirror, Mirror Off the Wall 166
Les Miserables 326
Miss Belle 101
Miss Constantine 254
Miss Lovecraft Sent Me 110
Miss Morison's Ghosts 297
The Mission 311
The Mist 386
Mr. Arcularis 24, 28, 69
Mr. Boogedy 155
Mr. Humphreys and His Inheritance 257, **258**
Mister Magoo 81
Mr. Magoo's Christmas Carol 81, 195

Mr. Magoo's Doctor Frankenstein 81
Mr. Magoo's Gunga Din 81
Mr. Magoo's Rip Van Winkle 81
Mr. Magoo's Sherlock Holmes 81
Mr. Magoo's William Tell 81
Mr. Mercedes 386
Mr. Mirgethwirker's Lobblies 21
Mr. Nightingale 273
Mr. R.I.N.G. 132
Mr. Scrooge 80
Mister Scrooge 80
Mr. Terrific 78
Mr. Tiger 51
Mr. Utterson's Encounter 42
El misterio de Madame Crowl 215
Misteryo 385
Mistress of Suspense 349
Monica and Friends 343
The Monkey's Paw 7, 8, 15, 69, 90, 91
The Monkey's Paw—A Retelling 46
Monodrama Theater 13, 19
The Monster 70
Monster Allergy 384
The Monster Bed 201
Monster Force 354
The Monster from Outer Space 74
Monster Mash 319
The Monster of Frankenstein 342
Monster Squad 200
The Monsters 49, 70
Monsters Among Us 385
Monsters Ate My Homework 321
Monsters in My Room 305
Moon of the Wolf 126, 138
Moon Probe 53
The Moon Stallion 268
Moonlight 384
More Than Human 364
Mortal Challenge 375
La morte in vacanza 22
Mosquito Squadron 154
The Most Dangerous Game 138
Most Haunted 356, 384
Motherland: Fort Salem 387
Movie Macabre 40
Movie Monsters 267
Movie of the Week 4, 112, 145
The Moving Maze 82
The Moving Toyshop 75
Mrs. Acland's Ghosts 222, 223, 224
Mrs. Amworth 3, 4, 278, 279, 280
Mrs. Bixby and the Colonel's Coat 282
Mrs. Moonlight 20

Mrs. Palfrey at the Claremont 253

Ms. Scrooge 331

Much Ado About Nothing 5

The Mummy 1, 9, 61, 74, 185, 382

Mummy Daddy 310

El muneco maldita 91, 212

Munster, Go Home! 77

Munster Masquerade 77

The Munsters 77, 99, 208

The Munsters' Revenge 78

The Munsters' Scary Little Christmas 78

The Munsters Today 78

Murder and the Android 28

Murder by the Book 119

Murder in the Mirror 54

Murder Me Twice 45

Murderous Vision 367

Murders in the Rue Morgue 25, 55, 75, 211, 300

Murrain 256, **257**, 259, 263

Music Scene 257

Musical TV Theater 342

My Babysitter's a Vampire 385

My Fair Munster 77

My Ghostwriter—The Vampire 306

My Left Fang 312

My Zombie Lover 316

The Mysterious Island 82

Mysterious Two 326

Mystery 278

Mystery and Imagination 2, 83, **84**, 89, 215, 232, 255, 283, 303

The Mystery in Dracula's Castle 154, 179

The Mystery of Collinwood 94

The Mystery of King Tut's Tomb 203

The Mystery of Pirate's Cove 202

The Mystery of the Haunted House 202

The Mystery of the Hollywood Phantom 203

Mystery of the Wax Museum 136

The Mystery of Witches' Hollow 203

Mystery on the Avalanche Express 203

Mystery Satellite 53

The Name of the Game 119

Nancy Drew 203

Nanny and the Professor 78, 197

Nanny and the Professor and the Phantom Circus 198

Napoleon and Samantha 179

Narciso Ibanez Serrador presenta a Narciso Ibanez Menta 90

The NBC Mystery Movie 111

NBC Television Opera Theatre 18

NBC Television Theatre 27

The Need for Nightmare 255

Needlepoint 300

NET Playhouse 28

The New Adventures of Mighty Mouse and Heckle & Jeckle 319

New Amsterdam 385

The New Avengers 66

New Blood 304

The New Exhibit 57

The New House 196

The New Invisible Man 61

The New Man 305

The New People 102

The New Saturday Superstar Movie 197

The New Scooby-Doo Movies 106

The New Scooby-Doo Mysteries 106

A New Woman 316

New York Television Theatre 82

The Next Step Beyond 51

Nezkuseny duch 343

Nick Carter 123

Nick Knight 339, 358

The Night America Trembled 21

Night Cries 149

The Night Flier 379

Night Gallery 108, 119, 196, 197, 386

The Night Killers 131

Night Must Fall 48

Night of April 14th 50

Night of Dark Shadows 94, 157

The Night of the Big Heat 24

Night of the Demon 85, 283

Night of the Marionettes 273, **273**

The Night of the Simhat Torah 335

Night of the Storm 127

Night Pleasures 175

Night Slaves 112

Night Stalker 132, 385

The Night Stalker 2, 4, 120, 130, 131, 132, **132**, 144, 314

The Night Strangler 2, 4, 130

The Night That Dracula Saved the World 208

The Night the Ghost Got In 13

Night Visions 384

Nightkill 324

Nightlife 339

Nightmare 72

Nightmare at 30,000 Feet 59

Nightmare at 20,000 Feet 58, 59

Nightmare Café 350

Nightmare Classics 321

A Nightmare Come True 377

Nightmare in Yellow 91

A Nightmare on Elm Street 1, 175, 317

The Nightmare Room 384

Nightmares and Dreamscapes: From the Stories of Stephen King 384

Nightworld 381

9 to 5 128

1984 21, 23, **23**

No Day at the Beach 311

No More Mr. Nice Guy 318

No Place Like Earth 82

No Place to Hide 324

No Sax Please: We're Egyptian 319

No Such Thing as a Vampire 96

Nobody's House 268

Nocturna 46

Non si sevizia un paperino 347

The Norliss Tapes 3, 4, 156, 158

Northanger Abbey 299

Nosferatu 1, 193

NOS4A2 387

Nostalgia punk 346

Nostradamus Berry 17

Not Like Us 374

Not of This Earth 374

The Not So Nice Mice 200

Notre-Dame de Paris 378

Notte in Casa usher 212

Nouvelles d'Henry James 141

Novela 18, 214

Nowhere to Hyde 106

Number Six 350

Number 13 69, 85, 240, 241, 312, 344

Nurse Will Make It Better 248, 249

Nursery Tea 281

Nuts in May 218

The Oblong Box 136, 300

Obras maestras del terror 14, 90

The Occult: Mysteries of the Unknown 205

An Occurrence at Owl Creek Bridge 45, 58

October Faction 387

The Odyssey 342

Of Late I Think of Cliffordville 57

Oh, Whistle, and I'll Come to You, My Lad 97, 225, 311

Oke of Okehurst 85

The Old College Spirit 312

The Old Curiosity Shop 342

Old Mrs. Jones 85

Oliver! 100, 158, 232

Oliver Twist 342

The Omega Factor 284

The Omen 58, 147, 368, 369, 370

Omen IV: The Awakening 369

Omnibus 20

On Camera 13, 27

On the Orient, North 308
Once an Eagle 171
Once Upon a Brothers Grimm 187
Once Upon a Time in the City of New York 315
One Deadly Owner 248
One Man 350
One Million Years B.C. 100
One on an Island 101
One Step Beyond 50, 135, 247
The One Who Waits 91
Only Skin Deep 321
Only Way Out Is Dead 113
The Open Door 84
Opening of the BBC Television Service 5
Ordeal in Space 32
Ordeal on Locust Street 50
The Order 385
The Originals 385
Orson Welles Great Mysteries 250, **250**
The Other Side of the Curtain 48
The Others 20, 46, 385
Otherworld 307
Otra vez Dracula 210, 214
Otra vuelta de tuera 141
Our Unsung Villains 47
Out of the Unknown 102, 295
Out of This World 68, 83
Outbreak 194
Outcast 386
The Outer Limit 17
The Outer Limits 71, **72**, 78, 349
The Outsider 387
Outward Bound 125, 267
The Oval Portrait 351
The Overcoat 33
Owen Marshall, Counselor at Law 119
The Owl Service 266

El pacto 91
Palabras cruzadas 211
Panic at Lakewood Manor 149, 188
Papa Benjamin 62
Paper Dolls 102
Paperhouse 267
Parasite Mansion 63
Pardon My Genie 266
Pardon My Ghost 33
Parents' Night 352
Parting Shot 352
The Passage 387
The Passion of Dracula 322
La pata del mono 90
Past Tense 30
Patterns 54
The Paul Winchell and Gerry Mahoney Show 14
Peculias para no dormir 92

Penda's Fen 219, **220**, 326
Pendulums and Hazel Twigs 247
Penelope Pulls It Off 326
Penny Dreadful 386
The People 121
People Are Alike All Over 56
The Pepsi-Cola Playhouse 25
Per sempre 346
Perchance to Dream 56
Perseus and the Gorgon 313
Perversions of Science 351
Pet Shop of Horrors 355
Petersen's Eye 25
Petto shoppu obu horazu 355
Phantom 90
Phantom Investigators 384
The Phantom Lover 85
The Phantom of Hollywood 185, **186**
The Phantom of Lot 2 186
Phantom of the Bridge 13
The Phantom of the Opera 90, 185, 328, 342, 355, 278
Phantom of What Opera? 110
The Phantom Rickshaw 26
The Philco Television Playhouse 21, 27
The Phoenix 268, 325
The Phoenix and the Carpet 268
A Photograph 220
The Photograph 54, 281
The Picture of Dorian Gray 18, 19, 29, 133, 144, 161, 185, 259
Pikovaya dama 7, 342
Piranha 374
The Pit 12
The Pit and the Pendulum 12, 89, 195
A Place of One's Own 85
A Place to Die 248
Places Where They Sing 249
Plague from Space 31
The Plague of the Zombies 185
Plan 9 from Outer Space 40
Planet of the Apes 58, 166
The Plastic Eaters 216
Play for Today 219, 222, 274
Play of the Week 67
Playdate 69
The Playground 307
Playhouse 90 54, 55
Pleas for the Damned 206
Pleasant Screams 321
Ploughing Day 172
Point of No Return 384
Poison 382
Poltergeist 145, 309, 370
Poltergeist: The Legacy 353
Poltergeist III 353
Ponds Theater 26, 47, 118
Poor Butterfly 102, 103
Poor Devil 156
Poor Girl 253

Port Charles 95
La porta sul buio 213
La porte dell'inferno 347
Portret Doriana Greya 19
The Poseidon Adventure 325
Possessed 51
The Possessed 2, 169
Possession 248
The Postman Always Rings Twice 346
Pottage 121
Potty Time 267
Poultrygeist 312
La poupée sanglante 212
The Power of the Ixodes 39
The Power Within 151
The Powers of Matthew Star 302
Preacher 386
The Prediction 62
The Premature Burial 63
Prescription: Murder 103
Press for Time 78
A Priceless Pocket 33
Priklyucheniya Sherloka Kholmsa I doktora Vatsona: Sobaka Baskerviley 303
Prime Cut 318
Primera fila 64
Prince of Darkness 246
The Princess and the Goblin 49
The Princess and the Goblins 49
The Prisoner 67
The Prisoner in the Mirror 63
The Probe 73
Producers' Showcase 24
Profundo rosso 212
Project Sahara 217
Promise Him Anything 144
Prophecy 350
Prototype 330
The Prudential Family Playhouse 20
Psycho 136, 310
Psycho IV: The Beginning 366
The Psychophonic Nurse 25
Pufnstuf 104
Le puits et le pendule 89
Pulitzer Prize Playhouse 22
Puppy Love 100
The Purge 385
The Purloined Letter 14, 15
Purple Playhouse 209
The Purple Room 62
Pyramids of Mars 73
Pyramus and Thisbe 5

Quatermass 37
Quatermass and the Pit 36, 100
The Quatermass Conclusion 38
The Quatermass Experiment 34, 38, 39, 97
Quatermass 4 37
The Quatermass Memoirs 38
Quatermass II 35

Quatermass 2 36
The Quatermass Xperiment 38
The Queen of Spades 12, 18, 26, 40, 92, 214
Quicksilver Highway 378
Quien puede matar a un nino? 92
Quiet As a Nun 277
Quinn Martin's Tales of the Unexpected 203
El quinto jinete 215
Quoth the Raven 110

Racconti di fantascienza 213
I racconti fantastici di Edgar Allan Poe 212
Rachel in Danger 277
The Railway Children 123
Raise the Titanic 294
Randall and Hopkirk (Deceased) 67
Rapunzel 48, **49**
Raquel 158
Rasputin 90
Raven 268
The Raven 91, 195, 371
Ravenswood 386
Raw Meat 326
Raxl, Voodoo Priestess 108
The Ray Bradbury Theater 122, 307
The Real Frankenstein: The Untold Story 383
The Real Ghostbusters 312
Re-Animator 365
Reaper Man 362
Rear Window 176
Rebecca 333
The Red Room 296
The Red Skelton Show 14
The Reflecting Skin 299
Reflections of Murder 141, 372
The Reluctant Vampire 321
Rendezvous 27
Rentaghost 267
Report from the Grave 321
Requiem for a Heavyweight 28, 54
La residencia 91
The Resurrection 317
El resurrecctionista 210
El retrato de Dorian Gray 19, 214
The Return 254
Return Flight 244
The Return of Count Yorga 121, 145
The Return of Dracula 110
The Return of Swamp Thing 353
The Return of the Curse of the Secret of the Mummys Tomb Meets Frankenduckulas Monster and the Wolfman

and the Intergalactic Cabbage... 319
Return of the Cybernauts 66
The Return of the Sorcerer 110
Return to Salem's Lot 194
Return to the Lost World 364
Return to Witch Mountain 190
The Returned 386
Les Revenants 385, 386
Revenge 43
Revenge! 118
The Revenge of Frankenstein 86
Revenge of the Stepford Wives 323
Revenge of the Zombies 40
Revolt of the Machines 29
Rheingold Theatre 32, 33
Rich Little's Christmas Carol 209
Ricochet 99
Riding with Death 165
Riget 355
Ripley's Believe It or Not 205
Ripper 73
The Ripper 132, 379
Ripper Street 386
Ritual of Evil 104
The Rival Dummy 20
The River 386
R.L. Stine's The Haunting Hour 385
The Road 71
Roald Dahl's Tales of the Unexpected 204, 281
The Robber Bridegroom 322
The Robert Herridge Theater 13
Robert Montgomery Presents 17, 20
Roberts Robots 267
Robin Redbreast 218, 219, 221
Robot! 210
Rock-a-Die Baby 130
The Rocket 91
The Rocking Horse Winner 278
Roger Corman Presents 373
Rogue Robot 286
Rollercoaster 153
Roman Holiday 95
Romance on the Orient Express 284
The Room in the Dragon Volant 60, 84, 85
Room 13 69, 85
The Room Upstairs 51
Root of All Evil 361
The Rose Garden 311
Rosemary's Baby 114, 147, 148, 336
The Rosenheim Poltergeist 247
Rossumovi Univerzalni Roboti 6
Rossum's Universal Robots 6, 22
Route 66 64
Royal Jelly 382

Rude Awakening 292
The Ruff and Reddy Show 104
Rumpelstiltskin 48, 371
Rumpole of the Bailey 218
Running with the Pack 314
R.U.R. 6, **6**, 212
Ryan's Hope 326

Saaya 385
The Sabbatical 254
Sabrina and the Groovie Goolies 107
Sabrina the Teenage Witch 107
Safe Sex 318
La saga de los Dracula 210
The Saint 51, 66, 156
Salad Days 20
Salem 386
Salem's Lot 3, 4, 191, 192, **192**, 194, 286, 366, 384
The Sandbox 82
Sandcastles 181
The Sandman 344
Santa Clarita Diet 386
Sapphire and Steel 285
The Sarah Jane Adventures 74
The Satanic Rites of Dracula 100
Satan's School for Girls 134, **134**
Satan's Triangle 4, 142, 143, 165, 204
Saturday Playhouse 28
Saturday Serial 38, 39
The Savage Bees 140, 149, 165, 188, 190
A Scaredy Fraidy 200
Scene of the Crime 375
Scenes from Twelfth Night and Macbeth 9
Schalcken the Painter 3, 4, 286, 287, 288, **289**, 290
The School for Scandal 5
School Play 225
Science Fiction Theatre 42, 49
Scoob! 106
Scooby-Doo 105, 106, 111, 200, 202, 277, 311, 328, 341
Scooby-Doo and a Mummy, Too 106
Scooby-Doo and Guess Who? 106
Scooby-Doo and Scrappy-Doo 106
Scooby-Doo and the Reluctant Werewolf 106
Scooby-Doo: Classic Creep Capers 106
Scooby-Doo! Mystery Mayhem 106
Scooby-Doo! The Mystery Begins 106
Scooby-Doo 2: Monsters Unleashed 106
Scooby-Doo, Where Are You! 4, 104, 106, **106**

Scorpion Tales 278
Scream and Scream Again 136
Scream Blacula Scream 145
Scream of Fear 117
Scream of the Wolf 137
Scream Pretty Peggy 136
Scream Queens 385
Scream: The TV Series 386
The Screaming Woman 122, 159
Screen Directors Playhouse 26
Screen One 356
Screen Two 298
Screenplay 334
Scrooge 196, 209, 277
Scrooge's Rock 'n' Roll Christmas 330
Sea Tales 254
Seasons of Belief 306
Seaton's Aunt 303
Second Chance 168, 386
Second City Firsts 238
Second City TV 372
The Secret Circle 386
The Secret Empire 206, 207
The Secret Files of Captain Video 29, 69
The Secret Garden 266
The Secret Identity of Jack the Ripper 338
The Secret of Crickley Hall 386
Secret Passions 336
The Secret World of Og 201
Sei donne per l'assassino 345
The Sense of the Past 9
The Sentry 132
Sepulchre of the Undead 206
Servant 387
Sesame Street 198
Sette orchidee machaite di rosso 347
Seven Blood-Stained Orchids 347
Seven Days in May 58
Seven Temporary Moons 32
79 Park Avenue 171
Sex and Violence 217
Sexton Blake 280
Sexton Blake and the Demon God 280, 281, **281**
Sexton Blake and the Hooded Terror 280
Shades of Darkness 303
Shadow Chasers 311
Shadow of a Scream 375
Shadow of Fear 155
The Shadow Out of Time 212
Shadowhunters: The Mortal Instruments 386
Shadows 267
Shadows on the Wall 92
Shaggy and Scooby-Doo Get a Clue! 106
Shark Attack 382
Shark Attack 3: Megalodon 382

Shark Attack 2 382
The Shattered Eye 83
Shattered Vows 304
She Waits 179
Sheaving Tide 172
Sherlock Holmes 123
Sherlock Holmes and the Baskerville Curse 330, 342
She-Wolf of London 357
The Shining 378
Shipshape Home 26
Shirley Temple's Storybook 48, **49**
Shock 41, 345
Shockers 352
Showdown 321
Shower of Stars 26
Showtime U.S.A. 22
Sightings 205
Sigmund and the Sea Monsters 198
The Sign of Satan 46
The Signalman 235, 237, **237**, 239
The Silence of the Lambs 382
Silent Night, Deadly Night 175
The Silent Scream 293
Silver Blaze 278
The Silver Key 344
Silverhawks 341
A Sin of Omission 296
The Single-Minded Blackmailer 52
Sister's Keeper 318
The Sitter 310
The Six Million Dollar Man 171
Six People, No Music 45
The Six Shooter 25
Six Sides of a Square 225
666 Park Avenue 386
The Sixth Finger 72, **72**
The Sixth Sense 110, 116, 117, 120
Sizwe Bansi Is Dead 222
The Skeleton in the Cupboard 352
The Skin of Our Teeth 24
Skinflint: A Country Christmas Carol 176
The Skull Beneath 40
Sky 267
Slasher 385
Sleeping Beauty 187, 252
Sleepwalker 249
Sleepy Hollow 386
Slimer! And the Real Ghostbusters 312
Small Blessings 316
The Smile 91
Smile, Please 110
Smith 244
Smoke 15
The Snow Queen 252, 268

Snow White and the Seven Dwarfs 155
Snowball Express 179
Snowbeast 166, **167**
Sodoma's Ghost 347
Soft Focus 69
Il sogno dell'altro 345
The Soldier and Death 313
Sole Survivor 177
Someone at the Top of the Stairs 248
Someone's Watching Me! 175
Something Evil 178
Something Is Out There 337
Something Scary 59
Something the Cat Dragged In 349
Something Wicca This Way Comes 363
Sometimes They Come Back 368
Sometimes They Come Back... Again 369
Sometimes They Come Back... for More 369
Somewhere in a Crowd 101
Son of Bespoke Overcoat 33
Son of Dracula 54, 185
Song of the Succubus 144
La sonrisa 91
The Sons and Daughters of Tomorrow 83
The Sorcerer 61
Soul World 362
The Sound Machine 282
South of Hell 386
Space Creature 74
The Space Eaters 316
Space Ghost 105
Space Ghost Coast to Coast 105
Space Patrol 266
Space Stars 341
The Spanish Moss Murders 132
Spasmo 347
Special Delivery 45, 91, 308
The Special London Bridge Special 158
Special Offer 259
Specialty of the House 45
Spectre 170, 374
Speed King 225
The Spell 167
Spell of Evil 248
Spend Spend Spend 218
The Sphinx 195
Spider-Man 187
The Spider Woman 137
Spine Chillers 296
The Spirit of Dark and Lonely Water 4, 272
The Spirit of Man 335
Split Decision 304
Split Personality 321
Spoket pa Canterville 17
The Spongers 218

Spooksville 386

Srendi Vashtar 281

The Stalls of Barchester 226, 230, 239, 241

The Stalls of Barchester Cathedral 226

Stan Against Evil 385

The Stand 373

La stanza numero 13 344

Star Boars 319

Star Tonight 27

Star Trek 74

The Star Wagon 28

Star Wars 345

The Staring Match 21

Starring Boris Karloff 61

Stars Over Hollywood 54

Starsky and Hutch 144

Startime 28

The Stately Ghosts of England 80

Stay Tuned, We'll Be Right Back 300

The Stepfather 370

Stepfather III 370

Stepfather 3: Father's Day 370

Stepfather II 370

The Stepford Children 324

The Stepford Husbands 324

The Stepford Wives 323

Stephen King's Golden Tales 306

Steptoe and Son 36

Steven Berkoff's Tell Tale Heart 350

Stigma 237, 239, 241, 271

Stillwatch 334

The Sting 109

The Stingiest Man in Town 26, 196

Stingray 266

The Stone Cutter 50

The Stone Tape 245, 246

Stones 224

Stop Susan Williams 206, 207

The Storm 20, 49, 40, 64

The Story of the Inexperienced Ghost 343

The Story of the Late Mr. Elvesham 345

Storyboard 68

The Storyteller 313

The Storyteller: Greek Myths 313

The Strain 386

The Strand Magazine 123

Stranded 364

Strange 385

The Strange and Deadly Occurrence 162

Strange Calls 385

The Strange Case of Dr. Jekyll and Mr. Hyde 15, 95, 129, 185, 321

The Strange Christmas Dinner 21

Strange Event in the Life of Schalken the Painter 92, 286

Strange Love 306

The Strange Man's Arrival 306

Strange Paradise 107, 108, **108**

The Strange Possession of Mrs. Oliver 167

The Strange World of Planet X 38, 39

The Stranger 39

Stranger in Our House 175, **175**

Stranger in the Family 82, 102

Stranger in Town 282

The Stranger Left No Card 282

Stranger Things 386

The Stranger Within 141

Strasidlo cantervilleské 342

Stredstvo Makropulosa 212

The Streets of San Francisco 203

La Strega 64

La strega 346

The String of Pearls 88

Struck by Lightning 207, **208**

The Student of Prague 5

Der Student von Prag 5

Studio 57 26

Studio Four 67

The Studio Murders 326

Studio One 20, 54, 64, 127

Subliminal Seduction 375

Substance "X" 31

Suicide Club 129

The Suicide Club 12, 60, 210

The Summer House 197

Summer of Fear 174

The Sunday Drama 278

Sunday Showcase 28

Sunset Boulevard 22

Supernatural 272, **273**, 359, 385

Supernatural: Haunting Stories of Gothic Terror 274

Supernatural: The Animation 385

Surface 385

A Surfeit of H2O 66

Suspect Device 374

Suspense 14, 27, 61

Suspicion 48

Suspiria 212

Svengali 329

Swamp Thing 353, 387

The Swarm 140, 165

Sweeney Todd 8, 88

Sweeney Todd: The Demon Barber of Fleet Street 209, 381

The Sweet House of Horrors 347

Sweet, Sweet Rachel 1, 116

A Swiss Affair 99

T. Bag and the Rings of Olympus 302

T. Bag and the Sunstones of Montezuma 302

T. Bag Strikes Again 302

T. Bag's Christmas Carol 302

T. Bag's Christmas Cracker 302

Tabitha 78

Tabitha and Adam and the Clown Family 197

Take Off with T. Bag 302

A Tale of Negative Gravity 26

The Tale of Sweeney Todd 380

A Tale of Two Cities 326

Tales from the Crypt 1, 48, 319, 320, **320**, 321, 351, 352, 371

Tales from the Crypt: Demon Knight 321

Tales from the Crypt Presents: Bordello of Blood 321

Tales from the Cryptkeeper 321, 354

Tales from the Darkside 2, 304, 306, **306**, 307, 310, 316

Tales from the Darkside: The Movie 306

Tales of Frankenstein 2, 52, 100, 137, 291

Tales of Mystery 67

Tales of Mystery and Imagination 351

Tales of the Haunted 300

Tales of the Unexpected 203, 204, 281, 298, 349

Tales of the Unknown 100

Tales of Tomorrow 18, 29, **31**, 52, 61, 135

Tales of Washington Irving 82

Tales That Witness Madness 51

Tall Tales and Legends 321

Tarantulas: The Deadly Cargo 149, 188

Target 49

A Taste of Evil 117

Taste of Fear 117

A Taste of Honey 24

Taste the Blood of Dracula 100

Il taxi fantasma 345

Teacher Creature 361

Teatro de misterio 210

Teen Wolf 385

The Telephone Box 211

The Television Ghost 10, **10**

El televisor 92

The Tell-Tale Heart 6, 12, 13, 15, 16, 19, 22, 46, 86, 195, 350, 371

Terminal Virus 374

A Terribly Strange Bed 13, 49

The Terror 24, 385

Terror at London Bridge 333

Terror from Within 249

The Terror of the Twins 67

Terror on Dinosaur Island 74

Terror Out of the Sky 149

The Test 213

Test Flight 30

Le testament du Docteur Cordelier 90
Testimone oculare 213
Teta 343
Texaco Star Theatre 11
The Texas Chainsaw Massacre 191
Thark 9, 23
That's Entertainment 186
Au théatre ce soir 64, 123
La théatre de la jeunesse 18
To theatro tis Defteras 64
There Was An Old Lady 118
Theseus and the Minotaur 82
They Shoot Horses, Don't They? 163
The Thing and the Captain's Ghost 187
The Thing from Another World 55
The Thing from the Grave 321
The Thing on the Doorstep 344
The Thing's the Play 187
Things to Come 13
Thingumajig 66
The Third Day 387
The Third Eye 301
Third Fate 40
The Third Pig 321
13 Demon Street 53
The 13 Ghosts of Scooby-Doo 106
The Thirteenth Chair 22
The 13th Hour 315
The Thirteenth Reunion 292
30 Coins 387
Thirty Minute Theatre 67, 282
30 Monedas 387
This House Possessed 324
Threat of the Thormanoids 29
Three Dangerous Ladies 279
The Three Little Pigs 321
Three Miles Up 350
The Three Ravens 313
3,2,1 92
Thriller 2, **63**, 129, 247
Through a Glass Darkly 96
Thundarr and the Barbarian 341
Thunder in a Forgotten Town 99
Thunder Rock 8, 26, 299
Thunderbirds 266
Ticket-of-Leave Man 209
The Tiger 51
The Time Element 28, 54
The Time Machine 9, 175
Time Out 59
Timeslip 266
The Tingler 197
Tiny Toons' Night Ghoulery 371
To Kill a King 247
To Lay a Ghost 83
To Serve Man 57

Tom Brown's Schooldays 266
Tomato Cain and Other Stories 281
The Tomb of Dracula 342
The Tomb of King Tarus 31
The Tommyknockers 371
The Tomorrow People 267
Tomorrow, the Rat 217
Tom's Midnight Garden 267
Too Easy to Kill 130
Top Cat 104
Topper 33, 153
Topper Returns 33, 153
Topper Takes a Trip 33
Torchwood 74
Torchwood: Web of Lies 74
Le tour d'écrou 141
Tourist Attraction 72
The Towering Inferno 215
The Tractate Middoth 11, 85, 89, 241
A Tragedy of Two Ambitions 250
The Trail to Christmas 25
Traitor 218
Il tram 213
Transferts 386
Tras la puerta cerrada 90, 91
I tre volti della paura 345
Treasure Island 266
The Treasure of Abbot Thomas 232, 239
Tremors 384
Trespass 141
Trick or Treat 305
Trilby 8, 21, 28, 259, 329
Trilogy of Terror 143, **144**, 168
Trilogy of Terror II 376
Trio of Terror 62
The Triumph of Death 97
The Trollenberg Terror 39
Trollhunters 385
The Trouble with Tribbles 75
Trucks 138
True Blood 384
Truly Madly Deeply 299
Tuesday's Documentary 255
Turma di Monica 343
The Turn of the Screw 20, 46, 89, 140, 253, 321, 375, 378, 382
Turno di note 345
TV de Vanguarda 64
20,000 Leagues Under the Sea 312
Twenty Thousand Leagues Under the Sea 31
The Twilight Zone 2, 4, 28, 54, 55, **57**, 58, 59, 71, 72, 79, 91, 108, 109, 115, 125, 133, 159, 177, 308, 379, 385
Twilight Zone: The Movie 59
Twist in the Tale 204, 353
The Twisted Image 61

Two 57
The Two Faces of Evil 294
Two-Fisted Tales 321
Two Ghost Stories 23
Two in the Morning 244
2001: A Space Odyssey 18, 30
The Two Wise Virgins from Hove 24
The Two Worlds of Charlie Gordon 26
The Tycoons 68

L'uccello dalle piume di cristallo 212, 213
U.F.O. 21, 54
UFO Abduction 380
The UFO Incident 165
The Ugly Little Boy 278
The Ultimate Impostor 154
L'ultimo dei Baskerville 123
Ultra Violet 361
Un, dos, tres 92
Un umo da ridere 347
Una note nel cimitero 346
Uncle Silas 86, 87
Under the Bed 73
Under the Car 366
Under the Mountain 301
An Unearthly Child 73
The Unexpected 25
The Unexplained 385
Unexplained Mysteries 385
Unfair Exchanges 298
The Unforeseen 49
The Unholy Threshold 38
The Uninvited 83
The United States Steel Hour 26
Universal Horror 382
The Unknown 49
Unknown Origin 374
The Unknown Peter Sellers 80
Unsealed Alien Files 385
Unsolved Mysteries 312
The Unspeakable 375
Until Death 346
L'uomo della sabbia 344
Urban Gothic 384

Valentine's Second Chance 201
Valley of the Dinosaurs 199
The Vampira Show 40, **41**, 194
Vampire 151
The Vampire 132, 144
Vampire Breath 351
The Vampire Diaries 2, 384
Vampire High 384
The Vampire Hunter 316
The Vampire Lovers 85
The Vampire Strikes Back 319
Vampire: The Masquerade 360
Vampirella 375
Vampires 221
The Vampire's Apprentice 200

Vampirina 385
Vampirismus 344
O Vampiro 343
Van Helsing 385
The Vandy Case 247
Vanishing Act 68
Veglia al morto 344
The Veil 61
Vek Makropulos 212
La Venere d'Ille 345
The Ventriloquist's Dummy 321
Die Verwandlung 92
Verdict from Space 30
Il verme 346
Das verraterische Herz 14
Vertigo 143
A Very Missing Person 123
Via delle Streghe 345
Vice Versa 6, 26, 70
The Victim 126
The Victorian Chaise-Longue 25, 68
A View from the Hill 240, 241
Viktoria 273
Il vincino di casa 213
The Vine of Death 54
Virgin 368
Virtual Seduction 374
Vision of Crime 61
Visions... 180
Visions of Death 180
Visit to a Small Planet 24
The Visitor 352
Visitor from the Grave 293
Voice in the Night 48
Volshebnaya lakva 46
Voodoo Doll 203
The Voodoo Factor 39
Voyage to the Bottom of the Sea 74, **75**

Wake in Fear 352
Wailing Well 311
Walkers 338
The Walking Dead 2, 385
The Walking Ghost 41
War and Remembrance 92
War of the Worlds 21, 356
Warlock 66
A Warning to the Curious 228, 229, 232, 312
Warrior Nun 387
The Wasp Woman 374
The Wasp's Nest 5
Watcher by the Dead 40
A Watcher by the Dead 344
The Waxwork 45
Waxworks 64
'Way Out 68, 96282
Wayward Pines 386
Web 39
The Wednesday Play 217
Weekend 212

Weird Fantasy 351
Weird Science 351
Welcome Home 83
Welcome to My Nightmare 310
Welcome to Planet Earth 375
Welcome to Planet Earth II 375
Welcome to the Deadhouse 351
Welcome to the Discworld 362
Well of Doom 62
The Wendigo 29, 69
Werewolf 74, **75**, 313, **314**
The Werewolf 132
Werewolf Concerto 321
Werewolf of Hollywood 316
The Werewolf of Woodstock 129, **130**
The Werewolf Reunion 273
Wessex Tales 250, 251
West Country Tales 254
Westinghouse Desilu Playhouse 28, 54
What a Night for a Knight 105
What Big Eyes 263
What Ever Happened to Baby Jane? 112, 124, 146
What We Do in the Shadows 385
What's New Pussycat 196
What's New, Scooby-Doo? 106
Wheels of Terror 365
When Michael Calls 4, 122
When Morning Comes 304
When the Bullet Hits the Bone 375
When We Are Married 5
Where Evil Lies 374
Where Have All the People Gone 162
Where Is Everybody? 55
Where the Woodbine Twineth 46
Whisper 110
The Whispers 386
Whistle and I'll Come to You 3, 4, 97, **98**, 225, 229, 241, 286
Whistle Down the Wind 222, 256
The Whistling Room 25
White Lady 335
White Zombie 40
The Whitechapel Murders 338
Who Can Kill a Child? 92
Who Framed Roger Rabbit 369
Whodunit 44
Who's Afraid of the Big Bad Werewolf? 106
Who's Who??? 66
The Wicker Man 172, 218, 224
The Wide World of Mystery 128, **130**, 131
Will the Real Martian Please Stand Up? 56
William and Mary 68, 96, 282, 310

William Shatner's A Twist in the Tale 352
William Wilson 69, 249
The Winds of War 92
The Wit to Woo 254
The Witch 24, 346
The Witch of the Eight Islands 25
Witch, Witch, Burning Bright 117
Witchblade 385
The Witcher 387
The Witches and the Grinnygog 301
Witches' Feast 110
Witches of East End 386
Witchfinder General 235
The Witching Hour 22
Witching Time 292
With Affection, Jack the Ripper 117, 145
Without Walls 349
The Wizard of Oz 188
Wolf 1
Wolf Creek 386
Wolf Lake 384
The Wolf Man 1, 52, 54
Wolves of God 67
The Woman in Black 340
The Woman in Black 2: Angel of Death 341
The Woman in White 387
The Woman Who Came Back 40
The Woman Who Stole a Ghost 304
The Woman Who Was No More 142
The Woman's Ghost Story 67
Wonders in Letterland 301
Won't Write Home, Mom—I'm Dead 249
The World Beyond 205
The World of Darkness 205
World of Dracula 206
World of Giants 53
World of Water 31
Worzel Gummidge 268
Worzel Gummidge Down Under 268
Wraxton Marne 39
Wrong Turn 366
Wynonna Earp 386
Wyrd Sisters 362

The X Files 358, 359, 362
The X Files: I Want to Believe 359

Yami no teio kyuketsuki Dorakyura 342
The Yattering and Jack 306
A Year at the Top 205
Yellow 321

The Yellow Pill 68, 83
The Yogi Bear Show 104
Young Couples Only 26
Your Favorite Story 26
Yours Truly, Jack the Ripper 63

Z Cars 338
Z Nation 385
Zack and the Magic Factory 201
La zarpa 91
Zenés szinha 342

Ze zivota hmyzu 7
The Zee Horror Show 355
Zoltan, Hound of Dracula 190
The Zombie 132